W9-BKG-687

Contexts, Intertexts, and Hypertexts

WRITTEN LANGUAGE
S E R I E S

Marcia Farr, senior editor

Contexts, Intertexts, and Hypertexts

edited by

Scott Lloyd DeWitt
The Ohio State University at Marion

Kip Strasma
Illinois Central College

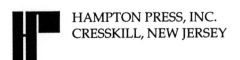

HAMPTON PRESS, INC.
CRESSKILL, NEW JERSEY

Printed in the United States of America

Library of Congress Cataloging-in-Publication Data

Contexts, intertexts, and hypertexts / edited by Scott Lloyd DeWitt, Kip Strasma
      p. cm. -- (Written language)
    Includes bibliographic references and indexes.
    ISBN 1-57273-214-8 (cl). -- ISBN 1-57273-215-6 (ppb)
    1. English language--Rhetoric--Computer-assisted instruction.
  2. English language--Rhetoric--Study and teaching. 3. Hypertext systems. I. DeWitt, Scott Lloyd. II. Strasma, Kip. III. Series: Written language series.
PE1404.C6339 1999
808'.042'0785--dc21   99-22897
                                                CIP

Hampton Press, Inc.
23 Broadway
Cresskill, NJ 07626

Contents

Acknowledgments

We thank a number of people who have supported us throughout the many stages of this book's completion. First, we thank the individual contributors who have all been amazingly patient during the processes of revising and editing, who endured and stuck by us when we asked for "just one more draft." Also, we thank the editors of the Written Language series at Hampton Press: Marcia Farr, Gloria Nardini, and Daiva Markelis, and the president of Hampton Press, Barbara Bernstein, for their careful editing comments and willingness to advance research in hypertext, writing, and computers.

A number of our own teachers deserve recognition: Douglas Hesse, Janice Neuleib, Jim Kalmbach, Ron Fortune, Ronald Strickland, Charles Harris, Rebecca Saunders, Elizabeth Crowley, Catherine Paeden, and Anne Rosenthal. Their visions in pedagogy are with us each day in our own classrooms.

Our colleagues gave a great deal of their time and offered endless encouragement toward helping us see this project through: Lynda Behan, Anne Bower, and Marcia Dickson at The Ohio State University (OSU) at Marion, and Beverly Moss at OSU at Columbus; Paul Resnick and Susan Becker at Illinois Central College.

Scott would like to thank Angela Wall, Penny Visser, Mary LeGare, H. Louis Ulman, F. Dominic Dottavio for his support of the

OSU-Marion Small Grant Program, and the OSU Ameritech Faculty Fellowship Program. He would like to thank Kip Strasma for his enthusiasm about this project and his ideas about computers and teaching writing. He would especially like to thank his family for their support throughout the years. Jim Ryan, "friend, confidant—for your light and laughter." And mostly, his partner, Danny B. Stout.

Kip would like to thank Scott DeWitt for his work and friendship. He would especially like to thank his family and family-in-law for their support. And mostly, his wife, Ann, "for her love and direction."

About the Contributors

Maureen Burgess is a doctoral candidate in the English Department at The Ohio State University. She has worked for several years as both an instructor and administrator in the department's Computers in Composition and Literature Program. Her current research focus is on student applications of "hypertextualities," physical, conceptual, and digital, in their study of narrative.

Scott Lloyd DeWitt is associate professor of English at The Ohio State University at Marion where he teaches first- and second-year writing, creative nonfiction essay writing, and computers and composition pedagogy. In 1993, he was awarded The Ameritech Faculty Fellowship at The Ohio State University in support of his work that investigates the influence of computer technology on invention in the writing classroom.

Kathleen Duguay is assistant professor of English at East Stroudsburg University of Pennsylvania where she teaches writing and literature courses. She formerly worked at North Adams State College where she taught in the English Department and served as coordinator of academic computing. She is also the founder of the New England Alliance for Computers and Writing.

Emily Golson is assistant professor of English at the University of Northern Colorado where she teaches undergraduate and graduate writing and rhetoric courses, directs the Writing Center, and trains graduate assistants.

Neil Lindeman is a graduate student at Brigham Young University where he has taught first-year composition and technical writing. He is currently working on his master's thesis, which traces the development of composition research methods using the work of Linda Flower.

Ann Margaret McKillop is assistant professor of education in the Curriculum and Instruction Department at the University of Maryland where she teaches courses in secondary language arts and technology applications in the classroom. Besides student-constructed hypermedia, her interests and research areas include composition, reader-response theory, media literacy, and interdisciplinary curriculum.

Deborah Balzhiser Morton is a doctoral student in rhetoric and composition at Illinois State University. Her research includes instructional technologies and iterative, participatory methods. She has taught courses in basic composition, composition, technical communication, and visual rhetoric. In 1995, she was selected to teach and collaborate on the research and development of master's degrees in professional writing, journalism, and public relations at the University of Western Sydney, Nepean, Australia.

Jamie Myers is associate professor of education, language and literacy education at the Pennsylvania State University where he teaches courses in qualitative research, social construction of knowledge, adolescent literature, Internet and other technology applications in the classroom, and semiotics. His scholarship explores the themes of collaboration, community, and critique within the construction of classroom structures for inquiry.

David Norton is currently a doctoral student at the University of Minnesota where he has taught technical writing, computers and composition, and online information management. Recently, his work on hyperphoric grammar won "Best Graduate Student Proposal" for the Association for Computing's SIGDOC96 conference.

Gary Ryan is a language arts teacher at Christian Brothers College High School in St. Louis, MO where he teaches American literature, composition, and writing with technology. In 1992, he was named as a founding board member of the Gateway Writing Project, one of the sites for the National Writing Project. He is also the first vice president of the Greater St. Louis English Teachers Association. In 1995, he was named to the Executive Board of the NCTE's Assembly on Computers in English.

Mary Lynn Saul is assistant professor of English at Worcester State College where she teaches freshman composition, introduction to literature, Chaucer, and the history of the English language. She has taught business writing, technical writing, and freshman composition on computer at various institutions for six years.

Kip Strasma is associate professor of English at Illinois Central College where he teaches writing, literature, humanities, and philosophy. He chairs the committee on computers and writing within the English Department and has helped shape the physiological and pedagogical direction of teaching writing with computers at Illinois Central College.

H. Lewis Ulman is associate professor of English at The Ohio State University where he has worked closely with the Computers in Composition and Literature Program (CCL) since its inception in 1987. He became the first faculty director of CCL in 1996. In addition to his administrative duties, he regularly teaches computer-supported writing courses as well as undergraduate and graduate courses on hypertext and the history and theory of writing technologies.

Beverly B. Zimmerman is assistant professor of English at Brigham Young University where she teaches professional and technical writing, project management, and a course in virtual rhetoric. She also specializes in ethnographic research in composition.

Introduction:
An Emerging Research

Scott Lloyd DeWitt
Ohio State University at Marion

Kip Strasma
Illinois Central College

OPENING CONTEXTS

With each new wave of computer technology comes disparate, often conflicting responses of enthusiasm and apprehension among writing teachers who have embarked on a journey that just 15 years ago seemed fictional, at best. Computers and composition studies, as a field of both inquiry and practice, still exists in relative infancy, yet the computer technology ascertains that change comes swiftly. Amidst the excitement and caution is a deepening pressure. Although writing teachers are blending technology with composition pedagogy and attempting to hold on to the integrity of previous advancements in composition, something new, something faster, something that promises to be more interactive or more intuitive or more integrated, pushes—rather impatiently—to become a part of how students learn to write. What is known about computers and composition shifts at such a phenomenal pace, due in part to a rapidly evolving computer industry that deliberately out-

1

dates itself with each new advancement; in part to a national, competitive push to make students computer literate in as many subject areas as possible (although often falling short of similar goals in training teachers); and in part to a driven, consistently producing group of scholars who urge boundaries outward to create a large, broad, and diverse research base that borrows heavily from disciplines seemingly separate from study in the humanities.

Revealed here are a number of tensions: How do we ever "keep up"? Or, for any mortal soul new to the field of computers and composition, how do we "get on board" an area of study that is moving at speed rail pace in the first place? What are the best ways to use technology, should one want to be "selective" in its use? What criteria should be used to make these decisions? Who is taking up what Haas (1996) referred to as the "concerted, focused attempt[s] to examine technologies of writing—historically, theoretically, empirically, and practically" (p. 25)? These questions are not new to compositionists committed to computer technology. Haas' question offered an apt example. Until recently, it was difficult to find extensive historical perspectives on computers and writing; prior to the recent publication of Hawisher, LeBlanc, Moran, and Selfe's (1996) *Computers and the Teaching of Writing in American Higher Education, 1979-1994: A History*, no single text devoted itself to an historical perspective of the field, save, perhaps, for Russell's (1991) *Writing in the Academic Disciplines, 1870-1990*, a text that minimally broaches computers and composition. Similarly, until the publication of *Literacy and Computers* by Selfe and Hilligoss (1994), only a few collections of theoretical and empirical essays existed on computers and composition, even though the journal *Computers & Composition* had begun to serve both ends quite early in its publication. And Haas' (1996) book takes the empirical agenda as far as it has been taken so far in the field. As these collections demonstrate, questions about computers and composition require writing teachers to construct a more complete picture of the writing process while asking how we can ensure that we examine as closely, as carefully, and as completely as possible the technology we embrace or discard. And how can this be done before we move on to that which seems (today, at least) bigger and faster?

Certainly, these questions encircle the role hypertext currently plays in the teaching of writing. Recent scholarship in computers and composition studies enthusiastically forwards new possibilities for writing within the context of hypertext. Calling hypertext both a new writing tool and writing space, scholars describe, at a theoretical level, how readers and writers may interact within hypertextual contexts and how composing processes might be altered as a result of reading and writing within hypertextual spaces. Still others explore the political nature of "text," "textual authority," and "intertextuality," promising new literacies that could extend from hypertextual thinking. Meanwhile, writing teachers explore the possibilities of hypertext in their classrooms; they use hypertext as a way to offer students concrete examples about abstract writing principles, they teach students how to use hypertext as a space where students can create a research base to be used in more traditional means of essay writing, and they assign students to read and write hypertexts as an end in their composition courses (DeWitt, 1996). These teachers, as a result, are witnesses, through their own trial and error, to an acute, first-hand understanding of how students interact with authored hypertext and hypertextual authoring programs, how composing practices work within hypertexts environments, and what new strategies for reading and writing instruction result from such interaction.

HYPERTEXT RESEARCH

Already the body of research on hypertext and writing is large and crosses freely from discipline to discipline, weaving a somewhat over-whelming fabric for anyone trying to grasp both the epistemological and pragmatic character of this new technology. The Association for Computing Machinery presents and publishes research that is graphic or human-computer interface-sensitive. Nielsen (1990, 1994) was concerned with the general uses of hypertext and hypermedia within and beyond the educational world; this is evident in his general properties for usability in hypertext systems (easy to learn, efficient to use, easy to remember, few errors, and pleasant to use), as well as in his extensive annotated bibliography of articles taken from such publications as the British *Hypermedia*, the *Proceedings of the ACM International Hypertext Conference*, and *The Journal of the American Information Science*. Delany and Landow (1991), although less international and technical, focus on key hypertext and hypermedia issues from within and beyond the humanities. Their collection of essays, *Hypermedia and Literary Studies*, describes Brown University's hypertext systems, features pioneering authors like Nicole Yankelovich, and includes narratives about linking literary works as well as curricular programs. Another grouping of research centers around literary and poetic concerns, as is illustrated by recent publications by Lanham (1989), Joyce (1988, 1995), Kaplan and Moulthrop (1990, 1993, 1994), and Johnson-Eilola (1994). And Bolter's (1991) *Writing Space* captures the coupling of historical perspectives and the theory of written discourse.

What this and other scholarship suggest is that hypertext research is made up of two distinct threads that, although immediately intertwined, can be separated all too easily: theory and practice. Much research, we find, painstakingly forwards theoretical perspectives that could lead to pedagogical practice, if a reader should decide to apply them in his or her classroom. Appearing at the same time as these abstract conclusions, writing teachers' narratives paint detailed portraits of assignments, activities, and classroom experiences that carry out and explore the practical, concrete dimensions of hypertextual writing but rarely develop a complex theoretical base. In the end, theory and practice of hypertext in our writing pedagogy often fail at a true union, in which one informs and enriches the other. Thus, we uncover another series of questions relevant to the study of hypertext and composition: Where are the connections located between theory and practice that are germane to this technology? Can these links be found within an already existing reciprocity between theory and practice? Or, have more prolific, more telling associations yet to be realized?

These questions begin to establish the foundation of this volume. Across the disciplines, we notice a scarcity of contextual studies on hypertext and writing, directed by composition specialists, that examine writing pedagogies and writing students in our writing classrooms. What drives this collection of chapters, really, is an absence, of sorts, within an ever-growing body of literature on hypertext and composition studies. Our review of the literature indicates that, although many researchers have embraced the ideas and platforms of hypertext in reaching a vast array of pedagogical goals, only a few have carried these concepts through to the classroom and reported what they found. McKnight, Dillon, and Richardson (1991) framed the gap in this research by explaining that scholars to date have "been content to discuss the apparent advantages of hypertext systems for most tasks, occasionally describing systems they have implemented and informally presenting their reactions to them . . . . [However,] in the absence of confirmatory data [from the classroom], any claims for the new medium should be treated with caution" (pp. 58-59). McKnight, Dillon, and Richardson's advice is both instructive and productive for compositionists as it directs its attention toward studies informed by praxis.

Typically, as compositionists integrate new, emerging technologies with their teaching, they become increasingly interested in studying how computers have changed how we teach and how students learn. Such inquiry in computers and composition espouses a multitude of approaches. Consider, for example, Hawisher's (1989) compilation of 42 research studies on computers and writing instruction that today, 10 years after its publication, illustrates how scholars and teachers rigorously test the grounds of how, if at all, computers change students' learning experiences. Hawisher's overview covers both quantitative and qualitative research of hardware and software, student experience, writing assessment, and writing within classroom contexts. Her findings are hardly conclusive, a point to which she readily admitted. In fact, much of what she found was contradictory. But because of the wealth of research that was available for her to survey, she was able to note patterns of similarities and differences as well as make future recommendations for further research.

A collection of essays devoted to studying the practical application of hypertext theory within the contexts of our writing classrooms has yet to appear on the scene of rhetoric and composition. This volume is directed toward scholars and teachers in computers and composition studies and connects the theoretical aspirations of hypertext with direct classroom applications, a union that has heretofore promised more potential than shown actualization. The writers' findings represented within, in all their diversity and similarity, open a space for dialogue at many levels. For example, as we review current scholarship, we are troubled to find deep theory elevated as a dominant movement in the research, not necessarily by proclamation, but instead by the absence of contextualized practical, hands-on research (see DeWitt, 1996, for an illustrative history of this point). There are several reasons why we find theory in its heightened position. Theoretical speculations on the *concept* of hypertext have a long and privileged history. Bolter (1991) noted that even the earliest forms of texts can be hypertextualized; he offered an interactive vision of the story of Oedipus structured in three overlapping dimensions, each subnarrative operating in a linear and nonlinear form. The theoretical concept of hypertext is evident to some extent in all forms of writing, although its modern definition owes itself to Bush's (1945) imaginary "memex" and Nelson's (1974) early vision of it connecting libraries, people, and information, the form of hypertext that most of us think about when the word is invoked. These theoretical speculations on the concept of hypertext seem more evident because of modern electronic technology that makes hypertext structure functional as well as semantic.

Perhaps another reason for heightened interest in the theoretical stems from the privileging of theory itself in our university systems where "few institutional structures reward pedagogical practices or answer educational needs of teachers" (Cahalan & Downing, 1991, p. 3). Phelps (1995) noted that these political slants may inform the very research modes used: Research often begins with theory, moves to practice, and "evolves normatively in the direction of greater depth" (p. 38). But one of the most important reasons why theory has been privileged over practice in hypertextualizing composition is the technology itself. Frankly, it has only been recently that hypertext has become an electronic, functional reality, which has not provided ample time for serious, pragmatic study of the technology needed to support the interactive and intertextual learning environments so prevalent in writing classrooms. This practical research has accelerated in the past few years with the massing of the World Wide Web (WWW) and related hypertextual browsing systems. But, even these studies have a theoretical "here's what I think" feel about them.

Although the survey of research represented here originated from a the gap between theory and practice, it cannot—in and of itself, as an end—strengthen the union between theory and practice of hypertext and student writing. We certainly reject any suggestion that pragmatic research is a more valid vehicle through which to generate, explore, and answer research questions and problems, and we do not intend to present these studies as a final destination of current discussions on hypertext. Instead, we present a group of "contextualized studies" of how hypertext has been used practically to classroom and student ends. In doing so, we begin to concretize the claims and promises that, in a very short time, have generated a great deal of attention around hypertext technology in the field. Furthermore, these studies force us to redefine what we mean by *writing, composition instruction,* and *hypertext,* disallowing us an ease in using these terms as if they possess uniform, unvarying meanings. In other words, this direction in the research compels us to isolate specific hypertextual applications and writing acts to better understand and describe how categorically this technology might influence student learning. There is no better way to see this than through the *context* of specific classrooms, the *intertexts* of theory in practical situations, and *hypertextualized* composition instruction in action.

We hope this collection is viewed as a contribution to an emerging research, serving to add to what Phelps (1988) called an ecology of our discipline. She contended that such is the ideal nature of our field,

> a site where different theories and practices can play against one another. From this perspective, a conceptual framework for composition serves not to eliminate competing approaches of views but to hold them in tension through their mutual relevance and difference. The interplay among them defines a "field" in the sense of a self-organizing system. Such a system is a dynamic process rather than an equilibrium structure; it maintains its integrity through continual self-transformation and possesses the capacity for novelty. At the same time, it is logically organized—differentiated, elaborated, hierarchical. . . . [A]n ecology of composition . . . articulate[s] its coherence as a field structured by its shared relevancies and oppositions yet [is] capable of continual evolution. (p. 4)

The research studies collected here begin to address what Phelps (1988) called the "conflictual relationship between theory and practice in composition" (p. 206) in such a way as to "elevate practice so that theory and practice are not only equal but equally essential" (Ede, 1992, p. 322). Although this text does not explicitly possess a pedagogical aim in the sense that the authors desire to prescribe ways to teach writing with hypertext, many of the studies that describe a pedagogical practice are drawn from classroom activities and research.

Many compositionists are eager to learn more about hypertext and its application to the writing classroom, but at the same time are circumspect about the broad claims and promises that have remained, to date, empty of contextualized findings. Although research from outside of computers and composition has informed our understanding of hypertext—we argue that this indicates a healthy field of study—a collection of research studies coming from within our community has yet to be offered. The unique position of this type of work can create a base that will continue to grow from theoretical questions and research problems arising out of our classrooms and interactions with our students. Consequently, such a collection will begin to inform fields outside composition, beginning to create new dialogues and exchanges. We forward that these research studies, adding to the existing body of literature, will thus problematize an existing reciprocity between theory and practice, pushing the conversation surrounding this technology beyond a place where theory and practice are so easily separated, and toward a more complete portrait of research in the field.

THE ROLE OF METHODOLOGY

One of the most productive dialogues to date on computers, composition, and research methodology grew out of Halio's (1990) controversial, "Student Writing: Can the Machine Maim the Message?" In the article, which appeared in *Academic Computing*, Halio laid out for the reader an experiment from which she claimed the graphic interfaces of Macintosh and IBM software directly affect students' writing. When read without critical attention, Halio's "findings" were indeed eye-opening, to say the least. Specifically, Halio claimed that students who use a Macintosh wrote at a significantly lower readability level than those who used an IBM, that writers using Macintosh computers chose subjects to pursue that were less serious than those using an IBM, and that students viewed the Macintosh as toy-like because of the accessible graphic tools (mainly font imaging and pictures) integrated in its word processing programs.

After publication of Halio's (1990) article, the debate that ensued was rapid and large, most of which occurred on USENET and LISTSERV groups, at the 1990 Conference on College Composition and Communication, and in a special section of *Computers & Composition*. In response to claims that her research was flawed (by a group of 20 scholars-researchers who took issue with the report), Halio defended her research as descriptive, not experimental, in nature and posited much of her article as anecdotal rather than empirical, claiming that her readers invoked a nonexistent methodology based on their reading of her study's frame and research questions.

We find the dialogue surrounding this publication instructive. First, most of Halio's critics were not convinced with her explanation; in fact, many took to task the journal's editors and reviewers for failing to scrutinize the research, deeming their publication negligent and irresponsible. But most of all, critics centered on what Kaplan and Moulthrop (1990) called "the methodological inadequacies of [Halio's] observations" (p. 254), outlining basic weaknesses in how comparable test populations and instruction were constituted and how student writing was assessed. Furthermore, various responses, including Halio's, indicate the profound dissimilitude that currently exists within the field regarding research methodology and epistemology. In other words, Halio was not speaking the same language as many other researchers who were quick to correct what they saw as methodological inconsistency. Without pointing blame, Halio's situation suggests, at least to us, that what is taken for validity by one group of knowledge-makers may not be acceptable for another; certainly, claims for how valid knowledge is reached alters from one discipline to another—and often within the discipline itself, as Halio's situation demonstrates. We are not condoning the activities or the conclusions of Halio's study; however, we are concerned about the dualistic notions that drove the criticism of the study and, more importantly, her defense of it. That is, as we worked on this collection of chapters, we became increasingly sensitive to the changing and often diverse notions of *method/methodology, qualitative, empiricism,* and *scientific,* for these notions mean very different things to different individuals, communities, and disciplines.

This volume is poised at the edge of these changes and debates about research methods and methodology. Readers may notice a certain absence at times of research terminology to which they are accustomed (at least from reading journals like *Research in the Teaching of English* or *Written Communication*). This is a conscious choice on our part. Instead of forcing writers into terminology and definitions of their research methods, we were more insistent on clear, detailed descriptions of their questions, predictions, activities, and students. In short, we placed a weighted emphasis on a categorical account of research rather than a categorization of it. The studies within, although indebted to "traditional" research methods and methodologies, "employ multivariate designs in order to examine the effects of a range of variables on writing. And, they are increasingly concerned with their study's ecological validity—whether its design accounts for or captures writing in authentic contexts" (Beach, 1992, p. 218). We asked researchers in this collection to place emphasis on research design where possible, but not to the exclusion of capturing the "authentic context." As Beach (1992) warned: "If researchers become enraptured with the technical aspects of design, they may ignore the theoretical assumptions underlying the study" (p. 233). (We would add that they may ignore the "context of the study" as well.)

A striking aspect of these collected works is a broadly defined common research vision. All utilize nonparametric research methods, those that "[examine] groups of writers as they are" (Beach, 1992, p. 219). In brief, the studies in this collection make use of qualitative designs, anecdotal evidence, and the strategies of ethnographic and/or case studies, even though they may not present themselves as "formal" examples of the category. Many blur the boundaries of rigid methodological categories and forms, employing a blend of these elements. Possibly two reasons for this blending resulted from our open call for papers. The first is rather simple: The thrust of research in composition studies in general has been moving away from interventionist-quantitative, scientific research toward more "naturalistic" research methods and tactics, and these scholars' articles within are part of this movement. The second possible reason for the overwhelming focus on qualitative approaches is more complex, but certainly understandable. The nature of research in a given field, both past and present, dictates the types of questions that will both be asked and answered in succeeding research studies (Cozby, 1989). Subsequently, the questions that a researcher asks during his or her investigation into a pedagogical or theoretical problem provides the exigency for the choice of methodologies employed.

At this early stage in research on hypertextualizing composition instruction, we note a high level of uncertainty in the field. As a result, these researchers asked questions that require what Brodkey (1987) called a "rhetoric of dialectics and (ethnographic) interpretation [that] deals with uncertainty, that is, offers arguments that display rather than obviate doubt" (p. 27). Their questions led to descriptive, contextualized studies that

> give a rich account of the complexity of writing behavior, a complexity that controlled experiments generally cannot capture. [They try] to show the interrelationships among multifaceted dimensions of the writing process by looking closely at writing from a new point of view in order to recognize important variables and to suggest new hypotheses for further study. (Lauer & Asher, 1988, p. 45)

Lauer and Asher argued that "to privilege one method of inquiry" or "to encourage individuals to choose among the modes of inquiry, maintaining literacy in only one" results in "an unfortunate and simplistic" view of research in the field (p. 7). Whereas we acknowledge a possible limitation in a common research vision in this collection, our aim was to invite scholars to create "designs appropriate for their own situations" (p. 3). Therefore, we offer this common, general research vision as an historical indicator. At the same time, however, we wish to celebrate the role of contextualized research in computers and composition studies and resist Lauer and Asher's perhaps representative assumption that qualitative research most often comes first because it investigates questions that need to be asked and tested in more "scientific" methodologies. The research presented here seeks to devalue an institutional hierarchy of research methodologies by valuing the dialogue of firsthand knowledge that occurs within the site of investigation (Brodkey, 1987; Newkirk, 1991).

Early on, as we began receiving proposals for this volume, our desire to construct them into an organizing structure was strong. We considered several possibilities: studies that moved from theory to practice and from practice to theory; studies that used exploratory versus constructive hypertexts; studies that examined students writing hypertext as an end in and of itself versus those that take up the ends of hypertext in the context of composing traditional, print texts. Such an organizing technique, we later discovered, places these studies within artificial categories that limited their appeal and their ability to converse with other studies in the collection. (We should also note here that publishing this collection as a hypertext crossed our minds more than once.) The contributions to this collection cross a broad spectrum and represent a multitude of educational levels, including kindergarten through grade 12, first-year college composition, upper division college writing, and graduate student training. A variety of platforms are also represented, including Storyspace, HyperCard, the WWW, Toolbook, and Guide. With the ever-increasing number of authoring programs, this variety seems to reflect the diversity in many schools. Interestingly, a large portion of the research collected within has been completed by graduate students and faculty whose primary teaching assignments are not exclusively graduate level but instead lower division, often introductory undergraduate courses, possibly suggesting an area of "cutting-edge" research where hypertext is tested again and again.

In "Sites of Conflict: The Challenges of Hypertextualizing Composition in the College Writing Class," Kathleen Duguay analyzes how students' approaches and practices in writing hypertext documents differed from how they approached and executed writing in a more traditional format in an upper level literature class and in a lower division composition class. Whereas students who used hypertext seemed to focus an excessive amount of time on the technical aspects of mastering the program, her analysis of collected data suggests that they showed a much keener awareness of audience and that they conducted research that tended to be driven by what the project needed rather than by a preconceived notion of an essay and simply gathering sufficient material to fill in the number of pages the instructor assigned. In "The Limitations of Hypertext in the Composition Classroom," MaryLynn Saul describes a collaborative assignment in which students composed conventional papers or hypertexts in a college composition classroom. Isolating her students' work with this one assignment, she compares four sections of college composition, two of which composed hypertexts and two of which composed conventional papers, in order to determine how differing assignments did and did not facilitate meeting the goals of her class. Her research highlights emerging conflicts between teaching writing and teaching technological operations.

Ann Margaret McKillip and Jamie Myers, in "The Pedagogical and Electronic Contexts of Composing in Hypermedia," propose that claims of more democratic structures and new freedom in composing processes may not be warranted based on their studies which explore the hyper/multimedia composing decisions of 16 Grade 7 students and 17 undergraduates in an English teacher education program. Authoring groups of students composed hyper/multimedia projects that included digitized images, sounds, video, and original quicktime movies. Their conclusions, based on videotaped data coded to indicate composing decisions in hyperlink pathways, highlight the strong influence of the teacher's pedagogy and traditional narrative structures, as groups strive to weave a meaningful pathway through a hyper/multimedia electronic space.

Scott Lloyd DeWitt examines how writing students used a hypertext application throughout the processes of inquiry, invention, and exploration. His study, "Defining Links," follows students enrolled in a developmental college composition course who constructed hypertexts while preparing to write a traditional, print documented essay. DeWitt's analysis of the course makes multiple correlations between students' hypertext-linking strategies and their self-constructed definitions of hypertext. He believes that hypertext facilitated students' learning by concretely illustrating and reflecting multiple cognitive processes for them, which in turn enabled them to consciously theorize about their own learning. By defining parameters for intersecting and interacting links, Emily Golson, in "Cognition, Meaning, and Creativity: On Reading Student Hypertexts," defines two kinds of links, intersecting and interacting, that appear in student-centered hypertexts. Drawing on schema and neural net theory, this author uses identifiable patterns of intersecting and interacting links to build an operational version of the reading process that rests on aesthetic as well as analytic comprehension of text.

David W. Norton, Beverly B. Zimmerman, and Neil Lindeman argue that one of the most difficult decisions students face in creating a collaborative hypertext document is how to link texts. "Developing Hyperphoric Grammar to Teach Collaborative Hypertexts" presents a hyperphoric grammar—a grammar for hypertext references—and a punctuation system that allows students and teachers a way of using the intended meaning of the linking referent to define the structure of the hypertext. This hyperphoric grammar helped the teacher and the students describe hypertext structures and to negotiate those structures by allowing them to plan relationships ahead of time and to signify those relationships.

Kip Strasma's chapter, "Hypertext Unplugged: Using Hypertext in Any Writing Context," resituates earlier conclusions toward two new contexts. His study suggests that nonelectronic hypertext concepts are a useful if not essential part of the "process" of designing an electronic hypertext—these concepts in print form make up part of the "hypermedia" context of hypertext, one that is often taken for granted. Following this argument, Strasma explores pedagogical uses for hypertext concepts in the composition classroom and presents suggestions from both his reading of theory and experience using hypertext in writing classes. Next, Gary Ryan explores how collaborative conversations are shaped by hypertext applications in a high school setting in, "Epistemic Conversations: Creating Socratic Dialogue in Hypertext." Drawing on the work of Plato, Vygotsky, and Ong, Ryan argues that conversation provides a structure into which students can pour their ideas and solidify cognitive structures in the crucible of discourse. While teaching high school English, he extended epistemic discussions into the computer medium by taking advantage of hypertext tools to expand his students' abilities to participate in the making of a text. His students, he argues, have created a writing environment that replaces status with flux, product with inquiry.

In the final study, "Inquiry into Hypertextualizing Teaching Assistants, Or How Do I Evaluate Hypertexts for Composition Teaching Assistants?" Deborah Balzhiser Morton investigates how hypertext systems can help composition teaching assistants (TAs) who are learning to teach first-year college writing. Morton's extensive project looks at how an introduction to hypertext helped prepare TAs for using the application in the classes they teach by integrating hypertext in TA training in such a way that the TAs themselves became "hypertextualized"—where hypertext became a part of their pedagogy rather than something "adding more to their list of worries." Her case provides a method for developing hypertexts for TAs as well as insights about TA needs and uses of hypertexts.

We conclude this collection with a response essay by H. Lewis Ulman and Maureen Alana Burgess, "Mapping the Emergent Structures of Hypertext." As they review the book's chapters, Ulman and Burgess identify a set of theoretical problems that includes an exploration of assessment, design, hypertext as an idea versus an implementation, and the uniqueness of this technology, especially in the context of what they refer to as "our business." Their piece places the articles in this collection within the broader contexts of what we can and should expect hypertext to become with continuing research and experimentation.

Overall, what we hope readers find in this collection is a diverse set of studies revealing the means and ends of hypertext in composition environments. Whether teaching in grade school or graduate school, using Storyspace or HyperCard, readers should find several chapters informative to their teaching theory and practice. Our aim is less to present a comprehensive view of research methods and methodologies and more to present a collection of studies that will contribute to an emerging dialogue surrounding hypertext, student writing, and research.

Chapter 1

Sites of Conflict: The Challenges of Hypertextualizing Composition in the College Writing Class

Kathleen Duguay
East Stroudsburg University of Pennsylvania

The concept of *hypertext* is attributed to Bush (1945), science advisor to Franklin D. Roosevelt in the early 1940s. In an essay published in the *Atlantic Monthly* called, "As We Think" Bush set out a plan for a machine he called the *memex*. Bush's idea for the memex called for the creation of a huge database that would allow users to browse efficiently through large amounts of material and make associative connections among documents. These "links" among documents would then be available for other researchers to follow or modify according to their needs. The memex was never actually built, but Bush's vision for linking texts together provided the framework for hypertext authoring systems that became possible with the invention of the computer.

Since the late 1980s, much has been written about hypertext in English studies. Researchers have argued that hypertext stands in marked contrast to traditional writing and the goals of traditional writing instruction. Traditional writing emphasizes the presentation of a clear, coherent thesis supported by examples and illustrations leading to a definitive resolution or closure. Hypertext documents, on the other hand, contain no distinct beginning, middle, or end; the reader is free to follow links in any order he or she chooses. Instead of a single thesis, a hypertext can offer multiple positions and viewpoints privileging none of them. Rather than providing the reader with resolution and closure, hypertext is open-ended, inviting the addition of new links.

Many educators and theorists in English have examined the impact that hypertext has had and could have on reading and writing instruction. These scholars are strong advocates for the positive impact of hypertext in teaching reading and writing. Landow (1992b) made a strong case for a "convergence" of critical theory and technology. In that text and other articles, Landow discussed his work with the Intermedia project at Brown University (probably the most ambitious instructional hypertext project ever undertaken) involving students and faculty in a joint venture to construct a hypertextual knowledge base. Slatin (1990a) argued that hypertext makes the interconnectedness of literary texts obvious and (Slatin, 1988) experimented with students reading and writing hypertext in writing and literature classes. Kaplan and Moulthrop (1990, 1993, 1994) also used hypertext in the classroom and examined the implications this technology has for reading and writing practices. Joyce (1988) found that using a hypertext program as a writing tool in a first-year writing course gave an alternative means of writing to students who had difficulty writing a traditional essay. Bolter (1991) claimed that the electronic writing space, most fully realized in hypertext, mirrors the way the mind works by making visible the connections that exist among ideas.

These theorists argued eloquently for the positive impact that hypertext has had and potentially could have on their students. Much of the work done by these scholars has focused on students reading hypertext. Here, I examine in some detail the work of four students who wrote their own original hypertext documents in a first-year composition course. On close examination of original hypertexts written by composition students, I have found that hypertext is a viable medium for composition instruction. Hypertext can expand and develop many of the goals of traditional writing instruction while offering new modes of composing.

I chose to work with first-year writing students and to focus my attention specifically on how students' writing strategies were changed, challenged, or unchanged by composing in hypertext. I carefully examined the products that the four students created and supplemented my reading of their hypertexts with writing process journals the students kept, interviews that I held with the students, and observations that I made of the students in class. The four students writing hypertext documents (Don, Lisa, Mike, and Jana) were part of a second-semester, first-year writing class and had already spent a semester reviewing and practicing the goals of conventional writing. These students had varied levels of skill and interest in using computers, but none had worked with a hypertext program prior to taking this class.

The hypertext authoring program we worked with was InfoAccess Corp.'s Guide. There exist a number of hypertext programs that have proven useful for writing hypertext webs both for the Mac and the IBM. Toolbook for the IBM is popular in educational settings. Toolbook closely follows the electronic book metaphor in its design. Guide, on the other hand, offers a very different conceptual framework for authoring hypertext. Guide does not use book terminology in describing options that authors can use in constructing a hypertext. A hypertext written using Guide is probably best conceptualized as a "web" of "nodes." "Nodes" are individual pieces of text or graphics that make up the "document set" of a hypertext. To create "links" between "nodes," a writer using Guide turns a word, group of words, or a spot on a graphic element into a "hot word" or "hot spot" on the screen and "links" it to some other text or graphic (node) in the "document set." Once the writer creates such a link, the selected text or graphic will become distinct in appearance from unlinked text on the page.

The three types of "links" available to the writer are expansions, notes, and references. The selected text will change to either bold, underlined, or italicized when the writer creates one of these links. In addition, the mouse pointer, when passed over one of these linked elements on the screen, will turn to an asterisk, a cross-hatch, or a hand, alerting the reader that the highlighted text is linked to something else. Each type of link has a distinct function for showing the relation between the hot word or graphic and the material to which it is linked. An expansion is best suited to hide lengthy pieces of explanatory or detailed text beneath other text in the document. For example, when a writer wants to give more detailed information about a word or concept, he can turn a particular piece of text into an expansion. When the reader clicks the mouse pointer on that text, the detail hidden beneath the highlighted text will appear on the screen. The "hot word" appears in bold to alert the reader familiar with Guide navigation that more information exists beneath the bold text. Expansions can be nested within other expansions so that, in theory, an infinite number of layers can exist below the surface of the document.

The second type of link is the note. Notes are best suited to providing brief definitions or explanatory information about the highlighted text or graphic. For example, a writer who is using a technical term or an uncommon word can provide the reader with an easily accessible definition by making a note for that word. A word that contains a note will appear underlined in the document and the mouse pointer will turn to an asterisk when passed over the underlined text. When the reader clicks the mouse pointer on the underlined text, a pop-up box appears on the screen containing the definition and will remain open as long as the reader keeps the mouse button down.

The third type of link is the reference. A reference can either link a word, phrase, or graphic to another "node" in the hypertext or to another location within the same "node." These links are best suited to establishing relationships between separate documents or parts of large documents. A "hot word" signaling a reference link appears in italics alerting the reader that clicking on that link will take him to another text or another location within the present text. For example, a writer discussing Samuel Taylor Coleridge's "Kubla Khan" could make Coleridge's name into an italicized "hot word" leading to biographical information residing in a separate "node." When the reader clicks the mouse pointer on "Coleridge," he or she will go to the "node" containing the biography.

The links just described can provide authors with sufficient tools to create quite sophisticated hypertexts. The students in my course knew how to create the three kinds of links after 2 weeks of in-class practice.

The following pages describe the similarities and differences that I found between conventional writing and hypertext writing as they appeared in the work of these four students.

CONVENTIONAL WRITING IN HYPERTEXT

A survey of textbooks used in first-year composition classes reveals a set of relatively standard goals for the course. These texts include sections on invention, prewriting, drafting, and revising. Most first-year composition courses tend to focus on theme or thesis writing where students are taught the importance of clearly and coherently presenting an argument or illustrating an idea.

In this section, I look at how students writing hypertext practice many of the same strategies of structuring and organizing their ideas as do students working on conventional writing tasks. The representation of these structures and organizations, however, are markedly different in hypertext writing than in conventional writing. I examine how the hypertexts written by my students were organized in order to express a central idea, how the writers used links as a means of developing and illustrating that central point, and how various pieces of text and graphics function as specific examples of the main idea.

Structure As an Organizing Principle

The hypertext composer, as does the conventional writer, creates a plan or structure that will effectively present the ideas he or she is trying to express in the text. In the following paragraphs, I illustrate how my four students used structure to assist potential readers in understanding the thesis or main idea they were trying to impart.

Don. Don's structure in his hypertext was quite complex in that it allowed for multiple pathways into and through the hypertext. As did the other students, Don provides a "Contents" page as the means of accessing his material. Don begins his hypertext by orienting his readers to the workings of the program. He includes an expansion link at the top of "Contents" that opens up to brief instructions on how the links in his document operate and how to identify them, "Text highlighted in black lettering denotes a reference button to click onto." Don was the only student in the group who provided instructions to his audience. In our interview I asked him why:

> KD: What was the purpose for the Instructions expansion
>   link at the top of your Contents page?
> Don: I thought most people who read it probably wouldn't
>   have seen a hypertext before. They'd want to know
>   what the different kinds of words meant and what they
>   were supposed to do with it. I didn't know when I
>   looked at the practice hypertext we used before we
>   started our own stuff.

Don's sensitivity to the needs of his reader points to a careful thought process of deciding what a reader will need in order to understand the hypertext.

This type of "reader-based" writing is also evident in the structure Don uses to illustrate his thesis. If we look at Don's Contents page (Figure 1.1), we see Don's conception of the organization of the main points in his hypertext. In our interview, I asked him why he included this page, and what he wanted it to accomplish:

> KD: What was the point of using a Contents page?
> Don: I guess I just wanted a place to put links to the main
>   files.
> KD: How did you decide which were the main files?
> Don: I wanted to show the uses that space exploration could
>   have for earth and the report on "Why the Space Station
>   Makes Sense" was my lead text, then the reports on
>   remote sensing and ecology were examples of how
>   space travel could help us on earth.

Figure 1.1. Don's "Contents" page

In the final response just quoted, Don states his thesis "the uses that space exploration could have for earth" and the main supporting points. As we see in the "Contents" page the first half of the list of the contents present us with "Introduction" (which links to "Why the Space Station Makes Sense"), "Remote Sensing," and "Earth's Ecology." These three links present the main idea, discussed in the "Space Station" document, and the links leading to the main supporting ideas. Furthermore, if we look at the diagram (Figure 1.2), a graphic representation of the linking structure of the hypertext, we can see that from the "lead text," "Why the Space Station Makes Sense," each of the other important supporting documents in the hypertext can be accessed. Like conventional writing, Don's hypertext also states a thesis, but does so implicitly rather than explicitly. Rather than the random collection of nodes of information from which readers make meaning, we see that hypertext writers can also make meaning by consciously structuring their material to support a thesis.

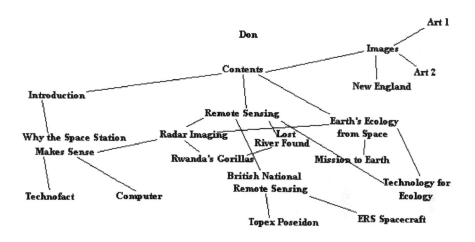

Figure 1.2. Diagram of links in Don's hypertext

Lisa. The structure of Lisa's hypertext is quite simple in contrast to Don's. Lisa includes a Contents page (Figure 1.3) with four reference links: "Introduction," "Genetic Testing," "Narcissus Cloned," and "Hall and Stillman." The rest of the hypertext is made up of four additional files, one for each of the links just listed. The hypertext has five files and nine links. Lisa did not include subordinate files that link from these four texts to further develop those points. Three of the files in turn have a "See Contents" link at the bottom of the page.

In this hypertext, the reader's experience is highly controlled with few choices as to where he or she can move in the document. Much of this effect is, of course, created by the paucity of material in this hypertext compared to Don's hypertext, for example. Despite these shortcomings, we still see a discernable intent in what Lisa has done. She wanted to present a thesis describing the debate on genetic engineering, specifically as it relates to cloning human beings. Although she does not provide much supporting material to develop her ideas, her hypertext structure functions in much the same way as a thesis in conventional writing. Reading through the documents in Lisa's hypertext reveals a focus on the issue of cloning human beings. Each node in the hypertext gives additional perspectives on the topic. Lisa fails to appropriately

Contents

INTRODUCTIONS

GENETIC TESTING

NARCISSUS CLONED

HALL AND STILLMAN

Figure 1.3. Lisa's contents page

illustrate or support the main point. Her hypertext fails as a piece of communication. Like inexperienced writers composing conventional texts who make an assertion without providing sufficient supporting evidence, Lisa only presents a few broad, underdeveloped points.

Lisa had many difficulties with learning and using the Guide program. Adding to her frustrations with the program itself, I found that her attitude toward her task worked against her ability to develop her topic more fully. In the following journal entry, Lisa describes her composing process in creating her hypertext:

> Today I entered a new file into hypertext. I'm finding it a little easier to deal with. There seems to be so many options and 'neat' things to do, but right now I'm just focusing on getting my research from paper into the text. I am setting a goal for myself so I can understand the more complex areas of hypertext.

I found two noteworthy points related to Lisa's development of her thesis. First, she seems overly focused on the technical aspects of the program, perhaps because she felt anxious about that part of the project. She does not seem to know which option to attempt first and ends up frozen in indecision. Her solution is to use only the reference link that she understood in order to "get her research into the text." Rather than work to explore and develop her thesis and use the hypertext form as a format to present those ideas, she wants to find a way to figure out the program.

Second, she describes her writing process as "getting my research from paper into the text." Although Lisa does paraphrase her source material in the pages of her hypertext, each section is only from one source. Unlike Don who provides alternate paths through the individual texts that make up his hypertext, Lisa's text follows a single sequential order. Her composing strategy to "get my research into the text" limits what she can do with her material.

My observations of Lisa in class indicated that she often avoided working on her hypertext. Instead of working on her problems with using hypertext and further developing her thesis during class time, she often asked to go to the library to do research instead. A combination of frustration with the program and ineffective approaches to writing made Lisa's experience with hypertext less than satisfying. I asked her about these problems in my interview with her:

> KD: You expressed some frustration in your journal entries. What frustrated you about the project?
> Lisa: I have been very frustrated because it is not going how I envisioned it.
> KD: How did you envision it?
> Lisa: I'm not really sure but it shouldn't be this hard to learn. I had to do things over too much.

Her expectations for working with hypertext were not met. She found the work much more difficult than she anticipated.

Mike. Mike's hypertext offers the least structured environment of the four student texts. Like Don's hypertext, Mike produced a number of pieces of writing linked together in a complex web. But, if we look at Mike's Contents page (Figure 1.4), we see that he did not provide major categories as Don did. In his journal, Mike described how he envisioned his organization: "I decided on the natural hierarchial format. I started with air and its effects on the environment and then the effects pollution has on the land or ground and then water." In his actual Contents page, however, he does not make this hierarchial format so obvious. His implicit thesis is the impact of pollution on the environment. The main categories on the Contents page are: "Air Pollution," "United States," and "Oceans." "Air Pollution" and "United States" have subcategories listed beneath them that relate to their respective categories. The structure is rather confusing for a reader accustomed to the more formal structure of conventional writing. It is only after reading through the hypertext that the reader understands this organization. Although Mike talks about creating a hierarchy, his text works more like an association of ideas.

If we look at Mike's journal, however, we see that he did not really intend the Contents page as an introduction to the hypertext at all: "I pasted a graphic of Michanglo's [sic] Creation (I downloaded from America Online) this is supposed to be symbolic of the world's environment." A copy of this page is shown in Figure 1.5. In addition to the graphic, the reader can choose a link to Contents or can click on the icon labeled Environment that leads to the document called "Air Pollution." In the fol-

Contents

Air Pollution
        industrial
        automotive
United States
        river
        wetlands
        toxic waste
        greenhouse
Oceans
Signature page

Figure 1.4. Mike's contents page

lowing journal entry, Mike describes how he sees his organization: "On 10\4 I started entering text in the file I named 'Air Pollution' this is supposed to be like an introduction, a place to start off." The Contents page, then, was not the crucial organizing strategy of Mike's hypertext. The "Air Pollution" text provides routes to all the other pieces of the hypertext.

Despite his apparent lack of overt attention to structuring his argument, the associative connections among the files in his hypertext support his thesis almost as effectively as the more careful structure that Don uses. The reader does have to work a little harder to understand Mike's structure than was necessary in working through Don's more careful organization. Browsing through Mike's hypertext, it is clear that his main point is to describe the damage done by pollution to the environment. In Don's hypertext, in contrast, the structure is set forth in the Contents page.

THE ENVIRONMENT

Figure 1.5. Mike's introductory page

Jana. The structure of Jana's hypertext was closer to Lisa's because Jana tried to control how the reader could move through her hypertext. Unlike the other students, however, Jana does not provide a Contents page to her own hypertext. Her Contents page (Figure 1.6) is a list of the titles of the four hypertexts on which the class had worked: "Ocean Life," "Genetics," "Environment," and "Space Exploration." Clicking on "Ocean Life" leads to Jana's own hypertext, specifically to a page on dolphins. "Dolphins," in Jana's hypertext, serves as the anchor for the rest of her files. All the other pages are linked from this page and only from this page, as can be seen by looking at the diagram of her hypertext (Figure 1.7).

Each of the linked files has a text link at the bottom, "Return to Previous Document." The reader can follow only the path that Jana has laid out. The reader clicks on a link in "Dolphins" and arrives at another document in the hypertext. Instead of being able to link to other files in the hypertext from that document, the reader must return to "Dolphins" in order to access another node in the hypertext. Like Lisa's hypertext, Jana's hypertext is rather thin in the amount of material it presents, and the structure of links is uncomplicated, leaving the reader a fairly structured path.

Interestingly, Jana was the most conscious of the difference between hypertext and the kind of writing to which she was accustomed. Jana's other writing assignments in the course were competent, not brilliant or especially complex, but she showed a clear grasp of the essential components of essay writing. She knew how to state a thesis and support it with examples, and she understood the conventions of using an introduction and conclusion. Her knowledge of composing actually worked against her ability to develop her hypertext document. In this excerpt from her journal, Jana describes her hypertext composing process: "I have created some links that I still need to put text into. I think that I am concentrating more on the format of my hyper text [sic] first and then I am going to sit down and enter all the text in." Jana, like Lisa, seems to be caught in an ineffective composing strategy. Instead of deciding how to link files in her hypertext together as she created them, as Mike does, Jana wanted to form a structure first and then add the files into her text. We saw Lisa follow much the same practice with similar results.

In essay writing, the conventions of introduction, conclusion, and thesis/support are well established. Jana focuses somewhat obsessively on the beginning, middle, and end features of writing conventional essays. In the following excerpt from her journal, Jana describes her concern with the differences between hypertext and conventional composing: "I still am finding it hard to stop myself from wanting to create a paper with a beginning and end." She also mentions her concern with these features a number of times in my informal discussions with her in class.

Table of Content

OCEAN LIFE

GENETICS

ENVIRONMENT

SPACE EXPLORATION

Figure 1.6. Jana's contents page

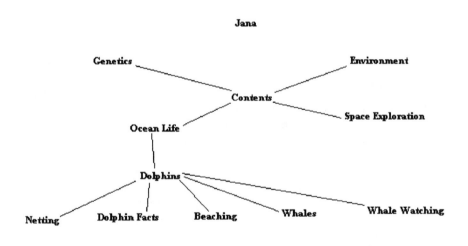

Figure 1.7. Diagram of links in Jana's hypertext

Rose (1985) suggested that writers who come up against writing tasks that do not conform to what they already know how to do, or writers who focus too much on rigid composing rules tend to exhibit a high degree of writer's block. Jana's concern with this difference between hypertext and conventional writing prevented her from trying alternative structures for her material and from generating more text from her sources.

Even though this over concern for beginning, middle, and end may have blocked the development of her hypertext, her document still carried out the assertion of a thesis and some illustration of her ideas. In the following journal entry she describes her intent:

> How did I decide that I was all done? Well, after reviewing all the information that I gathered I decided that I wanted my document to be a [sic] overview of what is causing the dolphin and whale populations to decrease. I could have gone into more detail and explain many more things but it would have taken me a lot more time than we had. I decided to stop where I did because it seemed to end right at the perfect place. After my last document it seemed to really rap [sic] it up nicely.

Her intent in the hypertext was to present an "overview of what is causing the dolphin and whale populations to decrease." She limited her development of this thesis by concluding it in a place that seems to bring closure rather than leaving her readers to find their own closure. Jana succeeded in finding the hypertext version of closure but at the expense of a more fully developed hypertext.

Linking As Illustration

The linking feature of hypertext programs is one of its most important components. Linking allows writers to represent graphically the relation between ideas in their writing. Hypertext linking allows writers more freedom and flexibility in how they present their text than does conventional writing. In conventional writing, each piece of text is used just once in the work even though certain pieces of text could illustrate more than one point. Hypertext allows a single example to be linked to more than one node in the hypertext. Linking in hypertext compares to presenting examples in conventional writing in that links function as pointers to the relations between the ideas in the hypertext, but hypertext can be used to express multiple viewpoints. In the following paragraphs, I illustrate how my students used linking as a means of supporting their ideas.

Don. Don was one of the two students who made numerous, complex links in his hypertext. As described in the last section, the Contents page has links to other key documents in the hypertext and functions to illustrate Don's main idea that space exploration is beneficial to life on earth. In addition to the links from the Contents page, many of the documents are cross-linked. My analysis of Don's hypertext examines a sample of the links that he uses to support his thesis that space exploration will benefit life on earth.

From the Contents page (Figure 1.1), the first link, "Introduction," opens to a page containing two graphics of the space shuttle. Between the two graphics, Don includes two brief paragraphs of text that he generated himself containing a further iteration of his thesis. The first sentence of paragraph one stated: "Earth, **viewed from space,** is a phenomenom [sic] that 20th century folks seem to take for granted." Clicking on the first link on the words "earth viewed from space" opens to a graphic of hurricane Hugo taken from space. A specific illustration of what he stated in the sentence.

In paragraph two Don states:

> A **report,** that I recently read and downloaded, best explains why space exploration should be persued [sic] in an ongoing and comprehensive manner. This report, **Why the Space Station Makes Sense,** shows the high degree of integration of all the disciplines of science with astronomy, space technology, and space exploration.

The text highlighted in bold indicates references in Don's text. Both the references link to the document "Why the Space Station Makes Sense." As we saw in the last section, Don identifies this as his "lead text"; the document that states his main point.

If we now turn to the Space Station document, we find a lengthy text describing the importance of space exploration, Don's thesis. Within that text, he adds crucial links to connect that "lead text" with the other important nodes in the hypertext. In the Space Station document, at the point where the author of that text described how research in space has contributed to the development of technologies on earth, Don designates a piece of text as a link: "The space program has been a key contributor to the information revolution from the very beginning." Clicking on this phrase sends us to a document called "Radar Imaging." If we look at the diagram of Don's hypertext (Figure 1.2), we can see that "Radar Imaging" in turn links to the two main subcategories listed on "Contents," "Remote Sensing," and "Earth's Ecology-From Space." These two topics represent the key areas of benefit that space exploration has for earth in Don's hypertext.

"Remote Sensing" and its associated links introduce the importance of various forms of satellite and other space-based earth-imaging techniques. The documents connected to that node are specific examples of these uses. For example, referring again to the diagram (Figure 1.2), we can see that Radar Imaging, a type of remote sensing, links to a specific example of the use of radar imaging, "Rwanda's Gorillas." The reader encounters this link in the "Radar Imaging" text at the point where the author mentions that radar imaging assisted the "study of heavily forested regions." If we click on that text, we go to the text "Rwanda's Gorillas," which describes how radar imaging was used to track the impact of an influx of human refugees on the Gorilla population. The links from "Earth's Ecology-From Space" focused on the ecological benefits to earth of space exploration and presents many of the same types of effective links as the examples just discussed. Don's hypertext nodes are an effective explication of a thesis and compares favorably in scope and breadth to a well-written, conventional student essay, but offers a richer relational set of ideas.

Jana. Jana's hypertext, as has already been seen, was much less complex than Mike's and Don's. As pointed out in the previous section, Jana had fewer individual files than did Mike and Don. Fewer documents, of course, leave fewer opportunities to make links among texts. "Contents" in Jana's text did not provide a list of the contents of her hypertext, but presented links to the other students' projects in the class, including a link to her own material.

Clicking on "Ocean Life" opens the first page of Jana's hypertext, a document entitled "Dolphins." "Dolphins" serves as a foundation for the rest of Jana's hypertext. From "Dolphins" the reader can link to each of the other documents in the set, although each subsequent document only goes back to "Dolphins" rather than cross-linking to other texts. If we look at the diagram of Jana's text (Figure 1.7), we see the possible paths the reader could take. "Dolphins" itself was a text written by Jana providing an overview of the dolphin situation. Within this text, highlighted words lead the reader to one of the other texts in the document set. Each of the linked texts only contains a link to return to "Dolphins."

Jana's thesis, as she states in her journal, is an "overview of what is causing the dolphin and whale populations to decrease." The five links she incorporates into the "Dolphins" text serve to support and illustrate this thesis. The first link on "netting dolphins" opens to a set of drawings illustrating netting practices that are dangerous to dolphins. The illustration serves as an example of the point made in the text. If the reader clicks on the first graphic, it will open the second graphic, which in turn links back to the first graphic. From there, the phrase "Return to Previous Document" leads back to "Dolphins," where the reader can proceed through Jana's introductory text and click on additional phrases.

The second link in "Dolphins" is the word "dolphins," which opens a text called "Dolphin Facts," listing information about dolphins. This link provides examples to further what she is saying in the "Dolphins" text at the point the word "dolphins" appears. A link at the bottom of the page "Return to previous document" takes the reader back to "Dolphins." The third link in "Dolphins" on "beaching" opens a document on the phenomenon of whale and dolphin beaching. The fourth link on the word "whales" links to a discussion of whales. The final link in "Dolphins" is "whale watching," which opens the "Whale Watching" document describing how these cruises can help save the whales. At the bottom of the page is a "Return to previous document." At the bottom of "Dolphins" itself is a link "Return to table of content."

The "Whale Watching" document serves an important purpose. It presents a possible solution to the problem of the decline of the dolphin and whale populations. The other files describe the problem. Jana tries to make the hypertext conform to the standards of conventional essays that, as she describes them, have a beginning and an end. She provided a limited amount of material that she structured very rigidly in order to lead the reader through the hypertext following *her* beginning, middle, and end. Her excessive concern with the form of the hypertext prevented her from developing more nodes of material and linking them in more sophisticated ways.

Lisa. Lisa's hypertext is also limited in what it accomplishes. As I already discussed, Lisa's hypertext consisted of five documents that had limited cross-linking. Even though Lisa does not provide the quantity of material that Don and Mike did, the links she does provide present various aspects of her main point, but none of them give further development of any of the specific points raised in the nodes.

The diagram of Lisa's hypertext (Figure 1.8) demonstrates the simple progression through the texts that she provided. The first document is "Contents" listing reference links to each of the four other files in the hypertext: "Introduction," "Genetic Testing," "Narcissus Cloned," and "Hall and Stillman." If we click on "Introduction," we go to a file containing a brief overview of the topic of genetic engineering that Lisa composed using some of the source material she had gathered. In this overview, she asserts her main point describing the state of genetic engineering as it relates specifically to cloning. Her intention in the hypertext is to describe the debate on the issue of cloning humans. The links from "Introduction" and from document to document provide additional aspects of genetic engineering as they relate to cloning.

There are two links in "Introduction." One is a navigational link, "See Contents," which also appears on each of the other documents. The other is a link from the words "creative discoveries" to a text called "Genetic Testing." "Genetic Testing" provides a summary of a *Scientific American* article on the state and uses of genetic testing. Lisa uses this text to illustrate how genetic testing can work to choose traits for cloning.

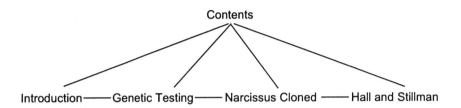

Figure 1.8. Diagram of links in Lisa's hypertext

From "Genetic Testing" are two textual reference links. The first on the word "researchers" links to a document called "Hall and Stillman" where Lisa describes the Hall-Stillman experiment, the cloning of the first human embryo. The last words of the "Hall and Stillman" text, "womb to produce a child," link back to the "Contents" page. Lisa does not provide a link back to "Genetic Testing," which makes it a bit cumbersome for the reader to return to that document to follow the second link. The second link in the "Genetic Testing" page, "individual's," links to the document called "Narcissus Cloned" where Lisa described the ethics involved in the cloning debate. "Narcissus cloned" contains only the link "See Contents" at the bottom.

Lisa, like inexperienced and underconfident writers writing conventional texts, presented a superficial, underdeveloped document. Hypertext will not make unskilled writers effective composers on its own.

Mike. Mike's hypertext, like Don's, is also quite complex with several documents linked through multiple paths. Although Mike does not employ the same careful structure that Don uses, his links still effectively illustrate his thesis. Mike's thesis describes the impact of pollution on natural resources. He combines his source material into paraphrases and summaries and creates nodes of material linked together to support his main topic. As seen in the last section Mike provides a "Contents" page, but it does not function as the organizing document of the hypertext. He identifies the document called "Air Pollution" as the introduction to his hypertext.

A few examples of Mike's use of links as illustrations for his thesis follow. If we look at the diagram (Figure 1.9), we see that once the

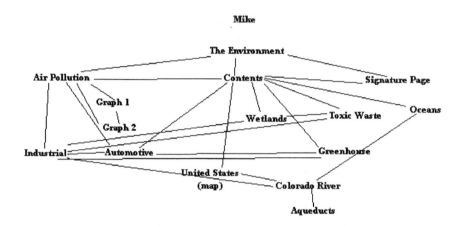

Figure 1.9. Diagram of links in Mike's hypertext

reader follows the link from the environment to "Air Pollution" all the other texts in the hypertext can be accessed. "Air Pollution," Mike's introductory text, has three links that provide information about air pollution.

The first on the word "industrial" opens a document by that name describing the impact of industrial pollution on air quality. The "Industrial" text serves as an illustration of a cause of air pollution. If we click on the phrase "see air pollution" at the bottom of the "Industrial" text, we return to the "Air Pollution" page and can choose the second subtopic "automotive." The word "automotive" in "Air Pollution" links to a text by that name describing the impact of car exhaust on air quality. Both the "automotive" and "industrial" links present examples of types of air pollution.

The links to "industrial" and "automotive" are accessible from the "Air Pollution" page or directly from "Contents." Also, under "Air Pollution" is a third reference link from the words "see graphs." This link calls up two graphical charts, so the reader can compare air pollution levels in 1983 and 1993. The graphs are in two different files; the reader clicks on the graph of 1993 (Graph 1) to open the graph of 1983 (Graph 2). Clicking on the 1983 graph takes the reader back to the word "graphs" in the "Air Pollution" document. The final reference link toward the bottom of "Air Pollution" on "E.P.A." opens a document called "Eco Groups," which is itself a link to a list of projects dealing with environmental protection efforts. As do the other links on this page, "see graphs" and "E.P.A." provide descriptive information about the main point of the "Air Pollution" page.

A number of Mike's other links function to illustrate his thesis on the problem of environmental pollutants. Although his links fulfill the function of explicating the thesis of the hypertext, the structure of the links follows a very different order than Don's, which we explore in the next section.

ALTERNATIVE WRITING STRATEGIES

In the last section, we looked at how hypertext writing can carry out some of the same practices as conventional writing. Despite its "nonsequential" structure, hypertext can, as does conventional writing, present and illustrate a main point or thesis. In this section I explore the unique features that hypertext composing offers writers. These new features, combined with the writing strategies described in the last section, make hypertext writing an expanded form of conventional writing that offers writers the opportunity to present text in an alternative form.

Associative Writing and Hierarchical Writing

Bolter (1991) made a distinction between hierarchical or conventional writing with the notion of what he called *topographic writing*. He traced the origins of his term *topographic writing*. Originally, the word *topography* was used in the description of a place. The term then evolved to refer to mapping and charting. In Bolter's view, topographic writing makes visible the multiple relations among ideas inherent in "verbal ideas." Bolter saw electronic writing, particularly hypertext, as both "visual and verbal." As Bolter described it, "It is not the writing of a place, but rather a writing *with* places, spatially realized topics" (p. 25). Topographic writing is a distinct characteristic of hypertext. Conventional writing, or hierarchical writing as Bolter described it, uses paragraphs, sections, and chapters to impose "order on verbal ideas." These "verbal ideas," in Bolter's scheme, attempt to "subvert" the author-imposed order of paragraphs, and so on. The associative links of hypertext, depicted topographically, make visible "alternative organizations that lie beneath the order of pages and chapters that a printed text presents to the world" (p. 22). Bolter further claimed that although the computer is not necessary for topographic writing (it can be done in conventional print), it is only in the computer environment where topographic writing "becomes a natural, and therefore also a conventional, way to write" (p. 25). In the following pages, I look at the associative links as seen topographically in the hypertexts of two of my students. Don and Mike used such associative links to provide alternative paths through their material.

Mike. Mike's hypertext was the most associative of the four hypertexts. As discussed in the previous sections, Mike does not use the same careful structuring of ideas as does Don. Figure 1.9 shows the topographic depiction of Mike's hypertext. Most of the nodes depicted in Figure 1.9 are not related in a hierarchical sequence. "United States," "Colorado River," "Wetlands," "Toxic Waste," "Greenhouse," "Oceans," and "Signature Page" all exist in the same plane, so to speak. These nodes cross-link and illustrate points from one to the next, but none of them function as a specific subordinate example of another node.

One of Mike's journal entries illuminated his attitude toward the process of hypertext composing: "As the text unfolded on the screen, note buttons started to appear, and other reference buttons." For Mike, the creation of the hypertext document was almost an automatic process. Links simply happened as "natural" outgrowths of the texts and graphics with which he was working. In Bolter's scheme, Mike's process of hypertext development is how topographic writing should work.

My discussions with Mike and my observations of him in class showed that he did little planning or formal structuring of the hypertext. The way he describes the "unfolding of text," and so on indicates the intuitive process that he followed in creating links in the text. He associated ideas rather than creating a carefully planned structure.

The downside to such a composing strategy, however, is that the meaning of the text is much harder to follow for readers accustomed to more traditionally structured texts. Perhaps for those of us thoroughly schooled in reading conventional text, it does take more work to understand associative writing. Despite the potential difficulties with associative writing, the writer's ability to link nodes of information to multiple texts allows a more complex representation of ideas. I suggest this higher level of complexity may be a more likely cause of reading difficulties.

Don. Don's hypertext also provides examples of associative writing, but not to the degree seen in Mike's hypertext. If we compare Figures 1.2 and 1.9, we can see the general top-to-bottom (general-to-specific) organization of nodes in Don's hypertext. In contrast, the movement in Mike's hypertext is lateral rather than from general to specific. Don's text, however, does illustrate the alternative representations of "verbal ideas" that exist beneath conventional text that Bolter described.

A reader approaching Don's hypertext can follow the links in a fairly hierarchical way by using the Contents page as the organizing force. The reader can choose the first link on "Introduction," follow that text to "Why the Space Station Makes Sense," to the documents "Techno Fact" and "Computer" that illustrate points of that text. The reader can then return to "Contents" and choose the next selection on the list, "Remote Sensing," and follow the subordinate links from that text. A reader could visit·all the documents in the text by reading through "Contents" as listed. In this way, the hypertext works much like a conventional essay.

The associative links that Don provides makes an alternative reading(s) possible. For example, if we follow the Introduction to "Why the Space Station Makes Sense," we can then link by association to "Radar Imaging," one of the subcategories under "Remote Sensing." From there, we can link to the third category of "Earth's Ecology-From Space." The associative links topographically illustrate relations among the ideas across categories, the spatial relationships among the ideas represented. Such an alternative organization enriches the development of the thesis. In a conventional text, these relations among ideas from different parts of the text require greater cognitive effort on the part of the reader to understand. In a conventional text, writers cannot show every connection among the ideas in a text and still form a clear, readable piece of writing. Because hypertext links are visible, hypertext writers can create larger numbers of connections among diverse parts of a hypertext that are much easier to see than such representations in conventional essays.

Synthesis Writing

The second-semester composition class I taught required that students learn to use research and incorporate source material into their essays. In composing hypertexts, my students used a combination of traditional library sources (books and journals) and Internet sources. Incorporating diverse writings into an essay is what Spivey (1997) referred to as "discourse synthesis." According to Spivey, discourse synthesis is a combination of reading and writing. Writers read source texts keeping in mind their writing goals while transforming the writing of others to help achieve their own writing goals. For beginning writers, such synthesis is often difficult because it requires that they combine varied sources along with their own prior knowledge to create a new representation of ideas.

Palumbo and Prater (1992) suggested we look at synthesis writing as it relates to the possible goals of hypertext/hypermedia. Palumbo and Prater defined synthesis writing as not just a combining of information from different sources but "the creation of a new whole from parts" (p. 69). Such knowledge-making in the context of creating and following paths has been identified as an important benefit for both readers and writers of hypertext.

In conventional writing, authors cannot string together whole texts directly quoted from sources or parts of texts and produce a successful piece of writing. Because of the sequential nature of conventional writing, writers must compile sources and then generate new prose to create a meaningful text for an audience. In hypertext writing, on the other hand, writers can show relation between sources by creating links that illustrate the connections among those ideas.

All four of my students use links as a form of synthesis. Two of them, Lisa and Jana, use traditional synthesis writing where the individual nodes of their hypertexts were made up of prose that they generated from their reading of source material. Mike practices conventional synthesis writing in most of his hypertext nodes, but also quotes some sources directly. Don links together whole texts or pieces of texts quoted directly from external sources; he includes only a few sentences that he composed himself. As shown previously, the students use hypertext links to illustrate points in their texts or to point to an association of ideas. In conventional synthesis writing, writers must make choices about what to include and what to reject from source material. The effect is that some ideas from external sources are emphasized or pointed to in order to further the writer's thesis. In hypertext synthesis, writers need to decide precisely where to place the target of a link in a given node. Mike's and Don's hypertexts were the most successful, probably because they were more complex than the other students in using links to create synthesis.

Mike. As already seen, Mike uses numerous associative links in his hypertext to demonstrate the relations among the nodes he incorporates into his document. Several of the links point to specific parts in the target document that connect more precisely to the part of the text we have linked from than the entire target document. Looking at the first paragraph of the document labeled "Toxic Waste," we see the words "wetland contamination" italicized. The italics indicate a reference link. Clicking on the highlighted words opens the document labeled "Wetlands." We do not arrive at the top of the text but at the beginning of Paragraph 6, which begins "In doing research for this paper I discovered that the effects of developmental pollutants on wetlands are awe-

some." He continues by describing some of those affects and their causes. The precise passage that Mike chose to emphasize here gives the
reader specific information on wetland contamination, the highlighted
words from "Toxic Waste." The beginning part of "Wetlands" describes
what a wetland is and efforts aimed at preserving them; the problem of
contamination is not introduced until the sixth paragraph. The link
emphasizes that precise relation between the link and its target rather
than just making a link to the beginning of the document and letting the
reader find the relevant part. Mike uses several other links of this type to
emphasize relationships among particular parts of his hypertext.

Don. Don uses this same device to create precise pointers to the
relations among ideas in the various documents that he chose to include.
Don's use of this kind of synthesis is more extensive than Mike's. Mike
only uses 5 such links, whereas Don uses 12. Turning to Paragraph 4 of
the document labeled "Lost River Found," we see the words "it could
lead to the discovery of important new sources of water" in italics
denoting a reference link. Clicking on that link opens the document
"Technology for Ecology" in the middle of the first paragraph. The reader sees the text beginning "In the United States, the average person uses
approximately 160 gallons of water each day." The passage goes on to
describe the discovery of water recycling systems used to conserve
water during space travel. There is a return link to "Lost River Found"
within that paragraph on the word "water."

As many of the other characteristics of hypertext writing that we
have examined in this chapter, hypertext synthesis writing involves
many of the same cognitive demands as conventional synthesis writing
as described by Palumbo and Prater. In conventional synthesis writing,
the writer must read and comprehend the source texts, decide what to
include in order to move toward the desired goals of the writing task,
and fit the source material into the context of what he or she already
knows. The hypertext synthesis writer must do these same things. In
addition, he or she must decide how links to specific parts of nodes will
advance the goals of the writing task, and how to employ useful navigation devices in the hypertext so that the reader will not lose track of the
purpose of the composition. Using pieces of text directly quoted from
sources works in hypertext because the links make apparent the connections that the conventional writer would make through generating his or
her own text based on outside sources.

CONCLUSION

The issues I raised here from the readings of my students' work leave much to think about as we consider the impact this new technology will have on writing. The way Don chose to approach the assignment clearly challenges some of the assumptions we make about what constitutes writing. Although Don did not synthesize information in the traditional way that we assume students will when writing essays, he did employ many strategies of traditional composing: linking ideas and concepts, using examples and illustrations, and synthesis through linking. His enthusiasm for the usefulness of the project he worked on forces us to take the alternative composing methods this student chose seriously. Lisa, on the other hand, had serious difficulties in working with the tools available in hypertext and could not seem to effectively employ either traditional composing methods or hypertext composing methods.

We, as writing professionals, need to look critically at the impact that technology will have on our profession so that we can adapt the uses of technology in teaching writing to best serve our students' needs. The choice between hypertext and conventional writing should not be an either-or decision. Clearly, hypertext will not replace conventional writing. Students will still need a thorough grounding in the processes of conventional writing in addition to instruction in the new options that hypertext has to offer.

Chapter 2

The Limitations of Hypertext in the Composition Classroom

MaryLynn Saul
Worcester State College

Hawisher and Selfe (1991b) advised that "[w]riting instructors who hope to function effectively in these new electronic classrooms must assess ways in which the use of computer technology might shape, for better and worse, their strategies for working with students" (p. 55). Such assessment continues today with new programs, including programs facilitating hypertext, which has been promised to bring exciting changes for the writing process. Landow (1994b) predicted that, "this new information technology [hypertext] has the power to reconfigure our culture's assumptions about textuality, authorship, creative property, education, and a range of other issues" (p. 32). Landow praised the characteristics of "multivocality, open-endedness, multilinear organization, greater inclusion of nontextual information, and fundamental reconfiguration of authorship, including ideas of authorial property, and of status relations in the text" (p. 36). He also asked the question, "What will the critic and theorist of literature do about hypertext?"

I also ask, "What will the teacher of composition do about hypertext?" Although not referring to teaching specifically, Kaplan and Moulthrop (1993) asserted that,

> we maintain that the representation of ideas through advanced tech-
> nologies [such as hypertext] still requires the production of text; it is
> still *composition*. This type of composition situates language—spo-
> ken, written, and iconographic—in a much richer context than the
> typed or word-processed essay can provide. A course in multimedia
> composition would still do the work of rhetoric, the critical study of
> semiotics in action, but it would do so in a broader technological
> context. (p. 264, emphasis in original)

Composition it may still be, but hypertext alters the techniques required
to be a successful writer. Hypertext may be described as a web of boxes
containing text that have been linked by the author. In reading the web,
a reader can follow one link from various choices that the writer has created, and thus the reader jumps from one box of text to another, in an
order determined only by the particular choices that reader makes.

Because hypertext does alter some techniques of writing and
reading, instructors may ask what type of composition is needed to
teach students for the future. Kaplan and Moulthrop cautioned against
an old-fashioned attitude, warning that "[i]f teachers of rhetoric and
communication embrace an exclusive, old-time print literacy, we could
see the computer put to work in writing courses as little more than a
rather expensive typewriter" (p. 266) and further that a "print-only
approach would also have dangerous consequences for our intellectual
development as a profession. If as teachers of literacy we allow ourselves to be defined in terms of one narrowly conceived skill, we shall be
opting out of an important set of cultural transformations" (p. 267).
Nevertheless, if we as teachers use the new technology, we must keep in
mind that we are teaching something new and different than we have
previously been teaching. What should we teach about the new technology and to what purpose?

In considering these questions, I analyzed my use of projects
using hypertext in the composition classroom in contrast to projects
using a conventional essay format to determine if the hypertext format
was as effective in meeting the goals of the class as was the conventional
one. In my case study, I used a hypertext project in two sections of freshman English at The Ohio State University (OSU) at the Columbus campus and a conventional paper project in two sections of the same course
at OSU at the Marion campus, all during the 1994-1995 academic year.
The two campuses are quite different, with approximately 55,000 students on the Columbus campus and 1,000 students on the Marion campus. Not only do the numbers contrast, but the students themselves
vary. In my sections on main campus, nearly all the students were fresh-
men, most immediately out of high school. There were a few (4 out of
20) minority students in each of these sections, primarily African

American and Asian American. In my sections on the Marion campus, many of the students (around half or more) were "nontraditional," or students who were returning after a number of years in the workforce. Many were single parents; all were white. The students' skills also varied. In my classes on main campus, the students ranged from very capable writers to some with moderate organizational and argumentational problems. In my classes at the Marion campus, there was a larger range of abilities from high school students who were getting a head start on college (including one who graduated that spring as valedictorian) and who were very capable writers to many who had just taken remedial writing courses. One student was even retaking the course because she had not passed the previous quarter.

In order to examine the effectiveness of hypertext, I used a variety of methods including observing the groups interacting in class, analyzing the quality of the finished projects, and an informal survey on students' attitudes toward the project. My main goal in teaching freshman composition is to teach students three main skills: to write a clear thesis statement, to maintain a consistent focus on this thesis, and to support the thesis with logical arguments. Obviously, my focus is on writing traditional essays, which was the focus of the writing program at OSU when I started teaching the class in 1986, and continues to be the preference there. I also believe that the class is intended to prepare students to write essays for other classes during their college career, and I have assumed that professors teaching those classes expect their students to write in this traditional form. I hoped that hypertext would add an interesting and fun strategy for working on these goals. I also thought hypertext, because of its function of creating links between pieces of writing, might help students see the connections in the different sections of their writing. In other words, I hoped that students would realize that one paragraph can have logical connections to more than one of the other points they are making, and that they have the choice of which connection they want to emphasize when writing a linear argument. Therefore, I hoped that hypertext would enable students to look at traditional arguments in new ways.

For the two sections that used the hypertext format, the reaction from the students was quite positive overall, despite frustration over learning a new program (as is discussed in depth later). All but one student responding to my informal survey on attitudes stated they felt favorably about the project and appreciated learning a new computer program, or appreciated familiarizing themselves more with the computers. This is consistent with the attitude of students in all the classes I have taught in computer labs who have expressed the desire to be computer literate and to keep current in the new programs.

However, after teaching both the hypertext project and the conventional project, I have begun to question how useful this program is in a freshman composition classroom. The students did work hard at making connections; however, the other goals seem to have been lost in the excitement and frustration of learning a new computer program.

NATURE OF THE COURSE

The course I taught was freshman composition, which is a five-credit course required of all incoming freshman, in either of two versions: 110, which is focused on argumentative essays; and 111, which is focused on responding to literature. Because OSU is on the quarter system, the course lasts 10 weeks. Typically four papers of 500 to 600 words are required during the quarter, and each paper undergoes usually three to four drafts. At least one rough draft is read and commented on by the instructor, and at least one draft is read by classmates. Student readers may be directed to comment on specific aspects of the writing. I commonly ask students to read for the focus, thesis, and support. The class also consists of reading and discussing essays by professional writers in order to examine writers' purposes and techniques. The focus of the discussions is on why the writers are successful or unsuccessful in conveying their ideas. The desirability of multiple drafts is explained in the Freshman English Program handbook (O'Hare, 1986-1987) for new instructors of 110, which I received when I first started teaching the course:

> One of the most important skills taught in English 110 is revision. In order to encourage students to develop the habit of critically-examining the prose they produce, many teachers of English 110 build into their syllabi a revision day that precedes the submission of each out-of-class essay done in the course. This is an effective means of getting students to regard writing as a process rather than as a product that is finished with the completion of a first draft. (p. 6)

There are two main reasons I require students to read and comment on each other's drafts. The first is to give the students the benefit of actual readers' reactions, readers who may not respond in the way the student writers expected. The second reason for this exercise is to improve the skills of students in critically examining writing in progress. The handbook also recommends using journals, freewriting, and critical responses to the assigned reading. Although my copy of the handbook is several years old and the writing program has changed in some ways, for instance by including more collaborative writing, the grading standards and the emphasis on revision have remained constant in the freshman English course.

The final draft of each conventional paper is typed and turned in along with all rough drafts for a grade. My methods of analysis of the writing of each group was based on the minimal composition skills as stated in the departmental handbook:

> a. An essay must present a clear central idea which provides focus for the composition.
> b. An essay must be clearly organized; logical development of thought must be readily discernible.
> c. Paragraphs within a composition must be unified, coherent, and adequately developed. They should contribute to the development of thought in the essay.
> d. An essay must offer supporting details which make the central idea clear and convincing.
> e. An essay must demonstrate a student's ability to use the language well; choice of words must be appropriate and specific. (p. 3)

This is what I always use as grading standards for "conventional" papers, meaning papers that are given to me on paper, typed, double-spaced, with 1-inch margins, written in a linear fashion with a definite introduction, body, and conclusion. Obviously, these standards were more difficult to apply, and in some cases simply did not apply, to the hypertext writing. The second skill, for example, on logical development and organization, can apply to hypertext, but in an entirely different way. Although organization in a conventional essay means the division of ideas into paragraphs and the order in which ideas are presented, in hypertext there is no predetermined order to read the boxes of text. A reader can jump around between boxes in a variety of patterns that the writer may or may not have anticipated. In addition, the "central idea" referred to in the first and fourth skills may or may not apply to hypertext. Because the text is broken up into multiple sections, and because the reader can read these sections in multiple patterns, hypertext seems to invite multivocality or various interpretations of the subject. What would appear disjointed and contradictory in a conventional essay can appear "logical" in hypertext.

Despite these challenges to assessment, I did analyze all projects, both hypertext and conventional, according to three measurements: focus, style of prose, and logic of argument. For focus, I expected both the conventional papers and the hypertext webs to concentrate on one particular idea, for example the advantages versus disadvantages of RU 486 (the "abortion pill"). Straying from this focus, for either format, would include providing much more background on how the pill works than is needed to evaluate the benefits and dangers of the medicine. By style of prose, I refer to the last composition skill previously listed. Whether the text is one continuous essay, or a box in a hypertext web, I expected students to use effective and specific word choice, using a minimum of clichés and awkward phrasing. In considering the logic of student arguments, I expected students to propose reasonable connections between cause and effect, and to use concrete evidence such as examples or statistics to support their statements. In the hypertext webs, this type of argument was most evident in individual boxes supporting a particular position on the topic.

ASSIGNMENT FOR THE PROJECT

For the hypertext project, students were required to choose and research a particular type of technology they thought needed to be stopped or restricted (see the assignment sheet in Appendix A). However, the topic itself was basically the same for each project, and both groups read the same essays, including a chapter from Mary Shelley's *Frankenstein*, and an article by Grossman advising readers, "Don't Just Say Yes to Technology." We also discussed as a class, criteria for weighing benefits against possible harm for any type of scientific research, including moral, financial, and health considerations. Because the topic was the same, some topics, such as sex change operations, were chosen by both hypertext and conventional groups. The main difference was the computer programs used by each group and the format the finished projects would take.

As previously stated, it became difficult to apply the same class procedure and standards to the hypertext project; however, I attempted to maintain continuity with the conventional papers that the students wrote for other assignments in the class. Although the project was obviously a significant departure from previous papers, primarily due to the need to learn a new computer program, I wanted the basic procedure of planning, writing, and revising to be maintained. I tried to keep the practice of revision built into the hypertext project by meeting with each group to look at the project and to allow them to ask questions. This served as the substitute for the rough draft the instructor usually reads. I also included a day where the groups viewed each other's projects, and could leave comments, in order to provide students with reactions of actual readers. The hypertext program used in the class was Storyspace, published by Eastgate Systems. Class time was provided to view sample hypertext webs and to practice the techniques of using the program before the project was begun.

In order to determine the students' attitudes toward the project and the new program, I required them to submit an informal survey at the same time as their finished projects (see Appendix C). I asked them to answer four basic questions: "How did each member contribute?" (in order to determine if contributions were equal); "What were the strengths and weakness of your project?" (in order to require them to analyze their own work); "What suggestions do you have for the next time I teach this project?" (in order to determine if any changes needed to be made); and finally, "What did you learn about writing?" (in order to determine if this project did in fact teach students anything about the writing process). I also asked them to suggest a grade for their project because I wanted them to look at their own writing critically. Naturally, no one suggested a grade lower than a B. Although I did not automatically give them the grade they requested, I did take into consideration their justification for the grade.

Even if I had not attempted to provide continuity in terms of procedure with the other assignments, I believe the students would have sought it for themselves. The students appeared to have difficulty in letting go of the conventional aspects of essays, such as introduction and conclusion. In fact, many groups included sections named "introduction" and "conclusion" even though I emphasized in class that in hypertext the reader can begin and end anywhere. Nevertheless, several groups seemed to want to control where the reader began and ended even if they could not control the path of reading the individual sections. This tendency of the students seems to defeat one purpose of writing in hypertext, which is allowing readers more choices.

For the sections of freshman composition that wrote conventional essays, I used the same basic topic (see the assignment sheet in Appendix B). I also required them to submit an informal survey with their projects, with the same questions as were required of the hypertext group (although I did not ask them to suggest a grade for their project, because previous students did not really analyze the merits to a significant degree). The number of group members was approximately the same for both the hypertext and the conventional groups; however, I assigned group members for the hypertext project and allowed students in the conventional project to choose their own groups. My usual practice is to assign groups, but one class, especially, on the Marion campus had some personality conflicts in groups assigned for other projects. Wishing to avoid any major group conflicts, I departed from my normal routine and allowed the students to choose their own groups.

CONCERNS ABOUT COLLABORATION

An interesting aspect of the survey results is that both groups expressed frustration. Half the students from the conventional project reported that the group project was difficult to do, whereas 9 out of 30 students from the hypertext project said they felt frustration during the project as shown in Figure 2.1. However, the source of the frustration was different for the two groups. Hypertext group members experienced frustration due mostly to the introduction of a new computer program they needed to master at the same time that they needed to research and write their webs, whereas the conventional group experienced difficulty in coordinating the schedules of group members in order to meet as a group (although I did provide some time for groups to work in class) and in working through differences in opinion about the subject of the project. Actually, I noticed from class observations that all the classes had problems coordinating busy schedules. Because most students, at both campuses, work as well as attend a full load of classes, scheduling meetings is always difficult. The conventional group may have commented more on this problem than the hypertext group because for the latter group the difficulty of learning the new computer program was so great it overshadowed the scheduling conflicts. Also, hypertext group members found ways of dividing projects and working individually more often, rather than needing to do all the work together. It may be that the idea that each member was responsible for writing different sections contributed to the idea of working separately.

In assigning the hypertext project, I strongly encouraged groups to take a group stand on the research subject. For instance, two of the hypertext groups chose as a topic the controversy over the drug RU-486, and I encouraged them to present their project from either a pro or con position. Both groups chose to take a pro stance on the subject, although one group was more successful than the other in arguing and presenting evidence for that position. Despite the potential for disagreement on the group's position on its topic, no one in the hypertext group expressed problems with disagreements among group members. The hypertext form itself apparently allowed for the variety of opinions within a group without conflict. Johnson-Eilola (1994) asserted that this possibility is one of the main advantages to using hypertext assignments:

> In a collaborative hypertext the preservation of multiple voices—
> especially when *collaborative writing* indicates the maintenance of
> individual (but internally and externally connected) voices—might
> be one way in which students can make their own voices part of the
> conversation. (pp. 214-215, emphasis in original)

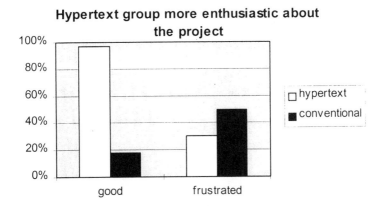

Figure 2.1. Hypertext group more enthusiastic about the project

One hypertext group demonstrated the possibility for this allowance for different voices within the group most obviously because they assigned certain members to answer the opinion section for each issue within the research topic, which was genetic engineering (much too broad of a topic of course). In one area, the group even included two contradictory opinion sections because there was disagreement about the subtopic.

This scheme works beautifully in hypertext, but cannot work so smoothly in a paper that is expected to be linear and to present a unified position. Even in papers where pros and cons on the topic are presented, usually the arguments against a writer's position are presented in such a way as to show the limitations or flaws in that position, thus reinforcing the main argument. However, in a group project where two members disagree on the point, neither member wants to have his or her position presented as the one that is discounted. This predicament is presumably what led to the frustration in the conventional group, who had to pick one point of view in spite of differing feelings among group members.

The conventional group also experienced frustration over basic techniques of managing group work effectively, and therefore seemed less enthusiastic about the project overall than the hypertext group. Although I am sympathetic to this group's frustration, I do not consider this a reason to stop using group projects. Ede and Lunsford (1985) wrote extensively on collaborative writing, and I agree with their summation that "In spite of the very real problems associated with successful group writing projects, the benefits of such writing seem to us to fully justify its use" (p. 126). I will not deny that writing as a group can be challenging and at times frustrating; however, the social skill of working as a team is a valuable one for students to learn. Ede and Lunsford surveyed working professionals, including consulting engineers, chemists, psychologists, managers, and technical writers, in order to determine the amount of team work required on their jobs. Of the 530 people responding to the survey, "87% reported that they have written as part of a team or group" (p. 122). Furthermore, more than 50% of the respondents viewed this type of writing positively, with 45% viewing it as "productive" and 14% as "very productive" (59% combined). Therefore, the skill, however challenging, is one our students will very likely need on the job. Because the conventional group reported problems with this skill, I infer that these students actually confronted the difficulties of group work and were forced to attempt to solve problems of collaboration, whereas the hypertext group could avoid some of this tension, and avoid the opportunity to learn more about collaborating, by dividing up the work so that each member wrote separate sections that might express opposing opinions.

Although I do not believe the students in the hypertext group learned much about collaboration, I do believe they learned something about research. Namely, they learned how to find information and how to incorporate this information into their writing. This learning was due to the structure of the assignment, because individual groups chose topics that they were interested in but knew little about, and was not due to the computer program they used. Thus, because the topic was the same, both the hypertext group and the conventional group learned this skill.

In deciding whether to continue to use group projects despite the potential for frustration, the advantage of having differing viewpoints should be considered. Although this was one of the main areas of frustration for my students in the conventional group, I have told my students in business writing (where collaborative writing is used for roughly half of the writing assignments) that this very difference of opinion is one of the advantages to working as a group. In fact, Ede and Lunsford advised teachers to assign groups in order to mix "ability levels, sexes, leadership qualities, etc." based on research that finds that "the most effective groups generally have members with a variety of viewpoints and skills" (p. 124).

One of my groups in business writing in fact found this to be true as group members struggled with an assignment in which they had to choose among five candidates to recommend for a promotion. Each group member was required to bring to class a memo supporting one of the candidates. In one group there was strong disagreement as to which candidate to choose as the students debated the pros and cons of each candidate. By the end of class they had finally agreed on one candidate, and they told me that this had been a difficult process, but on the other hand, they had very little to do in planning the group memo because they had covered all those points in the debate. Composing the memo for them was a much more straight forward task of typing out the arguments they had already made, whereas other groups were still working on forming the arguments supporting their choice.

None of the groups in the conventional project reported a similar experience, but they did have to meld together sections written by different members, and they did have to debate and choose a group perspective. In some cases, the positive experience of the business writing class was not duplicated in the conventional project because some group members had unbending personalities and dominated their groups. This may also be because this project was the only graded group project in the class, whereas in the business writing course the groups had learned to compromise with each other through several group projects before they worked on the recommendation. Nevertheless, conventional group members discussed their opinions on their topics frequently and learned to compromise (except for the two groups where one member dominated), whereas the hypertext group just added another section to accommodate a dissenting opinion. Although hypertext does have the advantage of allowing group members to express their differing opinions, because the students did not have to agree or compromise, there was less incentive for the members to really understand or even listen to each other's ideas. In other words, although a "good hypertext" may indeed include contrasting ideas, the students have not benefited from having to defend their own ideas.

A QUESTION OF EQUAL CONTRIBUTION

Although the hypertext project seemed to ease these tensions over disagreements, if that is even desirable, it did not ease one tension that is always inherent in group projects, and that is the problem of equal contribution of all group members, and, in connection to this, how each member's grade is determined. As Figure 2.2 shows, in the hypertext group, 70% of the respondents said contribution was equal as opposed to 22% who said it was not (not all students answered the question); on the other hand, in the conventional group, 73% of respondents said contributions were equal as opposed to 18% who said it was not.

From my experience using collaborative assignments in my business writing courses, this percentage of problems seems normal. Even though it is only a minority of groups that experience conflict over the inequality of contributions (typically, I would estimate, one out of

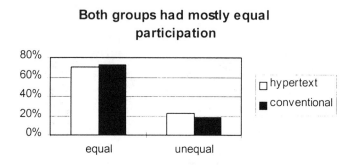

Both groups had mostly equal participation

Figure 2.2. Both groups had mostly equal participation

five), the experience can be particularly frustrating for the groups in which there are such problems.

The reason the hypertext format could resolve conflicts about group consensus but could not resolve conflicts about member contribution is that although each member could write different sections of the project, allowing for differing views, some members may have only written a small number of sections compared to the number written by other group members. Therefore, other group members believed that the members who wrote only one or two sections did not contribute equally. For instance, in one group, one person wrote only one section as compared to approximately four sections each for the other people in the group. From her viewpoint, her contribution was equal because she believed her section on the morality of postmenopausal birth was more difficult to write than the other sections that relied on more objective information. Nevertheless, the other group members did not believe the perceived difficulty of the section made up for the lack of further contributions. Although the student writing the section on morality did have a valid point—her section was indeed more difficult to write—her group members were not completely underestimating the value of her input because she waited until the last minute to write her section (due to some personal problems) and did not offer for her position as many arguments as needed to be convincing.

In another interesting example, one group member felt she was prevented from contributing more by the other group members, saying, "It was obvious that not everyone was given the opportunity to contribute equally"; yet from my observations of the group, this student seemed to misunderstand her group's intentions and thus failed to become more involved in the project. The hypertext group, overall, seemed to use a different sense of measuring the contributions of each member, basing their idea of contribution primarily on the number of boxes contributed (no matter how long or short the text in each box, no matter how difficult each bit of text was to write). On the other hand, the conventional group based its perception of member contributions on how much information each person wrote (again on quantity), and on how often the person worked with the group to revise the whole essay. Neither group seemed to base member contribution on the *quality* of what each person added to the essay. In any case, no matter what computer program is used, no matter what format the writing takes, based on my experience, the lack of motivation or loyalty to the group by certain students cannot ever be totally eliminated. It remains, for many instructors, the main complication of using collaborative writing in the classroom.

Some research has been done on how to resolve this continuing conflict, and Beard, Rymer, and Williams (1989) proposed a grading scheme for group projects that breaks up the grade for the project into

> *Group Report:* 50%. All group members receive the same grade on the written product. *Oral Interaction:* 25%. Members receive an individual evaluation of their participation in the group process. *Composing Process:* 25%. Members receive an individual evaluation of their contributions to the writing. (p. 33)

Beard et al. argued for the success of this grading process based on surveys measuring student acceptance of the fairness of the grading. They reported that "Students perceived that most of their group members fully participated in the various stages of the writing process . . . (83% [Agree and Strongly Agree])" (p. 40). "This perception of member involvement in the collaboration was significantly less prevalent in students' previous group experiences [which were presumably graded differently] (. . . 36% [Agree and Strong Agree])" (p. 40). For this goal of encouraging equal participation among group members, therefore, the key seems to be in the grading rather than in the format of the project.

LEARNING ABOUT WRITING

Not only do I think that students who worked on the conventional project learned more about working as a team because they had to reach consensus, but I also believe they learned more about writing because they had to work together to piece their individual sections into one unified essay. This is supported by both the results of my informal survey and my observation of the groups in action. In responding to the surveys, more students in the conventional project group reported learning about some aspect of writing than those who reported learning about their research subject (students could list more than one thing that they learned).

On the other hand, only a few students in the hypertext group discussed learning about writing as opposed to those who reported learning about their research subject or about computers, with 37% for each as demonstrated in Figure 2.3. In addition to the breakdown on whether they learned anything about writing, the conventional group listed slightly more aspects of writing than did the hypertext group—three for the conventional group, two for the hypertext group. Although no one in the conventional group reported they thought they had learned nothing about writing, one did in the hypertext group.

In answering this question, my students, as I did, may have used the traditional form of writing essays for their model of writing and what they learned about it. It is possible they may have learned techniques or skills for writing "good hypertext," however, this possibility is difficult to determine. The only evidence I can rely on to speculate on this potential is my impression of the quality of the hypertext webs the students completed. In a few groups, I believe the students produced extremely good webs that were interesting and easy to read. In a few other cases, students produced webs that were superficial in information and that presented difficulties in moving from one box of text to another. Overall, the ability of the students to write in hypertext was mixed; however, I believe this ability would improve if an instructor required more than one hypertext project in a course. It remains for the instructor to determine the importance of the ability to write in hypertext.

Another measure as to the learning process of the two groups is my observation of the groups working in class. Although I did not keep a detailed list of the group discussions I overheard, or record every question group members asked me, I can say that the focus of each group was different during class work. In the hypertext group, I heard less group discussions, but I was frequently busy assisting groups who were having problems that almost exclusively concerned using the computer. Typical questions for these groups focused on how to link sections, how to eliminate a box after they had accidentally added one, and how to copy writing from the word processing program into Storyspace. On the other hand, most of the conventional group's questions focused on organization, transitions, wording, and documentation; in other

Conventional group learned more about writing

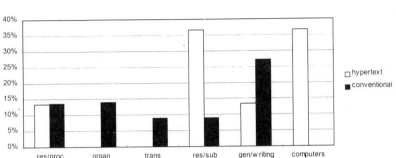

Figure 2.3. Conventional group learned more about writing

words, the kinds of skills I believed the class was designed to teach. A few groups did request help on computer problems, because the classes were still in a computer lab and using word processing programs.

In addition to the difficulties the hypertext group had with the computers, the suggestions they made for future classes, as can be seen in Figure 2.4, included an emphasis on more time in class to work on the project and more training on the program (other requests were for more help with topics and more time on the project overall).

I have realized after teaching in computer labs that whenever I use technology in the classroom, more time is required. Time is required for training, for practicing, and for solving the inevitable problems in the technology. Although both groups were using computers in computerized classrooms, only the hypertext group had to learn an entirely new program for the project. Because the program was so new and different from anything they had used before, it took time for these students to become familiar enough with the program to use it comfortably. So perhaps it is not surprising that these students requested more class time for the project, even though approximately half of the class sessions during the 3-week project were devoted entirely to group work. Because collaborative writing itself requires more time, including time in class, I question whether the additional time required to learn Storyspace is justified in a 10-week course where instructors have difficulty including as many topics and techniques about writing as they would like.

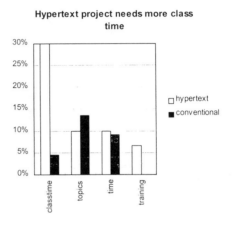

Figure 2.4. Hypertext project needs more class time

SUCCESS OF STUDENTS' PROJECTS

Another test of the effectiveness of using hypertext in the composition classroom is the success of the documents the students produced. Because the two types of projects were so different in format, I could not use the same criteria for analysis for both. However, there were some similar characteristics for which I was looking: I analyzed the focus, the argumentation, and the quality of style of the prose of both projects. Because of the different format in the hypertext project, for the evaluation of argumentation I analyzed the number of boxes that contained argumentative information versus the total number of boxes (so this figure reflecting the success of hypertext groups on argumentation measures how many groups used at least half of the boxes for argumentation and not the success of the arguments). For the conventional projects I analyzed the logic of the arguments. The goal I had for both projects was for the students to use the information they gained through research to support a position on the controversy; therefore, the amount and quality of argumentation was key. The comparison of the two groups on the point of argumentation was complicated by the distinctive characteristics of the two formats. I elected to measure the quantity of argumentation of the hypertext group because there was so little logical argument compared to the amount of pure information. However, in the conventional group, in most cases, nearly the entire essay was argumentative, and the information was integral to constructing the argu-ment. Nevertheless, this did not need to be the case; the hypertext group could have used argumentation as much as the conventional group. The reason the hypertext group did not use much argumentation seems to be due to the characteristic of hypertext of dividing the sections of text into separate boxes. Therefore, although the conventional group smoothly integrated the information with the various positions they held, the hypertext group was more likely to put evidence into boxes separate from their opinions.

I consider both focus (the ability to narrow the topic down to a manageable size and stay on point) and the quality of style of the prose (the ability to express thoughts clearly and effectively) to be basic char-acteristics of good writing. Although the results for both groups varied in quality because the ability of the writers varied in both groups, the conventional group produced more effective writing based on this crite-ria than did the hypertext group.

Of the conventional papers, all were very well focused, seven out of nine had a clear thesis, and eight out of nine had logical arguments as seen in Figure 2.5. For example, two groups wrote about the use of ani-mal testing, and both very clearly stated their positions: whereas one group was against the practice unconditionally, the other allowed the use of animal testing for medical reasons but not for cosmetic products.

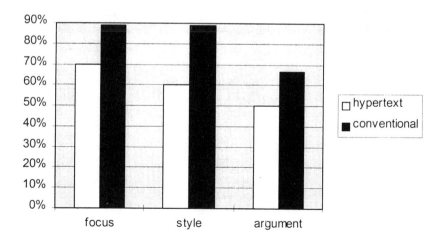

Figure 2.5. Conventional group scores better

The best use of research for logical argument was in the group that wrote about nuclear testing. This group's research provided a nearly overwhelming amount of information, but the group sorted through it to find the particular examples that would help make the case that testing was not only unnecessary but harmful to people and the environment. Deciding what was relevant was one of the aspects of the project on which I worked with the group. Originally the group wrote a rough draft that included much information about the development and original use of the atomic bomb, and we discussed how much background would be necessary to present this case against testing. I made a few suggestions, and group members read through the entire paper and eliminated the extraneous information.

Two other groups writing conventional papers worked on the topic of the use of the synthetic hormone for cows to produce more milk; both groups, from a primarily rural area where there are many farms, clearly took the side of the small family farmers who opposed the use of the hormone. These groups also used their research very effectively in order to support their arguments. One of these groups not only used facts found at the library, but also used personal experiences to support its cautious position.

On the other hand, I was disappointed that the groups in the hypertext classes did not use more argumentation, but rather the projects read like "an explosion of facts" (see Figure 2.6 for a breakdown of total boxes of text compared to number of argumentative boxes). It is not surprising, then, that more students reported learning about their research subject or computers rather than about writing. One example of this is provided by the group that wrote about sexual reassignment surgery. This group chose an interesting topic and raised important questions about whether it should continue, including the surgery's affect on the person's relationships (e.g., marriage), its cost, its side effects, and its morality. Although many of this group's sections concerned the negative aspects of the surgery, group members did not clearly take a stand against it. Like several other groups, this group viewed its project as laying out the facts and letting the reader reach his or her own conclusion, despite the fact that this is not how I presented the assignment. A selection from this group's portion titled "ethics" illustrates a refusal to take a position:

> Looking at both sides of the question, "Is having sexual reassignment surgery ethically wrong?" [sic] The side against would say yes for several reasons. One being that God created you as you are and changing that is going against God. . . . People for sex reassignment surgery would argue that the people using God's word to say why sex reassignment is wrong should remember that God also said

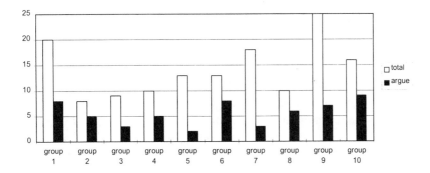

Figure 2.6. Few groups had a significant portion of argumentative sections in their webs

"Thou shalt not judge," so who are they to say what one person does to themselves is ethically wrong or not. . . . Each person is different and society should not label people who are different as wrong or not normal.

This group argues both sides of the issue, and the arguments are not well developed or supported. This ambivalent attitude was common in several of the hypertext projects. It is hard to explain why so many of the groups did not present clear positions. Part of the problem stems from the task of learning a new computer program, which was not easy to learn. So much of the students' energy and attention was devoted to this task that not much was left for focusing on writing. The nature of the assignment itself may also have been at fault, because the students were also learning about a new topic about which they previously knew very little. Yet, this exploration of a topic about which students knew very little was also true of the conventional group, who by and large managed to overcome this difficulty in order to stay focused on the basic position.

In the hypertext group, students who were struggling writers prior to the project, did not suddenly improve when writing in hypertext format. For example, the prose style and sophistication of the thinking did not always meet my standards for the class. An excerpt of one group can illustrate the problem:

Plastic surgery has been a controversial subject. People have used plastic surgery to improve their looks for many years. Plastic surgery can be a positive experience when used to help an accident victim or person with birth defects. Plastic surgery is sometimes abused by those who are unsatisfied with their appearance. This could be a big nose or small breasts. People of the world today are taking advantage of this technology to look and feel better about themselves.

On the other hand, many students in the conventional group combined their efforts to write a much better paper than they were able to write on their own. For example, one student, who had received two C- grades on previous papers, worked with a group that received a B on the final paper. An even better example is a group whose members consistently received C+ grades on previous papers written individually, yet wrote a paper together that merited a B grade. Clearly, while working as a group, they achieved more than they had been able to do by themselves.

In addition, these students' grades on individual assignments following the group project also improved (all received a B or A-), suggesting they may have learned something about writing during the group work that they were able to transfer to their own writing process. Mainly, the improvements in their writing consisted of a clearer thesis and more logical arguments to support the thesis, exactly conforming to my main goals for the course. By contrast, the same dramatic improvement was not evident for any student in the hypertext group. In almost all cases, in the hypertext group, the students' grades on the last paper were similar to grades on the first two (individual) papers. A typical example is one student who received a C+ on the first, a C on the second, and a C+ on the last paper, despite receiving an A on the group project.

STUDENTS' ASSESSMENT OF THE PROJECT

One last test of the success of the hypertext program in teaching writing was the students' comments about what they perceived to be the weakness of their projects. Although it was difficult for students to identify the problems in their own writing, some students did mention aspects of writing for which they had concerns. Conventional group members were mostly concerned with locating more information about their topic and the belief that they needed more facts and figures to add to the paper as seen in Figure 2.7.

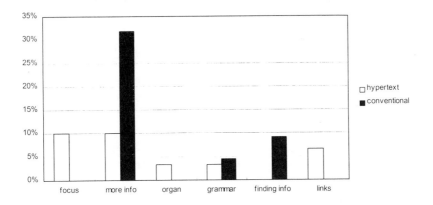

Figure 2.7. Hypertext group felt they were less successful on focus and organization

This may have been because I constantly emphasized the necessity of specifics in order to make a convincing argument, or because they realized after researching their topics that all the topics were more complex than they had anticipated. On the other hand, the hypertext group was concerned with focus, organization, and creating links (as well as with using more information). I believe students were correct in feeling that these aspects of the projects still needed improvement, and this may have been because the unusual format caused them confusion. After all, is a clear and limited focus necessary, or perhaps even desirable, in a hypertext web? How does one understand organization when there is no clear beginning or ending and no single path through the information contained in a web? One way of defining organization in hypertext may be the logical division of information into the various sections of text. The very characteristics of hypertext may have caused students more difficulty in mastering the skills of narrowing a focus and creating a logical organization.

CONCLUSION

In the end, I base my concerns about the use of hypertext in the composition classroom on the evidence of what students gained from the project rather than on their feelings about the project. Even though the hypertext group was enthusiastic about the project, I do not believe the hypertext format facilitated the goals of the course. A typical comment, if perhaps more strongly stated than others from the hypertext group, was "I would just like to say that this project was a refreshing change from the monotony of the other two papers. I had fun with this project while learning a lot about antibiotics and the storyspace program." This perfectly encapsulates what occurred in the hypertext projects: the students focused on learning a computer program and learning about the research topic, while very little thinking occurred about the process of writing. Although many students may see writing conventional papers as boring or "monotonous," they nevertheless still need to continue to practice and learn those "monotonous" techniques of writing that they have not yet mastered.

All in all, my experience with hypertext in the composition classroom has left me with more questions than answers. The first question that must be answered is, for what purpose should instructors use hypertext in any classroom, and especially in the composition classroom? Even though I do not consider the hypertext project I used successful in meeting the goals I had for my course, I think it is possible that hypertext could benefit the composition classroom. My at least partial optimism despite my experience is due to attending a seminar on hypertext and pedagogy. In meeting other instructors who have used hypertext in the classroom, I have learned new ways to use hypertext in writing courses. For example, hypertext may be a beneficial method of brainstorming or mapping out ideas for a conventional paper. The students then could see those connections between ideas that I was hoping they would see, but they also would proceed to choose which connections they want to privilege and how to create transitions from one idea to the next when bringing the pieces of writing together into a linear format.

Overall, I question what types of assignments work best when using hypertext as a tool for teaching composition. Although the project, as I created it, did not achieve my goals, perhaps other instructors, with different techniques, have had more success. As more instructors experiment with using hypertext in various types of courses, I hope to learn more about what hypertext can and cannot do for my students.

APPENDIX A: HYPERTEXT ASSIGNMENT

For this project, instead of writing a regular essay, you will create, in your responding groups, a hypertext web on some topic in science and technology. You will use the Storyspace program on the computers in this room, and the other Macintosh labs in Denney Hall (not available at other labs on campus). Refer to the directions for the program that I passed out in class.

For your topic, you should consider some technology or scientific research that you think goes too far, or at least should be examined or restricted. (If you prefer, you could examine a technology that others think goes too far, but you can argue that it does not.) Examples of possible technologies are

- genetic engineering
- food irradiation
- synthetic hormone give to cows to produce more milk

or any other topic that you find interesting. In other words, you want to ask yourselves the question: Just because we CAN do something, does that mean we SHOULD do something?

You may want to split up the topic for each group member to research. Each member may then want to write a text first on MacWrite Pro on his or her section, and you can work on putting the parts into the web and making the connections together. This is just a suggestion on how to divide up the work; if you think of a way that works better for you, go for it.

The project will be due on Tuesday, February 27 on disk. On Tuesday, February 20 I will talk to each group and preview the project—have any questions ready then. On Thursday, February 22 you will have a chance to see the other groups' projects and leave comments.

Along with the project, you should e-mail me a message by class time on February 27 explaining how you divided up the work on the project and who contributed what to the group effort. You should also evaluate your project, suggest what grade you think your group deserves, and explain why you think so.

APPENDIX B: CONVENTIONAL PAPER ASSIGNMENT

English 110c, Spring 1995
Dr. MaryLynn Saul

Assignment for Project #3

This project is a group project; groups should be three to four people. As a group you will write one paper of approximately five pages (one paper for the group). If you split the paper up into sections for each person to work on, you should meet as a group to go over the whole thing and smooth out the sections so they fit well together.

For your topic, you should consider some technology or scientific research that you think goes too far, or at least should be examined or restricted. (If you prefer, you could examine a technology that others think goes too far, but you can argue that it does not.) Examples of possible technologies are

- genetic engineering
- food irradiation
- unrestricted access to the internet
- procedures to allow women past menopause to have babies
- synthetic hormone given to cows to produce more milk

or any other topic that you find interesting. In other words, you want to ask yourselves the question: Just because we CAN do something, does that mean we SHOULD do something?

The rough draft will be due on Tuesday, May 9; I will look at what your group has put together so far, and give you suggestions for revision. Another draft will be due Tuesday, May 16, and you will read other groups' papers and make comments (bring or print out extra copies). **The final draft will be due Tuesday, May 23** (note the change from the syllabus).

Along with the project, you should e-mail me a message by class time on May 23 explaining how you divided up the work on the project and who contributed what to the group effort. You should also evaluate your project: what do you think are its strengths, weaknesses? I will add this message into your response grade (it does not count as one of the five responses you are supposed to do).

I look forward to seeing your finished projects! I would like to keep a copy of your projects to use with future 110c classes. I will ask you to sign a permission form if you are willing to do this.

APPENDIX C: SURVEY DIRECTIONS

English 110c, Fall 1994
Dr. MaryLynn Saul

Instructions for e-mail describing your project

Project #3 is DUE on November 22. By that day, by class time, you should e-mail me a message explaining how you created your project. Each member of the group should send me a separate message. You should address it to me, with copies to each of the other members of the group. (My e-mail address is msaul@magnus). If you don't have the addresses of your group members yet, exchange them today.

In your message you should include

- who did what parts of the project; how each person contributed (don't forget to include yourself)
- suggestions for improving the assignment for future classes
- what you learned about writing from this project
- advantages/disadvantages of writing in hypertext
- the grade you would give your project (examine it objectively)
- rationale for your grade
- what you would change about your project if your had more time (any weaknesses)
- anything else about the project you would like to comment on

APPENDIX D: CONVENTIONAL PROJECT SURVEY QUESTIONS

Either on e-mail or on paper, answer the following questions and turn in by the due date for the paper.

- Explain who contributed what to write the paper. What was each person responsible for?
- What did you learn about writing from doing this project?
- What are the strengths and weaknesses of your paper? What would you change about the paper if you had more time?
- What suggestions do you have to improve the project for future classes?

Chapter 3

The Pedagogical and Electronic Contexts of Composing in Hypermedia

Ann Margaret McKillop
University of Maryland

Jamie Myers
The Pennsylvania State University

It seems that all too often these days those of us who are not "online" or who are not "plugged in" are encouraged to rush out and join the technological revolution so that the world of information does not pass us by. And increasingly, schools are compelled to do the same so that students' future career choices are not curtailed by some form of computer illiteracy. However, we have found that as we have made the jump to cyberspace—whether it be engaging in online bulletin board discussions, creating World Wide Web (WWW) home pages, formulating simulations, or composing hypermedia documents—we have had to clarify our beliefs about the roles of teachers, students, and technologies to define what it is we hope to gain from computer-enhanced classrooms.

Our research, which specifically deals with the construction of hypermedia documents by students, confirms that the teacher's pedagogy shapes the students' experiences with technology and literacy. Furthermore, the socially constructed knowledge that students bring into the hypermedia environment greatly influences whether or how they utilize the potentials of the technology. Finally, although working in the hypermedia environment may open sites for critical literacy, it is more likely the students' willingness to take up the invitation that has the greatest impact on the authoring decisions and the development of critical literacy.

For our purposes here, *hypermedia* is defined as hypertextual documents—those allowing for non-sequential reading and writing (Jonassen, 1989)—that integrate multiple media. Thus, hypermedia involves the composing and organizing of electronic text, graphic, sound, and video computer windows to enable a reader to follow links that connect and display sequences of the media. Each window of information is often referred to as a space in which ideas are held, and the hyperlinks that move between these spaces are often displayed in a different color or font, or with boxes that act like graphic buttons. Hypermedia, then, is similar to a dismantled book with each page an intact space displayed one at a time with the possibility of multiple sequences through the pages. CD-ROM multimedia encyclopedias are examples of hypermedia; however, it is to student-constructed hypermedia documents that we refer in this chapter.

In examining the beliefs that guide our computer-enhanced classrooms, we have found it necessary to explicate a theory of meaning, a theory of learning, a theory of sociopolitical context, and a theory of action to contextualize our work. These four theories have helped us lay out our assumptions about what occurs when students author in hypermedia, thus informing our work for future encounters with this technology. By presenting a largely descriptive account of the students' hypermedia experiences and products in this chapter, we hope to inform those who might share our theories and beliefs about how technology might support more democratic forms and functions of literacy.

The ability of hypermedia to frame individual media "texts" and to author/read one or multiple sequences through the texts supports theories of the social construction of meaning. As A. Nielsen (1989) stated, "teachers and texts do not and cannot convey *knowledge* to students, but instead, provide the *means* by which students can create their own knowledge" (p. 6, emphasis in original). Because hypermedia involves the creation of visible links between the ideas in multiple texts and multiple media, it promotes this constructive process. Hypermedia also supports semiotic theories in which potential meanings are dispersed throughout all texts with interpretations arising as a result of the intertextuality constructed at each moment; thus each text space becomes interpreted with respect to the other texts in the hypermedia document to which we hyperlink. Pierce's classic definition aptly describes what is physically possible to construct in hypermedia: a "sign, or representamen, is something which stands to somebody for something in some respect or capacity" (cited in Innis, 1985, p. 1). Although any sign can be juxtaposed, or brought to bear, on another, intertextuality is based on an assumption that authors and readers share in culturally constructed systems of meaning, based on shared experiences with the world's texts. Thus, some connections between texts are more likely, however, these meanings are not the only possible meanings for particular texts. Multiple meanings are always possible. Shuman's (1993) definition of *reader response theory* might also serve as a definition of hypermedia projects: "It posits that all readers, by bringing their individual backgrounds and value systems to their reading, create their own texts as they shape their personal, highly individual transactions with the texts they are reading" (p. 30).

Our beliefs about learning involve a consideration of both the cognitive activities of the individual within the textual world of hypermedia and of the classroom social context in which computers and instructional activity with hypermedia are organized. According to Rosenblatt (1978), the nondeterministic belief that context, activity, and learner constitute each other to create a transactive meaning that is greater than the sum of the individual parts is crucial. Thus, computer programs that can be classified as computer-based instruction or computer-assisted instruction are troublesome because they are based on the assumption that meaning and knowledge can be reproduced through a single linear behaviorist pathway devoid of cultural context—a transmission style of teaching and learning (Dewey, 1938). This transmission, or "banking model" (Freire & Macedo, 1987) of education, which is predicated on the belief that the teacher's knowledge becomes the students' knowledge, "denies the students' indigenous culture and their potential for critical thought, subordinating them to the knowledge, values, and language of the status quo" (Schor, 1992, p. 33). Shifting the focus away from teacher-centered classrooms to student-centered classrooms through student-constructed hypermedia offers students a place to explore and critique ideas and requires the critical analysis and synthesis necessary to contextualize ideas in personally meaningful and multiple ways.

> The student is the subject of the process of learning to read and write as an act of knowing and creating. The fact that he or she needs the teacher's help, as in any pedagogical situation, does not mean that the teacher's help nullifies the student's creativity and responsibility for constructing his or her own written language and reading for this language. Learning to read and write means creating and assembling a written expression for what can be said orally. The

teacher cannot put it together for the student; that is the student's creative task. (Freire & Macedo, 1987, pp. 34-35)

Hypermedia projects offer a possible shift away from the traditional socio-political context of school that emphasizes the consumption of authorized knowledge distributed and displayed in the forms of print reading and writing. In his book *Word Perfect: Literacy in the Computer Age*, Tuman (1992) suggested that both opponents and advocates of technology in the classroom share a similar assumption—Print literacy is superior literacy or the only literacy to be considered. Tuman rightfully suggested that technology may impel us to redefine what literacy is now to what literacy may become in a "Word Perfect" world. We are in an age of postprint literacy primacy and, for better or for worse, see the emergence of computers as the predominant tool in the workplace for representing and communicating ideas. By simultaneously validating all forms of media, and privileging student-constructed representations, the traditional social relationships of power are shifted from the printed text and expert teacher to the collaborative inquiry of community members. But this individual cognitive emphasis must be melded with a social and cultural perspective. Meanings, whether experienced in an authoritative context or a constructivist context, are never individually determined, but are culturally grounded in a social negotiation of the signs we produce about and in shared experience. This position leads directly to our beliefs about political action.

We believe that the purpose of education is not simply preparing people for the workplace, but rather equipping people with the necessary critical skills to "read the world," make each other's readings problematic, and offer alternative readings. Critical theory in hypermedia means the juxtaposing of texts, images, and so on, to foster critique about the potential meanings of texts. Schor (1987) stated that "Critical learning is an act of study which can lead to a study of action" (p. 83). Through critically reading and questioning and juxtaposing texts in hypermedia format, students may see more clearly those aspects of society that they would seek to change. But even Schor recognized that projects meant for critical critique may not be taken up for that purpose. Thus, even though the electronic space may support critical constructivist, empowering, negotiating thought, the pedagogical context and the authoring traditions students bring to hypermedia may result in the use of the electronic space to reproduce culturally dominant meanings about the world.

Our research encourages us to invest a great degree of hope in the potential of hypermedia authoring. Our findings reported here indicate that some of this hope is well placed, and results that fall short reinforce our belief that technology alone cannot determine the nature of thought and action. It is always shaped by the pedagogical context in which students and teachers, authors and readers, and tools for representation, co-construct interpretive roles and responsibilities.

THE RESEARCH FRAMEWORK

The research frame of symbolic interactionism (Blumer, 1969) guided the two research studies. Central to this methodology is the belief that humans act toward things on the basis of the meanings they hold for those things and that these meanings are socially negotiated through ongoing interactions. Data within this research frame is highly qualitative in nature, consisting primarily of transcripts of interactions, interviews, and written documents that capture the everyday process of the experience as well as reflections back on the experience and the hypermedia projects produced. Although there may be ethnographic qualities to the study, we believe there to be a distinction between focusing on the "descriptive questions [of] values, beliefs and practices of a cultural group" that constitute ethnography and seeking answers to "process questions [about the] experience over time" that define grounded theory or symbolic interactionism (Morse, 1994, p. 224). Thus, critical to interpreting data to describe the sense students made of their authoring experience in hypermedia is the continual interaction of the inquirers with the participants in the research context. Such interaction allows the researchers to come to the fullest possible understanding of how the participants interpret each other and the world. This prolonged engagement (Lincoln & Guba, 1985) was accomplished because both of us were the respective teacher-researchers of the students involved in the construction of the hypermedia projects.

Our research was guided by the following questions: How do students compose in hypermedia? What influences are there on that process? As teacher-researchers, we worked with two different populations to seek understandings to these questions. McKillop worked with seventh graders on either a poetry or biography hypermedia project, and Myers worked with English education undergraduates on a literature-based hypermedia project. Work with each population informed the research with the other, especially related to the emerging findings of the influence of the pedagogical context on the nature of hypermedia documents authored by the students.

In both populations, students were organized into small groups to collaborate on hypermedia documents. They used several software tools to digitize media artifacts—sounds, images, videos, and texts—for use in constructing a StorySpace (Bolter et al., 1994) hypermedia document: SoundEdit Pro (1994) for digitizing voice-overs and music; Adobe Premiere (1994) for digitizing video and creating original quicktime movies; Ofoto (1993) or Adobe Photoshop (1993) for scanning images; and Microsoft Word (1994) or ClarisWorks (1994) for word processing.

The seventh-grade students involved in the study came from an English class at a local junior high school that is set up in interdisciplinary teams. During the course of the study, eight students worked on one non-integrated unit about poetry, and eight worked on a biography unit that was integrated with social studies. In all, 16 students collaborated in groups of 3, 4, or 5 during different class periods for 3 weeks. The classroom teacher selected the participating students based on her belief that some students might benefit academically or socially from being involved. The students ranged in ability from average to above average, as indicated by the previous semester's English grades. Having been released from their English class to work in a room adjacent to the school's media center, the students used one computer and shared a scanner and audio and video equipment with students from another class.

The undergraduates were secondary teacher education students in a block of three courses—Adolescent Literature, Secondary Language Arts, and Media Literacy—taken prior to a prestudent teaching experience. They formed six groups of three to explore themes in, between, and beyond three works of literature they read as part of their adolescent literature course and worked over a period of 4 weeks with a spring break interruption. Their classroom was well equipped with six computer workstations around the perimeter of the room, all linked on a network. From each workstation, the students could access the software and storage space they needed to complete their documents. They too shared a scanner and audio and video equipment.

DESCRIPTION OF THE PROJECTS

Of the two seventh-grade projects, the poetry groups started first. Dewey's (1938) belief that educators need to "arrange for the kind of experiences which, while they do not repel the student, but rather engage his activities are, nevertheless, more than immediately enjoyable since they promote having desirable future experiences" (p. 27) led to the following scenario:

Poetry Unit Proposal

You live in State College. The year is 2021, two years after a nuclear holocaust has decimated your community, your country, life as it was. Although many aspects of your life are still disrupted, your community feels the need for some sort of continuity and beauty. Your computer consulting firm (you do still have a few computers left that work) has been assigned the task of bringing the knowledge of poetry to school-age children. Areas that you will need to concentrate on include the following: how a poem looks, how a poem sounds, how a poem expresses an idea, how a poem uses language in a special way. While some poetry still exists from before the attack, you may need to write new poems of different types to provide students with the foundation they need. You may need to integrate or create film, sound, images, or original movies to complete your task. You will be working as a group for some sections of the project and as individuals for other sections. . . . Good luck.

Thus, within the context of composing their own original poetry, the students in the study were asked to relate the knowledge that they were constructing to other "students."

The biography groups were given the task of researching a famous person's life and composing a monologue to be presented in front of the combined social studies and English classes. To mirror what their classmates were constructing without the aid the computer, the students were instructed to write the monologue in first person. Although the students had initiated their research by the time they started working on their hypermedia projects, they had not composed their scripts nor even thought of how they would like to present the projects.

The undergraduate literature groups experienced several instructional activities focused on supporting the construction of a hypermedia interpretation of some significant idea(s) in, between, and beyond the three novels: *Ceremony* (Silko, 1977), *The Dollmaker* (Arnow, 1954), and *To Kill a Mockingbird* (Lee, 1960). The six small groups were encouraged to organize the media texts to support the construction of multiple meanings about ideas, thus author a hypermedia cultural critique. The following excerpt from a class transcript illustrates how the project was framed:

> Think back on our conversation today when you're searching for a purpose for what we might be trying to do with these three novels . . . the experiences in these three novels and the ideas in these three novels are beyond the novels, reaching far beyond the novels into the comments that we overhear on the street as Rick has said in terms of "I got a girl," into movies as Mike has implied, into music, everywhere these ideas show up. And what these ideas do . . . is they build this representation of what it means to be a spouse, or to have expectations, or to be frustrated, things like that . . . before I close with a poem I should try to explain that we think that the computer program StorySpace might provide a space in which you could explore ideas,

one idea that finds itself being represented in these novels and beyond these novels, because it allows you to put those representations into some relationship to each other to try to explore that idea. We've never used StorySpace before so we don't know whether or not it will actually facilitate exploring an idea like that as it is represented in various arenas of our life. (class transcript, 2/17/95)

DATA COLLECTION AND ANALYSIS PROCEDURES

Classroom data was collected by the use of video cameras, and episodes that became relevant were transcribed. A video/audio computer screen capture device called TelevEyes Pro (1993) allowed the video recording of small group work during the construction and during the presentation of finished hypermedia documents to the other members of each class. Relevant episodes from these videorecordings were also transcribed. The seventh-grade students kept a learning log journal, and were interviewed about their experience authoring the document. These sources of data were read and reread to excerpt segments that illustrated and explained influences on the students' hypermedia authoring decisions.

Two categories of decision making became relevant to describe the aspects of electronic authoring that supported the conceptual exploration and representation of ideas: the intent of the authors in incorporating media and the intent of the authors in organizing a single or multiple pathway through the project. The data excerpts further highlighted the influences on authoring decisions of teacher pedagogical instructions, of electronic constraints and possibilities, and of students' predilections toward traditional models of exposition. Thus, final data interpretation focused on explaining how the contexts of pedagogy, electronic media, and expository traditions structured how media was used and how pathways were constructed in the small group hypermedia projects.

A DESCRIPTION OF STORYSPACE HYPERMEDIA DOCUMENTS

The following description of the Poetry 4 project provides a sense of the characteristics of hypermedia documents written in the StorySpace software. Known as the "web view" because it graphically presents links (strings) between spaces (boxes), Figure 3.1 shows the topical organization of the project in a window titled **Presentation PD. 4 Poems**. Each space in this web view has two features: (a) the title of the space, which

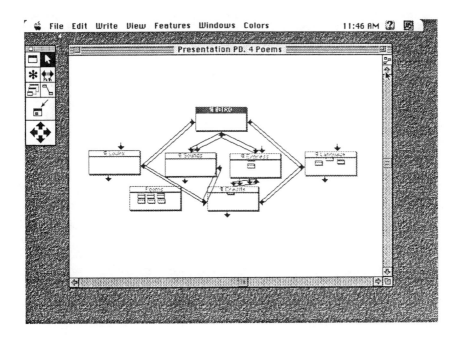

Figure 3.1. Web view of Presentation PD: Four poems

when clicked on, reveals a window for writing text and media called the writing space; and (b) the organizational space, in which subordinate spaces are represented by identical miniature boxes. The strings between boxes indicate author-generated hyperlinks between text/media contained in each of the writing spaces.

Not all of the links in a document are visible at one time because each space can contain more spaces inside spaces inside spaces and so on. When the reader double clicks in the organizational space, a new web view of the next hierarchical level of spaces and links is displayed. As Figure 3.2 illustrates, the title of this new window is the title of the writing space in the prior window—in this case, **Language.** The arrows above and below the spaces indicate incoming and outgoing links to other spaces in the document that are not visible in this web view because they are contained in a different hierarchical space.

A single click on the title of the space **Language** in Figure 3.1 reveals the writing space in which words, graphics, or video clips can be placed. Music can be included in a video clip or programmed to automatically play when the writing space is opened. Figure 3.3 displays the writing space for **Language.** When a writing space is displayed, links are

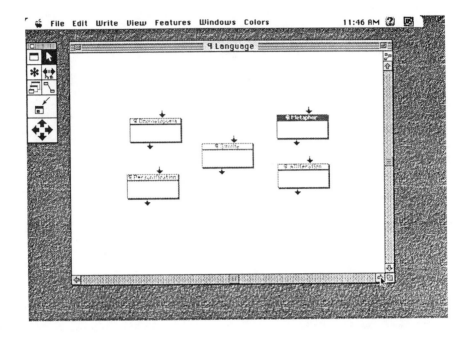

Figure 3.2. Web view of organizational space Language from Presentation PD: Four poems

not highlighted unless the author has selected a different color for the linked text. Links are made visible as boxes around words or in graphics, also illustrated in Figure 3.3, when the option key and the open-apple key are pressed simultaneously. Hyperlinks are constructed by using the link tool in the small tool palate to the left in Figure 3.3 to link highlighted words or media in any one writing space to another writing space or to specific highlighted words or media in another space. A tunnel tool allows the author to originate the link in one space, close that space, open other spaces, and end the link in the destination space. Links are only one direction, so they must be constructed in both directions if the author wants to give the reader a return path.

A single group of words or a graphic area can be highlighted to make multiple links going to different destinations. When the author does this, a dialogue box appears with choices for the reader to follow. Figure 3.4 illustrates this navigational dialogue box because the students linked the word *simile* to two writing spaces: *Language* and *Beluga*. Figure 3.5 shows the result of the reader having chosen to follow the *Beluga* link. As the space opens, the computer highlights the words the students linked to *simile* in the previous window: in this case, the entire

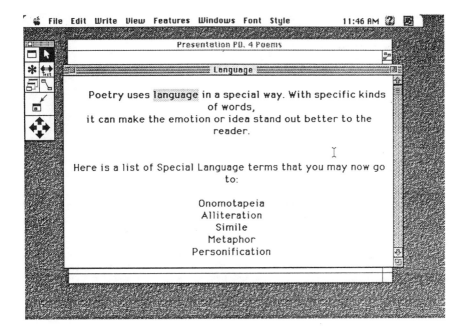

Figure 3.3. Writing space Language from Presentation PD: Four poems

poem is highlighted as an example of a simile. Text links require the author to select specific parts of text to connect and provide the reader with text "buttons" and highlighted destinations. It is also possible simply to connect whole writing spaces that require a different navigational tool located in the pull down menu.

StorySpace provides alternative views of projects that are called the "chart view" and "outline view." The outline view is the traditional Roman numeral outline of the hierarchically organized space titles. The chart view presents the titles of the spaces with lines representing their hierarchical organization; the organizational space is not graphically displayed as boxes but as lines between space titles. Figure 3.6 presents the chart view of **three novels** that was used to introduce the undergraduate literature groups to the authoring program. When the author creates a new space in the chart view, a line represents the hierarchical relationship of that new space; in Figure 3.6 **Why Me?** is subordinate to the space *Dollmaker.*

The author can rearrange the whole hierarchy of spaces in this chart view by dragging and dropping spaces. The reader clicks on the titles to read the writing spaces. As is highlighted later, the process of

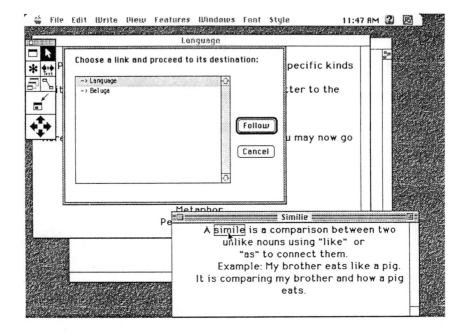

Figure 3.4. Dialogue box showing multiple outgoing text links from Simile, Presentation PD: Four poems

creating and moving spaces in the chart view, the ease of opening the writing spaces, and the hierarchical relationships represented by the lines reduced the authoring groups' desire to create text links between specific words and graphics contained in the writing spaces.

THE LURE AND IMPACT OF MEDIA

The students were very attracted to the electronic capabilities of the project because they could incorporate media in several different ways. Popular songs and music could be played alongside the display of a written text or image or there could be a combination. A sequence of images with transitions between each, and with music or a voice in the background, could be organized and compiled as a quicktime movie. This video production could then be added to a space in the project sequence of texts, images, and sounds.

The incorporation of the sound, image, and video media served different purposes. At a basic level, these media were meant to grab the

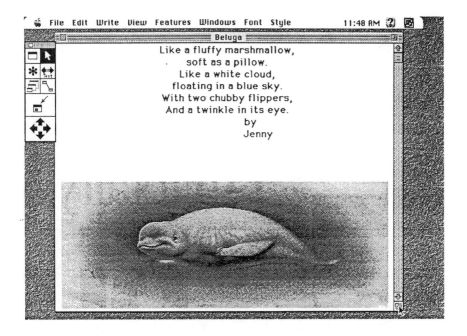

Figure 3.5. Writing space Beluga, text linked to Simile, Presentation PD: Four poems

attention of the reader and more fully engage him or her in the text. Beth (poetry project) and Tom (biography project) explain the importance of this function:

> Yeah . . . I think kids like to watch a movie because they would listen, because they want to see the pictures. I always like to see pictures in a book to help me imagine what goes with a poem. (Beth, interview, 5/23/95)

> I used pictures and made a movie with my poems because I think kids would pay more attention than reading a bunch of poems. (Beth, journal, 5/26/95)

> It's . . . to make it interesting. You know, we didn't want anything boring and we just want right away to capture their attention before they even got into our projects. (Todd, interview, 5/31/95)

The seventh graders added several quicktime video productions to their hypermedia projects. The first frame of the movie would appear in the

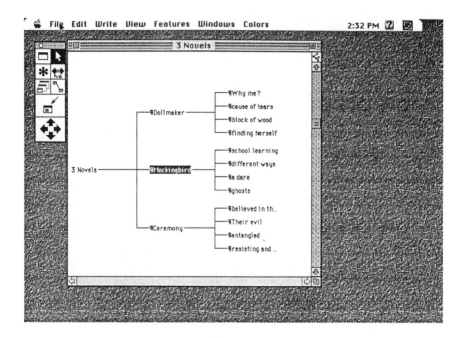

Figure 3.6. Chart view of three novels

selected space, and the reader would be able to activate a "play" control by clicking on the image. Only one group of undergraduates constructed an original quicktime movie, most likely because the teacher demonstrated the technique for just that group when they wanted to voice over a movie clip with a reading from one of the novels. However, the undergraduates also believed that the media increased the reader's attention by giving variety and a quicker pace to the experience of ideas. As the undergraduates shared their novel hypermedia products during two final class periods, engagement was visibly more noticeable when media portions were projected on the overhead screen.

Ron: I find the connections between the text are good, but I think the slow parts of the thing are where we don't have any video to connect with other than the text which we've all been discussing for so long.

Molly: You can see it.

John: Yes, something different from what you've already read.

Ron: already mulled over the text . . . we discussed it.

Kelly: Not only that but you get to see what somebody else thought, what they perceive as being the meaning. (Sharing of Bob group project, class transcript, 4/21/95)

Clearly the electronic capabilities of hypermedia offer authors strategies for creating texts that are more highly engaging than the traditional printed text and may offer important communication strategies beyond those available in print-only hypertext authoring.

Beyond the attention-grabbing function of the media, the authors used a media "text" for three purposes: to illustrate, extend, and in some cases, question the meanings presented by print or other media "texts." Pierce's semiotic theory, which defines the function of signs as an icon, index, or symbol, provided the basis for describing the meaning the authors intended to generate with a media sign. Media used as an icon presented an image, sound, or video that was meant to illustrate text already presented in a space. Indexical media did not attempt to illustrate a text, but together with the text, pointed toward a shared meaning represented by both "texts." Media that generated a symbolic meaning juxtaposed texts to create a third meaning not usually represented by, or shared between, either text. Most often, this third meaning was a greater possible understanding built on the ideas represented by the juxtaposed texts. At times, the third meaning involved alternative or oppositional ideas represented by the juxtaposed texts. The use of this distinction between iconic, indexical, and symbolic signs does not exactly follow the definitions of Pierce (Eco & Sebeok, 1983); however, it parallels the depth of representation implied by the sign functions and helps to illustrate how the student authors of the hypermedia projects used media in different ways to construct intended meanings.

We believe that in most cases the authors used the media to illustrate an idea already presented in one text. This iconic function for media may have been constrained by the pedagogical context because the teacher instructed the students to write a poem about a picture:

when I wrote "The Springs" I had to base it on like a picture so before I wrote it I thought of like something. Like I sat in my kitchen and I was looking at my toaster and I thought . . . I'm thinking about a toaster but I, I knew that wouldn't work so I just kind of thought about something that would work as a poem that other things were related to. And I just thought of that. And so then I wrote my poem and then drew the picture. (Cynthia, interview, 6/5/95)

In Figure 3.5 the image of a beluga whale presents an iconic use of an illustration. However, even without such an explicit direction to find images to illustrate the meaning of a text, most of the images in the undergraduate novel projects represented the characters or settings presented in quotes or written responses to the stories. The image of the Native American (see Figure 3.7) is inserted immediately after "Josiah" is named in the text. As iconic signs, images like these function to mirror or reproduce isomorphically the meaning of another sign; thus they do not offer much potential to embellish, extend, or shift critically the meaning of the original sign. Iconic signs basically replace the original "text" in the interpretive event.

> I think pictures are important. I like pictures because when I was little, I liked to look at pictures of things because it like, you know, I could imagine it but I sort of wanted to see . . . what the author was imagining. And sometimes . . . the stories are sort of hard to imagine . . . so if there's a picture it helped me imagine things. (Beth, interview, 5/23/95)

Although ideas were enriched to some degree by the addition of an illustrative image, images used in this way did not attempt to extend or layer the conceptual understanding of the meanings being illustrated.

Beyond these iconic uses of media, texts were often juxtaposed or linked to another "text" to suggest that both texts shared a common underlying iconic meaning. In *Finding herself* (Figure 3.8), the quote from The Dollmaker describes "Gertie" searching the sky for the North Star, however, the image presents a woman sitting at a butter churn. Separately, the two "texts" represent several possible meanings, but together, they become examples of a shared meaning. They point to a meaning that extends the understanding of either text into the experience of the other text, but they do not attempt to make the other text problematic.

A similar indexical meaning was constructed by Cynthia as she moved her poem, "The Springs," into a hypermedia electronic context. As Cynthia indicated in her interview, she originally wrote the poem and illustrated it with her own iconic drawing. When she began to consider juxtaposing her poem with a video clip, she moved away from the iconic function of her own illustration. The video began to function indexically because, along with the poem, it pointed to a shared idea that pushed the meaning of the poem beyond her original intention.

> [I was influenced by the video itself] a little bit because there's like a whole bunch of parts where the, the bear is holding the fish and eating the fish and then it threw it back in. It's like the fish are the neglected ones. The bear . . . I mean the springs are there pushing

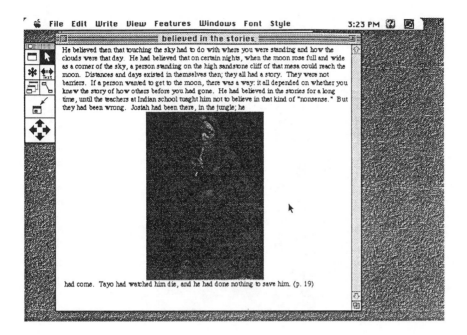

Figure 3.7. Iconic use of media in believed in the stories from das grup

them and they have no control over it and then the bears are picking them up and eating them or picking them up and then throwing them back in so they really can't tell them no don't do it. . . . It connected pretty well. . . . I had it [the title of the poem] as "The Springs" and . . . the springs were in like a lion and then the first four sentences are about the springs but the last four are about the fish and it's more the fish part is more I guess exciting, it's more . . . I don't know. It's the bigger part of the poem. And it's just like the springs are a part of what the fish are in and all the other animals are in so I decided to name it "The Crying Fish" plus because everybody else thought that was a lot nicer, I mean, not nicer. It just . . . had more of an impact on the fish than the springs. (Cynthia, interview, 6/5/95)

Cynthia's decisions about the meaning of her poem were affected by the juxtaposition of the video and her poem. Through the possibility of video, Cynthia sees that the focus of her poem may be different than she originally intended or that because of the video, it can be different than intended. Her renaming of the poem to "The Crying Fish" represents the shared meaning to which both signs indexically point. The electronic

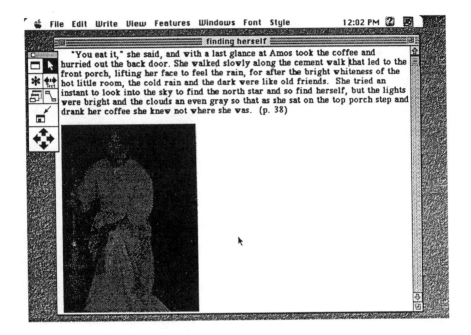

Figure 3.8. Indexical juxtaposition of media in finding
herself from Bob

context of hypermedia can clearly support the conceptual development
of students.

Media "texts" that functioned as symbols supported the construction of meanings that were greater than, or beyond, any of the individual
"texts" that were juxtaposed or linked together. The texts were meant to
work together to add up to some new idea rather than iconically illustrate
one meaning or indexically point two signs toward a shared meaning. In
several cases, authors believed they used media to represent ideas or feelings that could not be explained as well verbally in print or words.

> Like I don't think I could have expressed J. F. K. through words real-
> ly. Like whenever, I was like showing the movie, it could be the
> shot, that had a lot of impact that you said that it had on you and it
> had one (inaud.) of the movie and I don't think I could express that
> through words. (Jesse, interview, 5/17/95)

> Well um I just thought it would be fun. . . . I mean . . . it's harder to
> . . . talk about his life. 'Cause it's a lot easier to show pictures and
> stuff like that. (Pete, interview, 5/31/95)

Well . . . it shows like a sort of a rough couple . . . of his accomplishments in his life . . . that's on his grave. That's why I chose it. (Todd,
interview, 5/31/95)

Because Pete believes that pictures are easier to use than words, he
defines his conceptual space by an electronic possibility. Todd is able to
introduce the accomplishment through image instead of words, also,
because of the electronic space. Thus, the authors made use of the electronic capabilities of the hypermedia space to construct a sequence of
media texts with individual meanings that experienced together generate a larger conceptual understanding about the life of a person. As indicated by Mike's opening response to the presentation of a novel project,
the juxtaposed spaces of media served a symbolic function—that is, they
"emphasized" ideas beyond the novels.

> Mike: I felt with this that they emphasized struggle, especial-
> ly with the songs, that what they were talking about
> was everything from the struggle for human rights
> whatever to the struggle to just say hello to someone,
> you know what I mean.
>
> Ron: I thought that this organization of the space was good,
> in that (class laughter) it led to better connections
> between them because it kind of broke down the,
> where the finer lines were in all the novels good, and I
> thought some of the more powerful spaces were the
> ones that had actually no text in connection to any of
> the novels, especially the, I don't know, the one's
> where everything seems so unconnected, like they say
> hello and the film and gum and I was like, "What the
> hell is that?" (class laughter) and that's Boo Radley and
> you go "Oh, my God."
>
> Class: Yea. Yea. Yes.
>
> Mike: That's true. (Sharing Incredible Themes StorySpace,
> class transcript, 4/24/95)

Ron's description of the hypermedia space that juxtaposed the image of
a half a stick of gum and the song "Hello in There" by John Prine (Figure
3.9), without any text at all to explain any connection, illustrates how the
two texts worked together to symbolize a meaning beyond either one.
Nothing about the gum itself, and nothing about the song that describes
the loneliness of old people, would signify the identity of Boo Radley in
To Kill a Mockingbird. Together they generate a meaning beyond the conventional possibilities of either sign separately, thus they work symbolically. Likewise, an image of hands (Figure 3.10 of the space **hands**)

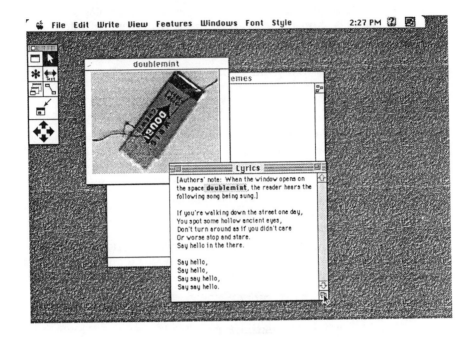

Figure 3.9. Symbolic juxtaposition of media in doublemint from Incredible Themes

linked from the quote and picture of a woman at a butter churn (**Finding herself,** presented in Figure 3.8) generates new symbolic meanings for the images that relate to the life of the character Gertie.

?:   I liked the picture of the . . . hands.

Ron: oh, that was beautiful.

?   That was one of our favorites.

Jo: Where was that from?

Hilda: It's just an advertisement . . . it's in all the magazines, they go through all these different pictures of hands.

Ron: That was just a nice one because you didn't even connect it—I mean it didn't have any text, really, it was connected to it directly and yet if felt, felt like it belonged there.

?:   It just fit.

Ron: You didn't need that "and here's a bit of text that this relates to." (sharing of Bob group project, 4/21/95)

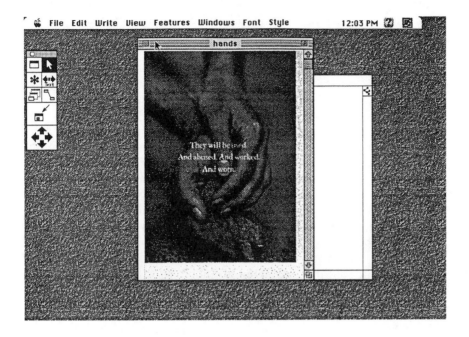

Figure 3.10. Symbolic juxtaposition of media in hands from Bob

The image of the callused hands is linked from the space **Finding herself** (Figure 3.8), which contains a quotation that does not mention hands. As the students indicate in the previous discussion, the image functions symbolically because its juxtaposition layers the meanings of both texts with another possibility.

Likewise, Amy searched carefully for pictures to fit her poem:

we needed a poem for an example of metaphor. When I wrote the poem I didn't think it would be a good piece. It turned out to be my best. I decided to make a movie with all of the subjects in my poem. I spent all my time finding *the* perfect picture for each. I wanted this to be a fantastic movie so my poem would stand out in the presentation. I looked through numerous books, newspapers, magazines, basically anything I could get my hands on. When I finally found all my pictures I scanned them onto the computer in their proper order [corresponding to the poem] and put them into "movie film." I then read my poem "Just People" slowly but clearly. To my surprise my recording was almost perfectly in sync with my pictures. (Amy, journal, 1995)

Although some of the media are clearly illustrative, the sequence beginning with a picture of a shark and audio text that suggests that the human will be the shark's dinner layers a new meaning on the subsequent image of a dinner plate replete with a fillet of fish. This humorous juxtaposition is followed by a final image of a man standing one legged with his arms outstretched; juxtaposed with the last line "we are just people," this image clearly functions symbolically by layering the possible meaning of the word "people" (see Figure 3.11).

Sometimes the greater understanding generated by the symbolic juxtaposition of texts made the meanings of the individual texts problematic. In Incredible Themes, a quotation from *Ceremony* describing the prejudice Tayo experiences from both Navajos and Whites because he is a half breed is juxtaposed with a song explaining why it's not a black-and-white world—that we all have mixed blood inside (see Figure 3.12).

In the excerpt from Snapple's novels given here, the sequence of spaces juxtaposes middle-class ladies condemning the squalid lives of Africans, to the squalid lives of White trash in Maycomb, to the condemning values of Mr. Daley about his hillbillies, to Calpurnia's opinion that "Yo're no better than others," to the disgrace of Indians in the Gallup Rodeo:

> Dan: . . . we highlight here squalid lives, ahmm, remember that was the cue, "It was easy to tell when someone bathed regularly as opposed to yearly lavations." ahm, this is talking about the Ewells, ahm, you know, kind of like the squalid community in Maycomb county. From there (text button highlighted contains the same text) right here we have *It was easy to tell* as our transition (button clicked to go to space **White trash** where highlighted text reads: "But the problems are not just overseas.") and, here we go (movie clip started: scene from the film version of *The Dollmaker* in which Reuben defends his brother against a Daley kid, is abused by Mr. Daley, is about to pull his knife on Mr. Daley, Gertie defends him, and Daley calls her a communist hillbilly.) Ahhhhhh, and while we're on the subject of hillbilly and white trash (text button—*Some people just take a better perspective on it* . . . —highlighted and followed to space **Calpurnia**.) ahmm, we went back *To Kill a Mockingbird* and this is Calpurnia saying, "Hush your mouth!! Don't matter who they are, anybody sets foot in this house 's yo' comp'ny, and don't you let me catch you remarkin' on their ways like you was so high and mighty!" Ummmmm, so, (text button highlighted) we on, the transition is *Yo' folks might be better'n the Cunninghams but it don't count for nothin' the way you're disgracin' 'em-* (button selected to go to space **Indian** where quote from *Ceremony* juxtaposed with light airy sounding song about the Sanjacinto mountain. Dan begins to talk over the song:) And, basically this is the scene in *Ceremony*, describing the Gallup ceremony, how

To a cat we are giants

towering above them.

To an ant we are mountains

blocking the warm sun.

**Figure 3.11. Just People original quicktime movie with voiceover
of poem**

To a shark we are dinner

just waiting to be eaten.

To another person . . . we are just people.

Figure 3.11. Just People original quicktime movie with voiceover of poem (con't.)

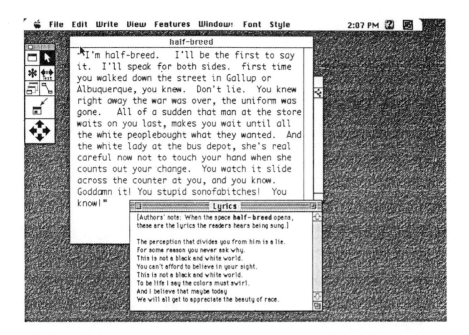

Figure 3.12. Symbolic Juxtaposition of media in half-breed from Incredible Themes

like all the white tourists come in and see the cute little Indians doing their dances and buying cute little Indian trinkets, ah, so, (song finishes playing with the words "Way above the desert snow, white winds blow.") Ahmm, and there, the transition was disgracing them, basically those were the key words, and here we highlight "They sold great amounts of liquor to Indians, and in those years when liquor was illegal for Indians, they made a lot more money because the bootlegged it." Ahm, we just thought that was disgrace. . . .

In this sequence of texts from all three novels, the juxtaposition makes problematic the meanings and values held by the people represented in each separate text. The electronic space allows the authors to comment on texts merely through physical juxtaposition rather than through explicit verbal deconstruction. The links work symbolically to layer new meanings on texts that would not be possible in traditional print narrative.

Although the data just cited presents a qualitative sense of how the authoring groups used media to construct meaning in the hypermedia documents, Table 3.1 provides a summary breakdown of the composing decisions.

Table 3.1. Summary Data of Media Type and Sign Functions.

Hypermedia Project Titles	Total # of Spaces	Spaces With Media Type						Media Sign Function		
		Exp	Text	Snd	Imag	Video	OQM	Icon	Index	Sym
Poetry 1	39	10	17	2	14	0	1	9	1	3
Poetry 4	34	12	9	3	9	1	3	8	2	3
Biography 3	65	36	11	3	29	0	9	15	6	3
Biography 4	20	1	1	9	8	1	11	11	4	2
Bertie	19	4	12	8	8	0	0	8	7	0
Snapple's Novels	28	8	17	6	6	6	0	6	5	8
Incredible Themes	15	4	6	9	6	0	0	3	4	4
Bob	25	4	17	2	7	3	1	4	6	2
2 chicks and dude	28	22	23	1	5	4	0	5	3	0
das grup	45	20	21	12	16	0	0	15	6	7

Media Types:
Exp: Exposition, narration, explanation, or interpretation in the form of text
Text: Poetry, artifact, quotations, documents
Snd: Sounds including voiceover and music
Imag: Images including photos and drawings
Video: Video clips
OQM: Original quicktime movies

Media Sign Function—juxtaposition in space or by linking:
Icon: Iconic: a text that illustrates another text
Index: Indexical: two different texts that point to a shared meaning
Sym: Symbolic: two different texts that generate a third, greater than meaning

The nearly equal number of spaces in Poetry 1 and Poetry 4 reflects the pedagogical imperative outlined in the scenario that requested the groups to produce a teaching tool that defined four specific aspects of poetry; thus, its imbedded structure is mirrored by both poetry documents. The 65 spaces in Biography 3 far exceed the 20 in Biography 4 because of the group sizes: Biography 3 had five students, whereas Biography 4 had only three. Of the remaining six projects dealing with the undergraduate literature experience, the difference in the number of spaces reflects various approaches to the authoring of the documents. Some groups, such as Bertie with 19 spaces, chose to integrate their text and media within a single space. Other groups, such as das grup with 45 spaces, linked text spaces to additional media spaces. Also a factor were the work habits among the undergraduates: some groups were far more industrious about collecting text and media to use in their projects, and some groups spent more time planning at the table than working at their computers.

The combined numbers of the first two columns in the breakdown of media types clearly shows that despite the potential for media inclusion, the documents are still highly print-oriented. Furthermore, when media was included, it primarily served the iconic function of reinforcing a meaning already communicated by the print. This is especially true for the seventh-grade projects. The undergraduate projects pushed at the meanings of the text to a greater extent as evidenced by the indexical and symbolic use of media in nearly half the cases.

A number of factors dictated which type of media were more likely to be included:

1. Images could be cut and pasted into the documents easily.
2. The procedure for adding sound to StorySpace documents was difficult for the students to manage and resulted in the loss of more than one work in progress.
3. The seventh graders were prohibited from using certain movies because of the ratings.
4. The students were captivated by the process of creating their own quicktime movies.
5. The biography projects lent themselves to a speech format that was easily embodied in the quicktime movies.
6. The undergraduates were not taught how to construct quicktime movies.

THE SHAPING OF HYPER PATHWAYS

The students retained the hierarchical authority of the author over the reader in the organization of pathways through their hypermedia projects. In most cases, the students clearly voiced their preference for one type of pathway over another; that is, the students did not haphazardly link their documents. Rather, they spent quite a bit of time delineating the links with an organizational structure in mind and were able to define what that structure was and why they used it. For the two biography projects, the assignment required individual monologues, so each member of the group composed a section of the hypermedia document about one historical person. These sections were combined in the final document and organized off of a single menu space. Students in the two poetry project groups chose to divide the responsibility for the authoring of spaces based on the assignment scenario that required the content of the final project to represent four areas of content knowledge about poetry. Although these groups also combined their work into one document organized from menu spaces, they created links that connected their individual work. The students in the six novel projects worked together on all spaces and negotiated the content, organization, and linking between the spaces they created.

Some projects were carefully sequenced with only one unidirectional path through the text and media elements of the exposition. Some projects allowed the reader to back up, but maintained a single pathway. Some projects offered menus of categorical information organized using expository frameworks of claim, chronological sequence, or definition example (classification); readers could choose to follow any of the multiple links provided within these categories. Only occasionally did links jump across categories to construct broader conceptual connections. Thus, one dimension of the organization of pathways was degree of choice. Little choice exemplified a linear exposition in service of a specific intended meaning, whereas greater choice indicated the intent of the authors to provide multiple "hyper" pathways, perhaps allowing readers more freedom to construct their own particular meanings.

A second dimension of organization was the intent of the authors either to transmit specific interpretations or to allow the reader to construct his or her own interpretation. This became evident in group projects that had only one pathway, yet did not explicitly present an intended interpretation. Instead, these pathways juxtaposed texts to offer the reader constructive opportunities for making meaning. These implicit possible meanings stood in contrast to other projects that attempted to transmit specific interpretations through both single and multiple pathways. Given these two dimensions, the projects contained few spaces that offered both multiple links and multiple possible interpretations to the reader. The vast majority of the pathways through the text spaces constituted authorized links and interpretations.

Within the Biography 4 project, Tom's J. F. K. monologue exemplifies documents that sequenced only one unidirectional path through the text and media elements of the exposition. In an interview, Tom was very decisive about how he wanted his monologue set up and how he wanted his readers to navigate his part of the document:

> I wanted to give . . . a little background. . . . I wanted to . . . show . . . how he [J. F. K.] grew up and then I wanted to show things that came in order, like he was in the war, then senator, President and I wanted to sort of go in order, you know. [Researcher: Chronological order?] Yea. I wanted to start with the war first, cause that's obviously where he started. (Tom, interview, 5/31/95)

Tom organized his section based on his belief that there is an intrinsic order to the information he was presenting, that certain information first will clarify other information later. Therefore, he chose a restricted linear single pathway with intended explicit meanings. Furthermore, when asked if he would structure all of his future projects in this order or in a similar fashion that restricted the reader's movement, Tom replied:

> It sort of depends like, for this person for a person [biography], I don't want them to skip around like go to when they die back to when they were a child, you know I can see something like say the unexplained [project mentioned earlier] for example you could . . . give the user or whatever a chance to go anywhere because there's really no order you want them to do cause they could go some place and learn like where they're [unexplained phenomena] found and another place like what is strange happening. . . . I mean they could go all over the place. This, with a person, it's sort of different, because it wouldn't really make sense if you skipped around, you just sort of want to go in one order, you learn from when they were young and they grow up. (Tom, interview, 5/31/95)

Thus, in Tom's view, certain topics "require" a given order, whereas others do not. He believes that biographies must be told in chronological order for the reader to get the best understanding of the material presented to her or him, but concedes that there are other orders better suited for other topics or genres. In addition, it is the electronic space of hypertext that allows Tom the freedom to exercise his sense of structure or to conceptualize organizations that use varying degrees of linearity, which in his mind are controlled by the directions of the assignment or the expository genre being presented.

Several projects allowed the reader to back up one space at a time but essentially maintain a single pathway. The students who constructed these projects wanted their readers to have the chance to review information in the previous space if necessary, but their organizational structure, and their reasons for it, remained linear in intent.

> Well I put this [movie] in because it was like his most famous accomplishment in his life and most people, they know that he wrote it but they don't know much about it and so . . . and this [Declaration movie] came after the Minister to France [movie] because this was after that and before his presidency. So it's sort of chronological order. (Todd, interview, 5/31/95)

When discussing why he chose to allow his readers limited choice—going forward or backward—in reading his document, Pete said, "Well in case they wanted to see something again or if they liked one of the videos they could go back and do it again without going back to the beginning of the whole presentation" (Pete, interview, 5/31/95). Pete understands the need for readers to have some freedom, but he allows them that freedom for reasons that have more to do with convenience than anything else. Again, this freedom is the direct result of working in the electronic space of hypertext. Ironically, the instrument that gives the author such decision-making freedom is also the tool that gives such control over to the reader. (Interestingly, Tom, Pete, and Todd were in the same group. One wonders what role proximity played in their decisions.)

The undergraduate group Bertie not only narrowed the pathway to a singular linear strand through each of the three novels, but group members also explicitly told the reader what was important. Here is an introduction to their strand about *To Kill a Mockingbird:*

> This StorySpace is concerned with the racism and injustices in the book. Again, it is important to listen to the words of the songs before reading the text because they help to support the quote. This is especially important when you go into the "truth" space because it is essentially telling the story of Tom Robinson.

Indeed, the authors not only try to enforce an interpretation on the reader, but they also tell the reader how he or she should go about formulating that interpretation—"listen to the words of the songs before reading the text . . ."

Bertie's approach differs from James, who leads the reader through a narrow path but leaves the opportunity to connect important ideas in the reader's hands. His single pathway, linear monologue links together the first person diaries "written" by Paul Revere with third person explanations of important events inserted between each "diary entry" (see Figure 3.13).

In an interview, James explained his strategy:

> I was just sitting around one night looking for my old stuff like years ago and I came across a diary that we had done either the last year or the year before from this Oregon Trail thing and I just thought it would be neat to do it this way. . . . Well [I explain the events in third person in between the diary sections] 'cause the diaries were basically overviews of what happened and this [the third-person insert] tells more about why how history progressed and I thought that would be helpful to people who were going to do a report themselves and they could find more information through looking at this. . . . Well they may be able to understand more of Boston's move to revolt because it shows information about how many people started doing tyranny and what they did during the revolution. I'd basically call it progression of events because it's more of a time line going through these events. . . . I felt that if they looked at it in a choice, they wouldn't know which part to do first. And where it was coming from. (James, interview, 5/31/95)

Like the other students, James is concerned that his reader has all the necessary information to help him or her understand later events. So his choice of how much freedom to give his readers is based on his belief that the reader may not be able to choose which pathway to take if he or she is not knowledgeable about the topic. For example, when faced with the option of reading about "The closing of the land bank," James questions how the reader is to know why this is an important strand. Therefore, because of his knowledge about the topic, James asserts authorial control, takes the choice out of the reader' hands, and guides the reader where he believes it makes most sense. Once again, the electronic context provides the author with the freedom to narrow the pathways for the reader, thus directing the construction of meaning.

Snapple's novels attempted to make the most of the constructivist nature of hypertext by suggesting implicit meanings the reader should create while reading. The authors of this project created a singular linear pathway, rather than a menu-oriented structure, that blatantly juxtaposed texts from all three novels to present their interpretation of major connecting themes.

> Dan: To give you a basic idea, just to be totally anti what we have learned in this class, we kind much guided the discussion. All of our links are sorta one way, so the idea is

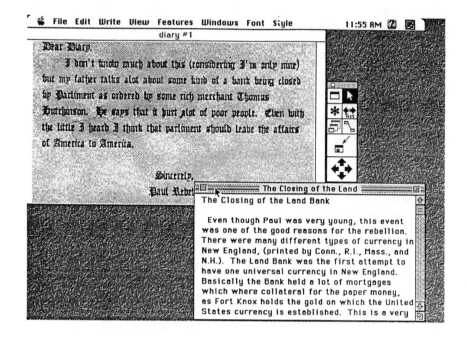

Figure 3.13. FIrst-person diary and third-person explication of events in Paul Revere from Biography 3

that the people doing the StorySpace have to make the links as to why those transitions were made, so they have to make the correlation between the transitions. Okay (Space **introduction** opened and text button "stuff of earth" selected to go to space **Creation** and highlighted text "Thought-Woman.") And we started off with religion among the three novels as our initial correlation between the three. And then (text button highlighted: "She thought of her sisters, N, and together they created the Universe") you see that's our highlighted box thingy. Now be careful, be sure to read all your boxes because theoretically they should all connect.

Like the group just discussed, this group defines for the reader the process for formulating an interpretation. The group's statement that "the people doing the StorySpace have to make links as to why those transitions were made, so they have to make *the correlation* between the transitions" indicates that this group still believes the electronic context can be used to intend a single meaning. Later on in the group's presentation, the authors realize that their intent to allow their readers to construct their own interpretation is diminished through their explicit elucidation of themes in the text of their StorySpace:

> Dan: And here we moved on to the father figure and here we have "When I asked Atticus about it, he said that we already had enough sunbeams in the family."
> (Highlighted text button.) Our transition is "He didn't mind much the way I was." (Text button selected to go to space **Josiah**.) Okay. And there we went to *Ceremony*. This is when Tayo had just told Auntie and Josiah they were going away, and Auntie didn't want them to go, and Josiah just said, Let' em, "You can't keep them forever." Ahmm, let's see, our own thought here was "These two quotes linked together helped to demonstrate the unconditional love that goes along with truly caring about someone. Atticus accepts Scout for who she is and Josiah realizes that Rocky and Tayo want the chance to see more of the world than just the reservation. Unfortunately, this kind of understanding and compassion isn't found among all the character's relationships." Sorry, we gave that one away a little

The statement "Sorry, we gave that one away a little" indicates that group members are aware that they have contradicted their stated philosophy, however, the actual linear structure of the project contradicts a philosophy in which the reader is invited to construct the meaning of the text. The pedagogical context of the three novels project very likely promoted this linear series of juxtapositions with implied authorial meanings. After all, the students were told on several occasions to focus on an idea and organize a pathway through the text spaces to explore that idea. In a sense, Snapple's novels best accomplished the directive. And, as authors, they were deeply involved in the social construction of meaning for the novels even if their produced text does not provoke the multiple possible meanings for their readers.

The undergraduate group 2 chicks and dude responded to the implicit nature of the links in Snapple's novels by suggesting that such implied meanings do not require much conceptual thinking from the authors.

Ann: Okay. We'll just start from the top (cursor moving in
        web view of entire story space, stops and opens space
        entangled.)
John: O.K. Let us mention, that unlike the snapple group [Jo
        laughs loudly], we took it upon ourselves after there
        was a quotation to write our feelings, to improvise, to,
        you know, use our brains.
[general class laughter, oohs and ahhs].

It is interesting that the students imply that drawing conclusions for the
reader involves more authorial understanding and is somehow more
beneficial to the reader than planning or designing a document that
attempts to help the reader construct his or her own interpretations. This
attraction to providing more expository explanation of literary interpretations suggests that traditional writing structures constrain the composing possibilities of electronic hypermedia, especially for undergraduates
who have a long history of writing analytic essays. Such a tendency is
also evident in several spaces of other projects including the following
excerpt from Incredible Themes:

Passive Female

[when space opened, song "I am a Rock" by Simon and Garfunkle
plays]
Gertie exemplifies a passive as well as active role in "The
Dollmaker." She can be viewed as a very strong and determined
woman. On the other hand, she can easily succumb to a passive
female identity.
    In the beginning of the novel, Gertie is depicted as a very
aggressive and obstinate individual. She stops a car by obstructing
the road with her mule. She repeatedly asks for a ride to the doctor's
office. She will not give up until her wish is granted.
    She is strong willed when she chooses to buy the Tipton Place.
Gertie is independent in that she will make her own decisions. She
doesn't want to confer with anyone about her choices.
    Her independence is again demonstrated when she leaves her
home for Detroit. She is not familiar with the city or anything outside of the country. However, she departs her homeland without her
husband and arrives in an unfamiliar environment. . . .

Projects that organized spaces in menu structures offered the
reader the opportunity to freely navigate through the linked spaces. The
menu structures used expository frameworks of claim, chronological
sequence, or definition example (classification). The undergraduate
groups Incredible Themes and Bob, organized their menus according to

themes that they constructed between the three novels. The 21 links from five main menu spaces in Bob give the reader a choice of examples from the novels about each theme category (see Figure 3.14).

2 chicks and dude and das grup organized their menus based on the three novels. Categorical spaces at the second level of the menu involve themes and characters with the last level of the menu giving media examples (see Figure 3.15). These two authoring groups also provided some underlying text and space links that connected ideas that cut across the main menu categories, although 2 chicks and dude only provided 3 such links as compared to 26 links underlying the spaces in das grup. But, however much choice the reader is granted through these categorical menus, the opportunity for meaning-making is curtailed when the authors transmitted to the reader explicit interpretations about the central text of a space, as evidenced in the following space from 2 chicks and dude, **cause of tears**:

> "Gertie cried on, her hands pressed against her face, the crumpled money spilling from her pocket. Just as she had been unable to tell her father any word of how she felt for him. She was tongueless to tell her mother that sorrow for Henley did not cause her tears, but her mother's unexpected gratitude, never mentioned through all these years. Maybe her mother had loved her. What a sin to have doubted it ever! She cried afresh over her own hardness of heart—Clovis going to war, and she thought only of money." (pp. 74-75)
>
> Because happiness could not be found in her relationship with her parents or her husband, Gertie sought it in another way—money. Money was her key to the happiness in her future that she lived for and dreamed about. The saved money would've brought her tears of joy even if her mother didn't say she loved Gertie. It just so happened that one came before the other and it was more overwhelming than Gertie was able to fathom.

By explicitly stating the meaning of the text, the group undercut the freedom to construct meaning that could be given to the reader through navigating the menu structure of the document and accumulating one's own meaning.

The two poetry projects also utilized the menu structure. In each case, the organization of the documents is largely the result of the pedagogically designed parameters of the scenario and the focus of the material presented to the students both in class and during the planning stages of the project. Additionally, the students designed for themselves the pathways they wanted to use in the sections they were responsible for. Amy describes in several journal entries how she decided to lay out her section:

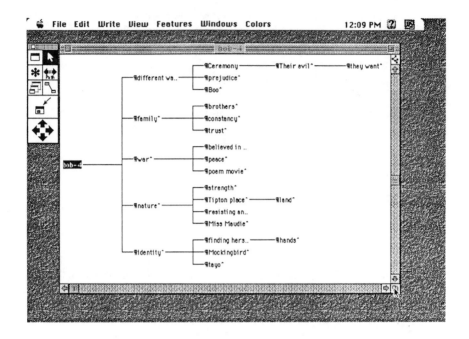

Figure 3.14. Chart view from Bob

I wanted to be in charge of the section on how poetry Uses Language in a Special Way. I decided to do this because there were many writing possibilities, like similes, metaphors, onomatopoeia, . . . alliteration, and personification. . . . I wrote a little about each of those [alliteration, etc.] because I wanted all of them to get individual attention. I decided to do that because you can go to one of them without having to read every single one of them. (Amy, journal, 1995)

Based on the pedagogical structure, then, Amy was able to conceptualize the electronic spaces and how she wanted to present and link them.

Another of the seventh graders explained in an interview the rationale she used to make links in her group's document between her sections and poems and other students' sections and poems:

Well [we linked by] clicking on the piece and picking like the word to link with something else. I guess it was, it was pretty neat how you could do that though. . . . But I guess picking the words that we had to use, you had to make words that made sense instead of just like picking any word so it was kind of hard to if there was like five

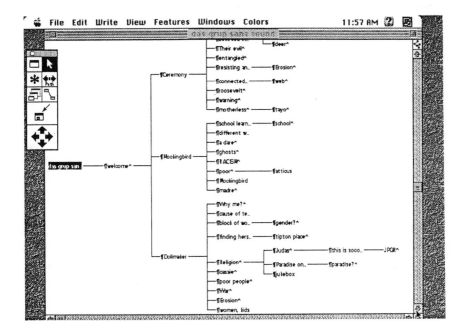

Figure 3.15. Chart view from das grup

things linked to one part you had to pick a certain thing to use.
(Cynthia, interview, 6/5/95)

Cynthia's statement that links must "make sense" shows that she is cog-
nizant that, as per the scenario, others will be reading the document and
depending on the group to link "correctly" the poetry elements and the
examples of each in the poems. But unlike the undergraduate group that
wanted people to infer a meaning from the single, implicit links, Cynthia
implies that there is more than one correct option for each element, thus
displaying her understanding of the explicit classification structure of
the document. But she also understands in a way that belies her 12 years
that too much static might interfere with the reader's ability to make
connections. Her statement that she "had to pick a certain thing to use"
indicates that she knows that not only is there more than one poem that
might exemplify the meanings of the poetry terms, but also that she
believes that not all the examples possible should be linked as they
might create dissonance for the reader. Thus, her use of the electronic
space is informed by her broadening conceptual understanding of the
topic at hand. Similarly, even the authors of a linear interpretive intent

with the three novels informed their construction of the electronic space with a growing conceptual understanding of the novels at hand.

This greater conceptual understanding was aided by and is also evident in Cynthia's description of the linking process, which began on a paper chart that included print copies of all the spaces and finished on the computer through the linking tool:

> [I'm not sure if we had it (the paper chart) when we did that part but] we took the introduction [if we had it and then we had like the language and the express of the sounds and everything and we thought well what . . . yeah we did have the beginning because we had this and then we had like personification and stuff.] And we looked at that and we said, you know, personification is part of that and something else . . . is part of this and that works for this poem and it worked for this poem and so we just kind of connected it what worked. If like something rhymed we put it in sounds or something like . . . some poems had two different parts like some sounds rhymed and some were personification so we had to see what was more like the biggest part of the poem. If it rhymed a lot or if the whole thing was personification. We had to decide. (Cynthia, interview, 6/5/95)

Obviously, the group's understanding of the topics at hand was aided by the process of linking, even if the reader's understanding from the act of following the links is not.

Within the biography projects, students planned their individual sections very differently. As already discussed, some students designed a restricted pathway for meaning and navigation by using single links and explicit "textual" connections. However, other students used the electronic possibilities to allow for various expository structures. Two boys created hybrid projects that combined both variable pathway links and single linear links. Both monologues opened onto a main menu of cut and pasted images (see Figure 3.16); these images were then selected and highlighted to create a pseudo-button navigational device that used the electronic possibilities of turning media into a navigational tool. This sophisticated use was not appropriated by any other group. Not surprisingly, each boy decided that certain information was better presented in one way than the other. In an interview, Ben explains why in his Saddam Hussein monologue he offers his reader several options in the "personal" section and no choices in the "political" section:

> So they [the reader] could find it [the space they wanted to read in the "personal" section] themselves and locate it and they can read it

Figure 3.16. Pseudo-button navigational link in Saddam Hussein from Biography 3

and see what they like on it. I think everyone should know about his political life and what happened during the war and how America was involved. And his personal life I thought people should just know a little more about him instead of just he was so bad or he was so versatile. . . . Political I thought should go in order, from how he got into it to when he was the President to the latest which was the Gulf War. The personal I thought wasn't as important, and they could choose whatever they wanted to know about him. (Ben, interview, 6/5/95)

Ben makes his decision about order based on the importance of the information: Less important information can be accessed randomly because it does not matter; more important information must be viewed in an order that makes sense, in this case, chronological order. (Note that unlike the other students, Ben sees no connection between or places little emphasis on early personal events and their impact on the reader's understanding of the later important political events.)

Mark's project on Colin Powell is similar in structure to Ben's. Mark's pseudo-button navigation tool allows the reader the choice between a space on the Gulf War that hot word links to related texts, a movie space about Powell's time "In Office," and an "Early Years" movie linking to two spaces about Powell's military honors. In addition, Mark jumps via hot word link to Ben's Saddam Hussein "Gulf War" movie "Because they both have to do with war." In an interview, Mark explains why and how he structured pathways as he did:

> More variety, actually more like a variety for people to go through. . . . I think it's pretty chronological, but the Gulf War, it's a lot funner if you can choose where to go, if you just like there, it's just like a report, a plain old report. There's reading through them, you have to go to the next one. You can go wherever you want, that's why I like the variety definitely and if you don't want to hear something then why do you have to listen to it? or go through it? . . . No, I think I gave them less [freedom] than I would have liked. I would have liked just doing everything, but it was kind of hard. Definitely on the freedom in listening to the speech [an electronic constraint that we actually changed right there during the interview], I mean if they wanted to get out during the middle then they should have been able to do that somehow. (Mark, interview, 6/5/95)

As much variety and freedom as Mark gives his reader, he clearly wants to give him or her more, but finds doing so difficult. Whether this is because he is unable to exploit the possibilities of the electronic space to the extent he would like or because his conceptual understanding of how to expand expository structures is limited, Mark obviously goes well beyond his fellow classmates in exploring the potential of the hypertext space.

The undergraduate project das grup made the most use of the electronic possibilities of hypermedia. Their menu based on the chart view of StorySpace (Figure 3.15) offers readers unlimited choice as to which space to read. Once in a space, the reader found text or space links to other spaces. This group authored the most links of this implicit nature. In all, 15 single links and 7 spaces with 11 multiple links created an underlying fabric of possible meanings between and beyond the three novels.

One example of this underlying linking is presented in Figures 3.17, 3.18, and 3.19. The cluster of four linked spaces from the three separate main menu novel categories used six links to provide multiple pathways for the reader to follow. Depending on in which space the reader started, a different sequence of experience would follow. Figure 3.17 begins in the **roosevelt** space, which is categorized within the novel

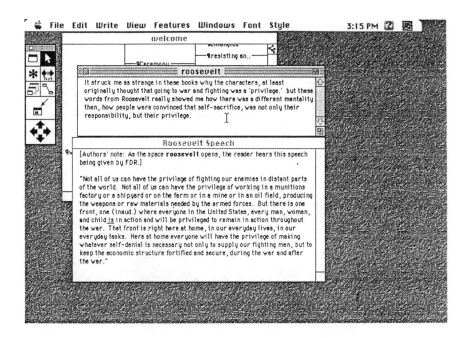

Figure 3.17. Writing space roosevelt with text of voiceover from das grup

Ceremony and juxtaposes an interpretation about the audio speech that is heard when the space opens.

The interpretation about the characters in "these books" connects to the experience of Tayo, Rocky, and other Native Americans who were convinced they would gain the rights of citizenship by fighting for the American nation. From **roosevelt**, the reader can follow one of two links to the **cassie** or **war** spaces shown in Figure 3.18. Roosevelt's words about "economic stability" are reinterpreted (a symbolic juxtapostion) in terms of Gertie's and Clovis' lives in *The Dollmaker*, or Roosevelt's words about "privilege" are made directly problematic by the image of the young boy and the question, "Does this look like privilege?"

Figure 3.19 presents the two possible destinations from the question about privilege in cassie. One is Roosevelt's speech, which a reader may not yet have heard, if they entered this set of underlying links from either **war** or **cassie**. The second destination is to the space **different ways**, which layers the issue of privilege onto a quote from *To Kill a Mockingbird* in which Calpurnia is scolding Scout when she says "and don't you let me catch you remarkin' on their ways like you was so high and mighty!"

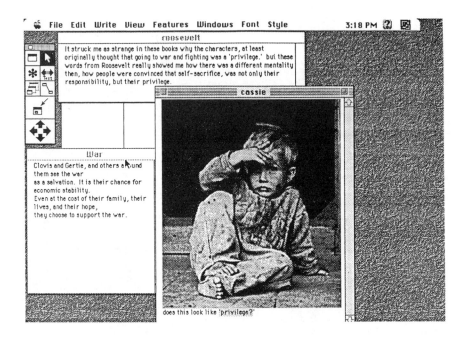

Figure 3.18. Links to cassie and war from roosevelt in das grup

Moving between these spaces in multiple ways involves the reader in different juxtapositions with potentially different resulting interpretations about the value of war, the idea of privilege; and connections between war, privilege, profit, opportunity, pride, and so on. Das grup's project was the only one containing underlying clusters of spaces, beyond the categorical menus, that linked in such a way as to provide the reader with a choice of pathways to follow and therefore, the possibility to construct more symbolic layers of meaning for the electronic hypermedia text.

Table 3.2 describes the organizational structure of the projects by delineating the types of pathways and links that were constructed. As indicated by the similar number of linear and multiple links, Poetry 1 and Poetry 4 utilized comparable menu structures that supported the definition-example exposition of their projects. Biography 3 and Biography 4's reliance on juxtaposed media can be explained by the pedagogical requirement for first-person monologue. The profusion of linear links and relative lack of multiple spaces in these two documents may be because the projects were developed by individuals to be housed in the same project. Although Bertie and Snapple's novels both used a

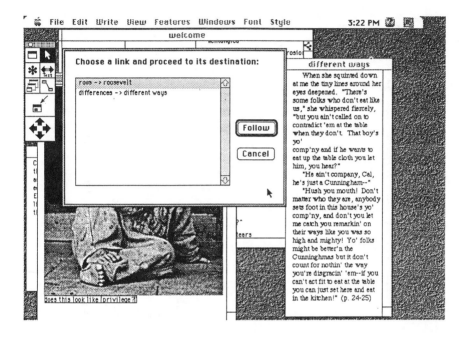

Figure 3.19. Links to roosevelt and different ways in das grup

linear pathway through spaces that juxtaposed text and media, Bertie used only space links to connect whole spaces. Snapple's Novels used only text links, which allowed this group to highlight excerpts to focus the intended meaning of their narrative. Incredible Themes did not use any linking at all but relied solely on the thematic structure of the chart view, mainly because they could not figure out how to use the link tool. Although Bob indicates the use of five spaces with 21 outgoing links, these were only space links that duplicated the thematic structure of their chart view. 2 chicks and dude and das grup used the hypertext potential of linking to build a set of connections between text experts and spaces which underlie the visible menu structure of the chart view. 2 chicks and dude created only 3 such links, whereas das grup had 22 links that readers could serendipitously find as they experienced particular spaces.

Table 3.2. Summary Data of Link Types and Path Types.

Hypermedia Project Titles	Total # of Spaces	Link Type Text	Link Type Space	Link Type Juxta	Path Type Linear	Path Type Multiple	Out links
Poetry 1	39	82	0	7	10	2–	9
Poetry 4	34	69	0	7	8	3–	11
Biography 3	65	98	0	28	39	4–	15
Biography 4	20	20	0	20	15	1–	3
Bertie	19	0	15	12	16	0	0
Snapple's Novels	28	23	0	15	24	0	0
Incredible Themes	15	0	0	9	0	0	0
Bob	25	0	24	10	3	5–	21
2 chicks and dude	28	3	0	6	3	0	0
das grup	45	14	12	18	15	7–	11

Link Types:

Text: a test link from a specific selection of text or image to another space

Space: a space link between two spaces

Juxta: a juxtaposition of media (print text is considered a media form) within one space

Path Types:

Linear: Space with only one outgoing link to follow (and possibly a return to a prior space)

Multiple: Space with more than one outgoing link

Out links: the number of total outgoing links in the total number of spaces categorized as multiple

CONTEXTUALIZING THE PROMISE OF HYPERMEDIA

The electronic and pedagogical contexts experienced by students trans-acted to shape the conceptual and physical work of authoring hyperme-dia. Even if a small group's product ended up as an attempt to represent a single meaning in a one-way only linear essay, the process of author-ing in the electronic space deepened the understanding of the concepts being represented:

> if I read over it before this I'd think . . . that poem rhymes and then once I learned all these other different things I could read over the same poem and say well that poem has a bunch of other things in it too. Maybe I would say something else first instead of saying it rhymes 'cause that was the only thing I knew then. And I'd say well that poem could be different by putting these words in it but the way it is there is, it's exciting because the words are better used or something. (Cynthia, interview, 6/5/95)

Without the hypermedia authoring, Cynthia would have continued to think of poems as representing one thing—metaphor, rhyme, sound—because the pedagogical context in which many of the poems were origi-nally written directed students to write a metaphor poem, then a rhyme poem, and so on. As a result of hypermedia authoring, students found the poetic devices in many poems and became much more sensitive to the way words can be used to create a desired meaningful effect.

Theoretically, we and proponents of electronic hypertext author-ing may put too much emphasis on the liberating benefits of the medi-um, at least for readers (Landow, 1992a). Almost all of the authors in our studies have sought to construct pathways that present particular intended meanings; they rarely left interpretation up to the readers. But, the long tradition of pedagogical contexts for authoring that students have experienced have almost entirely focused on getting the author's meaning and expressing themselves clearly in their own writing. The student authors did what they had always been expected to do with text; they constructed a narrative or expository pathway through multi-media texts. However, we did not frame the pedagogical context to pro-duce hypermedia products that could be modified by the new reader, which is an activity supporting the claims of liberation for the reader (Bolter, 1991; Lanham, 1989).

If we ignore the reader, and look only on these hypermedia pro-jects as an opportunity to support the conceptual development of the students about particular topics, then the activity was immensely suc-cessful. The electronic medium made it possible for the students to bring together in one space the vast array of media that play such a dominant role in defining the meaning of everyday life. Having all of the artifacts present in or easily accessed in *one space* may seem like a small point, but in reality, this issue of proximity is very important. Visual theorists understand this well; according to Stern and Robinson (1994), "Proximity is the tendency to group together those things that are located close to one another" (p. 40). This idea of grouping is not just spatial; rather, it refers to conceptual grouping. Add to proximity the planned links and organized structure of hypermedia documents and you have a very powerful tool for demonstrating and constructing intertextual relationships and meaning. In this sense, the authoring achieved the goal Myers implied in the following suggestion to students about their hypermedia projects:

> Think back on our conversation today when you're searching for a purpose for what we might be trying to do with these three novels . . . the experiences in these three novels and the ideas in these three novels are beyond the novels, reaching far beyond the novels into the comments that we overhear on the street as Ron has said in terms of "I got a girl," into movies as Mike has implied, into music, everywhere these ideas show up. And what these ideas do . . . is they build this representation of what it means to be a spouse, or to have expectations, or to be frustrated, things like that. . . . before I close with a poem I should try to explain that we think that the computer program StorySpace might provide a space in which you could explore ideas, one idea that finds itself being represented in these novels and beyond these novels, because it allows you to put those representations into some relationship to each other to try to explore that idea. We've never used StorySpace before so we don't know whether or not it will actually facilitate exploring an idea like that as it is represented in various arenas of our life. (class transcript, 2/17/95)

The authoring groups had little difficulty finding images, music, and video to represent important ideas in their projects. And the attraction to making their own quicktime movies with pictures and a voiceover was extremely captivating to both the seventh graders and the undergraduates. What did give the groups varying degrees of difficulty was the creation of hyperlink pathways through the spaces.

> I just wanted to say one other thing. When we got started on this a long time ago, we started with Jamie's flow chart and if we were to do it again we would work more on our own flow chart, but we used his to get started to figure out what we were doing really. Toward the end of the project we got better at manipulating the text

and finding our own stuff. (Marie, sharing das grup project, 4/26/95)

The pedagogical contexts we established with the undergraduates tended to make the linking aspect of hypermedia authoring more difficult, and understanding this allowed us to use different instructional strategies with the seventh graders, which tended to support the linking process.

Myers introduced the undergraduates to StorySpace by displaying a space he had already created on the three novels. He displayed the structure, or web view, of the space (Figure 3.1), showed students how to make new spaces, and directed them to make new spaces to enter their response to the four quotes from each novel that he had already provided. In the structure view, when an author creates a new space it shows up with a line visually linking it to the space one hierarchical level up, or the containing space. This line carries with it the impression of a link, thus without even using any linking tools, the structure view can signify a menu of ideas, categorized and linked together. The author can even move the spaces around to create a new set of categories with structure view links. This pedagogical move greatly impacted the undergraduates authoring, as many of the groups did not see any sense in creating additional links because the connections between spaces were already visible. In fact, the 21 space links giving the reader a choice of where to go out of five theme spaces created by the Bob group actually reproduce the structure links already visible in the structure view. The links created by Bertie and Snapple's Novels served as a single linear pathway through the spaces they left categorized by novels. The two chicks and Dude group created three underlying links, whereas only Das Grup created an extensive web of underlying links providing the reader with interpretive connections beyond the novel categories presented in the structure view of StorySpace.

Being aware of this constraining experience, McKillop did not use the structure view, but kept students in the space view of StorySpace (Figure 3.2). In this view, the containers act as categorical holding spaces, and only text or space links created by the students show up as arrows into or out of the spaces. To support the seventh graders' construction of links, McKillop created large wall charts with the printed out spaces. Then students were directed use pen or marker to select words or images to connect from space to space. This planning on paper allowed students to see all of the spaces that could only be seen a few at a time electronically on the computer monitor. In addition, the focus on using only text links supported the electronic and conceptual development of interpretive pathways.

> I think it was to see the connection . . . you write and you read but
> you don't . . . see the connection. We had to link so you had to read
> it first and then you saw those but then you thought there was like if
> you write a . . . metaphor and you find that there's alliteration or
> personification and it's just like instead of just writing a poem,
> another poem will fit it. (Beth, interview, 5/23/95)

Beth explained how looking for text to link involved her in considering
the conceptual connections, or intertextuality, of every word in a space;
"it can have all five special languages and that. And it helped you learn"
(Beth, interview, 5/23/95).

The pedagogical context blocked the undergraduates from utilizing the power of hypermedia to author links. Their initial experience
with the StorySpace file used by Myers for instruction was so blocking
that most of them interpreted the whole hypermedia project as something they would do as teachers to direct their own students' learning.

> Dan: If you as a teacher you present this to a class, the prob-
>   lem is the difference between guiding and directing,
>   and with the multimedia project it seems more like,
>   instead of letting the students find the ideas, you give
>   the ideas to generate the discussion about. . . .
>
> Ron: The way you present this to a class is similar to the way
>   Jamie is presenting it to us, as in here is your tool, here
>   is how you use them, and I mean he provided us with a
>   general outline of some ideas but you can branch off of
>   that and use that as you want, and instead of having a
>   teacher go to the StorySpace and create things that are
>   shown to the students, the teacher presenting the
>   StorySpace to the students where they create things to
>   show to the teacher. (class transcript, 2/20/95)

Ron was clearly in the minority when he expressed his idea that
StorySpace and hypermedia authoring were tools for students to construct their own understandings. The traditional pedagogical context in
which the teacher directs the thinking of students had framed the project
as computer-based instruction in which students are led through a particular sequence of experiences by a computer rather than by the teacher.
This event counters Landow's (1992b) belief that "hypertext answers
teachers' sincere prayers for active, independent-minded students who
take more responsibility for their education and are not afraid to challenge and disagree" (p. 163). Even the seventh graders, who seemed to
be very much in charge of the construction of their own meanings in the
hypermedia projects they created, were guided to construct an instructional experience about poetry for students who knew nothing.

Ultimately, sufficient evidence exists to support the conclusion that all of the students using hypermedia deepened their understanding about the subject matter they sought to represent in the electronic medium. This does not mean that the meaning they socially constructed is somehow empowered or critical of any cultural status quo. In only a few exceptions did the undergraduates push their interpretations about the books beyond the books and by juxtaposing media from the world launch into a critique of cultural values or examination of their own values (J. Myers, 1992). Ohmann (1985) argued that rather than being a democratizing agent, technologies such as hypertext are potentially oppressive tools controlled by the dominant society. The belief that authors and readers in a hypertext system are controlling a text is just an illusion. Hypermedia as a technology cannot determine revolutionary change; it will serve the sociopolitical contexts that authors bring into the creative process. And in school classrooms, claims that the teacher-student relationship is one that will be "reconfigur[ed]" by the new technology as the teacher becomes "more a coach than a lecturer, and more an older, more experienced partner in a collaboration than an authenticated leader" (Landow, 1992b, p. 123) will only be realized if the pedagogical context offers such a possibility.

Even Bolter (1991), who is one of them most ardent supporters of how the new technology will change literacy, argued that the writing space is not just a physical space, but also a mind set, a psychological construct that allows one to work within, and without, the conventions of the physical writing space. In most every case, the authors in our studies brought to the hypermedia electronic space the traditional mind set of linear exposition. In fact, the undergraduates were even resistant to the electronic space as they defended the value in writing a traditional paper.

Dan: I'm not saying that I enjoy writing when I had to do it, but I think it's important to maintain that type of literacy. I think that with the computer age and I think yes we do need to keep up with the times, but at the same time I think we have to keep a fluency of writing down, just for the sake of our own humanity, for our own intelligence, for our sake of our own sense of style, I think that with computerization we tend to obliterate style altogether just to get the ideas down. I think a lot of that is lost.

Deb: A paper makes you take that quote and put it into a context . . . it makes you connect themes, connect ideas. I guess I can say that there are strengths and weaknesses, but what are they, how do you define them, and you can give one quote and say this is a strength, but when you look at the whole book and you see a strength or a weakness, it just makes you support your ideas, it makes you think more about them, when I think that the quote just gives you a surface level.

Ron: StorySpace isn't just the quotes. I think that what you're still talking about in the last part of being a paper is not excluded from being in StorySpace. You can make spaces and write down about the thing.

Deb Right . . . but, there is something about a theme that makes you think more than I think StorySpace.

Ron: Well that's because you've never done it before. I think they're very similar. I think StorySpace can allow you to break off into different areas other than writing, but I think it can include writing.

Peg: I think all of us are kinda of well you have to put in a quote and then you give your response. I don't see why we can't just open a box and say gee this is what I thought today and just totally write into a paper. I think we're all stuck up on write a quote and then respond to it. You don't have to do that on there. In fact it'd be kinda cool if we all wrote something totally out, you know, just this is what I think because this is what my experience was, you know, you can put that in there. I don't see anything wrong with it. (class, 2/20/95)

As Peg emphasizes again how Myers' pedagogy constrained the initial understanding of composing in StorySpace, she also reinforces the use of StorySpace as a word processor in which you can just go ahead and write the familiar types of linear expositions the technology is supposed to move literacy beyond. Charney (1994) highlighted how the assumptions made about the reading and writing processes by jubilant advocates of hypertext are in direct conflict with "rhetorical theory, cognitive psychology, and document design," all of which confirm that reading and writing in the hypertext environment may "increase the burdens on both readers and writers" (p. 241). Likewise, Haas and Neuwirth (1994) contended that believers in the technology as an all-powerful mind set are in danger of granting too much control to the machine by not examining how the background of actual readers and writers determines much of their interaction with the computer.

We believe, based on our work with 13- and 20-year-olds, that the electronic contexts of hypermedia offer authors important tools for constructing relevant and engaging interpretations about their world. The addition of multimedia allows authors to layer meanings onto a text and thereby promote a deeper consideration and understanding of ideas through the creation of a broader multimedia intertextuality; this understanding is generated by the hundreds of images and sounds that authors consider, but ultimately do not use, as they look for texts to use in their projects. The ability to link specific sections of a text, including images, to other texts involves the authors in visually representing intertextuality. The traditional contexts for writing brought by the authors need not be seen as a limiting factor in the construction of hypermedia documents. It may indeed be foolish to believe that authors should not attempt to intend a meaning; not to do so would imply that an author need not take a position, argue a point, or put forward a set of values for others to consider. The freedom of interpretation implied by hypertext advocates, if possible, would in fact be dangerous in a democratic society because it suggests that ideas are just out there floating in the ether, open to any interpretation one would like to make. Hypermedia may in fact do just the opposite quite well, as some authoring groups demonstrated how they could juxtapose and link texts to present oppositional ideas, thus creating the moment of tension in values and beliefs that underlies the negotiation of meaning necessary to naming and renaming our shared experiences in a continually growing, collaborating, democratic society. However, we must remember that the technology alone did not cause this to happen; rather the pedagogical context together with the electronic context constructed the values and social relationships that defined the experience of literacy.

Chapter 4

Defining Links

Scott Lloyd DeWitt

Ohio State University at Marion

One might argue that I am about to state the obvious, especially at this moment in the history of hypertext and composition studies: A characteristic that distinguishes hypertext from all other types of text is the opportunity to create and/or use electronic links. Yet, much like Slatin's (1990a) *College English* thesis—"Hypertext is very different from more traditional forms of text"—it must be stated. Links bring users from one text to another, from one hypertext to another. They dissolve and resolve textual boundaries. They present choice and embody transition. Links effectuate cognitive stereoscopy ("a-ha!") as well as cognitive dissonance ("what?") (Bleich, 1986, p. 99). They are what allow a hypertext to be recenterable or acenterable.

They are the defining property of "what hypertext is."

Hypertext linking plays a constitutive role, both explicit and implicit, in how research describes hypertext. For example, Conklin (1987) asserted that sophisticated links distinguish hypertext from mere window systems and file systems. Researchers' descriptions of hierarchical and associative organization and access of information pivots on hypertext's linking (Baird, 1988; Bevilacqua, 1989; Byles, 1988; Carr, 1988; Howard, 1988; Jonassen, 1988; Kearsley, 1988; Shneiderman & Kearsley, 1988; K. Smith, 1988). Joyce's (1988) exploratory and constructive hypertexts describe two types of relationships users can have with hypertext linking. Slatin's exploration of sequence, prediction, and coherence grows from the notion of linking in hypertext. Bolter, Delany, Landow, Shirk, McDaid, Smith, and Moulthrop spend substantive time in their work defining hypertext, asserting it cannot be separated from a discussion of hypertext linking (see DeWitt, 1996, p. 10).

The title of this chapter, "Defining Links," offers an intentional play on words. *Defining* as a present participle identifies a task, an act—in this case, something we need to do to better understand the nature of links: "In this chapter, I will be defining links in students' hypertexts." However, *defining* as an adjective qualifies a particular attribute of hypertext links—in this case, that they define relationships as well as the experience of discovering relationships for both hypertext creators and users: "In this chapter, I will argue that hypertext links are *defining* in nature."

I did not originally set out to study student writers and links, per se. I conducted a large-scale study that sought to examine how students employ strategies of inquiry and problem formulation for writing while using a hypertext application. I operated from the premise that experienced and successful writers use not only a wealth of information available to them, but also the connections and relations they see among and within this information as a means of inventing continuously throughout the writing process. They observe and respond to the worlds around them. Also, I considered many of the claims researchers make about how learners can benefit from classroom hypertext applications, namely:

- Hypertext gives students a new, powerful tool for accessing and creating knowledge.
- Hypertext can help students make connections between seemingly unrelated ideas.
- Hypertext promotes organized and integrative thought.
- Hypertext encourages collaborative learning.
- Hypertext gives students easier access to their own writing.

These are the very areas of difficulty encountered by first-year college writing students, particularly those enrolled in intensive or developmental programs.

I designed a hypertext component for a unit of a freshman writing course, then analyzed that section of the class as teacher-researcher. The unit included short inventive and exploratory readings and writings, class discussions, in-class writings, in-depth reading assignments, and summary writing, all of which led to a major writing assignment—a documented essay. Students created a hypertext of their inventive writing that later served as a database that they explored to find topics and discover relationships. As teacher-researcher, I recorded daily occurrences in the classroom. Also, I analyzed the students' hypertexts, their writing, and carefully examined the transcripts from interviews I conducted with students near the completion of the project.

In the end, the overall project, originally a doctoral dissertation, looked at hypertext and invention from multiple perspectives, extending outward to curriculum development, cognitive learning theory, the pedagogy of technology, reading theory, association psychology, and 19th-century rhetorics. This chapter, however, presents a small segment of that study. In order to better understand how students used hypertext throughout the processes of invention and inquiry, I found it necessary to understand how students defined hypertext for themselves. This chapter concentrates on associations between how students define hypertext links and the role these links play in their self-constructed definitions of hypertext itself. In order to give this reading of my study necessary context, I describe the research project design in its entirety.

ESTABLISHING CONTEXTS: THE WRITING COURSE AND ITS PROGRAM

The writing program at Illinois State University (ISU) describes Language and Composition I (English 101) as

> a course intended to foster students' development as active writers within various academic and public intellectual communities. To do this, students must be able a) to identify topics significant to a specific readership or to make that readership attentive to the individual writer's interests; and b) to produce texts appropriate to the forums (the "places of publication") for which they are intended. Both abilities, which are complexly intertwined and mutually reinforcing, are developed through practice in *reading* texts and practice in *writing* texts that exhibit the pertinent conventions. Conventions include such things as acceptable types of evidence, strategies of argument, and patterns of organization and development, as well as "lesser" matters of style and format. (Departmental handout: "To the Composition Faculty: A Conceptual Overview of Language and Composition I")

Although descriptive in theory, the program is prescriptive in its course requirements: students must complete eight papers (including one ungraded diagnostic essay, one that entails source documentation, and one modeled after the ISU junior-level writing exam) and 15 writings about reading.

The particular course I was teaching was a section of Intensive Language and Composition I (English 101.10). The Department of English offers a special writing track for those who are identified as students who initially may have difficulty in a first-year writing course. Students who receive a 2 or less out of 5 on the ISU writing entrance exam, or who receive ACT English subscores of 21 or below and a score of 3 or less on the ISU writing entrance exam are placed in English 101.10. Although students who are enrolled in an Intensive English 101 section complete the same program requirements and receive the same credit hours as those enrolled in regular English 101, English 101.10 students must attend class 5 hours a week instead of only 3. Enrollment in English 101.10 is 20 per class, and teachers are assigned two undergraduate teaching assistants (UTAs) to aid them with individualized conferencing (UTAs are selected based on a rigorous interviewing process and their successful completion of Language and Composition I with a grade of "B" or higher and an overall GPA of 3.0).

English 101.10 students are by no means considered remedial. They do, however, need more contact hours of individualized writing instruction to develop their written language abilities within the university setting. The program's philosophy further espoused that these students would best be served by not only additional contact and experience with the written discourse of the university setting, but also by the individualized attention they receive by enrolling in an intensive class. These sections of composition were designed to be taught using the models and theories of Bartholomae (1986); Bartholomae and Petrotsky (1986); Hull, Rose, Fraser, and Castellano (1991); and Hull and Rose (1989).

THE TECHNOLOGICAL ENVIRONMENT

I taught English 101.10 in the Department of English's professional writing classroom, a networked classroom of Apple Macintosh SE 20 computers. The core software in the classroom consisted of Microsoft Word 4.00D, HyperCard 2.0, PageMaker 3.01, all of which was driven by Macintosh System Software v6.0.7. Each workstation was networked to the other workstations via a high-capacity classroom server/storage hard disk using AppleShare Network Software. The classroom disk was organized in levels of folders through which students had capabilities to organize their own storage space. At the onset of the course, students were taught the use of the Macintosh computer system using the "Macintosh Tour," through which they learned the concepts of inserting and deleting, editing, pull-down menus, mouse use, and windows. They were introduced to Microsoft Word 4.00D and the workings of the professional writing classroom network within the first week of classes. After these thorough introductions, students had acquired enough of the basics of the Macintosh system and the network to learn more advanced features of the computers on their own and by using the documentation available to them in the classroom and on line. Students were expected to complete all of their writing using the computer. For the most part, students turned in their writing online via the classroom network, and it was returned to them with written comments in the same way. Also, most handouts were distributed through the network instead of in paper form. By the end of the first complete unit of study, students were familiar with most of the computer classroom's capabilities and features.

THE UNIT

The section of Language and Composition I I planned to use for my research was organized thematically around the broad topic, "Current Issues." Topics for units included, "Taking a Closer Look at ISU," "Defining Family," "The Chaos of the AIDS Pandemic," and "Representations in Popular Culture." The course held rigorous expectations for students in terms of developing their critical reading and writing skills. All units included many short inventional reading and writing assignments that led to a major writing assignment.

The unit studied in this research project, "Freedom of Expression and the University Community," covered issues of free speech specifically on college campuses (see Appendix A). The topic was a pressing and timely current social issue with much written dialogue occurring in the popular press and media that also paralleled volatile situations on campus. The pedagogical and theoretical intent of this unit was consistent with other units taught in the course. The unit placed much emphasis on strategies of problem formulation with reading and writing placed at the heart of systematic inquiry. The unit was designed paying close attention to the sequencing of assignments and classroom activities so that the skills of reading and writing fed into, enriched, and extended the abilities of each other. The classroom was designed as an interactive learning environment—student-focused and student-centered. Students were asked to write with real-world purposes, for real-world audiences, and within real-world forums and communities.

Freedom of expression and First Amendment rights is one of the many topics that students often approach simplistically and superficially: Students are unsure of how to problematize the issue and think critically about it. At the heart of this composition course is a theoretical framework that posits that exploring a topic through reading and writing will help students become critical thinkers. Therefore, students read many short articles on the topic of freedom of speech and expression from varying points of view. Also, students wrote responses to these articles, to class discussions, and to real-world situations concerning issues of First Amendment rights. The final writing project assignment required students to conduct a survey of college community individuals on some aspect of freedom of expression and to write both a report of their findings and an essay to a particular audience interested in their results. I hoped that students would accomplish several things in the unit's final writing assignment:

1. They would learn to form a general research question that would drive their exploration into a topic.
2. They would learn to write a survey questionnaire and to use the results as a source for writing.
3. They would learn to make generalizations based on specific information they had obtained.
4. They would learn to use the same pool of information for different types of writing (format, purpose, audience).

The unit consisted of 15 class days and exceeded the course requirements with three journal entries and two major writing projects.

English 101.10 offered me flexibility in teaching a hypertext program, HyperCard, to my students. Having never taught HyperCard before, I was uncertain of how quickly the students would adapt to the new computer program, and I was uncertain of the troubleshooting that I would have to do throughout instruction. Because this course met 5 days a week, I was confident that student learning in the class would not be jeopardized by integrating into the course the use of a new computer application.

HyperCard offers its users a number of authoring and scripting capabilities in addition to word processing, paint, draw, and tools to create backgrounds, fields, and buttons. With these capabilities, users can create graphically complex cards with multiple scrolling fields within a rich network of links that can be specially scripted to meet particular needs. Also, scanned images, sound, and video can be incorporated into a user's stack. HyperCard is known for being easily learned and used by those with little technological expertise. However, foregrounding my pedagogical objectives, I chose to narrowly focus what I taught students about HyperCard. For example, graphically designing cards and learning HyperCard's scripting language is important for those whose focus is learning the full features of the program. But I feared that it would take too much attention away from the intended writing instruction of this course.[1] I focused HyperCard instruction by

1. designing a common card for all students to use that was clearly titled for the unit and contained a scrolling field and an area to store buttons (Figure 4.1).
2. teaching students how to use the word processing features of the scrolling field.
3. showing students how to add and delete cards.
4. demonstrating for students how to navigate through their cards using the "Go" menu.
5. instructing students on the basic steps necessary for creating buttons and links between cards.

Students were assigned to create a HyperCard stack that included the following:

- A copy of the U.S. Constitution's First Amendment and ISU's Equal Opportunity/Affirmative Action statement.
- A summary and a response to three assigned rhetorical situations about university life and freedom of expression (see Appendix B). The situations focused on verbal harassment; libel; and boycotts, protests, and demonstrations. Each offered conflict from multiple perspectives to what could appear on the surface to be a simple, cut-and-dried case.
- A written summary of "Chapter 2: An Open Community" from the Carnegie Foundation's *Campus Life: In Search of Community.*
- A written response to the following question: "Consider your role in the university community at ISU. What do you feel is the most pressing issue concerning this role and First Amendment rights and freedom of expression?" (Figure 4.2).

---

[1]In its support of scholarly endeavors, the department grants those conducting research on student writing a great deal of freedom when designing courses in which the research will take place. Easily, I would have been allowed by the director of writing programs and the department to employ variations on some of the "requirements" for the course. However, in designing the course as a whole, before beginning this research study, I had followed the department's guidelines, which I felt provided students with a sound background of writing instruction. Because in my research I was studying one unit in the context of the entire semester, I felt it necessary to continue using the department's guidelines throughout so as not to disrupt the course's sequence. Therefore, I intentionally placed constraints on myself as both teacher and researcher.

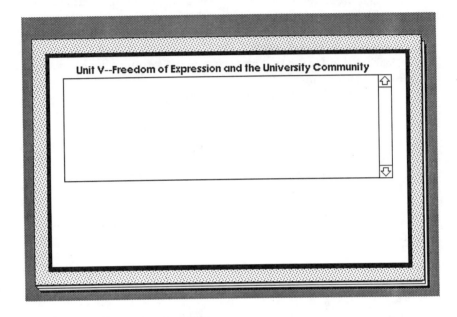

Unit V--Freedom of Expression and the University Community

Figure 4.1. Common card designed for students

They were also encouraged to include the following assignments in the stack:

- Written responses to two articles they were asked to find on their own on a topic of interest for the unit.
- Written responses to two articles from an alternative reading list of 27 articles.

As students continued to work with HyperCard, building their stacks, they were presented with the unit's major writing project. They were directed to their HyperCard stacks:

> For the past week (and actually, for the past semester), you have been writing about different issues of freedom of expression. And for the last week, you have stored and organized much of your writing on a HyperCard stack. From this writing, your HyperCard stack itself, and your own personal experience, you need to generate a topic for this paper.

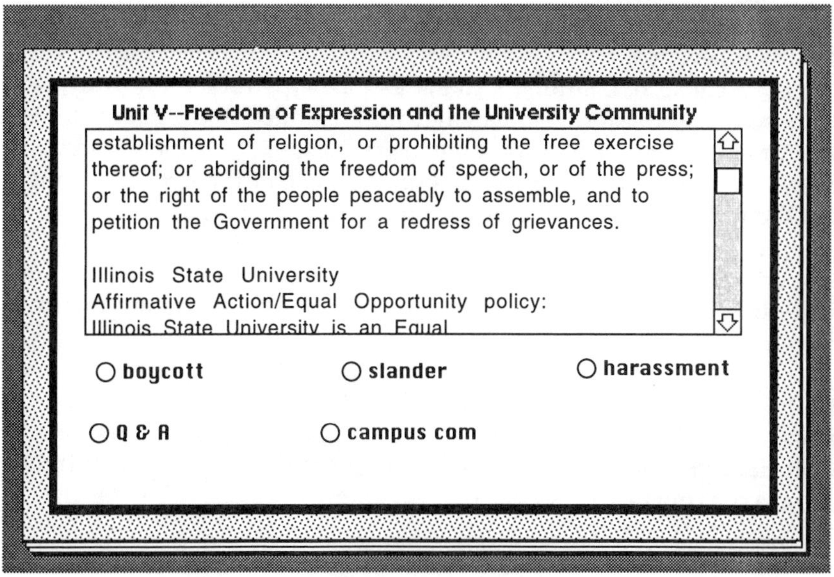

**Figure 4.2. The common card with student-generated text
and buttons/links**

In other words, students were asked to draw on their experience from
the writing assignments themselves and from their experience creating
their hypertexts. Also, they were asked to search their hypertext as a
database to help generate a topic for the unit's major writing project.

COLLECTION OF DATA

Throughout my research project, I participated in copious note-taking
and journal writing that provided me with the data I needed to study
the course and the writing program. I kept a daily log of classroom
occurrences throughout the unit of instruction. Also, I kept a written
record of all classroom instruction that occurred throughout the unit.
And finally, after each class session, I recorded in a journal my thoughts
about and reactions to the class session. (I often used this journal to formulate responses to my students about their work. See Appendix C.)
The writing that I recorded as teacher provided me with descriptions of
classroom instruction and student inquiry and learning in context that
became an invaluable resource to my role as researcher. Furthermore,

exploring the classroom as a site for inquiry and learning provided me with the context in which I could ask specific questions about students' use of HyperCard.

I chose five students to act as participants for my study. All were second-semester freshman and were enrolled in the course for the first time. They agreed to grant me interviews that took place on Day 12 of the unit. The interviews focused on their use of HyperCard throughout the unit. I reserved classroom time so the interviews could be conducted within the setting where the students had worked on HyperCard. The subjects' names were Devin, Daniel, Marie, Yvonne, and Matthew (I promised students anonymity—these are not their real names).

My rationale for choosing participants for this project stemmed from students' overall attitude toward the course as opposed to an assessment of students' writing abilities, their final written products, or their final grades. I looked at three aspects of students' overall attitude toward the course:

1. Attendance: Those students chosen as participants for my research missed no more than two class meetings throughout the entire semester, had missed only one class by the final quarter of the semester, and had missed no class meetings throughout the studied unit.
2. Course requirements: All the students chosen for my research successfully completed the course requirements of 8 major writing projects and 15 journal assignments. Furthermore, all the students turned in their work by the designated due date, and no one requested an extension for turning in work late.
3. Class participation: All the students chosen as research participants received an "A" for class participation based on a departmental rubric. Also, all the students chosen as participants frequently made appointments outside of class during office hours and regularly requested additional written feedback to their writing.

I believe there exists a direct parallel between students' overall attitude toward the class and their overall learning experience. Therefore, I chose participants whose experience I perceived as matching both the fullness of the project I developed and my investment as the researcher in that project. For example, because of their excellent attendance, those students chosen as participants were those who took advantage of the time allotted to them in class to work in the technological environment in which they were being studied. Also, they clearly took advantage of the classroom itself as a learning environment by showing a commitment toward a rigorous course that met 5 days a week at 8 a.m. for 16 weeks for which they received 3 hours of university studies credit. These students also benefited considerably from the course's theoretical framework, specifically that of the course's sequence, by completing all course requirements and completing them on schedule. And finally, those students chosen for my research created a positive classroom learning experience by participating at a high level of sophistication. They frequently participated in classroom discussions and activities, offered insightful comments and asked critical questions in class, and prioritized matters of reading and writing during class time.

While writing in class, the students worked directly on the classroom's network and used their floppy disks for back-up purposes. Because of the classroom disk storage facilities and network of the computerized classroom, I was easily able to gather the work they had stored in our class folder. Within the designated class folder on the classroom disk, each student had his or her own folder designated by last names. Students were not given special access privileges and/or security options for their folders so that I, as well as the other students in the class, could have easy access to their work. From their folders, I collected students' HyperCard stacks and the first drafts of their writing projects from the unit. Analyzing students' writing and their HyperCard stacks provided me with the data to begin answering my first two research questions:

1. How would students organize and link their reading and writing using HyperCard?
2. How could the overall design of the students' stacks be described and classified?

Toward completion of the unit, the five students I selected as research participants granted me interviews concerning their experiences with HyperCard and the writing projects on which they were working. These interviews were conducted with each individual participant at a computer workstation in the classroom during periods of the day when no classes were meeting. I recorded the interviews on tape with each one lasting approximately 25 minutes. These recordings provided me with an account of students describing their own experiences in the context of the learning environment. Analyzing the transcripts from these interviews provided me with the data to begin answering my next two research questions:

3. How would students describe how they organized and linked their reading and writing using HyperCard?
4. How would students describe and classify the overall design of their own stacks?

Students were asked to define HyperCard in their own words to see if they had constructed a theoretical framework of the concept of hypertext. Next, students were asked to give a "tour" of their stacks and describe their rationale for constructing the stacks in the manner that they did. Students described what they had written on a particular card, clicked on an available button, and described where the link would take them and why. Also, they were asked to describe their link classification, or in other words, how they decided to linguistically represent the links within their stacks. This also added to the students' perceived theoretical framework of the concept of hypertext. And finally, students were asked to explain how they used the stack they created throughout their invention processes while working on their writing projects.

The information I had obtained while conducting this study (descriptions of the classroom learning environment, analyzing students' writing and HyperCard stacks, and interviewing students about their experience using HyperCard in the composition classroom) provided me with the data to answer my all-encompassing research question:

5. How would students use their HyperCard stack throughout the processes of inquiry and problem formulation?

HYPERTEXTUALIZING COMPOSITION

Current theory in hypertext and composition studies leans toward embracing hypertext as a new form of writing. Current practice, subsequently, explores the possibilities of having students write hypertexts as their major writing assignments in composition courses. Asking students to write hypertexts in addition to meeting the existing course requirements for a specific unit of one major writing assignment, two writings about readings, one of which should be a summary, all of which can be evaluated by the standards written by the department, was not going to be possible. So I asked myself, "Should these 'requirements' limit or restrict our freshman writers from experiencing the benefits of hypertextual classroom applications?" My answer was, of course, "No." Instead, what I needed to do was take a closer look at the processes that students go through in meeting these departmental requirements and design an application for hypertext based on these processes. After experiencing the convergence of current critical theory on hypertext and how the writing program is defined by the Department, I then asked myself, "Can hypertext help students make connections between the reading and writing assignments we give them that will in turn feed into their invention processes that lead to major writing assignments? In other words, can students hypertextualize and therefore gain better access to their own traditionally written texts—texts that they use for invention while making meaning and creating knowledge?"

By asking students to create HyperCard stacks of their own writing in combination with meeting the departmental requirements, I was able to achieve a positive integration of hypertext in the composition classroom. First of all, the patterns of good behavior that students had developed thus far in the class for approaching writing tasks were not disrupted. As stated earlier, the unit was designed before deciding on a hypertext application. Therefore, the unit's assignments and activities paralleled the work that students had completed thus far in the semester. For example, students read to write. They critically read the writing of others, analyzing both the content and formal structures of the writing. Students learned to explore within and outside of themselves when developing topics for writing. Students viewed revision positively as an opportunity to rethink their ideas as they continued in their reading and writing processes. Students worked and interacted with the technology as a tool, not as either a stumbling block or as a cure-all. Overall, the integration of hypertext in this particular case reinforced the idea that the reading and writing they completed for a unit in the classroom should not be viewed as a series of "assignments" but instead as a means of inquiry, invention, exploration, forming content, and formal schemata, or, in other words, as a process of coming to know.

This integration of hypertext in the current composition curriculum also allowed me to fulfill many responsibilities expected of me in my position as writing instructor at the university. Students completed the department's requirements for the course. The writing that students completed for their HyperCard stacks was modeled after suggested assignments for writing about reading (journals). This included written responses to readings and summary writing. Because each of these writings was contained on a separate card within the stacks, I was able to evaluate them as separate pieces of writing (in fact, users of HyperCard will find they can print "fields" of text, bringing their writing from an electronic writing space to print).

This use of hypertext in the composition classroom again reinforced for students that reading and writing is a way of coming to know, and that successful writers complete a great deal of reading and writing before they complete a desired end product. Indeed, some of the reading and writing within their stacks was graded and was considered in meeting department requirements. However, the creation of the stack itself to facilitate invention was not evaluated. Never before was it possible, or desirable, to evaluate students' reading and writing as it relates to invention. Grading students' inquiry would mean grading student process. Instead, the chunks were graded as product as they fulfilled a department requirement. The creation and use of the hypertext was treated as process: The hypertext itself was not graded and was treated solely as a space of exploration.

DEFINING HYPERTEXT

At no time during HyperCard instruction did I offer the students a theoretical definition of *hypertext*. Instead, I directed their attention to what HyperCard does and how it operates by demonstrating its capabilities using a DataShow projection device. Also, I gave the students writing assignments that they were to complete using HyperCard. When I taught them how to make links within their stacks, the classroom discussion did not focus on theoretical issues of linking electronic texts but instead stopped with valuing the ease of getting from one text to another. While students in the class used the program, I was eager to help those who encountered difficulties or who asked for assistance. However, I did not spend time explaining authoring rules or linking principles, nor did I offer students advice on creating their HyperCard stacks. By not telling students how they "should" use HyperCard and by not articulating an objective definition of hypertext, I was able to see if they could articulate insightful definitions of hypertext merely by experiencing its application.

In order to avoid asking a leading question, or at least in order to lead all of the interview subjects in the same direction, I asked them all the same question, one that I had written before the interviews:

> How do you define HyperCard? For example, if you were talking about using this program in your English class and a friend asked you, "What is HyperCard?" what would you say?

Key words defined a commonality: *organize, connection, manage, accessible, relationship, sort.* Similarly, common to these definitions was an unavoidable metaphor—that of the notecard. HyperCard is based on the idea of the index card, and students' experience with notecards in high school English classes extended the metaphor with the program being used in a composition course.

For both Matthew and Devin, HyperCard acted as a means of making and organizing relationships. Matthew said:

> I guess I would kinda explain it as like they are like cards hooked together to help you sort out your thoughts. You can switch from card to card in certain organized ways. Certain thoughts would be put together that relate to a topic but you can also hook together other topics that might be related in a different way. You just write about one thing or way that you feel, and if it has any relationship to any other thing that you want to write down, you just write that down, and make the connection. It's kinda like a stapler—you staple your ideas together with the buttons. You can staple them all together or you can staple just certain ones together.

Devin described negotiating between the general and the specific for organizing his writing. He said:

> This is a way to organize information that is basically the same topic but it's different things depending on who you are talking about or what the specific thing is that you are thinking about a general topic. You know, like we were focusing on a very broad topic, freedom of speech, but then we looked at all of these smaller ideas that were connected to it. HyperCard lets you organized the information so that you can connect different ideas together that would normally be difficult to see the connection. HyperCard allows you to go back to square one to clear your eyes of the smaller ideas and topics and look again at the bigger picture. It's not that HyperCard actually does that for you. You are still doing it. This is just a tool that makes it easier in the long run.

It is significant that Devin at first makes an assertion that recognizing connections between the ideas found in his writing would "normally be difficult to see" if he were not using HyperCard. He then believes that he has stated that the technology has actually made the connections instead of him and clarifies that he is "still doing it" and that "this is just a tool that makes it easier in the long run."

C. Smith (1991) argued that defining hypertext is a matter of negotiating between hypertext as information system and hypertext as facilitation. Hypertext as information system exists as a body of text to be searched, restructured, and reconfigured. Its purpose is to be explored so that users can gain a wealth of knowledge from the texts they encounter. Hypertext as information system, then, positions the application as exploratory in nature, a place where text is managed and retrieved. Although users can access information associatively, intuitively, and hierarchically according to their needs, hypertext as information system foregrounds the system over the user. Hypertext as facilitation, on the other hand, foregrounds the users and the users' experience over the system. It begins to view hypertext in the context of use, as a space where students make relationships and construct meaning, activities that feed into and enrich other processes. Hypertext as facilitation, then, positions itself as exploratory in nature, but more importantly, it positions itself as constructive as its application adds to and enhances learning experiences.

The challenge for effective application of hypertext to student inquiry, invention, and exploration becomes achieving and maintaining a positive balance of hypertext as information system, a space where a body of information exists, and hypertext as facilitation, how that space is used to feed into and enrich writing processes. Devin's defined experience exemplifies the students' use of HyperCard as information system and facilitation:

> I felt like I was at an advantage over all of my mixed up ideas when I had this to work with. I get really confused, and I forget things that I think or that I have written, and this let me keep it all together. I could manage better. I really don't remember getting all confused during this assignment like I have with others. And I think that I saw things different. Like, it really is all the same thing, free speech. I mean that it's all related, not the same. Just different ways of looking at it.

Although not as specific and articulate as Matthew and Devin, Daniel and Marie defined HyperCard in terms of ease of entering information into the program and using the program as a storage space. Daniel said:

> It's like using notecards. Except because it's a computer, you get to use word processing, which means you don't need to worry about mistakes, and it's easy to change. And it's faster, if you can type good. You get down what you're feeling and what your thoughts are on the card. You can like write it, as informal as you want. It's a quick way to get your ideas down and save them. You can go back and read them and use what you wrote down. And then you make buttons so you can move around easier.

Marie adds:

> You know how you always used to have to use those little note-cards? Well, you type the stuff on the HyperCard program. It gives you so many cards and then you can link them. You can have as much on a card as you want, and like I said, you can link them together so that you have all of your ideas together. I think it's kinda like when you do research papers and you have all of those note cards. This would be much easier doing it this way, I think, better than the old way. You are using the computer. You have everything on the disk, and you don't have to save. All of your notes are automatically saved because of HyperCard.

If Daniel and Marie were mostly influenced by the ease of creating a HyperCard stack, and Devin and Matthew defined HyperCard in terms of organization and relationships, then Yvonne combined the benefits of both views and looked at HyperCard as a means of gaining access to her own writing. She said:

> Instead of using index cards, you are using HyperCards. It's more accessible instead of leafing through the index cards. You've got it on computer. Your buttons are like key phrases, you know, so that you don't have to go through the whole stack to find what you are looking for. Once you give a button a key phrase, you can just use that button to get through the stack and get to a card and get to whatever information you have on it. When we first learned this, just putting writing in there, I thought that this was stupid. I didn't understand why we were learning a new program to just put some of our writing on there. I still had to use the menu and go to "previous" or "next" to look up my information. And I thought that this was going to be easier to get to our stuff, but it really wasn't. But once we did the buttons, it was easier. Programming the buttons makes my writing more accessible.

Many educators are concerned with hypertext being applied as merely database management and information retrieval systems. Yet Yvonne demonstrated a positive concept of hypertext as information system by allowing it to facilitate her reading and writing experience.

One could argue that these students' definitions hardly represent the dynamic nature of what hypertext is or what it does. Also, they lack such key terms as *associative, nonlinear, hierarchical,* and *intuitive.* On the other hand, these students defined HyperCard in a matter true to their experience with the program. And more importantly, they have defined the program in terms of how it facilitated their reading and writing experience.

A significant part of Language and Composition I is teaching students to analyze situations for writing. This includes not only purpose, exigency, and audience, but also the forums in which public nonfiction prose appears. For the most part, students learn that these forums for writing, not the teacher or the assignment, dictate the length of the final written product. But as a rule of thumb, students in Language and Composition I produce papers between three and five pages in length.

However, students enrolled in this course were well aware of the writing requirements that awaited them not only in future English courses, but also in other courses across the disciplines. When asked if they could imagine any application for HyperCard outside of Language and Composition I and whether they would use the program again, all of the research study's subjects referred to "the research paper" as their exigency for using the program in the future. Key phrases that occurred during the interviews included, "longer papers," "more information to deal with," and "managing all the research."

Devin: Like if I have a bunch of ideas that I want to get down, you know. And I know that as I go on in school that I am going to have lots of big papers to write, so I think that I could use it for that. I mean, I used it here for a pretty short paper. I bet that I could use it a lot when I get, you know, like a thirty page paper assignment and have more information to deal with. I bet that I could use it to study for a test, too. I could put all of my notes on it and study at the computer and use the buttons to get to different notes. And maybe the connections would make me remember things better. Like when I was writing, I could remember things better, and where they were better, when I used this. So I bet that it would work for taking a test, too.

Marie: When I have to write research papers, I will use HyperCard to help me. I have trouble managing all the research. I could put my thoughts and ideas together by linking them and it would be a lot easier rather than having to write it down and scribble it out, you know, do it over, I mean, I would use this. It's a lot easier.

Matthew: I think that a lot of people have problems, I mean you are always told to brainstorm before you do some project, and I think that this is a good way to brainstorm for any project, to get different ideas out and connect them, and you don't have to worry about putting them in paper form. Like you can write whatever you want, and when you want to write about a different topic, you just get a new card, and if it's related, you get a new button and connect them. It helps to get ideas out of your head whether or not you are going to use them in your paper or not, they all help in the long run.

Yvonne: It's rather time consuming to input the data and create the buttons. But once I got better at it I suppose it wouldn't take as long. I think it could help me with my writing. Maybe if I was writing a longer paper, a 10-page paper or something more involved, and I had a lot of stuff to work with, this would give me access to my data quicker and better.

Daniel: Ya, for some of the bigger papers that I know that I will have to write later on in school. I have a problem with arranging all of my stuff, notes and stuff, neatly so that I can use them when I start writing the actual paper. I can see using this for that. I'm sure that I will be writing big papers in a couple of years. I think it will be a big help.

Certainly, overwhelming and confusing our students with vast amounts of information is not one of our pedagogical goals in teaching writing. But students will encounter situations where they need to gain control over multiple texts they are processing. Slatin (1988) pointed out that the complex processes of writing and research necessitate that students manage large amount of materials and make connections and relationships between and within. He said, "That's what a liberal education is supposed to be for. It's also what hypertext and hypermedia systems are for" (p. 127).

REVISING HYPERTEXTS

Those who design their composition courses as interactive learning settings spend a significant amount of time responding to student writing. Much of the responding takes place in the form of written comments on student drafts. These comments serve as a dialogue between teacher and students about the written text itself which, we hope, enhances students' learning processes about composing. But when students need more immediate attention to their writing, sometimes the student-teacher conference is the most effective means of offering feedback to student writers.

The student-teacher conference was an integral part of the learning setting in the researched Language and Composition I course. I often workshopped with students in the classroom as they worked on drafts of their major writing assignments. Also, students often made appointments during my office hours to discuss their work in progress. In almost all cases, these conferences took place using the computer; I would read and respond to students' writing as we both sat at a student workstation in the classroom or at my office computer. As a teacher, I viewed my role in the conference setting as both an imagined audience for the writing and as someone with a higher level of expertise in written communication based on my own reading and writing experience. Therefore, my contribution to the dialogue about students' writing often took the form of questions that would force the students to rethink the texts they had produced. Students had grown accustomed to this type of exchange throughout the semester.

As mentioned earlier, for the most part I remained "hands off" when students were working with the HyperCard program. If students, while working in class, had questions about or needed feedback on their short writing assignments, I eagerly conferenced with them. However, at no time during these conferences did we include discussion of their use of HyperCard. Again, I felt as a researcher that it was important to see how and to what extent hypertext applications actually facilitated student learning.

The interviews I conducted with my research subjects mirrored the student-teacher conferences to which they were accustomed. What became pointedly clear during my interviews with my research subjects, however, is that students were both willing and eager to rethink and resee their experience with HyperCard, exhibiting behavior Birnbaum (1986) characterized as "reflective thought," behavior that is "rooted in expectation of mastery rather than anxiety about failure" (p. 32). This reflective behavior showed up during the interview; when questioned, for example, about how they had organized their HyperCard stacks, students' responses often led to a revision of their stacks. However, I realized that these students would have benefited from student-teacher conferencing about how they used the program during the process of creating their stacks. Students felt somewhat abandoned by me as teacher; throughout the semester I never hesitated to intervene and offer them assistance with how the technology in the classroom could serve as a more proficient tool to them as writers.

When asked about the frustrations they experienced with HyperCard throughout the unit, Daniel and Matthew both agreed that their frustration did not necessarily rest with the program itself as much as it did with how independent they were forced to be while learning its application. Daniel admitted:

I felt a bit lost through this whole thing. Well, not the whole time. I mean at first, when you showed us how to enter the stuff on the cards, it didn't make much sense that we were learning this program. It does everything that the other program [Microsoft Word] does. Well, not even as much. But then you showed us how to make buttons, and it started to make more sense. But you really didn't tell us much. I thought that you would be coming around and looking at our stacks and talk to us. I think you could have given me advice on how to make it better.

Matthew's reaction was similar:

I think that it would do a lot of good if it [HyperCard] was incorporated more into the class. Like talking like this about it. I'm already thinking about some of the things that I wrote and how I made buttons. So if we had the chance to talk to you about this, like we do our papers in class, I think that would be different.

Daniel's comments are interesting in that the concept of hypertext "started to make more sense" when he experienced the program's linking capabilities, showing that his experience rather than his teacher defined "what is hypertext" for him. And Matthew's insight is telling as he articulates that there exists a relationship between "what I wrote and how I made buttons." Daniel's developing understanding of the program and Matthew's connection of his writing and its connections could have become points of departure for further discussion in a student-teacher conference.

Specific examples of students rethinking and reseeing their stacks during the conference-type interview show how students benefited from discussing their use of HyperCard. For example, Yvonne's stack was somewhat simplistic in its level of connectivity. In fact, she failed to see connections that I perceived as clear and obvious. But a dialogue with Yvonne and a simple open-ended question helped her see a missed relationship. Yvonne explained her response to the question pertaining to her role at the university and First Amendment rights that was accessed by the button "Q & A":

Basically my response was that this is a white university, and as an African American, it is my duty and responsibility to promote other minority causes and benefit all of the minorities at ISU. We are not being represented very well by the masses.

But the only other link this card had was with a card that contain ISU's anti-discrimination policy. As we reviewed her other writing, I, as a reader, was surprised that she did not make other connections within her stack, connections that I saw.

Scott: Let's talk about your response to the question that I asked you to respond to about your role at ISU. One of the things that you wrote about was being African American on a primarily white campus. Do you see any connections between your response there and any other of the writing you have done?

Yvonne: Probably "Boycott" and "Harassment." They could link up with my response on "Q&A." Because boycotts and civil rights are definitely connected, and we [African-American students] have all experienced some type of harassment at this school. So I could make some connections there. That would help.

Another similar exchange would have proven to be beneficial had it occurred while she was creating her stack:

Scott: One thing that I am thinking is, for example, you get back into this stack 2 years down the line, or someone else in the class wants to learn something about what you have written. If they saw "Q &A," would that tell them what was on the card?

Yvonne: No it wouldn't. That's a name just for me.

Scott: But how about in the future?

Yvonne: I guess I wouldn't really know what was on it.

Scott: What would you name this button today so that 2 years down the line you would know what was on this card?

Yvonne: Let me go back and look at it. Maybe "My role at ISU." That's better than "Q&A" for sure.

Of course, in this pressured setting, Yvonne is not thinking about the limitation of the number of characters she can use to name a button, but the exchange between the two of us helped her to improve the design of her HyperCard stack, and in turn could provide for a more positive facilitation.

REREADING AND LINKING

As students continually completed short, inventive writing assignments using HyperCard, they were instructed how to make links, or buttons, that would connect their ideas stored on separate cards. With HyperCard's "New Button" feature, creating an electronic link between two cards consisted of a quick and simple execution, using just a few commands. However, to make purposeful links within their stacks, students needed to have invested themselves a great deal into their own writing.

This investment came most strongly in how students spent a significant amount of time rereading their own written texts that they had produced as part of their inquiry into the topic of "Freedom of Expression and the University Community." In order to make purposeful links between cards, students had to be not only familiar with the text they had produced on the cards, but, as readers they also had to have actively made connections between the content of the different pieces of writing. And these two operations, of course, required students to reread the writing that they had already produced.

The participants for this study had spent a great deal of time rereading their written texts. They were familiar with not only what they had written, but also with where the writing was located within their HyperCard stack. During the interviews I conducted with these students, no one at any time hesitated while giving me a "tour" of their HyperCard stacks. Students, starting on any given card, were asked to simply click a button, describe the text composed on the target card, and explain the rationale for the electronic link between the two. This process continued until we had exhausted all of the writing that the students had completed using the program. I attribute their knowledge of and familiarity with their own written texts to them creating links within their HyperCard stacks and to using their HyperCard stacks for searching for topics about which to write.

Carefully reviewing the links that students created within their HyperCard stacks provided another means by which to study students' experience with the program. I was concerned that students would link every card to every other card without actively making meaningful connections between the ideas. With the "Copy" and "Paste" features of HyperCard, it would have been easy for students to design a set of buttons and copy the entire set to each card with little meaning behind these links (the "Copy" command in HyperCard not only copies the button as an icon, but it also copies the programming built into the button).

However, of the five students with whom I worked closely, not one student made gratuitous links in his or her stack. When asked to create buttons within their stacks, these students in fact made links that connected their ideas. They scrutinized the links they made, and the links were, in their eyes, purposeful. Therefore, creating links became a meaning-making act, not merely an execution of a series of commands. Because these links were purposeful to the students, they experienced cognitive stereoscopy, a "re-cognition . . . [of] one perspective superimposed on another in such a way that the one perspective does not appear to be prior to the other" (Bleich, 1986, p. 99).

The links or buttons that students made in their HyperCard stacks can be investigated at yet another level. HyperCard does not automatically name buttons for users according to key phrases found or highlighted in a text. Instead, the user is responsible for purposefully naming buttons. HyperCard asks students to name the buttons that represent the links they have made (unfortunately, the buttons' names could only contain 10 or fewer characters with HyperCard 2.0, a limitation that has been eliminated from subsequent versions). Naming buttons in HyperCard served as a representation of the connections the students encountered when they experienced cognitive stereoscopy. But in order to name buttons, students were required to complete a cognitive process that in composition studies we pursue often. Naming buttons forced students to summarize and synthesize the texts they were connecting. As they continued to make purposeful connections between their written texts, students were engaged in on-going summarizing and strategic backtracking.

However, the classification systems students employed for naming buttons differed greatly. When naming buttons, students chose to represent the link between cards according to the content of ideas on the cards or based on the assignment they were completing. Buttons named according to content were descriptive in terms of definition, or in terms of situations and issues being addressed. Buttons named according to an assignment described the type of writing assignment completed or borrowed a key term from the assignment itself. All five students involved used a combination of both types of classification.

Examples of these two types of classification will better illustrate how students chose to name buttons in their HyperCard stacks. Matthew created a button that would lead to his response to the rhetorical situation about a comedian invited to campus who was deemed offensive to much of the student population. He named this button "Comedy?" Because he was limited to the number of characters that he could use when naming a button, Matthew used the question mark to represent what wouldn't fit in the button name: "This means, like, isn't this just comedy, a joke? If I could, I would have named it something like, 'Seriously offensive, or just plain comedy?' So that's why I named this "Comedy?" Matthew was not only involved in ongoing summarizing when naming the button, but was also pushed toward summarizing due to the program limiting the number of characters allowed on a button label.

When Marie was summarizing and responding to all three rhetorical situations, she viewed each as very different and saw very few connections between the two. But when she began to link her responses in her HyperCard stack, and juxtaposed them with the First Amendment to the U.S. Constitution and ISU's Affirmative/Equal Opportunity policy, she saw that what they had in common was that "they were, like, stretching the First Amendment and the school's policy too far." Therefore, Marie linked all three situations to the card that contained the First Amendment and ISU's antidiscrimination policy and named the buttons, "Too far." In doing so, Marie participated in ongoing summarization, but more importantly, she was involved in strategic backtracking. Her summary of the buttons as "Too far" depended directly on their connection to the First Amendment and ISU's antidiscrimination policy.

Devin, Daniel, and Yvonne chose to name buttons that reflected the assignments they were working on rather than the content of the writing on a card where a button would take them. For example, students were asked to respond to the following question: "Consider your role in the university community here at ISU. What is the most pressing issue concerning this role and First Amendment rights and freedom of expression?" Yvonne named the button in her stack that took her to this card, "Q & A." She said, "You gave us a question and you asked us to respond to it, so I named it, 'Question and Answer,' you know, 'Q & A.'" Daniel also named the button that represented this writing according to the assignment, but he named this button "Role." He said, "You asked us to write about our role here and freedom of expression. So I just named this 'Role.' That's what the assignment was about, my role." Students were also assigned to write a summary of "Chapter 2: An Open Community," from the Carnegie Foundation's (1990) Campus Life. Devin named the button that directed him to this writing "Summary." He said, "This button takes us to the summary of the article that we had to do for our journals." Other common assignment-oriented buttons included "Situation 1," "Situation 2," and "Situation 3."

One point becomes clear when looking at the assignment-oriented classification of buttons. When students described the writing that was found on the cards to which these buttons directed them, they also described the writing in terms of the assignment. For example, both Daniel and Yvonne included in their descriptions that they completed this writing because I, the teacher, had assigned it: "You gave us a question. . . . You asked us to write . . . ." And Devin includes that this writing assignment is part of his journal for the unit. How they named the buttons reflects their attitudes toward the purpose of the written texts they produced.

It would seem that those students who named buttons according to the content of the card, or the ideas between which they saw a connection, had a deeper understanding of the issues with which they were dealing than those students who identified their buttons according to the assignments that they were completing. And some correlation does exist. For example, those students who named their buttons according to the assignment explained the content of the card in terms of the assignment. And often their investment in the issue at hand is superficial. Consider how Devin describes the writing on the card that is accessed when he clicks on the button, "Situation 3," the rhetorical situation that focuses on slander, liable, and freedom of expression:

> Situation 3 is about a history teacher, his name is Cliff, he got accused of, by a young lady, that he had said something about abortion. And basically the situation never happened, so the guy thought that he had to go through all the pain and embarrassment over something that never happened and his dean didn't want to tell him about the student because he felt that he wouldn't be able to grade her fairly.

Devin begins, "Situation 3 is about . . . " and indeed, on the surface these assignments presented narratives, or stories. But Devin's explanation of the situation is not only simplistic, it is not an accurate account of the assignment's narrative (see Appendix B). Cliff, the teacher, is not accused of speaking about abortion. He is accused of inviting a speaker to class to discuss the topic. Furthermore, during the interview, Devin fails to account for his response to the situation and his analysis of it in terms of First Amendment rights.

However, the fact that students named buttons according to content does not necessarily mean that they experienced a deeper understanding of the issues at hand. For example, consider again the rhetorical situations to which students responded. Daniel did not name the button according to the assignment; he named the button according to the content of the writing on the card. A button in his stack named "Watterson" took Daniel to the rhetorical situation that focused on violent verbal threats and harassment. The setting of this rhetorical situation was Watterson Towers, a residence hall on ISU's campus. This button was named according to the story that illustrated the issue of violent verbal threats and harassment, not on the issue itself. Daniel's investment in this rhetorical situation as a story and not as a sociopolitical issue was articulated when he described the writing on the card:

It's a story about a female RA in Watterson who was harassed by two males. She was alone, and they said some pretty harsh things to her. She wasn't sure what she should do, so she let it go at first. Then she told her boss and they were going to press charges. She was going to take them to SJO.

The difference rests with Daniel's investment as a reader and a writer in a fictional account rather than the issues that the fictional account is attempting to illustrate. How he named the button reflected his experience with the text as a reader and a writer.

Regardless of whether students named buttons according to ideas or assignments, one concept of linking in HyperCard remained constant: These subjects used HyperCard for their own personal purposes, and this again was reflected in their classification and naming of buttons. In fact, all five students attested to the fact that they named their buttons to facilitate their own personal use of the stack. Key phrases that affirmed this during the interviews include "a quick reference," "I knew in my mind," and "something that would help me remember what was on the card." Daniel expanded on his use of button names: "The way that it's set up right now, it's just for me personally. It would be pretty confusing for others to look at these buttons and try to figure out what they meant without having any idea what was on the card, or on the stack." Yvonne added, "It's just for my use. The way they are named now, I know what is on there and it's just for me."

But even as students named buttons for their own personal association, they did so keeping a certain level of immediacy in mind. Students who named buttons according to the assignments, for example, "Situation 1," could not expect the label to trigger at a later date the same type of association that it triggered while they were working on the unit. Even some abbreviations could fail to make a purposeful connection. Yvonne named the button that would take her to her summary of the Carnegie Foundation piece, "Camp. Com.," short for "Campus Communication." Devin explained that his button names could expand the immediacy of their use in terms of other members of the class: "I think that anyone in the class would know what it is that I have on these cards by the names, but only because we all did the same assignments."

CONCLUSIONS, IMPLICATIONS, AND CONTINUING QUESTIONS

This study begins to question many of the promises and broadly accepted benefits forwarded by current research on hypertext and student writing. Consider, for example, the claim that hypertext offers students the opportunity to develop high-level thinking skills as they encounter texts and make purposeful connections. Hypertext itself will not teach students advanced-level thinking skills. But its concept can indeed augment sound pedagogy that does. Although I resist and am critical of blanket, technocentric promises of hypertext, I am comfortable going so far as to say that actual experience with the technology can augment the pedagogy that we embrace and can further promote the acquisition of critical thinking skills.

I find it difficult in this research study to differentiate between how students were influenced by the pedagogy that viewed writing as systematic inquiry and how students were influenced by hypertext as a technology that could facilitate systematic inquiry. Again, it becomes necessary to identify specifically how students were actually influenced by hypertext, and how other factors may have affected them. Throughout the semester I had already introduced students to hypertextual techniques—without technological application. Students read many essays and articles on a topic being pursued in a thematic unit. These readings were written from varying perspectives and employed many different forms and conventions. Students completed short writing assignments about the readings, including response and summary writing. Students also participated in class discussions and some type of small group activity. In the end, they were asked to address the unit's major writing assignment, making connections between the reading and writing activities they had participated in throughout the unit. In other words, the unit's short reading and writing assignments—intended to facilitate inquiry—created a sense of chaos for students, and the unit's major writing assignment forced students to make meaning by developing a sense of order from the chaos.

I reviewed the basic structure of each unit that students had already completed as I asked during our interviews how they felt hypertext changed their invention processes:

> When we started this assignment, it was really no different from any other assignment that we completed over the semester. You did a great deal of reading and writing some responses to the readings and different situations. There were class discussions. And we did this so that you could begin to generate some ideas toward forming a paper topic. But in this case, you did all of the writing and brainstorming using HyperCard. Has this changed your way of thinking throughout this invention process or the way that you approached your major writing assignment?

The five study participants believed that HyperCard had in some way changed the way they approached the processes of inquiry and invention. Responses ranged from stating that HyperCard made the process easier to explaining that HyperCard actually made the students see connections that they normally would not have seen. Yet, if students believe that hypertext helped them to see and make relationships, what do they believe prevents them from seeing and making the same relationships without the use of hypertext? One participant claimed that hypertext helped her to gain access to her own writing. What normally prevents her from gaining—or how did she lose—access to her writing?

Because of the approach I took toward my research questions, I am unable to analyze specifically how hypertext changed students' approaches to reading and writing assignments. The technology did suddenly shed light on my pedagogy throughout the semester and more concretely illustrated or reflected students' learning processes for them. Because students were able, without hesitation, to describe how they thought HyperCard had facilitated their processes of inquiry and invention, they were consciously theorizing about their own learning processes. In the end, hypertext served as a model or a representation for their own thinking and learning processes. Specifically, hypertext served as a technological representation of what it means to participate in critical inquiry, and generally the concepts of hypertext facilitated the teaching of this skill.

In many ways, hypertextualizing composition instruction means rethinking how both we as teachers and the English studies programs to which we belong operate. By the ways in which they define their very purpose, English studies programs face considerable challenges as they continue developing in a technological age. I explained that a number of guidelines, policies, and conceptual overviews that exist in the department significantly shaped how I taught hypertext and how I integrated the application into my pedagogy. Although I was at liberty as an instructor to use these policies as guidelines and was allowed to develop new approaches to teaching in the classroom, it is important to look at conflicts that may arise in a writing program by hypertextualizing instruction as well as how working within these self-imposed constraints opens the door to other interesting questions. For example, a question worthy of consideration is whether departmental, program, and course definitions truly limit pedagogical hypertext applications. Had I not imposed departmental constraints on myself, I would have had the opportunity to create a much larger unit of study that included different types of writing. Perhaps students could have created hypertext portfolios that included all of the unit's writing, including draft work and writing process self-reflections.

At the same time, aligning with or working against departmental, program, and course definitions, recognizing an existing pedagogy as sound or outdated, can offer guidance and structure to effective integration of hypertext and writing instruction. Balancing hypertext instruction and the composition pedagogy that I knew was important to students' writing development was essential. Remaining hands off for the most part in hypertext instruction raised many questions, even as it provided insights into how students used and defined the program. I learned in the interviews I conducted that students were eager to conference with me about their use of HyperCard. A number of questions arise about the form such a conference should take. For example, we need to decide at what point we intervene in students' use of the program and contemplate the types of questions we should ask students during a conference and how these questions will facilitate learning.

As a teacher, I also questioned the place that theoretical discussions of hypertext had in a developmental writing course. Asking ourselves, "What part do these discussions play in the design of a course?" could offer direction for a number of questions for further research. How could theoretical discussions of hypertext change the way students use the application? How should these discussions be integrated into writing pedagogy? Will any writing pedagogy be displaced by integrating this theory into the classroom? What student experiences are limited by avoiding theoretical discussions of hypertext? In my study, students' exposure to HyperCard was limited to one unit that occurred late in the semester. How would students' experience with hypertext change if they had more sustained exposure to the program as well as an opportunity to participate in an ongoing dialogue about its use in terms of their writing processes? Studies focusing on these types of questions can begin to articulate full, rich integrations of hypertext and composition pedagogy.

I do believe that incorporating theoretical discussions of hypertext into the unit students were working on would have significantly changed how they defined hypertext for themselves. For example, I pointed out that all of the study's participants used the idea of the notecard when defining HyperCard. Of course, this is the metaphor on which HyperCard is based. But these students were defining a specific program, HyperCard, not the concept of hypertext. In their definitions of HyperCard, key terms used to describe hypertext are missing—*associative, nonlinear, hierarchical, intuitive*. Did students not experience these hypertextual concepts, or were they just not given the base from which to articulate them? In turn, are these terms that quickly roll off the tongues of anyone researching hypertext's static representations of a dynamic technology?

Finally, I found a direct correlation between students' reading and the links that they made in their HyperCard stacks. The most significant finding is that students, when creating links, spent a considerable amount of time rereading their own writing in order to make purposeful connections within their stacks. What deserves further attention, however, is how the types of reading in which students participated while creating links was different from the type of reading in which they participated while exploring their stacks after links had been made. Students read for connections when creating links, forcing them to summarize, synthesize, and backtrack in order to create the links. Students returned to their stacks, reading for depth, meaning, and ideas, while continuing to develop their topics for writing. Both types of reading fed into their processes of inquiry, but were very different in purpose.

CERTAIN REFLECTIONS

The purpose of this study was to begin thinking about hypertext applications and hypertext instruction in composition courses. As with much of my research of late, I find that I am asking more questions than I am providing answers. Yet I see value in ending on somewhat unsure footing. To do so promotes further reflection on the methodology I have embraced and the methods I have used in my work. Although ending with so many questions might be disconcerting, I actually find myself stimulated by this situation. I have avoided looking at student texts alone as a way to understand their learning. Instead, I have looked at student writing—the process and the product—from multiple perspectives all within the context of my own pedagogy. The complex nature of this union is almost certain to raise questions that push me toward the continuation of my research on how computer technology influences how I teach and how students learn.

APPENDIX A: UNIT'S MAJOR WRITING ASSIGNMENT

Unit V
Freedom of Expression
and the University Community
Writing Projects 5&6

INTRODUCTION TO THE ASSIGNMENT

The writing that you do for Unit V is going to focus on "Freedom of Expression and the University Community." For Projects 5 and 6, you are going to conduct a survey on some facet of First Amendment rights and the university. Then you will write about your findings.

You probably noticed on the top of the page that this assignment is in two parts:

Project 5 will be a report on your survey results. I will teach you a basic report format in which you clearly present the results of your survey. This part of the assignment is purely informative.

Project 6 will be a written presentation of your results to a specific audience. You will discuss the results of your survey in a formal essay directed to someone who needs the information that you have gathered. If possible, you should also incorporate support from the readings you completed for this unit. While this part of the assignment is also informative, you will have to take into consideration why the audience is interested in the information, and what use the information has to the audience. Also, this part of the assignment might very easily become a highly persuasive piece of writing.

GENERATING A TOPIC

For the past week (and actually, for the past semester), you have been writing about different issues of freedom of expression. And for the last week (excluding days hampered by computer bugs) you have stored and organized much of your writing on a HyperCard stack. From this writing, your HyperCard stack, and your own personal experience, you need to generate a topic for this paper.

First of all, your topic for this paper must be about freedom of expression and some facet of college life. You should begin by asking yourself a question: "What would I like to know about (*fill in the blank with some specific focus on freedom of expression and college life*)?" Then you will write a short survey about this question, hand out your survey, and analyze the results in hopes of answering your question.

There are plenty of topics that you can explore. First of all, review your HyperCard stack for ideas. You should be able to generate a good list of survey questions based on some of the writing you did in the HyperCard stack. Also, think about what interests you the most about freedom of expression and college life.

Also, think ahead. Remember that your survey needs to serve some purpose and that you will be presenting your survey results to a specific audience that is interested in what you have discovered. You will find, especially with Project 6, that you will not succeed with this assignment if your survey has no purpose and no predetermined interested audience.

WRITING A SURVEY QUESTIONNAIRE

Your questionnaire must meet a few requirements:

1. Your questionnaire must be targeted for a specific population. Therefore, you must ask a series of questions that will give you the demographic information that you will need: gender, age, year in school, residence on campus, major, etc. (no need for a name—keep this anonymous). For example, you may want to survey differences between two different residence hall floors and the differences between men and women on those floors. Or maybe you want to survey freshman and senior art majors. You will need to gather this information.

2. Your questionnaire must ask at least 10 questions about the topic you are investigating. You will probably want to make these questions multiple choice (possibly with space for comments.) This will make tabulating the results easier.

3. Your questionnaire needs to be distributed to at least 25 respondents. You can print a laser copy and take it to a local copy shop, media services, or Milner library (if you need to save paper, use a smaller font—Times will give you more words per page).

APPENDIX B: STUDENT ASSIGNMENT SITUATIONS

Situation 1

Comedian Mickey Hay has been scheduled to perform on campus. The ISU entertainment committee is excited about Hay coming to campus. He is popular among college-age students and should be a big money-maker for the campus. However, Hay is a controversial comedian and is known to offend many different groups of people. He tells racist jokes. He promotes stereotypes of Jewish people. He uses derogatory language to describe disabled people. He compares women to farm animals. He sings a song called, "Killed a Fag Last Night on the Way to Burger King," and asks the audience to sing along.

Many students have written letters to the editor of the *Vidette* expressing their disgust that the university is sponsoring the concert, but the letters have not appeared. After an investigation, it is learned that the editor of the newspaper is a big fan of Hay and is planning on attending the concert. The editor claims that she has never seen the letters that were supposedly left at the *Vidette* office.

A coalition of student organizations forms: Feminist Alliance, Black Student Union, Jewish Student Union, Campus Religious Life, Gay and Lesbian Alliance, Office of Disability Concerns, Alliance of Latin American Students, Progressive Student Union, and many more. They try to make an appointment to speak with members of the Entertainment Committee, but the committee won't speak to them. They try to speak to the editor of the *Vidette*, but she claims she is too busy and can't make an appointment with them until after the concert.

The group organizes a boycott of the concert and demonstrates on the quad during the noon hour. They pass out over 10,000 flyers condemning Hay's concert. They challenge the student body to boycott the concert. They ask the president of the university and the director of affirmative action to speak out against the concert. And they demand that the Entertainment Committee be more sensitive to the students of ISU when they schedule acts.

Many students still attend the concert. However, ticket sales are 40% below the projected sales figures. The Entertainment Committee and the *Vidette* criticize the coalition in an editorial claiming that the school lost money on the concert and that the coalition is responsible for the loss.

Question:

What is your gut reaction to the above situation? React to the above passage briefly in writing. How, if at all, does the First Amendment to the Constitution (or any other Amendment) apply to this situation? Does freedom of expression include damaging boycotts? Did everyone in this situation have an equal, fair, and impartial opportunity of freedom of expression?

Situation 2

Three male students living in Watterson Towers wait for a female RA to make her rounds. She is known for being tough on the men who live in the hall. When she walks by them, they stand behind her whispering: "You're not going to write me up, are you bitch?" "Why are you such a cunt to us, man?" "Maybe you'd loosen up a bit if you came and spent the night with me." The men laugh and then say in a conversational tone of voice, "Hey! See ya later. Have a good night."

After an evening of being extremely frightened and somewhat confused, the RA reports the incident to the hall coordinator. The RA feels that she has been threatened. But the two of them are concerned that they won't have a case because no one else heard the men make these comments to her. Two days later, however, another student, a male, who was sitting on the floor around the corner when the incident occurred, comes forward and claims that he heard the entire incident. He says that he would have come forward earlier, but he was afraid that he would be tagged a "narc" and harassed by the three men. He says that he does not want to be involved, and that if his name comes out, he will deny ever having heard the incident. The RA and hall coordinator promise confidentiality.

The three men are confronted by the hall coordinator and the RA. At first the three men deny that they made the comments toward the RA. When they are told that there is a witness, they then change their story. "It was just a little joke," they chuckled. "Didn't the witness hear them all laugh?" They say that they are the victims, the powerless ones. She is the authority figure in the building. They say if the RA wanted to, she could write them up and enforce resident hall rules on them. Why is she playing the innocent party? Also, if she was really offended or afraid, why did she wait so long to bring it up? And besides, weren't they just exercising their freedom of expression? They didn't mean to be offensive, and they didn't threaten her. They can't help it if she gets upset by a few "adult" words. Finally, they promise that they will fight for their freedom of speech rights if the RA and hall coordinator try to press charges.

Question:

What is your gut reaction to the above situation? React to the above passage briefly in writing. How, if at all, does the First Amendment to the Constitution apply to this situation? Does freedom of expression define what can be considered threatening? Did everyone in this situation have an equal, fair, and impartial opportunity of freedom of expression?

Situation 3

A young university history instructor, Cliff, is called into his superior's office. Apparently, the parents of one of Cliff's students has filed a complaint with the dean. These parents claim that their child, a female, was upset because Cliff brought to class a speaker from a local pro-choice organization to speak about the topic of abortion. The parents claim that the guest speaker spoke only of the positive side of abortion. The speaker told the class that they should consider abandoning their religion if their church was not pro-choice. She also gave out information to students about Planned Parenthood and local agencies that would help them find the means to have an abortion if they chose to do so.

Cliff's superior and the dean both need to respond to the parents, so they feel it necessary to interview Cliff in hopes of finding more information about the incident.

Cliff is shocked. Cliff claims that the student and the student's parents have lied to the dean. He denies that the incident ever occurred, and he can prove that the student and parents fabricated the entire scene. Cliff points out that there are a few students in the class who have consistently received poor grades, but the low grades are a result of laziness and poor attendance. Cliff's supervisor and the dean believe Cliff, and they convey their findings to the student's parents.

Cliff feels that he has been harassed. He has had to defend himself against false accusations, and he feels that his role in the classroom has been seriously undermined by a student's dislike for him. Cliff asks for the name of the student who he feels maliciously tried to damage his career and/or disrupt his teaching of the course. The dean refuses to release the name claiming that the student has a right to confidentiality. Also, if the student's name were released to him, the dean feels that Cliff might not be able to be fair and impartial when assigning grades to the student's work. However, the Dean assures Cliff that the university is behind him and that his teaching record has not been tarnished in the least.

Question:

What is your gut reaction to the above situation? React to the above passage briefly in writing. How, if at all, does the First Amendment to the Constitution apply to this situation? Does freedom of expression include lying/slander? Did everyone in this situation have an equal, fair, and impartial opportunity of freedom of expression?

APPENDIX C: RESPONSE TO STUDENT WRITING

English 101.10-01
S. DeWitt

I was both pleased and surprised by some of your responses to Situations 1 through 3. For the most part, your answers are interesting (some a bit short), and I learned much from them. However, many of you did not take the time to "step outside of yourselves." In other words, you didn't take the time to think about how others may feel. Instead, you were very self-centered in some of your responses. If you recall the assignment for the situations, you were to first give your gut reaction (a place where I expected you to be somewhat self-centered if you needed to). Then you were to answer specific questions about the situations. Did you do that?

Here are some things that you can think about (merely MY reactions to your writing and the situations that I myself have had to deal with in the past):

The comedian: Many of you *dismissed* the fact that people on this campus might be offended by Hay's form of comedy ("It's just a joke"). No matter what your opinion, dismissing people's ideas without thinking about or responding to them does not provide for a positive exchange of ideas. And why else are you at the university? And what have you learned in this class? Also, many of you argued that Hay has the right to freedom of expression. But then you either ignored the point about the Vidette or turned around and said that the editor of the paper did not have to print the letters from the angry students. Others of you argued that people have the right to see what comedy they want. Then you said that those who organized a boycott were wrong for trying to persuade others not to see the show. What is the purpose of the boycott? Isn't this a means of persuasion? Isn't persuasion one of the main tenants of freedom of expression? Don't those who participate in a boycott do so by choice?

The RA: If someone is afraid to say something because of fear for personal safety and emotional well-being, what does freedom of expression really mean? This situation was about fear. But many of you didn't even think about this. NOT ONCE! One of you made the point, "If this RA was a man, I don't think that such a big deal would have been made of this." What about the male student who overheard everything? Was he not afraid to speak? Why did he ask for his name to be kept confidential? The point, "If this RA was a man . . ." is interesting. My response is that the RA wasn't a man. What we saw was three men who made these comments to one woman. And one man who overheard the situation was afraid to say anything to defend the woman. Also—let's not forget what was said: "You're not going to write me up, are you bitch?" "Why are you such a cunt to us, man?" "Maybe you'd loosen up a bit if you came and spent the night with me." How many of you said that she had no reason to be offended or afraid? How many of you said that there were no sexual advances made? And I guess if this is your idea of a joke, I don't much understand your sense of humor.

Cliff the history instructor: Most of you had very logical, well thought-out responses to this situation. And no, slander and libel are NOT protected by the First Amendment. I think, however, that many of you again dismissed the potential dangers of this situation because "the damage," that being Cliff's reputation as a good teacher being tarnished, never happened. What you failed to realize is that "the damage" came darn close to happening—because of a lie. And for this reason, I personally do not think we can simply ignore similar situations because "they never happened." Here is something else to think about that I personally am torn about. Cliff doesn't get to find out who the student is. Yet, Cliff has to stand in front of his class every day not knowing who this student is who tried to hurt him. I imagine that Cliff is quite preoccupied. But I can, as hard as it is, understand why this student's name is kept from Cliff. Cliff's responsibility as a teacher is to grade fairly and impartially. And I don't know if he could have done this with the lying student.

Chapter 5

Cognition, Meaning, and Creativity: On Reading Student Hypertexts

Emily Golson
University of Northern Colorado

When writing in hypertext, students engage in a complex interplay between verbal and nonverbal expression that influences the shape their pieces will take. In order to facilitate this shaping, students develop strategies to guide them in connecting emergent meanings to ever changing perceptions of form. Hypertext links provide visible manifestations of these strategies. As students construct these links, they leave behind trails of simulated cognition as fascinating as the texts themselves. The links, the trails of cognition, and the shaping raise many questions, among which are the following. "What guides the shaping?" "Is it possible for readers to predict which direction or shape a text will take?" "Do we have the language to discuss this shaping?" "If so, can this language help readers adjust to unpredictable links or shapes?"

This chapter offers one interpretation of the cognitive, discursive, and spatial operations that occur while reading student-created hypertexts. The interpretation proceeds from a definition and illustration of two types of links found in student hypertexts to a discussion of the ways in which these links both affirm and contradict recent attempts to connect hypertext to schema and neural net theories of learning and comprehension. The application of theory to text—the definition of links and the filtering of theory through this definition—allows for the construction of an operational version of the reading process that rests on an aesthetic as well as analytic comprehension and generation of text. By emphasizing the interplay between the aesthetic and the analytic, we can then work toward a better understanding of the discursive and emotional forces that promote meaning, thus setting the stage for future discussions of hypertext literacy.

The hypertexts cited in this study were created in an advanced creative essay course taught yearly from 1991 to 1994. Students enrolled in this course were given elementary instruction in HyperCard 2.1 for the Macintosh. Those who elected to explore the growing claims for the creative possibilities of writing in hypertext were encouraged to substitute a hypertext document for a traditional essay in their course portfolio. Once proficient in the application, students developed their hypertexts independent of classroom instruction, with occasional consultation with the instructor. Eighty students chose the hypertext option during a 4-year period and 40 eventually submitted hypertext documents in lieu of a print essay. These students spent approximately 45 hours composing texts that ranged from 50 to 150 screens. In addition to their documents, these students also wrote a two- or three-page reflection on their experience. Of the 40 students involved in the study, approximately 30 were satisfied with their texts and all indicated they would opt to create more text if given the opportunity.

The texts varied in form and content. Most students wrote hybrid pieces, linking personal journals and scholarship, commentary and narrative, and visual perceptions and verbal explorations. Although the "finished" documents were sometimes difficult to follow, repeated readings revealed consistent avoidance of the traditional verbal-nonverbal, discursive-expressive categories of print texts in favor of texts that incorporated multiple and varied forms of logical and artistic expression. Further study of these documents revealed that students tended to create two types of links. Texts with large numbers of *intersecting* links tended to present empirical information or pre-existing knowledge in a highly structured form, and those with large numbers of *interacting* links tended to present expressive material in chaotic but not wholly unpatterned displays. Large numbers of either type of link tended to determine whether the text contained factual or imaginary material, but no one text contained only one type of link. The following explanation focuses on portions of two student texts that provide clear illustrations of intersecting and interacting links, with occasional references to links contained in four other sample texts.

INTERSECTING AND INTERACTING LINKS

Student hypertexts are created from *intersecting* and *interacting* links that provide structure and variance in the text. *Intersecting* links do not suggest meaning; they signal the existence of commonly accepted bits of graphic and verbal information in an expanding flatland of bytes and screens. They give knowledge a spatial fixity and standardized correspondence and facilitate comprehension by connecting screens featuring empirical details, established information, or logical conclusions in multiple, continuously expanding, easily recognizable schema. In doing so, they encourage a view of knowledge as one large, infinite system of engineered bytes that allow for the rapid processing of information and the accumulation of aggregative meaning, but that do little to enhance the readers' or writers' abilities to perceive nuance. Within the context of this definition, intersecting links signal well-marked departures to expected destinations. One example of an *intersecting* link is the File option of most application programs. The reader or writer knows that the option will lead to a screen that offers pathways to actions facilitating program operations.

Texts with large numbers of *intersecting* links usually allow information to flow through a balanced binary branching structure in which information is nested in either-or hierarchical choices of equal yes-no values (Landow, 1994a; Landow & Delany, 1993). The simplicity of binary choice supports a vision of comprehension that is primarily hierarchical and a vision of knowledge that is empirical and factual. The typical reader approaches these texts with a simple question and searches for the shortest pathway to "the answer." Opening screens usually feature categories of links roughly analogous to a table of contents in print texts, and subsequent hierarchies and subsets of information conform to the opening screen's announced plan. New meanings do not emerge from the processing of connections; rather, comprehension is enhanced and controlled through the exploration of aggregative details that fill out a basic schema or add a related recognizable schema to an already existing structure. Links have clearly identifiable functions and fit tightly into the well-constructed whole. For the most part, there are no surprises, no invitations for reflection. Such texts are fairly easy to navigate and provide quick answers to well-defined, simple problems (see Table 5.1).

In contrast to texts with large numbers of *intersecting* links, texts with large numbers of *interactive* links promote a random rather than structurally coherent use of space through unpredictable patterns of association. By inviting readers to pursue unknown paths where familiar situations cloak unexpected realizations, *interacting* links force readers to build momentary coherence from momentary disparity, thus

Table 5.1. Characteristics of Links.

Intersecting Links	Interacting Links
Structural Characteristics	
• Clearly labeled	• No clear labels
• Departures and arrivals signaled by clearly defined verbal and graphic signs	• Departures signaled by suggestions rather than clear promises
• All links contribute to a scheme	
Characteristics of Knowledge	
• Schema attached to knowledge domains	• Sense of wisdom through experience
• Factual or empirical information	• Fleeting vision of transformed shapes
• Standard correspondences between and among schema	• Ambiguous and/or metaphorical
• Stresses coherence	
• Links to knowledge contexts outside of text	
• Meaningful ideas subsumed in an already existing cognitive structure	
Characteristics of Problem Solving	
• Metacognition: stresses development of metamemory systems	• Define local problems
• Pragmatic: knowledge transfer to complete task outside the text	• Chaotic, vagrant, inventive, sensual
• Clarifies essentials of the problem	• Flexibility of approach
• Classifies action sequences as opposed to offering random choices	• Constantly redefines problems
• Correlative subsumption	• Partial synthesis
• Derivative subsumption	• Transfer to other local problems
• Strong meaningful context outside of text drives the reading	• Situated meanings and unexpected realizations
• Attending the facts and conditions	• Experience within/without text drives reading
	• Search for deep meaning to solve problem of what text is about
Characteristics of Thinking/Shaping	
• Master strategy the same	• Master strategy constantly changing
• Follows prescribed shape	• Intuitive and logical play off one another

allowing for insight, change, and movement to the next unpredictable pattern of association. Sometimes, *interacting* links lead to seeds of meaning rather than fully or even partially articulated propositions. And sometimes they suggest figurative rather than literal connections both within and without the text. *Interactive* links encourage generation by strengthening or weakening associative connections between nodes, thereby promoting nuances of thought. By positing questions and forcing surprises through unexpected suggestions, felicitous phrasings and, as Charney (1994) defined them, "chance conjunctions and odd juxtapositions" (p. 259), and by bringing distant and unexpected portions of text to close proximity with one another (Landow, 1994a), texts with large numbers of *interactive* links provide a dense structure devoted to teasing meaning among, between, and beyond links. Unlike *intersecting* links that abide by a singular, commonly recognized cognitive system, *interacting* links create and recreate their own systems so that entire webs are never as they seem (see Table 5.1).

One example of an *interacting* link is the phrase "hole in the air" that in a student prose poem entitled "The Wild" serves as a metaphor for fading images of home, town, and text. The metaphor appears in the opening screen when the speaker threatens to throw his computer through a hole in the air. This screen fades to other portions of the text chronicling struggles with family, town, and writing in electronic environments. In a typical thread, readers depart from a section on family through a button labeled Home to a description of a small Texas town that then leads to a section on fading memories. Thus, with the press of a button, the fleeting experience of working with memory is reinforced by the fleeting experiences of working with electronic text. The metaphorical linking of technology to text, the fusion of operation and meaning, highlights the fragile existence of text and life and echoes throughout the remaining portions of the piece (Golson, 1995).

Texts with large numbers of *interacting* links promote generation by compelling readers to break familiar mental acts and avoid premature judgments. By constantly positing moments when meaning is unstable, these texts force readers to find a problem before attempting a solution, thereby employing a cognitive process that Bruner (1961, 1971) described as requiring incompleteness, anomaly, trouble, inequity, and contradiction. Once defined, the problem's solution may involve the activation of *mediation connections*, defined as implicit connections that occur inside the reader but not necessarily in the text (Jenkins, 1963). Thus, texts with large numbers of *interacting* links differ from those with large numbers of intersecting links because they situate problems inside rather than outside the text and rely on impulses coming from outside the text to guide readers toward resolution.

When poorly designed, both types of linking exhibit noticeable weaknesses. *Intersective* linking can frustrate readers by failing to deliver promised information or to indicate where useful information is located. In contrast, because of the multiple possibilities for implicit as well as explicit connections, *interactive* linking can be difficult to process. At times, continuous streams of unstable meaning can prompt readers to question the validity, relevance, or purpose of the entire text. Readers may wonder, for example, if the ambiguities really exist and if the connections are valid. They may also worry about the paths not taken, paths that would have yielded clearer or at least less disparate meaning. Poorly designed *interactive* linking can trap readers in swirling eddies of contradiction, force readers to participate in mindless games, or encourage readers to view meaning-making as a vagrant activity. Sometimes, as readers try to make sense out of multiple meanings, they may suspect they are pursuing the illusion of knowledge rather than knowledge itself. When at their best, however, *interactive* links can assist readers in pursuing the scent of meaning through ever-increasing threads of fleeting words and pictures to form a truly postmodern vision of contents of the text. Similarly, when at their best, *intersecting* links can assist readers in defining and clarifying knowledge domains, pursuing defined tasks, and solving problems.

Texts with large numbers of *interactive* links are roughly analogous to Joyce's (1988) *constructive* hypertexts, texts that Joyce defined as developing "a body of information which they [readers/writers] map according to their needs, their interests, and the transformations they discover as they invent, gather, and act upon that information" (p. 11). Texts with of large numbers of *intersecting* links bear some resemblance to *exploratory* hypertexts, which Joyce defined as texts that "enable writers and readers to control the transformation of a body of information to meet their needs and interests" (p. 11). However, texts with large numbers of *intersecting* links can differ from Joyce's exploratory hypertexts in small but crucial ways. For example, although these texts encourage writers and readers to "understand the elements that make up a particular body of knowledge and to plot their progress through these elements" (p. 11), acts that Joyce considered crucial to the reading of exploratory hypertexts, they also tend to emphasize the aggregation and structuring of information rather than the creation and transformation of information, as Joyce would have us believe. When transformation does occur, it moves through the mediation of *interactive* links and results in the creation of a new schema that overlays rather than replaces the old schema. This often occurs in student texts, suggesting that students see the two types of links as offering inclusive rather than exclusive approaches to knowledge, comprehension, and structure.

To sum up thus far, when given the opportunity to generate hypertexts on topics of their choice, students rarely create purely constructive or exploratory hypertexts. Rather, most create hybrid pieces, with *interacting* links providing meaningful and not so meaningful insights and *intersecting* links anchoring these insights into a temporary schema or well-organized knowledge domains. Whereas one section of a text might contain *interacting* links that reflect the momentary perception of the topic and thereby mirror emerging thought, another section might contain *intersecting* links that place commonly accepted knowledge in easily recognizable structures. Although the movement between interacting and intersecting presentations may seem chaotic, careful analysis suggests that nonverbal shapes as well as verbal associations may influence structure and meaning.

CREATIVE POSSIBILITIES FOR TEXTS EMPHASIZING INTERSECTING LINKS

The "Cary Grant" piece presented here is an example of a text made up of *intersecting* links. This text was composed early in the data-gathering phase of this study, and it mirrors a model hypertext document designed for a Yale University ornithology class called "The Surface Anatomy of a Bird" (Lynch, 1988). As with "Surface Anatomy," "Cary Grant" is a well-structured hypertext document. The text consists of 90 screens with two major threads, one an autobiography of Cary Grant and the other a six-stranded, cross-linked section featuring the following categories: Cary Grant's co-stars, Cary Grant's films with Howard Hawks, Cary Grant's Oscar-winning films, Cary Grant's films with Hitchcock, Cary Grant's films with Hepburn, and Cary Grant's other films.

The text has a pyramid shape that complements the discursive context. The pyramid structure provides visible support for schema theory, which argues for the organization of previously acquired verbal knowledge in identifiable constructs. (Anderson, 1977; Rumelhart & Ortony, 1977; Schank & Abelson, 1977). According to cognitive specialists, schemata, a collection of schema, are templates that are used to organize and retrieve information. As organizing structures, schemata can be process oriented (e.g., how to make a cake), visual (e.g., describing the parts of the human body), or may represent goals (e.g., completing a shopping trip). Schemata may be hierarchical, associative, sequential, or spatial as long as they allow for the structure and systematic retrieval of information. As blueprints for problem solving, in their simplest form, schemata allow us to fill in the blanks.

Most of the "Cary Grant" text does not invite debate. Comprehension is almost immediate as browsing requires low cognitive overhead. *Intersecting* links form a well-defined information retrieval system by assuming a hierarchical construction in which schemata are brought to the text to form systems and subsystems of information. In such a structure, as Gagne and other cognitivists explained with reference to print texts, meaningful ideas are subsumed in already existing cognitive structures. New information is added through alternating subsystems of derivative and correlative subsumptions (Ausubel, 1968; Gagne, 1985; Novak, 1965). The hierarchical structure of "Cary Grant" allows for quick retrieval of answers to questions of increasing specificity, such as which films Howard Hawks directed (The Hawk icon on the Index screen) or a synopsis of a film (the Filmstrip icon on the Howard Hawks screen), and so forth.

All screens are designed to promote rapid browsing (see Figure 5.1). Links are clearly labeled. Departures are signaled by icons whose functions have been identified on either the home or subsequent screens. Arrivals are announced by headings that pick up on keywords, icons, or definitions appearing on the home or some other navigational screen. Chunks of information are located in well-defined spaces and careful arrangement allows each screen to provide a simple message (see Figure 5.2). Graphic and verbal data are aesthetically balanced, with different size fonts signaling different levels of hierarchical information. Abundant white space supports the quick delivery of a simple message.

"Cary Grant" suggests a view of meaning-making that C. Smith (1994) called *thin cognition*, such as the act of finding specific answers to specific questions. It assumes a reader who employs one problem-solving strategy, such as the breaking of large problems into subclasses and chaining them together (Wickelgren, 1974). The *intersecting* links in the text that lead to solutions to predefined problems contain no meaning within themselves; they simply realize a navigational structure. Thus, in order to find the academy award-winning films that Cary Grant made with Alfred Hitchcock, the reader presses Films made with Alfred Hitchcock and then presses Oscar-winning films. The motivation for the question, the reason for reading the text, and the correlation between the two answers exist outside the reading and seldom add to making further meaning in the text.

Unlike "Surface Anatomy," however, the "Cary Grant" text is not limited to factual information. At times free-branching associations subvert the hierarchical design. The biography section, for example, contains links to other actors' comments about Cary Grant, thus adding carefully selected insights to the factual approach. In addition, the biography section contains buttons labeled **More**, that link to the writers'

The Films of Cary Grant
Index

Click here to see a list of
Cary Grant's various
co-stars in his many films.

Click here to learn about
Cary Grant's films with
director Howard Hawks.

Click here to learn
about Cary Grant and
the Oscars.

Click here to find out about
Cary Grant's films with
director Alfred Hitchcock.

Click here to find out about
Cary Grant's films with
actress Katherine Hepburn.

Click here to find
out about Cary
Grant's other films.

To Return to General Index

Figure 5.1. The navigation screen of "Cary Grant" text

opinions of Cary Grant. Hence, even though the text is highly factual and structured according to a schema, there are sections that suggest rather than articulate additional meaning and sections that deviate from the announced schema to present unexpected associations and conclusions. I read these sections as awkward attempts to generate new insight rather than present commonly acknowledged information.

CREATIVE POSSIBILITIES FOR INTERACTIVE LINKING

Often student writers of texts with intersecting links will subvert recognizable schema to achieve a fuller range of association, information retrieval, problem finding, and solution activities. When the subversion becomes rampant, the texts begin to take on a different look as large numbers of *interacting* links branch chaotically to, from, and sometimes through a recognizable pattern of *intersecting* links. One section of a rambling text called "Womyn," for example, contains five threads. One thread links descriptions of fences. Another connects descriptions of the different ways in which women feel fenced in. Another thread links ref-

The collaboration of Cary Grant and Director Alfred Hitchcock.

Director Alfred Hitchcock was born in London in 1899. Interested in drawing and graphic arts, Hitchcock became involved in film by trying to design a new system for title cards for the American film company, Paramount, which was looking for new recuits in England. This would lead him to exposure to German, American and English filmmaking techniques and, finally, to directing. Hitchcock would become known as the "master of suspense," dicirecting many films which would thrill audiences for years.

Four of Cary Grant's films were directed by the master of suspense and mystery, Alfred Hitchcock. In 1941 Hitchcock directed Grant in <u>Suspicion.</u> Their next endevor was with <u>Notorious</u> (1946). <u>To Catch A Thief,</u> in 1955, was the duo's third film. Grant and Hitchcock's final film together, and probably the most famous for both, was <u>North By Northwest</u> (1959).

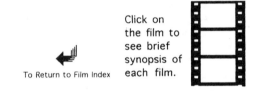

Click on the film to see brief synopsis of each film.

To Return to Film Index

Figure 5.2. An example of a well-designed screen with clearly identified intersecting links

erences to the ways in which language can be used to fence in women. Another thread links descriptions and discussions of rape. And another thread links discussions of paranoia. The text is constructed in such a way that readers may experience being fenced in and become aware of the use of language as a form of fencing before they reach the descriptions of fences. The descriptions of fences, connected by a series of *intersecting* links, provide a resting place, a place of low cognitive overhead (see Figure 5.3). When I read this portion of the text, I share in local level, nondebatable knowledge that anchors other parts of the text. The remaining sections connect *interacting* links. Repeated readings of these sections generate variable patterns of strong and weak associations. Mediation connections, already defined as cognitive threads to experience outside of the printed text (Jenkins, 1963), determine the weight of each association, which changes with each reading. The order in which the sections are read provides an additional level of variance to the weight of associations. Thus, as I reconstruct depth, breadth, and sequence of meaning , I experience variant versions of paranoia, fences, women and rape.

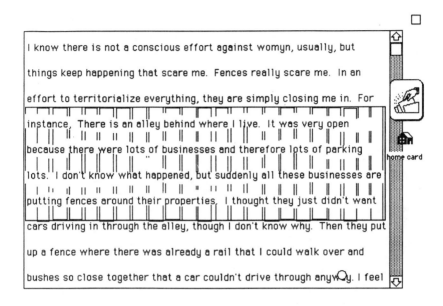

Figure 5.3. Sample screen from descriptions of fences. All screens in this thread contain fence graphic. Readers click anywhere on the fence to move to next fence

The promotion of variant versions and many types of linkages requires the use of numerous commonly recognized cognitive strategies, among which are the following:

1. Flexibility: the ability to move from classifying to defining, to breaking the problem into parts, to identifying contradictions or discrepancies.
2. Discrimination: the ability to identify and avoid superficial meanings which can be misleading or unproductive.
3. Synthesis: the ability to integrate various levels of association (Gagne, 1985).
4. Reflection: the ability to search for "deep meanings" (White & Wittrock, 1974) that in this case may be defined as the momentary strength of an association.

Texts with large numbers of *interacting* links also require readers to tolerate partial solutions at a local level. For example, the fence at the end of the alley might suggest a feeling of security rather than support an emerging higher level premise, such as all fences create paranoia. Thus, the local level solutions may lead to more contradictions rather than provide clues to what the text is about. Finally, texts with large numbers of *interacting* links require that readers be patient, for the expected solution may never be forthcoming or may appear in an unexpected form. The "Womyn" text, for example, contains many contradictory solutions.

SHAPES OF EMOTIONS

Interacting links create random patterns that can illicit nonverbal emotional reactions. In "Womyn," for example, descriptions of fences are identified by a graphic image of a circle and are linked in a circle. Descriptions of feelings of being fenced in are identified by the graphic image of a fence. The "feelings of being fenced in" thread branches through the text, with selected branches leading back to the fence(circle) descriptions and other branches leading to the rape and paranoia threads. One branch of the fenced-in section leads nowhere, forcing me to retrace my steps or to quit the text. In addition to fences and small circles, one button labeled **continue** links to a thread that explores the ways in which language fences in women. Readers following the language thread do not return to any of the other four threads but continue to other sections of the text.

The text's structural and operational patterns suggest emotional reactions that complement discursive meaning. As I read "Womyn," for example, I circle one area of the text in the fence section and reach a dead-end in the section on feelings of being fenced in. This activity arouses my own feelings of insecurity and frustration, thereby enhancing the meaning of the fences, fenced in, and paranoia sections. As the emotional reaction to the nonverbal shaping of impression and experience builds, discursive meaning emerges with complementary levels of irony. The text opens to a button labeled **press me**, accompanied by a simple invitation to explore the text (see Figure 5.4). The invitation is later complemented by references to "press me" in both the rape and fenced-in sections, suggesting the negative consequences of pressing and being pressed. As the speaker presses against a rough wooden fence in the fenced-in section, she feels a sharp sense of pain when a sliver penetrates her hand: This pressing and pain is duplicated in the penetration portion of the rape section.

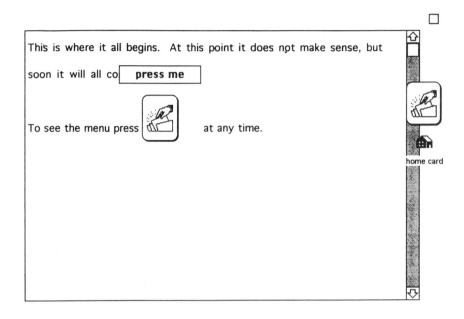

Figure 5.4. The opening screen for the "Womyn" text

DISCURSIVE MEANING AND EMOTIONAL REACTION: THE EXPRESSIVE COMPLEMENT

"Womyn" exemplifies student texts that successfully integrate recognizable schema with random associative patterns in partially constructed webs, thus allowing for expanses of thick cognition as well as moments of thin cognition. But "Womyn" not only provides opportunities for exercising multiple and complex cognitive processes, that in turn enhance comprehension, it also stimulates the senses. As I work through multiple, unscheduled departures and arrivals, I experience a heightened awareness or high-energy state. Large numbers of *interacting* links encourage me to become cagey, prescient, prompting me to search for meanings that will subvert or distort emerging interpretations. The sensitivity to change is heightened by the constant clicking of buttons and flashes of light. This readiness may be interpreted as an enabling objective that, according to Gagne (1985), prepares audiences for unexpected outcomes.

One of the unexpected outcomes is the irony that echoes through the discursive, emotional, and physical experience of the text.

The opening invitation to **press me**, for example, is accompanied by the statement "at this point, it does not make much sense, but soon it will all come together." As the text comes together—intellectually, emotionally, and physically—in rapes, interminable paranoia, and loss of innocence, as meaning and sensation become so overwhelming that it is the shaping, the intuitive moving to the right or to the left in an attempt to find a schema, a patch of solid ground, that guides my reading of the text (see Figure 5.4).

CLOAKED, DORMANT, AND CONTRADICTORY LINKS: THE CREATION AND SUBVERSION OF ART

Interactive links can be subdivided by rhetorical function, thus allowing for a better understanding of how links obscure or divert aesthetic and analytic comprehension. Thus far, I have been able to identify three types of *interactive* linking: *cloaked, dormant,* and *contradictory.* The press me opening of "Womyn," is a good example of a *cloaked* link in which hidden meanings become apparent with the activation of the link. In some texts, *cloaked* links lie dormant until the reader discovers their interactive possibilities through further reading of the text. In a text called " Pierre," for example, the author describes a love affair between Pierre, an artist living in Paris, and a beautiful woman, who at any given moment, depending on the reading, is attracted or not attracted to Pierre. The text's dominant thread features a background of a starry night (see Figure 5.5). Initially, the background appears to add ambiance and continuity to the piece. Later, however, when I arrive at a screen where Pierre is contemplating the night sky, I discover that some stars actually link to multiple interpretations of Pierre's love affairs, thus enriching Pierre's story and adding further operative potential to all night sky screens. Eventually, the potential for linkage in any night sky background dominates my reading, and I must discover which night sky screens contain *interactive* links.

Dormant and *cloaked* links raise the level of expectation for texts. They suggest possibilities that may or may not exist and direct the reader to examine every word and every graphic for possible meaning. Texts with large numbers of *dormant* and *cloaked interactive* links can suggest interpretations that may or may not have existed in the author's mind. To counteract these instabilities, student texts invariably contain a stable section or pattern, a schema that forms a resting place for the tired or idle reader. Just as the "Womyn" text contains a pattern of *intersecting* links describing fences, for example, so the "Pierre" text contains a thread of *intersecting* links that describes Pierre's paintings. The thread is

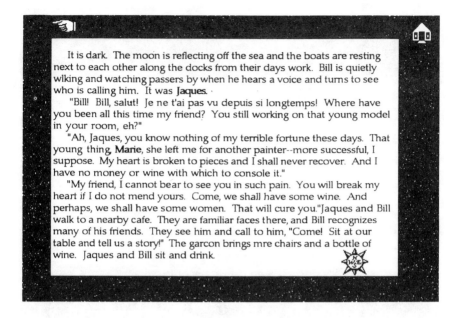

It is dark. The moon is reflecting off the sea and the boats are resting next to each other along the docks from their days work. Bill is quietly wlking and watching passers by when he hears a voice and turns to see who is calling him. It was Jaques.

"Bill! Bill, salut! Je ne t'ai pas vu depuis si longtemps! Where have you been all this time my friend? You still working on that young model in your room, eh?"

"Ah, Jaques, you know nothing of my terrible fortune these days. That young thing, Marie, she left me for another painter--more successful, I suppose. My heart is broken to pieces and I shall never recover. And I have no money or wine with which to console it."

"My friend, I cannot bear to see you in such pain. You will break my heart if I do not mend yours. Come, we shall have some wine. And perhaps, we shall have some women. That will cure you."Jaques and Bill walk to a nearby cafe. They are familiar faces there, and Bill recognizes many of his friends. They see him and call to him, "Come! Sit at our table and tell us a story!" The garcon brings mre chairs and a bottle of wine. Jaques and Bill sit and drink.

Figure 5.5. A sample screen showing the starry night. The figure shows stars linking other parts of the text

circular, like the fence thread in "Womyn." Two *interactive* links lead the reader out of this section. One leads to a screen that describes Pierre's desire as a secret infatuation, thus implying that Pierre is in love with an aesthetic vision of women. Another leads to a thread that branches into the backgrounds of the women described in Pierre's paintings, thus implying that Pierre has had many affairs with real women. Repeated readings indicate that it is difficult to tell how many infatuations, if any, are with real women and which of these real women actually accept or reject Pierre.

Cloaked and *dormant* links tend to add to the richness of the text by increasing the readers' level of awareness. *Contradictory* links, however, may yield mixed results (see Figure 5.6 for an example of a weak *contradictory* link). In a section of a text called "Criminal Justice," for example, summaries of Durkheim's and the author's opinions are cross-linked to photographs of Durkheim and the author with buttons labeled *authorities*, thus giving the author an authority equal to and sometimes inseparable from Durkheim's authority, an assertion supported by post-modern thought. In other examples, however, *contradictory* links may lead to superficial chastisement rather than profound insight. When

Figure 5.6. An example of a weak contradictory link

readers of a text entitled "The Wildside" are asked if they want the main character to commit suicide, for example, a yes button simply leads to a screen that reads, "Our man wouldn't do that!" This contradiction is not supported by current or subsequent readings of the text.

SUCCESSFUL AND UNSUCCESSFUL INTERACTIVE LINKING

Successful *interactive* linking depends on the inclusion of multiple links that integrate the figurative, literal, and operational levels of the text and generate continuous strands of strong and weak associations that both surprise and enlighten the reader. Failure to provide this type of variability can lead to disaster. A text called "Happy Endings," for example, a parody of Margaret Atwell's "Happy Endings," provides a simple example of a nonvariable approach to *interactive* linking. The text invites readers to trace the fate of two characters, John and Mary, through multiple events, many of which contain two other characters, James and Madge. As John and Mary's life stories change with each screen, the notion of choice changes. At first, choice seems terribly important. As I read the text, I look for clues to help me make positive choices for Mary. But the text contains no clues. Multiple readings indicate that certain partners prompt selected events, and selected events, in turn, lead characters to selected fates. Mary may end up living happily ever after, or she may lead a tragic life, but there is no way to intuit the shape of the text nor is there any indication of intellectual or emotional richness in the text.

"Happy Endings" is not a well-written text. It contains no strong or weak associations: Each link is of equal value. The one-to-one relationship of screen to character, character to character, and character to event leaves little room for nuance or for increased insight. By preferring plot to a rich interplay between words, thoughts, and/or sensual associations, the author limits meaning. When carried to extremes, texts with associations of equal value turn the act of reading into a mindless game.

SCHEMA AND NEURAL NET THEORY

By defining types of links, we can better understand how portions of the text play off one another, but we cannot understand how we actually read the text. Scholars have theorized how such reading works, but few have applied theory to an actual text. Davida Charney (1994), for example, drew on *schema theory* to advance a skeptical view of the ways in which hypertext aids reading comprehension. According to Charney, there are two visions of hypertexts: romantic and pragmatic. The romantic vision encourages the creation of texts with incoherent expectations or texts that fail to confirm expectations, or texts that invite confusion by failing to signal relations among ideas. In contrast, the pragmatic vision, as exemplified in hypertext manuals, erroneously assumes readers know what information they need and in what order the information should be read. Both, according to Charney, require a cognitive investment that is not equal to the return. In response to Charney, C. Smith used neural net theory to argue for hypertext's ability to facilitate thinking processes through its rich and varied representation of association. Drawing on neural net research, Smith suggested that hypertext can simulate what Kintsch and van Dijk (1978) once described as an initial, enriched, but incoherent and possibly contradictory text base that is context-free.

Smith used Kintsch's cognitive matrix to illustrate how hypertext allows for constantly changing relations among ideas. As Smith explained, Kintsch's model consists of a matrix of numbers, each number representing the strength of association (weight of link) between the two nodes. When an activation vector is applied to the text, numbers in the matrix and corresponding weight of association changes accordingly to prescribed mathematical rules. Smith viewed reading hypertext as an activation process "rippling through the net, revealing local 'hot spots' of relevance, showing in high relief the portions that pertain" (p. 272). She did not discuss when or how the text stabilizes, as Kintsch's comprehension model suggests, but referred to the result as a relief with large-grain patterns of relations.

Smith's vision of temporary, large-grain patterns of relations seems to make sense. In "Womyn," for example, as patterns emerge, fade, and re-emerge slightly altered, the text appears to replicate the neural net environment that Smith posited. But unlike the Kintsch model, or Smith's modification of the Kintsch model, " Womyn" also posits the existence of at least one inalterable pattern (the fences), a schema that has the potential to be present throughout every reading. This schema forms the background for the continual generation of patterns of strong and weak associations. In short, "Womyn" references both schema and neural net theory.

Although both schema and neural net theory suggest a useful context for understanding potential difficulties in reading a hypertext, neither provides a language that completely supports the generative aspect of reading and writing hypertexts. Careful reading of student texts reveals that each approach has its weaknesses. Schema theory provides a context for designing hypertext manuals or texts that present a body of commonly recognized information, but it does not, as Smith noted, offer insight into the physical, social, cultural, or historical worlds that contribute to thinking nor does it account for the emotional processes, such as doubt, intuition, and contradiction, that contribute to "thick cognition" (C. Smith, 1994). When applied to student texts, schema theory does not allow for brief interpretive interludes in "Cary Grant" or the rich emotional vision present in "Womyn." In contrast, Smith's version of Kintsch's neural net theory posits an initial incoherent text analogous to hypertext and emphasizes the existence of a constant flux of strong and weak associations. Smith's approach adds a dimension of variability to the rigid structuring of schema theory, but it does not account for how meaning is generated by the interaction of the variable and invariable patterns in texts similar to "Womyn." Indeed, Smith's use of the Kintsch model could be misleading as Kintsch used neural nets to describe comprehension. The act of reading hypertext, as we all know, involves both comprehension and generation, for just as the associative process continually draws new inferences that, once comprehended, contribute, if only momentarily, to the interpretation that guides or shapes the reading or generative interpretation of the next portion of the text, so the reader, through the very act of choosing which link to follow, generates as well as comprehends portions of the text.

TOWARD AN OPERATIONAL VERSION OF READING A HYPERTEXT

Thus far, we have established that when composing in hypertext, students may favor a schematic as opposed to a variable generative approach, but the reading of these texts incorporates both, thereby propelling as well as facilitating the reading/writing, learning experience. Although Smith's version of Kintsch's neural net model provides a possible context for describing what a hypertext is, it does not provide an operative language to describe how student-produced hypertexts can be read. By identifying *intersecting* and *interacting* links, we can articulate a system of comprehension that includes generation and is more descriptive of how writers and readers make meaning from the text. The following description of an operational version of reading is based on the ways in which *intersecting* and *interacting* links behave in student hypertexts.

Imagine a matrix similar to Kintsch's, an associative network containing knowledge of both language and world, with each column and row corresponding to a node, each intersection containing a number representing the strength of association. The matrix, representing the first draft of a text, contains at least one instance of several identical, higher number *intersecting* links or schema of previously constituted knowledge. These higher number *intersecting* links form a raised pattern with random weaker associations forming other patterns at will. Each reading or revision carries number values from previous associations. As readers and writers work through the text, they further refine their understanding of the text by creating random patterns, patterns that carry with them some version of a schema that is constantly being enhanced. By the end of the reading/writing session, the matrix has changed. Strengthened associations are now indicated by larger numeric values and weakened associations are indicated by smaller numeric values. A second reading brings continued change. The preceding is analogous to Smith's image of moments of stabilization, moments when primary meanings, as defined by higher numbers, stand out in graphic relief to secondary associations.

Analysis of the "Cary Grant," " Womyn," and other student texts suggests that the moments of stabilization may be governed by at least three discernible impulses. As portions of text grow at odd moments, when either a "felt sense" (Murray, 1982) or "moments of feeling on the threshold of thought" (C. Smith, 1994) begin to emerge, premonitions are impelled by at least one of the following forces: an impulse to complete a pattern or schema of *intersecting* links, an impulse to branch from one pattern of *intersecting* or *interacting* links to another, or an impulse to return to a preceding schema. In many cases, these impulses stem from predetermined images of geometric shapes or some other visual rather than verbal construct. In other words, they proceed from some sense of metatext. As the readers/writers make choices, emerging shapes complement verbal constructs, working together to form new interpretative schema or directions. Some schema change with each reading. Some schema fade, but all schema and all preceding knowledge echo throughout the text. This shaping, this process of closing circles or constructing branches define the moments that Joyce (1995) referred to as moments of transformation of meaning and knowledge. They play an important role in text design and in the comprehension and generation of meaning, and therefore should not be separated from cognitive or discursive discussions of portions of the text, for they confirm the complex interplay between verbal and nonverbal conscious and intuitive forces.

CONCLUSION: THE VALUE OF READING AND WRITING HYPERTEXT

When a reader reaches for a hypertextual shape, he or she is affirming the existence of compositional forces that are different than those that generate print texts. Some of these forces may not only work against the so-called "linearity" of the print tradition, but they may also work against the binary and spatial limitations of hypertext itself. Although it is possible to question the value of writing in hypertext and the wisdom of putting "enormous technological and creative effort at the service of what might be quite rare and ephemeral associations" (Charney, 1994, p. 259). It is also possible to view the creation and reading of hypertext as a developing aesthetic for a new type of literacy or a postmodern argument for an alternative way of constructing and representing knowledge.

If we accept the preceding argument, we cannot expect to read student hypertexts as simple problem-solving structures nor can we view them as visible confirmation of neural nets. Rather, we must view them as emerging forms that constantly incorporate these and perhaps other possibilities. Thus far, I have benefited from reading my students' hypertexts in three ways. First, by reading a medium that generates associations of differing values, I have gained entry into a reading structure that supports a postmodern approach to cognition that is more in keeping with contemporary thought. Second, with each transferral of newly learned cognitive strategies to each new text and each reading of an existing text, I improve my ability to handle number and quality of ideas. And finally, with the development of a sensitivity to nonverbal as well as verbal data, I not only experience how shape complements discourse but am also exposed to enriched possibilities for creativity. At the moment, I am still in the beginning stages of reading my students' texts, yet as the above study illustrates, there are moments when I not only understand but intuit the shape of their creative acts, and in so doing, actively participate in the development of a hypertext literacy.

ACKNOWLEDGMENT

I thank students at the University of Northern Colorado for sharing my enthusiasm for hypertext and for giving me permission to study and reproduce their work.

Chapter 6

Developing Hyperphoric Grammar to Teach Collaborative Hypertexts

David Norton
Beverly B. Zimmerman
Neil Lindeman
Brigham Young University

Much has been written about how hypertexts embody current postmodern concepts about reading, writing, texts, and language. Hypertext advocates Stuart Moulthrop, Jay Bolter, and George Landow argued that hypertexts promote reader-centered exploration, dreamlike association structures, and decentered texts. Likewise, much has also been written about how hypertexts allow collaboration. Goldman-Segal (1992), referring to "Learning Constellations," a multimedia tool, stated that collaborative virtual environments "foster connectedness, interdependence, intimacy, cooperation, and multiple points of view" (p. 257). Landow (1992a) argued that group hypertext projects can be a tool for teaching collaborative authorship that allows students to work as groups in constructing new meanings. Joyce (1995) stated that collaborative hypertexts provide a "new cosmology of learning and teaching" where learners become "co-equals in an interpretive community" (p. 121).

Although much has been written about postmodern and collaborative hypertextuality, there have been few attempts to study students writing collaborative hypertexts. This study attempted to answer the following questions: "What happens when students—in this case college students who had never before written hypertexts—write a collaborative hypertext?" "What structures will students create when they write a collaborative hypertext?" "How will students discuss these hypertexts?"

In 1993, we developed a hypertext composition course for first-year college students. Using Landow's description of bootstrapping and Bolter's software Storyspace, we adapted our current first-year writing course, English 115, to use hypertext to teach students the concepts of nonlinearity, collaborative writing, and critical thinking. During the 2 years that the course was taught, we conducted an ethnographic study[1] to observe how writing hypertexts influenced students' understanding of structure and the role of readers, writers, and texts. Based on student feedback, the course was continually redesigned in an attempt to solve one of the most difficult questions of negotiated hypertext structuring: how to identify and express the structuring function of a link.

DEVELOPING A CURRICULUM

At the heart of the current first-year writing course is a social constructionist methodology that encourages students to consider their writing as part of an academic conversation. In the hypertext version of the

---

[1]Guba and Lincoln (1989), in suggesting criteria and procedures for scholarly inquiry, argued that investigators in educational research should pursue the study in a natural setting, acknowledge the researchers as instruments in the study, employ qualitative inquiry methods, and incorporate and use the researchers' own experience and expertise. To preserve as much as possible the natural setting of the writing classroom, we employed an ethnographic or participant-observer approach to gathering data, and analyzing and reporting the results of our study. To gather the data, we audiotaped every class period, videotaped key class periods, kept reflective journals and observational field notes, asked students to complete a formal and informal evaluation of the course, interviewed students in the course, and "grounded" our findings in the current literature in the field of composition.

To analyze our data, we transcribed our journals, observational field-notes, and videotapes, then analyzed them for reoccurring themes. Based on these themes, we conducted class discussions and interviews with students. Then we compared our research with existing literature. To make sure students received the best instruction we could, we implemented changes in the pedagogy while the courses were in progress. Our observations took place at a private university of approximately 28,000 students located in the intermountain west. Our writing course comprised of approximately 50 students over three semesters.

course,[2] students wrote both linear paper versions and electronic hypertext versions of three types of assignments: a personal essay, a research project, and a textual analysis. However, primary emphasis of the study was placed on the research project assignment, which is described here. The original goal of the hypertext course was to replicate Landow's (1992a) bootstrapping pedagogy while at the same time fulfilling the requirements of the course.

Following as closely as we could the pedagogy Landow described in which students took linear essays and created hypertexts, Norton[3] taught the class during a summer term pilot study. He gave his class a general subject on which to do research, then divided the students into groups or teams of four and allowed them to choose specific issues or themes related to that subject. Each student wrote an individual research paper that discussed a topic connected to his or her team's issue or theme. Then students linked their texts together as a team and created an introduction for their theme. Finally, the class created the class research project by linking together the team's hypertexts.

Each student had a role in creating the team hypertext: A manager organized team meetings and ensured the team met class deadlines; an editor made final decisions on the appearance of the hypertext links; a technical engineer made backups of the work, imported graph-

---

[2]In order for our course to be successful, we felt we needed to do the following:

1. Meet current department guidelines for the course that requires students to complete three writing assignments—a personal narrative about an educational experience, a library research paper, and a critical analysis of a text.
2. Teach students to create nonlinear hypertexts.
3. Facilitate collaboration among the students.

Throughout the course, we found it necessary to revise the original syllabus and other class assignments several times in order to provide more time for students to write and link their work during class time. As a result, some of the regular class discussion about course readings was carried on outside of class through the use of e-mail.

As part of our university's evaluation of all first-year writing courses, students submitted a final portfolio of their written papers. The portfolios were then graded by two other teachers (who did not teach hypertext composition). The results of the portfolio evaluations from our class were then compared to the scores of all of the other portfolios from the nearly 100 first-year composition courses taught each semester at our university.

Appendix B summarizes the objectives and assignments for the hypertext English 115 course we developed.

[3]Working closely with Dr. Zimmerman, David Norton developed and taught the hypertext courses. All three of us gathered and analyzed the data presented.

ics, and tested links; and an issues captain decided what issues to discuss and who would discuss them. During subsequent semesters, Norton revised this research project assignment continually as we observed students negotiating the structures of their hypertexts.

Students Must Clearly Distinguish Between Linear Structures and Hypertext Structures

At the end of our pilot study, it became clear that some students had difficulty moving from writing linear texts to writing the hypertexts. For example, when the students' papers were included in the departmental evaluation of English 115 portfolios, students in the hypertext course scored a full point lower than the average scores for other classes taught that term. On a 12-point scale, with the average portfolio score being a 9, students in the hypertext section received an average score of 7 to 8. Although we felt part of the reason the scores were low was because valuable class time was used in teaching students to use the computers,[4] we also wondered if students were interpreting the papers and hypertexts as the same task. As a result, we rewrote the curriculum to distinguish more clearly between linear writing and hypertext writing.

Norton again taught the hypertext class the following fall semester. This time, he discussed papers and hypertexts as separate kinds of writing with different purposes, techniques, and processes. He emphasized that, although students could use much of the same content in both, the paper each student would turn in was its own assignment quite distinct from the collaborative hypertext. More importantly, throughout the course, Norton distinguished between linear structures and hypertext structures to enable students to form notions of appropriateness both for good papers (sequential, focused arguments) and collaborative hypertexts (interrelated, chunked arguments). Moreover, because the students knew how to use the computers, they spent more time writing. The pedagogy had very positive results. At the end of the semester, the students' paper portfolio scores rose to the averages received by the rest of the composition courses.

During class discussion and in interviews after they had finished their group work, students commented on how writing hypertexts differed from writing linear texts. For example, we found one student referred to hypertext writing as "more modularized." Another student

---

[4]Because many of the students were unfamiliar with the computer hardware and software, much of the class time was spent helping students become familiar with the equipment. Following the pilot study, we limited enrollment in the course to students who were familiar with the Macintosh computer environment.

commented that writing a hypertext actually made him focus more than when he was writing a paper. Other students used the medium to consider points that seemed irrelevant in linear texts. One student said, "You can also include little things, little side notes, that you couldn't do within a paper. It just wouldn't fit." Another added, "Yeah, it might stick out in a paper, but it wouldn't in a hypertext." Another student stated that the hypertexts allowed him to cover the topic more holistically.

The students, however, seemed dissatisfied with the procedure we had established. Our transcribed fieldnotes and videotapes showed that students continually asked the question, "Why can't we write the hypertexts first?"

Students Should Create Hypertexts First, Then Write Linear Text

We decided to have students write their papers first, then divide their text into pieces and connect it with the papers of the other class members. Our understanding of Landow's (1992a) pedagogy and Barrett's (1989) ideas led us to believe that students' linear papers could be combined into group hypertexts that would be enlightening to the writers as well as to other readers. There was also a practical reason for having students write their papers first. Linear papers, especially research papers, have a specific style and structure. We thought that by teaching the students to write their papers first, the linearity would provide some structure for the students when they imported their papers into Storyspace. We envisioned each paper as a path through the hypertext and we thought that students could simply link those paths together to create a team hypertext. We were apprehensive about letting the students create hypertexts out of their research before they wrote their papers because we did not want to impose a specific hypertext structure on the students and because we were not sure how Norton would grade the variety of hypertext research projects that might be turned in.

Having students move from a written paper to a hypertext worked well for the personal narrative unit where students consistently created links between common experiences; however, students seemed confused with the library research paper. For example, one student stopped her argument almost mid-sentence. When asked why, she said that she was just going to connect it to someone else's hypertext and that person would complete the idea for her. Students also found that the linear structure prevented them from developing a collaborative hypertext. When they started to create their hypertexts, they felt restricted in form by the three- to five-page logical argument assignment.

In an interview, one student, Ken, described his problem with structure this way: "You can't stretch topics if you're going to do it in a hypertext. You gotta get it all into one paragraph. Or one window." Arnold stated that the hypertext "makes you think more about what you write, instead of continuing with just one thought, because you have to think about [he held up his hands, creating a space in the air] how they will fit together."

In a class discussion we asked students to further evaluate their experience. Doug stated: "I think we should create the hypertext first, then write a paper." Almost all the other students agreed that trying to "bootstrap" a hypertext out of a linear paper restricted them in form and content, and seemed like busy work. In fact, when we reviewed their drafts from the research project and the textual analysis project, we found students wrote twice the amount of text they needed for their research papers, and then cut out some of the most interesting text to keep for their hypertexts. We again revised the curriculum, this time to allow students to create their hypertexts first and then write their papers.

Students Need a Method for Indicating the Structure of Their Links

From the beginning, students seemed unsure about the function of hypertext links. Our videotapes also showed that each time the students began linking their personal work and team work together, someone would ask, "What should I link to? What's a good link?" Instead of answering the question, we asked the students to decide as a class and to decide as teams how they would link their hypertexts together. The editors from each team met and decided where links would be placed and how they would look on screen. Then each team began linking the writing together.

Despite the fact that the student editors met beforehand and decided how the class hypertext's links would look, the teams created a wide range of hypertext structures. For example, some teams had cut their papers up into topical sections, then scattered them like a deck of cards and relinked each writing space so that it was difficult to see where one student's work started and another ended. Other teams kept their papers intact, as four long writing spaces, then linked to specific paragraphs, ensuring that the reader would know exactly who wrote what. Some teams had a starting point with a long list of every writing space available; other teams had a more hierarchical structure with individual windows for each member of the team.

As the students huddled around one computer to create the class hypertext, several students again asked, "How are we supposed to link to the other teams' work?" The teams that had chosen a hierarchical structure wanted to know where the other teams' hypertexts started; the teams that had chosen a nonhierarchical structure wanted to spread out their neighbors' work and thread links between key words and ideas. Still others thought the hypertexts should be organized by author.[5]

In a taped class discussion with students at the end of the fall semester, we asked what their number one problem had been. The response was overwhelmingly: "How do we determine the links when we can't see what the others are doing?" "If everyone is working on many layers, how do we communicate?" In essence, students were asking what the standards (or structures) should be for negotiating connection, sequence, and emphasis in a text that could start anywhere and seemed to be endless.

Charney (1994), in discussing hypertext literacy, pointed out that strategies for structuring linear texts are "the product of centuries of experimentation" (p. 245). As readers and writers become familiar with a certain type of text or genre, they learn to expect certain patterns or frameworks called *schemas* for those texts. Thus, readers learn to expect a specific schema based in part by signs that are provided in the text. But hypertexts are a recent invention. Readers have not developed schemas for hypertexts and authors do not always provide cues. Without these cues, Charney argued, figuring out a hypertext simply becomes a "guessing game" (p. 259).

---

[5]An excerpt from a tape transcript shows some of the confusion the students felt while trying to link two teams' hypertexts together. Members of the four teams are identified by T1, T2, T3, and T4.

> November 2, 1994. The class is divided into two groups of two teams huddled around the computers. One of the students asks, "What should we link?"
>
> Teacher: You figure out what's most important and go from there.
>
> Students laugh and look at each other.
>
> Pause
>
> Teams 1 and 2 begin looking at each other's work and deciding how to start.

John (T1):   Do we want to make a window, then say we're . . .

Jane (T1):   I think we should just link them and not make it [a new window].

John (T1):   Yeah, but see they don't have what we have.

Jane (T1):   Show them what we have.

John (T1):   See this is what we have. From the papers, when we link, they go into here. So then they [readers] know where they can go—that we're switching papers.

Ted (T2):   Right.

Brian (T2):   Bring that up one more time. Okay, we'll just create a new one [window].

John (T1):   What are these things?

Our students were unfamiliar with the hypertext genre and were unable to articulate cues that would help readers understand the hypertext's structure. Because our students lacked prior understanding, they needed some "epidiectic" structuring in order to conceptualize how the act of linking created a structure for their hypertexts, and they needed cues to discuss and negotiate those structures with each other.

We did not want to suggest to students that "thematic" structuring was preferred to "hierarchical" or "authorship" structuring; rather, we wanted students to consider each others' priorities and find ways to accommodate each other. We concluded that the question that continually arose in class—What should we link?"—was a request by students for a method—a grammar—to describe how a community's mosaic was related. We decided we could only address that question by developing terms to describe how links refer to each other.

We were aware that other systems for negotiating the relevance of links already existed. Charney (1994) identified two different camps of hypertext developers: the "pragmatics" and the "romantics" (p. 241). Using her distinction, we tried to evaluate hypertexts developed by both camps. For example, professional hypertext developers (William Horton, Jakob Neilson, and WinHelp developers), in their pragmatic approach to delivering information, create very hierarchical structures. On the other hand, literary theorists (Joyce, Moulthrop, Kaplan, and Bolter) propose a concept of hypertextuality that is either a thematic or

---

Brian (T2): That's what they click on to go to the next paper.
John (T1): Oh.
Brian (T2): That's like to go to my paper; that's like to go to his; that's to continue.
John (T1): Hmm.
Brian (T2): So where do you want to link to?
John (T1): Uh well . . . I don't know . . .
Brian (T2): What are your papers about anyway?
John (T1): Mine is about . . .

Each student gives a description of his paper.

Brian (T2): So, where do you think yours will link the best?
John (T1): I think probably with the (describes an idea in terms of the space three planes. Ah yeah, well it might be easier as a writer to have everything on one plane because you can see where everything's going. But then when we try to build it together with someone else, it makes it more difficult.
Bill (T3): It's getting a little hard to figure out where we're going to.
Jeff (T4): See what we've done is linked all of our quotes together to the works cited so if they want to read the works cited, they can go directly to the quote we use.

"rhizomatic" structure. The difference between the two camps were vast, but both groups seemed to agree—as Landow (1991) noted, "links represent useful, interesting—in a word, significant—relationships" (p. 82). This was a starting point then, a touchstone whereby students could evaluate links.

We wanted to develop a system not bounded by the theories and practices of one camp or the other. This required a different approach. We decided to examine the practices and products of several hypertexts to determine if there were common structures between hypertexts as varied as Joyce's *Afternoon* and a commercial Help system?

CREATING A GRAMMAR OF EXISTING HYPERTEXTS

Hypertext developers describe their software using paper and place metaphors to explain how their products work. For example, there are card stacks, pages, topics, infobases, maps, paths, story boards, webs, and home pages. Each metaphor shapes a hypertext differently, yet they all seem to have similar features. Once a user becomes accustomed to a hypertext program, negotiating the program is simple. This similarity between software products suggests that certain standards are in fact being used. However, the standards do not seem to be specific to the interface metaphors used by software developers. For example, some products like Folio, Envoy, and Acrobat treat online documents like scrolls of paper that you can jump up or down through; other tools like HyperCard, WinHelp, Storyspace, and many multimedia viewers chunk the documents into pieces sized for the computer screen. In addition, the World Wide Web (WWW) allows you to do both to some extent. How the software treats a body of text influences the way people navigate that text because the writer and the reader of a hypertext must conform to the requirements set by the software. Nevertheless, the overall purpose for all hypertext software is to link things together. In fact, the main reason someone would want to write a hypertext document rather than a linear document is to show complex, significant relationships and connections.

Despite the differences between interface metaphors used by various software programs for different purposes, all the links or references to other places in the hypertexts had a limited number of functions. In the book, Cohesion in English, Halliday and Hasan (1976),[6] described two categories of references: exophoric and endophoric.

---

[6]Following the suggestion of William Eggington, a professor of language and linguistics at our university, Norton consulted the work of Halliday and Hasan. Because links refer to other nodes, he focused on their discussion of reference.

Exophoric references are situational and based on context; endophoric references are textual and sequential. Although these categories were not proposed for a hypertext environment, they gave us a language for describing the way hypertext links function. It is important to note that not all links reference the way pronouns do. The linking system is more complex and can be generally described in four ways: to establish sequence, to create associations, to reference starting points, and to initiate computer actions. Table 6.1 summarizes the hyperphoric grammar, a grammar for hypertext references, developed during this study.

Like all grammars, these categories for hypertext references overlap and emphasize certain attributes over others. However, we felt this grammar could be effective because it described existing hypertexts. In addition, the grammar let us describe how both the software and the textual links organize the hypertext. That is, we could discuss with students the software interface and the document as related components of an overall structure. Because the grammar provided terms to answer the question, "What is the purpose of this existing link?" it helped us discuss "What should we link?" with students as they wrote their collaborative hypertexts.

In addition, as part of the grammar system, students used specific markers for different types of links. These markers or "punctuation" helped collaborators understand the intent and relevancy of the links in the hypertext, provided a sense of cohesion, and reduced the feeling of getting lost. The punctuation also put control of the links with the group of student collaborators, not with the software. The punctuation signaled the purpose of the link, and by so doing, helped readers understand the structure of the hypertext before they made a jump. Examples of the punctuation markers we created are also included in Table 6.2.

TEACHING HYPERPHORIC GRAMMAR

After hyperphoric grammar was developed, Norton again taught the hypertext writing course. This time, he did not make the students write a linear paper first and he taught them hyperphoric grammar before they created their class hypertext. Norton used the grammar to emphasize the distinctions between linear structures and hypertext structures. For example, he gave the students a short writing sample and briefly explained Halliday's description of how pronouns give linear texts coherence. Then he discussed how pronouns refer "backward" and "forward" to other words in the text, making a linear pattern of reference. He pointed out that occasionally pronouns refer to contextual events not

Table 6.1. Hyperphoric Grammar.

Referent	Function	Diagram
Chronophora	Provides sequences; refers to texts that are categories, subsets, or linear transitions. The two types are listed below:	□ ↕ □ ↕ □
Anachronophora	Provides sequence back one step at a time	□ → □
Catachronophora	Provides sequence forward one step at a time	□ ← □
Primaphora	Refers to a starting point or location; is not bound by sequence	□ ← □ □
Paraphora	Provides nonsequential association between two texts; categorized by relationship to the node link from. The two types are listed below:	[A] → [A] · [B]
Endoparaphora	Provides dependent parallel information regarding a word, sentence or idea; adds to context; depends on origin node for context.	[A] → [a]
Exoparaphora	Provides independent parallel information regarding a word, sentence or idea; range from context specific correlations to arbitrary connections; unlike any other referent, does not have to function within hierarchy or sequence.	[A] → [A]
Compuphora	Performs an action or computer command other than jumping from one place to another; may start video clips, sounds, or search tools.	□ → [Email]

Table 6.2. Punctuation Used By Students to Signal Type of Link.

Referent	Punctuation	Example
Chronophora:		
Anachronophora	"{" placed in front of word, with a "{" at the end if the link is more than one word.	{Several of the issues mentioned so far { clarify the point I've been trying to make.
Catachronophora	"}" placed in front of word, with a "}" at the end if the link is more than one word.	There are } several aspects to this issue }.
Primaphora	"^" placed in front of word, with a "^" at the end if the link is more than one word.	You have now completed the discussion of hypertests. ^click here to return to opening screen^.
Paraphora:		
Endoparaphora	")" placed in front of linked word, with a "(" at the end if the link is more than one word.	The man at the store told)him that he would take)the horse and buggy(.
Exoparaphora	"}" placed in front of linked word, with a "{" at the end if the link is more than one word.	Throughout }history people have found Plato's cave allegory to be elitist.
Compuphora	"~" placed in front of word, with "~" placed at the end if the link is more than one word.	Click ~here to send me an e-mail response~.

specifically mentioned in the text, but this practice requires that the readers understand the writers' context. Then he introduced the Latin prefixes Halliday used and related them to "forward," "back," "in," and "out," suggesting to students that these terms described the structure of the "links" that pronouns make with the names and ideas to which they refer. To simplify Halliday's terms, Norton shortened the descriptive terms to "endos," "exos," "catas," and "anas." Then he had the students map the links between pronouns and their antecedents or objects of possession and had students define those links.

Then students used Netscape to view several home pages on the WWW. Norton explained that the back and forward buttons on these pages functioned much like the pronouns in the examples they had just read. He asked the students, "Why do you use this home button?" "What does the home button refer to?" After the class described the function of a home button, he explained how the links and the buttons in the hypertext functioned like pronouns by referring to other places in other texts. However, unlike a pronoun in linear text, a pronoun—or any other word in a hypertext—could be linked to a home page, a page beyond the writer's hypertext, a page "within" a page, or to another application. These buttons could refer forward and backward as well.

Then, Norton introduced hyperphoric grammar, explaining how each link in the grammar functioned. He asked students to categorize the links they followed on the WWW. Finally, he assigned students to create a simple hypertext using the grammar system.

RESULTS OF USING HYPERPHORIC GRAMMAR

We found the grammar enabled the students to quickly grasp the concept of nonlinearity. Students stopped asking questions about what to link and began to find ways to include all the links we had defined. Besides making our task of teaching hypertexts easier, hyperphoric grammar provided a vocabulary for describing particular hypertext structures we had observed among student writers. In addition, the grammar enabled students to negotiate the structure of their group hypertexts and provided us with a way to begin to establish criteria by which we could evaluate the collaborative hypertexts students created.

Describing the Structure of Student Hypertexts

During the summer and fall terms, we observed two general trends that individuals and groups used to create their hypertexts. Originally we described these writing patterns as hierarchical or "tree" structures and diffused or "strawberry patch" structures. Hyperphoric grammar provided us with a better vocabulary for describing and analyzing the structure of our students' hypertexts. We began by counting the type, level, and color of the hypertext links in each hypertext document; that is, the number of links created in the individual, team, and class hypertexts. Then we classified each link on the student, team, and class levels using the categories in hyperphoric grammar.

Using this method, we determined that students who wanted to emphasize their arguments—and, to some degree, a sense of individual authorship—carefully constructed a cata-anachronophoric pattern. Sometimes their structures were simple linear link patterns; other times, students created multilinear, hierarchic patterns. They connected their individual work to others who had used similar structures because they could find clear beginnings and endings. Figure 6.1 shows a hypertext students created exhibiting this pattern

Students who wanted to emphasize the relationships between issues or topics that their groups were working on, used linking patterns that, at first, seemed to not have any consistent pattern. However, when we analyzed their hypertexts using hyperphoric grammar, we realized that they had created cata-primaphoric patterns with supporting exo-anaphoric and endo-anaphoric links (with an occasional endo-primaphoric pattern). In effect, these students used a consistent pattern; however, the pattern gave them the flexibility they needed to show the interconnectivity of their group work. Figure 6.2 shows a hypertext students created exhibiting this pattern.

NEGOTIATING HYPERTEXT STRUCTURES

Students always face structural constraints when they develop a piece of writing. For the students in English 115, the assignments required them to take a stance on an issue. The teacher and class decided on a topic (such as jazz music), then the teams divided the topic into subtopics (such as U.S., African, and European influences on jazz music), and finally each student did research on the subtopic to develop an informed opinion on it. Students who did well on the assignment found it very difficult to argue a point without creating some kind of overall structure.

Another important constraint was that the students worked in teams. Their group hypertexts were negotiated documents. Each link, at least at the team level, was discussed or at least followed a prenegotiated pattern. Negotiating the links required students to address questions such as, "What would the reader need here?" "What are the main arguments and issues that we have in common?" "How do we organize these sepa-

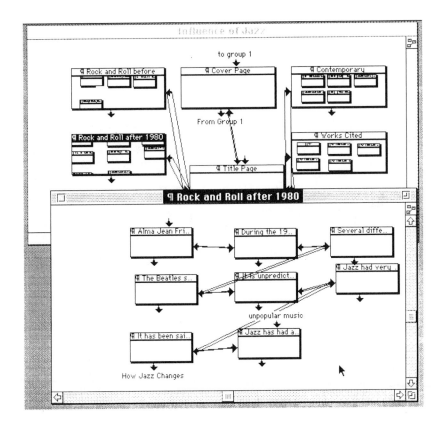

Figure 6.1. Cata-anachronophoric patterns

rate nodes of text to represent our ideas?" These are difficult issues in creating a group hypertext—especially when the teams work separately.

Consequently, even though many of the students from the summer and fall semesters chose a cata-primaphoric pattern for their personal hypertexts, the majority of the team links made between student nodes were cata-anachronophoric. In fact, when we asked students how they created the collaborative links, one student summed up the approach used by almost all the students. He said, "First we create the pyramid, then we add whatever links go between." In other words, they first created catachronophoras and anachronophoras, then they added any primaphoras or paraphroras they could.

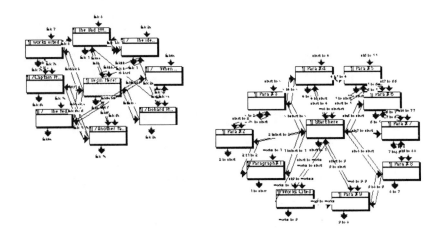

Figure 6.2. Cata-primaphoric pattern

During the winter semester, the number of primaphoric links increased in the team hypertexts. Anachronophoras, which during the fall semester had been integral to team and class structures, were used by the winter semester students as "return" links for individual student catachronophoras (links that were not negotiated) and for endoparaphoras and exoparaphoras. Table 6.3 shows the number and types of links students used each semester.

Table 6.4 shows that winter semester students also used more of all of the types of links in their team hypertexts. Thus, it appears that hyperphoric grammar enabled students to negotiate more complex

Table 6.3. Summary of Hypertext Links.

Type of Link	Student		Group		Class		Totals	
	Fall	Winter	Fall	Winter	Fall	Winter	Fall	Winter
Anachronophora	98	264	6	0	4	0	108	264
Catachronophora	168	332	38	60	12	5	218	397
Primaphora	87	120	1	62	0	1	88	183
Endoparaphora	0	68	0	16	0	0	0	84
Exoparaphora	25	88	3	16	0	5	28	109
Total Links	378	872	48	154	16	11	442	1,107

Table 6.4. Linking Patterns Employed by Collaborators.

Averages Per Collaboration[a]	Fall	Winter
Anachronophora	1	0
Catachronophora	12	13
Primaphora	.20	3.5
Endoparaphora	0	0.8
Exoparaphora	.75	4.2

[a](Team + Class)/Number of Teams

hypertext structures than before. Students were able to maintain a cohesive organization for their teamwork and still create the complex associations that separate hypertexts from linear texts.

Perceiving the Reader-Writer-Text Relationship

Perhaps most interesting was how students saw their contributions to the collaborative hypertext. Students in the fall semester class seemed to consider themselves more as individuals working on the project than as a unified team. This is evident in the way they described their team hypertext documents. For example, one team made it clear from the start that each part of the hypertext was written by a particular member of the team; they placed little emphasis on the collaborative aspects of their work (see Figure 6.3).

The winter semester groups, in contrast, used language that to some extent, downplayed the individual nature of their work and emphasized the collaborative team aspect of the hypertext document. Figure 6.4 shows examples taken from an opening menu to a team hypertext on African-American spirituals that makes no mention of the individual students. We believe this indicates the students were rethinking their relationship to the other members of their team and the class. Their home page served two functions: It provided a place of reference for structure, and it helped the students express a group identity. Students in this group considered their work together as "our hypertext" instead of "Steve's paper" and "Brian's paper." Understanding the interconnective nature of different types of links may have suggested to some of the winter semester students that their roles had changed as writers—they were no longer just autonomous authors, they were collaborating writers who had a common task, body of knowledge, and method of communication.

*In Steve's paper, Clashing Cultures, he tells of the white man's view of the indian as opposed to the Indian views themselves. Also discussed is the actions [sic] taken by the white man because of their views of the Indian.
*The main ideas in Brian's paper, North American Indian Education, are the difference between the success of when the Indians controlled their education and when the white man controlled their education.
*Jessica's paper, Conflicting Views, deals with the different views between the Indian tribes and how they viewed the education process proposed by the government. Dr. Carl Marburger was a main leader in getting the Indians to have a say in the process.

Figure 6.3. Team hypertext showing little emphasis on collaboration

This section of our class hypertext will address the controversy regarding the origin of the African American Spiritual. Was the spiritual developed as a result of the unique African culture or was it a direct consequence of the expansion of European practices and influences? There have been experts who have spoken in compliance with the idea that the spiritual was founded chiefly through the aid and example of Europe. In addition, there are those who argue again this "European-influence" assumption. There is no solid evidence for either argument . . . so who is correct? After researching this topic to a greater extent (through this hypertext), may you can discover your own conclusion.

Furthermore, many authorities convict the African American people of "borrowing" from other cultures to create their own style of musical expression. Whether this is true or not, it is rarely acknowledged that the African characteristics of music made an enormous impact on the development of American music. This section will further discuss the significance of the African influence on the creation of American music as a collective group.

Click on the desired topic:
}What is a spiritual}
}Where did spirituals originate from}
}To what extent does the African influence play a role in the development of spirituals?}
}What is the influence of Africans on the development of the various forms of American music?}

Figure 6.4. Team hypertext showing emphasis on collaboration

Signifying the Function of Links

Because they were working in groups, each class soon discovered they needed to distinguish between the function of different types of links. Most teams found ways to distinguish between links made by the team and individuals. In every semester, almost all students, without prompting, chose different colors to signify different types of links. In effect, color equaled links. And once students began to recognize the issues involved in structuring a hypertext, they began choosing different colors for different things.

During the pilot study and fall semester, the students discovered the need to differentiate between links when they were well into the project. Consequently, they did not plan for different types of links. Often the color schemes chosen by students conflicted with the schemes chosen by other teams. Students thus had a hard time deciding how they should link their hypertexts together. Students who used and understood the grammar, however, were able to immediately decide how colors were to be used. They used the punctuation to distinguish between references and used color to distinguish between links made by an individual, a team, or the class. And they distinguished these link levels before they started creating their hypertexts. This suggests that the winter semester students had an understanding of hypertext structure that previous classes did not get until after they were well into their hypertexts. Because the students (in this case, the student editors) negotiated ahead of time that a particular color would be used for team-level links ("all exoparaphoras will be punctuated and colored blue"), the students had a sense that their team's work needed to be both structurally and thematically coherent.

When we asked students to respond via e-mail to the question, "What makes a good link?" Scotty replied, "The devices that we employed help the reader to stay on top of the hypertext. They also help the writer to build a logical pattern that fits the ideas behind the report in a most effective way." Steve's e-mail reply stated:

> I think a good link must be visible and stand out well to the reader. Links should have coherence and be related in some way to the original text from which the link is coming from. There should be a distinct correlation between the two. This relation should be made visible to the reader or at least a hint towards it before the actual link is made. Personally I do not like to go into something if I do not know where it is going to take me in the first place. Just as in a written paper, the ideas and connections between two things must be clearly stated and obvious to the reader.

Tyler's e-mail also recognized the importance of signifying the purpose of links:

> One of the greatest trials I had with the use of Storyspace and computer hypertext was the correct use of links. At first, I was completely mystified over how they would connect text and how to actually accomplish the task. I learned the importance of clear, understandable, and readable links while doing the class project. I discovered that my links, even though understandable to me, had to be user friendly and comprehendible to someone who had never used Storyspace before.

IMPLICATIONS OF THE GRAMMAR

We believe that using hyperphoric grammar helped students write much more complex hypertexts and allowed them to negotiate meaning with each other—even when they could not see what the other groups were doing until after they completed their individual hypertexts. The grammar provided cues or ways of looking at the structure of the hypertext to see how the individual texts would eventually fit with the texts of other members of the group. Thus, the structure the students chose was informed by an understanding of how their work would relate to the work of the other team members and the class.

This grammar, like all descriptive systems, emphasized certain qualities of hypertexts over others. We did not address issues like document layout, information chunking, and what subject matter is most useful to hypertexts. However, providing a vocabulary to describe links seems important, not only to assist educators in teaching collaborative hypertext composition but also to assist users who increasing use collaborative hypertexts on the WWW. We see the grammar as providing useful structural descriptors for all types of hypertext communities.

CONCLUSION

The main purpose for our study was to teach collaborative hypertext composition so that students could create relations between separate texts. The pedagogy that evolved during this study resulted from several insights. First, we needed to help students distinguish between linear structure in traditional written texts and hypertext structures—even when both the linear text and the hypertext required students to complete a similar assignment (i.e., research a topic). We first focused on the way linear sentences link similar ideas together, then we compared that structure with hypertext linking patterns.

Second, we found that students felt restricted in content and form when they were required to write a linear text and then convert it to a hypertext. When we reversed the process, however, the students developed structures that functioned in both media.

Third, in order to collaborate, students needed to be able to describe and discuss the structures of their hypertexts. By developing a grammar or method for describing links in existing hypertexts, we were able to teach how links function to create structure in hypertexts as well as in linear texts. Our students could then use the grammar and punctuation system to describe their personal linking patterns and to negotiate with a group to create a collaborative hypertext, even though they were not able to see the other groups hypertext until after they had completed their own hypertext. Our pedagogy helped us teach both linear texts and hypertexts concurrently, helped the students see the purpose behind each activity, and provided everyone in the classroom with a common understanding of hypertexts.

Finally, we used the grammar to describe consistent patterns students used with and without the grammar. We also found students using the grammar created hypertexts that indicated they viewed their work as a communal effort and their hypertext as a collaborative document.

Our course, this preliminary study can not be generalized beyond our particular situation. However, the study clarifies specific questions that should be addressed in future studies. For example, how effective is a descriptive system in helping understand the structure of hypertexts? Can a descriptive system, such as the one we have created, help us to determine what makes one link better than another? Can teachers use this descriptive system to establish criteria for evaluating and grading collaborative hypertexts?

When we first began our study, the WWW was relatively new and unknown and the major groups of hypertext compositionists were developing hypertexts for literature courses. Now, many people have an interest in hypertexts and collaboration via the WWW is taking many forms. As more people use hypertext programs to create web pages, they need guidance in creating cues that will help readers to use their hypertexts more effectively.

APPENDIX A: FURTHER DESCRIPTION OF LINKS

In hyperphoric grammar, there are four general categories of links: chronophoras, primaphoras, paraphoras, and compuphoras. In addition, chronophoras may be subdivided into anachronophoric and catachronophoric links, and paraphoric links may be subdivided into endoparaphoric and exoparaphoric links.

Chronophoric Links

Chronophoras are links that provide sequence. They refer to nodes that are categories, subsets, or linear transitions. Building a logical argument requires chronophoric references. Chronophoras are the most frequently used references in hypertexts. When writers create logical paths through their hypertexts, they create chronophoric, typically catachronophoric (or forward) references. When interface designers create tree directories, maps, and history features for their products, they are describing the chronophoric structure of their hypertext. Of course, paper documents also use chronophoric references in the form of time or sequence transitions. There are two types of chronophoric references: anachronophoras and catachoronophoras.

Anachronophoric Links. Anachronophoras provide sequence back one step at a time. For example, if A, B, and C are nodes in the sequence: A—► B —► C then B refers anachronophorically to A. But C does not refer anachronophorically to A.

Catachronophoric Links. Catachronophoras provide sequence forward or toward one step at a time. For example, if A, B, and C are nodes in the sequence: A —► B —► C, then A refers catachronophorically to B. But A does not refer catachronophorically to C.

Primaphoric Links

Primaphoras refer to a central starting point or location. They are not bound by time sequence. These links are the spokes in hub-and-spoke hypertext structures. The Home button on a Web browser, the contents button on a Help system, and a link to a home page are all primaphoric references. Most hypertext software provides some kind of a primaphoric referent that gives the hypertext a macrostructure. Hypertext writers may rely on the software for primaphoric references or supply their own.

Paraphoric Links

Paraphoras provide a parallel association between two nodes. For example, explanations, definitions, keywords are linked by association. Paraphoras can be used for everything from providing context to making radical shifts in an argument. For example, a paraphoric link on the word "him" in "the man at the store told him that he would take the horse and buggy" could remove the ambiguity of the sentence by explaining who "him" refers or connects to.

Paraphoric references consist of two types, endoparaphoras and exoparaphoras, that—like dependent and independent clauses—are categorized by their relationship to the node from which they link.

Endoparaphoric Links. Endoparaphoras provide dependent parallel information regarding a word, sentence, idea, or node. Endoparaphoric references add context that may already be known by some, but not all, readers. Pop-up menus and definitional windows contain endoparaphoric references. For example, if writers are discussing HTML and they add a link explaining that HTML stands for HyperText Markup Language, they have created an endoparaphoric link. Because the definitional node depends on the original node for context, the referent still functions hierarchically and sequentially.

Exoparaphoric Links. Exoparaphoric links provide independent parallel information regarding a word, sentence, idea, or node. They include the "See Also" links that range from context specific correlations to arbitrary or whimsical connections. For example, the information provided by a status bar in a word processing program could be considered exoparaphoric.

Exoparaphoric links are interesting to postmodern hypertext writers because—unlike any other referent—they do not have to function hierarchically or sequentially. Hypertext paraphoras like their predecessors—footnotes, endnotes, and cross-references—can subvert the hierarchical structure of a text. They encourage exploration and require reader involvement.

Compuphoric Links

Compuphoras perform an action or computer command other than jumping from one place to another. Compuphoric references start video clips, open e-mail dialogues, and start search tools. They add a degree of animation to hypertexts and make possible hypermedia or software application features.

APPENDIX B: SUMMARY OF HYPERTEXT FIRST-YEAR WRITING COURSE

Table B.1. Summary of Hypertext First-Year Writing Course.

Stage	Objectives	Reading	Writing
Developing your own voice/ Listening to others	Understand that texts (voices) are connected	Narrative	One-page analysis of hypertext
		Essays	Personal narrative (create context)
	Chunk text and link coherently	Other student's essays	In-class essay
			Short essay on reading
	Interact with text Critique texts		Education hypertext (answers the question: "What is education?")
Responding to other voices/ conversing to create knowledge	Understand the readers make decisions	Research from library	In-class essay (describe and respond to jazz pieces
	Understand readers can write	Each other's essays	Group essays on aspects of jazz
	Discern persuasive intent	Essays on ethos, logos, pathos, logical fallacies, and worldview (to evaluate sources)	Research/negotiation Hupertext (linking group essays)

Table B.1. Summary of Hypertext First-Year Writing Course (con't.).

Stage	Objectives	Reading	Writing
Responding to other voices: interpretation and evaluation	Understand that technology is a text	Short essays which require interactive annotations	Short response analysis (about research and negotiation process)
	Understand readers interact with text	Essays which students will analyze for connotation, context	Hypertextual analysis
	Understand text on the page is not all there is (literary devices)		Hypertext (analyze same hypertext from first day)

Chapter 7

Hypertext Unplugged: Using Hypertext in Any Writing Context

Kip Strasma
Illinois Central College

It seems anachronistic (now) to place hypertext next to print technology, especially as this book goes to print with radical increases in electronic hypertext technologies involving the World Wide Web (WWW)–HTML web editor programs, java, and multimedia technologies that promise to digitalize print even further. My voice is from the start marginal, as most authors or studies referring to hypertext have its "electronic" manifestation foremost in their minds; this argument is easily made of Nelson (1984), Conklin (1987), Douglas (1996), Moulthrop (1992), and Kaplan (1991), but can also be asserted (in a mechanical sense) of Bush (1945). Their excitement and that espoused of new, computerized writing spaces, authored programs for humanities, and authoring capabilities in Bolter's (1991) *Writing Spaces*, Lanham's (1991) *The Electronic Word*, Landow and Delany's (1991) *Hypermedia and Literary Studies*, and Joyce's (1995) *Of Two Minds: Hypertext, Pedagogy, and Poetics*, evidence the strong hold that the recent electronic capabilities and platforms have on current notions of hypertext.

When working with these writers and texts, I am repeatedly drawn to the notion that electronic hypertext reminds me of something I have always known in my reading, teaching, and writing—like a distant memory that is called into clarity with the turn of an event. Hypertext has been awakened by electronic technology, while the memory is that layers and layers of intertextual links embedded in our everyday and literary uses of language. As McKnight, Dillon, and Richardson (1991) remind us, "hypertext hasn't *suddenly* arrived. . . . What *has* developed rapidly in recent years is the ready availability of enabling technology . . ." (p. 1, emphasis in original). Evidence from the print record illustrates their point, for the elements of hypertext are present in most documents:

- Non-linearity is present in indices and popular magazines.
- Recursivity operates among footnotes and endnotes in academic papers.
- Common links between sign and signification that involve the reader are very much part of the constructive, intertextual reading process celebrated recently by reader-response and postmodern theory.
- Nodes exist as "chunks" of information, such as a page in a book or in the stanzas of a poem.
- Multiple paths are constructed by authors and readers—or hundreds of years in the forms of encyclopedias, novels, and dictionaries. A phone book is a massive hypertext.

Hypertext as an *idea* is not new, but its use as a *functional* medium in electronic form is only a few years old. In our own time where electronic technology is making it faster, easier, and more responsive, hypertext has drawn overt attention toward its structural presence; this presence reminds us that we can consciously highlight hypertext dimensions in our pedagogies that inform invention, revision, and portfolios, especially print-rich contexts.

Furthermore, I am drawn to the productive uses of hypertext as a concept because of its utility as the first stage in designing electronic applications of hypertext. For example, while discussing a Netscape document for a midwestern television station with the director of computer systems, it became apparent that the task was less technical than textual. The main objective was to determine how the information would be connected or anchored, which required the use of a map or diagram. A "white board" stood against the wall outlining the major nodes of information linked by lines to and from them and other nodes. Although the information within the nodes was important, more attention was paid to the overall structure or shape of the WWW site than anything else. This experience happened again just recently as Illinois Central College began preparations for its own website; only this time the white board was replaced with 11- by 17-inch paper. Both of these experiences, along with my own note cards and elaborate diagrams that have preceded the development of HyperCard, Storyspace, and Netscape hypertexts, remind me that hypertext should be approached as much more than an electronic phenomenon.

I preface this chapter with these reflections because they justify the relatively nonelectronic context of the activity represented, namely, a conceptualization of hypertext without its electronic functionality—by "conceptualization," I mean an imitation of hypertext through using some or all of its elements in print or otherwise nonelectronic technology. As previously noted, conceptual hypertext (usually in print form) often forms the planning stages of electronic hypertexts. Anyone who has designed a hypertext program, interactive novel, or website can attest to this. Some even believe that whatever is designed in electronic hypertexts can be more effectively achieved in print.[1] Another justification for the context of this study originates from the question of whether the computer is all that is needed for the productive use of hypertext in writing classes, which is related to the practical reason for framing the study in this way: to demonstrate that hypertext can be used teleologically in writing classes as a form of conceptualization, thus, broadening the scope of its utilization to classrooms that do not have access to computers and rejecting notions that hypertext is only a way of accessing and storing information. One final justification stems from the pedagogical efficiency that accompanies the task of not instructing students how to use a computer program, a task that may be inappropriate when time resources are not justified.[2] Conceptual hypertext builds on transparent knowledge that students have accumulated in their previous writing and research experiences. As many of the electronic programs and platforms borrow their metaphorical orientations from print that I use in my simulation (maps, card surfaces, scripts, and the like), this chapter illustrates how students use them productively without the mediating aspects of electronic technology.

---

[1]The debate between print-based (conceptual) interactivity and electronic (functional) hypertext is by no means resolved. Ong (1982) noted that any revolution in media communication produces a dependence on previous forms; this may well be the case with electronic hypertext. Indeed, I argue that conceptual hypertext may form the groundwork for success in electronic hypertext.

[2]As this book goes to press, this point is even more poignant because of the recent development of WYSIWYG editors for WWW documents; these are often cumbersome and difficult to "multitask." We are still several years away from the more "transparent" applications needed for instruction with HTML hypertext.

THE THEORETICAL INTERTEXTS

Several related theoretical intertexts inform the approach to conceptual hypertext that I illustrate here. Together, they attempt to structure my primary inquiry: When asked to compose a constructive hypertext using only the tools of conceptual hypertext (in this case, note cards, paper records, and paper for overview maps), how do students' levels of textual complexity and perceptions of successful representation for a particular audience change based on how they apprehend the information? To help clarify this question, I need to begin with the distinction that Chatman (1981) described as "a salient property of narrative":

> That is, all narratives, in whatever medium, combine the time sequence of plot events, the time of *historie* ("story-time") with the time of the presentation of those events in the text, which we call "discourse-time." What is fundamental to narrative, regardless of medium, is that these two orders are independent. (p. 118)

Chatman explained how novels and films differ in their use of description and point of view. But his generalization about the relationship between representation and duration in narrative suggests that hypertexts are also be affected: Students using conceptual hypertexts have a content or "story time" based on how they perceive the information or "discourse times." (Specifically, I designed an assignment using Association for Computers and Writing [ACW] listserv responses to a specific query made by one listserv participant.) Chatman's notions are central to understanding how hypertexts, in any form, are constructed, for a writer is faced with both connecting and representing information for a particular audience of exploratory readers.

The fact that writers and readers do this with different levels of difficulty or complexity and audience understanding is reflected already in electronic hypertext. It is commonplace now to think of hypertexts as exploratory or constructive (as my use of Joyce's, 1995, terms already suggests): between an already authored hypertext that delivers information (in finished form for a reader to peruse) and the processes of authoring one—or in Joyce's words, as "an invention or analytical tool [to aid the writer rather than the reader in managing the information]" (pp. 41-42). As the writing task indicates (Appendix A), students in this study were asked to construct a hypertext for exploratory purposes, one that presents the information in a helpful way for readers' navigation. Joyce (1995) also noted that, "[m]ore than with exploratory hypertexts, constructive hypertexts require a capability to act: to create, change, and recover particular encounters within the developing body of knowledge" (p. 42). How students do this with different levels of complexity and success, and audience awareness is at the center of this study. Joyce's distinction helps frame the overall shape of a document by focusing on its designer- or user-based purposes, both of which are critiqued by the study of nonelectronic contexts in this investigation.

Furthermore, I draw on another theoretical intertext to illustrate differences in complexity through the number and kinds of hypertext links. In an earlier presentation (Strasma, 1995), I proposed a grammar of links that included intra- and extratextual links (within and to other nodes or texts), as well as hierarchical, associative, and jump (random) categories at each level.[3] Links can form a tight structure, follow a thematic path, or operate at random in and outside of a document. The first two kinds of links, hierarchical and associative, suggest more complex thinking than random that can appear anywhere in a text; associative links, on the other hand, do not require the same level of thinking as hierarchical. C. Smith (1994), borrowing from Kintsch's theory of discourse comprehension, noted that comprehension "has two stages, construction and integration":

> Construction [association] yields a loosely structured text base, or mental representation of the discourse combining text knowledge and aspects of world knowledge, in the form of propositions. Integration [hierarchy] consolidates this mental representation, eliminating unrelated and less applicable propositions to disclose the relevant propositional structure. . . . (pp. 272-273)

Based on this distinction, the level of abstraction required for integration surpasses that of construction because it shows relationships at multiple levels. Thus, those documents that present information in a hierarchical fashion yield complexity not represented through the mere combining of textual knowledge.[4] It is possible to conclude that some links are more

---

[3]It is necessary to pause here to carefully define these terms. *Random links* can "jump" to anywhere in a hypertext with no apparent reason; accordingly, they form the simplest form of linking when writing a hypertext. One links for the mere pleasure of linking. *Associative links* combine common ideas related to a unified subject; they are, thus, more complex because such linking requires an understanding of the information at hand. The most complex links, *hierarchical*, combine ideas or nodes within an overall structure in various levels of abstraction. Hierarchical links require not only an understanding of the information at the concrete level but an understanding of the abstract relationships of that information to overall whole.

[4]This argument suggests three different levels of hypertextual complexity based on the use of hypertext links: those that are represented randomly, by subject,

complex than others; depending on the context of the document, hierarchical links represent integration and complexity, for example, that associative and random links cannot.

I began my low-electronic technology study with one final intertext, "terministic screens," which argues that language shapes perception. For Burke (1966), a term or word describes the implicit observations within language that influence what and how we know; he noted that "we must use terministic screens, since we can't say anything without the use of terms: whatever terms we use, they necessarily constitute a corresponding kind of screen; and any such screen necessarily directs the attention to one field rather than another" (p. 50). Burke's metaphor for how language directs attention is a series of filters—green, red, or yellow—that change the contrast of black-and-white photographs. A number of parallel frameworks easily come to mind, such as denotation and connotation (in poetry), direct talk and doublespeak (in politics), and truth and epistemology (in philosophy). What is unique about Burke's observation is its subtle simplicity that explains how some terms or patterns produce a stronger impact than others at the levels of meaning, image, and imagination, that is, how some "screen" more strongly and some weakly: ". . . [T]erms can be cycles of terms that imply one another, and all such terms can be variously translated into terms of either images or ideas, and any such image or idea can serve as a point of departure, providing a new perspective peculiar to its own point of view" (p. 62).

To illustrate further, I conducted a quasi-experimental study (Strasma, 1991) in which students responded to the quotation, "freedom is not the right to do whatever we want, but the courage of doing what we ought," in three different writing assignments. Incorporating Burke's reasoning, each assignment presented a unique "screen" represented as the author; an environmentalist talking about Earth Day, a communist discussing the end of the Cold War, and VFW member advocating an amendment against flag burning. The responses were coded for the level of agreement and/or disagreement (as prompted by each assignment) with the screening terms, resulting in significant findings:

---

and in a logical structure. It is an argument that can be further evidenced anecdotally by recalling any hypertext composing session such as the one introducing this chapter. Linking or anchoring information thematically, although more difficult than random linking, can be done through indexing, keywords, and so forth. But hierarchical linking requires an understanding of the relationship between the information and the entire document.

- Most students were ambivalent in their agreement and/or dis- agreement with the environmentalist's observations resulting in a 2.97 average score (based on a 5-point coding scale).
- Almost all students agreed with the VFWs member's disagree- ment with flag burning, resulting in a 4.57 average score rep- resenting the *strongly agree* category (based on a 5-point cod- ing scale).
- Many students agreed with the communist, resulting in a 3.83 average score indicating the *agree* category (based on a 5-point coding scale).
- Even though the students wrote about the same amount in the different assignments, many more students agreed than dis- agreed (almost two to one against disagreement).

Although various terms might be equally or more effective in demon- strating how language directs attention through "screening," this quasi- experimental study shows that the language operative in rhetorical tasks influences students in opposing directions—and with different degrees of identification or compulsion. The originating screen for the quote or "terministic screen" altered in different ways what they observed from that point forward. In most cases, students carried out the implications of the original terms without exception or, in many cases, qualification.

In the present context, I built a similar construct by collecting and editing a series of statements about the future of English depart- ments from ACW listserv members; I used 10 selections, including the original post requesting information; one thematic collection of respons- es on print; one on English departments; and one rhetorical challenge from an experienced reader/writer (see Appendix B). Overall, my aim was to see how the sequence of the listserv messages would impact the structures of students' hypertext conceptualizations. In other words, I wanted to see how conceptual hypertext's recursivity, visualization, nonlinearity might reinvest students' understandings of more traditional notions that now inform composition instruction—specifically, how the conceptual hypertext activity could alter their writing processes and final writings.

THE PEDAGOGICAL CONTEXT

I teach at a 2-year community college in the midwestern United States. The particular class I worked with (Composition II) included 14 first- year students from a second-semester writing class devoted to the study of research and argumentation. The particular class was a Quality

Undergraduate Education for Students who Transfer (QUEST)[5] course for students preparing to transfer to 4-year state and private institutions. Courses in the QUEST program are those in the first 2 years of an undergraduate degree at competing public and private institutions in the United States. Students completing Composition II, the second-semester course after Composition I, successfully satisfy the transfer requirements in writing for these senior institutions. Composition II includes several writing activities that involve the use of primary and secondary research for the purposes of composing well-reasoned and argued papers for a variety of audiences and disciplinary forums. Sections of Composition II that I teach also utilize portfolio assessment and collaborative group projects.

Students in my QUEST Composition II class were asked to complete the conceptual hypertext assignment at the beginning of the term as part of their first writing activity on collecting and utilizing research for composition. Students in groups of three or four were asked to compose a hypertext document that included 10 cards (nodes) of information that made sense and would help others in the class access the information meaningfully (see Appendix A for the complete assignment). Each of the 10 statements was printed on a 3- by 5-inch note card with the author's name and affiliation. Individuals in each group received a complete set of cards in a specific arrangement stressing a rhetorical, topical, or random sequence. These arrangements are reported in Figure 7.1. The rhetorical grouping stresses one opposing statement (by placing it second after the query) made by one of the listserv members that the question about the future of English might be an assignment rather than a genuine concern, as reflected on note card eight in Suzanne Webb's listserv comment challenging the intentionality of the request. On the other hand, the topical arrangement foregrounds one of the key ideas shared by most of the note cards: the future of print (again, by placing it in a preferential order); this arrangement poses a unique challenge to the "terministic screen" found of the original and rhetorical request for

---

[5]The QUEST program includes students who have received a 20 or better on the ACT examination and/or are in the top half of their graduating high school class. Typically, QUEST courses are only made available for QUEST students, thus, forming a more familiar context for instruction, although commonly five or more sections of QUEST Composition II are open to the 175 QUEST students in the program. Particular information about the 14 students who participated in this study is summarized in Appendix C, while general information about the QUEST program can be found in Appendix D. Groups were arranged randomly based on the geography of the classroom (proximity of students seated next to one another).

information. Finally, the last, random groupings represent constants against which the other groups are compared.[6]

Figures 7.2 through 7.5 represent the maps that groups drew to represent conceptual hypertexts in the activity. To illustrate them, I have combined several forms of information collected before and after the study. Specific descriptions of each group's background and activity are briefly noted in Appendix C; other materials have been amalgamated in the following descriptions. Students in the first group summarized their document by citing the way that the cards "talk about how the English department will be in the future," thus, stressing the overall subject matter of the design (at four levels) in addition to the question-and-response design expected from the sequence of their research cards. It is also interesting to note the use of numbers on the cards; when I asked the group about this, members said the numbers helped them keep track of the cards and did not identify any particular sequence for a reader (see Figure 7.2).

Organization of 10 not(d)e cards according to group number and chronological order of cards when presented to each group. The information on each card and their original order appear in Appendix B.

Group I (Rhetorical)
1, 8, 10, 2, 6, 9, 4, 3, 7, 5

Group II (Topical)
1, 2, 7, 10, 3, 4, 5, 6, 9, 8

Group III (Random)
4, 9, 8, 10, 3, 7, 1, 6, 5, 2

Group IV (Random)
8, 7, 1, 4, 6, 10, 2, 3, 5, 9

**Figure 7.1. Sequence of information to highlight
"Terministic screens"**

[6]These sequences represent the interpretation of "terministic screens" utilized in this study; it operates on the assumption that the sequence of interaction may direct students' attention from that point forward regardless of the remaining content.

Visual representation of the hypertext document as drawn by four members of the first group that received the "rhetorical" sequence of research cards.

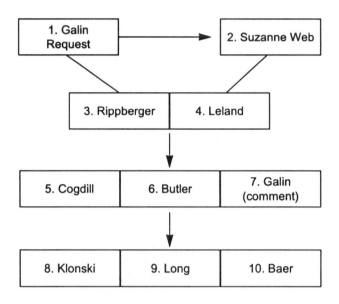

Figure 7.2. Design of document from Group I

In their justification for their arrangement, Group I presented the following explanation:

> The reason as to why we placed the cards in the order they are is because they link together this way. Some of the cards had similar things to say about the future of the English language and English Department in the next 50 years. . . . Others simply said electronics and computers would take the place of actual text in books and other materials. It only makes sense to put them into groups on particular topics, then fit them into the whole story, so it can make sense to the next person who may read it.

The students' words are reflected in the representation of the document, which shapes the information into hierarchical "chunks" according to associative units: rhetorical, curriculum, print, and communication concerns (from top to bottom). But the "story" or rhetorical component surrounds all these units, thus, fitting them together into a coherent whole.

When I asked one of the group members how the document worked, she responded that "the reader begins at Galin's request and can move in two directions, but we divided the cards into different levels to stress the ideas of the cards." This observation is developed further in the group's description of its composing processes for the document:

> Also, we now have a much better understanding as to what was really going on involving the cards. Before the cards were in a specific order, we couldn't really understand as to what was going on, but now we have a clear view by grouping cards together by what they have in common with each other.

This statement supports the students' shape for the document, and it illustrates the engagement group members experienced while constructing their conceptual hypertext map. Of all the groups, based on my observations and notes, Group I composed the most material and seemed to work the most intensely. I discuss this and other tentative conclusions in the next section.

Group II received the card sequence that stressed the "topical" organization. In this arrangement, the sequence of the information presented one of the dominant themes from the ACW conversation at the opening positions of the card sequence, namely, the topic of the future of print and other media; because this topic counters that of the question originally posted (about the future of English departments), it placed a conflicting "terministic screen" to the second group. The results from this group's collaborative work (Figure 7.3) show that their arrangement resembles that of the first group, albeit in a more linear form. Note how the numbers serve as an indication of sequence and not as an indexing function used by the first group.

Group II members did not identify the cards by author but by the subject matter contained on them, a possible response to the sequence's "terministic screen." Yet, their brief descriptions help tie the information in such a way that it begins to look like the same rhetorical story or narrative used by Group I, contrary to the information sequence presented to them (e.g., "topical" sequence). Furthermore, the arrangement of the actual document as recorded in this map is very linear with only one card offering more than one reading path, which further supports the linear narrative shape of the document. In the justification statement, Group II noted that "cards 9 and 10 sort of sum up everything. We used a question-answer approach or paired combination system." This statement not only suggests that the last cards work as a conclusion, as if the document reflected a more typical, academic paper, but also the inherent structure of question and response. Their approach seems to dominate the shape of the document, forcing a rather closed path through the information. Interestingly, when

Visual representation of the hypertext document as drawn by three members of the second group that received the "topical" sequence of research cards.

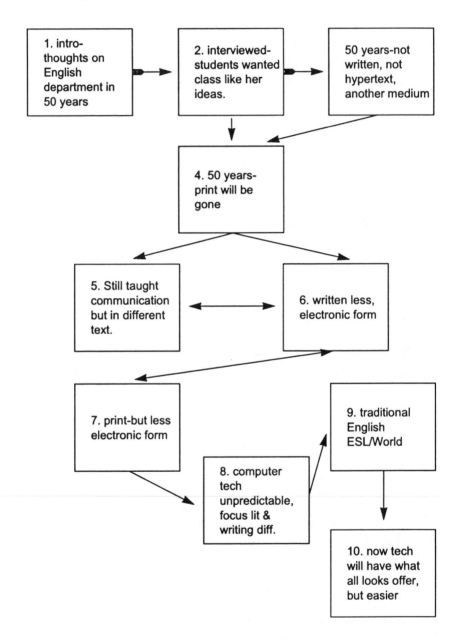

Figure 7.3. Design of document by Group II

asked about multiple links between Nodes 3 and 4, one student commented that it did not "make a difference which way the reader went because
the information was the same." In other words, the reader could progress
to Nodes 5 or 6 and still get to Node 7, but if Node 6 is selected, Node 5 is
bypassed altogether; hence, the reader need not have all choices, indicating
that the document is even more rigid that it initially appears. Questions as
to why this group selected such a narrow path for the reader, why it opted
to represent the "rhetorical" issues over the "topical" ones, and how the
group created a narrative context for the information are addressed later.

The remaining two groups received random sequencing of the
information cards. Of all the groups, Group III crafted arguably the most
interesting document in terms of its aims and structure. At a glance, it is
obvious that the level of complexity achieved by this group surpasses
that of the first two discussed (see Figure 7.4). Other groups assumed
that the starting place for the reader would be Card 1, but Group III did
not index its nodes by numbers at all, choosing to rely on the authors'
identification. This group noted an entry point labeled "start" and a concluding point that the group called a "floating summary." At a deeper
level, this group has structured multiple links and paths for the reader,
which members explained was the reason for the floating summary that
could be accessed at different times during the reading experience. In
the group's words, the "floating summary [allowed] readers to end the
experience at their own judgment." One other aspect of the mapped document is the small circle not connected to any card. I asked the group
about this, and the students said there was no other way to draw what
they wanted to do, which was to show several possible links at one time.
In their justification for the shape of their document, Group III wrote,
"The reader should start up at the top with Galin's card and follow
arrows to responses. Backtracking is necessary to maintain an understanding of how each card is related to others.[7] We did not present all
possible routes from card to card due to a lack of time." Group III's
choices of "route," "backtracking," and other "possibilities" further evidence the richness of the document's complexity. As only limited
instruction was given about hypertext prior to the assignment (a choice
made early on to avoid unnecessary intervention on my part), the shape
of this hypertext introduces the question of why Group III's document
differed so radically from the others. In the description of the document,
Group III students noted that the Galin cards presented a frame for the
text:

---

[7]This difference is crucial because the group went beyond representing information to representing relationships in its conceptual map, a key indicator of complexity. More follows.

Visual representation of the hypertext document as drawn by three members of the third group that received the "random" sequence of research cards.

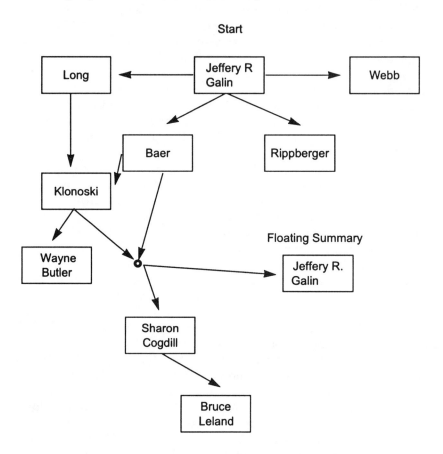

Figure 7.4. Design of document by Group III

> In the group of cards we were given, there were two obvious cards with obvious functions. One began with, "I have an odd request"; the other was written by the same person and provided an obvious conclusion. We then looked through the remainder for replies to the request.

Thus, they also saw or imposed an inherent rhetorical structure in the cards that may have surfaced, as in the other groups' documents, from the rhetorical content of the cards, which seemingly was unaffected by the random sequence of the cards at the outset.

The last group provided the least amount of detail regarding the final document (see Figure 7.5) shaped during class, perhaps because two of the group members were absent from class on that day or because group members appeared to lack interest in the activities. I include it here to complete this initial discussion of this study's findings. Group IV's structure appears enigmatic, for the numbering sequence, suggesting a linear path for the reader, does not obviously follow the pattern of the links represented by the lines; in fact, this group did not use arrows to represent the direction of links at all, which presents an interesting contrast to the other groups and suggests this group's document is the least "reader-based" of all. For example, once the reader moves from the first node to Webb's criticism of the assignment, the reading experience is finished because there is no way to access other nodes or to loop back into the conversation.

This may seem as if the two group members did not think through their document carefully, but the evidence from their descriptions suggests that they saw the cards operating as one-to-one comments, replies, or associations that worked like a series of separate dialogue interchanges:

1. The card is requesting replies from people.
2. This card is a reply to the question on Card 1.
3. This card is a comment on the statement on Card 7.
4. This card is a response to Card 3.
5. This card is a reply to the question on Card 1.

And so on. Thus, it seems evident that the map works less as a representation of a complete document with a continuous flow than as representations of individual relationships shared by the information on the cards.[8] Group IV's document has the linear look of the Group II documents, but there is no indication of a progression between cards or path through the information. Although this group was less concerned with how to show relationships among all the cards, pairs of cards suggests that this group more than any other may have been screened by the rhetorical question and response screen.

Together, these observations from my investigation suggest some tentative conclusions:

---

[8]This is a finding taken up in the conclusion. Almost all groups noted that the task helped them to "make sense" of the information in a "constructive" way.

Visual representation of the hypertext document as drawn by two members of the fourth group that received the "random" sequence of research cards.

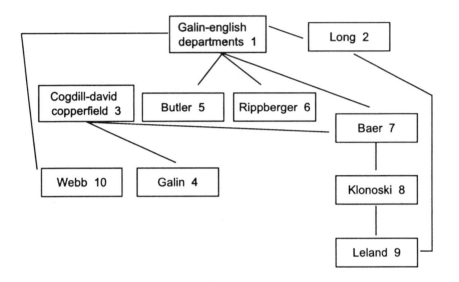

Figure 7.5. Design of document from Group IV

- All groups began their documents with Node 1 requesting information from others regardless of the predetermined sequence ("terministic screen"). This was the starting point and most significant node in the structures represented by the maps.
- Each of the groups included multiple associative and some hierarchical links in their documents, albeit in different numbers and at conflicting levels of complexity.
- The students who reportedly had little experience with hypertext successfully mastered the concept of hypertext enough to represent nonlinear links and paths, although the evidence from Group IV challenges this generalization. (There were some differences in the reported knowledge about hypertext among the groups' members.)
- Each document also referred to the cards by either number, content, or author. This may likely be due to the efficiency of the labeling, but I think it is important for how the information was perceived by the groups.

- All the groups reported learning something about the "topic" during the process of trying to shape them into a hypertext document.

ANALYSIS THROUGH THEORETICAL CONTEXTS

Earlier, I discussed several theoretical notions that informed my classroom activity. The last sought whether the sequence of the cards would influence the shape of the final documents, an indicator of whether the supposed "terministic screens" influenced the way that the information was perceived by the students. It is not entirely evident that the rhetorical, topical, or random screening sequences had any individual influence on student choices. There is evidence that the rhetorical screen was strong, however, because all groups used it to orient their documents regardless of the chronological sequence of the nodes. Certainly, Group I's document represents the two rhetorical cards most prominently. Readers must pass through these nodes prior to moving to the others. Confirming data comes from Group II's document, which possessed the topical sequence; despite the original sequence, this group's document featured the same two cards from Galin and Webb in the first and second nodes of the hypertext. Group III numbered these same nodes 1 and 10, whereas Group IV framed its document with Galin's and Webb's comments. I conclude from this evidence that the rhetorical content of these two nodes so strongly influenced the students in their choices that the order or sequence was of little influence. This rhetorical content ended up being the strongest "terministic screen" of the assignment because of its presence in the content of the nodes.

Such a strong screen shows the dominance of the content over sequence or chronology, a finding counter to my earlier study on more traditional exposition. Students read through the sequence screens to the question and response strategy suggested by the content of the information on the cards themselves. In one way or another, all the documents used the question and answer approach as the primary way to shape the documents, falling back on the topical or chronological shapes secondarily. This implies that of the screens, the rhetorical, informed by the content, was the strongest in terms of its influence on the shape of the documents, while the topical ranked second. Another conclusion comes into view when Burke and this investigation are read in the context of Woolley's (1992) observations about the interactive novel that applies to hypertext as well: "The main problem with the concept of [hypertext] is its assumption that narrative is in some sense independent of the imaginary realm it navigates" (p. 157). Woolley denoted here that narrative coherence is not separate from the language that makes up a narrative. Thus, the rhetorical cues (question and response over a period of time on the ACW listserv) in the content of the individual and various cards guided students' structures of coherence. The carrying out of such rhetorical implications evidences one clear conclusion about both conceptual and electronic hypertext because the language of hypertext form is still linear.

The second theoretical context involved the conceptions and representations of the conceptual hypertext narratives. Originally, I speculated that students might construct several discourse times from a single story time. As the figures illustrate, there is a great deal of variety in how groups conceived of the story time and represented it as a discourse time. Each group worked very hard to align a discourse time in its documents to the perceived story time and sometimes used the process to understand the story time itself. This is most evident in the statement by Group I students that did not know what was going on until they arrived on a structure that allowed them to represent the conversation (discourse time) according to the perceived content (story time). In addition, some groups tried to represent several discourse times in the same conceptual hypertext. Group III's conceptual hypertext is the more obvious example because of the attempt to represent multiple relationships among nodes through different "routes" and "backtracking." Group I's is less apparent, but while interviewing a Group I informant, I learned that the reader could progress from one level to the next through any of the nodes on a particular level, suggesting that multiple discourse paths were designed into the document, even though they do not obviously appear in the map of the document. When I asked how it was possible to move from one level to another, since there are four levels of several cards, the student responded, "The reader can access other levels from any card within that level." I countered with, "So this map does not fully represent how the hypertext works?" "No," he replied, "it is more of an outline of the connections." Their hypertext only hinted at multiple discourse times or reading paths. What I find the most interesting is that students learned a great deal from one another's discourse times or representations by comparing and contrasting them. This suggests that a productive pedagogical activity can be generated around such comparisons for exploring multiple ways to structure the same information. The writing processes typical of more linear, text-based essays (in multiple phases and drafts) is enriched by practice with constructing hypertext drafts because of the attempt to structure several discourse stories—so much so that it might be an excellent place to begin when attempting to instruct students on the global principles of the writing process.

My third curiosity implied that different levels of complexity may be present in the separate hypertexts—measured in terms of the sort of document as well as the number and kind of links. The maps, interviews, and other materials demonstrate that students worked constructively to produce a hypertext document for themselves and readers. For example, in Group III's follow-up interview, the informant confirmed that the students were using the assignment as an opportunity of invention, of making sense of the information as a constructive text. Other groups talked about how they wanted to make the information or relationships evident to readers. As noted earlier, this is where one difference between levels of complexity seems evident. Some groups tried to represent only the information in the nodes and included few links that might represent relationships. At least one group tried to represent a vast array of relationships, which I think is evident in the number and kinds of links. For example, in terms of the kinds of links made in the documents, there is a wide range of difference (see Table 7.1). Group III's document provides the largest variety in links and reading paths, although all the documents show evidence of associative or hierarchical links.

The links are measured in terms of how the nodes relate to one another. An associative link connects nodes that share the same idea, usually indicated by multiple connections or arrows to or from one node (Group I). Hierarchical links relate levels of nodes to one another in the form of connections to and from clusters within the entire document (Group III). Random nodes, presented in Group III's document only, can go to anywhere in the document. The presence of several and various links initially suggests that for at least two groups, a high level of integration is represented in the constructive documents. Students composed their documents as wholes with parts that "made sense." But why the groups have a dividing line of complexity (between Groups I and III and II and IV) is not entirely evident. It seems to be unrelated to "terministic screens" or even the content of the material from the ACW listserv but may stem from a lack of understanding of the information

Table 7.1. Number of Hypertext Links According to Kind.

	Group I	Group II	Group III	Group IV
Hierarchical	4	6	6	1
Associative	6	3	12	5
Random	0	0	2	0

about English departments and technology. Nevertheless, my own observations indicate that the most complex conceptual hypertexts came from the most engaged groups (suggesting questions about conceptual hypertext and collaborative techniques). Also, as the summaries of the documents in the earlier section suggest, most of the students perceived their writings as a story or narrative with a beginning, middle, and end. At least some students in this study seemed to work within and beyond such a structure. All of this leads to the conclusion that when composing their conceptual hypertexts, students as a whole were able to achieve moderate levels of complexity. When revised later, especially after comparing and contrasting discourse times, second drafts might become even more complex. There is some indication that audience did play a role, for those groups that mentioned an audience in their descriptions of the documents also had the most complex documents.

CONCLUDING CONTEXTS FOR CONCEPTUAL HYPERTEXTS IN WRITING CLASSES

The purpose of any study is to provide a broad and deep analysis of any human activity, resulting not so much in sweeping generalizations but in emerging awareness and questions. It is evident from the conceptual hypertext activity studied within that, when composing under the constraints of a typical writing assignment, students were able to produce conceptual hypertexts of a complex nature regardless of how the information was presented to them. Even though the proposed "terministic screens" did not appear to directly influence the shape of student hypertexts, it is clear that the rhetorical "terministic screen" present in the information borrowed from the ACW listserv was strong. Thus, the sequence of information seems to be less important during the composing of the conceptual hypertext (in terms of how the information is presented prior to a composing situation) than, say, it might be during the reading of a produced or exploratory hypertext, such as a HyperCard stack, Storyspace document, WWW document, or Book on Tape.[9] What is most important is how the information fits together for the designer (writer-based) in accordance with his or her perception of the users' needs (reader-based). Thus, students were able to see that content can

---

[9]When reading a "finished" hypertext, especially in a functional, electronic form, the order of the material is very important. True, some authors provide more open-ended paths than others. Yet, for the most part, the presentation sequence influences the reader who must choose among already arranged nodes, links, and paths than it is for the writer in charge of construction such operations.

suggest its own structure within the context of a document that simultaneously will be organized according to readers' needs and purposes. This sort of double vision is an essential part of writing, and the writing process that hypertext helps to highlight and demonstrate.

Certainly, the one conclusion that continually delighted me was the level of interest in the activity itself—resulting, perhaps, from the enigmatic presentation of information in hypertext form. Many students had a high level of excitement with the assigned task, which may not seem so odd to most of us who have used collaborative activities; but the fluid and open context that hypertext enables makes the groups' work that much more engaging. Although hypertext alone will not guarantee this sort of activity, it can be a refreshing departure from more traditional forms of pedagogy; there are intonations that the "concealed secret" inherent to the activity studied may have influenced students' engagement in a positive way. This conclusion is clearly evidenced by the lively discussion in the third group and the serious concentration of the first and second groups.

Furthermore, although the reading and writing of hypertext in any form has yet to make a serious entrance into required writing classes at undergraduate institutions, findings from this study initially suggest that its inclusion may be justified as an invention, collaborative, or revision heuristic. I appeal here to the first group's epistemic discoveries made during the process of constructing a new discourse time for the data, as well as the remaining groups' willingness to work as teams toward the common purpose of "making sense" of the ACW quotes for themselves and, in at least two cases, readers. The findings from my investigation suggest that it can be included successfully as part of existing writing process and collaborative activities. Indeed, an entire assignment can be conceived out of the stages described within: editing comments from a listserv, shaping them into constructive, conceptual hypertexts—even programming their interfaces with electronic platforms such as HyperCard or Guide. Or, any single element can be abstracted for practice in linking and shaping information; the fact that each group or student may compose a different arrangement provides rich opportunities for discussion about arrangement and access of information. And, of course, the actions of students described here are an essential part of designing any electronic hypertext, whether web page or interactive novel. Although we can create electronic hypertexts entirely with computer interfaces, such as may be the case with the new web journal *Kairos*, more than likely such work results from a combination of media that includes conceptual hypertext. This media-rich context for teaching hypertext presents students with several strategies for composing instead of offering one to the exclusion of others.

More generally, my conclusions hint that hypertexts can initiate genre and media awareness, for writing with conceptual hypertext reveals the "situatedness" of any narrative by positioning that narrative against contrasting forms. During some of the discussions with students about the activity in class, it was evident to all how each group "realized" the information in a unique way. Ultimately, the value of early applications of hypertext may be providing a new way to conceive of the writing process, a claim that the writers of the electronic software Storyspace make themselves. The development of meta-awareness in outlining and revision processes has long been a central concern in writing classes. Thus, is not only because of hypertext in its conceptual (or functional) mode that these aims are achieved, but through its reflective use in the contexts of existing reading and writing principles common to our own classrooms: invention, genre, collaboration, form, content, audience, and so on. In other words, this study does not show that hypertext will deliver students from their writing ailments. Yet, the processes described by students within show how rich even a brief, limited use of hypertext can serve as an instructional tool for learning the best way to organize and shape information.

APPENDIX A: WRITING TASK

For our first activity of the term, I would like you to work with a series of statements written by members of the Association for Computers and Writing listserv. A listserv is an electronic mail forum for discussing ideas related to issues of interest to the users. Your task is to read through the 10 selections and make annotations on parts that seem important or interesting. After you have read and annotated, I will assign you to a group within which you will work to shape a hypertext document that presents the information in a meaningful and helpful way for you and a group of student readers. Note that there are no correct answers to the task.

In addition to the document, I would like you to hand in a series of reflections (one to two pages—these can be written individually or as a group) on what happened in the group that you think was important in determining the make-up of the document. Specifically, describe in detail how the document works and how you came to the decisions about what the document would look like. You will have part of this and the next class period to complete these tasks. I will collect your cards and writings at the end of the second class. Finally, please write the number and group members' names on each of the writings.

Thanks and have fun. See me for questions.

APPENDIX B: INFORMATION COLLECTED FROM ACW LISTSERV BY NODE

Node / Card 1—"I have an odd request. I just got a call today from the co-editor of a campus magazine at Pitt asking if I would be willing to be interviewed for an article they are doing for the fall. The editor wanted to know what I thought English and English departments would look like in 50 years.
I would greatly appreciate any thoughts on this question. My interview is next Thursday."
    Thanks in advance, Jeffery R. Galin

Node / Card 2—"Maybe in 50 years there will be a place in English departments where books are not the object of study, or print not the object of study, or print is just a component in some other kind of multimedia discourse, not hypertexts, since hypertext is an attempt by a print-based literacy to adapt to another medium."
    Richard Long, Daemen College

Node / Card 3—"I would love to believe the claims of Joyce, Landow, Bolter, and others that print media is dead and that society will fundamentally change as it did with the introduction of the Guttenberg press. But, I agree with someone who said that print literacy will not be gone in 50 years."
    Jeffery R. Galin

Node / Card 4—"And I agree for as long as print resolution is superior. But in defense of screen reading remember that print is a technology that supplies very high resolution (2,000 dpi), portability, and a physical interface (pages, ink smells, binding noises, etc.) When screen resolution increases from its current 72 to 75 dpi to about 1,000 (sooner than many expect), we will have another portable reading technology with hypertextual links to whole libraries, infrared networks, and a physical interface that substitutes graphics, music, CPU noises, etc. for the smell of printer's ink. In short, the new reading technology will have all that books offer and more—the switch will be easy."
    Ed Klonoski, University of Hartford

Node / Card 5—"What we know as written communication will diminish and will be replaced by electronic forms. The interactivity of these electronic forms will make the communicative act more like round table discussions, seminars, and the like."
Eugene Baer

Node / Card 6—"If you read David Copperfield these days, you'll notice in a way you might not have before how many of the metaphors of the book are metaphors of print, books, reading. So we'll teach print I bet, but we'll teach it in a context of other discourses.

I suppose it will be good in the future if we teach electronic media *production*—like whatever forms multimedia production takes.

How are we going to prevent our own obsolescence? Aren't we already obsolete to most of the American public?"
Sharon Cogdill, St. Cloud, Minnesota

Node / Card 7—"But seriously—besides discussing the influence that computer technology will have (as unpredictable as the present influences were 50, or even 25, years ago), you might mention some of the structural changes that have taken place in a few schools which may point toward what the rest of us will do: The splitting of literature and writing into separate departments and the change of some English departments to cultural studies departments."
Bruce Leland, Western Illinois University

Node / Card 8—"This must be a journalism assignment. I got a similar request last fall, but focused on what pedagogy would be like. Further, I was assured that my remarks were mere fodder for a class project, not an interview that would be written up and published. Imagine my surprise upon walking into my HEL class (that apt acronym) and having my students greet me with questions about why couldn't we have class the way I said classes ought to be."
Suzanne Webb, Dept. English, Speech, and Foreign Language

Node / Card 9—"People will still need to be introduced to and taught the communicative skills of the culture, it just won't be text the way we recognize it."
Wayne Butler, Associate Director for Instruction

Node / Card 10—"It seems to me that the English department of the future will include (as my department at this community college does) ESL/World Englishes/English as an International Language along with 'traditional' literature, writing, and rhetoric."
M. K. Rippberger, English as a Second Language

APPENDIX C: DETAILED DESCRIPTIONS OF STUDENTS AND GROUPS

1. Survey questionnaire
   a. What was your experience with Composition I?
      I asked this question to determine the kinds of writing that students completed in our program. Although the department has a centrist syllabus, the number and duration of assignments varies from instructor to instructor. Most students had completed at least six papers using a variety of modes or strategies. (The department allows instructors to select one of two textbooks, with *Reading Critically, Writing Well* [RCWW] by Axelrod and Cooper (St. Martin's Press) being the most popular among QUEST instructors.) Students' papers reflect the tenor of *RCWW*'s critical reading and generic writing strategies, including readings from professional and student essays, along with analysis of genre strategies (autobiography, explanation, comparison/contrast, evaluation, proposal, etc.). As a whole, their experiences were upbeat and positive.
   b. Have you ever worked with hypertext before?
      Only two students had any experience with hypertext. One (Group I) indicated that he uses the WWW occasionally and that he knew that it worked in a hypertext fashion. The other student (Group III) possessed deeper knowledge of hypertext, for he talked of HyperCard and "stacks" during our interview.
   c. Do you regularly use a computer for writing?
      All students noted they used a computer for writing their papers, probably because of their required instruction in word processing in Composition I, or because some Composition I classes meet in computer classrooms. Three quarters of the students said they had access to a computer at home.
   d. Do you like to work in groups that produce only one document?
      Because the activity involved collaborative work, this question aimed at assessing students' perceptions of working together. All students had completed group work before, but not all had written collective documents. When I asked group informants about their perceptions on what happened during their collaborations, two noted they were primarily responsible for helping move the students along; these groups were contrasted by the other two who worked more equally during the time allotted for producing the document.

h. Do you work outside of being a student?

More than 60% of the students work in addition to being a student, as community college students often do to supplement their college and transportation costs. In my experience, QUEST students balance their work and study better than open-admission students due to the required advisement.

i. To what school do you plan to transfer?

As first-year students, many did not have a specific college in mind, although three were able to suggest a range of possibilities—most of which were state schools in the area.

j. For what career or degree are you preparing?

QUEST students receive an associate in arts and sciences degree on completion of the 2-year program, unless their program of transfer requires specific courses. Nevertheless, two students voiced interest in music, one in nursing, three in the sciences, and the rest "undecided."

2. Group characterizations

a. Group I

As noted within, this group worked the most diligently on its document; this group was also one of the more egalitarian groups. Group members provided complete documentation and took the largest amount of time for writing their document. Often quite and reserved, this group was "on-task" almost the entire time. My observation notes indicate that this group was unsure of its task at first and spent a several minutes planing and discussing the assignment. There were three females and two males in this group, the latter serving as the most experienced with hypertext but no obvious leadership role. One of the group members had experience using electronic hypertext.

b. Group II

Group II was quiet in its workings with the assignment, although group members went immediately to task without discussing the assignment. One member of the group served as the leader and recorder, providing more direction than the others. This student had little experience with hypertext but eagerly took on the role of leading the group to the completion of its document. There were three members in this group, all female.

c. Group III

This group appeared somewhat casual about its composing tasks; members were often in conversation about topics related and unrelated to the task. They also spent the most amount of time orienting themselves to each other. Led by two individuals, one with the most experience using hypertext, this group of three (two males and one female) quickly composed its document after a lengthy discussion; once completed, the group debated how to represent one particular node in its diagram. I wanted to intervene with a suggestion, but did not.

d. Group IV

With two students absent, one male and one female, this group of two males was very quiet. It appeared they had divided up the tasks of the assignment sequentially and agreed to work on them individually, suggesting a parallel form of collaboration in contrast to the shared work by the other three groups. Although they did complete their document, the supplemental information (justification and description) was either brief or not included. This was the least successful of all the groups.

APPENDIX D: DESCRIPTION OF QUEST PROGRAM

QUEST is an enriched version of the associate in arts and science degree course of study. What makes the QUEST program unique?

- Special classes that provide an opportunity to take an active part in the classroom.
- Team-taught, multidisciplinary courses.
- A more diverse general education requirement, resulting in a well-rounded graduate.
- A lounge where QUEST students, faculty, and mentors can go to talk, debate, have lunch, make new friends, listen to informal workshops, and most importantly, develop a sense of identity and belonging.
- A community of learning to replicate some of the intellectual climate of a residential college or university.
- An orientation to ease transition from high school to college.
- Provides a smooth transition from a community college to a 4-year college.

Although QUEST does give students a wider range of general education requirements, courses recommended for virtually any Associate in Arts and Science degree course of study in the catalog can be met through QUEST (adapted from the 1995-1997 *Illinois Central College Catalogue*).

Chapter 8

Epistemic Conversations: Creating Socratic Dialogue in Hypertext

Gary Ryan
Christian Brothers College High School

In *Writing Space*, Bolter (1991) argued that the computer's virtual landscape breaks down traditional barriers between writers, readers, and the text. Because the reader can actually manipulate the text itself, or any other element on the screen, readers have an opportunity never before possible. In fact, although readers of traditional texts can mark up and deface the text, they cannot enter into the text and actually become another writer. Perhaps this experience of being able to alter the text is the most fundamental rhetorical element available to readers of electronic texts, and Bolter argued that every action a reader takes in the electronic medium is an act of writing because that reader shares a responsibility for the text:

> This sharing of responsibility points the way in which electronic writing will continue to develop: we can envision an electronic fiction in which the reader is invited to alter existing episodes and links and add new ones. In this way the reader becomes a second author, who can then hand the changed text over to other readers for the same treatment. . . . The promise of this new medium is to

explore all the ways in which the reader can participate in the making of the text. (p. 144)

Here, then, is the perfect virtual classroom, a discourse community of writers and readers, naturally orbiting a single textual environment where the writer or reader has the ability to converse with the text. Although Bolter was talking about creating fiction, I discuss here the processes of creating meaning through collaborative writing.

With this in mind, my goal as a high school English teacher is to create "epistemic conversations" by opening all written documents to recursive revision by an expanding community of writers to create a superior body of knowledge, a knowledge based on mutual agreement, interaction, and composition; thus, I argue that, just as an essay may provide a snapshot of the line of argument of an individual's learning on a particular topic, the membranous structure of a hypertextual composition may show us the social and collaborative structure of a community of learners creating knowledge, just as in the Athenian grove.

Yet, not all writing environments can recreate an Athenian grove where students and teachers wandered around in the flow of philosophical insight. In some writing environments, individuals just seem to be adrift in virtual isolation. For example, at my school, after more than a decade of teaching high school language arts, I became convinced my students were too often turning in essays that were at best isolated documents meant exclusively for viewing by the isolated teacher. Therefore, for the past decade, I have incorporated a significant amount of revision and peer editing into designing the process in which my students write in order to capture that elusive quality of inquisitive and thoughtful conversation in writing; I have come to understand the important social fabric of peer review in the development of writing because students cannot experiment with language in isolation. Thus, the traditional essay—perhaps because of its very structure, the linear-hierarchical style, where the reader is led step by step through the argument, and each piece of evidence is made clear and relevant—simply does not contain the flexible rhetorical space that logical experimentation requires. Indeed, conversation in the format of the essay would be as cumbersome as writing footnotes to footnotes, or scrawling some neo-Medieval illuminations into the margins of the text. My goal has become to open up the text of the essay to rambling inquiries—babbling, schmoozing, questioning, extrapolating—and accidental collaborative collisions—bickering, teasing, cajoling—in order to create a conversational logic out of a group text. I do not necessarily mean chit-chat; I mean focused conversations, like that between teachers and students—Socratic dialogue.

For the most part, conversations between teachers and their students are epistemic, conversations that search for versions of truth.

Epistemic conversations turn mere information into knowledge, for the conversation humanizes irrelevant data into a narrative. Teachers, like Socrates, repeatedly argue that true knowledge develops only in the interactions of real individuals in real contexts. Conversations between students and teachers do just that; they bring narrative structure to disorganized facts and help to synthesize the thoughts of all (the class) in a dialectic of conversation. Knowledge, then, is a product that develops one step at a time, as a matter of mutual agreement, or as Berlin (1987) explained, out of the interaction of individuals "engaging in rhetorical discourse in discourse communities—groups organized around the discussion of particular matters in particular ways" (pp. 165-166). It matters less how these conversations are displayed; the important element is that organized discussion provides the paradigm for understanding. All this explains the reason my students' initial essays lacked qualified musings (i.e., they were born in *isolation*).

By contrast, Socrates' teaching method can be seen as the paradigm for the epistemic approach to learning today, for we still learn by talking, listening, and debating. In Plato's *Phaedrus*, we see Socrates' typical teaching style as having a simple conversation with another person but with a series of penetrating questions, showing that his young friend has never truly examined life and that the young man has taken what was cleverly written in a book for truth. In this way, Socrates plays the part of a mentor, preparing his student for a better understanding of the world. He wins the student over to his argument, not by rhetoric alone, but through intimate dialogue, passion, and friendship. Without this constant reference to its original social context, the written word appeared to Socrates incapable of defending itself in the dialogic marketplace of conversations:

> If [humans] learn this it will implant forgetfulness in their souls: they will cease to exercise memory because they rely on that which is written, calling things to remembrance no longer from within themselves, but by means of external marks; what you have discovered is a recipe not for memory but for reminder. And it is no true wisdom that you offer your disciples, but only its semblance; for by telling them of many things without teaching them you will make them seem to know much, while for the most part they know nothing. (p. 157)

For Socrates, writing was a semblance of knowledge, the true knowledge that only resides in other people and that can only be communicated through intimate, intense conversation. Writing takes knowledge out of context by separating the writer from the word and placing it on the page. Writing has a profound effect on the human consciousness because, as Ong (1982) explained in *Orality and Literacy*, writing stores "what is known outside the mind" (p. 79). Socrates worried that what was outside the mind would be outside the community as well, and the kind of community and knowledge that Socrates was interested in required both knowledge in the mind and the mind in the community.

I can just imagine Socrates' reaction to the summer reading essays. I'm sure he would have taken my students aside and said, "Let's talk." This is what teachers do. Two thousand years after Socrates, Vygotsky (1962) performed work that renewed interest in the importance of community for learning and established the basis for collaborative learning. In his landmark work, *Thought and Word*, Vygotsky proved that we talk before we think; in fact, speaking precedes meaning. Thought comes into existence through social action. Conversations create meaning; thinking to ourselves develops out of our trying to make connections and establish relationships between things through the process of conversing with another. Like Socrates, Vygotsky came to the conclusion that the road to knowledge was produced by the collective experience. Humanity's power to think conceptually, Vygotsky suggested, is due to the possibility of a dialogue with others at crucial stages in cognitive development. Without a sense of verbalizing in a community, thought can be severely hindered. Like Socrates, we require conversations to understand. Vygotsky explained, "We must talk to others before we can think in language to ourselves" (p. 41). In fact, thinking, concluded Vygotsky, is talking to others.

Socrates lived in a time when writing was a new technology; we, too, live in a time of technological transformation, one that can bring talking back to the isolated writer in innovative ways. The big news in computers and writing is not better thesis statements and better empirically based essays; the big news is chat rooms, networking software, web pages, e-mail, and students enjoying wallowing in language. For me, this is the new picture of the successful computer writing environment where collaboration, talking, and dialoguing can be viewed as a way to radically alter the writing process. Hawisher (1989) echoed my enthusiasm in a recent essay that tracks a sort of paradigm shift to a new way to conceive of computers; she suggested that we are "building a research base that relies less on technocentric perspective than on a view informed by the interaction of technology with the culture in which it exists" (p. 64). The message here, in other words, is very clear: Look at the culture.

THE STUDY

In this chapter, I argue that the HyperCard stacks my students created sustained them in their academic inquiries and helped to produce a vigorous community of writers and readers. I demonstrate this and a set of procedures that teachers can employ to create community in a virtual medium in their own classrooms by summarizing the experiments I conducted in my own classes with hypertext. In the fall of the 1994-1995 school year, I set up a goal to use HyperCard to expand each student's ability to participate in the making of the text by altering existing episodes and links and adding new ones. I had set up the study for 22 Grade 11 American literature students who were enrolled in a private, midwest all-male high school. The hypertext composition study was designed to answer the following research questions:

1. Would using a HyperCard writing and reading environment expand the student's ability to participate in the making of the text by altering existing episodes and links and adding new ones? If so, exactly how?
2. Would writing in a hypertextualized environment about U.S. authors help students learn or understand the course material in the same fashion that classroom conversations promote group learning? If so, exactly how?

The study was to last the entire school year of 1994-1995. However, this was just the pilot program for a new pedagogical method to address the course material. I repeated the project the following fall semester of 1995 with a similar set of junior honor students. Some classes did not use HyperCard in completing their assignment, and I have watched these comparison groups and documented their learning in my fieldnotes, so I could better judge what was different about this group or how they compared.

In an attempt to isolate and identify the potential influences of students' participation in writing a hypertext and to gather data that would help me answer central research questions, I chose three different methods of data collection to use in this study. With this triangular approach, I hoped to identify changes that might occur in both cognitive and affective domains and secure both objective and subjective data: evaluations of student performance, students' stimulated recall on surveys, and case study materials.

Evaluation of Essays

For the past 3 years, my students had written three major essay assignments for their American literature class: an analysis of a novel, a research paper on a U.S. author, and an analysis of a short story or poem by a U.S. author. For this study, all three assignments were evaluated using a general rubric adopted by the state of Missouri for students in Grade 11. The rubric included an emphasis on a main idea that was clearly stated, followed by several subordinate themes that were logically articulated, and above all, a logical progression of ideas and coherence. In order to establish some credibility for these scores, I asked several colleagues to help me code and grade these essays. In developing the standards for these three essays, the members of the scoring team, through a number of controlled scoring sessions, centered on five criteria (focus, organization, development, style, and correctness) that we thought to be both crucial and typical of our students' expected skills. An emphasis was also placed on the need for superior and creative research. Throughout the scoring, the team did not know which students participated in the hypertext project. Abbreviated versions of our rubrics for excellent and rudimentary included:

A clearly excellent essay: main idea clearly stated; subordinate themes logically articulated; includes logical progression of ideas and coherence; body of paper contains evident beginning, middle, and end; develops strong support for the argument, using many specific quotes and points of analysis; sophisticated sentence structures and effective transitions; free of major errors in grammar and mechanics; very few minor errors.

A rudimentary essay: clearly noncompetent; main idea poorly stated or nonexistent; unclear organization; little or no use of paragraphing to set off and develop subordinate ideas; supporting detail irrelevant or lacking; word choice awkward and imprecise; systematic errors in grammar and mechanics.

After many scoring sessions, we came to view proficient essays to have a clear premise and a highly structured hierarchical argument and weak essays to be marked by digression, repetition, ambiguity, and incompleteness. In other words, we wanted roughly a five-paragraph version of the kind of 15-page compositions we had painstakingly learned to write in graduate school.

As always, I graded the papers; only this time, all three essays were scored by a team of teachers using the same rubric. I began this project by wondering if comparing similar writing assignments throughout the course of 1 year would be an appropriate method by which to judge how the introduction of a hypertext changed my students' writing processes. For many years, two traditional essays, scored according to a rubric I had adapted for our school from guidelines suggested by the state of Missouri for Grade 11, had bracketed the school year. The first traditional essay was assigned at the beginning of the first semester and the second traditional essay was to be completed at the end of the second semester. I hoped the later essays would be a good indication of learning.

Student Attitude Surveys

Surveys were given to the students before and after the hypertext assignment to assess their previous writing experience—the types of writing and writing process assignments required in previous grades— and their attitudes about these different experiences. The survey was designed to see what effect the hypertextualizing of their compositions had on their attitudes toward their work, their chosen authors, and the types of writing they created. On the surveys, the students were asked to respond on a 5-point scale ranging from 1 (*strongly agree*) to 5 (*strongly disagree*) to a series of descriptive statements on multiple revisions, peer reviews, and the use of hypertext tools. I gave the survey twice, once before and once after the HyperCard assignment, and each time I included a space for open-ended comments, where the students were asked to comment on "the use and creation of the *Literary Journal* hypertext in class." By the second year, I required the students to take extensive fieldnotes of their own because I became convinced that talking about their writing was an important factor in their understanding of the assignment and the course content. These student fieldnotes became part of a larger case study on one individual class of 22 students.

The Narratives of Individual Students

Employing the qualitative methods of "action research" (which includes using fieldnotes to support my observations of composing behaviors in the classroom and during individual conferences, collecting student writing in process, and performing a systematic analysis of student composition development), I developed case studies or individual narratives for these students. I researched the literature on hypertexts, created the hypertext and experimented with it in my classroom, and interviewed colleagues and scholars and creators of hypertext. Finally, I consulted with colleagues and fellow researchers to gauge the accuracy of my findings and to discover new avenues for further inquiry. The traditional evaluations, the interviews, and the student attitude surveys were significant indications of the study's success, but the case studies told the human story of this collaborative effort and reinforced the results of the other investigations.

When the Researcher is Part of the Context. It is important to understand that I was actively involved in leading these students through careful readings of their individual authors and source material, in creating the hypertext, and in showing the students alternate possibilities to augment their essays. I was also actively learning. Consequently, I could not entirely extract myself from the context of the composition. As I wrote and observed, as I questioned and evaluated, I tried to create a triangulation of evidence, so I could be sure that what I was observing would be also noticed by other, more objective, observers. I read the fieldnotes of all the students and other members of the research team, teachers outside of the triangulation who had observed my classes and evaluated compositions, and periodically summarized this data in entries called "Reflections." Later, I would synthesize these notes into a discussion of the greater principles of hypertextualizing composition. As F. Smith (1982) noted in *Writing and The Writer*, "Another instrument is always required to observe the instrument observing the image" (p. 2). Implied in this remark is the impossibility of watching yourself in the act of creating. However, I was not interested in creating a community in which I played no part.

Whenever possible, I paired students from the first focus group with those in the second who shared a similar author or points of interest. For example, the seniors who had investigated the beat poets would help the junior students with their investigations the following year. This became one of the most promising aspects of the program as many students dedicated their free time to the tutoring of student writers. Some of these discussions were captured on film and will later, when we have the necessary technology, be preserved in our hypertext. By exchanging fieldnotes and forming focused discussion groups, I was trying to foster in these students an awareness of the sociocultural process permeating this project. These sessions often revealed the submerged issues underneath the reading and writing of the hypertext.

As the study evolved, I also learned to change my mind and experimental techniques as I evaluated the data. I learned to say, "Ah, very interesting; let's look at this." For example, when reviewing small group discussions that I had videotaped, I noticed that students needed some time to talk through the writing they had just finished composing and were about to recite. This impulse of students to talk out loud as they wrote was a phenomenon I had not expected to find. At first, I almost wanted to remind them to read their work and not comment, but I later came to the conclusion that this was a very necessary step and that these students were giving their writing a context through conversation, perhaps, in much the same way early cave painters discussed their figures of bison and deer with the tribe. Verbal context seemed essential. I was also pleasantly surprised to see how much they liked keeping fieldnotes on their investigations. Unfortunately, I did not do this very much until the second and third years of the program, but it now occupies a significant place in my curriculum. By now it was very obvious to me that students needed to talk about their writing in order to continue composing; however, it was a challenge to transfer a temporal, social event into HyperCard.

LITERARY JOURNALS

In order to answer my original questions about hypertext, for the second essay, I changed the original assignment about an author to one that included the process of these students' investigations of a U.S. author and of the time period in which he or she lived. The focus of the assignment was no longer the traditional essay but rather their investigation. Much more emphasis was placed upon the notes and rambling scaffolding musing, rather than on the traditional end product of the finished text. The students wrote and created the hypertext called *Literary Journals*. Approximately 5 weeks of the second quarter of the fall 1994 semester and the second quarter of the spring 1995 semester was spent in individualized study based on their investigations of U.S. authors. These students were given the following assignment:

> Each student has been assigned an author and asked to imagine that author's daily life. First, the student will research that author's life and write a brief biographical summary. Second, the student will focus on a particular decade of the author's life, looking closely at three to five events in this time frame. The student will then be expected to keep concise notes, including bibliographic information on his or her readings. Third, the student will immerse himself in particular places and events, actually taking on the persona of his author by writing a diary and recording the highlights of 10 years.

As these students created their "journals," they also placed their compositions in a HyperCard stack called *Literary Journals* that I designed for this experiment. The HyperCard stack was a hypertext that allowed for the creation of links to other documents. These students were encouraged to add to their initial compositions in a variety of ways—footnotes, biographical material, comments on other students' work, and supplementary material. In this way, while the hypertext would not have a clear premise and a highly structured hierarchical argument, it would contain all the building blocks that make up the proficient essay, although in a rather informal order.

Designing the Equipment

It is important to point out that reading, writing, and thinking in a hypertextual environment is not necessarily something new, but is rather an evolutionary process. People have been reading and writing nonlinear text for a long time, but what is new is the computer's capacity for storage and retrieval. The three students represented in the next section are exemplars of a natural evolution, from writing primarily in manuscripts, to composing on the computer with the intent of publishing in print, to composing exclusively for a virtual environment. Because hypertext is a nonlinear reading and writing environment, it is important to recall that a hypertext can be considered a collection of documents related in some fashion. These documents do not have to be physically sequential as in a bound book. The kind of hypertext that I envisioned best for my students was a vast and variable community of texts. Traditional essays of criticism and/or scholarship could easily be a part of the accumulation, but the hypertext would also provide the opportunity for new kinds of "essays." For example, a reader could journey through a sequence of cards in *Literary Journals,* stopping at points to leave notes in the fieldnotes' commentary window, thus entering into the discussion and becoming another writer. There would be no limit to the varieties of extensions to each student's individual compositions and their annotations: texts alluded to and/or used by various authors; photographic materials; sounds; essays on the facts revealed by annotations. It would make little sense to impose any limit on the number and kind of these networked texts. Everything would grow in relation to the natural investigations of the students involved in the project.[1]

The primary design structure for *Literary Journals* was taken from *DataMaster,* a hypertext tutorial on data modeling created by Schmidt (1992-1996) and agpw, inc. Essentially, *Literary Journals* is an

---

[1] I am indebted to David Warren, PhD for these insights on the nature of hypertext and the community of authors.

electronic book created to help the students better understand American literature through writing and research. The principal audience for *Literary Journals* is students responsible for creating their own *Literary Journals* for this assignment. *Literary Journals* is also an attempt to include other interested individuals—teachers, parents, and other students—in an ongoing electronic dialogue with the writers or creators of these journals. *Literary Journals* is, in one sense, a living document: a multimedia learning environment created by one class that forms the basis for future students' research and additions. I made it known from the beginning that each student was crafting a text for the illumination of the students who would come later. As a consequence of this attitude, students from previous years were eager to help these younger writers by explaining possible interpretations of the chosen author's work and by being peer reviewers and active listeners of the novice students' work in progress. This endeavor enabled us to create an individual learning experience for each student supported by social interaction. Unlike in the case of the textbook, the scholars who created these HyperCard stacks were available, walking our hallways.

How to Read the Book

Literary Journals requires a personal computer for its use. However, students can read *Literary Journals* like they would a book, by going chronologically through the text, reading one card at a time in sequence. But on every screen students have choices to make and things to do (see Figure 8.1).

Students were encouraged to follow their impulses. It was a new way of learning based on inquiry. In direct contrast to traditional academic texts, readers should not be concerned if they are not following some predefined path. They only needed to stay interested, to follow the criss-cross patterns of their own minds. Instead of a single argument the reader is forced to follow, a reading is created by the individual inquiry. Unlike the textbook, there are no page numbers.

The Grammar of the Hypertext. The basic unit of this document is the card (a screen of information). Every idea has its own card. *Literary Journals* organizes sets of cards to create threads of discussion around the U.S. authors and the individual events students have chosen to write about in their essays. For example, when David pretended to be William Faulkner writing a journal, he created a card titled "The Second Pillow" that discusses the end of the story "A Rose for Emily." From this card, a reader might go on to the next card, "Nobel Prize Speech," or the reader might click on a word in bold letters and enter the Faulkner game room,

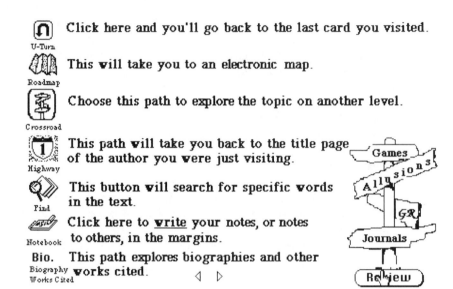

Figure 8.1. An example of the "reader's choices"

or even perhaps compose a new trail of documents on his own. Figure 8.2 shows an example of a card in the HyperCard stack that a student created, complete with the buttons that served as links to footnotes, biographical information, games, and commentaries from his own field-notes and the notes left from previous readers.

The card shown in Figure 8.2 is a good example of how the electronic space of the computer has allowed me to begin to capture the ephemeral qualities of natural thought by making visual the bread crumb patterns of a student's inquiry. On the right, where I have pasted a text field, is the student's response to the original assignment—to investigate a U.S. author and to write a journal as if they were that author; and then, on the left, I have placed buttons to incorporate fieldnotes, footnotes, and games. In this way, I have restructured the nature of the community of text by inviting potential readers to participate in the associative elements surrounding the creation of the text on the right. Had a reader pressed on the road sign, he or she would have been transported to a transcript of a discussion between David, the teacher (me), and another student on Faulkner's experiments in narration as seen in the novel, *Light In August*, and the short story "A Rose for Emily."

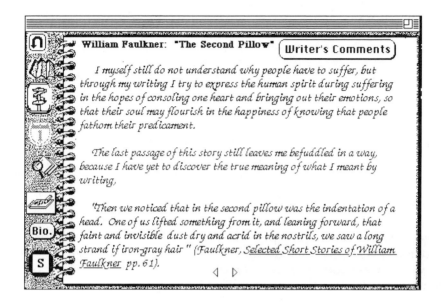

Figure 8.2. Example of student created card with links

1/20/96:
Teacher: . . . Faulkner seems to be one of those authors that created because he had to write . . . about those people . . . just to feel some of wonderful emotions. I think that is what writing does, it allows you to pretend to be other people.

David: Faulkner said once that the authors in his lifetime had destroyed their manuscripts because they withdrew all human emotions from them.

Teacher: Wow! Don. What was that you were telling me about the different narrators in *Light in August*?

Don: Well . . . I was saying how he seems to provide a different narrator for each major character in the book. For example, Joe Christmas...

Teacher: . . . But isn't the story told in the third person?

Other cards might include music composed by a student for a particular author or scene from the journals. Although traditional texts are exclusive, hypertexts are inclusive. The reader decides the order of reading and is partly responsible for creating the logic of the text. For example, a reader might want to finish Don's thought. If so, the reader could type the comment into the conversation or into the pop-up "Notes" field. Later readers would then benefit from this type of illuminated conversation.

Students involved in the program become self-powered vehicles, free to drive almost anywhere they please. In *Literary Journals*, the students decide whether they stay on the main route or explore the sights, whether they follow the suggested itinerary or create their own. If students only drive the main route, they should achieve a better understanding of the course material. In addition, *Literary Journals* provides the opportunity for students to explore ideas more fully, to play games related to the current topic, and to review what they have been studying. I have found that all of the students in the study were comfortable playing these computer games, perhaps because the linguistic levels begin rather low and the expectations for prerequisite knowledge are nonthreatening. Yet, playing these games gives the reader confidence to continue reading. Students are comfortable with games. Games are also a great way to learn information, and the computer gives the creators of these games a unique opportunity to dialogue.

Dialogic Questions. Each student in the program created at least one game with five questions. These questions started by requiring the lowest levels of critical thinking (i.e., recalling facts) and progressed to the higher levels of reasoning and synthesis. Talking with these students in the composition of these games became one of the best opportunities to evaluate a student's thinking process and understanding of the course material. In considering possible responses to the questions, the students had to develop a heightened sense of purpose and audience, particularly while they were creating the dialogic answers to multiple-choice questions. A simple multiple-choice question becomes a dialogic node as the wrong selections are "answered" by the writer with a tempting prompt, that perhaps will nudge the player toward the correct answer. Some quizzes are quite challenging, having two correct answers (see Figure 8.3).

The playful challenge of games and the conversational narrative kept students motivated and moving toward their potential. What is great about these games we have created is that they are language games, and the students are completely immersed in writing, reading, and critically thinking in writing; this is yet another example of hypertext's rhetorically superior space, a space not available in the static print of the traditional five-paragraph essay. The computer's capability to provide instantaneous pop-up text windows creates a virtual space for arguments not possible in print. None of the traditional rhetorical avenues open to high school students would be open to this type of dia-

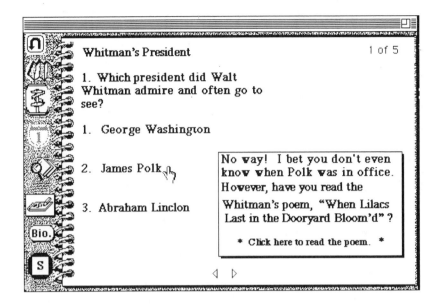

Figure 8.3. Example of "dialogic question in quiz"

logue with their readers. The obvious glee these students took in creating these questions, and particularly, in their responses to the answers, was rather infectious. Often students would create games to respond to the games they had just played. But there was much more than play going on here.

Furthermore, because these questions required students to imagine possible answers and the submerged scaffoldings of thought required to answer correctly, they engaged in a type of epistemic conversation with their audience. The games were not only created to test the reader's knowledge but also to help the reader respond correctly at the next opportunity. In this way, the students' participation in the creation of the text has made them take responsibility for their learning in ways absent in traditional terms. By conferencing with these students as they created the questions and, most importantly, the answers, I have been able to build on the critical thinking skills these students already possessed, and I have been able to get a glimpse of the nodes of information trapped inside the informal logic of their thoughts. The games exposed better than anything else the truly unique analyzing skills, the metaphorical dexterity, and the insightful wit these students possessed. The conversational narratives, at times silly, ambiguous, and incomplete, were also important ports of entry, where students, both writers and readers, could participate in the natural flow of ideas and be helped to levels of critical thinking and sudden flashes of insight not possible without proper help. These games provided a perfect vehicle for epistemic conversations, for they promoted critical thinking in a learn-by-doing experience with an identifiable community—those pranksters in the game. Students were not just doing exercises in a decontextualized workbook; they were playing Ted's game. Or they were playing against Ted.

As these games indicate, the overall significance of hypertextualizing composition through *Literary Journals* is that for the first time the "text" matches the pedagogy that we all want. The text is no longer didactic, linear, and finalized, but amorphous, aphoristic, and full of fragmented potentiality. The text begins to show the messy composing process that supports the more formalized composition on the right. By hypertextualizing composition in this fashion, we are not only changing the nature of literacy but also the classroom paradigm, by shifting from product to process. Good educations are essentially great conversations; the hypertextual canvas provides a more dynamic picture of the relationship between students and teachers. Student compositions do not only offer a snapshot of the individual student's thinking, the text also offers a snapshot of the learning community. This is an extremely important concept because quite often the nature of the text drives the curriculum.

FINDINGS

In this section, I look more closely at the three methods of data collection used to answer the central research questions: an evaluation of my students progress and performance in a series of traditional essays, a student attitude survey, and case studies of individual students. My data collection revealed that hypertextualizing the composition provided a unique and important vehicle for evaluating student learning.

Evaluation of Essays

The essays composed later in the year almost always received higher scores. These were not controlled, holistically scored tests, but compositions that developed over months. Therefore, the fact that the grades got better as the students and I conferenced on the paper through drafts, reflected a better understanding of the course work on the part of the student. Many of these later essays reflected several months of reading, writing, and revising, as the students groped for a better understanding of their authors' work. The traditional academic essays did provide an important insight into student learning, but these essays did not answer important questions about the methods of brainstorming, revising, and editing used to create these compositions. However, a comparison of the traditional essays with the hypertexts was quite interesting.

Three important elements were apparent in different levels in all of the compositions: unity, voice, and interactivity. The scoring team came to view unity as being one of the primary "events" of the traditional essay—with its attendant head, body, and foot. At first, unity seems to disappear in the hypertext composition, yet I later argue that the lack of unity is only an illusion created by the metaphor of the single author, working alone to create a personal composition. Ironically, compositional unity does not often seem to be connected with conversations, or even conferences between students and teachers. Voice, which is traditionally muted into the third-person omniscient in the traditional essay, becomes the trademark of the hypertextual experience. Voice is easily seen in conversations, but it is enhanced by facial gestures and a sense of personal interaction. The narrative quality is also the most difficult for students to learn, and perhaps this lack of humanization of the earliest uses of the technology marked what Socrates feared—the loss of real personal interaction. In our hypertexts, there was always room for dialogue. Students created the different aspects of their compositions in a variety of voices; for example, the biographies were almost uniformly written in a reserved third-person point of view, whereas the games often included slang and the clipped syntax of the conversational first person point of view. The narrative quality of these hypertextual additions to the composition seemed to anticipate and invite reader response. Remarkably, instead of creating chaos, these extratextual elements somehow seemed to refocus the reader to the real importance of the assignment—to investigate a U.S. author's life and work—by making visual the connection between passages in an author's work and some biographical fact. Finally, what the hypertexts seem to reveal is a conversational unity, the kind of complex thought that only develops in the give-and-take of conversations—arguments, counters, bickering, forgiving. Conversational unity can be seen in the small bits of video conferences, in the comments in hypertexts, in the playful dialogic questioning of the games, and even in the final traditional essays, where the drafting, conferencing, and peer review synthesized into a final expression. Traditional essays look for information; hypertexts look for communication. Hypertexts are never finished texts but the aphoristic suggestions of potential texts.

Student Attitudes

I used two methods of data collection to find out what students' attitudes were toward hypertext. I developed a student attitude survey to gather data and to expose general trends. The survey was filled out on the first day of class, and was repeated at the end of the year when all compositions were completed. I also had students keep elaborate fieldnotes on their work in progress. During the course of the school year, I would meet with students to share fieldnotes and to periodically reflect on the experience of creating these hypertexts. The primary finding of the student attitude surveys was that the students generally enjoyed working with hypertext. Before this study, few of the students had ever heard of the concept of hypertext. None of the original focus groups tested had used or known of hypertext before using it in this study. The next year, only 3 of the 21 students in the focus group had ever used or known of hypertext before this class. Of the 140 students in the general population surveyed, only 5 had used or known of hypertext before this study; and of those 5 students, 2 had misunderstood the question, one gave the cryptic remark "1/22/92," and two correctly associated the term with the Internet. The general knowledge base of the group surveyed was summarized by one succinct reply, "I don't have a clue what hypertext is." One student expressed interest in hypertext by commenting, "From what I have heard in the past, hypertext helps the students see their works as potentially publishable, not solely written for the critique of the instructor. In a sense, writers begin to present their work in a unique, more profound approach than before."

The student attitude survey revealed that the students did indeed have an enjoyable experience. Each student surveyed strongly agreed or agreed with qualification that hypertext creates enthusiasm for the learning task, encourages student inquiry, engages students in thought-provoking conversations, encourages students to be independent thinkers, arouses students' natural curiosity, permits students to search for meaning, improves critical thinking skills, encourages students to construct meaning, allows students points of view to be valued, and encourages students to consider different points of view. The written responses were also enlightening. Two common responses shed significant light on the nature of this project. First, hypertext was easy to use, "an extremely rapid means of offering sufficient information on a certain topic." Second, it provided an experience to "get help on the project from people their age."

It was obvious from my own observations that the students liked working with the hypertext. Many students particularly liked the ability to retrieve information quickly, but these students also placed a great deal of emphasis on the ability to see the information from the point of view of other students their age. This last concept seems to suggest that there is a distinct desire to see information personalized. This is a trend quite evident in the Internet, where the proliferation of individual, personalized websites abound. Here again the social nature of the computer rises to the surface. There also seems to be a developmental pattern to the use of hypertext in our study, a progressive movement away from impersonal and decontextualized information toward the personalization of information and communication. I noticed this first with the focus group the first year, but it became pronounced in the second year. I have come to consider this shift from impersonal to personal as a reflection of the larger shift in the students' conception of audience and purpose. At first, the students viewed the audience as primarily the teacher, but as students became acquainted with their material and established a credible persona for their chosen authors, they got more confident in trying out creative approaches to the material and communicating about it with others.

I also looked at students' fieldnotes. These comments were most helpful in determining student attitude and writing process. During the first 3 years as this project developed, I increasingly became convinced that student fieldnotes provided an important evaluative tool. Almost all the fieldnotes were positive, and the great work the students produced was perhaps a direct reflection of their enjoyment of the assignment and with working with the new technology. There is an implicit recognition of free inquiry and expression of ideas and information in a very personal way. Through observation and conversations with my students, I came to believe that this joy existed, not only because it was a great assignment, but perhaps because it reflected a greater structure in which students could think freely. Perhaps my students had problems producing straight lines of arguments because they were used to writing only as a response to authority and in finding information out "there," rather than in themselves. The linear structure of the typical academic essay forces students to squeeze their thoughts into an artificial pattern. It is no wonder that students do not take ownership or responsibility in creating their compositions. Hypertexts, on the other hand, occupy a more flexible space than printed essays. Electronic texts, like ours, tend to follow a pattern identified by Bolter (1991):

> The text is a continuous prose paragraph, displayed on the computer screen for the reader to read in the traditional way. Some of the words are in boldface; the style indicates that there is a note on the word or phrase, something more to be said. To retrieve the note, the reader points with the cursor at the text in the boldface and presses a button. A second window then opens on the screen and presents a

new paragraph for the reader to consider. The reader examines the note and may then return to the original paragraph. . . . In a printed book, it would be intolerably pedantic to write footnotes to footnotes. But in the computer, writing in layers is quite natural and reading the layers is effortless. All the individual paragraphs may be of equal importance in the whole text, which then becomes a network of interconnected writings. (p. 15)

Instead of fragmenting the students' perspectives on the material, this fragmentation of the text actually seems to have freed their consciousness to be able to produce rather straightforward synthesis of the author's work. Hypertext is a more natural way of reading. My students did not find reading nonlinear texts difficult or uncomfortable, provided that the retrieval of pertinent information was immediate. Anytime a reader lost his or her way, the hypertext became a failure, a nonreading and nonwriting space. Then we had to fix the links. I argue here that this textual liberation enabled my students to produce essays of great skill and focus because they were able to follow their own inclinations.

CASE STUDIES OF WRITERS AT WORK

Each year, I selected several students and collected additional data on them in order to develop individual case studies; furthermore, I spent a considerable portion of each year trying to put their experiences into a narrative. Each of the following students represent a single year in the life of the project, but beyond that, I believe they also reveal an evolution of sorts, for these three important stories show the significant patterns of thought requisite to creating true hypertextual compositions. Together their journal writings, games, and other compositions in the *Literary Journals* evidence the collaborative rapport among students and instructor.

Student 1: Todd—A Beginning Writer Struggling Alone for Greatness

Not all writers are prepared for advanced compositions. Beginning writers need a place to present text that will have the chance for community support. Todd is a great example of a student writer who blossomed during this experiment. He did not participate regularly in class, but he had been writing poetry in a notebook he kept for his own enjoyment. Here, from my fieldnotes, is a picture of Todd evolving into a published poet:

Todd is busy writing poetry. His mother told me yesterday that Todd has just discovered a passion for writing because of this project. He has never received better than a "C" in any of his previous language arts courses here at school. Although he is a bright individual, Todd often sleeps through his classes and is passive in his approach to academics. However, this outpouring of talented poetry seems to have begun in response to his independent investigation of Walt Whitman. In the selection below, the passages in quotations are Todd's. The rest is a paraphrasing of Whitman's writings about the Civil War:

April 13, 1861
When I look at war, I don't see innocence—men fighting for causes, but I see families being ripped apart. This family of our nation, our family of men, being ripped at the seams. "The brutality of war tears at my inner being which lies on a pillow of serenity" (Todd). I must turn from this war, from the brutal truth that it tells. I must turn to poetry of men; I will work once more on Leaves. But first, I recall lines from a favorite poet, from another time: "Oh how tranquil waters are in chaos, not so much as with a small stone, but a gathering of stones which do not ripple the peace but ravage it."

It is obvious that the possibility for other types of writing assignments, in connection with the unique publishing in hypertext, contributed to Todd's ability to write. This student, who previously had been just barely trying in school, produced the best critical essay of the spring semester, a critique of the poetry of William Carlos Williams. It is important to note that Todd did not use the hypertext before he wrote his *Literary Journals*, for at that time Todd was not interested in the project. It was only after he had produced wonderful entries and had begun to see the possibilities of publishing in this environment that he began working with our hypertext. Hypertext gives beginning writers like Todd the nonthreatening forum of expression they need to build skills toward more complex, abstract compositions. In this way, the student who wrote that "hypertext helps the students see their works as potentially publishable, not solely written for the critique of the instructor" was right.

Moreover, Todd was a good example of the student who engaged in serious revision and produced final essays that were generally more organized and clear on the more abstract academic subjects of the spring semester. Todd wrote very few drafts in the beginning of the year, but as the year progressed, he produced more revisions and engaged in a wider range of rhetorical strategies. Todd's final expository essay on William Carlos Williams' poem, "Danse Russe," went through eight major drafts. His thesis statement changed almost as many times, and his analysis went from a simple summary to an elegant explication of the final imagery:

> This moment of freedom in "Danse Russe" is given in "spare" details. He tells a lot about his escapade using very few words. In ninety two, quick, yet descriptive words Williams conveys several things. First, he tells us that others in the household are asleep, and it is early morning. He gives the sense that he has not yet gone to bed. Then, he gives the location of his room and describes what he is doing—dancing nakedly. The mirror is the central object in the room, with perhaps little furniture and a little light coming in from behind the shades. Possibly, shadows of trees filter into his room. Next, he sings softly and admires every part of his body when he states, "If I admire my arms, face/my shoulders, flanks, and buttocks/against the yellow-drawn shades—." And lastly, he poses a question, "Who shall say I am not/the happy genius of my household?" He is inviting the reader of the poem to answer his question.
>   . . . Perhaps in this poem, Williams is describing something that frequents the minds of many people after seeing movies or reading stories or poetry. It is as though a person wants to take on the role of someone else and take on the part of another person. . . . In this case, Williams fantasizes that he is a famous ballet dancer and stumbles into thoughts about his own life. Perhaps a little like Whitman in his "Song of Myself," Williams in the poem "Danse Russe" seems to be rejoicing over his freedom to dance naked and to proclaim that he is "lonely." Through his cryptic and spare verse in his poem, he teases the reader. No one can say that he is not "the happy genius of his household."

I reflected on Todd's progress in my notes:

> 2/12/96
> I am tempted to say that Todd's writings on Whitman helped him complete this analysis on Williams, yet that would only be conjecture for Todd never said that. In fact very little is known about Todd's writing process during this time, for he kept it to himself. I learned some wonderful information from a chance conversation with his mother and I gathered much valuable material from my fieldnotes, but the documents themselves are remarkably mute. I know Todd went through at least eight drafts of his final essay because I worked on most of them with him. Unfortunately, Todd did not keep a complete writing portfolio of all his drafts, thus we are left with only the final draft as evidence of his efforts on this work. I have had to reconstruct Todd's writing processes through my fieldnotes on our conferences and other interviews.

This is essentially what was problematic about Todd's essay. Although it was brilliant, there was no way of showing other students how he got there. Yet, this has been the traditional method of writing instruction, showing students models of excellent writing. Also, this has been the traditional method of evaluating writing, by looking at finished pieces.

Ultimately, my experience with Todd left me bewildered. Of course, Todd had written a wonderful essay, an essay I would proudly show to my students the following year. However, somehow I felt we had missed an opportunity to show the process by which this wonderful essay had come to life. Even though we had lived through eight different drafts of the essay, we had missed the opportunity to capture the process. Showing exemplary models is a common teaching strategy, and not essentially a bad thing; but, what does this say about teaching? After Todd, I came to the conclusion that teaching is not believing too much in the finished product but in celebrating the potential paper.

Student 2: David—A Skillful Writer And Desktop Publisher

David is one of the most dedicated students I have ever taught. He embraces the ideals discussed in our mission statement; he is a self-educating, compassionate individual, who is always ready to collaborate with another student. Here is a typical day from David's file.

> David is busy, first editing on paper some remarks he has made concerning a letter he wrote as Faulkner to a publisher. Here is a portion of that letter:
>
>> "He writes not of love but lust, of defeats in which nobody loses anything of value, of victories without hope, and worst of all without pity or compassion. His griefs grieve on no universal bones, leaving no scars. He writes not of the heart but of the glands."
>>
>> The writer must learn again how to manipulate the most immortal aspect of man, his soul, and withdraw all the emotions that keep it alive, so man can rise and be fulfilled by his soul.
>
> When he is finished, David finds a note that I have left concerning Faulkner's stylistic creativity and letters. He reads my comments, creates a new card, and extends the discussion by giving examples of the revisions he's made from his own paper. In this way, our discussion has been left for other students to possibly follow.

David was a successful writer and collaborator before he began writing in hypertext, but the hypertext gives a better perspective of the kinds of activities that makes David successful. David completed several excellent essays, beyond the requirements of the class. He contributed these essays and his fieldnotes to the hypertext, creating a direct path along his writing process. A future student can follow along with David's thoughts as he created a superior analysis of Holden Caulfield's character. However, more important than his finished composition, David contributed the composition choices he had to make. A student could hit the bold letters below and instantly trace the steps David went through as he constructed his essay. These additions to David's text also marked a subtle shift in composition pedagogy, away from an emphasis of the brilliant mind as an example apart from the community—which is how most of my students view models of excellent student papers—towards an examination of the mind in society.

In his self-examination of his composing process, David writes:

> I am proud to present to you, a revised copy of my *The Catcher in the Rye* essay, regarding Jane Gallagher's function in the story. I have also included all of my **drafts** which aided me while writing this **final revised copy** of the essay. I will explain to you the revisions I have made in the essay.
>
> I added a paragraph before **the first quote**, which deals with Allie's death and the effect it has on Holden. I proceeded to explain how Jane enters Holden's life and the immediate effect she plays on his life. After the first quote, I explained the point of the quote more thoroughly, and made an effort to connect my ideas that I expressed in the paragraph preceding the quote. I also used a transition sentence from this paragraph into the next quote.
>
> Following **the second quote**, I correlated the new ideas with the preceding ideas. I also further explained the situation involved in the quote and removed the third quote from the paper because I felt it did not reinforce my analysis and explanation very well. You commented about the quote I removed. "Slightly out of context, what leads up to this?" In place of removing the paragraph, I relayed what happened in my own words in the seventh paragraph (including quotes as paragraphs). **I further analyzed Holden's situation with Jane** and hinted that Holden was beginning to realize Jane was becoming an adult and could protect herself. I reinforced this explanation with two quotes . . .
>
> . . . Thank you for the chance to revise the essay, because your comments made sense to me, and I wanted to see what you would have to say about my revised paper.

In my field notes I wrote:

> 2/11/96
> Of course, David could make comments on each of these points in other windows. Bold words lead to the quotes in the text, which also

contain bold words of importance, which when clicked open commentary windows. In this way, a text is layered with critical comments.

David has obviously learned many of the revision strategies of
professional writers. He is comfortable using the computer for composition, and he is an accomplished collaborator. Evident in David's
analysis is his dialogic process, as he struggled with one of my critical comments and added transitional phrases that would help pull
the potential reader of his essay along a distinct line of argument.
David thinks about audience. David was already a good writer
before he wrote in hypertext, and it may not have significantly contributed to the development of his writing proficiency; however,
hypertext has given us a clear picture of his composing processes.
Perhaps more importantly, in creating his HyperCard journals on
William Faulkner, in crafting the dialogic quizzes, and in participating in the videotaped epistemic dialogues, David has allowed other
students a clear image of an accomplished writer at work.

Interestingly, David is still most comfortable creating linear
texts, texts that have a clear premise and a highly structured hierarchical argument. Like most competent writers making a transition
into writing with the computer, David continued doing what he had
been doing with pen and then with PageMaker, only now he works
exclusively with the computer. Because David's literary tastes are so
inexhaustible, he seems like the perfect candidate for writing in
hypertext, but whether he will continue to do so is anybody's guess.
Interestingly, hypertext does not always appeal to the most intelli-
gent, or the most creative, or the most driven writers. Each medium—pen, paper, PageMaker, and hypertext—requires a subtle
change in the level of consciousness for the writer to feel at home.

Student 3: Jeff—Cyberwriter

Jeff was a student in the 1995-1996 American literature class. Jeff was
also a student who displayed a natural affinity for writing in hypertext.
Here is his personal evaluation of the experience of writing hypertext:

> For the short time I have used, and experimented with the
> HyperCard application I have started to feel the excitement and
> energy of creating with it. I could never understand Mr. Ryan's
> extreme enthusiasm in this project until I began to create one of my
> own stacks. I have found creating my *Literary Journal* a journey. I
> usually don't like to use the much over used word "Journey" in
> explaining an event that I am a part of, but in this case it is very
> appropriate. There are so many different possibilities or "paths"

working with this program that it makes it exciting, and pushes you to keep going. I have worked with different programming languages, but the language that HyperCard uses seems to be adaptable even for someone who has never programmed.

Doing my *Literary Journal* using HyperCard has made my project more attractive, fun to read, and very user friendly. The assignment called the *Literary Journal* is an English assignment meant to learn more about a certain author by doing research about the life and works of the author. This HyperCard stack started primarily as a *Literary Journal* about J.D. Salinger, the author of the famous novel, *The Catcher in the Rye*. Well I have taken it from there and plan on turning it into a tool in which people can use to help them with an English assignment. I believe no matter how computer illiterate a person is, looking up a topic on a computer-based interface will always seem more fun. Even if it is used for the same reason as an encyclopedia. . . . If you sort of like computers you will most definitely like using this for an assignment.

Jeff is well-suited to writing hypertext, not only because HyperCard has made his project "more attractive, fun to read," but also because he finds the landscape "very user friendly." Jeff is comfortable being a cyberwriter because he seems to intuitively grasp what Selfe (1989) called "the multilayered grammars of the computers," the basic formats of the computer landscape "which govern such things as arrangement, structure, form, and appearance of text" (p. 5). Particularly striking is Jeff's expression of his composing process as a journey, for in hypertext, the traditional genre of academic composition—the linear-hierarchical style, where the reader is led step by step through the argument and each piece of evidence is made clear and relevant—gives way to a much more informal logical structure, a logic of multilayered nodes of thought strung together like synapses by the reader's choice of forking paths. Jeff's hypertext is filled with choices, buttons, and bold text that could lead the reader in extra-textual directions. Instead of merely giving his readers a transitional phrase, Jeff offers a multilayered billboard that announces in an attractive manner the subtle contextual links that support the content of the individual journals Jeff has created in the persona of J. D. Salinger. Figure 8.4 is an example of one such node.

Here's what I noted:

1/15/96
Digressive Text: Jeff if just flying through these cards. He seems to read along, decide where to make a word bold, and goes on to link the word to a card. At another computer, Tony and Bob are reading journal entries. They read two or three pages, Bob gets bored and so they play some literary games. Tony wants to create a game, Bob

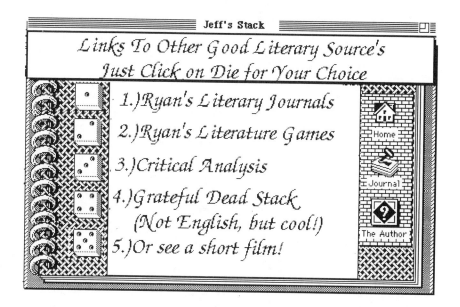

Figure 8.4. Jeff's billboard

says no. It seems common for students to go through the hypertext in this fragmented, digressive manner, only spending several moments on a single screen, always looking for a new idea to pursue. Often two or three students are reading together!

Could it be that Jeff just naturally thinks hypertextually? Is hypertext just the right logical structure into which Jeff's thoughts fit? Could it be that Jeff's previous experience with computers and programming has conditioned his mind towards hypertextual material? Does the space of the text produces a cognitive change in consciousness? . . . Then Jeff's natural affinity for digressive writing might be a sign of the future.

Ong (1982) said that "The difference that literacy makes, is evident in a culture's 'texts.' Oral cultures produce poems, stories, mythology, lore, and dramatic performances; they do not produce philosophic essays" (p. 209). The shape of a culture's consciousness can be seen in its texts. The American mind of the soundbite is not the same American mind that listened to the 6-hour Lincoln-Douglas debates, as documented in Postman's (1985) *Amusing Ourselves to Death: Public Discourse in the Age of Show Business.* Ironically, many elements that appeared as weaknesses in the evaluation of the traditional essays, the two critical analysis papers, appear in this context as strengths. Instead of a treatise, the reader is treated to a conversation, a rather informal rambling of related topics.

This nonlinear, multiple reading of a hypertext gives form to a new rhetorical order, an order described by Carter (1993) in his examination of the informal logic of hypertext composition. Speaking at a conference on computers and writing, Carter contended that hypertexts feature the natural flow of language usually expressed in public discourse, characterized by digression, repetition, ambiguity, and incompleteness. One might recall these were the qualities that the scoring team found so frustrating in its analysis of the traditional essays. However, Carter argued that these characteristics, rather than revealing a lack of logical order and arrangement, are indeed a misreading of the logical display often found in hypertextualized composition. Carter suggested that we need to throw out standard notions of linear arrangement in order to fairly evaluate the logic of these new compositions:

> If this question of display, or arrangement, is relevant to the field of informal logic, it is absolutely central to the field of hypertextual discourse. Sequence, as we have historically experienced and described it in traditional media, is radically different in hypertext. Rather than force our existing expectations upon hypertextual writing, we must look at the way arguments are actually constructed within hypertext in their own right. Since the audience determines reading order, I would not suggest that there is no longer such a thing as arrangement; on the contrary, it is perhaps the most dynamic element in hypertext. But it no longer belongs to the writer . . . the only true measure of an effective argument is whether it gains the adherence of the audience. (pp. 30-31)

As teachers born in what many theorists are calling the late age of print, we have been cultured to regard the linear argument as supreme; yet, we must, as Carter explained, look for and find the strength of an argument in hypertext, "not in the sequence of its elements, but rather in their structural relationships. By structure I mean the relationships between essential parts of the argument: the premises, claims, raw data, possible rebuttals, and so on" (p. 31). Structure in the hypertextual argument may be developed in several ways: The implied premise might be clearly identified, or the hypertext writer might offer the reader the possibility of exploring "what is normally unstated in the argument" (p. 31). Often you will find a grid of identified buttons that offer the reader links to various parts of the main argument; or perhaps sometimes a rather idiosyncratic grove of icons, buttons, and bold letters will entice the reader from the main path of the argument toward several branching points of evidence or allusions. This is what is meant when theorists suggest that in hypertext a writer creates a rhetorical space. And why not? As Bolter argued, "Why should a writer be forced to produce a single, linear argument or an exclusive analysis of cause and effect, when the writing space allows a writer to entertain and present several lines of thought at once?" (p. 114). It might well be that students who cannot produce linear arguments get practice in logical thinking by presenting their informal arguments in hypertext.

This presentation of multiple lines of argument might be seen in the way the student writers in this study created annotations to their existing text. For example, in his field notes, one student tried to explain the relationship between T. S. Eliot and Ezra Pound by putting in this explanation of the revisions of the second section of "The Wasteland:"

> November 21, 1995
> In this revisions Ezra told Eliot that he really didn't understand what the poem was trying to say. . . . The original poem was about a game of chess, and how the game of chess coincides with life. The poem was originally titled, "In The Cage," but when Pound read it he figured that the title "A Game of Chess" would be more fitting. The actual content of the poem was also changed. In the first draft the poem related chess to life, but in the second draft Pound's revisions made the poem more clear and the poem basically described a chess game and its many different types of moves.

This fragment of an explanation is a good beginning for a later essay, the kind of beginning that perhaps Todd made in his connection of the incidents of Walt Whitman's life with the imagery of his later poems. However, the author of this statement has no intention of finishing this thought, nor need he do so. Some of the best moments of expression in hypertext are those aphoristic moments of enlightenment that beg for the reader to finish the thought, to offer a suggestion and converse. This is why every screen has notebook buttons enabling passers-by to drop messages to later explorers. Of course, this rhetorical freedom is contagious, for the writer is inviting the reader to vigorously participate in the creation of the text. The reader is thus invited to expand and revise the hypertext. Jeff, like the best composers of hypertext, has created links that offer the readers the opportunity to create their own links and additions. Jeff said recently, "I want to keep at least an original copy of my HyperCard stack somewhere, but mixed up with a million things...all sorts of documents. Everything changing, like those children's' books where you pick the plot turns." But what kind of dialogue would this create?

CONCLUSION: ENTERING THE CONVERSATION

The mere presence of a hypertextual environment does not move students rapidly beyond their level of intelligence. On the contrary, most of the students could only enter the discussion, as they do in normal conversations, at their previous level of understanding of the material. All of the students loved playing and creating the electronic games, where the linguistic levels start at a low level and progress; yet very few of the students in this study group could sustain a discussion on Pound's revisions of Eliot's poetry. Those students that did write superior traditional essays only accomplished them after an intense period of conferencing with other students and teachers. In this way, creating a hypertext prompted the classroom context to change. We started reading groups around selected authors and themes. We are recording these discussions on film, and later we will analyze the discussion. We are just beginning to understand the differences between oral conversations and conversations in hypertext. Using a HyperCard writing and reading environment did expand the students' abilities to participate in the making of the text by altering existing episodes and links and adding new ones. Furthermore, the composing of *Literary Journals* has created an opportunity for literacy where none existed before because students were able to enter the literary discussion on their own informal level, and thus, achieve practice in logical argument.

Creating and participating in these epistemic conversations promoted serious discussions among the students and with me. They were not unlike the conversations between Socrates and his students. Socrates argues again and again that true knowledge develops only in the interactions of real individuals in real contexts. Conversations between students and teachers do just that, bringing narrative structure to disorganized facts and helping to synthesize the thoughts of all (the class) in a dialectic of conversation. Knowledge then is a product that develops one step at a time, as a matter of mutual agreement. Consequently, these students learned the course content through group use. Nowhere in their learning were these students left to themselves with only books.

Through helping my students create a hypertext, I have discovered a better method of conversation with my students. I hope that the narrative of my study helps others to do the same. Throughout, my goal has been to create hypertext tools that will help my students to experience the course work in an active manner that reflects inquiry, the alertness of natural thought, to stimulate them to thoughts of their own. We may not have recreated the Athenian grove, but we have created a writing and reading space that is fun, active, passionate, and epistemic. We babble; we paint; we read; we write; we think. Through the experience of trying to build in conversation into our hypertext tools for learning, I have discovered more about myself as a teacher. Now instead of teaching 140 students the same subject, I help to teach 140 individual students to teach each other.

Chapter 9

Inquiry Into Hypertextualizing Teaching Assistants: Or, How Do I Evaluate Hypertexts for Composition Teaching Assistants?

Deborah Balzhiser Morton
University of Minnesota

Hypertext advocates in composition and English promote hypertexts as classroom tools while seeming to either ignore or neglect the fact that teaching assistants (TAs), with minimal teaching and/or graduate experiences, often teach such classes. TAs worry about pedagogy and, perhaps, whether they really belong in graduate school; they worry about putting together a coherent syllabus and not looking like fools in front of their students when the computer classroom does not "work" as planned. Rather than hypertextualizing these courses and adding more to the list of TA worries, I suggest that we begin by hypertextualizing TAs. Before we encourage or expect TAs to introduce hypertexts into their classrooms or have TAs use hypertexts for some pedagogical purpose unknown or vague to them, we should help TAs conceptualize and understand their own uses of hypertexts.

This chapter is about creating hypertexts—not the use of HTML or style guides but about processes for discovering and methods for creating usable and effective hypertexts for given contexts. My specific issues concern TAs as an audience. My general issues concern the art and science of designing effective hypertexts and the information you can learn through the process. In this chapter, I advocate iterative, participatory development of hypertexts or a form of what some call either *prototyping* or *user-centered design* (UCD). I also discuss that my research fails to prove the hypothesis that hypertext effectively supplements the course-specific TA orientation. Finally, I suggest directions for further research.

UCD and its resulting analyses can help administrators shape courses and hypertexts for them and their TAs. Schriver (1992) explained that information from early studies of cognition and composing empowered "teachers with detailed accounts of writers at work that both support and challenge their intuitions about composing processes" (p. 192). In the same way, detailed accounts of TAs creating their courses and using hypertexts could inform administrators through a depth of information—that both supports and challenges administrative intuitions—about course outcomes, about how TAs create their courses, and about how they may or may not use hypertext to do so.

Hypertext seems to be an appropriate medium for TA orientations. Atkinson (1993) reported that "technology-based media are especially useful for employee communications, training, and sales materials" (p. 260). Similarly, Horton (1990) reported that hypertexts are good for teaching concepts, for problem solving, for loose collections of interrelated documents, and for modeling and teaching organization. TAs are in a sense being trained and are participating in employee communications; they are learning concepts, solving problems, needing strategies for organizing new information and materials, and receiving new materials.

While at a midsize, midwestern state university, referred to here as Midwest University, I designed a hypertext to help orient TAs to their course. The hypertext prototype, *Orientations, Hypertext, and Multiplicity*, is a database of information about, Language and Composition II, a course most TAs will teach and that supplements the week-long, TA orientation. As envisioned, *Orientations, Hypertext, and Multiplicity* would eventually include materials for other courses taught by TAs, noncourse-specific materials (i.e., core readings, policies, procedures, frequently asked questions), course-specific materials for faculty other than TAs, and noncourse-specific materials of interest to all departmental faculty.

The hypertext was designed to be accessed with a World Wide Web (WWW) browser, connect to the department's home page, and for its documents to be downloaded along with other Internet resources. *Orientations, Hypertext, and Multiplicity* contains four sections: Departmental Policies and Governing Statements, Sample Syllabi, Some

Paper Assignments, and Some Exercises and Assignments. Its approximately 175 documents—more than 350 screens of text—were generated by administrators, instructors, and students.

In designing a hypertext for composition, I had to consider that a large percentage of those teaching such courses are TAs whose priorities do not include hypertextualizing composition. I wondered if TAs introduced to a hypertext to aid in course preparation say they would use that hypertext and if so under what conditions. For those who claim that they would use the hypertext, I wondered what types of information and organizational patterns would be best, if and how it would change attitudes toward hypertext, if it would be helpful in conceptualizing courses or TAs' own uses of hypertexts, or if TAs would put those uses into affect if provided with the means to do so.

CONTEXTS

Orientations, Hypertext, and Multiplicity emerged from foundational hypertext literature, administrative needs, and conversations with colleagues. Bolter (1991) pointed out that "electronic writing in general is still in its infancy" (p. 5). Consequently, much of its literature in composition and English studies is necessarily theoretical in terms of where it might go or descriptive in terms of specific applications. For example, *Evolving Perspectives on Computers and Composition Studies* (Hawisher & Selfe, 1991a) provides us with information about hypertext in terms of its history (e.g., Shirk, 1991), its definition (e.g., McDaid, 1991; Shirk, 1991), its redefinition (e.g., McDaid, 1991; C. Smith, 1991), and its promise (e.g., McDaid, 1991; Moulthrop, 1991; Shirk, 1991; C. Smith, 1991). As seen in *Hypermedia and Literary Studies* (Delany & Landow, 1991) other literature explores theory (e.g., Dickey, 1991; Harpold, 1991; Slatin, 1991) or provides local applications (e.g., DeRose, 1991; Friedlander, 1991; Graham, 1991). These works, along with Bolter's (1991) *Writing Space* and Lanham's (1992) *The Electronic Word* create a base of materials particular to the benefits of hypertext and the written word.

At least two critics would have us believe that our existing hypertext research blinds us with hope and leaves us in want of details on which to base decisions. Dobrin (1994) may have us believe that much of what is written about hypertext is "hype," referring particularly to Moulthrop and Kaplan (1994), Charney (1994), and C. Smith (1994) in *Literacy and Computers* (Selfe & Hilligoss, 1994). Dobrin viewed such studies as attempts to fit applications into particular ideologies: "We hear of one application in the classroom, but it is of hypertext experimentally pressed into the service of an ideology, not of a general class-room application" (p. 307). Dobrin found this approach problematic because it assumes hypertexts should be used before critical analyses of them have been done: "We do not hear anything of hypertextual tools that might be useful in the teaching of literacy. The authors simply assume that we will have to bring hypertext into the curriculum because they can see that hypertext is important" (p. 307). Much existing hyper-text literature matches ideologies to hypertext as an ideal rather than discusses what happens when the match is made, at least until recently. In a similar vein, Johnson (1995) posited hypertext as a romantic phe-nomenon: "The emergence of hypertext has been driven by a romantic view that enamors developers of hypertext and thus blinds them to the practical and social aspects of this new electronic phenomenon" (p. 13).

I agree with Dobrin and Johnson; we do need to analyze and question hypertext applications if we are to effectively hypertextualize composition or even if we are to determine that we should or could hypertextualize it. We do need to see "technologies instead of being used by them," as Kalmbach (1988, p. 174) said. We need, as Dobrin sug-gested, details. Works such as those criticized by Dobrin and Johnson should be recognized as an impetus for the more analytic studies they seek. It is predictable that literature about a new medium describes that medium and theorizes about its effectiveness. Lauer and Asher (1988) pointed out, however, that such research is more than just an impetus: "Historical research traces and reinterprets the sources of beliefs, prac-tices, and problems. Rhetorical theory guides empirical research, which in turn helps verify theory, a reciprocity that other fields lack" (p. 7). Careful analyses along with more critical research can give us such a rec-iprocity in hypertext research.

IMPETUS

Orientations, Hypertext, and Multiplicity emerged from the hypertext foundational literature, particularly works connecting hypertexts with cognition. Based on such literature, including works like those Dobrin and Johnson critique, I believed that hypertext could help readers bal-ance individuals with communities, diversity within boundaries, as well as fixity with multiplicity.

From a cognitive grammar perspective, Langacker (1987) explained:

> we construct our conception of the "real world" bit by bit, stage by stage, from myriad and multifarious sensory and motor experience.

It consists of the organization we impose, through the progressive and interactive application of interpretive procedures on both primary experience and higher-order cognitive structures that derive from previous processing. (p. 114)

Langacker explained that meaning and reality are multiple because people bring their individual experiences to any situation and take their own meaning and reality away from combinations of experiences. This is of particular interest to those preparing instructors for their classrooms because each instructor brings multifarious experiences and memories about what a composition classroom should be, which may not match administrators' ideas about the shape of courses in their program.

It is not my intention to reiterate foundational hypertext literature or composition pedagogies, here. Instead, I explain how the nonlinear and associative nature of hypertexts coupled with administrative needs led to *Orientations, Hypertext, and Multiplicity.*

INDIVIDUAL WITHIN COMMUNITY—SELF

Each TA seeks various course materials for specific reasons. Unfortunately, time constraints of an orientation limit the number of examples that can be discussed and, consequently, those that are discussed could read as prescriptions to the course. TAs in transition try to balance the self with others in the discourse community, beginning with the expectations of their program. Bizzell (1982) explained that "Academics are, perhaps, too ready to assume that such operations as 'describe' or 'analyze' are self-evident, when in fact they have meanings specific to the academic discourse community and specific to disciplines within that community" (p. 230; see also Morton, 1994). Bizzell referred to undergraduate writers, but I extend her point and refer to TAs. Often, TAs are expected to know the discourse community and its operations when they do not—at least not as fully as might be assumed.

In the United States, teaching is often as invaluable an experience to postbaccalaureate education as research is for the degree because it facilitates the practice of both rhetorical and philosophical aspects of, in this case, writing and pedagogical theories. Through this practice, TAs push boundaries, question theories and practices, then postulate new ones. To begin their education and situate themselves within discourse communities, TAs need to be oriented to the expectations and theories held by their program. Although most TAs arrive with about the same level of formal education, they come from diverse backgrounds and with diverse ideas about writing and the world of academics. For example, each understands grading criteria and classroom expectations differently. Theoretically, a database of course-specific documents demonstrates that there are a variety of approaches to the course and that TAs can and should create their own.

DIVERSITY WITHIN BOUNDARIES—CONTENT

Orientations, Hypertext, and Multiplicity grew from the belief that a database of various course-specific materials from a variety of approaches balances diversity within boundaries. The objectives and goals of the course remain constant and form boundaries. Diversity rises from the number of perspectives (i.e., different syllabi, assignments, and emphases) applied from the course objectives and goals. Landow (1992b) claimed that hypertext "links one block of text to myriad others," thereby destroying the "physical isolation of the text, just as it also destroy the attitudes created by that isolation" (p. 63). TAs can see from the diverse materials that they should synthesize the materials and adapt them to their own needs and approaches. *Orientations, Hypertext, and Multiplicity* houses a number of documents from a variety of perspectives, destroying the narrow narrative and offering diverse perspectives.

FIXITY WITHIN MULTIPLICITY—STRUCTURE

In Barthes' (1974) notion of ideal textuality, no single document takes precedence over others, at least not implicitly as determined by the creator. *Orientations, Hypertext, and Multiplicity* was envisioned in the same manner: One sample syllabus, for instance, would not become more important than any other, especially because they are all accessed from the same place and users choose which one(s) to read. Bolter (1991) helped characterize such notions when he described electronic museums: "At its best and at its worst, the electronic museum is a space through which the visitor moves at will, sampling the exhibits, lingering over the ones that interest him or her and ignoring those that do not" (p. 231). There are multiple navigational possibilities: "there is no compulsion, no required order, and no requirement that any or all the exhibits must be visited. . . . It is organized as a network, rather than a hierarchy." He suggested that networks are favored in contemporary American culture, as evidenced not only in the way we construct books, libraries, and museums but also in our social and political lives (p. 231).

TAs need to learn balance between the fixity and multiplicity, the constraints and the freedoms in their courses. Landow (1992b) suggested, "Hypertextual materials, which by definition are open-ended, expandable, and incomplete, call such notions [linearity and fixity] into question" (p. 59).

Hypertext seems like an appropriate medium, in part, because its advocates claim that it can facilitate the way people read. We know that readers "skim; they skip; they read just enough to reach a personal level of satisfaction with their knowledge or until they read a personal level of frustration with the document or product" (Redish, 1993, p. 17). Hypertext handles multiplicity in that readers can access only what they need or what is of interest to them.

Hartman, Diem, and Quagliana (1992) explained that to learn effectively, people must engage in learning activities that factor in prior knowledge, context in which material is presented and organized, the availability of appropriate schemata, and a framework with which to integrate the information. On the basis of Redish's (1993) insight about readers, Hartman et al.'s (1992) explanation of cognition, and Langacker's notion of cognitive grammar, I determined that hypertext could effectively support TA orientations. After TAs complete an orientation session that emphasizes a core of what each TA should know, a hypertext could be available for them to access what is of particular interest to them.

ADMINISTRATION

Aside from theoretical assumptions, underlying administrative concerns for *Orientations, Hypertext, and Multiplicity* include helping TAs in transition from a common syllabus to a lack of a common syllabus, from close guidance to minimal guidance, from the course content and emphasis in one class to that of another, and from one set of students to another. Additional concerns include time, money, and the availability of materials. I present them here because they influence a hypertext and its implementation: "the rhetorical situation governing the development of an in-house manual is far more complex than traditional research allows. In-house writers must understand that rhetorical situations include far more than just users and their needs with new systems" (Mirel, 1988, p. 287). In user-centered approaches, context is not comfortable dutifully receding into the background. Administrative concerns define much of the context of a course and its offering. What follows are some issues defining the rhetorical situation of *Orientations, Hypertext, and Multiplicity*.

The Course

Orientations, Hypertext, and Multiplicity was created for TAs of Language and Composition II, with Language and Composition I as its prerequisite. All undergraduates at Midwest University must successfully complete Language and Composition I before registering for course work beyond 30 hours. Many programs at the university also require successful completion of Language and Composition II prior to being accepted or prior to graduation.

According to the writing committee, the courses both "emphasize reading/writing connections," "seek to help students develop search, research, invention, and revision strategies," "emphasize shaping writing for specific forums," and "use a mode of instruction that is interactive, process-oriented, student- and task-centered, and computer-assisted." Both courses are also informed by "research in rhetoric, writing and cognition, by theories of language as a social construct, and by current research in composition pedagogy." Because TAs usually teach Language and Composition I at least once before teaching Language and Composition II, they have at least minimal experience with the approaches.

The most significant difference between the courses is that the first emphasizes public discourse, whereas the second emphasizes academic discourse. The writing committee notes three other differences about Language and Composition II: Students write longer papers, papers require the use and documentation of source materials, and the course requires a five- to seven-page research paper. Additionally, the first course is portfolio-based, whereas the second may not be. Helping TAs internalize these approaches and differences for their own course development challenges administrators.

The Orientation

Language and Composition II was traditionally taught by full-time faculty, but for many reasons it is now taught largely by TAs. Intensive orientation sessions for TAs of Language and Composition II are limited because resources are limited. These limitations are compounded for Language and Composition II TAs because they are moving from highly to minimally structured means of gathering and creating course materials and concepts.

Most TAs assigned to Language and Composition II have some, albeit limited, experience in both graduate school and with teaching. While teaching Language and Composition I, TAs become used to being closely guided. They complete one graduate-level course in research methods and one theoretical course, Introduction to the Composing Process. They are also closely guided as they complete a week-long orientation session and register for a one-credit course that meets weekly to discuss teaching in the program. During the orientation session, TAs are provided with a suggested syllabus, related assignments, and sample student work. In the one-credit course, TAs turn in weekly journals about their classroom experiences, are assessed on at least one set of marked papers, and receive classroom evaluations at least twice a semester. Because of their reliance on previous structure, TAs tend to be nervous when conceptualizing the next course on their own.

The Access

A hypertextual database makes a collection of materials readily available to TAs at any time they have access to the Internet and the WWW: during class, office hours, or other more convenient times. Departmental information can be obtained from the department office; however, it is available only during departmental hours with costs for all materials—used or unused—carried by the department. Also, although departmental information may be obtained from the office, materials such as sample syllabi, assignments, and essays cannot. TAs would have to contact past instructors for examples, which is impractical and time-consuming. It would also be expensive for the department to copy and distribute several syllabi with their supplemental materials. The hypertext provides a collection of materials and saves time that would be better spent on conceptualizing the course than on gathering materials. The director of writing reported that because of the lack of resources and conceptual preparation, TAs relied on friends' syllabi or put together assignments in an ad hoc fashion without thoroughly conceptualizing the whole course or appropriate pedagogies for their choices.

Increased availability of information is particularly useful because TAs cannot always articulate questions about a course until they are directly involved with it. TAs often complete the orientation before thinking of questions. With the availability of an Internet database, TAs could return to it after the orientation session in order to research, for example, past paper topics or approaches to the course. TAs who think of questions on Saturday do not have to wait until Monday morning, which may be too late, to access course-specific materials to finish preparing an assignment. In another scenario, TAs might access the collection prior to the orientation in order to define and prepare their course and to arrive with possibilities for implementing the course objectives. As a result, questions can be articulated prior to the orientation, or at least more easily formulated during the orientation.

Development Through Iterative, Participatory Methods

Composition faculty who incorporate computer technology in their curricula should commit to studying its usability. Johnson (1995) claimed that "if hypertexts are to have widespread impact, then they must be designed to fit the active, functional contexts of users," which entails "long-term commitments to studying the usability" (p. 18). Hillman, Willis, and Gunawardena (1994) revealed that "regardless of the proficiency level of the learner, inability to interact successfully with the technology will inhibit his or her active involvement in the educational transaction" (p. 34).

I recommend an iterative, participatory method as the approach to which we commit. In *A Practical Guide to Usability Testing*, Dumas and Redish (1993) explained iterative approaches. Some refer to this approach as *prototyping* because it involves creating a prototype, testing it (and recreating and testing, again, as many times as necessary), and then creating the actual materials. Others might call this *formative evaluation*, which "is a form of diagnostic testing in which testers look at the product and its accompanying information, see how well people are performing tasks, find weak spots, improve the product and information, and then repeat steps" (Duin, 1993, p. 310). Usability testing often stirs notions of testing a product after it has been developed. Participatory methods, however, involve users from the onset.

Composition faculty who use a process approach are already familiar with the idea behind iterative approaches. They assign drafts, provide instructor feedback and opportunities for peer feedback, and require revisions. In terms of course or curriculum development, some assume that considering objectives, developing materials, using them in class(es), and then revising them for the next term would be considered iterative, participatory design. There are two main differences. First, an iterative, participatory approach that is user-centered would take outlines and course materials to students, potential students, administrators, advisors, and the like before the course was developed and during development. The course would develop, then, from the interactions with others rather than being revised only after such interactions. Second, when using the method in terms of hypertext, faculty must also learn the grammar of the medium (e.g., hypertext) and, perhaps, of the method (e.g., UCD).

RESULTS ANU DISCUSSION

In the remainder of this chapter, I describe the creation of *Orientations, Hypertext, and Multiplicity* and provide examples of the types of information composition faculty might expect from various steps. Creating *Orientations, Hypertext, and Multiplicity*, included the following steps:

1. Asking users to define the problem (user analysis).
2. Planning a solution by creating a prototype.
3. Developing a method for testing the prototype.
4. Implementing the solution by testing the prototype on my own and with experts.
5. Evaluating the prototype through tests with users.
6. Revising the prototype.
7. Testing the prototype once more. (See Appendix A for the detailed steps.)

As with any case study, the data from my testing is not generalizable; *Orientations, Hypertext, and Multiplicity* is tailored for TAs at Midwest University. I also provide brief explanations of goals for various stages in the iterative, participatory design and testing of hypertexts.

Administrators and faculty might find parallels and similarities in the audience and need. As such, my data may become part of a brainstorming session or framework for their context. Administrators and faculty might also gain insights into the types of queries they might conduct at their locations.

USER ANALYSIS

The purpose of user analyses is to find practically significant information. User analyses are a form of descriptive research, which Hayes et al. (1992) said help formulate hypotheses. Here, data from user analyses will be used to hypothesize about what constitutes an effective hypertext for a given context. Similarly, user analyses provide the same type of information as case studies: "they are detailed and try to capture something of the complexity of events, they provide opportunities for discovering unexpected relations" (Hayes et al., 1992, p. 91).

Like audience analyses (Lauer, Montague, Lundsford, & Emig, 1985) and forum analyses (Porter, 1986), user analyses provide information for document development, in this case a hypertextual document. Through audience analysis we learn about audiences and their backgrounds and through forum analysis we learn *"from,* not just *about,* the audience" (Porter, 1992, p. 138).

When conducting user analyses, look for patterns. Be sure to consider the range of answers, especially if the sample size is small. Open-ended questions, in-depth interviews, and focus groups work well for learning from and about users. Depth interviews are "highly focused." According to Berger (1991), they "get at matters such as hidden feelings or attitudes and beliefs that respondents may not be aware of or that are only dimly in their consciousness" (p. 57). Focus groups are a "kind of collective depth interview, and it is hoped that the discussion will lead to important insights" (p. 91). Communication processes and the tendency for people to discuss ideas in groups give focus groups external validity, or truth outside of the immediate questions or context. Albrecht, Johnson, and Walther (1993) explained:

> One of the advantages of the opinions generated through focus group interaction (over the opinions elicited from individual respondents) has to do with the isomorphism of group opinions to those of individuals in the population at large. This observation does not pertain to the qualitative nature of the comments made by focus group members, but refers to the process of opinion formation and propagation in normal life. (pp. 53-54)

In-depth interviews and focus groups compliment each other. Individual interviews might first be conducted so that focus group participants have already thought about the topic. This approach might be selected for identifying questions to explore more fully through dialogue. On the other hand, conducting the focus group interview first might identify information that begs for more specific, individual answers that might be gained through follow-up in-depth interviews.

When conducting user analyses, be sure that you know what you are looking for, but don't be so rigid in that purpose and in making observations that you close yourself off from unanticipated insights. In my user analyses, I aimed to discover what materials TAs would expect to find in a hypertextual database for orienting them in their course and their attitudes toward the course. I also sought categories for these materials so that they could become the organizing principle for navigating the hypertext.

My User Analysis

Based on what I learned from interviews about TAs, I suspected that TA attitudes toward the course or hypertext could influence its effectiveness. Most TAs admitted they were at least a little nervous about teaching Language and Composition II. When pressed about their nervousness, many explained they did not know how to conceptualize their course. One TA gave a representative response:

> I felt somewhat constrained by our common syllabus [for Language and Composition I], but now I know why I had it. It had a syllabus, assignments, exercises, and grading scales. It had examples. I didn't have to put it together. I know now I couldn't have, at least not effectively. Now, I have a course description and a syllabus from [another TA]. I'm not sure what I'm supposed to assign or what I am supposed to do with them [the students].

Similarly, three interviewees from the focus group claimed they came to have an intimate understanding of Language and Composition I but were unsure about how to construct Language and Composition II. When pressed further, one TA said "I know that the course is about academic discourse and that [students] should write four or five papers. But what are they supposed to write? That's what I am unclear about, I guess." The remaining focus group members shook their heads in agreement.

During the second set of interviews, I pressed for more specificity about topics mentioned earlier. So, for example, when TAs said they wanted more information about assignments, I asked, "What kinds of information do you want? What can the department provide for you? Would you prefer the closely guided approach as you have now?" Only one TA wanted to have a prescribed course. He said, "This is how I finance my schooling. I do not plan on teaching—yes, I want the department to figure it out for me so that I can go in and do it. This doesn't mean that I don't take it seriously: I'm just not in it like some of the other people around here. I need to spend more time on my classes." Although he is only one person, he is one person in a small group. In a large group, more TAs could be "in it" for the educational funding. What I learned is that the orientation, online or otherwise, needs to address different needs and priorities of TAs, including being in it for the tuition and token living dollars.

Overall, TAs expected to at least know the objectives of Language and Composition II assignments and to understand how they relate to the course as a whole. Four TAs wanted detailed materials without feeling constrained by them. In other words, they wanted to "use the goals and objectives of the assignments as heuristics for designing [their] own." Another TA states: "I understand we are learning how to be effective teachers, which involves planning our own courses. I think that the absence of materials is not the most effective answer, though." She continues:

> There are materials for [Language and Composition II] but there could be more in depth materials so that we can understand if we are approaching the course as the department would have us. Since we are not yet experts, the materials could have more depth. For example, it would be helpful to see assignments that have been used, along with student papers that have been generated by those assignments. I am sometimes surprised by what students write in response to the assignments. I would like to see what a typical paper might look like for any given assignment. Also, what type of assignments might help lead to that paper assignment? What do I do with them in class so that they are not wasting their time in being there?

It is important to let your purpose guide your interviews but to also be flexible so that you can learn not just verify. For instance, about one third of the TAs responded not about the course and its content but about the classroom. "I just got used to teaching on the IBMs and now I have to learn the Mac," replies one TA. Another responds, "What do I think about the course? We have a course outline and will have an orientation session. I am concerned more with the computers, like what should I do when someone gets lost?" He chides, "What if a student gets lost and it takes me too long to figure out what they are doing? Then they really think that I know what I am talking about." Overall, TAs in the focus group came to the consensus that they were not so much concerned with using the computers but that they were nervous about the networked classroom. Many were confident in their ability to use the computer but not with navigating through the server or in doing so in a confident, graceful manner in front of students.

When asked about their attitudes toward hypertext, most responded with, "What is hypertext, exactly?" After I explained hypertextuality, I received two types of responses: intrigue ("That sounds as though it would be helpful") or hesitancy ("I need to see one"). In follow-up questions about what is intriguing or good about such a hypertext, I again received two types of responses. TAs either repeated what I had said or they said little more than, "it seems pretty good."

Discussion of User Analyses

An emergent pattern was that insecurity seems to drive much TA concern—insecurity about knowledge of course content, their reception by faculty and students, and the computer classroom. It seems that if nothing else, a collection of course-specific materials could increase confidence. The analysis from TAs supported the analysis about TAs. TAs seem to want course-specific documents to refer to when planning their course. They want documents that demonstrate "proven" approaches as well as specifics about their context. Remember, however, to consider the range of responses. The TA who wanted the department to provide a ready-made course was an outlier, the only one who responded in that way. If there were more subjects, however, more TAs might share his view. In this case, the outlier seeks the same end as the others—detailed information. In this case, the outlier and the others seem to agree that demonstrates that a database of information could be helpful.

Careful consideration reveals that course-specific materials in a hypertext cannot directly help TAs overcome insecurities about their networked computer classroom. Moreover, their shallow responses and ambivalent opinions about hypertext suggested they needed to see a prototype before responding more thoughtfully. At this stage, comments about the course were more telling than those about hypertext and I coded these to create the prototype. I believed that exposure to hypertext would help TAs become familiar with the network and feel more confident.

Coding

Coding data helps reveal patterns or relationships. Some examples of what coded data can reveal are identified by Grice and Ridgeway (1993): information about pertinence, appearance, readability, clarity of writing, task orientation and supportiveness, and entry points (the ability to quickly access information).

For applicable results, we must establish reliability, or repeatability of results. Reliability generally comes through interrater agreement of coded data, where independent researchers and main researchers' coding are compared for accuracy. In UCD, information from user analyses is designed into a product and then tested with the users and other investors in their context. In user-centered design, accuracy is "best verified by review of the information and by testing its use in context. Accuracy is difficult to achieve, but is largely a matter of taking great care" (Grice & Ridgeway, 1993, p. 433). In iterative, participatory development, researchers reach reliability by developing the results into a product and then giving that product back to the users to verify. The prototype is tested and revised and re-tested and revised until the end users and other involved parties agree that there is reliability.

Completeness will be identified when end users and administrators come to consensus—or near consensus based on needs and resources—about the prototype. Grice and Ridgeway (1993) said that "With hands-on tests of information supplied to typical users, you can see large gaps and omissions, but you can never guarantee that everybody will always have enough information" (p. 433). Because the completeness factor can ultimately never be satisfied, we consider a document complete when "no more problems can be identified, or until the kinds of problems detected are considered trivial" (Rubens & Rubens, 1988, p. 214).

PROTOTYPE 1

The data from my user analysis, experiences, and secondary research provided four categories for *Orientations, Hypertexts, and Multiplicity*. Departmental Policies and Governing Statements, Sample Syllabi, Some Paper Assignments, and Some Exercises and Assignments. Shirk (1992) explained that other organizational patterns for hypermedia could be imposed by the designer, brought about by the learner, or made possible by the medium itself.

The first prototype was a fairly open system. In completely open-ended hypertexts, each document links to every other document in the system. *Orientations, Hypertext, and Multiplicity* was not completely open in that all documents did not link to all other documents. Instead, the documents within a module were linked, but the modules themselves were separate.

Testing Prototype 1

I tested *Orientations, Hypertext, and Multiplicity* through verification and retrospective measures, particularly post hoc, individual interviews. Concurrent measures, in the form of protocol analysis, could be used in place of retrospective measures, but I used my time during tests to note screens and actions rather than to note users' thoughts. I used post hoc interviews to gain insights into users' thoughts.

Other useful methods for prototyping include post hoc focus groups, because they can provide dynamic dialogues about the prototype. Time constraints prevented me from being able to arrange post hoc focus groups, however. Another recommendation for prototyping is comparative testing, which Duin (1993) explained compares "two ways of presenting the same information" (p. 315). Comparative testing could be used to compare TAs using documents from the office versus those in the hypertext, to compare using documents in the office with talking to previous TAs, or, finally, to compare two online means for organizing information.

If resources allow, videotaping the screen and keyboard as well as the facial expressions of users could compensate for the memory loss in retrospective measures. This, however, requires two videorecorders for each subject as well as time to review the tapes. Hayes et al. (1992) pointed out that "retrospective reports also give generally accurate information about the participant's processes although they may be more subject to forgetting than concurrent processes" (p. 248). Retrospective measures may take a bit more time in that more revisions might be required to compensate for memory losses, but this may still be less time than would be spent examining video or audio. On the other hand, by using protocol analysis and videos, I could have paid attention to the talk-aloud aspects and later reviewed the nonverbal cues. Again, because of time constraints, I could not. Bauersfeld and Halgren (1996) pointed out that "many of the traditional field study techniques do not lend themselves to these time constraints" (p. 177). When prototyping and testing, careful attention must be paid to the trade-offs of your choices. I did not have time to review videos, so I chose not to use them.

My Tests From Prototype 1

Four trends comprised nearly 60% of the responses to my first proto-type: (a) the system was too open-ended, (b) syllabi constituents should have been grouped together, (c) links needed annotations, and (d) connections between related material needed to be more clear. Most of the remaining feedback (33%) was local rather than global (i.e., missing or nonfunctional links, or inconsistencies in terms or explanations).

When I asked about content, only 6% responded to the content; I usually received feedback related to structure. When I asked if the hypertext should contain any other types of categories or information, two TAs asked for samples in the Sample Assignment section to connect to their syllabus of origin. Typical responses include: "It is really good to have all of these syllabi" or "I like having people's assignments because it gives me different ideas."

Because I received little feedback about the content and categories, I asked directly, "Are the categories what you expected?" All the TAs responded "yes." I did not, however, factor these responses into my analysis because it could not be clear if TAs really felt that the content was what they expected. They could have answered "yes" because they felt pressured to answer, because the prototype contained relevant information (even if it was not complete or enough), or because the prototype contained similar information to their Language and Composition I course packet so that is what they expected. Their responses could also relate to other confounding variables. A researcher should be suspect of his or her own investigation if all users mainly comment about how much they "liked it." If this happens, continue with another method of inquiry or a different set of questions.

As TAs used the prototype, they did not ask for a category that was not already included. They may have asked for a specific document within categories, particularly within the Sample Syllabi section, but they did not ask for materials that did not fit into the categories provided.

Prototype 1 and Retooling the Prototype

From the four trends discovered through my tests, I retooled the prototype. Here, I explicate how my results reshaped *Orientations, Hypertext, and Multiplicity*.

Open Versus Closed. My results corroborate research that has been completed since the onset of my project. Weise (1995), for example, explained that a drawback of "complete user control" is that "there is no guarantee users will actually see everything they are required to see to understand the material" (p. 30). Even though my prototype was not completely open-ended, as advocated by Landow and others, the allotted control—users could connect to any document—was inappropriate.

Often, TAs wanted to either return to previously visited documents or go to another document in the same category, but it seemed that too many choices either hindered navigation or lead to confusion. The most common question users asked during testing was, "How do I get back to [where I was]." This question identifies a need for a clearer navigational path. The next most frequent comment was, "There should be [a particular document or type of document]." Because the documents users requested existed elsewhere in the hypertext, I concluded that this was a structural rather than a content-related problem. The structure seemed to be too complex to easily find given material. I decided that a more closed system was appropriate. Figure 9.1 demonstrates the links between items in the more closed system. Note that all documents do not link to all other documents. Instead, one can see patterns where categories emerge.

Figure 9.2 demonstrates that materials are arranged hierarchically. As might be typical in a book, there are sections and subsections.

Before I made changes, Plagiarism connected to Grading Standards, Instructor Sample Syllabi, and every other document in the text. Because I made changes, Plagiarism connects to the Table of Contents and to Departmental Policies and Governing Statements (and it should, probably, also connect to individual assignments).

Constituents. TAs at Midwest University wanted more than just the whole syllabi; they wanted to connect constituent parts of different syllabi together. For example, some TAs want to compare various late work policies from different syllabi, such as those seen in Figure 9.3, when creating their course and writing their policy. As a result, the

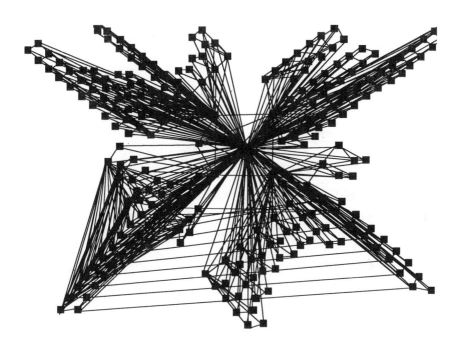

Figure 9.1. Designing a more closed system

revised prototype contained collections of syllabi constituents. These constituent are included in the section called Instructor Sample Syllabi, as seen in Figure 9.2.

Four TAs commented they do not want to "open up each syllabus just to see one part and then go back and do it all again for the next part." They wanted all the sample late work policies to be available in one place. One TA noted that she spreads sample syllabi on the floor so that she can easily compare the parts that interest her. She was particularly interested in comparing approaches and organization of schedules, which she did by physically cutting schedules from sample syllabi and placing them next to each other. With only whole syllabi, TAs could not easily compare the information of current concern. Placing constituents such as schedules into one document provides an easy way for TAs to download or print only the information that they wanted. Each of these documents contains the late work policies, for example, from all of the sample syllabi. Figure 9.3 shows two late work policies to demonstrate the type of information in these sections.

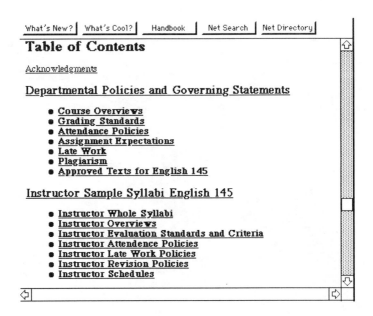

Figure 9.2. Viewing the hierarchy and constituent parts

Annotations. Links needed to be annotated to facilitate navigation. TAs expected details about links in order to make decisions about whether to chose that link. They wanted to make more educated decisions about choosing or ignoring links. The prototype contained 23 sample syllabi. To provide some context, each syllabus was named based on the TAs approach to the course as illustrated in Table 9.1.

During the tests, all of the TAs began looking at Sample Syllabi, but none chose to look at more than six. Seven TAs opened the Sample Syllabi section but had difficulties. Five got frustrated and quit looking at syllabi all together. Many had a hard time returning to the syllabus after connecting to other documents. When opening the Sample Syllabi contents list, one TA remarked, "How the hell am I supposed to know which one I want to read? " then, "I am not wasting my time looking at all of those to see if they are relevant to me or not."

These descriptive names of course syllabi were not enough to help TAs identify information about the syllabi. It seemed that TAs needed annotated links in order to make decisions about which links to choose. As a result, each link to a syllabus received a brief annotation to

LATE WORK

As stated in PIPS #105, late work is not accepted in English 145. If you are in class when an assignment is made, but cannot be here when the assignment is due then send it with a classmate, drop it in the folder on my door before class, or call me ahead of time to make arrangements. Possible extensions must be negotiated in advance (and advance is not 5 minutes before class!). I reserve the right to lower assignment grades for late work. Late work affects your final participation & course grades--don't make it a habit.
To view this whole syllabi see Writing and Thinking

THE (DREADED) PAPERS

Please turn in your papers on time. I consider a paper late if it is turned in after the class period on the day it is due -- and I will take 1/3 of a grade off for each day it is late. Furthermore, if you can't turn something in to me and have to turn it in somewhere else (my office or the instructor's box in Stevenson 401) please tell me where your paper is. If you turn a paper in to my office on a Friday and I don't know about it until Monday it is already a whole letter grade off (if it is a C paper, then it will become a D).
To view this whole syllabi see First, What is Similar and Dissimilar?

Figure 9.3. Comparing constituent parts of materials in the hypertext

help users in assessing the relevance or benefits of that link. Figure 9.4 shows such annotations.

Connections. TAs found it difficult to determine which links were of value to them and which connections they should make. TAs wanted to be able to connect assignments from one section of the proto- type to the corresponding syllabi in another section. "When I read an assignment, it would be nice to have it connect to its course," says one TA who represents the views of five others. These comments were valu- able because the documents in question were already connected. Furthermore, by asking for a document to connect to the course when it already does, TAs are asking for clear and previously made connections. It seemed that because of the difficulties above and perhaps because of confounding variables, TAs did not want to explore on their own or they wanted a system to identify emphasis or rate relevance. They had a task to do and they did not want to spend their time finding connections.

Table 9.1. Adding Descriptive Names.

• Basic Information	• Strengthening Writing and Analyzing Abilities in Academic Context
• Writing Strategies Approach	
• Writing and Thinking	
• Interrogate Existing Knowledge	• Language and Its Function in Our Lives
• Conventions, Communities and Forums: Fall	• First, What is Similar and Dissimilar?
• Analyzing Audiences, Comparing Conventions, and Arguing Intelligently	• A new Way of Seeing
	• Conventions and Expectations
• "from-to"	• A Semester for English 145 Teachers and Other Lost Souls
• Situated in Academic Conversations	

Landow (1992b) and other hypertext theorists praise hypertext for its open-endedness and its ability for facilitating connections, and by implication critical thinking, but here serendipitous connections hindered rather than helped. It seemed obvious, then, that TAs needed a cognitive map to help facilitate task completion.

TESTING PROTOTYPE 2

Retooling a prototype is not enough. Reliability is not achieved until there is consensus that the system is satisfactory. After the prototype is retooled, it must be tested again. If consensus is not achieved with the second prototype, more changes and tests become necessary. During the testing for Prototype 2, I received consensus from the users, the director of writing, and members of the writing committee that the system and its retooling were satisfactory.

During post hoc interviews, I asked TAs if their attitudes about hypertext changed as a result of using the prototype. I also asked whether their attitudes about hypertext would affect their use of *Orientations, Hypertext, and Multiplicity* or a similar hypertextual database. Those who asked, "What is hypertext" during preliminary interviews claimed to have a greater understanding of hypertext after using one. Most TAs responded similarly: "Using a hypertext is easier than I thought—it sort of demystified it all." Additionally, all but one respon-

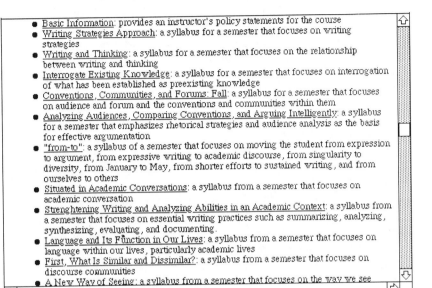

Figure 9.4. Naming and annotating links

dent said they would use such a hypertext if one were available. The respondent who admittedly would not use the hypertext also admitted to being intimidated by computer classrooms and resistant to teaching in such an environment. Opinions of those already familiar with hypertext did not seem to change.

My results reinforce Dumas and Redish (1993) and others who claim that users need to be included from the onset. By going to users first, I determined what and how materials should be included. My first user tests revealed difficulties from a user's perspective. These provided information that would have otherwise gone unnoticed, or at least unnoticed for timely consideration. The usability tests revealed that the second prototype was a helpful tool containing needed information in an adequately structured way.

FOLLOW-UP

It may seem that once the prototype is created and consensus reached that a project is complete. It is important to follow up, however, to verify the effectiveness of the end product. Post hoc interviews and focus group interviews are effective for follow-up. If possible, follow up with initial users as they might add insight. Then, if possible or relevant, follow up with new users as well. With new users, perform user testing as with the first prototype. Because the group of TAs continually changes and each group brings multifarious experiences, a new group of TAs could have different needs, constituting changes to the hypertext. Follow-up may be particularly important with a hypertext for TAs, especially because technologies advance so rapidly. Furthermore, each new cohort of TAs may have more confidence concerning technology or they may have more technological savvy.

From post hoc telephone interviews, I found that no TAs used the hypertext. When asked why, they explained they had too many other worries. The TA who cut constituents from syllabi and spread them across the floor said that she did not take advantage of hypertext because having the sections connected in one online document was different than spreading them across the floor. Her complaint was that she could view only one screen full of information at a time (frames may be able to address this to some degree). When I explained that if she printed the document she would be able to see them all at once and would save the time of cutting up syllabi she said, "I never thought of that."

Other common responses include:

- I didn't think about it [the hypertext, after using it in the study].
- I am not interested in hypertext. It was all right for someone interested in hypertext, but not for me.
- After testing the hypertext, I thought that I might utilize it, but when I really thought about it, I thought "why?"
- I did not want to think about the course that much. I just want a tried and true syllabus.
- I don't have a computer at home and I hate using the computer labs; therefore, it is just as well for me to go to the office and gather materials. If I have to go there anyway, the hypertext hasn't helped me. I would want to use it for convenience sake.
- I didn't know how to get there [to the website of the hypertext].

The most common response was that in hindsight, what TAs really wanted when preparing their syllabus was dialogue and interaction. TAs wanted to talk to others about their syllabi and their experiences with them. They wanted to ask questions and both hear and see responses. They wanted to discuss ways of implementing various exercises and assignments. TAs really wanted to know what others were thinking about in preparing their syllabi in a given way. The hypertext did not address the hows and whys of the syllabus and it did not give them an opportunity to interact with people who could address those hows and whys.

DISCUSSION

Overall, anxiety, lack of knowledge, extra effort, and interaction seemed to be the most common reasons that TAs did not use *Orientations, Hypertext, and Multiplicity.* The first three barriers include anxiety about the medium or the computer classroom, a lack of knowledge about the grammar and usage of the medium, and not wanting to make an extra effort in order to use it. Proper training or orientation to the hypertext and computer classroom could help reduce anxiety and increase knowledge about the grammar and usage of the medium. Even so, we must consider that as "making students computer-literate on networks may not enable them to find a voice once they leave the classroom" (Wahlstrom, 1994, p. 182), hypertextualizing TAs may not make them willing and able to use hypertext for conceptualizing and creating their courses. It may also be the case that even with proper training hypertexts may still sit unused.

The most common reason TAs did not use *Orientation, Hypertext, and Multiplicity* was that they wanted dialogue and interaction when preparing their courses. Simply showing syllabi for comparison, for example, does not really help a nervous TA understand the hows and whys of pedagogical or practical choices. Sure the context for the courses and assignments might be given in overviews, but that does not help TAs address concerns such as "How do I implement this?" and "What types of responses might I expect from students?" Perhaps, adding justifications and discussions could improve the hypertext.

On the other hand, a more expansive hypertext that explains the hows and whys may still not encourage use; it may be interaction with their peers rather than content that TAs seek. Textual hows and whys may not be able to replace dialogue and synchronous discussions, be they face to face or telephone. Kaufer (1993) claimed that asynchronicity of media is effective because it

> frees communication partners from this constraint [co-temporal communication] and enables communication partners to be involved with the same communicative transaction but at different times. The written word made it possible for individuals to engage

in communicative transactions, if not at their leisure, at least not at exactly the same time. (p. 100)

Kaufer did not consider variables such as nervous TAs switching from IBM-compatible classrooms to Macintosh classrooms or conceptualizing and creating their own. Perhaps, without such barriers asynchronicity would be freeing; however, my results suggest that synchronous communication might be more effective for the TAs in the study. In fact, the wait between conversations allows time for anxiety to build and because of time constraints TAs generally have only a few days to put together their courses; thus, a wait between conversations becomes less tolerable. Further research must be done in order to examine TAs and their interactions—synchronous and asynchronous, computer-mediated and unmediated—as they become enculturated into their discourse community.

SUGGESTIONS FOR FURTHER RESEARCH

Perhaps synchronicity is not the key. Perhaps interaction is the key. Moore (1993) explained three types of pedagogical interactions: learner-content, learner-instructor, learner-learner. Hillman et al. (1994) added interface to Moore's list. *Orientations, Hypertext, and Multiplicity* addresses interface and content, but instructor and learner have been largely ignored (unless one considers accessing other TA documents as interacting with peers—I don't consider it interactive). Further research might focus on the role of interaction in hypertexts (interaction at a substantive level, not as a mere manner of selecting links). New advances in the generation of WWW documents could possibly be used to add interaction. Then, added to technological interaction, what roles does hypertext play in interaction with faculty and peers, if any, in an orientation for TAs?

Another aspect to consider is that unless a context for understanding a course is presented to instructors, they rely only on their own contexts. Although this is not new, I repeat it as a reminder that if we want to orient TAs to paradigms practiced within their departments, we must provide materials for doing so. Although some may argue that hypertexts can facilitate connections, we must consider that there is a difference between potential for connections and actual connections. The TAs in my study demonstrate that at least when approaching the hypertext with a specific task and need for information, the TAs want to follow a cognitive map, not create one. Further research would explore cognitive mapping as a supplement for TA hypertexts and orientations.

I conclude that participatory development is an effective process for developing and evaluating hypertexts. Johnson-Eilola (1994) claimed there is a "need for a fuller understanding of the nondeterministic, complex, and interwoven nature of the technological, individual, and social aspects of writing and reading in hypertext" (p. 204), and UCD is a way for getting at these aspects. My process addressed social and individual aspects of hypertextualizing TAs and I still found that there were more social and individual aspects to consider.

Rather than narrowing our efforts to testing particular aspects about a hypertext, I argue that we broaden our research to include social and individual aspects of technology. I claim that even though a prototype seems to be effective by consensus, it may not be utilized. Confounding variables may interfere with the use of an effective medium. Baym (1995) listed types of variables: "the factors of temporal structure, external contexts, system infrastructure, group purposes, and participant and group characteristics have been put forward as the most salient preexisting forces on the development of computer-mediated community" (p. 149). All of these variables should be considered during development.

Just because TAs did not use *Orientations, Hypertext, and Multiplicity* on their own does not mean that they wouldn't. Anxiety about the computers could interfere more than the TAs admit or realize. "Fear is an important element in every novice computer user's first attempts to use a new machine or new software: fear of destroying data, fear of hurting the machine, fear of seeming stupid in comparison to others, or even to the machine itself" (Hillman et al., 1994, p. 10). Consequently, TAs who are introduced to and who use hypertext during their orientation and their TA preparation course might have different reactions to hypertexts than those introduced to hypertexts only during their orientation. Moreover, once hows and whys are added to the hypertext TAs might react differently. Also, if hypertexts were introduced in a context where connections would facilitate discussions, such as in a seminar or on a listserv, the environment might facilitate information the TAs seek.

Dumas and Redish (1993) pointed out that "it is very difficult to test both whether *people will* use the documentation and how they will use it in the same test" (p. 77). My user analyses and usability testing allowed me to create a prototype and to find out how to revise the prototype for the situation. I learned that TAs wanted sample syllabi and assignments. I also learned that TAs wanted syllabi constituents to be located both within its syllabus of origin and in a document with like constituents. I found that TAs who were anxious about hypertext felt better about them after having used one. I also found that a hierarchical system works best for the TAs at Midwest University and that they preferred links to be annotated. Finally, I found that TAs said that they would use such a hypertext if one were available.

Because my user testing demonstrated that *Orientations, Hypertext, and Multiplicity* is an effective hypertext, I hypothesize that my means for implementing it might have been ineffective. What needs to be tested, now, are ways of implementing such hypertextual systems. I have identified both anxiety and the need for dialogue as two variables affecting the usability of a hypertextual orientation tool for TAs. What would help overcome those barriers? Would different ways of implementing the hypertext change its usability? Would different ways of implementing a text into a course can change its usability as it relates to the class? What are different ways for implementing the hypertext? What other confounding variables exist? Can they be overcome? How can we teach TAs the grammar of hypertext without overburdening users? Do teaching assistants seek dialogue with their peers and how would this affect their use of an orientation hypertext?

What I did not find was an effective means for determining if or how TAs would use the hypertext. Mirel (1988) claimed that "testing whether a manual is used and determining the effects of that use are separate aspects of usability" (p. 291). She explained: "Broadly speaking, 'actual use' usability testing looks at the connection between the use of an in-house manual and larger organizational efforts to integrate a new system into the workplace" (p. 291). Studying both actual use and larger organizational efforts regarding integration are crucial for successfully hypertextualizing TAs.

ACKNOWLEDGMENTS

Thanks to James Kalmbach, an impetus of this chapter, and to Lise Hansen for enduring many early drafts.

APPENDIX A

User Analyses

1. In interviews, 18 TAs were asked open-ended questions about their attitudes toward both the course and hypertext, as these might be confounding variables. After these questions, the TAs and three members of the writing committee were asked about the information or materials they would expect in a hypertext created to help orient them. Interviews were held at the convenience of subjects—in TA offices, the computer lab, TA homes, or over the telephone. All of the TAs were teaching Language and Composition I and were potential teachers for Language and Composition II. Consequently, TAs needed course-specific materials.
2. Five TAs from the initial 18 participated in a focus group about their attitudes toward hypertext as an orientation tool. Due to time constraints after nine interviews were completed, each of those TAs were invited to participate in the focus group. The five participants agreed to participate and were available at the designated time. The interview took place in the computer lab where the TAs would teach their course.

Coding

3. The data was coded. I looked for the types of materials that TAs said would be useful and I used these as categories and materials for the hypertext.

Prototype 1

4. The prototype was created from the interview data.

Testing Prototype 1

5. Usability tests regarding the categories in and navigational structure of the hypertext were conducted with 15 TAs and one member of the writing committee. First, the hypertext and its sections were demonstrated. Then, TAs were observed using the hypertext to help them prepare for Language and Composition II, particular attention was given to places that were seemingly frustrating or confusing. When questions were

asked, I answered with, "What would you do if I weren't here?" If TAs tried to work out the answers but asked the questions a second time, I answered. These tests took place either in the computer lab or in TA homes, which ever the TAs preferred. The loss of subjects was due to scheduling difficulties.

TA Orientation

6. TAs selected to teach Language and Composition II went to their orientation where they were introduced to their course and classrooms.

Retooling the Prototype

7. Changes are made to the prototype based on the usability tests.

Testing Prototype 2

8. Usability tests were conducted with 11 TAs—those selected to teach Language and Composition II and others who could still potentially teach the course. The loss of subjects was due to scheduling difficulties.

Suspected Confounds

9. Using both open- and close-ended questions, the 11 remaining TAs were about their attitudes toward the course, teaching the course, and hypertext.

TAs Prepare & Teach Their Courses

10. TAs prepared their syllabi and course materials.
11. TAs taught their courses.

Follow-up

12. After that semester and an additional semester, eight TAs are asked about the hypertext created to help orient them to Language and Composition II. The loss of subjects was due an inability to contact all of the subjects.

APPENDIX B

The specific modules or chunks of information emerged as follows:

Departmental Policies and Governing Statement contains materials approved and established by the director of writing and the writing committee. "Course Overview" defines the course. Other governing materials include "Grading Standards" for individual papers, portfolios, summaries, and responses to readings; "Attendance Policy," which contains university and departmental policies as well as answers to questions about why such policies exist; "Assignment Expectations," which defines various assignments; "Late Work," which states the department's stand; "Plagiarism," which describes the nature of plagiarism; and "Approved Texts," which lists approved textbooks for the semester.

Sample Syllabi overviews Language and Composition II by linking syllabi that were created by previous instructors.

Some Paper Assignments contains sample assignments and papers, including one student's work for the whole semester and essays displaying instructor comments.

Some Exercises and Assignments contains exercises and assignments designed to develop reading, writing, thinking, and articulation skills. These are organized into the following categories: "Audience and Forum," "Brainstorming and Planning," "Defining," "Categorization," "Titles," "Reading and Writing," "Source Documentation," "Revising," "In-Class Writings," and "Handouts: Not Assignments or Schedules."

Chapter 10

Response:
Mapping the Emergent Structures
of Hypertext

H. Lewis Ulman
Maureen Alana Burgess
Ohio State University

Reading, because we control it, is adaptable to our needs and rhythms. We are free to indulge our subjective associative impulse.

* * *

Once a reader is enabled to collaborate, participate, or in any way engage the text as an empowered player who has some say in the outcome of the game, the core assumptions of reading are called into question.
    —Sven Birkerts (1994)

Like colors and chameleons, hypertext appears differently depending on the background against which it is viewed. Consider, for instance, the two epigraphs just cited, which appear in adjacent chapters of Birkerts' (1994) *The Gutenberg Elegies*. Both chapters discuss electronic media from the perspective of print. The first laments the "vocal tyranny" of books on tape. "With the audio book," Birkerts argued, "everything—pace, timbre, inflection—is determined for the captive listener. The collaborative component is gone; one simply receives" (p. 147). Proponents of hypertext might sense a sympathetic sensibility here, a reader open to loosening the conventions that separate readers' and writers' roles. But then we read not 20 pages later an elegy for "the idea of the author as a sovereign maker" (p. 158), a complaint that hypertext "promises to spring me from the univocal linearity which is precisely the constraint that fills me with a sense of possibility as I read my way across fixed acres of print" (p. 164). Not an out-and-out contradiction of the earlier argument, perhaps, given the focuses of the two essays on different media, but evidence nevertheless of what shape-shifters media and our constructions of them can be when we view them in different contexts. Moreover, although 50 years have passed since Vannevar Bush imagined the Memex, and 25 years have gone by since Ted Nelson envisioned the docuverse, electronic hypertext is still an emerging technology, a rapidly moving target that threatens to render pronouncements about its nature, applications, and efficacy are all but obsolete before they can be mounted on a World-Wide Web (WWW) server, much less appear in print.[1]

Part of the difficulty here stems from the fact that definitions of hypertext involve at least three distinguishable, although complexly interrelated, dimensions:

1. A *theory of textuality* designed to help us imagine alternatives to the symbolic artifacts, cultural institutions, and social relations of print culture; for instance, as suggested earlier, hypertext is often viewed as blending the roles of readers and writers.
2. A wide variety of *material, enabling technologies* and associated *symbol systems* used for writing and reading hypertexts, technologies such as HyperCard, Storyspace, Hyperstudio, Claris Home Page, and the various material and symbolic components of the WWW—fiber optic cables, routers, HTML, HTTP, URLs, browsers, and servers.
3. *Textual forms* and *works* composed and read with hypertext systems, including Storyspace webs such as Joyce's (1992) *Afternoon*, HyperCard stacks such as Larsen's (1993) *Marble Springs*, and WWW texts such as Moulthrop and Cohen's (1996) *The Color of Television*, works that enact the expressive and communicative possibilities of hypertext.

---

[1]We do not mean to imply that other media such as print are static. Rather, we are pointing to the distinctiveness of transitional periods marked by rapid changes in technologies of writing. Technological change may always be occurring, but we tend to think of the material history of writing as punctuated by periods of especially significant change—the shift from orality to literacy in ancient Greece, from manuscript to print in early modern Europe, and from print to electronic media on a global scale in our own time.

Within the conceptual space defined by these three dimensions of hypertext, a set of theoretical problems has arisen.

1. *The problem of uniqueness.* In attempting to distinguish hypertext from other forms of textuality, scholars have tried to identify unique features (e.g., nonlinearity) of hypertext. Although such arguments are often overstated and overgeneralized, it is worthwhile to examine what is truly unique about the features and uses of a given hypertext system, if only because our effort to understand hypertext in this way can lead to a fuller understanding of textuality in general. There are, however, more applied problems and promises at stake. How, for instance, do we determine whether something students do with hypertext can be done only, or can always be done better, with hypertext?

2. *The problem of distinguishing ideas and implementations.* As DeWitt points out in his chapter in this volume, students in his study defined hypertext in terms of HyperCard, the particular program they were using in class. As a result of this synechdochic extension, the students' ideas about hypertext as a form of textuality were determined by the specific technological implementation of hypertext they were using. How do we draw comparisons and develop a body of knowledge when we must constantly distinguish between the idea of hypertext and its multiple implementations? Is the problem any different for other media such as print?

3. *The problem of context.* Hypertext as a theory of textuality or as an enabling technology is often discussed in terms of design features and their potential uses. But we also need to study technology as it is actually used, for only then can we see what it becomes in the hands of users. What are the key elements of the contexts important for studying how hypertext is used? Where, how, and to what effect are hypertext systems being used?

4. *The problem of affordances and constraints.* According to Norman (1993), the affordances of any technological artifact consist of "its possible functions: A chair affords support, whether for standing, sitting, or the placement of objects. . . . Different technologies afford different operations. That is, they make some things easy to do, others difficult or impossible" (p. 106). Because technologies such as hypertext systems are used in complex contexts, how do we tease out the particular affordances of a given technology from all other factors affecting,

say, writing pedagogy? How can we determine what aspect of a hypertext system makes some learning activity easy or hard? These questions require a shift in emphasis from one-dimensional, causal explanations of how technology affects learning to explanations that analyze particular hypertext systems in use in order to understand how individual learners exploit, or are constrained by, specific feature of the systems.

5. *The problem of assessment.* What criteria do we look for in hypertext works? Are there conventions against which to measure how closely a given hypertext meets a standard? If not, how do we assess hypertexts when every hypertext system and every hypertext work is essentially a prototype? Are there rhetorical heuristics against which to measure hypertext designs? Is the problem any better defined than assessment of writing in print?

6. *The problem of design and instruction.* Given the problems involved in assessing hypertexts, how do we design hypertexts? How do we teach students and colleagues to design hypertexts? How does students' knowledge of composing in print affect their learning of hypertext authoring, and how does their exposure to hypertext affect their writing in print?

7. *The problem of determining our business.* An apocryphal story tells how steamboat companies that insisted they were in the steamboat business went under, while others who recognized they were in the transportation and freight business switched to railroads and survived. What is the "business" of teachers of composition in this time of rapid change in writing technology? Print literacy? Or communication and verbal art in multiple media?

In the introduction to this volume, DeWitt and Strasma argue that much previous work on hypertext has been characterized by an abundance of theory and speculation accompanied by a dearth of empirical studies of hypertext in pedagogical contexts; or, in terms of the problems previously described, by fascination with the idea of hypertext at the expense of detailed study of its implementation and use, particularly in writing courses. By contrast, each study in this volume addresses theoretical questions in the context of a particular pedagogical problem and setting. Here at the end of volume, we assess these studies collectively from the broader perspective of the theoretical problems just outlined and ask in regard to each problem, "What have we learned? How have these studies filled in our understanding of the emerging structures of hypertext?"

THE PROBLEM OF UNIQUENESS

Several of these chapters speculate about the unique aspects of hypertext. For instance, McKillop and Myers suggest that hypermedia in general may be more highly engaging than print, and Strasma suggests that writing in hypertext may help "initiate genre and media awareness." However, the studies are not generally designed to compare broad effects of hypertexts to those of print; rather, they focus on how different hypertext programs facilitate writing, reading, and research processes in particular educational settings.

In other words, these studies yield situated comparisons of writing in print and in hypertext. Indeed, in every case the studies in this collection were conducted in contexts that involved traditional print. Hypertext was often introduced as a adjunct strategy for exploration and invention. In such contexts, part of the problem of assessing the significance of one's findings involves determining how specific aspects of particular hypertext technologies change the dynamics of writing and learning. Taken together, the variety of hypertext technologies (conceptual, HyperCard, Storyspace, WWW) and educational settings and goals that informs these studies reminds us that global pronouncements about the unique aspects of hypertext are of limited usefulness in applied pedagogical research.

THE PROBLEM OF DISTINGUISHING IDEAS AND IMPLEMENTATIONS

Taken together, these chapters remind us to distinguish between our general idea of hypertext and the particular implementation we use in our classrooms. We need to recognize that we have chosen not only to teach with hypertext but also to employ a particular hypertext technology and to ask our students to use that technology in particular ways. As Strasma points out in this volume, "hypertext as an idea is not new, but its use as a functional medium in electronic form is only a few years old." We add that hypertext as an idea is not fixed, and it has been implemented in various electronic and print forms (note that one of the studies in this volume employs conceptual hypertexts constructed with paper index cards (Strasma), whereas the rest employ various electronic hypertext technologies, including HyperCard, Storyspace, and the WWW).

Strasma describes hypertext in electronic and nonelectronic media as involving nonlinearity, recursivity, links between sign and signification, nodes, and multiple reading paths. Even if we accept, for the sake of argument, that this cluster of features accurately describes hypertext (some authors would substitute *multi*linearity for *non*linearity), we need to recognize that these features can be implemented quite differently in various hypertext software and by teachers and students using that software. We highlight three aspects of hypertext implementation that these chapters helped us think about more critically.

First, many of the studies in the volume invoke Joyce's distinction between constructive and exploratory hypertexts and make a case for the importance of students writing their own hypertexts. Although that approach is the norm in this book, it offers a stark contrast to the emphasis on browsing that is so common in applications of the WWW in education.

Second, although hypertext links work in pretty much the same way in most hypertext programs (clicking on an anchor—a word or a button—takes the reader to a target somewhere else), the teachers in this collection show that this simple feature can be used in complex ways. Indeed, several of the chapters provide rhetorical taxonomies of hypertext links (Strasma; Golson; DeGuay; Ryan; Norton, Zimmerman, and Lindemann). These analyses remind us that the link is as much a *techne* (art) as a technology (Lanham, 1996).

Third, the particular implementations of hypertext in these studies remind us that any given use of educational technology is shaped by factors other than the features of the technology, including factors such as the learning curve involved in using particular features of computer software and the appropriateness of those features to specific learning tasks. For instance, none of the studies report using some significant features of the programs employed in the studies. None of the studies employing HyperCard mention Hypertalk, the scripting language that allows authors to extend the capabilities of HyperCard stacks well beyond the features available through the program's menus and commands. Scripting would allow writers to incorporate other media more flexibly and to design more richly interactive stacks. Similarly, the studies that employ Storyspace do not mention that program's ability to assign keywords to writing spaces and to create paths through the writing spaces in a document according to selection criteria such as author, keyword, date of creation or modification, character strings, and so on— allowing the program to be used, in effect, as a database. This feature would support pedagogical goals like those outlined in DeWitt's study, in which hypertext was used primarily as a tool for invention. We understand that these features might not have fit the schedules or pedagogical goals of the classes described in this volume. At the same time, the features just described do offer ways for teachers to extend Joyce's notion of constructive hypertext. As our idea of hypertext becomes more and more influenced by the WWW, we need to remember the still largely unexplored possibilities of other hypertext technologies.

THE PROBLEM OF CONTEXT

In his contribution to this volume, Ryan notes the shift in studies of computers and writing from a focus on technology as agent or instrument to technology as context. All the studies in this volume employ research methods (quasi-experimental, qualitative, case study, and so on) that attempt to account for, and in some cases control, the various contexts affecting student learning. These teacher-researchers worked in a wide range of educational contexts, including junior high school classes in English and social studies, college composition and education courses, and training programs for new graduate teaching associates in English. Some were surrounded by technologically rich environments, whereas others could allow only four students to construct hypertext projects because of limited site licenses or hardware capabilities.

In addition, the authors note how the design and success of projects based on hypertext are affected by students' prior experience with various media (McKillop and Myers, DeGuay, Strasma); the course content, the teacher's pedagogy, and students' attitudes (Strasma); students' processes of comprehension (Golson); the writing requirements of other college classes (Saul); and the effect that competing sources of information such as conversation have on uses of hypertext reference materials (Morton). In each case, the most important consideration is the fit between the pedagogical goals of the course or situation and the affordances of the technologies employed.

Finally, several studies in the volume raise questions about various social contexts that affect students' use of hypertext, including changing roles of readers and writers; changing distribution of expertise and authority among teachers and students; and the effect of digital media on the representation and construction of cultural difference (see especially McKillop and Myers). However, studies of non-networked technology in individual classrooms or other limited settings do not have the breadth of focus to address broad cultural dimensions of students' use of hypertext, and as hypertext on the WWW increasingly enables the formation of a global community of discourse, we will need cross-cultural studies of students reading and writing hypertext on the WWW—representing themselves and their communities and communicating with people in other communities within the electronic contact zones of the Internet. Furthermore, we need to view our use of hypertext in individual classrooms within the context of broad demographic studies of access to computing.

THE PROBLEM OF AFFORDANCES AND CONSTRAINTS

These studies have also impressed on us the difference between the features of hypertext programs and the affordances of those programs for the teaching of writing. We might think of features such as the link commands in HyperCard and Storyspace as functional controls of the software, whereas affordances determine how we use those feature to accomplish tasks in specific contexts. Features, then, might be defined in terms of technical operations, affordances in terms of goals. Flip open a reference manual, and you will find a list of features, whereas you will find affordances described in tutorials and templates. Features take on value only in contexts of use, and thus become affordances. So what do we learn about the affordances and constraints of the particular technologies used in the studies in this collection? How were the features of those programs assigned value by students and teachers? McKillop and Myers found that the seventh graders in their study included Quicktime video and sound in their hypertexts because they felt such inclusions would be more engaging to their audience (other students), whereas the undergraduate education majors focused on a text-based web in Storyspace to introduce adolescent literature. Golson argues that hypertext links lend themselves to two types of affordances: well-designed texts characterized by interacting links "allow readers to tap into the generative possibilities of language, thereby expanding the readers' meaning-making capacity or reinforcing the readers' insight," whereas texts characterized by intersecting links "can assist readers in defining and clarifying knowledge domains, pursuing defined tasks, and solving problems." Strasma claims that "limited use of hypertext can serve as an instructional tool for learning the best way to organize and shape information."

It is also important to note that the affordances of hypertext technology may be determined by individual circumstances as well as by particular writing tasks such as those previously noted. For example, the affordances and constraints of hypertext may be different for students of differing abilities, as Ryan notes: "Hypertext gives beginning writers like Todd the nonthreatening forum of expression that they need to build skills toward more complex, abstract compositions." Other factors that might determine the affordances of hypertext features for individual students are their familiarity with digital and other media, their experience as readers and writers, and their individual learning styles. Can we generalize these claims about affordances? Probably not. Rather, they can serve as heuristics that must be adapted to specific contexts. As with all teaching models, hypertext pedagogy must be adapted to individual teachers' and students' circumstances.

THE PROBLEM OF DESIGN AND INSTRUCTION

Put another way, the uses of hypertext described in this book constitute models of *techne* rather than technology; the collection offers a wealth of strategies for teaching with hypertext that other teachers can adapt to their own classrooms. First, we find several analyses of linking that can provide students with heuristics for developing and organizing their hypertexts (Strasma; DeGuay; Ryan; Norton, Zimmerman, and Lindemann). Second, the chapters present a wide range of assignments, including Ryan's *Literary Journal*, in which successive classes of students expand upon the same hypertext, and DeWitt's use of hypertext as a method of teaching students how to collect data and formulate claims while writing a conventional paper. Third, the studies provide models of individual students' composing processes (DeWitt) and those of collaborative groups working on hypertext projects (Strasma; Saul; Norton, Zimmerman, and Lindemann). Fourth, we find analyses of hypertext structures, including Strasma's account of his students' conceptual hypertexts and Morton's discussion of open versus closed structures and of the optimal granularity of nodes (teaching assistants in her study wanted all the late policies together in a single document rather than embedded in many syllabi). Finally, even the authors' research method provide insights for teaching. Morton's discussion of usability testing offers a rich model of design (prototyping) that might be adapted to student work on hypertexts.

Given the experimental nature of the medium, however, we need to recognize that following these models will not always result in texts that work in the ways that teachers and students imagine. After all, it is a truism that most experiments fail when measured against final goals but succeed in generating new knowledge for further experimentation. In short, trial and error is part of the learning process. Hypertext pedagogy needs to provide students with opportunities to experiment, to abandon experiments, and to reflect on what they have learned from their experiments.

THE PROBLEM OF ASSESSMENT

Formal assessment (grading) is elided in these studies, but we can ask how the students and teachers evaluated the success of their hypertexts, given the contexts in which they were working. What measures of quality emerged from these uses of hypertext? In some cases, teachers appear to measure student texts against a model of hypertext structure. Golson claims that the best hypertexts written by the students in her study incorporate both schematic and generative approaches to comprehension, as evidenced by their incorporation of the two types of links that she identifies (intersecting and interacting). Similarly, Strasma values the most complex hypertexts, those that employ the most of all three kinds of links he identifies (hierarchical, associative, and random). These measures of quality focus on products. By contrast, Ryan employs measures of quality that focus on students' processes of composing. He evaluates portfolios that include student reflections about their hypertext authoring, and he conducts attitude surveys to assess how students feel about their work in this new medium.

How should we balance concerns with process and product in a medium that is still in its infancy, lacking the conventions that underlie so much of our assessment of conventional printed texts? How do we evaluate experimentation? DeGuay's chapter can help us think through such questions of assessment. One of her students was overwhelmed by technical and conceptual problems and did not produce a text that took advantage of all the possibilities of hypertext authoring outlined in DeGuay's model—complex linking structures and multilinear paths. Another student brought to the class a high level of technical expertise and considerable skill in academic writing, and, as one might expect, created a complex, well-written hypertext, according to DeGuay's criteria. In her analysis of the first student's experience, DeGuay raises the question of whether it is valuable to have students struggle with the complications of the medium. To put her concern another way, we might ask which student had the more valuable learning experience.

We have argued that hypertext must be evaluated in the context of experimentation and use. This perspective suggests the value of portfolio assessments that emphasize student reflection on their processes of design and evaluation of what they have learned rather than focusing exclusively on what they have produced.

THE PROBLEM OF DETERMINING OUR BUSINESS

None of the courses described in this volume were focused exclusively on hypertext; all were focused on writing or involved regular writing in traditional print media. Those facts led us to reflect on the relation of new media to the traditional goals, methods, and materials of writing instruction. Can hypertext be an alternative mode of discourse equal to print in status and expressive range, or is it merely another arrow in the pedagogical quivers of writing teachers? Many of the chapters in this volume agree with Strasma's claim that the inclusion of hypertext in "required writing classes" can be justified as an "invention, collaborative, or revision heuristic." Furthermore, authors who conducted research in writing classes seem to agree with Strasma that, under ideal conditions, hypertext can support meta-awareness of the very concepts of central concern in writing classes. But it is worth noting that none of the chapters propose allowing students to work exclusively in hypertext in the required writing course if they so choose.

This positioning of hypertext as an adjunct to traditional media accurately reflects the current relationship of hypertext to academic discourse in general. Clearly, we are not yet in a position to say that our business is the teaching of communication and verbal art in any media that fit a given rhetorical situation. Our own skills and experience, as well as those of our students, dictate that we think of our work primarily in terms of traditional discursive forms and practices. But until we get to the point of accepting hypertext as a *techne* or discursive form equal to traditional forms of academic discourse, it is worth asking our students to consider what their business as writers might become during their lifetimes. Although in the short run they need to privilege learning to write in forms that they will be expected to produce in their other school and college courses, learning to treat the choice of media as a rhetorical choice among media and technologies with different affordances may be the more important lesson in the long run.

FURTHER INQUIRY

As we suggested earlier, it is striking that the WWW is seldom mentioned and is employed in only one of the studies in this book. The relative absence of the WWW here reminds us, of course, that print publication is hard put to keep pace with technological innovation in digital media, and we certainly need further empirical studies of students reading and writing on the WWW in order to understand how that medium might expand our understanding of the possibilities of hypertext for composition. However, the absence of the WWW is significant in other ways.

Consider, for instance, that whatever we thought hypertext was on the basis of our experience with HyperCard and Storyspace has been changed dramatically and forever by the WWW. Certainly the WWW retains familiar characteristics of hypertext such as nodes, links, multiple reading paths, and multimedia, but the social, economic, and political dimensions of the WWW are of a different order altogether than anything associated with the standalone hypertext programs of just a few years ago. Now it seems that hypertext is becoming synonymous in many people's mind with the WWW, and many teachers are embracing the WWW as an instructional medium. However, the chapters in this volume remind us that the WWW, at least in its current implementation, is still for most users a relatively restrictive hypertext environment compared to HyperCard or Storyspace, lacking, for example, a scripting language with the range of features found in HyperTalk, the easy-to-use database capabilities of Storyspace, and the multiple working environments and representations available in Storyspace. Although WWW authoring programs are beginning to incorporate some of these features, one lesson that teachers of writing should learn from the advent of the WWW is that elegant and phenomenally successful solutions to particular hypertext problems (e.g., worldwide linking of multimedia documents) may not always provide the best environment for using hypertext in the teaching of writing.

In keeping with the textual experimentation reported in this collection, comparative studies should continue to ask students to work in multiple electronic and print media, to think about what hypertext and other media are not just in terms of particular technologies but also in terms of what they have been and can be in the context of varied and ongoing textual experimentation and use.

References

Adobe Photoshop 2.5. (1993). Mountain View, CA: Adobe Systems, Inc.

Adobe Premiere 4.2 (1994). Mountain View, CA: Adobe Systems, Inc.

Albrecht, T. L., Johnson, G. M., & Walther, J. B. (1993). Understanding communication processes in focus groups. In D. L. Morgan (Ed.), *Successful focus groups: Advancing the state of art* (pp. 51-64). Newbury Park, CA: Sage.

Anderson, R. C. (1977). The notion of schemata and the educational enterprise: General discussion of the conference. In R. C. Anderson, R. J. Spiro, & W. E. Montague (Eds.), *Schooling and the acquisition of knowledge* (pp. 415-431). Hillsdale, NJ: Lawrence Erlbaum Associates.

Arnow, H. (1954). *The dollmaker.* New York: Avon Books.

Atkinson, F. (1993). Presenting information through multimedia. In C. M. Barnum & S. Carliner (Eds.), *Techniques for technical communicators* (pp. 253-272). New York: Macmillan.

Ausubel, D. P. (1968). *Educational psychology: A cognitive view.* New York: Holt, Rinehart & Winston.

Baird, P. (1988). HyperCard opens an electronic window on Glasgow. *Electronic Library, 6,* 344-353.

Barrett, E. (Ed.). (1989). *The society of text: Hypertext, hypermedia, and the social construction of information.* Cambridge: MIT Press.

Barthes, R. (1974). *S/Z* (R. Miller, Trans.). New York: Hill & Wang.

Bartholomae, D. (1986). Inventing the university. *Journal of Basic Writing, 5,* 4-23.

Bartholomae, D., & Petrotsky, A. (1986). *Facts, artifacts, and counterfacts: Theory and method for a reading and writing course.* Portsmouth, NH: Heinemann/Boynton-Cook.

Bauersfeld, K., & Halgren, S. (1996). "You've got three days!" Case studies in field techniques for the time-challenged. In D. Wixon & J. Ramey (Eds.), *Field methods casebook for software design* (pp.177-195). New York: Wiley & Sons.

Baym, N. K. (1995). The emergence of community in computer-mediated communication. In S. G. Jones (Ed.), *CyberSociety: Computer-mediated communication and community* (pp. 138-163). Thousand Oaks, CA: Sage.

Beach, R. (1992). Experimental and descriptive research methods in composition. In G. Kirsch & P. A. Sullivan (Eds.), *Methods and methodology in composition research* (pp. 217-243). Carbondale: Southern Illinois University Press.

Beard, J. D., Rymer, J., & Williams, D. L. (1989). An assessment system for collaborative-writing groups: Theory and empirical evaluation. *Journal of Business and Technical Communication, 3*(2), 29-51.

Berger, A. A. (1991). *Media research techniques.* Newbury Park, CA: Sage.

Berlin, J. (1987). *Rhetoric and reality: Writing instruction in American colleges 1900-1985.* Carbondale: Southern Illinois University Press.

Bevilacqua, A. F. (1989). Hypertext: Behind the hype. *American Libraries, 20,* 158-162.

Birkerts, S. (1994). *The Gutenberg elegies: The fate of reading in an electronic age.* Boston, MA: Faber & Faber.

Birnbaum, J.C. (1986). Reflective thought: The connection between reading and writing. In B. T. Petersen (Ed.), *Convergences: Transactions in reading and writing* (pp. 30-45). Urbana, IL: NCTE.

Bizzell, P. (1982). Cognition, convention, and certainty: What we need to know about writing. *Pre/Text, 3*(3), 213-243.

Bleich, D. (1986). Cognitive stereoscopy and the study of language and literature. In B. T. Petersen (Ed.), *Convergences: Transactions in reading and writing* (pp. 99-114). Urbana, IL: NCTE.

Blumer, H. (1969). *Symbolic interactionism: Perspective and method.* Englewood Cliffs, NJ: Prentice-Hall.

Bolter, J. (1991). *Writing space: The computer, hypertext, and the history of writing.* Hillsdale, NJ: Lawrence Erlbaum Associates.

Bolter, J. D., Joyce, M., & Smith, J. B. (1994). *StorySpace 1.3.* Watertown, MA: Eastgate Systems.

Brodkey, L. (1987). Writing ethnographic narratives. *Written Communication, 4*(1), 25-50.

Bruner, J. S. (1961). The act of discovery. *Harvard Educational Review, 31,* 21-32.

Bruner, J. S. (1971). *The relevance of education.* New York: Norton.

Burke, K. (1966). *Language as symbolic action: Essays on life, literature, and method.* Berkeley: University of California Press.

Bush, V. (1945). As we may think. *The Atlantic Monthly, 176,* 101-108.

Byles, T. (1988). A context for hypertext: Some suggested elements of style. *Wilson Library Bulletin, 63*(3), 60-62.

Cahalan, J. M., & Downing, D. B. (Eds.). (1991). *Practicing theory in introductory college literature courses.* Urbana, IL: NCTE.

Carnegie Foundation for the Advancement of Teaching. (1990). *Campus life: In search of community.* Princeton, NJ: Princeton University Press.

Carr, C. (1988). Hypertext: A new training tool? *Educational Technology, 28*(8), 7-11.

Carter, L. (1993). Written argumentation in hypertext: A study in structure and arrangement. In *Ninth conference on computers and writing: Presentation summaries* (pp. 30-31). Ann Arbor: University of Michigan Board of Regents.

Charney, D. (1994) The effect of hypertext on processes of reading and writing. In S. Hilligoss & C. Selfe (Eds.), *Literacy and computers: The complications of teaching and learning with technology* (pp. 238-263). New York: Modern Language Association.

Chatman, S. (1981). What novels can do that films can't. In W.J.T. Mitchell (Ed.), *On narrative* (pp. 117-136). Chicago: University of Chicago Press.

ClarisWorks 2.0. (1994). Santa Clara, CA: Claris.

Conklin, J. (1987). Hypertext: An introduction and survey. *I.E.E.E. Computer, 20*(9), 17-41.

Cozby, P. C. (1989). *Methods in behavioral research.* Mountain View, CA: Mayfield.

Delany, P., & Landow, G. (Eds.). (1991). *Hypermedia and literary studies.* Cambridge, MA: MIT Press.

DeRose, S. J. (1991). Biblical studies and hypertext. In P. Delany & G. P. Landow (Eds.), *Hypermedia and literary studies.* Cambridge, MA: MIT Press.

Dewey, J. (1938). *Experience and education.* New York: Collier.

DeWitt, S. L. (1996). The current nature of hypertext research in composition studies: An historical perspective. *Computers and Composition, 13,* 69-84.

Dickey, W. (1991). Poem descending a staircase: Hypertext and the simultaneity of experience. In P. Delany & G. P. Landow (Eds.), *Hypermedia and literary studies* (pp. 143-152). Cambridge: MIT Press.

Dobrin, D. (1994). Hype and hypertext. In C. L. Selfe & S. Hilligoss (Eds.), *Literacy and computers: The complications of teaching and learning with technology* (pp. 305-315). New York: Modern Language Association.

Douglas, J. Y. (1996). "Nature" versus "nurture": The three paradoxes of hypertext. *Readerly/Writerly Texts, 3*(2), 185-207.

Duin, A. H. (1993). Test drive—Evaluating the usability of documents. In C. M. Barnum & S. Carliner (Eds.), *Techniques for technical communicators* (pp. 306-335). New York: Macmillan.

Dumas, J. S., & Redish, J. C. (1993). *A practical guide to usability testing.* Norwood, NJ: Ablex.

Eco, U., & Sebeok, T. (Eds.). (1983). *The sign of three: Dupin, Holmes, Pierce.* Bloomington: Indiana University Press.

Ede, L. (1992). Methods, methodologies, and the politics of knowledge: Reflections and speculations. In G. Kirsch and P. A. Sullivan (Eds.), *Methods and methodology in composition research* (pp. 314-329). Carbondale: Southern Illinois University Press.

Ede, L., & Lunsford, A. (1985). Let them write—together. *English Quarterly, 18*(4), 119-127.

Freire, P., & Macedo, D. (1987). *Literacy: Reading the word and the world.* Cambridge, MA: Bergin & Garvey.

Friedlander, L. (1991). The Shakespeare project. In P. Delany & G. P. Landow (Eds.), *Hypermedia and literary studies* (pp. 257-271). Cambridge, MA: MIT Press.

Gagne, R. (1985). *The conditions of learning.* New York: Holt, Rinehart & Winston.

Goldman-Segal, R. (1992). Collaborative virtual communities: Using "Learning Constellations," a multimedia ethnographic research tool. In E. Barratt (Ed.), *Sociomedia: Multimedia, hypermedia, and the social construction of knowledge* (pp. 257-296). Cambridge, MA: MIT Press.

Golson, E. (1995). Perils and promises of paths not taken: Studies of student hypertexts. *Computers and Composition, 12*(3), 295-308.

Graham, D. (1991). The emblematic hyperbook. In P. Delany & G. P. Landow (Eds.), *Hypermedia and literary studies* (pp. 273-286). Cambridge: MIT Press.

Grice, R., & Ridgway, L. S. (1993). Usability and hypermedia: Toward a set of usability criteria and measures. *Technical Communication, 40*(3), 429-437.

Guba, E. G., & Lincoln, Y. S. (1989). *Fourth generation evaluation.* Newbury Park, CA: Sage.

Haas, C. (1996). *Writing technology: Studies on the materiality of literacy.* Mahwah, NJ: Lawrence Erlbaum Associates.

Haas, C., & Neuwirth, C. (1994). Writing the technology that writes us. In S. Hilligoss & C. Selfe (Eds.), *Literacy and computers: The complications of teaching and learning with technology* (pp. 319-333). New York: Modern Language Association.

Halio, M. P. (1990). Student writing: Can the machine maim the message? *Academic Computing 4,* 16-46.

Halliday, M.A. K., & Hasan, R. (1976). *Cohesion in English.* London: Longman.

Harpold, T. (1991). Threnody: Psychoanalytic digressions on the subjects of hypertexts. In P. Delany & G. P. Landow (Eds.), *Hypermedia and literary studies* (pp. 171-181). Cambridge: MIT Press.

Hartman, A., Diem, J. E., & Quagliana, M. (1992). The many faces of multimedia: How new technologies might change the nature of the academic endeavor. In E. Barrett (Ed.), *Sociomedia: Multimedia, hypermedia, and the social construction of knowledge* (pp. 175-192). Cambridge: MIT Press.

Hawisher, G. E. (1989). Research and recommendations for computers and composition. In G. E. Hawisher & C. L. Selfe (Eds.), *Critical perspectives on computers and composition instruction* (pp. 44-69). New York: Teachers College Press.

Hawisher, G. E., LeBlanc, P., Moran, C., & Selfe, C. L. (1996). *Computers and the teaching of writing in American higher education, 1979-1994: A history.* Norwood, NJ: Ablex.

Hawisher, G. E., & Selfe, C. L. (Eds.). (1991a). *Evolving perspectives on computers and composition studies.* Urbana, IL: NCTE.

Hawisher, G.E., & Selfe, C.L. (1991b). The rhetoric of technology and the electronic writing class. *College Composition and Communication, 42,* 55-65.

Hayes, J. R., Young, R. E., Matchett, M. L., McCaffrey, M., Cochran, C., & Hajduk, T. (1992). *Reading empirical research studies: The rhetoric of research.* Hillsdale, NJ: Lawrence Erlbaum Associates.

Hillman, D. C., Willis, D. J., & Gunawardena, C. N. (1994). Learner-interface interaction in distance education: An extension of contemporary models and strategies for practitioners. *The American Journal of Distance Education, 8*(2), 30-42.

Horton, W. K. (1990). *Designing & writing on-line documentation: Help files to hypertext.* New York: Wiley.

Howard, A. (1988). Hypermedia and the future of ethnography. *Cultural Anthropology, 3,* 304-315.

Hull, G., & Rose, M. (1989). Rethinking remediation: Toward a social-cognitive understanding of problematic reading and writing. *Written Communication, 8,* 139-154.

Hull, G., Rose, M., Fraser, K. L., & Castellano, M. (1991). Remediation as social construct: Perspectives from an analysis of classroom discourse. *College Composition and Communication, 42,* 299-339.

Innis, R. E. (1985). *Semiotics: An introductory anthology.* Bloomington: Indiana University Press.

Jenkins, J. J. (1963). Mediated associations: Paradigms and situations. In C.N. Cofer & B. S. Musgrave (Eds.), *Verbal behavior and learning* (pp. 210-257). New York: McGraw-Hill.

Johnson, R. R. (1995). Romancing the hypertext: A rhetorical/historio-graphical view of the "hyperphenomenon." *Technical Communication Quarterly, 4*(1), 11-22.

Johnson-Eilola, J. (1994). Reading and writing in hypertext: Vertigo and euphoria. In C. L. Selfe & S. Hilligoss (Eds.), *Literacy and computers: The complications of teaching and learning with technology* (pp. 195-219). New York: Modern Language Association.

Jonassen, D. H. (1988). Designing structured hypertext and structuring access to hypertext. *Educational Technology, 28*(11), 13-16.

Jonassen, D. H. (1989). *Hypertext/hypermedia.* Englewood Cliffs, NJ: Educational Technologies Publications.

Joyce, M. (1988). Siren shapes: Exploratory and constructive hypertexts. *Academic Computing, 3*(4), 10-42.

Joyce, M. (1992). *Afternoon, a story* [computer disk]. Watertown, MA: Eastgate Systems.

Joyce, M. (1995). *Of two minds: Hypertext pedagogy and poetics.* Ann Arbor: University of Michigan Press.

Kalmbach, J. (1988). Reconceiving the page: A short history of desktop publishing. *Technical Communication, 35,* 277-281.

Kaplan, N. (1991). Ideology, technology, and the future of writing instruc-tion. In G. E. Hawisher & C. L. Selfe (Eds.), *Evolving perspectives on computers and composition studies* (pp. 11-42). Urbana, IL: NCTE.

Kaplan, N., & Moulthrop, S. (1990). Other ways of seeing. *Computers and Composition, 7,* 89-102.

Kaplan, N., & Moulthrop, S. (1993). Seeing through the interface: Computers and the future of composition. In G. P. Landow & Paul Delany (Eds.), *The digital word: Text-based computing in the humani-ties* (pp. 253-270). Cambridge, MA: MIT Press.

Kaufer, D. S. (1993). *Communication at a distance.* Hillsdale, NJ: Lawrence Erlbaum Associates.

Kearsley, G. (1988). Authoring considerations for hypertext. *Educational Technology, 28*(11), 1-24.

Kintsch, W., & Greene, E. (1978). The role of culture—Specific schemata in the comprehension and recall of stories. *Discourse Processes, 1,* 1-13.

Kintsch, W., & van Dijk, T. (1978). Toward a model of text comprehen-sion and production. *Psychological Review, 85,* 363-394.

Landow, G. P. (1991). The rhetoric of hypermedia: Some rules for authors. In P. Delaney & G. P. Landow (Eds.), *Hypermedia and liter-ary studies* (pp. 81-103). Cambridge, MA: MIT Press.

Landow, G. (1992a). Bootstrapping hypermedia: Student-created docu-ments, intermedia, and the social construction of knowledge. In E. Barratt (Ed.), *Sociomedia: Multimedia, hypermedia, and the social con-struction of knowledge* (pp. 195-217). Cambridge, MA: MIT Press.

Landow, G. (1992b). *Hypertext: The convergence of contemporary critical theory and technology.* Baltimore, MD: Johns Hopkins University Press.

Landow, G. P. (1994a). Introduction. In G. P. Landow (Ed.), *Hypertext theory* (pp. 2-32). Baltimore, MD: Johns Hopkins University Press.

Landow, G. P. (1994b). What's a critic to do? Critical theory in the age of hypertext. In G. P. Landow (Ed.), *Hyper/text/theory* (pp. 1-50). Baltimore, MD: Johns Hopkins University Press.

Landow, G., & Delany, P. (1993). Managing the digital word: The text in an age of electronic reproduction. In G. Landow & P. Delany (Eds.), *The digital word: Text-based computing in the humanities* (pp. 13-28). Cambridge, MA: MIT Press.

Langacker, R. W. (1987). *Foundations of cognitive grammar: Theoretical prerequisites* (Vol. 1). Stanford, CA: Stanford University Press.

Lanham, R. A. (1992). *The electronic word: Democracy, technology, and the arts.* Chicago: University of Chicago Press.

Lanham, R. A. (1996). *A hypertext handlist of rhetorical terms* [computer file]. Berkeley: University of California Press.

Larsen, D. (1993). *Marble springs* [Computer disk]. Watertown, MA: Eastgate Systems.

Lauer, J. M., & Asher, J. W. (1988). *Composition research: Empirical designs.* New York: Oxford University Press.

Lauer, J., Montague, G., Lundsford, A., & Emig J. (1985). *Four worlds of writing* (2nd ed.). New York: Harper & Row.

Lee, H. (1960). *To kill a mockingbird.* New York: Warner Books.

Lincoln, Y., & Guba, E. (1985). *Naturalistic inquiry.* Beverly Hill, CA: Sage.

Lynch, P. (1988). *The surface anatomy of birds* (hypertext document). New Haven, CT: Yale Center for Advanced Instructional Media. Biomedical Communications. Yale University School of Medicine, Yale University.

McDaid, J. (1991). Toward an ecology of hypermedia. In G. E. Hawisher & C. L. Selfe (Eds.), *Evolving perspectives on computers and composition studies* (pp. 203-223). Urbana, IL: NCTE.

McKnight, C., Dillon, A., & Richardson, J. (1991). *Hypertext in context.* New York: Cambridge University Press.

Microsoft Word. (1994). Redmond, WA: Microsoft.

Mirel, B. (1988). The politics of usability: The organizational functions of an in-house manual. In S. Doheny-Farina (Ed.), *Effective documentation: What we have learned from research.* Cambridge, MA: MIT Press.

Moore, M. (1993). Three types of interaction. In K. Harry, M. John, & D. Keegan (Eds.), *Distance education: New perspectives* (pp. 19-24). New York: Routledge.

Morse, J. M. (1994). Designing funded qualitative research. In N. K. Denzin & Y. S. Lincoln (Eds.), *Handbook of qualitative research* (pp. 220-235). Thousand Oaks, CA: Sage.

Morton, D. B. (1994). Socially constructed individuals: Integrating writing theories. *English in Texas, 25*(4), 7-12.

Moulthrop, S. (1991). The politics of hypertext. In G. E. Hawisher & C. L. Selfe (Eds.), *Evolving perspectives on computers and composition studies* (pp. 253-271). Urbana, IL: NCTE.

Moulthrop, S. (1992). Infomand and rhetoric. *Writing on the Edge, 4*(1), 103-127.

Moulthrop, S. (1994). Rhizome and resistance: Hypertext and the dreams of a new culture. In G. Landow (Ed.), *Hyper/text/theory* (pp. 299-319). Baltimore: John Hopkins University Press.

Moulthrop, S., & Cohen, S. (1996). *The color of television. Media ecology: A journal of intersections* [Online]. Available: http://raven.ubalt.edu/features/media_ecology/lab/96/cotv/cotv01.html [1998, October 8].

Moulthrop, S., & Kaplan, N. (1994). They became what they beheld: The futility of resistance in the space of electronic writing. In C. L. Selfe & S. Hilligoss (Eds.). *Literacy and computers: The complications of teaching and learning with technology* (pp. 220-227). New York: Modern Language Association.

Murray, D. (1982). Teaching the other self: The writer's first reader. *College Composition and Communication, 33*(2), 140-147.

Myers, J. (1992). The social contexts of school and personal literacy. *Reading Research Quarterly, 27*(4), 297-333.

Neilsen, A. (1989). *Critical thinking and reading: Empowering learners to think and act.* Bloomington, IN: ERIC.

Nelson, T. H. (1974). *Dream machines.* Redmond, WA: Author.

Nelson, T. H. (1984). *Literary machines.* Palo Alto, CA: Author.

Nielsen, J. (1989). *Hypertext and hypermedia.* San Diego, CA: Academic Press.

Nielsen, J. (1994). *Multimedia and hypertext.* Cambridge, MA: Academic Press.

Newkirk, T. (1991). The politics of composition research: The conspiracy against experience. In R. Bullock & J. Trimbur (Eds.), *The politics of writing instruction: Postsecondary* (pp. 119-135). Portsmouth, NH: Heinemann/Boynton-Cook.

Norman, D. A. (1993). *Things that make us smart: Defending human attributes in the age of the machine.* Reading, MA: Addison-Wesley.

Novak, J. D. (1965). A model for the interpretation and analysis of concept formation. *Journal of Research in Science Teaching, 3,* 72-83.

O' Hare, F. (1986-1987). *Freshman English program, The Ohio State University: A handbook.* Columbus: Ohio State University.

Ofoto 2.0.2. (1993). Larkspur, CA: Light Source Computer Images.

Ohmann, R. (1985). Literacy, technology, and monopoly capital. *College English, 47*(7), 675-689.

Ong, W. J. (1982). *Orality and literacy: The technologizing of the word.* New York: Methuen.

Palumbo, D. B., & Prater, D. (1992). The role of hypermedia in synthesis writing. *Computers and Composition, 10*(2), 59-70.

Phelps, L. W. (1988). *Composition as a human science: Contributions to the self-understanding of a discipline.* New York: Oxford University Press.

Phelps, L. W. (1995). Images of student writing: The deep structure of teacher response. In C. Anson (Ed.), *Writing and response: Theory, practice, and research* (pp. 37-67). Urbana, IL: NCTE.

Porter, J. E. (1986). Intertextuality and the discourse community. *Rhetoric Review, 5*, 34-47.

Porter, J. E. (1992). *Audience and rhetoric.* Englewood Cliffs, NJ: Prentice Hall.

Postman, N. (1985) *Amusing ourselves to death: Public discourse in the age of show business.* New York: Penguin.

Redish, J. C. (1993). Understanding readers. In C. M. Barnum & S. Carliner (Eds.), *Techniques for technical communicators* (pp. 14-41). New York: Macmillan.

Rose, M. (1985). Complexity, rigor, evolving methods, and the puzzle of writer's block: Thoughts on composing-process research. In M. Rose (Ed.), *When a writer can't write: Studies in writer's block and other composing-process problems* (pp. 227-260) New York: Guilford.

Rosenblatt, L. (1978). *The reader, the text, the poem.* Carbondale: Southern Illinois University Press.

Rubens, P., & Rubens, B. K. (1988). Usability and format design. In S. Doheny-Farina (Eds.), *Effective documentation: What we have learned from research* (pp. 213-233). Cambridge, MA: MIT Press.

Rumelhart, D.E., & Ortony, A. (1977). The representation of knowledge in memory. In R.C. Anderson, R.J. Spiro, & W. E. Montague (Eds.), *Schooling and the acquisition of knowledge* (pp. 95-135). Hillsdale, NJ: Lawrence Erlbaum Associates.

Russell, D. R. (1991). *Writing in the academic disciplines, 1870-1999: A curricular history.* Carbondale: Southern Illinois University Press.

Schank, R., & Abelson, R. (1977). *Scripts, plans, goals and understanding.* Hillsdale, NJ: Lawrence Erlbaum Associates.

Schmidt, B. (1992-96). *Datamaster.* St. Louis: agpw.

Schor, I. (1987). *Critical teaching & everday life.* Chicago: University of Chicago Press.

Schor, I. (1992). *Empowering education: Critical teaching for social change.* Chicago: University of Chicago Press.

Schriver, K. (1992). Cognition and context. In G. Kirsch & P. A. Sullivan (Eds.), *Methods and methodology in composition research* (pp. 190-216). Carbondale: Southern Illinois University Press.

Selfe, C. (1989). Redefining literacy: The multilayered grammars of computers. In G. Hawisher & C. Selfe (Eds.), *Critical perspectives on computers and composition instruction* (pp. 3-15). New York: Teachers College Press.

Selfe, C. L., & Hilligoss, S. (Eds.). (1994). *Literacy and computers: The complications of teaching and learning with technology*. New York: Modern Language Association.

Shirk, H. N. (1991). Hypertext and composition studies. In G. E. Hawisher & C. L. Selfe (Eds.), *Evolving perspectives on computers and composition studies* (pp. 173-176). Urbana, IL: NCTE.

Shirk, H. N. (1992). Cognitive architecture in hypermedia instruction. In E. Barrett (Ed.), *Sociomedia: Multimedia, hypermedia, and the social construction of knowledge* (pp. 79-93). Cambridge: MIT Press.

Shneiderman, B., & Kearsley, G. (1988). *Hypertext hands-on: An introduction to a new way of accessing and organizing information*. Reading, MA: Addison-Wesley.

Shuman, R. B. (1993). The past as present: Reader response and literary study. *English Journal, 82*(5), 30-32.

Silko, L. M. (1977). *Ceremony*. New York: Penguin Books.

Slatin, J. (1988). Hypertext and the teaching of writing. In E. Barrett (Ed.), *Text, context, and hypertext* (pp. 111-129). Cambridge, MA: MIT Press.

Slatin, J. (1990a) Reading hypertext: Order and coherence in a new medium. *College English, 52,* 870-883.

Slatin, J. M (1990b). Text and hypertext: Reflections on the role of the computer in teaching modern American poetry. In D. S. Miall (Ed.), *Humanities and the computer: New directions* (123-135). Oxford: Oxford University Press.

Slatin, J. (1991). Reading hypertext: Order and coherence in a new medium. In P. Delany & G. P. Landow (Eds.), *Hypermedia and literary studies* (pp. 153-169). Cambridge, MA: MIT Press.

Smith, C. F. (1991). Reconceiving hypertext. In G. E. Hawisher & C. L. Selfe (Eds.), *Evolving perspectives on computers and composition studies* (pp. 224-252). Urbana, IL: NCTE.

Smith, C. F. (1994). Hypertextual thinking. In C. L. Selfe & S. Hilligoss (Eds.). *Literacy and computers: The complications of teaching and learning with technology* (pp. 264-281). New York: Modern Language Association.

Smith F. (1982). *Writing and the writer*. New York: Holt, Rinehart & Winston.

Smith, K. (1988). Hypertext—Linking to the future. *Online, 12*(2), 32-40.

SoundEdit Pro 3.0. (1994). San Francisco, CA: MacroMind/Paracomp.

Spivey, N. N. (1997). *The constructivist metaphor: Reading, writing, and the making of meaning.* New York: Academic Press.

Stern, R., & Robinson, R. (1994). Perception and its role in communication and learning. In D. Moore & F. Dwyer (Eds.). *Visual literacy: A spectrum of visual learning* (pp. 31-52). Englewood Cliffs, NJ: Educational Technology.

Strasma, K. (1991). *Saddam Hussein, Keneth Burke, and "composition."* Unpublished master's thesis, Illinois State University, Normal, IL.

Strasma, K. (1995, March). *A rhetoric of hypertext links: Connections to, from, and within hypertext documents.* Paper presented at the Conference on College Composition and Communication, Washington, DC.

TelevEyes/Pro. (1993). Dedham, MA: Digital Vision.

Tuman, M. (1992). *Word perfect: Literacy in the computer age.* Pittsburgh, PA: University of Pittsburgh Press.

Vygotsky, L. S. (1962). *Thought and language.* Cambridge, MA: MIT Press.

Wahlstrom, B. J. (1994). Communication and technology: Defining a feminist presence in research and practice. In C. L. Selfe & S. Hilligoss (Eds.), *Literacy and computers: The complications of teaching and learning with technology* (pp. 171-185) New York: Modern Language Association.

Weise, E. (1995). User control in hypermedia instructional applications: A literature review. *Technical Communication Quarterly, 4*(1), 23-34.

White, M., & Wittrock, M.C .(1974). Learning as a generative process. *Educational Psychologist, 11,* 87-95.

Wickelgren, W.A. (1974). *How to solve problems.* San Francisco: Freeman.

Woolley, B. (1992).*Virtual worlds: A journey in hype and hyperreality.* Cambridge, MA: Blackwell.

Author Index

Subject Index

Historical Perspectives in Marketing

Essays in Honor of
Stanley C. Hollander

Edited by

Terence Nevett
Central Michigan University

Ronald A. Fullerton
Southeastern Massachusetts University

Lexington Books
D.C. Heath and Company/Lexington, Massachusetts/Toronto

Library of Congress Cataloging-in-Publication Data

Historical perspectives in marketing.

  Includes index.
  1. Marketing—History.   2. Hollander, Stanley C.,
1919–   . I. Hollander, Stanley C., 1919–   .
II. Nevett, T. R. (Terence R.)   III. Fullerton, Ronald A.
HF5415.H544 1988   380.1'09   87–45770
ISBN 0–669–16968–4

Published simultaneously in Canada
Printed in the United States of America
International Standard Book Number: 0–669–16968–4
Library of Congress Catalog Card Number: 87–45770

The paper used in this publication meets the minimum requirements of American National
Standard for Information Sciences—Permanence of Paper for Printed Library Materials, ANSI
Z39.48–1984. ⊚™

88 89 90 91 92 8 7 6 5 4 3 2 1

To Stanley C. Hollander

Contents

Preface

This book reflects the surge of interest in marketing's past, which has occupied students of both marketing and history in recent years. It also reflects the impact of, and the affection held for, the scholar in whose honor these contributions were written—Stanley C. Hollander. Of all the interests of this wide-ranging scholar, marketing history has been the greatest.

Well-meaning friends and colleagues warned us not to become involved with this book. While there was unanimous agreement that this was a truly suitable way to honor Stan Hollander, they felt the practical problems involved in coordinating the efforts of so distinguished a group of authors would prove insurmountable. They were wrong, for which we would like to thank all those whose work appears in this volume. Every single manuscript arrived in time to meet our less-than-generous deadlines; the comments of reviewers and editors were graciously acknowledged and acted upon. We could not have asked for more.

We also wish to express our appreciation of the perceptive and insightful critiques provided by our reviewers. Since some of our authors acted as reviewers as well, we thank them while respecting their anonymity. We can, however, publicly acknowledge the contributions of Professors A. Fuat Firat of Appalachian State University and Alberto Lima of Michigan State University, the latter being one of Stanley Hollander's former students.

Lastly, we wish to thank the staff of Lexington Books for their help and encouragement. Together with our contributors and reviewers they overcame our trepidations and helped make our job both pleasant and rewarding.

Terence Nevett, Lansing, Michigan
Ronald A. Fullerton, Warwick, Rhode Island

Introduction

Why Marketing History?

It is time to develop a historical perspective on marketing. Marketing is one of the mainsprings of modern Western life, energizing and helping shape the cultural and political as well as the social and economic aspects of our existence. But it did not achieve this position yesterday. It has a history far longer and richer than commonly thought—and hitherto neglected by both marketers and historians. This book is an effort to begin serious and systematic exploration of the historical heritage and significance of marketing.

Marketing's history includes the development and impact of actual marketing practices and institutions, and the articulated thought about these. Both thought and practice are covered here. During the twentieth century more and more of the formal published thinking has come from the academic discipline of marketing; practicing marketers certainly think, but are restrained from publishing by competitive and time considerations. Formal marketing thought has been enriched by heavy borrowing from such disciplines as economics, social psychology, statistics, and psychology; it is beginning to draw upon the humanities as well. When marketing scholars speak of marketing "thought", they are referring to the findings of the discipline, which include far more than the high-level generalities that are conventionally associated with "thought." While some of these findings can seem mundane, even trivial, they have often had far more impact upon everyday life than most of the grand theoretical effusions of, say, economics. They are important.

Marketing's history has been neglected by historians and scholars of marketing alike. For historians, this has meant slighting one of the *central* elements of successful industrialization and of the modes of life and consumption which have predominated in the Western world for the past century and a half—and which are now spreading rapidly in some other parts of the world. How can we understand the development of modern life, of modernity itself, if we ignore *or oversimplify* one of its major formative elements? Yet many historians continue to assume that industrialization was basically a matter of increased production, ignoring the classic suggestion of Gilboy (1932) that increased marketing was required as well. Of those historians who do take marketing into account most, unfortunately, tend to define it far too narrowly. Typically, marketing is equated with advertising alone—and the efficacy of advertising overvalued. The complex interplay of product design, pricing, wholesale and retail distribution, and promotional efforts other than advertising (e.g., salesmanship) with advertising—an interplay in which advertising frequently plays a minor role—is thereby ignored.

Among the relative handful of American historians who have focused upon marketing history in recent years, advertising has been by far the most popular topic (e.g., Fox 1984; Marchand 1985; Pope 1983; Schudson 1984), followed by department stores—especially those which advertised and otherwise promoted themselves heavily (e.g., Miller 1981; Williams 1982). These are valuable studies, but deal with only a fraction of marketing. Only the work of Braudel (1982) and McKendrick, Brewer, and Plumb (1982) suggests marketing's full scope, but these cover neither the nineteenth and twentieth centuries nor the United States. There remains a great deal for historians to do, literally hundreds of dissertations and monographs for the United States alone.

There is also a great deal for marketing scholars to do with marketing history, and for two reasons. First, because it is their own heritage, to which they can bring insights few if any historians would possess; and second, because marketing cannot be fully understood apart from its history.

Marketing is a complex topic. It needs the richness and subtlety of well-done historical analysis if it is to be adequately understood. As one of the contributors to this book pointed out some years ago, there is no substitute for historical analysis in determining what the strengths and weaknesses—the actual achievements—of marketing efforts have in fact been and most probably will be (Savitt 1980). Historical analysis encourages us to confront the inevitability as well as the complexity of change, topics for the understanding of which the now-predominant U.S. social science-based analyses provide pitifully inadequate guidance (Fullerton 1987). While the social sciences have added greatly to the analytical power available to marketing academics and practitioners, their predominantly normative and ahistorical thrust has also inadvertently limited it by discouraging historical analysis. Among the consequences, as Stanley Hollander has long admonished, is too much reinvention of the wheel, which in turn has engendered a sometimes unjustified sense of progress among marketers.

That historical analysis can complement and enrich our present array of analytical approaches to marketing will become evident during the course of these pages. Long before this book was conceived, however, Stanley Hollander was demonstrating incisively, repeatedly, and wittily the multiple strengths of historical analysis in marketing. To historians, moreover, he was demonstrating the value of historical analyses that utilized as source material the past findings of marketing scholars.

Stanley C. Hollander and Marketing History

Stanley Hollander has done more than anyone else to further the study of marketing history. One of the best-known U.S. marketing scholars for the past thirty years, he was written authoritatively on a variety of topics— retailing, government regulation of marketing, marketing and third world economic development, international marketing, and the teaching of ethics. He has been a scholar in the classical sense of the word, a Renaissance man among marketers. For in addition to all of his other scholarship, he has explored marketing history, producing a rich stream of work which has now been flowing for nearly four decades; it is detailed in the Appendix. The stream began with pamphlets on the history of sales promotion and of labels (1953; 1956). These were written partly to help finance Hollander's doctoral studies, which themselves produced a valuable historical perspective on U.S. discount retailing. The stream continued with studies of a national buying club in existence from 1916 to 1953 (1959) and of Henry Ford's innovative commissary (1960), four important essays on the evolution of retail institutions (1960; 1966; 1977; 1980), thoughtful articles on nineteenth century U.S. efforts to repress traveling salesmen (1964), studies of surrogate shoppers (1971) and past episodes of consumerism (1972/1973); and has rolled on down to the recent analyses of sumptuary legislation (1984), past services' marketing (1985), and historians' views of consumption (1986). As this is being written, Hollander is researching the marketing reform ideas embodied in the U.S. Industrial Commission Report of 1901. His work has been published in major historians' outlets as well as marketing ones, evidence of its acceptance by both disciplines.

In addition to his own writings, Hollander has helped to further the study of marketing history by others. Some of his recent work is collaborative with doctoral students, for example. He has been the prime mover behind the marketing history conferences held at Michigan State University in 1983, 1985, and 1987, and future conferences which he has firmly scheduled for 1989 and 1991. Attended by an international group of scholars, including historians and historical sociologists in addition to marketers, these conferences have inspired a small but increasingly sophisticated—and growing—body of historical work (Hollander and Savitt 1983; Hollander and Nevett 1985; Nevett and Hollander 1987).

As the chapter in this book by Rassuli argues, Hollander's historical oeuvre constitutes a significant contribution to marketing knowledge. His work has demonstrated that marketing—as we know it today—does indeed have a history, a rich and interesting one. It has demonstrated the power of historical analysis to generate concepts that illuminate current marketing institutions and practices, to suggest what future ones may be like, and to improve the caliber of marketing conceptualization.

Hollander has frequently employed historical analysis to generate hypotheses, concepts, theories, and scenarios of the future, an approach which has traditionally been used—to good effect—more by historical sociologists (e.g., Max Weber, Werner Sombart, Immanuel Wallerstein) than by historians. The concept of the surrogate shopper, for example, was derived by Hollander from a "now almost completely forgotten marketing functionary [of the period 1850–1940], the . . . 'professional shopper' " (Hollander 1971, 218). Generalizing from this specific historical phenomenon, he was able to produce a useful concept for understanding some aspects of present-day buying behavior; the concept's enduring value is shown by the fact that is has recently been updated and elaborated by Solomon (1986) in the leading U.S. marketing journal. Hollander's historical examination of consumerism, done at the seeming apogee of U.S. consumer discontent (1972/1973), generated the scenario that consumerism would recur periodically in the future just as it had in the past—that it was not unique to the early 1970s as many marketers believed.

Hollander has often challenged prevailing views in marketing with historical evidence. As do many professional historians, he has emphasized the *complexity* of actual temporal phenomena as against easy generalities and simple conceptualizations. His 1954 doctoral dissertation (which has recently been honored by inclusion in a reprint series) set the tone. Written when discounting by E. J. Korvette and other new retail firms was being widely touted as a revolutionary innovation in U.S. retailing, it presented massive evidence that various and numerous forms of discounting had been widespread for decades. It then pressed the case further by arguing that since discounts had been granted to so many individuals and groups for so many reasons for so long, the widespread belief that the one price (for all) policy had prevailed in U.S. retailing since the early twentieth century could not possibly be true.

Hollander did not deny that there was *something* new about post–World War II discounting, or that the one price system had become widespread; rather, he was refuting the simplistic—and therefore misleading—views of these phenomena which had become widespread. At the same time, he was implicitly challenging researchers to devise more accurate conceptualizations.

In a *Journal of Retailing* article published in 1966, Hollander showed how this could be done. His subject was the then-popular theory of the "retail accordion," according to which dominance in U.S. retailing has changed back and forth between retailers offering broad assortments and those offering specialized and narrower ones. The historical evidence revealed a much more complex picture that did not substantiate the simple sweep of the "accordion," said Hollander; he then proposed an elegant metaphorical conceptualization which it did substantiate—the "retail orchestra":

> Instead of comparing retailing to an accordion, we might picture it as an orchestra or band of accordion players . . . The orchestra will never consist entirely of only expanded or contracted accordions . . . [Instead,] the retail population will continue to resemble the composition of a well-designed shopping center (Hollander 1966, 31, 54).

Far from being the enemy of marketing theory he is sometimes said to be, Hollander in his historical oeuvre has encouraged the development of better theories, theories better able to comprehend and explain the complex realities of actual marketing. He has provided a valuable corrective to the tendencies of (some, not all) marketing scholars to oversimplify, whether in the quasi-comic book form of some textbooks, or in the uncritical aping of otherworldly approaches from the discipline of economics in journals.

About This Book

The contributions that make up this book reflect not only Stanley Hollander's passion for marketing history, but also the diversity and range of his scholarship and the strength of his personal influence. Directly and indirectly, through his own work and through encouraging others, he has constantly pointed the way to new areas of research and provided new perspectives on existing ones. His distinguished career as a teacher is reflected in the fact that several of his former students are among the contributors to this volume. The sheer diversity of what our contributors have regarded as "Hollander historical subjects" is in itself a tribute to the wide-ranging interests and amazing scholarship of this remarkable figure.

In the book's first section, which we have called "The Evolution of Marketing Thought," William and Isabella Cunningham assess Hollander's enormous contribution to the discipline of marketing, and the teams of Jagdish Sheth and Barbara Gross, and Shelby Hunt and Jerry Goolsby present complementary accounts of how thinking on marketing has developed over the course of the twentieth century. Sheth and Gross take a broad view, looking at the overall picture and identifying parallels in the study of marketing and of consumer behavior, which has become a discipline in its own right during the past two decades. Hunt and Goolsby concentrate on the once-dominant "functional" approach to marketing, tracing its rise and eventual fall from favor, and suggesting reasons why it is unlikely ever to regain its prominent position. (The reader may care to compare this view with that expressed by Ronald Savitt in the context of economic development—and keep in mind that Stanley Hollander has always enjoyed and encouraged scholarly controversy.)

The next section, "Marketing in its Historical Context," presents three contrasting views of the historical development of marketing, each demonstrating the value of Hollander's insistence that there are valuable lessons to be learned from history. George Fisk is concerned with the nature of historical change in marketing systems. He introduces concepts and theories of change from the biological and physical sciences which have promise in illuminating change over time in marketing. Ronald Fullerton distinguishes marketing in the generic sense, which has existed as long as trade, from the distinctive and powerful type of marketing that has developed in the modern Western world. Fullerton links Modern Western Marketing to capitalism, theorizing that the demise of the latter would also bring that of the former. Kathleen Rassuli, representing the latest generation of Hollander students, discusses some of the issues raised by her teacher's work in the area of marketing history, and uses the history of the early English book trade to demonstrate some of the lessons to be learned from marketing phenomena of the past.

Hollander has long been interested in the subject of economic development. In our third section, "Marketing and Economic Development over Time," two contributors illustrate how a historical perspective can help shed light on a process which has long occupied policymakers as well as scholars in several disciplines. Ronald Savitt contends that since development is essentially evolutionary, it can only be understood as a manifestation of historical change. E. Jerome McCarthy uses historical examples to present the concept of an index of orientation towards marketing; the index can help explain why there is or is not much economic development in a country.

"Historical Perspectives in Retailing," the fourth section, represents an area of study with which Stanley Hollander has been particularly associated over the last forty years; the three contributors to this section demonstrate once again the rewards awaiting the marketing student who searches out the lessons of marketing history. Edward W. Cundiff examines the evolution of retailing from a perspective which is at once historical and cross-cultural. Philip Kotler uses the history of the U.S. convenience store as the basis for predictions about its likely future. Roger Dickinson evaluates the price experiences of U.S. retailers in the 1950s, suggesting some of the implications of these experiences for the present day.

"Advertising: The Archaeology of Marketing" is the book's concluding section. The relationship of advertising to marketing history, we suggest, is similar to that of archaeology to other areas of historical study: it provides those artifacts without which it is impossible to construct an accurate picture of past events. Richard W. Pollay presents a definitive account of the major collections of past advertising housed in North America, while Terence Nevett assesses the influence of American ideas and practices on British advertising in the period before 1920.

All the chapters have been specially written in honor of Stanley Hollander. The contributors offer him the fruits of their labor with gratitude and with great affection.

References

Braudel, Fernand. 1982 (1979). *Civilization and Capitalism, 15th–18th Century: vol. II: The Wheels of Commerce,* translated by S. Reynolds. New York: Harper & Row.

Fox, Stephen. 1984. *The Mirror Makers: A History of American Advertising and its Creators.* New York: Morrow.

Fullerton, Ronald A. 1987. "The Poverty of Ahistorical Analysis: Present Weakness and Future Cure in U.S. Marketing Thought." In A. F. Firat, N. Dholakia, and R. Bagozzi, eds.. *Philosophical and Radical Thought in Marketing.* Lexington: Lexington Books. 97–116.

Gilboy, Elizabeth W. 1932. "Demand as a Factor in the Industrial Revolution." *Facts and Factors in Economic History.* Cambridge: Harvard University Press. 620–639.

Hollander, Stanley C. See Appendix.

Marchand, Roland. 1985. *Advertising the American Dream: Making Way for Modernity, 1920–1940.* Berkeley: University of California Press.

McKendrick, Neil, J. Brewer, and J. H. Plumb. 1982. *The Birth of a Consumer Society: the Commercialization of Eighteenth Century England.* Bloomington: Indiana University Press.

Miller, Michael B. 1981. *The Bon Marche: Bourgeois Culture and the Department Store 1869–1920.* Princeton: Princeton University Press.

Nevett, Terence, and S. C. Hollander, eds. 1987. *Marketing in Three Eras: Proceedings of the Third Conference on Marketing History,* East Lansing: Department of Marketing and Transportation, Michigan State University.

Pope, Daniel. 1983. *The Making of Modern Advertising.* New York: Basic Books.

Savitt, Ronald. 1980. "Historical Research in Marketing." *Journal of Marketing* 44 (Fall). 52–58.

Schudson, Michael. 1984. *Advertising: the Uneasy Persuasion.* New York: Basic Books.

Solomon, Michael R. 1986. "The Missing Link: Surrogate Consumers in the Marketing Chain." *Journal of Marketing* 50 (October). 208–218.

Williams, Rosalind H. 1982. *Dream Worlds: Mass Consumption in Late Nineteenth Century France.* Berkeley: University of California Press.

Appendix
Stanley C. Hollander's Writings on Marketing History

1953   *Sales Devices Throughout the Ages.* New York: Joshua Meier Co.,

1954   "Discount Retailing: An Examination of Some Divergences from the One-Price System in American Retailing." Ph.D. diss., Economics Department, University of Pennsylvania. (Published in reprint by Garland Press, New York, in 1986.)

1956   *History of Labels.* New York: Alden Hollander. (Publisher was not a relative.)

1959   *The Rise and Fall of a Buying Club.* East Lansing: Bureau of Business and Economic Research, Michigan State University.

1960a   (with Gary Marple) *Henry Ford: Inventor of the Supermarket?* East Lansing: Bureau of Business and Economic Research, Michigan State University.

1960b   "The Wheel of Retailing." *Journal of Marketing* 24 (July). 37–42.

1963   "A Note on Fashion Leadership." *Business History Review* (Winter). 448–451.

1964a   "Anti-Salesmen Ordinances of the Mid-Nineteenth Century." In S. A. Greyser, ed., *Toward Scientific Marketing.* Chicago: American Marketing Association. 334–351.

1964b   "Nineteenth Century Anti-Drummer Legislation in the United States." *Business History Review* (Winter). 479–500.

1966   "Notes on the Retail Accordion." *Journal of Retailing* 42 (Summer). 29–40.

1971   "She 'Shops for You or With You': Notes on the Theory of the Consumer Purchasing Surrogate." In George Fisk, ed., *New Essays in Marketing Theory.* Boston: Allyn & Bacon. 218–240.

1973   "Consumerism and Retailing: A Historical Perspective." *Journal of Retailing* 48 (Winter). 6–22. (Special issue of the *Journal* edited by Roger Dickinson.)

1976   "Traveling Salesmen." *Dictionary of American History.* New York: Charles Scribner's Sons. 105–106.

1977a   "Comments of the Retail Life Cycle." *Journal of Retailing* 52 (Spring). 83–86.

1977b   "George Huntington Hartford, George Ludlum Hartford, and John Augustine Hartford." In J. A. Garraty, ed., *Dictionary of American Biography.* New York: Charles Scribner's Sons. 276–278.

These papers are concerned exclusively or near-exclusively with marketing history. Many of Hollander's other writings also have historical dimensions.

1980a   "The Effects of Industrialization on Small Retailing in the United States in the Twentieth Century." In S. Bruchey, ed, *Small Business in American Life*. New York: Columbia University Press. 212–239.

1980b   "Oddities, Nostalgia, Wheels and Other Patterns in Retail Evolution." In R. W. Stampfl and E. Hirschman, eds., *Competitive Structure in Retail Marketing: The Department Store Perspective*. Chicago: American Marketing Association. 78–87.

1980c   "Some Notes on the Difficulty of Identifying the Marketing Thought Contributions of the Early Institutionalists." In C. W. Lamb, Jr., and P. M. Dunne, eds., *Theoretical Developments in Marketing*. Chicago: American Marketing Association. 45–46.

1983   "Who and What is Important in Retailing and Marketing History." In Stanley C. Hollander and Ronald Savitt, eds., *Proceedings of the First North American Workshop on Historical Research in Marketing*. East Lansing: Department of Marketing & Transportation Administration, Michigan State University. 35–40.

1984a   "Herbert Hoover, Professor Levitt, Simplification and the Marketing Concept." In P. Anderson and M. Ryans, eds., *1984 Winter Educators' Conference Proceedings*. Chicago: American Marketing Association. 60–63.

1984b   "Sumptuary Laws: Demarketing by Edict." *Journal of Macromarketing* 4 (Spring). 3–16.

1985a   "A Historical Perspective on the Service Encounter." In J. Czepiel, M. Solomon, and C. Surprenant, eds., *The Service Encounter*. Lexington: Lexington Books. 49–64.

1985b   (with Terence Nevett) *Marketing in the Long Run: Proceedings of the Second Workshop on Historical Research in Marketing*. East Lansing: Department of Marketing and Transportation, Michigan State University.

1986a   (with Kathleen Rassuli) "Desire—Induced, Innate, Insatiable?" *Journal of Macromarketing* 6 (Fall). 4–24. (Analyzes historians' views of consumption.)

1986b   "The Marketing Concept: A Deja Vu." In George Fisk, ed., *Marketing Management Technology as Social Process*. New York: Praeger. 3–28.

Part I
The Evolution of Marketing Thought

Introduction

Hollander's seminars in the History of Marketing Thought have long been a feature of the doctoral program in marketing at Michigan State University, so it is fitting that William and Isabella Cunningham and Shelby Hunt, distinguished former students, should be among the contributors to this section.

William and Isabella Cunningham offer a concise and eloquent assessment of Hollander's contribution to the discipline of marketing. Through his broad learning and enormous analytical power, which have never been diluted or distracted by intellectual fads, Hollander has vastly increased the respect that the academic world grants the discipline of marketing. He has through his own example generated respect for all those who contribute to marketing thought.

The next two chapters in this section offer elegantly formulated and complementary accounts of the way marketing thought has evolved during the twentieth century. Jagdish Sheth and Barbara Gross identify four main stages in this evolutionary process. First, as the study of marketing emerged as something distinct and separate from economics, came the classical schools, embracing the commodity, functional, institutional, and—somewhat later—regional approaches. Distinguished by an emphasis on aggregate market behavior and borrowing from economics and sociology, the classical approach remained dominant until the early 1950s when it gave way to the managerial schools, which included the managerial, systemic and exchange approaches. Though they still borrowed from the social sciences, the focus shifted from aggregate to individual behavior and to the control of markets of the benefit of producers. The third stage, that of behavioral marketing, emerged in the 1960s. Including the organizational dynamics, consumerism, and buyer behavioral schools, it also focused on individual behavior but tended to draw from the behavioral sciences, particularly psychology, rather than the social sciences. Lastly the authors identify adaptive marketing, which is seeing the focus of marketing thought shift back to aggregate behavior, drawing from both the social and behavioral sciences.

Examining how the study of consumer behavior has developed over the same period, Sheth and Gross detect ways in which it has been influenced by the changes in marketing thought which have affected both the areas studied and the methodologies employed. During the classical period, consumer behavior study was directed toward consumption economics, dealing with such areas as aggregate demand and standards of living, household budgeting, conspicuous consumption and reference groups, and retail patronage. The preferred research methodologies included case studies, market surveys, and analysis of census data. The managerial period saw consumer behavior scholars focusing on the individual consumer and the household, and concerned with opinion leadership, the diffusion of innovations, brand loyalty, and the use of demographics and socioeconomic status as market segregation criteria. Research methodologies included the development of operations research models with longitudinal panel data, and econometric models with cross-sectional data.

In contrast to the earlier stages, the shift to behavioral marketing was inspired by the changing emphasis of consumer behavior study rather than the other way around. Consumer behavior scholars borrowed from social, cognitive, and organizational psychology to develop comprehensive models of consumer and organizational buying behavior; from clinical psychology to develop new concepts in motivation research, personality research, and psychographics; from cognitive psychology for work on information processing and involvement; and from psychological approaches to the study of attitudes. At the same time consumer behavior was also turning to the social sciences for laboratory experimentation techniques, focus group interviews, projective techniques, and cross-sectional mail and telephone survey techniques. By this point, the authors believe that consumer behavior, with its strong methodological and theoretical base, had become a mature subdiscipline growing increasingly independent of marketing.

As attention is once again being directed towards aggregate behavior, Sheth and Gross identify four areas with which marketers will become increasingly concerned: the globalization of markets, customer retention, consumer perceptions of competition, and behavior modification strategies. This in turn will lead consumer behavior research to concentrate on cultural influences on buying behavior, consumer satisfaction and dissatisfaction, comparison shopping, perceptions of competitive advertising and pricing, and the study of actual behavior and the techniques by which it can be modified. At the same time, the authors foresee an impending conflict of interest. On the one hand, the issues of concern to marketing will involve aggregate behavior and borrowing from the social sciences. On the other, there are many consumer behavior researchers, particularly those trained in psychology, whose *forte* is individual behavior, and who may well regard the social sciences as lacking in scientific rigor. What may eventually result, therefore, is the emergence of consumer behavior as an independent discipline.

Shelby Hunt and Jerry Goolsby present a somewhat different classification, dividing marketing thought into the commodity, institutional, functional, and managerial approaches. They trace the history of the functional approach, which having been influential for almost five decades, is now rarely mentioned by contemporary writers. Using a life-cycle analogy, they place the introductory stage in the first two decades of the present century. At that time writers such as Shaw and Weld were concerned with middlemen, pointing out the usefulness of marketing institutions in distribution— something that economists had largely ignored. The growth stage occurred from 1920 to 1940, which saw a rapid increase in the teaching of business in general and marketing in particular at university level. This created a need for textbooks, most of whose authors followed the functional approach, while elsewhere the functionalists generally tended to win academic debates with proponents of the commodity and institutional approaches. An important factor in helping to strengthen the functionalists' position was the Great Depression, which tended to divert attention from the production of goods and services and toward the problems of marketing them. At the same time, however, the commodity approach was falling out of favor because of its heavy agricultural orientation, while the study of institutions was beginning to seem less relevant than the study of the functions they carried out.

Hunt and Goolsby date the maturity stage as lasting approximately from 1951 to 1970. During this period the functional approach was refined by such writers as Alderson, Bucklin, Baligh and Richartz, and McGarry. The last named, however, also set the stage for its decline by suggesting it was too narrow and mechanistic to deal with the essentially dynamic nature of marketing. The six functions he proposed—contractual, merchandising, pricing, propaganda, physical distribution, and termination—may be regarded as representing the tasks of marketing management rather than functions in the hitherto accepted sense. When in 1960 McCarthy's *Basic Marketing* organized the subject on overtly managerial lines using the four Ps, the end was truly in sight, although the functional and managerial approaches coexisted for the next decade.

The authors ascribe the downfall of the functional approach to two main factors. One was the publication of the Gordon and Howell and Pierson reports which prompted business schools generally to adopt a more professional and managerial orientation in their teaching. The other was the changing nature of competition in American and overseas markets, which again focused attention on marketing, leading to the emergence of the marketing manager and thus to still further emphasis on the managerial and analytical aspects of marketing teaching.

The functional approach undoubtedly played a key role in the development of marketing thought. Its day is over, however, and the authors cannot foresee any circumstances in which it might regain its former prominence. Nevertheless, in his chapter in the section on Marketing and Economic Development, Savitt argues persuasively that it still has a role to play in the study of the process of economic development by helping us toward a better understanding of the role of marketing.

1

Stanley C. Hollander
The Scholar Behind Marketing and
Retail Theory

William H. Cunningham
Isabella C. M. Cunningham

Although marketing is coeval with society itself, its practices for many years were derided and dismissed by people who scorned marketing's practitioners as charlatans, social parasites who cynically preyed upon a naive and gullible public. The truth is, of course, that the early marketing innovators like Stanley Marcus or Joe C. Thompson have proven as critical to the development of today's economic and social lifestyle as were the inventors of the automobile and the sewing machine. The serious—and now so extensive and richly varied—literature of marketing has come about comparatively recently. And it is due in large measure to the work of Stanley C. Hollander that marketing is recognized as an academically respectable subject.

Until Hollander, retailing, even though it was widely acknowledged as the driving force and central focus of marketing, had not had lavished upon it the scholarly attention enjoyed by other and more esoteric topics. Only someone with the knowledge and vision of a true marketing scholar would think of devoting a career to developing a historical tradition for marketing and establishing the theoretical base for an understanding of retailing. In the more than fifteen books (many of which have been reprinted many times) and dozens of articles (frequently anthologized) Hollander has written or helped edit, the evident breadth of his historical vision and depth of his reading immeasurably enrich his writing.

It does not come amiss here to mention Hollander's humor. It is of a wry, British sort, caviare to the general, perhaps, spread very thin, but greatly welcomed by those well read in the subject but largely unaware of much except a tedious seriousness informing it. Of a book dealing with E.A. Filene, Stanley Hollander writes urbanely that it is "gossipy, somewhat malicious and therefore interesting." That he accepts traditional retailing practices with less than total awe is apparent when he comments tongue-in-cheek that retailers "believe that people who slink around the store in warm weather wearing loose, bulky coats with many inner pockets are up to no good; that gift sales will peak before Christmas, and that impulse goods should be displayed in high traffic locations." These two examples of Hollander's wit are found in his article "Retailing Theory: Some Criticism and Some Admiration," in Donald W. Stamfl and Elizabeth C. Hirschman's *Theory in Retailing: Traditional and Nontraditional Sources* (Chicago: American Marketing Association, 1981). Even Hollander's *titles* are amusing: "Let Us Contemplate our Navels—The Need for a Sociology of Marketing and Marketology" runs one; "If Small is Beautiful, Is a Very Small Sample Even Prettier?" asks another. Let it be understood that Stanley Hollander is that very rare academic: a serious scholar who is sophisticated enough not to treat his subject—or himself—with disproportionate seriousness. By his publications, by his willingness to share with his students his matchless knowledge of the literature, and by the uncompromising high standards of research he demands, Stanley Hollander has properly come to be known as the giant of marketing.

His theoretical generalizations have so far gone seriously unchallenged. "The Wheel of Retailing"—to date appearing in twenty-one anthologies—is a classic example of Hollander's ability to make thesis, antithesis, and synthesis result in unique and convincing conclusions to explain the complex socioeconomic phenomena of marketing. (How many scholars in the field, we wonder, are comfortable enough with Hegel to employ his thinking so effectively and appropriately in such a strikingly new area?)

The truth is that Hollander brings to bear on marketing as broad a range of scholarly interests as any classical scholar possesses when he studies a potsherd from antiquity. Repeatedly, Hollander has tied marketing practices and consumer behavior to economic theory—a macro perspective, so important in science, largely ignored by other marketing scholars. But although he is superbly versed in sophisticated economic theory, he is equally attentive to the homely example. Frequently in his lectures he would allude to the teacher of retailing under whom he studied as an undergraduate at New York University in the late 1940s—the man always came to class perfectly turned out, complete with hat and walking stick. There, said Hollander, recalling the experience to his own students, was proof that the personal presentation in certain types of trade is as important as what is said or sold.

While others were puzzled about how to quantify or classify cultural differences, Hollander simply—and, so the facts show, correctly—assumed they were important and pursued his research across national barriers long before International Marketing was included in the course offerings of academic departments. He has been concerned with causality, managerial practices, leadership, and environment—not necessarily in the order of their importance—as key elements in the development of his theory.

He has kept himself admirably informed on social changes and up to date on the newest academic research. Each of Hollander's publications is a response, a comment, or a positive critique enhancing our understanding of the subject under examination.

While insisting upon provoking thought, Stanley Hollander has held steadfast in eschewing sensationalism. He provides his students not with superficial evaluation but with rigorous, in-depth examination of empirical results. His obvious respect and affection for retailing have persisted undiminished for forty years. His knowledge, experience and, above all, his patience, have proved invaluable to his students and colleagues.

We academics have not yet, perhaps, fully appreciated just how significant a debt we owe to Stanley Hollander. We take for granted that marketing is a recognized discipline and indeed a science. Unlike our predecessors, we have not been obliged to defend our subject's academic respectability. The memory of peddlers, small store operators, and fast-talking salespeople has long been disassociated from the complex mathematical models we use in our courses. As a matter of fact, many of us are more concerned today about experimenting with the psychological involvement consumers may feel than we are about trying to understand the complicated interaction of marketing activities in a global economy.

Hollander has never forgotten and remains attentive today to what, precisely, differentiates theory from experimentation and a science from a catalogue of axioms. From the time of publication of his first article, appearing in 1948 in the *Journal of Retailing,* until the present day, Stanley Hollander has taught his colleagues about the paramount importance of macrophenomena as integral components of social research.

Stanley Hollander has remained indifferent to fads. He has stressed continually to the graduate students under his supervision the importance of a thorough background in art, economics, history and social history, literature, and language when developing their new insights into marketing phenomena.

He reminds us that enlightened and informed thought is superior to the mere amassing of survey data. Hollander is and will continue to be a stablizing influence in the field of marketing. His contribution is permanent.

2

Parallel Development of Marketing and Consumer Behavior: A Historical Perspective

Jagdish N. Sheth
Barbara L. Gross

Introduction

The history of consumer behavior with respect to substantive focus, research methodology, and influence from external disciplines has largely paralleled the history of marketing thought. The focus of marketing has historically been directed toward the market, with an emphasis on understanding the needs and behavior of consumers. As a result, the study of consumer behavior has been closely aligned with the study of marketing. Although traditionally an area of inquiry within the larger discipline of marketing, consumer behavior began in the 1960s to emerge as a subdiscipline, and is currently showing signs of becoming a discipline distinct from marketing. Four eras of marketing thought and research may be identified, each associated with different "schools of thought" and each influencing the focus of consumer behavior research.[1]

The first era of marketing's history was dominated by the classical schools of marketing thought. These schools of thought emerged in the early 1900s, as marketing divorced itself from the founding discipline of economics. The classical schools focused on aggregate market behavior and borrowed from such social science disciplines as economics and sociology. The second era of marketing thought was dominated by the managerial marketing schools. Emerging in the early 1950s, the managerial schools shifted the focus of marketing to individual behavior, yet continued the tradition of borrowing from the social sciences. The third era of marketing thought has been dominated by the behavioral marketing schools, emerging in the 1960s and continuing to influence marketing research today. The behavioral marketing schools have borrowed from the behavioral sciences, including several branches of psychology, in an effort to gain greater insight into individual behavior. Finally, the fourth era of marketing thought is associated with what we have termed the adaptive marketing schools, and is currently emerging. The adaptive schools are shifting the focus of marketing back to aggregate market behavior and borrowing from the social sciences as well as from the behavioral sciences.

It appears that each era of marketing thought has motivated interest in specific areas of consumer behavior. Further, each era has influenced the preferred research methodologies applied to consumer behavior. Figure 2–1 provides a summary of the specific schools of marketing thought associated with each era, and identifies emphases in consumer behavior that parallel the emphases of the marketing schools. The consumer behavior emphases identified as paralleling the adaptive marketing schools represent predictions for the future of consumer research.

Classical Marketing Schools and Parallel Consumer Behavior

The emergence of marketing as an independent discipline, divorced from the founding field of economics, has been eloquently documented by Bartels (1962). Three schools of thought were identified as emerging in the early 1900s. These have come to be known as the classical schools of marketing thought, and are specifically referred to as the commodity school, the functional school, and the institutional school. Additionally, we include the regional school as contributing to the first era. All four schools emphasized descriptive research focusing on aggregate market behavior, and borrowed heavily from the social sciences. Specifically, they were influenced most by demand theory in microeconomics, including concepts of consumer surplus and monopolistic competition (e.g., Marshall 1890; Chamberlin 1933); and by theories of spatial markets, trading areas, and rural versus nonrural market definitions in economic geography and economic demography (e.g., Marshall 1890; Ohlin 1933).

The commodity school has been the most enduring of the classical schools of thought. Writers identified with the commodity school have focused on the objects of market transactions as the central subject matter of marketing, and have attempted to differentiate various classes of products on the basis of their physical characteristics and associated consumer buying behavior. The focus of the commodity approach was originally on manufactured products and agricultural commodities, with the relevance of the commodity school to services not recognized until later.

The commodity school is perhaps most identified with the work of Copeland (1923), who generated the still popular convenience goods, shopping goods, specialty goods trichotomy. Even earlier, however, Parlin (1912) identified a threefold classification of goods as convenience goods, shopping goods, and emergency goods. Several subsequent writers (e.g., Holton 1958,

MARKETING AND CONSUMER BEHAVIOR FOCUS ON:

AGGREGATE MARKET BEHAVIOR	INDIVIDUAL BEHAVIOR

MARKETING AND CONSUMER BEHAVIOR RELIANCE ON:

SOCIAL SCIENCES

Era One	Era Two
Classical Marketing 1900-1950	Managerial Marketing 1950-1975
a. Commodity School b. Functional School c. Institutional School d. Regional School	a. Managerial School b. Systemic and Exchange School
Parallel Consumer Behavior 1930-1970	Parallel Consumer Behavior 1960-1975
a. Consumption Economics b. Retail Patronage	a. Opinion Leadership and Diffusion of Innovation b. Brand Loyalty c. Family Life Cycle d. Demographics and Socioeconomics

BEHAVIORAL SCIENCES

Era Four	Era Three
Adaptive Marketing 1975-Present	Behavioral Marketing 1965-Present
a. Macromarketing School b. Strategic Planning School	a. Organizational Dynamics School b. Consumerism School c. Buyer Behavior School
Parallel Consumer Behavior 1980-Present	Parallel Consumer Behavior 1960-Present
a. Cross-cultural Consumer Behavior b. Retaining Existing Customers c. Consumer Perception of Competition d. Behavior Modification and Focus on Behavior	a. Consumer Buying Behavior b. Motivation Research c. Personality d. Psychographics e. Attitudes f. Information Processing g. Involvement

Figure 2–1

1959; Luck 1959; Bucklin 1963; Kaish 1967) attempted to refine the Copeland classification by providing more precise definitions. In contrast, Aspinwall (1958) provided an independent classification based on the color spectrum (red, orange, and yellow goods). His classification was specified in terms of replacement rate, gross margin, degree of adjustment, time of consumption, and searching time.

In contrast with the other classical schools, the commodity perspective continues to hold the interest of contemporary marketing researchers. Most notably, Holbrook and Howard (1977) recently expanded the Copeland classification to include a fourth category termed preference goods. Enis and Roering (1980) and Murphy and Enis (1986) adopted and refined this classification, demonstrating its relevance to services and ideas as well as goods. They also distinguished between the consumer perspective and the marketer perspective in defining the four types of products, and related the classification to marketing strategy.

Emerging concurrent with the commodity school, the functional school promoted a focus on marketing activities or functions as the central subject matter of marketing. Shaw (1912), generally acknowledged as the founder of the functional approach, identified marketing functions performed by middlemen to include sharing the risk; transporting the goods; financing the operations; selling; and assembling, assorting, and reshipping. While not intending to provide an exhaustive list of marketing functions, Shaw's early contribution aroused the interest of other authors who sought to provide more conclusive classifications relevant to all marketing organizations (rather than just middlemen). This resulted in a number of alternative classifications (e.g., Weld 1917; Cherington 1920) and an unfortunate lack of unanimity.

By the mid-1930s, Ryan (1935) reported that at least twenty-six books and articles had been published that dealt with marketing functions, and that fifty-two distinct functions had been proposed by various authors. The lack of consensus among authors advocating the functional approach led Fullbrook (1940) to admonish that most authors had failed to recognize the distinction between the pervasive and inherent functional requirements of the marketing process (appropriately regarded as functions) and the specific activities involved in the performance of marketing functions (not appropriately regarded as functions). McGarry (1950), holding a similar view, proposed a classification consisting of the contactual function, the merchandising function, the pricing function, the propaganda function, the physical distribution function, and the termination function. Central to McGarry's classification was the idea that marketing functions may be accomplished via a variety of specific activities.

The functional school has received little attention since McGarry's contribution. However, a relatively recent article by Lewis and Erickson (1969) attempted to integrate the functional approach with the systems perspective, and identified two major functions of marketing as obtaining demand and servicing demand.

The third school of thought, the institutional school, emerged concurrent with the commodity and functional schools, focusing on the agents or organizations that perform marketing functions. The early stimulus for the institutional school was the belief among consumers that middlemen add excessive costs to products without a concomitant addition of value. Thus, early authors evaluated the roles of marketing intermediaries to determine whether the economic contributions of these organizations could justify their existence. Often regarded as the founder of the institutional school, Weld (1916) argued that middlemen such as wholesalers and retailers provide essential value added services by fostering time, place, and possession utilities (an approach also taken by Butler 1923). Further, Weld argued that marketing efficiency is enhanced through functional specialization, analogous to the efficiency achieved through production specialization. Other early authors seeking to justify the role of marketing middlemen (e.g., Breyer 1934) emphasized the role of middlemen in overcoming the various obstacles and resistances to the exchange of goods.

With these early authors having offered cogent justification for the existence of marketing intermediaries, subsequent contributors to the institutional school largely focused on the structure and evolution of distribution channel systems. As examples, Converse and Huegy (1940) discussed the potential benefits and risks associated with vertical integration, Balderston (1964) sought to provide a normative approach to optimal channel design, and McCammon (1965) identified various types of centrally coordinated channel systems and suggested reasons for their emergence. Both Bucklin (1965) and Mallen (1973) proposed theories to explain and predict the inclusion of intermediaries in channels of distribution. Bucklin introduced the principles of postponement and speculation to explain the creation of intermediate inventories between producers and consumers, and hence the use of indirect versus direct channels. Mallen proposed the concept of functional spin-off, hypothesizing that marketers will choose between performing functions themselves and subcontracting (spinning off) to functional specialists so as to minimize the overall cost of performing marketing functions.

Finally, the regional school viewed marketing as economic activity designed to bridge geographic or spatial gaps between buyers and sellers. The regional school is less well known than the commodity, functional, and institutional schools, and is often overlooked in discussions of schools of marketing thought. However, it is another early school that emphasized aggregate market behavior and borrowed from the social sciences.

Emerging somewhat later than the other classical schools, the origins of the regional school may be traced to the writings of Reilly (1931) and Converse (1943, 1949). These authors developed mathematical formulas termed "laws of retail gravitation" for determining the boundaries of retail trading areas and for predicting where consumers are most likely to shop. Their early work was continued by Huff (1962, 1964), and subsequent authors also examined wholesaler and manufacturer trading areas (Vaile, Grether, and Cox 1952; Revzan 1961; Goldstucker 1965). Grether (1950, 1983), a proponent of the regional approach for nearly half a century, enriched the contribution of the regional school substantially by using the regional perspective to analyze interregional trade (i.e., predict the flow of goods and resources among geographic regions varying in resource abundance).

As the classical schools dominated marketing thought prior to World War II, their reliance on social science disciplines, focus on aggregate markets, and use of research methodologies appropriate to the study of aggregate markets influenced the early study of consumer behavior. Early consumer researchers largely focused on consumption economics and retail patronage. Researchers focusing on consumption economics examined such issues as aggregate consumer demand and standards of living (e.g., Waite 1928; Zimmerman 1936; Wyand 1937; Norris 1941); household budgeting (e.g., Katona and Mueller 1953, 1956; Foote 1961); and the phenomena of conspicious consumption and consumption of necessities versus luxuries (Katona 1953; Katona, Strumpel, and Zahn 1971). Additionally, the focus of consumption economics contributed to early work on reference group influence as a determinant of consumer behavior (e.g., Bourne 1957; Stafford 1966). Researchers focusing on retail patronage examined such concepts as self-service (Robinson and ay 1956); retail gravitation (Reilly 1931; Huff 1962); and the wheel of retailing (Hollander 1960). Research methodologies favored by early consumer researchers included case studies, market surveys, and analysis of census data. As demonstrated by Bartels (1962) and by Lockley (1974), interest in conducting consumer research studies and in examining market research methodology proliferated during this period.

Managerial Marketing Schools and Parallel Consumer Behavior

The classical schools, with their emphasis on describing aggregate market behavior, gave way to the managerial marketing schools, with their emphasis on controlling individual behavior in the marketplace. These schools, referred to specifically as the managerial school and the systemic and exchange school, emerged in the 1950s in the midst of the unprecedented economic boom following World War II. Due to enhanced production capability and a proliferation of new product introductions, it was found that the supply of products exceeded the demand in most markets. Thus, it was desired to control market behavior for the benefit of producers.

The managerial school of thought advocated a managerial approach to marketing, maintaining that the market can be managed for the benefit of the marketer (e.g., Howard 1957; Kelley and Lazer 1958). Pioneering authors generated such well-known and enduring concepts as the marketing mix (Borden 1964); product differentiation and market segmentation (Smith

1956); the product life cycle (Levitt 1965; Smallwood 1973); and the marketing concept (McKitterick 1957; Keith 1960; Levitt 1960). Additionally, considerable emphasis was given to generating concepts and theories relevant to specific elements of the marketing mix. Early examples included the concepts of skimming and penetration pricing introduced by Dean (1950), the hierarchy of effects model of advertising developed by Lavidge and Steiner (1961), and the "need satisfaction theory of personal selling" advocated by Cash and Crissy (1958). Each of these areas and concepts continues to generate substantial research today.

The systemic and exchange school emerged in the late 1950s, advocating that marketing must be viewed as a system and that marketing exchanges or transactions are the central focus of marketing activity. The launching of the systemic and exchange perspective has been dually credited to McInnes (1964) and to Alderson (1957, 1965; Alderson and Martin 1965). McInnes (1964) proposed that markets result when the makers and users of products seek to satisfy their needs and wants through exchange. Alderson and Martin (1965) proposed the "law of exchange" to explain why two parties decide to enter into a transaction. Subsequently, others such as Kotler (1972a) and Hunt (1976) gave more explicit focus to the exchange perspective by arguing that transactions or exchanges should be considered the central subject matter of marketing. Bagozzi (1974, 1975, 1978, 1979) refined and elaborated on the concept of exchange, attempting to develop a theory of exchange to serve as the foundation of marketing thought and practice.

Although the managerial schools, like the classical schools, relied on the social sciences, authors associated with this era were generally influenced by more recently developed concepts and research methodologies. To illustrate, scholars associated with the managerial schools eagerly borrowed concepts and methods from the emerging field of managerial economics (e.g., Dean 1951). This branch of economics focused on the theory of the firm, rather than on demand theory, and contributed such influential concepts as monopolistic competition and product differentiation. The managerial schools were also influenced by research in communications on opinion leadership (Katz and Lazarsfeld 1955; Katz 1957); research in rural sociology and economic anthropology on diffusion of innovation (Rogers 1962); and research in sociology on social stratification and household structure (Loomis 1936; Warner and Lunt 1941; Glick 1947; Kahl 1953).

Accompanying the shift in emphasis within marketing was a similar shift in emphasis within consumer behavior. Rather than focusing on aggregate market behavior, consumer researchers began to focus on individual consumers or households as the unit of analysis. Like marketing as a whole, however, consumer behavior continued to borrow from the social sciences. As a result, research emerged on such topics as opinion leadership and diffusion of innovation (Silk 1966; Arndt 1967; Bass 1969; Myers and Robertson 1972); brand loyalty (Cunningham 1956; Frank 1962; Harary and Lipstein 1962; Kuehn 1962); life-cycle stages of households (Wells and Gubar 1966; Murphy and Staples 1979; Gilly and Enis 1982); and market segmentation based on demographics and socioeconomic status (Martineau 1958; Coleman 1960; Levy 1966; Wasson 1969; Sheth 1977). Preferred research methodology included developing stochastic and other operations research models with longitudinal panel data (to predict brand loyalty), and developing econometric models with cross-sectional data (to measure the impact of demographic and socioeconomic variables on buying behavior).

Behavioral Marketing Schools and Parallel Consumer Behavior

As the focus of research shifted away from aggregate markets and toward individual behavior, the marketing discipline observed that the behavioral sciences could contribute much to marketing's understanding of individual behavior in the marketplace. Thus, marketing scholars searched the literatures of various branches of psychology for concepts and research techniques to facilitate this understanding. In contrast with the other eras discussed in this paper, consumer behavior rather than marketing is credited with initiating the shift in perspective. Thus, during this era, rather than marketing leading consumer behavior, the study of consumer behavior led and influenced the study of marketing. At least three identifiable schools of thought emerged. These may be referred to as the organizational dynamics school, the consumerism school, and the buyer behavioral school (focusing on organizational buying behavior as well as on consumer behavior).

Authors associated with the behavioral marketing schools have been influenced by economic psychology, with its emphasis on customer expectations (Katona 1951, 1953); by clinical psychology, with its emphasis on subconscious motivation (Hall and Lindzey 1957); by organizational behavior, with its emphasis on power, conflict, and bounded rationality (March and Simon 1958; French and Raven 1959; Emerson 1962; Pondy 1967); and by social psychology, with its emphasis on the desire for cognitive consistency (Festinger 1957; Heider 1958). Consistent throughout these behavioral science disciplines is the finding that it is often perception, rather than objective reality, that drives human behavior. Thus, marketers concluded that much behavior relevant to marketing (e.g., among competitors, customers, and channel members) is driven by individual perception.

The emergence of the organizational dynamics school, with its emphasis on the behavior of distribution channel members, is generally credited to the work of Stern (1969), and particularly to his early papers on the topics of power and conflict in channels of distribution (Beier and Stern 1969; Stern and Gorman 1969; Rosenberg and Stern 1971; El-Ansary and Stern 1972). However, the behavioral approach to investigating interorganizational relationships in marketing may be traced to even earlier work by such authors as Ridgeway (1957) and Mallen (1963). Largely receiving impetus from Stern's work, a number of authors since the early 1970s have investigated the impact of power (Hunt and Nevin 1974; Lusch 1976; Etgar 1976; Frazier 1983b); conflict (Etgar 1979; Brown and Day 1981; Eliashberg and Michie 1984); and various influence strategies (Angelmar and Stern 1978; Frazier and Summers 1984; Frazier and Sheth 1985) on channel performance and relationships. Additionally, a number of authors have endeavored to develop general models of interorganizational relations (Robicheaux and El-Ansary 1975–1976; Stern and Reve 1980; Achrol, Reve, and Stern 1983; Frazier 1983a). The political economy perspective introduced by Stern and Reve (1980) and Achrol, Reve, and Stern (1983) has provided a framework for integrating the economic focus of the institutional school with the behavioral focus of the organizational dynamics school.

The consumerism school emerged in the late 1960s in response to the growing consumerism movement in the United States. Consumerism, as a social movement, focused on issues of consumer welfare, sought to correct the perceived imbalance of power between buyers and sellers, and criticized specific firms and industries as being guilty of negligence or malpractice (Beem 1973; Kotler 1972b). Concerned with the implications of consumerists' criticisms for marketing practice (Drucker 1969), a substantial amount of research effort has been devoted to investigating such issues as deceptive advertising (Jacoby and Small 1975; Gardner 1976; Armstrong, Gurol, and Russ 1979); the provision of product information (Day 1976; Resnik and Stern 1977; Houston and Rothschild 1980); marketplace treatment of disadvantaged consumers (Kassarjian 1969; Ashby 1973; Andreasen 1975); and consumer satisfaction, dissatisfaction, and complaining behavior (Day 1977; Hunt 1977; Day and Hunt 1979; Oliver 1980; Churchill and Surprenant 1982; Oliver and Bearden 1983).

As in other eras, the shift in emphasis associated with the behavioral marketing schools was paralleled by a similar shift in consumer behavior. As mentioned previously, however, the shift in emphasis within consumer behavior actually preceded and influenced the shift in marketing. Since its emergence in the early 1960s, the buyer behavior school has contributed the bulk of research to date on consumer behavior and organizational buying behavior.

As it became accepted that buying behavior is psychologically driven, the focus of consumer behavior turned toward examining the inner world of the individual buyer (Bauer 1960; Dichter 1964; Howard and Sheth 1969). Concepts borrowed from social, cognitive, and organizational psychology were used as building blocks in developing comprehensive models of consumer and organizational buying behavior (Andreasen 1965; Nicosia 1966; Howard and Sheth 1969; Engel, Kollat, and Blackwell 1968; Webster and Wind 1972; Sheth 1973); and concepts borrowed from clinical psychology served as the bases of motivation research, personality research, and psychographic research (Evans 1959; Dichter 1964; Kassarjian 1971; Wells and Tigert 1971; Wells 1975). Psychological approaches to the study of attitude (Rosenberg 1956; Katz 1960; Fishbein 1967; Fishbein and Ajzen 1975) influenced attitude research in consumer behavior (Wilkie and Pessemier 1973; Sheth 1974a; Mazis, Ahtola, and Klippel 1975; Lutz 1977; Locander and Spivey 1978); and research on information processing and involvement in cognitive psychology (Krugman 1965; McGuire 1976) influenced the study of consumer information processing and high- and low-involvement choice behavior (Bettman 1979; Olshavsky and Granbois 1979; Antil 1984). Further, research methodologies appropriate to the study of individual psychological phenomena were borrowed by consumer researchers from the behavioral sciences. Such methodologies included laboratory experimentation; focus group interviewing, depth interviewing, and projective techniques (used in motivation research); and cross-sectional mail and telephone survey techniques (used in attitude and psychographic research).

It should be noted that the behavioral marketing schools have been largely responsible for increasing the scientific sophistication of the marketing discipline, with the buyer behavior school in particular deserving much of the credit. Further, with a strong theoretical and methodological base available from the behavioral sciences, the emergence of the buyer behavior school propelled the status of consumer behavior to that of a subdiscipline with adequate maturity to assert considerable independence from marketing. The growing independence of consumer behavior has been evidenced by the establishment of a separate association for the study of consumer behavior (the Association for Consumer Research) and an interdisciplinary journal devoted to consumer research (the *Journal of Consumer Research*).

Adaptive Marketing Schools and Parallel Consumer Behavior

Most recently, marketing has begun to shift its emphasis back to the study of aggregate market behavior. Substantial attention has recently been focused on opportunities and threats generated by such environmental forces as regulation, technology, and global competition. This has resulted in the emergence of the adaptive marketing concept, derived from management thinking which maintains that it is more effective to adapt the organization to fit environmental realities than to attempt to adapt the environment to fit the organization (Toffler 1985). Schools of thought identified with this era are the macromarketing school and the strategic planning school. Researchers associated with these schools of thought have continued to borrow from the behavioral sciences, but have also borrowed concepts from the social sciences relevant to the study of environmental contingencies. Such concepts include environmental scanning (Steiner 1979), stakeholder analysis (Freeman 1984), and competitive analysis (Porter 1980, 1985).

The macromarketing school emerged in the 1970s in response to the growing interest across business disciplines in the impact of business on society and in the impact of societal forces on business. Regarding marketing as a social institution, the macromarketing school is associated with work that examines the effects of marketing on society, examines the effects of societal forces on marketing, adopts the perspective of society, and/or studies marketing systems at the societal level (Hunt and Burnett 1982). While other schools of thought (particularly the managerial school) have recognized that environmental factors influence marketing, they have generally regarded these factors as uncontrollable (McCarthy 1960). Thus, these schools of thought have afforded little research attention to environmental factors. In contrast, the macromarketing school has sought to give in-depth attention to societal forces, analyzing their impact on marketing as well as marketing's impact on them. While the macromarketing perspective may be traced to early writings by Holloway and Hancock (1964) and Fisk (1967), the macromarketing school did not emerge in full force until the latter 1970s. The development of macromarketing as a school of thought has largely followed from the University of Colorado's organization of the first in a continuing series of macromarketing seminars (Slater 1977), and from the founding of the *Journal of Macromarketing*.

The strategic planning school is currently emerging as the newest school of marketing thought (Sheth and Gardner 1982). Authors associated with this perspective emphasize the importance of analyzing environmental dynamics and of proactively adapting the organization to the environment. Many contributions of the strategic planning school have come from consulting firms and their clients. Such contributions include produce portfolio models developed by General Electric and the Boston Consulting Group; experience curve models developed by the Boston Consulting Group; and the Profit Impact of Marketing Strategies (PIMS) program, initiated by General Electric and currently under the management of the Strategic Planning Institute. Further, a substantial number of marketing researchers have recently advocated strategic planning and environmental management perspectives in their writings (e.g., Abell 1978; Montgomery and Weinberg 1979; Anderson 1982; Cook 1983; Henderson 1983; Sheth and Frazier 1983; Wind and Robertson 1983; Zeithaml and Zeithaml 1984; Day 1986). The Spring 1983 issue of the *Journal of Marketing* was devoted to articles on marketing strategy (Cunningham and Robertson 1983); and an increasing number of marketing texts are being written from a strategic planning perspective (e.g., Luck and Ferrell 1979; Jain 1981; Cravens 1982).

As the environmental forces fostering the adaptive marketing perspective become more pronounced, we predict that at least four areas of consumer research will emerge or escalate in importance. First, as markets have become increasingly global (Levitt 1983), a growing emphasis has been placed on international marketing. This has fostered a concomitant interest in cross-cultural consumer behavior and increased research on culture as an influence on consumption and buying behavior (Sheth and Sethi 1977; Plummer 1977; Green et al. 1983; Belk 1984a; Sherry 1986). We predict that this interest and emphasis will increase as globalization continues.

Second, with maturing markets and intensified competition, the emphasis of marketing appears to be shifting away from the acquisition of new customers and toward the retention of existing customers (Albrecht and Zemke 1985; Desatnick 1987). Thus, we predict that the focus of consumer research will shift as well. For example, interest in consumer satisfaction and dissatisfaction may be expected to increase. In particular, more in-depth research on complaining behavior, word-of-mouth communication, and other consumer responses to dissatisfaction is anticipated (Richins 1983; Resnik and Harmon 1983; Bearden and Mason 1984; Folkes 1984).

Third, with maturing markets, interest in the competitive environment has intensified (Kotler 1980). Thus, we predict that interest will be fostered in consumer perceptions of marketing competition. The need for research on this topic has already become apparent as marketing has sought to take a customer-oriented approach in its efforts to define product markets and analyze market structure (Day, Shocker, and Srivastava 1979; Srivastava, Alpert, and Shocker 1984). Additionally, with much competitive effort currently directed toward psychological positioning (Ries and Trout 1981), consumer researchers may be expected to aid marketers in evaluating their positioning strategies. Insights relevant to marketing may be provided by examining such phenomena as comparison shopping, consumer perceptions of competitive advertising, and consumer perceptions of competitive pricing.

Finally, with the accelerated pace of competitive and technological change, a recent trend in marketing practice has been to use behavior modification strategies rather than persuasion strategies in attempting to influence consumers (Markin 1977; Nord and Peter 1980). Traditional persuasion strategies endeavor to first effect attitudinal change, with behavioral change following. In contrast, behavior modification strategies endeavor to first effect behavioral change, with attitudinal change following. In light of this trend, we predict that the future emphasis of consumer research will be less on the study of perceptions, cognitions, and attitudes, and more on the study of actual behavior and behavior modification techniques. Early focus on behavior modification has included research on foot-in-the-door techniques (e.g., Scott 1977; Hansen and Robinson 1980) and research on the effectiveness of incentives in stimulating purchase and repeat purchase behavior (e.g., Scott 1976). Additionally, some recent work has taken a classical conditioning perspective (Gorn 1982; Allen and Madden 1985; Bierley, McSweeney, and Vannieuwkerk 1985). Evidence of a growing interest in actual consumption behavior is provided by several recent calls for research on consumption experience (Jacoby 1978; Sheth 1982; Holbrook and Hirschman 1982; Belk 1984b; Holbrook 1985; Sheth 1985); and by the current interest in naturalistic inquiry (Hirschman 1986).

Along with these forecasts, however, we also predict that as the adaptive perspective gains support in marketing, consumer behavior may be faced with a serious dilemma. As an integral part of marketing, the subdiscipline of consumer behavior will undoubtedly wish to continue to investigate issues relevant to marketing's needs. This will necessitate an emphasis on aggregate consumer behavior and increased borrowing from the social sciences (Kollat, Blackwell, and Engel 1972; Sheth 1974b; Nicosia and Mayer 1976; Engel 1981; Kassarjian 1982; Sheth 1982; Zielinski and Robertson 1982). However, we expect that many consumer researchers will be reluctant to abandon their emphasis on individual behavior and the scientific traditions gleaned from the behavioral sciences. Prior to specializing in consumer behavior, many consumer researchers received their scientific training in psychology. As a result, they are most skilled in investigating individual behavior. Further, influenced by the behavioral sciences, the field of consumer behavior has embraced logical positivism as its dominant scientific philosophy. Many consumer researchers therefore regard the alternative philosophical approaches and research methodologies embraced by the social sciences as lacking in scientific rigor.

Given these traditions, it is not certain that consumer behavior will automatically follow marketing as it has in the past. It is perhaps more probable that consumer research will become polarized. While marketing will almost certainly continue to study consumer behavior from its own perspectives and investigate topics relevant to its own needs, the science of consumer behavior may emerge as an independent discipline continuing to focus on individual consumer behavior.

Notes

1. Although there currently exists considerable controversy as to what is appropriately considered a "school of thought" (as opposed to a theory or paradigm), we have chosen to avoid this debate. Instead, we have followed the tradition of Bartels (1962) in referring to the various approaches to the study of marketing as schools of thought.

References

Abell, Derek F. 1978. "Strategic Windows." *Journal of Marketing* 42 (July). 21–26.

Achrol, Ravi Singh, Torger Reve, and Louis W. Stern. 1983. "The Environment of Marketing Channel Dyads: A Framework for Comparative Analysis." *Journal of Marketing* 47 (Fall). 55–67.

Albrecht, Karl, and Ron Zemke. 1985. *Service America!: Doing Business in the New Economy.* Homewood, Ill. Dow Jones-Irwin.

Alderson, Wroe. 1957. *Marketing Behavior and Executive Action: A Functionalist Approach to Marketing Theory.* Homewood, Ill.: Richard D. Irwin.

———. 1965. *Dynamic Marketing Behavior: A Functionalist Theory of Marketing.* Homewood, Ill.: Richard D. Irwin.

Alderson, Wroe, and Miles W. Martin. 1965. "Toward a Formal Theory of Transactions and Transvections." *Journal of Marketing Research* 2 (May). 117–127.

Allen, Chris T., and Thomas J. Madden. 1985. "A Closer Look at Classical Conditioning." *Journal of Consumer Research* 12 (December). 301–315.

Anderson, Paul F. 1982. "Marketing, Strategic Planning and the Theory of the Firm." *Journal of Marketing* 46 (Spring). 15–26.

Andreasen, Alan R. 1965. "Attitudes and Customer Behavior: A Decision Model." In Lee E. Preston, ed., *Research Program in Marketing: New Research in Marketing.* Berkeley: Institute of Business and Economic Research, University of California. 1–16.

———. 1975. *The Disadvantaged Consumer.* New York: The Free Press.

Angelmar, Reinhard, and Louis W. Stern. 1978. "Development of a Content Analytic System for Analysis of Bargaining Communication in Marketing." *Journal of Marketing Research* 15 (February). 93–102.

Antil, John H. 1984. "Conceptualization and Operationalization of Involvement." In Thomas C. Kinnear, ed., *Advances in Consumer Research.* Provo Utah: Association for Consumer Research. 11:203–209.

Armstrong, Gary M., Metin N. Gurol, and Frederick A. Russ. 1979. "Detecting and Correcting Deceptive Advertising." *Journal of Consumer Research* 6 (December). 237–246.

Arndt, Johan. 1967. *Word of Mouth Advertising: A Review of the Literature.* New York: Advertising Research Foundation.

Ashby, Harold J., Jr. 1973. "The Black Consumer." In William T. Kennedy, ed., *New Consumerism: Selected Readings.* Columbus, Ohio: Grid. 149–176.

Aspinwall, Leo. 1958. "The Characteristics of Goods and Parallel Systems Theories." In Eugene J. Kelley and William Lazer, eds., *Managerial Marketing: Perspectives and Viewpoints.* Homewood, Ill.: Richard D. Irwin. 434–450.

Bagozzi, Richard P. 1974. "Marketing as an Organized Behavioral System of Exchange." *Journal of Marketing* 38 (October). 77–81.

———. 1975. "Marketing as Exchange." *Journal of Marketing* 39 (October). 32–39.

———. 1978. "Marketing as Exchange: A Theory of Transactions in the Marketplace." *American Behavioral Scientist* 21 (March/April). 535–556.

———. 1979. "Toward a Formal Theory of Marketing Exchanges." In O. C. Ferrell,

Stephen W. Brown, and Charles W. Lamb, Jr. eds., *Conceptual and Theoretical Developments in Marketing.* Chicago: American Marketing Association. 431–447.

Balderston, F. E. 1964. "Design of Marketing Channels." In Reavis Cox, Wroe Alderson, and Stanley J. Shapiro, eds., *Theory in Marketing.* Homewood, Ill.: Richard D. Irwin. 176–189.

Bartels, Robert. 1962. *The Development of Marketing Thought.* Homewood, Ill.: Richard D. Irwin.

Bass, Frank M. 1969. "A New Product Growth Model for Consumer Durables." *Management Science* 15 (January). 215–227.

Bauer, Raymond A. 1960. "Consumer Behavior as Risk Taking." In Robert S. Hancock, ed., *Dynamic Marketing for a Changing World: Proceedings of the 43rd National Conference of the American Marketing Association.* Chicago: American Marketing Association. 389–398.

Bearden, William O., and J. Barry Mason. 1984. "An Investigation of Influences on Consumer Complaint Reports." In Thomas C. Kinnear, ed., *Advances in Consumer Research.* Provo, Utah: Association for Consumer Research. 11:490–495.

Beem, Eugene R. 1973. "The Beginnings of the Consumer Movement." In William T. Kelley, ed., *New Consumerism: Selected Readings.* Columbus, Ohio: Grid. 13–25.

Beier, Frederick J., and Louis W. Stern. 1969. "Power in the Channel of Distribution." In Louis W. Stern, ed., *Distribution Channels: Behavioral Dimensions.* Boston: Houghton Mifflin. 92–116.

Belk, Russell W. 1984. "Cultural and Historical Differences in Concepts of Self and Their Effects on Attitudes Toward Having and Giving." In Thomas C. Kinnear, ed., *Advances in Consumer Research.* Provo, Utah: Association for Consumer Research. 11:754–760.

———. 1984. "Manifesto for a Consumer Behavior of Consumer Behavior." In Paul F. Anderson and Michael J. Ryan, ed., *1984 AMA Winter Educators' Conference: Scientific Method in Marketing.* Chicago: American Marketing Association. 163–167.

Bettman, James R. 1979. *An Information Processing Theory of Consumer Choice.* Reading, Mass.: Addison-Wesley.

Bierley, Calvin, Frances K. McSweeney, and Renee Vannieuwkerk. 1985. "Classical Conditioning of Preferences for Stimuli." *Journal of Consumer Research* 12 (December). 316–323.

Borden, Neil H. 1964. "The Concept of the Marketing Mix." *Journal of Advertising Research* 4 (June). 2–7.

Bourne, Francis S. 1957. "Group Influence in Marketing and Public Relations." In Rensis Likert and Samuel P. Hayes, Jr., eds. *Some Applications of Behavioural Research.* Paris: Unesco. 207–257.

Breyer, Ralph F. 1934. *The Marketing Institution.* New York: McGraw-Hill.

Brown, James R., and Ralph L. Day. 1981. "Measures of Manifest Conflict in Distribution Channels." *Journal of Marketing Research* 18 (August). 263–274.

Bucklin, Louis P. 1963. "Retail Strategy and the Classification of Consumer Goods." *Journal of Marketing* 27 (January). 50–55.

———. 1965. "Postponement, Speculation and the Structure of Distribution Channels." *Journal of Marketing Research* 2 (February). 26–31.

Butler, Ralph Starr. 1923. *Marketing and Merchandising*. New York: Alexander Hamilton Institute.

Cash, Harold C., and W. J. E. Crissy. 1958. *A Point of View for Salesmen*. Vol. 1 of *The Psychology of Selling*. New York: Personnel Development Associates.

Chamberlin, Edward Hastings. 1933. *The Theory of Monopolistic Competition*. Cambridge, Mass.: Harvard University Press.

Cherington, Paul T. 1920. *The Elements of Marketing*. New York: Macmillan.

Churchill, Gilbert A., Jr., and Carol Surprenant. 1982. "An Investigation Into the Determinants of Consumer Satisfaction." *Journal of Marketing Research* 19 (November). 491–504.

Coleman, Richard P. 1960. "The Significance of Social Stratification in Selling." In Martin L. Bell, ed., *Marketing: A Maturing Discipline*. Chicago: American Marketing Association. 171–184.

Converse, Paul D. 1943. *A Study of Retail Trade Areas in East Central Illinois*. Urbana: University of Illinois Press.

———. 1949. "New Laws of Retail Gravitation." *Journal of Marketing* 14 (October). 379–384.

Converse, Paul D., and Harvey W. Huegy. 1940. *Elements of Marketing*. Englewood Cliffs, N.J.: Prentice-Hall.

Cook, Victor J., Jr. 1983. "Marketing Strategy and Differential Advantage." *Journal of Marketing* 47 (Spring). 68–75.

Copeland, Melvin T. 1923. "Relation of Consumers' Buying Habits to Marketing Methods." *Harvard Business Review* 1 (April). 282–289.

Cravens, David W. 1982. *Strategic Marketing*. Homewood, Ill.: Richard D. Irwin.

Cunningham, Ross M. 1956. "Brand Loyalty—What, Where, How Much?" *Harvard Business Review* 34 (January-February). 116–128.

Cunningham, William H., and Thomas S. Robertson. 1983. "From the Editor." *Journal of Marketing* 47 (Spring): 5–6.

Day, George S. 1976. "Assessing the Effects of Information Disclosure Requirements." *Journal of Marketing* 40 (April). 42–52.

———. 1986. *Analysis for Strategic Market Decisions*. St. Paul, Minn.: West Publishing Company.

Day, George S., Allan D. Shocker, and Rajendra K. Srivastava. 1979. "Customer-Oriented Approaches to Identifying Product Markets." *Journal of Marketing* 43 (Fall). 8–19.

Day, Ralph L., ed. 1977. *Consumer Satisfaction, Dissatisfaction and Complaining Behavior*. Bloomington/Indianapolis: Department of Marketing, School of Business, Indiana University.

Day, Ralph L., and H. Keith Hunt, eds. 1979. *Refining Concepts and Measures of Consumer Satisfaction and Complaining Behavior*. Bloomington/Indianapolis: Department of Marketing, School of Business, Indiana University.

Dean, Joel. 1950. "Pricing Policies for New Products." *Harvard Business Review* 28 (November). 45–53.

———. 1951. *Managerial Economics*. Englewood Cliffs, N.J.: Prentice-Hall.

Desatnick, Robert L. 1987. *Managing to Keep the Customer*. San Francisco: Jossey-Bass Publishers.

Dichter, Ernest. 1964. *Handbook of Consumer Motivations: The Psychology of the World of Objects*. New York: McGraw-Hill.

Drucker, Peter. 1969. "The Shame of Marketing." *Marketing/Communications* 297 (August). 60–64.

El-Ansary, Adel I., and Louis W. Stern. 1972. "Power Measurement in the Distribution Channel." *Journal of Marketing Research* 9 (February). 47–52.

Eliashberg, Jehoshua, and Donald A. Michie. 1984. "Multiple Business Goals Sets as Determinants of Marketing Channel Conflict: An Empirical Study." *Journal of Marketing Research* 21 (February). 75–88.

Emerson, Richard M. 1962. "Power-Dependence Relations." *American Sociological Review* 27 (February). 31–41.

Engel, James F. 1981. "The Discipline of Consumer Research: Permanent Adolesence or Maturity?" In Kent B. Monroe, ed., *Advances in Consumer Research*. Vol. 8. Ann Arbor, Mich.: Association for Consumer Research.

Engel, James F., David T. Kollat, and Roger D. Blackwell. 1968. *Consumer Behavior*. New York: Holt, Rinehart and Winston.

Enis, Ben M., and Kenneth J. Roering. 1980. "Product Classification Taxonomies: Synthesis and Consumer Implications." In Charles W. Lamb, Jr. and Patrick M. Dunne, eds., *Theoretical Developments in Marketing*. Chicago: American Marketing Association. 186–189.

Etgar, Michael. 1976. "Channel Domination and Countervailing Power in Distributive Channels." *Journal of Marketing Research* 13 (August). 254–262.

———. 1979. "Sources and Types of Intrachannel Conflict." *Journal of Retailing* 55 (Spring). 61–78.

Evans, Franklin B. 1959. "Psychological and Objective Factors in the Prediction of Brand Choice: Ford Versus Chevrolet." *Journal of Business* 32 (October). 340–369.

Festinger, Leon. 1957. *A Theory of Cognitive Dissonance*. New York: Row, Peterson and Company.

Fishbein, Martin, ed. 1967. *Readings in Attitude Theory and Measurement*. New York: John Wiley & Sons.

Fishbein, Martin, and Icek Ajzen. 1975. *Belief, Attitude, Intention, and Behavior: An Introduction to Theory and Research*. Reading, Mass.: Addison-Wesley.

Fisk, George. 1967. *Marketing Systems: An Introductory Analysis*. New York: Harper & Row.

Folkes, Valerie S. 1984. "Consumer Reactions to Product Failure: An Attributional Approach." *Journal of Consumer Research* 10 (March). 398–409.

Foote, Nelson N., ed. 1961. *Household Decision-Making*. Vol. 4 of *Consumer Behavior*. New York: New York University Press.

Frank, Ronald E. 1962. "Brand Choice as a Probability Process." *Journal of Business* 35 (January). 43–56.

Frazier, Gary L. 1983a. "Interorganizational Exchange Behavior in Marketing Channels: A Broadened Perspective." *Journal of Marketing* 47 (Fall). 68–78.

———. 1983b. "On the Measurement of Interfirm Power in Channels of Distribution." *Journal of Marketing Research* 20 (May). 158–166.

Frazier, Gary L., and Jagdish N. Sheth. 1985. "An Attitude-Behavior Framework for Distribution Channel Management." *Journal of Marketing* 49 (Summer). 38–48.

Frazier, Gary L., and John O. Summers. 1984. "Interfirm Influence Strategies and Their Application Within Distribution Channels." *Journal of Marketing* 48 (Summer). 43–55.

Freeman, R. Edward. 1984. *Strategic Management: A Stakeholder Approach*. Boston: Pitman Publishing.

French, John R. P., Jr., and Bertram Raven. 1959. "The Bases of Social Power." In Dorwin Cartwright, ed., *Studies in Social Power*. Ann Arbor: Research Center for Group Dynamics, Institute for Social Research, University of Michigan. 150–167.

Fullbrook, Earl S. 1940. "The Functional Concept in Marketing." *Journal of Marketing* 4 (January). 229–237.

Gardner, David M. 1976. "Deception in Advertising: A Receiver Oriented Approach to Understanding." *Journal of Advertising* 5 (Fall). 5–11, 19.

Gilly, Mary C., and Ben M. Enis. 1982. "Recycling the Family Life Cycle: A Proposal for Redefinition." In Andrew A. Mitchell, ed., *Advances in Consumer Research*, Vol. 9. Ann Arbor, Mich.: Association for Consumer Research.

Glick, Paul C. 1947. "The Family Cycle." *American Sociological Review* 12 (February). 164–174.

Goldstucker, Jac. 1965. "Trading Areas." In George Schwarzt, ed., *Science in Marketing*. New York: John Wiley & Sons. 281–320.

Gorn, Gerald J. 1982. "The Effects of Music in Advertising on Choice Behavior: A Classical Conditioning Approach." *Journal of Marketing* 46 (Winter). 94–101.

Green, Robert T., Jean-Paul Leonardi, Jean-Louis Chandon, Isabella C. M. Cunningham, Bronis Verhage, and Alain Strazzieri. 1983. "Societal Development and Family Purchasing Roles: A Cross-National Study." *Journal of Consumer Research* 9 (March). 436–442.

Grether, E. T. 1950. "A Theoretical Approach to the Analysis of Marketing." In Reavis Cox and Wroe Alderson, eds., *Theory in Marketing: Selected Essays*. Chicago: Richard D. Irwin. 113–123.

———. 1983. "Regional-Spatial Analysis in Marketing." *Journal of Marketing* 47 (Fall). 36–43.

Hall, Calvin S., and Gardner Lindzey. 1957. "Freud's Psychoanalytic Theory." In *Theories of Personality*. New York: John Wiley & Sons. 29–75.

Hansen, Robert A., and Larry M. Robinson. 1980. "Testing the Effectiveness of Alternative Foot-in-the-Door Manipulations." *Journal of Marketing Research* 17 (August). 359–364.

Harary, Frank, and Benjamin Lipstein. 1962. "The Dynamics of Brand Loyalty: A Markovian Approach." *Operations Research* 10 (January-February). 19–40.

Heider, Fritz. 1958. *The Psychology of Interpersonal Relations*. New York: John Wiley & Sons.

Henderson, Bruce D. 1983. "The Anatomy of Competition." *Journal of Marketing* 47 (Spring). 7–11.

Hirschman, Elizabeth C. 1986. "Humanistic Inquiry in Marketing Research: Philosophy, Method, and Criteria." *Journal of Marketing Research* 23 (August). 237–249.

Holbrook, Morris B. 1985. "Why Business is Bad for Consumer Research: The Three Bears Revisited." In Elizabeth C. Hirschman and Morris B. Holbrook, eds., *Advances in Consumer Research,* Vol. 12. Provo, Utah: Association for Consumer Research.

Holbrook, Morris B., and Elizabeth C. Hirschman. 1982. "The Experiential Aspects of Consumption: Consumer Fantasies, Feelings, and Fun." *Journal of Consumer Research* 9 (September). 132–140.

Holbrook, Morris B., and John A. Howard. 1977. "Frequently Purchased Nondurable Goods and Services." In Robert Ferber, ed., *Selected Aspects of Consumer Behavior: A Summary from the Perspective of Different Disciplines.* Washington, D.C.: National Science Foundation, Directorate for Research Applications, Research Applied to National Needs.

Hollander, Stanley C. 1960. "The Wheel of Retailing." *Journal of Marketing* 25 (July). 37–42.

Holloway, Robert J., and Robert S. Hancock, eds. 1964. *The Environment of Marketing Behavior: Selections from the Literature.* New York: John Wiley & Sons.

Holton, Richard H. 1958. "The Distinction Between Convenience Goods, Shopping Goods, and Specialty Goods." *Journal of Marketing* 23 (July). 53–56.

———. 1959. "What is Really Meant by 'Specialty' Goods?" *Journal of Marketing* 24 (July). 64–66.

Houston, Michael J., and Michael L. Rothschild. 1980. "Policy-Related Experiments on Information Provision: A Normative Model and Explication." *Journal of Marketing Research* 17 (November). 432–449.

Howard, John A. 1957. *Marketing Management: Analysis and Decision.* Homewood, Ill.: Richard D. Irwin.

Howard, John A., and Jagdish N. Sheth. 1969. *The Theory of Buyer Behavior.* New York: John Wiley & Sons.

Huff, David L. 1962. *Determination of Intra-Urban Retail Trade Areas.* Los Angeles: Real Estate Research Program, Graduate School of Business Administration, Division of Research, University of California, Los Angeles.

Huff, David L. 1964. "Defining and Estimating a Trading Area." *Journal of Marketing* 28 (July). 34–38.

Hunt, H. Keith, ed. 1977. *Conceptualization and Measurement of Consumer Satisfaction and Dissatisfaction: Proceedings of Conference Conducted by Marketing Science Institute with Support of National Science Foundation.* Cambridge, Mass.: Marketing Science Institute.

Hunt, Shelby D. 1976. "The Nature and Scope of Marketing." *Journal of Marketing* 40 (July). 17–28.

Hunt, Shelby D., and John J. Burnett. 1982. "The Macromarketing/Micromarketing Dichotomy: A Taxonomical Model." *Journal of Marketing* 46 (Summer). 11–26.

Hunt, Shelby D., and John R. Nevin. 1974. "Power in a Channel of Distribution: Sources and Consequences." *Journal of Marketing Research* 11 (May). 186–193.

Jacoby, Jacob. 1978. "Consumer Research: A State of the Art Review." *Journal of Marketing* 42 (April). 87–96.

Jacoby, Jacob, and Constance Small. 1975. "The FDA Approach to Defining Misleading Advertising." *Journal of Marketing* 39 (October). 65–68.

Jain, Subhash C. 1981. *Marketing Planning and Strategy*. Cincinnati, Ohio: South-Western Publishing Company.

Kahl, Joseph A. 1953. *The American Class Structure*. New York: Rinehart & Company.

Kaish, Stanley. 1967. "Cognitive Dissonance and the Classification of Consumer Goods." *Journal of Marketing* 31 (October). 28–31.

Kassarjian, Harold H. 1969. "The Negro and American Advertising, 1946–1965." *Journal of Marketing Research* 6 (February). 29–39.

———. 1971. "Personality and Consumer Behavior: A Review." *Journal of Marketing Research* 8 (November). 409–418.

———. 1982. "The Development of Consumer Behavior Theory." In Andrew A. Mitchell, ed., *Advances in Consumer Research*. Ann Arbor, Mich.: Association for Consumer Research. 9:20–22.

Katona, George. 1951. *Psychological Analysis of Economic Behavior*. New York: McGraw-Hill.

———. 1953. "Rational Behavior and Economic Behavior." *Psychological Review* 60 (September). 307–318.

Katona, George, and Eva Mueller. 1953. *Consumer Attitudes and Demand. 1950–1952*. Ann Arbor: Survey Research Center, Institute for Social Research, University of Michigan.

———. 1956. *Consumer Expectations, 1953–1956*. Ann Arbor: Survey Research Center, Institute for Social Research, University of Michigan.

Katona, George, Burkhard Strumpel, and Ernest Zahn. 1971. *Aspirations and Affluence*. New York: McGraw-Hill.

Katz, Daniel. 1960. "The Functional Approach to the Study of Attitudes." *Public Opinion Quarterly* 24 (Summer). 163–204.

Katz, Elihu. 1957. "The Two-Step Flow of Communication: An Up-to-Date Report on an Hypothesis." *Public Opinion Quarterly* 21 (Spring). 61–78.

Katz, Elihu, and Paul F. Lazarsfeld. 1955. *Personal Influence: The Part Played by People in the Flow of Mass Communications*. Glencoe, Ill.: The Free Press.

Keith, Robert J. 1960. "The Marketing Revolution." *Journal of Marketing* 24 (January). 35–38.

Kelley, Eugene J., and William Lazer, eds. 1958. *Managerial Marketing: Perspectives and Viewpoints*. Homewood, Ill.: Richard D. Irwin.

Kollat, David T., Roger D. Blackwell, and James F. Engel. 1972. "The Current Status of Consumer Behavior Research: Developments During the 1968–1972 Period." In M. Venkatesan, ed., *Proceedings 3rd Annual Conference of the Association for Consumer Research*. College Park, Md.: Association for Consumer Research. 576–585.

Kotler, Philip. 1972a. "A Generic Concept of Marketing." *Journal of Marketing* 36 (April). 46–54.

———. 1972b. "What Consumerism Means for Marketers." *Harvard Business Review* 50 (May-June). 48–57.

———. 1980. *Marketing Management: Analysis, Planning, and Control.* Fourth ed. Englewood Cliffs, N.J.: Prentice-Hall.

Krugman, Herbert E. 1965. "The Impact of Television Advertising: Learning Without Involvement." *Public Opinion Quarterly* 29 (Fall). 349–356.

Kuehn, Alfred A. 1962. "Consumer Brand Choice as a Learning Process." *Journal of Advertising Research* 2 (December). 10–17.

Lavidge, Robert J., and Gary A. Steiner. 1961. "A Model for Predictive Measurements of Advertising Effectiveness." *Journal of Marketing* 25 (October). 59–62.

Levitt, Theodore. 1960. "Marketing Myopia." *Harvard Business Review* 38 (July/August). 45–56.

———. 1965. "Exploit the Product Life Cycle." *Harvard Business Review* 43 (November/December). 81–94.

———. 1983. "The Globalization of Markets." *Harvard Business Review* 61 (May-June). 92–102.

Levy, Sidney J. 1966. "Social Class and Consumer Behavior." In Joseph W. Newman, ed., *On Knowing the Consumer.* New York: John Wiley & Sons. 146–160.

Lewis, Richard J., and Leo G. Erickson. 1969. "Marketing Functions and Marketing Systems: A Synthesis." *Journal of Marketing* 33 (July). 10–14.

Locander, William B., and W. Austin Spivey. 1978. "A Functional Approach to Attitude Measurement." *Journal of Marketing Research* 15 (November). 576–587.

Lockley, Lawrence C. 1974. "History and Development of Marketing Research." Chap. 1 in Robert Ferber, ed., *Handbook of Marketing Research.* New York: McGraw-Hill.

Loomis, Charles P. 1936. "The Study of the Life Cycle of Families." *Rural Sociology* 1 (June). 180–199.

Luck, David J. 1959. "On the Nature of Specialty Goods." *Journal of Marketing* 24 (July). 61–64.

Luck, David J., and O. C. Ferrell. 1979. *Marketing Strategy and Plans: Systematic Marketing Management.* Englewood Cliffs, N.J.: Prentice-Hall.

Lusch, Robert F. 1976. "Sources of Power: Their Impact on Intrachannel Conflict." *Journal of Marketing Research* 13 (November). 382–390.

Lutz, Richard J. 1977. "An Experimental Investigation of Causal Relations Among Cognitions, Affect, and Behavioral Intention." *Journal of Consumer Research* 3 (March). 197–208.

McCammon, Bert C., Jr. 1965. "The Emergence and Growth of Contractually Integrated Channels in the American Economy." In Peter D. Bennett, ed., *Marketing and Economic Development (The 50th Anniversary International Symposium of Marketing and Allied Disciplines).* Chicago: American Marketing Association. 496–515.

McCarthy, E. Jerome. 1960. *Basic Marketing: A Managerial Approach.* Homewood, Ill.: Richard D. Irwin.

McGarry, Edmund D. 1950. "Some Functions of Marketing Reconsidered." In Reavis Cox and Wroe Alderson, eds., *Theory in Marketing*. Chicago: Richard D. Irwin. 263–279.

McGuire, William J. 1976. "Some Internal Psychological Factors Influencing Consumer Choice." *Journal of Consumer Research* 2 (March). 302–319.

McInnes, William. 1964. "A Conceptual Approach to Marketing." In Reavis Cox, Wroe Alderson, and Stanley J. Shapiro, eds., *Theory in Marketing*. Homewood, Ill.: Richard D. Irwin. 51–67.

McKitterick, John B. 1957. "What is the Marketing Management Concept?" In Frank M. Bass, ed., *The Frontiers of Marketing Thought and Science*. Chicago: American Marketing Association. 71–82.

Mallen, Bruce. 1963. "A Theory of Retailer-Supplier Conflict, Control, and Cooperation." *Journal of Retailing* 39 (Summer). 24–32, 51.

———. 1973. "Functional Spin-Off: A Key to Anticipating Change in Distribution Structure." *Journal of Marketing* 37 (July). 18–25.

March, James G., and Herbert A. Simon. 1958. *Organizations*. New York: John Wiley & Sons.

Markin, Rom J. 1977. "Motivation in Buyer Behavior Theory: From Mechanism to Cognition." In Arch G. Woodside, Jagdish N. Sheth, and Peter D. Bennett, eds., *Consumer and Industrial Buying Behavior*. New York: Elsevier North-Holland, Inc. 37–48.

Marshall, Alfred. 1890. *Principles of Economics*. London: Macmillan.

Martineau, Pierre. 1958. "Social Classes and Spending Behavior." *Journal of Marketing* 23 (October). 121–130.

Mazis, Michael B., Olli T. Ahtola, and R. Eugene Klippel. 1975. "A Comparison of Four Multi-Attribute Models in the Prediction of Consumer Attitudes." *Journal of Consumer Research* 2 (June). 38–52.

Montgomery, David B., and Charles B. Weinberg. 1979. "Toward Strategic Intelligence Systems." *Journal of Marketing* 43 (Fall). 41–52.

Murphy, Patrick E., and Ben M. Enis. 1986. "Classifying Products Strategically." *Journal of Marketing* 50 (July). 24–42.

Murphy, Patrick E., and William A. Staples. 1979. "A Modernized Family Life Cycle." *Journal of Consumer Research* 6 (June). 12–22.

Myers, James H., and Thomas S. Robertson. 1972. "Dimensions of Opinion Leadership." *Journal of Marketing Research* 9 (February). 41–46.

Nicosia, Francesco M. 1966. *Consumer Decision Processes: Marketing and Advertising Implications*. Englewood Cliffs, N.J.: Prentice-Hall.

Nicosia, Francesco M., and Robert N. Mayer. 1976. "Toward a Sociology of Consumption." *Journal of Consumer Research* 3 (September). 65–75.

Nord, Walter R., and J. Paul Peter. 1980. "A Behavior Modification Perspective on Marketing." *Journal of Marketing* 44 (Spring). 36–47.

Norris, Ruby Turner. 1941. *The Theory of Consumer's Demand*. New Haven, Conn.: Yale University Press.

Ohlin, Bertil. 1933. *Interregional and International Trade*. Cambridge, Mass.: Harvard University Press.

Oliver, Richard L. 1980. "A Cognitive Model of the Antecedents and Consequences of Satisfaction Decisions." *Journal of Marketing Research* 17 (November). 460–469.

Oliver, Richard L., and William O. Bearden. 1983. "The Role of Involvement in Satisfaction Processes." In Richard P. Bagozzi and Alice M. Tybout, eds., *Advances in Consumer Research*. Ann Arbor, Mich.: Association for Consumer Research. 10:250–255.

Olshavsky, Richard W., and Donald H. Granbois. 1979. "Consumer Decision Making—Fact or Fiction?" *Journal of Consumer Research* 6 (September). 93–100.

Parlin, Charles Coolidge. 1912. *Merchandising and Textiles*. 5–6.

Plummer, Joseph T. 1977. "Consumer Focus in Cross-National Research." *Journal of Advertising* 6 (Spring). 5–15.

Pondy, Louis R. 1967. "Organizational Conflict: Concepts and Models." *Administrative Science Quarterly* 12 (September). 296–320.

Porter, Michael E. 1980. *Competitive Strategy: Techniques for Analyzing Industries and Competitors*. New York: The Free Press.

———. 1985. *Competitive Advantage: Creating and Sustaining Superior Performance*. New York: The Free Press.

Reilly, William J. 1931. *The Law of Retail Gravitation*. Austin: The University of Texas.

Resnik, Alan J., and Robert R. Harmon. 1983. "Consumer Complaints and Managerial Response: A Holistic Approach." *Journal of Marketing* 47 (Winter). 86–97.

Resnik, Alan J., and Bruce L. Stern. 1977. "An Analysis of Information Content in Television Advertising." *Journal of Marketing* 41 (January). 50–53.

Revzan, David A. 1961. *Wholesaling in Marketing Organization*. New York: John Wiley & Sons.

Richins, Marsha L. 1983. "Negative Word-of-Mouth by Dissatisfied Consumers: A Pilot Study." *Journal of Marketing* 47 (Winter). 68–78.

Ridgeway, Valentine F. 1957. "Administration of Manufacturer-Dealer Systems." *Administrative Science Quarterly* 1 (March). 464–483.

Ries, Al, and Jack Trout. 1981. *Positioning: The Battle for Your Mind*. New York: McGraw-Hill.

Robicheaux, Robert A., and Adel I. El-Ansary. 1975–76. "A General Model for Understanding Channel Member Behavior." *Journal of Retailing* 52 (Winter). 13–30, 93–94.

Robinson, Lawrence R., and Eleanor G. May. 1956. *Self-Service in Variety Stores*. Boston: Harvard University, Graduate School of Business Administration, Division of Research.

Rogers, Everett M. 1962. *Diffusion of Innovations*. New York: The Free Press of Glencoe.

Rosenberg, Larry J., and Louis W. Stern. 1971. "Conflict Measurement in the Distribution Channel." *Journal of Marketing Research* 8 (November). 437–442.

Rosenberg, Milton J. 1956. "Cognitive Structure and Attitudinal Affect." *Journal of Abnormal and Social Psychology* 53 (November). 367–372.

Ryan, Franklin W. 1935. "Functional Elements of Market Distribution." *Harvard Business Review* 13 (January). 205–224.

Scott, Carol A. 1976. "The Effects of Trial and Incentives on Repeat Purchase Behavior." *Journal of Marketing Research* 13 (August). 263–269.

———. 1977. "Modifying Socially Conscious Behavior: The Foot-in-the-Door Technique." *Journal of Consumer Research* 4 (December). 156–164.

Shaw, A. W. 1912. "Some Problems in Market Distribution." *Quarterly Journal of Economics* 26 (August). 703–765.

Sherry, John F., Jr. 1986. "The Cultural Perspective in Consumer Research." In Richard J. Lutz, ed., *Advances in Consumer Research*. Provo, Utah: Association for Consumer Research. 13:573–575.

Sheth, Jagdish N. 1973. "A Model of Industrial Buyer Behavior." *Journal of Marketing* 37 (October). 50–56.

———. 1974a. "A Field Study of Attitude Structure and Attitude-Behavior Relationship." In Jagdish N. Sheth, ed., *Models of Buyer Behavior: Conceptual, Quantitative, and Empirical*. New York: Harper & Row. 242–268.

———. 1974b. "The Next Decade of Buyer Behavior Theory and Research." In Jagdish N. Sheth, ed., *Models of Buyer Behavior: Conceptual, Quantitative, and Empirical*. New York: Harper & Row. 391–406.

———. 1977. "Demographics in Consumer Behavior." *Journal of Business Research* 5 (June). 129–138.

———. "Consumer Behavior: Surpluses and Shortages." In Andrew A. Mitchell, ed., *Advances in Consumer Research*, Ann Arbor, Mich.: Association for Consumer Research. 9:13–16.

———. 1975. "Presidential Address: Broadening the Horizons of ACR and Consumer Behavior." In Elizabeth C. Hirschman and Morris B. Holbrook, eds., *Advances in Consumer Research*, Provo, Utah: Association for Consumer Research. 12:1–2.

Sheth, Jagdish N., and Gary L. Frazier. 1983. "A Margin-Return Model for Strategic Market Planning." *Journal of Marketing* 47 (Spring). 100–109.

Sheth, Jagdish N., and David M. Gardner. 1982. "History of Marketing Thought: An Update." In Ronald F. Bush and Shelby D. Hunt, eds., *Marketing Theory: Philosophy of Science Perspectives*. Chicago: American Marketing Association. 52–58.

Sheth, Jagdish N., and S. Prakash Sethi. 1977. "A Theory of Cross-Cultural Buyer Behavior." In Arch G. Woodside, Jagdish N. Sheth, and Peter D. Bennett, eds., *Consumer and Industrial Buying Behavior*. New York: Elsevier North-Holland. 369–386.

Silk, Alvin J. 1966. "Overlap Among Self-Designated Opinion Leaders: A Study of Selected Dental Products and Services." *Journal of Marketing Research* 3 (August). 255–259.

Slater, Charles C., ed. 1977. *Macro-Marketing: Distributive Processes from a Societal Perspective*. Boulder: Marketing Division, Graduate School of Business Administration, University of Colorado.

Smallwood, John E. 1973. "The Product Life Cycle: A Key to Strategic Marketing Planning." *MSU Business Topics* 21 (Winter). 29–35.

Smith, Wendell R. 1956. "Product Differentiation and Market Segmentation as Alternative Marketing Strategies." *Journal of Marketing* 21 (July). 3–8.

Srivastava, Rajendra K., Mark I. Alpert, and Allan D. Shocker. 1984. "A Customer-Oriented Approach for Determining Market Structures." *Journal of Marketing* 48 (Spring). 32–45.

Stafford, James E. 1966. "Effects of Group Influence on Consumer Brand Preferences." *Journal of Marketing Research* 3 (February). 68–75.

Steiner, George A. 1979. *Strategic Planning: What Every Manager Must Know.* New York: The Free Press.

Stern, Louis W., ed. 1969. *Distribution Channels: Behavioral Dimensions.* Boston: Houghton Mifflin.

Stern, Louis W., and Ronald H. Gorman. 1969. "Conflict in Distribution Channels: An Exploration." In Louis W. Stern, ed., *Distribution Channels: Behavioral Dimensions.* Boston: Houghton Mifflin. 156–175.

Stern, Louis W., and Torger Reve. 1980. "Distribution Channels as Political Economies: A Framework for Comparative Analysis." *Journal of Marketing* 44 (Summer). 52–64.

Toffler, Alvin. 1985. *The Adaptive Corporation.* New York: McGraw-Hill.

Vaile, Roland S., E. T. Grether, and Reavis Cox. 1952. *Marketing in the American Economy.* New York: The Ronald Press Company.

Waite, Warren C. 1928. *Economics of Consumption.* New York: McGraw-Hill.

Warner, W. Lloyd, and Paul S. Lunt. 1941. *The Social Life of a Modern Community.* New Haven, Conn.: Yale University Press.

Wasson, Chester R. 1969. "Is It Time to Quit Thinking About Income Classes?" *Journal of Marketing* 33 (April). 54–57.

Webster, Frederick E., Jr., and Yoram Wind. 1972. "A General Model for Understanding Organizational Buying Behavior." *Journal of Marketing* 36 (April). 12–19.

Weld, L. D. H. 1916. *The Marketing of Farm Products.* New York: Macmillan.

———. 1917. "Marketing Functions and Mercantile Organization." *American Economic Review* 2 (June). 306–318.

Wells, William D. 1975. "Psychographics: A Critical Review." *Journal of Marketing Research* 12 (May). 196–213.

Wells, William D., and George Gubar. 1966. "Life Cycle Concept in Marketing Research." *Journal of Marketing Research* 3 (November). 355–363.

Wells, William D., and Douglas J. Tigert. 1971. "Activities, Interests and Opinions." *Journal of Advertising Research* 11 (August). 27–35.

Wilkie, William L., and Edgar A. Pessemier. 1973. "Issues in Marketing's Use of Multi-Attribute Attitude Models." *Journal of Marketing Research* 10 (November). 428–441.

Wind, Yoram, and Thomas S. Robertson. 1983. "Marketing Strategy: New Directions for Theory and Research." *Journal of Marketing* 47 (Spring). 12–25.

Wyand, Charles S. 1937. *The Economics of Consumption.* New York: Macmillan.

Zeithaml, Carl P., and Valarie A. Zeithaml. 1984. "Environmental Management: Revising the Marketing Perspective." *Journal of Marketing* 48 (Spring). 46–53.

Zielinski, Joan, and Thomas S. Robertson. 1982. "Consumer Behavior Theory: Excesses and Limitations." In Andrew A. Mitchell, ed., *Advances in Consumer Research,* Ann Arbor, Mich.: Association for Consumer Research. 9:8–12.

Zimmerman, Carle C. 1936. *Consumption and Standards of Living.* New York: D. Van Nostrand Company.

3
The Rise and Fall of the Functional Approach to Marketing: A Paradigm Displacement Perspective

Shelby D. Hunt
Jerry Goolsby

Acknowledgment

Professor Stanley Hollander, who was on the senior author's dissertation committee and in whose honor this paper was drafted, might (will undoubtedly?) disagree with certain (almost all?) aspects of this chapter. Ironically (most fortunately?), Stan authored a paper entitled "The Marketing Concept: A Deja Vu" (1986) in the *Festschrift* honoring Reavis Cox. In his acknowledgment he notes:

> I am not entirely certain that Reavis Cox will agree with all of the points in this chapter, but he always encouraged considerable diversity of opinion among his students. Once, after I gave a paper at an AMA session in which he presided, someone approached him and in an attempt at academic one-upmanship said, "Your own student disagrees with you." I was prepared to defend my paper as purely Coxian, but Reavis ended the matter by saying, "That is the point of education."
> Dear Stan, Déjà Vu; Déjà Vu?

The Functional Approach

Historically, four different approaches have dominated the study of marketing: (1) the commodity approach, (2) the institutional approach, (3) the functional approach, and (4) the managerial approach. One of these, the functional approach, has been described as "most contributing to the development of a science of marketing" (Converse, Huegy, and Mitchell 1952, 62). On the other hand, many popular marketing textbooks do not even list "function" in their indexes (Pride and Ferrell 1985; Berkowitcz, Kerin, and Rudelius 1986; Kotler 1986; Kinnear and Bernhardt 1986). McCarthy and Perreault's book (1986) is one of the few that discusses the functional approach in its introductory chapter. Why has the functional paradigm, which guided marketing thought for over half a century, almost vanished?

The purpose of this chapter is to analyze the anomaly of the "most significant" contribution to marketing science being so disregarded in current literature. We will do so by using the metaphor of the life cycle. That is, it is often claimed that products go through a life cycle of introduction, growth, maturity, and decline. Likewise, the functional approach to the study of marketing has gone through similar stages and an analysis of these stages will explain the rise and fall of the functional approach.

The Introductory Period: 1900–1920

The beginning of the twentieth century chronicles the beginning of university education in the business area and the concomitant development of formal instruction in marketing. The first course in marketing officially offered at an American university was "The Distributive and Regulative Industries of the United States" offered in 1902 at the University of Michigan and taught by Professor E. D. Jones (Bartels 1976, 22). Other courses were soon offered at the University of Pennsylvania, the University of Pittsburgh, the University of Wisconsin, and Ohio State University. Little is known about the teaching materials used in these courses, although it may be safe to assume that they were ad hoc in nature, since no formal body of literature on marketing existed.

Credit for the first scholarly article on marketing and the beginning of marketing's formal literature is commonly given to Arch W. Shaw for his article entitled "Some Problems in Market Distribution" (1912). This is not to say that there had not been previous publications (primarily in trade journals) on such things as selling and advertising. Rather, many believe that this article was the first systematic exploration of marketing in the sense that we use the term "marketing" today. Shaw was a businessman (founder of the Shaw-Walker Company, a manufacturer of office equipment), a publisher (founder of the magazines *System* and *Factory*), and economist. He despaired that his fellow economists focused all their attention on manufacturing and production since he believed that "the problems of market distribution are no less worthy of systematic study."

Shaw was particularly interested in distributors (he used the term "middlemen") and observed that institutions such as banks and insurance companies seemed to perform many of the activities that had historically been done by distributors. Shaw developed his "functions of middlemen" (see Appendix for lists of all authors' functions) as an effort to identify the useful services that middlemen historically perform. He pointed out that the rise of banks as "functional middlemen" could be explained by noting that they have assumed the traditional middleman's function of "financing the operations." Further, the rise of insurance companies could be explained by pointing out that they have assumed the traditional middleman's function of "sharing the risk." Shaw believed that conventional middlemen were retaining their competitive positions best in the functions of selling, assembly, assorting, and reshipping.

L. D. H. Weld was the second writer in this introductory period to propose a set of functions of marketing, defining the term as "the services that must be performed in getting commodities from producer to consumer" (Weld 1917, 317). In 1916 Weld delineated eight "functions of wholesale middlemen," and then in 1917 identified seven "marketing functions" (see Appendix). Like Shaw, Weld was an economist. However, while Shaw's background was in the industrial area, Weld's background was agriculture. His agricultural orientation explains the fact that one of his functions of wholesale middlemen was "establishing connections with country shippers." Weld was primarily concerned with explaining how agricultural products are marketed and justifying the existence of middlemen in the system. Weld's research tended to point out the useful services provided by marketing intermediaries such as those who trade in agricultural futures. The research was so controversial that he was called before a legislative investigating committee in Minnesota, which tried to prove that he had been instructed by the trustees of the University of Minnesota to teach his "dangerous doctrines about the efficiency of grain marketing" (Bartels 1976, 258).

In summary, the functional approach to marketing is as old as the formal study of marketing, itself. The originators of the functional approach, Shaw and Weld, did so because economists had ignored the topic of distribution, because distribution problems were deemed to be important, because there were changes developing in distributive institutions, and because of a desire to point out the usefulness of marketing institutions in distributing goods and services. Their lists of marketing functions differed, in part, because Shaw had an industrial marketing background and Weld's background was in agriculture.

The Growth Period: 1921–1940

The two decades between 1921 and 1940 represented a growth period for the functional approach to marketing. This growth accompanied the rapid rise of marketing as a subject taught at the university level, which itself paralleled the rapid rise of business education at the university level. For example, whereas only 1,500 students were graduated from schools of business in 1920, there were more than 18,000 graduates of such schools in 1940 (Hugstad 1983). The rapid rise of university education in business and marketing prompted the development of more formal teaching materials and textbooks on the subject.

The 1920s gave rise to seven textbooks on marketing. Duncan (1921) offered a list of marketing functions in his book, but adopted the institutional approach as its organizing structure. His institutional orientation probably explains why he felt moved to include such items as "the functions of the warehouse industry" in his list of functions. Like Duncan, Brown (1925) also included a list of functions of marketing. Unlike Duncan, however, Brown organized his book using a commodity approach and the functions of marketing were de-emphasized.

The other five writers authoring marketing textbooks in the 1920s adopted the functional approach for organizing and studying the subject. Cherrington (1921) believed the elementary activity of marketing was to bring buyer and seller together in a trading mood, using merchandise functions, auxiliary functions, and sales functions. He stressed that marketing should focus on functions rather than institutions because "functionaries are constantly changing, whereas functions are not" (1921, 50). Clark (1922) was the first author to group the various functions into the categories of exchange, physical supply, and facilitating functions. Clark acknowledged that his list of functions was derived from those of Weld. He was the only author of this period to acknowledge the fact that his list of functions was not an original contribution.

The functions of marketing outlined in Ivey's *Principles of Marketing* (1923) were virtually the same as those put forth by Cherrington. Ivey emphasized the marketing of manufactured goods and used functional analysis to explain the rise of specialized "functional middlemen." He noted that "before the industrial revolution each person whose task it was to get goods from the producer to the consumer performed a part of each function" (1923, 7).

Converse (1921) was one of the few authors of this time period who did not believe that all "functions" are always necessary: "The elimination of the middleman may or may not eliminate his function. Some of the functions may be transferred to others, while others may be eliminated." He believed that "the functional approach involves a consideration of the ways in which functions are performed, of the utility in the various functions, and of the agencies which can perform the functions to the best advantage" (1930, 31).

The final textbook of this period, Maynard, Beckman, and Weidler (1927), like Clark, adopted the organizing framework of exchange, physical supply, and auxiliary functions. However, to Clark's list they added the function of "collection and interpretation of market information." When modern writers refer to the "traditional functions of marketing," they customarily are referring to the lists and groupings of Maynard, Beckman, and Weidler.

In addition to textbook writers, other book and journal contributors such as Macklin (1924), Breyer (1934), Ryan (1935), and Fullbrook (1940) discussed the merits of the functional approach, offered their own lists of marketing functions, and generally promoted functional analysis in this growth period. The debate between the functionalists and those preferring a commodity or institutional approach to marketing study was decisively "won" by the functionalists. The functional approach to the study of marketing dominated five decades, as exemplified by the fact that the functionalist textbooks of Clark, Converse, and Maynard, Weidler, and Beckman (and their subsequent revisions) were the best-selling textbooks in marketing.

The reasons for the growth and eventual dominance of the functional approach were several. First, the United States was moving away from a purely agricultural economy toward a modern industrial society. Since the commodity approach to the study of marketing was heavily agriculturally oriented, it was less appropriate for the times. Second, most marketing scholars believed that the study of "functions" was somehow more fundamental than the study of the institutions that carried out those functions.

The third factor favoring the development and acceptance of the functional approach to the study of marketing was the onset of the Great Depression in the 1930s. The problems of excess supply in the production area in the United States economy prompted academicians and businesspeople alike to focus increasing attention on problems in the marketing of goods and services, rather than their production. Further, the Depression and its resulting financial consequences led to the merger of the National Association of Marketing Teachers with the American Marketing Society to form the American Marketing Association in 1937. In the prior year the two associations had joined forces to initiate the *Journal of Marketing*. Marketing had now become officially institutionalized and the functional approach was thought highly useful in analyzing problems of efficiency, competition, and government regulation in those years of economic distress.

The Period of Maturity: 1941–1970

The 1941–1970 period reflects the maturity phase of the functional approach's life cycle. As such, one would expect to find further refinements in the approach and, also, the seeds of its decline. The work of Alderson (1965) illustrates such further refinement. He adopted the methodological approach of anthropological functionalism to explore marketing systems. In so doing, he considered the functions of marketing that had been identified by previous writers as the "subfunctions which together constitute the function of marketing as a whole" (1965, 11).

Bucklin's *A Theory of Distribution Structure* (1966) can also be considered to be a further refinement of the functional approach to marketing. Bucklin's purpose was to explain the evolution of channels of distribution. His approach, which he identified as microeconomic-functionalist, was to identify the service outputs of the channel of distribution in terms of delivery time, lot size and market decentralization, and then to determine the functional activities necessary to produce those outputs: transit, inventory, search, persuasion, and production. He proposed that the purpose of the commercial channel of distribution was to minimize its total cost for any given set of outputs desired by the consumer.

Baligh and Richartz (1967) extended the mathematical development of the functional approach. They developed a mathematical model of the channel of distribution, drawing upon the original work by Balderston (1958). The Baligh and Richartz model is based on the key concepts of cooperation, competition, and their impact on "contactual" costs. The fundamental premise underlying their theory is that "exchange transactions are not costless and that in consequence there exists the possibility that these costs can be reduced" (Baligh and Richartz 1967, 6).

McGarry's well-known article on marketing functions (1950) both provided a refinement in the functional approach and, at the same time, the seeds of its demise. McGarry believed that the traditional functions of marketing gave a perspective that was too narrow in scope, too mechanistic, and did not grasp the dynamic task inherent in any marketing system. He proposed:

> The term "function" should be so defined as to meet the purpose for which it is used. The function of the heart is not simply to beat, which is its activity, but rather to supply the body with a continuous flow of blood. The term "function" should be restricted to the *sine qua non* of marketing, those things without which marketing would not exist.

McGarry (1950) proposed six functions of marketing: contactual, merchandising, pricing, propaganda, physical distribution, and termination. Note that these functions are much closer to what typical marketing managers actually do than such "traditional" functions as finance, risk, standardization, and grading. Without knowing it, McGarry was presaging the rise of the managerial approach to the study of marketing and the demise of the functional approach.

The publication of McCarthy's *Basic Marketing* (1960) is widely cited as the "beginning of the end" for the functional approach. McCarthy organized his text along managerial lines using the Four Ps of price, place, promotion, and product. The emphasis of the book was on the problems of the marketing manager, rather than looking at the characteristics of marketing systems and their functions.

The 1960s represent a transitional period wherein books adopting the managerial approach existed side by side with those using the more traditional functional approach. Some authors attempted to merge the two approaches. For example, Staudt and Taylor (1965) proposed a list of "managerial functions of marketing." This approach was also taken in the 1965 edition of Converse, Huegy, and Mitchell. Nevertheless, by 1970 the functional approach had lost its dominant position.

The Period of Decline: 1971–Present

The 1960s' gradual decline in the use of the functional approach to teach marketing became precipitously steep in the 1970s. No new textbooks adopted the functional approach; only revisions of previously published, functionally oriented textbooks were available. By 1980, even the revisions of the functional textbooks were out of print and the triumph of the managerial approach was virtually complete. Why was the functional approach abandoned, when it had apparently served the marketing discipline so well for more than forty years? Two environmental factors can jointly explain the demise of the functional approach to marketing.

First, programs and courses of instruction across all areas of business education changed radically in the 1960s and 1970s. Many of these changes were precipitated by two classic studies conducted on business education: the Gordon and Howell (1959) report funded by the Ford Foundation and the Pierson (1959) report commissioned by the Carnegie Foundation. Neither study could find much good to report about business education in the United States. In particular, they found the "core" courses (such as marketing) to be too descriptive in content and not sufficiently analytical. Further, they strongly urged business schools to adopt a more professional-school, rather than vocational-school, approach: "Collegiate business education should educate for the whole career and not primarily for the first job. It should view the practice of business professionally in the sense of relating it to what we have in the way of relevant systematic bodies of knowledge" (Gordon and Howe 1959, 8).

Business schools in the United States responded dramatically to the recommendations of the foundations' reports. All of the areas, including marketing, attempted to decrease the descriptive content of their courses, increase their analytical and intellectual content, and adopt a more professional/managerial orientation. Consistent with the criticisms of the foundation reports, the functionally oriented textbooks in marketing were drearily descriptive.

Further, although they were not narrowly vocational, neither were they truly professional/managerial. Thus, the switch to a managerial orientation in textbooks was consistent with the trends in other business disciplines and prompted by the widely accepted criticisms of current business education made by the foundation reports.

The changing nature of competition in the American economy in the later part of the 1950s and in the 1960s also helps explain the demise of the functional approach. After World War II the United States was the only major nation of the world whose industrial structure was still intact. With ready markets in Europe and Asia, the most pressing problems for American industry lay in the area of production, not marketing. However, beginning in the 1950s, competition increased dramatically both within the United States and in the world markets. As a consequence, American industry once again turned its attention toward problems in the marketing arena. This led to the development and subsequent acceptance of the "marketing concept" and the rise of the professional marketing manager in American industry.

It is fair to say that the concept of the "marketing manager" with the responsibility of integrating pricing, promotion, product, and channels of distribution decisions, was virtually invented in the 1950s. Previous to this time, although there had been sales managers and advertising managers in abundance, these people were not marketing managers in the sense that the term is used today. Further, although there were many managers with the label "marketing," they seldom had "integrating" responsibilities. Therefore, the decline of the functional approach and the rise of the managerial approach to the study of marketing can be succinctly explained by pointing out that (1) the functional approach was too descriptive for the times; (2) the managerial approach was more analytical; (3) the managerial approach was professional, rather than vocational; and (4) the rise of professional marketing management in American industry created a strong demand for managerially trained marketing executives.

The fact that the marketing functions approach is no longer used to organize marketing textbooks does not imply that specific functions are no longer taught—for many of them still occupy prominent places in textbooks. For example, the functions of demand creation, buying (particularly consumer buying) and market information (market research) receive extensive treatment in most modern texts. Further, the functions of transportation and storage (physical distribution) receive some attention. However, the functions of finance, risk, standardization, and grading receive little or no treatment.

Conclusion

What is the prognosis for the functional approach to the study of marketing? Is it likely that it will, like the phoenix, rise from its own ashes? We suspect

6. Transporting.
7. Storing.
8. Financing.
9. Risk taking.
VI. C. S. Duncan (1921). *Marketing.* New York: Appleton & Co. "Functions of Marketing."
    1. Functions of middlemen.
    2. The transportation function.
    3. The functions of organized exchanges.
    4. The functions of the warehouse industry.
    5. The functions of commercial grading and inspection of commodities.
    6. The function of market news.
    7. The function of market price.
    8. The function of financing distribution.
VII. Fred E. Clark (1922). *Principles of Marketing.* New York: Macmillan. "The Marketing Functions."
    1. Functions of Exchange.
       a. Demand creation (selling).
       b. Assembly (buying).
    2. Functions of Physical Supply.
       a. Transportation.
       b. Storage.
    3. Auxiliary of Facilitating Functions.
       a. Financing.
       b. Risk Taking.
       c. Standardization (and grading).
VIII. Paul Wesley Ivey (1923). *Principles of Marketing.* New York: Ronald Press. "Functions of Marketing."
    1. Assembling.
    2. Grading.
    3. Storing.
    4. Transporting.
    5. Risk taking.
    6. Financing.
    7. Selling.
IX. Theodore Macklin (1924). *Efficient Marketing for Agriculture.* New York: Macmillan.
    "Classification of Marketing Services and the Utilities Which They Create."
    Elementary Utility is created by the farmers' services through their individual farm operations in contrast to marketing services below.

Utility of:	Created wholly or patly by marketing services of:
1. Place	1. Assembly
	2. Grading and Standardizing
	3. Packaging
	4. Processing
	5. Transporting
	7. Financing
	8. Distributing
2. Form	1. Assembly
	2. Grading and standardizing
	4. Processing
	7. Financing
3. Time	1. Assembly
	2. Grading and standardizing
	3. Packaging
	4. Processing
	6. Storing
	7. Financing
4. Possession	1. Assembling
	2. Grading and standardizing
	3. Packaging
	4. Processing
	6. Storing
	7. Financing
	8. Distributing

X. Edmund Brown (1925). *Marketing*. New York: Harper & Brothers. "Functions of Marketing."

1. Purchasing.
      Assembling.
2. Selling.
      Distributing.
3. Traffic control.
   a. Shipping.
   b. Delivery.
4. Storing and Warehousing.
5. Standardization.
   a. Sorting.
   b. Grading.
6. Financing.
      Utilization of credit facilities.
7. Risk taking.
      Underlies all business activity.

XI. Harold Maynard, W. C. Weidler, and Theodore Beckman (1927).
Principles of Marketing. New York: Ronald Press Co.
"Marketing Functions."
1. Exchange.
    a. Demand creation and selling.
    b. Buying (assembly).
2. Physical Supply.
    a. Transportation.
    b. Storage.
3. Auxiliary Functions.
    a. Finance.
    b. Risk bearing.
    c. Standardization and grading.
    d. Collection and interpretation of market information.
XII. Paul D. Converse (1930). *The Elements of Marketing.* New York:
Prentice-Hall.
"Typically Marketing Functions."
1. Buying (possession utility).
    a. Determining needs.
    b. Finding a seller.
    c. Negotiation.
2. Selling (possession utility).
    a. Creating demand.
    b. Finding a buyer.
    c. Advice to a buyer as to use of product.
    d. Negotiation.
    e. Transfer of title.
3. Transporting (place utility).
4. Storing (time utility).
5. Standardizing and grading (possession utility).
6. Assembling (place utility).
7. Dividing (time utility).
8. Packing (time utility).
        General business functions involved in marketing.
9. Financing.
10. Risking.
11. Recording.
XIII. R. F. Breyer (1934). *The Marketing Institution.* New York: McGraw-
Hill.
"The Marketing Functions and Utilities."
Marketing Functions   *Utility Created, Direct or Indirect*

1. Quality Determination Function
2. Storage function.
3. Contactual function.
4. Negotiary function.
5. Measurement function.
6. Packing function.
7. Transportation function.
8. Financing function.
9. Payment function.
10. Risk bearing function.

1. Form (direct or indirect). Possession (indirect).
2. Time (direct).
3. Possession (indirect).
4. Possession.
5. Possession (indirect).
6. Form (indirect).
7. Place (direct).
8. Time (indirect).
9. Possession (indirect).
10. Possession (indirect). Form (indirect). Time (indirect). Place (indirect).

XIV. Edmund D. McGarry (1950). "Some Functions of Marketing Reconsidered." *Theory of Marketing*. Reavis Cox and Wroe Alderson, eds., Homewood, Ill.: Richard D. Irwin. 265.
"Functions of Marketing."
   1. Contactual.
      The searching out of customers.
   2. Merchandising.
      Adopting products to users' wants.
   3. Pricing.
      For acceptance of customers.
   4. Propaganda.
      Persuasion to select the product.
   5. Physical distribution.
      Basically transportation and storage.
   6. Termination.
      The change in the custody of and responsibility of goods.

XV. E. Jerome McCarthy (1964). *Basic Marketing—A Managerial Approach*. Homewood, Ill.: Richard D. Irwin.
"Functions of marketing."
   1. Exchange functions.
      a. Buying.
      b. Selling.
   2. Physical distribution functions.
      a. Transporting.
      b. Storing.
   3. Facilitating functions.
      a. Grading.
      b. Financing.
      c. Risk taking.

  d. Market information.
XVI. Paul Converse, Hix Huegy, and Robert Mitchell (1965). *Elements of Marketing*. New York: Prentice-Hall.
  "Marketing Functions"
  1. Movement of ownership—creating possession utility.
    a. Buying.
      1. Awareness of needs.
      2. Selection of means of satisfying needs.
      3. Seeking sources of supply.
      4. Negotiating prices and terms.
    b. Selling.
      1. Stimulating consciousness of needs.
      2. Creating desire for means of satisfying needs.
      3. Making goods or services available to prospective buyers.
      4. Adjustment of offering to needs.
      5. Negotiating price and terms.
    c. Transfer of title and payment.
    d. Risking.
  2. Movement of goods—creating place and time utility.
    a. Transporting.
    b. Storing.
    c. Grading.
    d. Dividing.
    e. Assembly of orders.
    f. Packing.
  3. Marketing Management.
    a. Formulating policies.
    b. Providing organization.
    c. Providing equipment.
    d. Financing—providing capital.
    e. Supervising and controlling activities.
    f. Risking.
    g. Securing information, especially by accounting and research.
XVII. Thomas A. Staudt and Donald A. Taylor (1965). *A Managerial Introduction to Marketing*. Englewood Cliffs, N.J.: Prentice-Hall.
  "Managerial Functions of Marketing."
  1. Market Delineation.
      Determining who the relevant buyers are and other relevant quantitative factors that serve to define the market.
  2. Purchase Motivation.
      The assessment of those direct and indirect factors which underlie, impinge upon, and influence purchase behavior.
  3. Product Adjustment.

Those activities which are engaged in to match the product with the market in which it is to be purchased and consumed.

4. Physical Distribution.

The actual movement of goods from points of production to points of consumption.

5. Communications.

The transmitting of information and messages between buyers and seller to the end that the most favorable action climate for the seller is created in the marketplace.

6. Transaction.

The activities which must be performed between the time a meeting of the minds occurs among the parties concerned and the actual transfer of ownership.

7. Post Transactional.

The activities which assure satisfaction of the product in use, and the follow-through activities which provide feedback for more effective performance of marketing operations on a continuing basis.

References

Alderson, Wroe. 1965. *Dynamic Marketing Behavior*, Homewood, Ill.: Richard D. Irwin.

Balderson, F. E. 1958. "Communication Networks in Intermediate Markets." *Management Science*, 4 (January). 154–171.

Baligh, Helmy H. and Leon E. Richartz. 1967. *Vertical Market Structures*. Boston, Mass.: Allyn & Bacon.

Bartels, Robert. 1976. *The History of Marketing Thought*. Columbus, Ohio: Grid.

Berkowitz, Eric, Roger Kerin, and William Rudelius. 1986. *Marketing*. St. Louis: Times Mirror/Mosby College.

Breyer, R. F. 1934. *The Marketing Institution*. New York: McGraw-Hill.

Brown, Edmund. 1925. *Marketing*. New York: Harper & Brothers.

Bucklin, Louis. 1966. *A Theory of Distribution Structure*. Berkeley, Calif.: University of California Institute of Business and Economic Research.

Cherrington, Paul. 1921. *The Elements of Marketing*. New York: Macmillan.

Clark, Fred. 1922. *Principles of Marketing*. New York: Macmillan.

Converse, Paul D. 1921. *Marketing Methods and Policies*. New York: Prentice-Hall.

———. 1930. *The Elements of Marketing*. New York: Prentice-Hall.

Converse, Paul D., Hix Huegy, and Robert Mitchell. 1965. *Elements of Marketing*. New York: Prentice-Hall.

Duncan, C. S. 1921. *Marketing*. New York: Appleton & Co.

Fulbrook, E. S. 1940. "The Functional Concept in Marketing." *Journal of Marketing*, 9 (January). 229–237.

Gordon, Robert, and J. E. Howell. 1959. *Higher Education for Business.* New York: Columbia University Press.

Hollander, Stanley C. 1986. "The Marketing Concept: A Deja Vu," in George Fisk, ed., *Marketing Management Technology as a Social Process.* New York: Praeger Publishers. 3–29.

Hugstad, Paul S. 1983. *The Business School in the 1980s.* New York: Praeger Publishers.

Ivey, Paul Wesley. 1923. *Principles of Marketing.* New York: Ronald Press Co.

Kinnear, Thomas, and Kenneth Bernhardt. 1986. *Principles of Marketing.* Glenview, Ill.: Scott, Foresman & Co.

Kotler, Phillip. 1986. *Principles of Marketing.* Englewood Cliffs, N.J.: Prentice-Hall.

Macklin, Theodore. 1924. *Efficient Marketing for Agriculture.* New York: Macmillan.

Maynard, Harold, W. C. Weidler, and Theodore Backman. 1927. *Principles of Marketing.* New York: Ronald Press Co.

McCarthy, E. Jerome. 1960. *Basic Marketing.* Homewood, Ill.: Richard D. Irwin.

———. 1964. *Basic Marketing: A Managerial Approach.* Homewood, Ill.: Richard D. Irwin.

McCarthy, E. Jerome, and William D. Perrault, Jr. 1968. *Basic Marketing.* Homewood, Ill.: Richard D. Irwin.

McGarry, Edmund D. 1950. "Some Functions of Marketing Reconsidered," in Reavis Cox and Wroe Alderson, eds., *Theory in Marketing.* Homewood, Ill.: Richard D. Irwin.

Otteson, Schuyler F., William D. Pauschar, and James M. Patterson. 1964. *Marketing: The Firm's Viewpoint.* New York: Macmillan.

Pierson, Frank C. 1959. *The Education of American Businessmen.* New York: McGraw-Hill.

Pride, William, and O. C. Ferrell. 1985. *Marketing.* Boston, Mass.: Houghton Mifflin.

Ryan, F. W. 1935. "Functional Elements of Market Distribution." *Harvard Business Review* 13 (October). 137–143.

Shaw, Arch. 1912. "Some Problems in Market Distribution." *Quarterly Journal of Economics.* 26, 706–765.

Staudt, Thomas A., and Donald A. Taylor. 1965. *A Managerial Introduction to Marketing.* Englewood Cliffs, N.J.: Prentice-Hall.

Venkatesh, Alladi, and Hikilesh Dholakia. 1986. "Methodological Issues in Macromarketing." *Journal of Macromarketing* 6 (Fall). 36–52.

Weld, L. D. H. 1916. *The Marketing of Farm Products.* New York: Macmillan.

———. 1917. "Marketing Functions and Mercantile Organization." *American Economic Review* (June). 306–318.

Williamson, Oliver E. 1975. *Markets and Hierarchies: Analysis and Antitrust Implications.* New York: The Free Press.

Part II
Marketing in Historical Context

Introduction

The contributors to this section are concerned not so much with marketing thought—though hopefully there is some connection between what academics say and what practitioners do—as with the evolution of marketing as a historical phenomenon. From different perspectives the three authors present concepts of historical change, explore changes which have occurred in the character of marketing, examine examples of marketing practice from previous centuries, and suggest some implications for the future.

George Fisk discusses concepts of change over time and space which have been developed by physicists and biologists; these, he believes, have promise for illuminating at least some aspects of marketing's evolution. Fisk discusses four concepts of change: revolutionary, evolutionary, random, and deterministic. Patterns of change in marketing systems, he believes, correspond to those in biological and physical science, and share a common origin. Scientific concepts and theories, therefore, may reasonably be used to explain the processes that lead to change in marketing. Fisk introduces four types of theory: energy-entropy theories, information-learning theories, evolution-environmental theories, and self-organizing systems theory. He explains how these relate to marketing activity over time.

Fisk's arguments are provocative. Some will dispute them. But the discussion makes it very clear that natural scientists are facing up to and attempting to understand the stupendous complexity of change in nature over time; they are tackling "chaos" itself. Marketing change over time is also fearfully intricate. Should the discipline of marketing continue to rely, unreflectively, upon the now-hoary belief, derived from classical British economics, that time and complexity must be largely assumed away in theorizing—or upon the even hoarier belief (it dates to the philosopher Occam, who died in 1349) that parsimony is essential to good theory? Such are the kind of questions Fisk's essay stimulates.

Ronald Fullerton also takes the concept of temporal change as his starting point, drawing attention to the inadequacy of the U.S. social-science approaches commonly used by marketers in explicating it. He suggests, however, that German social science, particularly that infused by the philosophy of historicism, has had a historical emphasis which provides a means of understanding historical phenomena in terms of both continuity and change.

Except in its abstract "generic" sense, he argues, marketing is an historical phenomenon. Particularly if we adopt a systems perspective, it may be seen to have changed over time. Focusing upon the distinctive variant of marketing, developed in the Western world since 1500 A.D., Fullerton argues that it has not always existed, does not exist today in many parts of the world, and may not exist in the future. If we can understand its past evolution, we may find pointers to what lies ahead. The key, he theorizes, is to be found in Western marketing's almost symbiotic relationship with capitalism. The features that characterize the capitalist entrepreneur correspond closely to those that characterize the successful marketer, although writers on capitalism, by focusing closely on aspects of production, have tended to overlook this important implication. Since capitalism is shown to be a historical phenomenon, whose changes over time have been reflected in Western marketing, its near-inevitable eventual demise would also bring that of the marketing most familiar to us.

Kathleen Rassuli is concerned with the lessons to be learned from the practice of marketing in the past. After outlining some of the important issues raised by Hollander's work in marketing history, she devotes the second part of the chapter to a specific historical situation in which we can see marketing techniques and strategies being practiced. Rassuli examines the English book trade in the years following the introduction of the printing press (1470–1535 A.D.). The early printers were far from operating in a sellers' paradise, as is sometimes asserted. Their potential market was limited by the low level of literacy and the high prices they were obliged to charge to cover the high cost of paper. At the same time they were facing competition on three fronts from the second-hand manuscript trade, from hand copying, and from continental printers. William Caxton, who set up the first press in England, is shown to have flourished in such an environment by following sound marketing principles. His business is analyzed in depth.

4

Interactive Systems Frameworks for Analyzing Spacetime Changes in Marketing Organization and Processes

George Fisk

Introduction

In classical physics, Albert Einstein hypothesized that space and time are linked into a four-dimensional mathematical structure called "spacetime." Since Einstein's geometric approach to gravity was supported and then amended to describe additional, more recently discovered, forces in nature, "spacetime" is a concept now employed to measure distances in which oscillatory patterns exist over time (Freedman and van Nieuwenhuizen 1985, 74–81). Spacetime, in other words, refers to mathematically describable patterns of change over time.

Exploring the concept of spacetime can offer us new insight into, and new understanding of, the development of marketing over historical time. This chapter suggests a radically new perspective for researching, analyzing, and thinking about historical changes in marketing systems. The perspective draws heavily upon recent work in the natural sciences, particularly theories of fluctuation, to probe spacetime change and relate the findings to the analysis of marketing activities over time. The paper focuses upon four basic concepts of change which arguably apply as well to marketing organizations as to biological and physical phenomena: (1) revolutionary change, (2) evolutionary change, (3) random change, and (4) deterministic change.

The rationale for the approach taken here is as follows. In all biosocial processes, historical patterns are formed by the rhythms of life, interrupted by political and culturally punctuated events such as wars, inventions, and organizational revolutions. The patterns of observable change in marketing organizations are either revolutionary or evolutionary, random or deterministic, corresponding to patterns which have been observed in the biological or in the physical world. Although it is not possible to prove that patterns of marketing change arise from the same biological or physical interactions that produce biological evolution or celestial mechanics, the very existence of marketing metaphors such as "the fashion cycle" suggests that concepts which have a common origin in physical structure and processes have been transferred to marketing use. Because of their use in marketing, as well as the logic of their common origins and structure, it is assumed without proof that the processes of the physical and life sciences are homologous with the processes underlying change in marketing. Witness marketers' frequent reference to such terms as "price equilibrium."

In other words, it is assumed that all these processes stem from common origins rather than simply having the analogous property of appearing to be similar in pattern. On this assumption, the theoretical explanations and concepts of change drawn from twentieth century paradigm shifts in the physical and biological sciences are used to explain the processes that give rise to cyclical and historically one-directional changes in marketing.

Concepts of Change

It has been said that if one can find the right perspective for a class of problems, the individual solutions to these problems will be trivial. The purpose of this chapter is to move toward such a perspective by providing frameworks leading to the selection of theories with which to analyze the processes that underlie patterns of change in marketing history. Then, by examining variables considered in theories of fluctuation, the *processes* underlying *patterns* of historical change in marketing are explained.

History is defined here as the search for the necessary antecedents of a set of past events. The well-known scientist Stephen J. Gould (1987, 10) has referred to this as "Time's Arrow" to distinguish it from what he terms "Time's Cycle." "Time's Cycle" refers to repetitive—cyclical—occurrences over time. Gould posits "Time's Arrow" and "Time's Cycle" as the two ends of a dichotomy. In following "Time's Arrow," historical change is one-directional: an event cannot precede its necessary antecedent. Gould views history as "an irreversible sequence of unrepeatable events" (Gould 1987, 10). Historical explanation permits analyses to move linearly with time in using prior activities to predict and explain events which are believed to have followed.

The changes in marketing history which this chapter considers have occurred over a very short period in the Earth's overall history. They can be best understood as linear—by reference to Gould's metaphor of "Time's Arrow." Some changes in marketing over time are not really history as defined here, but rather are repetitive recurrences. Equally important in our discussion, therefore, are "Time's Cycles," which are embedded in such marketing metaphors as "the fashion cycle" and the Wheel of Retailing. In "Time's Cycle," events have no causal impact upon history because their apparent motions are but parts of repeating cycles. The Product Life Cycle that traces the growth, maturity, and decline of sales for a class of products exemplifies this deterministic sequence.

Gould's dichotomous polarities of cycle and arrow metaphors permit us to consider, in a single chapter, the recurring deterministic cyclical regularities and random irreversible unrepeatable events that we conventionally call history.

To help explain this dichotomy we introduce here Gould and Eldridge's Hypothesis of Punctuated Equilibrium. Proposed in 1972, it asserted that in the natural world there have been long periods of stasis or equilibrium punctuated by bursts of change. Today the reality of Punctuated Equilibrium is accepted, but the search for the *process* by which it is produced continues in the study of both living and extinct species. Our theoretical focus here is on *processes* rather than *patterns* of change because the processes give rise to the patterns we call history. Examination of the processes responsible for generating patterns of change is made in the following theory section.

Applications to Marketing

Under the conditions postulated by Punctuated Equilibrium—long periods of stasis interspersed with bursts of change—how can we apply to marketing history explanations of change derived from the physical and biological sciences? To begin, we must distinguish between distinctive historical events and recurrent behaviors that can be predicted accurately from "lawful" interactions. In other words, we must distinguish between patterns based on random events and those based on deterministic invariant but lawful relations.

Events are predictable with great accuracy if they are subject to deterministic laws, but if the accuracy of measurement is subject to uncertainty, small differences in initial conditions may lead to very large differences in final outcomes. For example, deterministic laws of gravitation predict eclipses centuries in advance, but sales, orders, and numbers of customers served cannot be predicted using marketing "laws" of retail gravitation and the like. Historical theories must allow for random change as well as deterministic lawful theories of change.

Before considering theories of fluctuation, the four concepts of change already introduced will be explained in greater detail to give the rationale for these theories. These concepts of change are derived from the two dichotomous perspectives discussed previously: "Time's Arrow" versus "Time's Cycle" and random versus deterministic change. The four concepts of change are:

1. Revolutionary change, which is sudden and discontinuous.

2. Evolutionary change, which consists of mutations produced by populations interacting over time and space.

3. Random change, which refers to changes for which necessary antecedents are unidentified.

4. Deterministic change, in which necessary antecedents are related "lawfully" to their consequences.

Revolutionary Change

Marketing investigators treat as revolutionary the sudden appearance of innovative products like personal computers. Revolutionary change includes sources of random disturbance that create discontinuity or disequilibrium in marketing systems. Product failures, innovations, new institutional arrangements, market crashes, and a list of similar marketing phenomena are members of the set of revolutionary changes sharing the characteristics of unpredictability, deviation from established patterns, and suddenness. Revolutionary change that entails sudden discontinuity or divergent behavior may alter concept, structure, and process at the same time.

Thus, following Ramaprasad (1982, 387), a change in concept, structure, or process rather than the effect of such a change may be defined as revolutionary. In dynamic systems' analysis, random transformations are classified as revolutionary. Market crashes and the emergence of fads are marketing examples of revolutionary change.

Evolutionary Change

Evolutionary change is the result of mutation and symbiosis. Boulding (1981, 23) defines evolution as the "ongoing ecological interaction of populations of species . . . which affect each other under conditions of constantly changing parameters".

Evolutionary changes in the successive epochs of marketing history appeared first with gift and barter exchanges during the food gathering and hunting stage of development thousands of years ago. These exchanges later evolved into barter and money exchanges. With the growth of agriculture, an "agora" or central trading place appeared for periodic exchanges, followed by the era of fairs and market center days. Fixed trading places employing money and credit transactions preceded the industrial epoch, which commenced in the 1800s. Electronic funds transfers and credit exchanges characterize today's information epoch. The effectiveness and efficiency of transaction energy inputs have climbed steadily through each of these epochs of exchange technology. The current era of the global village in which money transfer is simply an electronic impulse now startles no one; the transfers and movements of goods that such transactions initiate have collapsed the time separations between the initiation and conclusion of a marketing exchange. Transaction technology today is the result of a long evolutionary process.

Revolutionary versus Evolutionary Change

Revolutionary change is an element of evolutionary change in the sense that revolution requires a series of historical antecedents and that its consequences become elements of antecedent for future changes. Revolution is characterized by a sudden shift in the direction of some elements of a social system. Disruptive changes often accelerate cyclical or periodic change, thus providing the distinction between a rapid revolutionary disruption and a slow evolutionary mutation.

For example, a change in retail selling method such as the recent burst of home shopping or warehouse club shopping evokes sudden changes in retail structure and process. The revolution is in the innovative concept that combines telephone and television viewing in a way that lures consumers to call in their orders. If home shopping eventually results in a turn of the Wheel of Retailing, this consequence is an element of evolutionary change. If it continues to accelerate, home shopping will certainly produce disruptive changes in retailing, but however disruptive, these consequences are catalogued here as evolutionary because they are effects rather than causes of change in structure or process.

When in the course of time the accumulation of consequences induces a change in retailing structure, the transformation in structure is an element of the revolutionary change that may now be described as the cause of the transformation state.

Many revolutionary changes in marketing are presently under way. These include the spread of bar-code inventory management and pricing, *kanban* "just-in-time" delivery of materials in progress, twenty-four-hour continuous trading in commodity markets, and innovations in services marketing. Such changes are revolutionary because they are creating changes in the *structure* of marketing organizations. The structural changes range from reporting by cellular telephone-computers to global marketing of standardized products across diverse cultures around the world without resort to centralized trading exchanges.

Revolutionary changes in marketing are analogous to the changes that occur in biological systems. Isomorphism is of course not causality. However, mutations in gene structure that add new properties to existing gene structures create the same kinds of tests of organization for environmental suitability that can be observed in marketing organizations. The changes are homologous environmental tests of organization, not analogous formally similar principles. They may therefore aid in explaining changes in marketing by reference to changes in biological systems, namely birth-death processes. Species birth-death processes are often noted in such marketing metaphors as "the death and burial of sick products" (Alexander 1964).

Random Change

The second dichotomy of "lawful versus random" change introduces another dimension of change into the spacetime framework: uncertainty introduced by the variability in each of the interacting supply, demand, and environmental determinants of marketing activity. Uncertainty has always entailed business risk, since neither revolutionary change nor evolutionary change is easily predictable. It is now known that merely collecting more information about a phenomenon cannot identify clearly the relationship between cause and effect. The indeterminacy of outcomes is well known to sales forecasters. Such randomness caused by the interaction of differing determinants of demand has come to be termed "chaos" (Crutchfield et al. 1985, 46). "Chaos," however, can be explicated. How can this be?

Deterministic "Lawful" Change

The behavioral sciences have lagged in recognizing that "chaos is deterministic, generated by fixed rules that do not themselves involve any elements of chance . . . There is order in chaos: underlying chaotic behavior are elegant geometric forms that create randomness in the same way as a card dealer shuffles a pack of cards" (Crutchfield et al. 1985, 46). What appears to be disorder is actually deterministic "lawful" change. Since random effects can be explained by the interaction of a few variables, the possibilities of prediction are promising when determinism governs the rules by which known variables assume geometric forms.

Five Self-Evident Propositions About Change

Five self-evident propositions based on the foregoing concepts of change may be presented as axioms for understanding the two dichotomous frameworks presented previously:

1. Evolutionary change in marketing may be revolutionary and revolutionary change evolutionary, in their effects on marketing organization or process.

2. Evolutionary and revolutionary changes may be outcomes of either random or deterministic forces in spacetime.

3. Interactions between deterministic system elements may produce random effects.

4. Random forces are demonstrably ordered in all sociocultural and socio-biological systems of which marketing activity is a subset.

5. The predictability of evolutionary and revolutionary change in marketing can improve if modeling of interactions between marketing organizations and their environment measures random forces more accurately.

Measuring Spacetime Change

Time and Space Analyses of Change

The time span of marketing history is most brief in terms of the age of our planet. This limits the length of time runs against which to test the theories presented here. At best, historical analysis of marketing could go back to precommercial societies, but Vernon Mund's standard work, *Open Markets* (Mund 1948), begins much later, around 1200 B.C., and concludes with the twentieth century United States. Among the analyses with the longest time span considered is Wendel (1986), which begins with the origin of cities and ends in twentieth century America.

For managerial and public policy purposes, attention is focused upon even shorter periods. Barger's (1955) exemplary public-policy-oriented study analyzes employment, output, and distribution costs for the eighty years ending in 1949. In management control and evaluation, which do make heavy use of "historical" analysis, temporal control units customarily partition operating periods into daily, weekly, monthly, and annual reporting periods to compare fluctuation in marketing performance. The spatial control units within sales and marketing organizations commonly include local market areas, regions and territories, national, international, and finally, global markets. Thus to study change, activities are, by convention, partitioned into time and space units such as those shown in table 1.

It should be noted that all the measures in table 1 oscillate over time and space. Since fluctuation, not equilibrium, is the constant state, we need theories of spacetime fluctuation. We are also concerned with the marketing processes by means of which marketing institutions and processes appear, grow, decline, and disappear. The emergence of a steady state or an equilibrium is simply a snapshot of an ongoing process taken at a point in time. From the perspective of spacetime, equilibrium is simply a cross-section snapshot frozen in time and space. We therefore need evolutionary theories of interaction between organizations and environment.

To relate marketing flows to the physical and biological sciences it is necessary to transform economic conceptualizations of marketing flows into common units of measurement that can be transferred to measure performance in any discipline. The obvious candidates are thermal and caloric energy, information units, or other process units amenable to transformation.

For example, the delivery of food supplies may be measured by calories consumed by humans. Thermal energy delivery may be approximated by surrogate measures of energy consumed in the conduct of primary, secondary, and tertiary industry. Since energy delivery defines the birth/death rates limits for consuming populations in any geographically bounded space, the energy available in the area of supply during the consumption cycle is measured by the production and distribution of energy.

When provided with an economic value per energy unit, the value of aggregate production and distribution can be transformed back into economic magnitudes. Accordingly, periodic studies of changing supply, demand, and price movements used in management accounting can be translated into energy equivalents. As reported in news media weekly, monthly, and annually, such information could, if translated into energy units, become valuable to research workers in explaining the dynamics of market processes and in forecasting historical developments that effect the marketing operations of producers and traders. The property of interest here is the possibility that these money values can be transformed into approximate measures of energy or information.

In this manner, seasonal studies of change may examine the fluctuations in prices and profits which are associated with biologically-related changes in supplies of agricultural products whose caloric values can be closely approximated. Commodity exchange price studies conducted by agricultural college research bureaus for crops marketed could be transformed into energy units for purposes of historical comparison, the added accuracy of physical measures substituting for the unstable values of money over time.

Not all historical changes are transformable into energy or information equivalents, however. For example, seasonal studies are also important in fashion and department-store-type merchandise, automobiles, and other products, yet in these cases conversion into energy or information terms presents greater conceptual problems. The physical and dollar volume of sales are related not only to the consumer appeal of styling and the whim of fashion, but also to the transformation of psychological consumer preferences. These may be comparable over long time runs, but they cannot be translated into either energy units or into the biological rhythms of production as in agricultural commodities. Hence most studies of seasonal variation will continue to be statistical analyses of the sales for a single commodity rather than biophysical system interaction studies.

Cyclical studies may also emphasize social phenomena such as the Consumer Life Cycle, Product Life Cycle, Fashion Life Cycle, and institutional cycles of marketing intermediaries such as the Wheel of Retailing (Hollander

1960). While Product Life Cycle and innovation diffusion curves are expressed by a common mathematical formulation, the Gompertz logistic growth trajectory, much work needs to be done to transform these units into energy, information, or other phenomena comparable across the biological, physical, and social sciences. Since these problems do not appear insurmountable, it is appropriate to consider the applicability of theories of change drawn from the physical and biological sciences in an effort to advance the vision of what marketing history can become, rather than what it is at present.

Interactive System Theories for Analyzing Change

Four theories that provide new perspectives for analyzing spacetime change have appeared within the last century: (1) energy-entropy theories, (2) information-learning theories, (3) evolution-environmental theories, and (4) self-organizing systems theories.

Energy-Entropy Theories

Life-support processes require expenditure of energy. From primitive food gathering to the complex exchange of high-technology goods, marketing efforts deliver standards of living. Hence the amount of energy made available by the collecting, sorting, and dispersing activities of marketing regulates the size, growth, and level of living of a given population. The history of marketing can be seen as the history of time variation in delivering caloric and thermal energy supplies to consuming populations whose upper limits are defined by this energy-delivering capacity.

Georgescu-Roegen's (1971) *The Entropy Law and the Economic Process* introduced entropy to the social sciences. In the absence of war and pestilence, the energy-entropy framework of food supply defines the birth/death rates of populations. The equilibrium *(E)* between a population and its food supply occurs when the energy utilization rate *(U)* of the average organism *(N)* is in balance over time:

$$(U)\ (N) = (E)\ t$$

where *t* represents the time interval (Berryman and Stenseth 1984).

The history of per capita caloric energy expenditure correlates with the history of well-being. If the population is unable to regulate its growth, energy equilibrium can be maintained only by a decrease in the utilization rate *(U)*. In Sub-Saharan Africa per capita energy consumption is moving toward zero. Elsewhere it is rising as levels of living improve.

At the macromarketing societal level of aggregation the social task of marketing is to deliver a standard of living. Thus energy supply can be related to the supply of rural goods and urban goods made available through distribution networks. Food and extractive industry products may be termed rural goods. The supply of urban goods, including manufactures and services provided by the market sector, are exchanged within an economy for rural goods. Historical analysis of marketing behavior is facilitated by a spatio-temporal model of changing patterns of rural-urban goods exchanges within a society. David Young (1984) has proposed such a model to explain the forces underlying the rise and decline of early civilizations.

Young modeled, first, the biophysical environmental constraints on the flow of matter and energy through society by means of an environmental multiplier. Next he modeled the rate of change in population density by calculating birth, death, and migration rates. The amounts of rural products available for distribution were estimated by multiplying population environ-mental and technological productivity functions. These flows, necessary to generate urban-goods production, were used to estimate flow rates of ma-terials into manufacturing and services production. Using diffusion processes to estimate the flow of urban goods back to rural consumers, Young was able to model the symbiotic exchanges between the rural- and urban-goods sectors. From a historical standpoint, the significance of his analysis lies in the ability of the spatiotemporal model to analyze the rise and fall of early civilizations. Taxation is the key variable explaining the population oscilla-tions in states exercising power over jurisdictions in which rural-urban ex-changes are in steady-state relationships. By means of equations, Young estimated energy flow for a single state in its early stages and the longevity of such states in interaction with larger states that repeatedly dominated their smaller neighbors. Marketing scholars interested in historical time runs have much to learn from such mathematical archaeology.

When the time dimension is limited to a single energy epoch such as the Industrial Revolution or the Information Age, the provisioning technologies of marketing can be measured in finer detail. For example, world modeling attempts to study the contradiction between exponential population growth and finite energy resources. Multisector models include different production coefficients for retail trade, for wholesale trade, and for transportation, each of which can be followed over the periods for which simulated data are exercised interactively.

One example is to be found in the trade sector models of Roger Layton (1981). Studies of limits to growth have led to the recognition that social limits rather than physical limits constrain effective performance of markets. In the marketing literature this debate is largely ignored despite the persua-sive arguments of such scholars as Moneison (1981) and Bartels (1986).

Information-Learning Processes

Since information directs the mobilization and allocation of resources, it is appropriate to relate learning and information to energy production, distribution, and consumption. Disciplines as divergent as cell biology, electrical engineering, and psychology explain the creation, conservation, and transfer of information needed to direct the mobilization and allocation of resources by marketing activity.

Norbert Weiner introduced the concept of information as a social control mechanism in 1948. It was immediately recognized by management analysts as pertaining to internal and external communication in organizations. Weiner coined the term "cybernetics" to describe how communications were employed to steer and control the activities of purposeful organizations. Cybernetics, he said, is "the process of receiving and using information in the process of adjusting to the contingencies of the outer environment, and living effectively within that environment" (Weiner 1954, 17–18). Eric Jantsch (1981, 102) asserts that "in sociocultural evolution, information transfer becomes extended to include information about the organization, not just matter and energy, but of information itself." When information is used to shape marketing exchange by directing the mobilization and allocation of resources, the terms used define the market mechanism of supply, demand, and price.

In applying cybernetic theory to marketing systems, the role of price and inventory information in resource allocation is much discussed in the economic literature on the attraction of supplies to spatially distributed markets. In the present Information Era the range of data communicated has expanded to include orders, credit reports, market research analyses, and marketing audits. These and other data are communicated to management via accounting and marketing research departments for the purpose of "feedback," a necessary step in the cybernetic steering function that controls resource deployment. Effective resource allocation, of course, requires managers to deploy marketing and other resources to their most promising profit and sales opportunities. Thus communication, feedback, and control are the essentials of the "cybernetic mechanism" by means of which markets direct the deployment of resources. These processes are related to the spacetime application coordinates in table 1.

Evolution-Environmental Theories

Introductory marketing texts customarily identify categories of environmental influences that provide opportunities and threats to the firm in pursuit of sustainable competitive advantage. The idea of marketing-niche strategy is indeed borrowed from the concept of ecological niche or foothold. Alderson's survival theorems were premised on the notion of niche (Alderson 1957). Later writers modified this concept, and the well-known product strategy matrix of Bruce Henderson's Boston Consulting Group is essentially an analysis of firm performance relative to environmental opportunity for growth. At the microanalytic level of the firm, the drive for growth is premised on the belief that only through growth can the firm continue to attract the resources needed to maintain its competitive vitality and survival. However, growth is always constrained by the resources available in the environment.

The notion of ecological niche is also related to cities as central places where buyers and sellers can meet to conduct market exchanges. At macroanalytic levels the concept of evolutionary change examines how a species grows when conditions for births permit population additions to exceed population subtractions. For example, populations of retail stores expand during recurrent periods of rising gross margins in the Wheel of Retailing. In microanalysis, focus shifts to firms and types of firms whose customer populations provide growth opportunities and whose competitors provide the threats creating the environmental conditions facing the organization.

Environmental theories also seek to explain the evolutionary changes in structure that extend beyond "information." Boulding (1981, 17) explains that the "know-how" inherent in structure is used to direct energy to transport and transform materials in such a way as to expand the human-occupancy niche through the production of artifacts. He writes: "The pattern jogs along in an immensely complex interaction of things, organizations, and people, with biological, meteorological, and geological environments, structures, and populations" (Boulding 1981, 17).

Self-Organizing Systems Theory

The theory of fluctuation with which evolution is concerned has been advanced by the idea of self-organizing systems proposed by Ilya Prigogine and his associates in 1977 (Nicolis and Prigogine 1977). The theory links new organized states to lawful reactions and to chance via random fluctuations. It is a most promising concept for the analysis of spacetime change. Although neither marketing theorists nor marketing historians have yet sufficiently mastered the knowledge of the physical sciences required to make use of the theory, physicists have presented specific applications of it to marketing (Allen 1981).

According to the theory, a change in the structure of an existing organization may be produced by the random fluctuations of any of the interacting system variables when the system is near the points at which a new organization could emerge. *Between* the points at which a new organization could emerge an economic system is regulated by deterministic laws, but *near* the points at which change is possible, the random fluctuation determines the branch that the system follows in its reorganization.

These points, called bifurcation points, "introduce the concept of 'history' into the explanation of the state of the system" (Allen 1981, 29). A system organized according to solution "C", for example, has had a history of passage through bifurcation points "A" and "B". "Evolution involving both determinism and chance has been called 'order by fluctuation' (Nicolis and Prigogine 1977) and we see that this extension of the physical sciences offers a new paradigm which is potentially of great importance for the human sciences" (Prigogine, Allen, and Herman 1977).

The key concept here is that change in process and structure cannot be explained by traditional equilibrium analysis, which treats movement away from equilibrium as destabilizing and the return toward equilibrium as the move toward stability. Nonequilibrium order through fluctuation is an empirical reality observable in chemical and physical interactions as well as in sociocultural and sociobiological systems. Table 4–1 is illustrative of observable changes in marketing systems. Evolution in these systems occurs through their common origins as energy- and information-processing systems, not by formally similar principles.

Once self-organization takes over from random interactions, the emergence of complex order sets the evolutionary process in motion. Continuous-entropy production and dissipation of the entropy by the organization structures is initiated by random interactions. Then organization structures dissipate owing to their interaction with the existing environmental forces. This self-creative process is called autopoesis, and is observable in all biological systems. Autopoesis refers to the characteristic testing of biological cell renewal against its physical environment in a random fashion, leading to the formation of a structure that is continuously subject to modification by environmental possibilities.

Evolutionary change develops from continuous exchange between organism and environment. When internal reinforcement of fluctuations drives systems over an instability threshold, internal amplification and breakthrough fluctuations assemble a new structure. If it is environmentally viable, it persists. Thus evolutionary change can become revolutionary. The marketing historian's task is to note the underlying regularities such as the constraints on resource availability that lead to formation of novel organization structures. These may be plotted in time-space bifurcation paths.

Implications for Future Study

The next step in refining interactive frameworks for analysis of spacetime change in marketing is to construct matrices for comparing the interactive

Table 4–1.

Applications of Spacetime Measures to Marketing Activities: Spatial Dimension of Market Area Analyzed By Time Period and Level of Aggregation

Local Market Area	Regional Market Area	National Market Area
Periodic Micro	*Periodic Micro*	*Periodic Micro*
Reports on inventories, sales, costs, and profit for allocating effort to products and markets served by establishments.	Reports on inventories, sales, costs, and profit for allocating effort to divisions and functional activities and products to local markets within region.	Reports for allocating efforts to bases of allocation: Customers, products, functional activities, etc. for all served markets within a domestic economy.
Seasonal, Cyclical, and Trend Micro	*Seasonal, Cyclical, and Trend Micro*	*Seasonal, Cyclical, and Trend Micro*
Marketing resource mobilization policy and strategy decision for a single trading area.	Marketing resource mobilization policy and strategy decision for all trading areas in a geographic region.	Marketing resource mobilization policy and strategy decision for all trading areas in all regions served by a marketing organization.
Catastrophic Local	*Catastrophic Regional*	*Catastrophic National*
Bankruptcy	Population out-migration.	Depression

MACROMARKETING ORGANIZATIONS

Local Market Area	Regional Market Area	National Market Area
Periodic Macro	*Periodic Macro*	*Periodic Macro*
Industry and public policy decisions on area development, resource commitments to provisioning technologies.	Industry and public policy decisions on regional development, resource commitments to provisioning technologies.	Industry and public policy decisions on domestic economy development, resource commitments to provisioning technologies.
Seasonal, Cyclical, and Trend Macro	*Seasonal, Cyclical, and Trend Macro*	*Seasonal, Cyclical, and Trend Macro*
Efforts to shape the environment of the trading area to marketing opportunities and threats.	Efforts to shape the environment of the region to marketing opportunities and threats.	Efforts to shape the national environment to marketing opportunities and threats.

system constructs just described along the spacetime dimensions identified earlier in this chapter. The purpose of such an effort would be to determine the range of applicability of each of the frameworks to each of the conditions under which they might be managerially applied to marketing systems. But having thus plowed up the prairie, it is appropriate to leave the dust storms to the care of the next generation of Ph.D. dissertation writers and to the marketing historians who will supervise their theses.

References

Allen, Peter M. 1981. "The Evolutionary Paradigm of Dissipative Structures," in E. Jantsch, ed., *The Evolutionary Vision*. Boulder: Westview. 25–72.

Alderson, Wroe. 1957. *Marketing Behavior and Executive Action.* Homewood: R.D. Irwin.

Alexander, Ralph S. 1964. "Death and Burial of Sick Products." *Journal of Marketing* 28 (April).

Barger, Harold. 1955. *Distribution's Place in the American Economy Since 1869.* Princeton: Princeton University Press.

Bartels, Robert. 1986. "Marketing: Management Technology or Social Process at the Twenty-First Century?" in G. Fisk, ed., *Marketing Management Technology as Social Process.* New York: Praeger. 30–32.

Berryman, Alan, and S.C. Nils. 1984. "Behavioral Catastrophes in Biological Systems." *Behavioral Sciences* 29 (April). 127–137.

Boulding, Kenneth E. 1978. *Ecodynamics.* Beverly Hills: Sage.

———. 1981. *Evolutionary Economics.* Beverly Hills: Sage.

Crutchfield, James P., J.D. Farmer, N.H. Packard, and R.S. Shaw. 1986. "Chaos." *Scientific American* (Dec.). 46–57.

Freedman, Daniel Z., and P. van Nieuwenhuizen. 1985. "The Hidden Dimensions of Spacetime." *Scientific American* (March). 74–81.

Georgescu-Roegen, Nicholas. 1971. *The Entropy Law and the Economic Process.* Cambridge: Harvard University Press.

Gould, Stephen J. 1987. *Time's Arrow Time's Cycle.* Cambridge: Harvard University Press.

Hollander, Stanley C. 1960. "The Wheel of Retailing." *Journal of Marketing* 24 (July). 37–42.

Jantsch, Eric. 1981. *The Evolutionary Vision.* Boulder: Westview Press.

Layton, Roger. 1981. "Trade Flows in Macromarketing Systems, Part I." *Journal of Macromarketing* 1 (Spring). 35–48.

Moneison, David D. 1981. "What Constitutes Usable Knowledge in Macromarketing." *Journal of Macromarketing* 1 (Spring). 14–22.

Mund, Vernon A. 1948. *Open Markets.* New York: Harper & Row.

Nicolis, G., and I. Prigogine. 1977. *Self-Organization in Nonequilibrium Systems.* New York: Wiley.

Prigogine, Ilya, P.M. Allen, and R. Herman. 1977. "The Evolution of Complexity and the Laws of Nature" in E. Laszlo and J. Bierman, eds., *Goals in a Global Community.* New York: Pergamon.

Ramprasad, Arkalgud. 1982. "Revolutionary Change and Strategic Management." *Behavioral Science* 27 (October). 387–392.

Wendel, Richard F. 1986. "Cities as Agencies of Distribution: the Vital Role of Exports" in G. Fisk, ed., *Marketing Management Technology as Social Process.* New York: Praeger. 87–102.

Young, David A. 1984. "A Spatiotemporal Model of Civilization." *Behavioral Science* 29 (April).

Wiener, Norbert. 1954. *The Human Use of Human Beings: Cybernetics and Society.* Garden City: Doubleday.

5
Modern Western Marketing as a Historical Phenomenon: Theory and Illustration

Ronald A. Fullerton

> "One must never lose sight of the fact that even such manifestations of civilization as modern capitalism are unique historical phenomena *(historische Individuen)* which appear but once on the stage of history."
> —Werner Sombart, *Der moderne Kapitalismus*
> (Vol. III, 1928, translated by the author)

> "Novelty, newfangledness, must be matters of excitement for an aggressive commercial and capitalist world: ever-increasing profit is not made in a world of traditional crafts and stable fashions . . . Aggressive consumption lies at the heart of successful bourgeois society."
> —J.H. Plumb, "The Acceptance of Modernity" (1982), in N. McKendrick, J. Brewer, and J.H. Plumb, *The Birth of a Consumer Society.*

Introduction

Stanley Hollander has shown us that marketing as we know it now does indeed have a history, a long history. It is a product of a protracted, still-ongoing, historical evolution. The evolution of marketing has not been a simple unilinear progression, but rather a vexedly complex process that cannot be adequately penetrated by the standard analytical methods which contemporary U.S. marketers have adopted from the Anglo-American social sciences. Such methods are founded upon assumptions which either ignore or oversimplify temporal change (Fullerton 1987b). The methods of historians are illuminating, but tend to shy away from the theorizing and abstract conceptualization *which we need at this point* to make the process of marketing history clearer and more challenging as a research subject to both marketers and historians.

A more suitable approach becomes possible through adopting method-

Special thanks to A. Fuat Firat, Erdogan Kumcu, and Ronald Savitt for their suggestions.

ologies devised by German social scientists, who have had a dynamic-historic emphasis for well over a century. Marx and Schumpeter are well-known representatives; differing on many points, both stressed the historical and therefore fluid nature of major social and economic systems and structures. The German methods allow formal yet flexible conceptualization and theoretical explanation of social, cultural, and economic phenomena in change over time; they permit a sophisticated awareness of the simultaneous working of continuity and change. The theories and concepts intend to reflect known historical evidence, but in their presentations factual details are less central than they are in most historians' works.

This chapter consciously follows the German tradition. In particular, it follows the social science philosophy of historicism. Summed up in the work of Mannheim (1924), Meinecke (1972 [1936]), and Troeltsch (1922, 1923), historicism is based on profound reflection upon historical change; the philosophy has been related to marketing issues by Fullerton (1987a). Unlike the positivist assumptions in which most marketers have been trained, historicism stresses the fluid, evolutionary, and *ultimately transient nature of all social, cultural, and economic systems and structures*. In historicist analysis, equilibrium can never be the norm; flux is—complex and often unpredictable flux. The contemporary U.S. sociologist Wallerstein, whose work is imbued with historicism, captures its essence very well in this passage about major economic structures: "Structures are those coral reefs of human relations which have a stable existence over relatively long periods of time. But structures too are born, develop, and die" (Wallerstein 1974, 3).

During their course of existence, social and economic structures form systems which are held together by shared core values. These values may be absolutes, *but only for a time*. "The Absolute itself is in a process of becoming," writes Mannheim; "it is itself spatially bound . . . There are no formulations *(Forderungen)* which are valid for all times, but rather the Absolute reconstitutes itself in a new, concrete form in every age" (Mannheim 1924, 56, 58, translated by the author). Core values, systems, and structures, then, are historical phenomena, and so too are the theories and concepts which explicate them.

This chapter conceptualizes Modern Western Marketing—the vigorous marketing which we take for granted—as a historical phenomenon, then proposes a theory to explain why Western marketing has evolved as it has. This theory builds upon interpretations of capitalism by Max Weber and Werner Sombart, two of Germany's greatest social scientists. Historical illustrations of the theory are followed by a discussion of its implications for the future of Western marketing.

Marketing as a Historical Phenomenon

In its generic sense of voluntary-exchange relationships undertaken to fulfill human needs and wants, marketing goes far back into history, even into prehistory (Nevett and Nevett 1987; Pryor 1977; Walle 1987). Yet it is undeniable that many differences distinguish present from past marketing. Some are trivial, others fundamental. The further back one traces marketing in a cultural area, the greater the differences are likely to be. *Thus the pervasiveness of marketing activities, their degree of development, their vigor, their effectiveness—in brief, their very ethos—differ markedly across time and across societies; and with these differ the extent of marketing's social, cultural, and economic impact.* In addition to differences across time, there can be enormous differences in marketing in different geographical/cultural areas even at the same points in time, for example between Communist Eastern and capitalist Western Europe today (Naor 1986).

The best way to conceptualize all of this is to think in terms of marketing systems, each representing a major variant of marketing. Such systems differ not only in their practices and institutions, but also in the core values which foster these. Following historicist reasoning, marketing systems are posited to be unified by "a single central value, which unites within itself . . . all the other values" (Troeltsch 1923, 94). In contemporary Communist Romania the marketing system's central value is the belief that only the highest levels of government can establish the priorities by which "major and critical resources are allocated" (Naor 1986, 29).

Marketing systems are historical phenomena—they begin, they evolve, and change; ultimately they end. Each has a unique identity. That in Romania, for example, can be dated to the establishment of a Communist government there in the 1940s, which helped give its unique identity. As will be shown, the marketing system of the economically advanced West began much further back, several hundred years ago, with the contemporaneous beginnings of capitalism and what historians call the "modern" era of European history about 1500 A.D.

Modern Western Marketing as a Historical Phenomenon

Modern Western Marketing is a specific variant of marketing which has developed in the economically advanced capitalist societies of Western Europe and North America; in recent years it has spread to the Pacific Rim. It has been distinguished by its aggressive growth orientation and by what Max Weber termed "purposeful rationality" *(Zweckrationalitaet).* "Purposeful rationality" means that actions are undertaken consciously and for specific and practical purposes; nothing is left to fate or chance, and results are monitored against intentions. Taboos and traditions are not permitted to stand in the businessperson's way. Operationally, Modern Western Marketing can be defined as the vigorous cultivation of existing markets and equally vigorous efforts to open up new ones through insistent promotion, frequent introduction of new products, careful study of market demand, and ongoing efforts to control and coordinate distribution channels. Existing channels may be bypassed in the quest for larger markets.

The exchange process here is characterized on the seller side by impatiently assertive goals and by approaches which fuse creativity and rationality. On the buyer side it is characterized by an aggressive, never-satisfied, urge to consume. Modern Western Marketing is the most highly developed marketing in the world, and the most effective at providing a high material standard of living. Its impact is and has been enormous, not only upon the societies in which it has flourished but also upon much of the rest of the world, to which it serves as both an aspirational paradigm and as a reminder of economic backwardness (Berger 1986).

It did not always exist. The marketing attitudes and practices as well as the marketing environment in Western Europe five hundred years ago were closer to those of today's most somnolent and backward "less developed country." Marketing efforts were minimal and feeble—when they were present at all. Consumption urges were, in the aggregate, equally feeble. Powerful tradition repressed entrepreneurial urges (Berger 1986).

Modern Western Marketing is a historical phenomenon, not a universal one. This fact is of more than antiquarian interest. That this variant of marketing did not always exist in the past implies very strongly that it may not always exist in the future. Though the past may lack compelling interest for some marketers, the future should not. In the case of Modern Western Marketing, an evaluation of its past evolution will aid in understanding its current state and likely future. The theoretical key to such an evaluation lies in the relationship between Modern Western Marketing and capitalism. For it is capitalism which provides the central value of Modern Western Marketing.

The Theory of Capitalism and Modern Western Marketing

The Concept of Capitalism

Although many historical writers date the phenomenon of capitalism to the late 1400s, the word itself was not used until 1854. Its core meaning of employing resources (capital) to secure profit through a market exchange process is widely accepted, but around this has developed an efflorescence of definitions which have quite different emphases (Dobb 1962). To the present-day Marxist sociologist Wallerstein (1974, 16; 1980, 27, 31), capitalism is essentially a method of appropriating surpluses through which one social class controls and exploits another. To many American businessmen it is a paradise (now lost) in which government refrains from bothering free enterprise. Some see vigorous competition as the central fact about capitalism; others argue that capitalism inevitably represses competition.

So varied, contradictory, and controversial are the ways of defining capitalism, some scholars despair of the value of the word. As the great historian Braudel (1977, 46) noted, however, it simply has no adequate substitute. The phenomena which can be subsumed under it are too important to be either ignored or scattered. Moreover, there is substantial agreement that capitalism has been a basic, if not the basic, driving and creative force behind the spectacular material development of modern Western civilization (Berger 1986, 19). During the past five centuries, while monarchs have strutted and poets scribbled, capitalist businessmen have quietly created the dynamic, materially advanced, intensely commercialized Western culture which has become the dominant paradigm for most of the world.

But how? Through which mechanisms did this happen? Here the vast literature on capitalism is of surprisingly little help. Karl Marx emphasized the productive—supply—powers of capitalist enterprise, and so have most subsequent historians and economists whether Marxists or not (Dobb 1963, 8–10; McKendrick, Brewer, and Plumb 1982, 96–97). Demand for the products that the capitalists released in such abundance has either been presented as a given (e.g., in the "Production Era" myth in introductory marketing texts) or, at the other extreme, asserted to have been forced upon the public through, in Marx's words, "conquest" and "exploitation" (Marx and Engels 1978 [1848], 475).

Neither view is satisfactory. The few historical works which have examined marketing activity as an explanatory factor for the commercialization of society, however, suggest what practicing businesspeople have long felt: that demand is developed mainly mainly by conscious, energetic, and purposeful human activities—by active marketing efforts to discover, meet, and (sometimes) stimulate it (Fullerton 1975, 1977, 1979, 1988; McKendrick, Brewer, and Plumb 1982). Some of these efforts have been aggressive, but it is absurd hyperbole to describe them in Marx's martial terms.

Capitalism and Modern Western Marketing— Closely Related

The theory advanced here is that there is a close relationship between Modern Western Marketing and capitalism: *The marketing developed in the modern Western world is the concrete manifestation of capitalist ideals.* Modern Western Marketing, energetic and effective, cannot be understood apart from capitalism; it developed with capitalism, has over time changed in response to changes in capitalism, and may vanish if capitalism follows the prediction of many and vanishes itself.

To elucidate this process, the important points about capitalism are those emphasized in the definitions given by Werner Sombart (1863–1941) and Max Weber (1864–1920). The complementary nature of these definitions was noted nearly sixty years ago by Fechner (1929). To Weber and Sombart, the essence of capitalism is a powerful system of beliefs to which business-men believe that they must conform whether they want to or not (Weber 1976 [1904–1905], 180–181; Sombart 1954 [1927], 68–69; Parsons 1928, 651; 1929, 35, 43). The goal of the capitalist, according to Weber (1976 [1904–1905], 17) is "the pursuit of profit, and forever *renewed* profit, by means of continuous, rational . . . enterprise . . . It rests upon the expec-tation of profit by the utilization of opportunities of exchange." An emphasis on the ongoing, theoretically infinite, nature of the capitalist enterprise is also central to Sombart (1967 [1915], 172–173). Profit under capitalism is calculated rationally, that is by taking balances expressed in numerical (i.e., monetary) terms. Profit is essential according to Weber, not because the capitalist is greedy—he may or may not be—but rather because "an indi-vidual capitalistic enterprise which did not take advantage of its opportun-ities for profit making would be doomed to extinction" (Weber 1976 [1904–1905], 17). Extinction of the enterprise is the worst fate that can befall its owner(s) under the capitalist value system. *Since the capitalist businessman feels compelled to make his venture an ongoing, self-sustaining one, and since he can only achieve this goal through ongoing success (i.e., profit) in the market exchange process, he must discover and practice the most effec-tive marketing possible.*

Here then is the crucial point in the relationship between capitalism and Modern Western Marketing: Capitalism engenders energetic and ambitious marketing, which in turn enables capitalism to realize its goal of self-sustainment. One is unthinkable without the other; one reinforces the other.

The need of capitalism for effective marketing becomes even more evi-dent in light of Sombart's great insight (1927, 68) that "the goals of the capitalist enterprise are . . . without bounds *(unbegrenzt)*". The capitalist entrepreneur is not content to merely sustain his enterprise into an infinite future, but also to make it grow, to unleash the "enormous energy" (1927, 69) inherent in the capitalist labor arrangements. Sombart finds capitalism to be fired by the same restless, never-satisfied, all-embuing aggression and ambition which from the 1500s through 1800s impelled Western Europeans to surpass all previous and then-contemporary civilizations in exploration, science, and technology. Capitalism's enormous ambitions, moreover, are made more potent by the rational and calculating discipline of its entrepre-neurs. To Sombart, the capitalist entrepreneur unites in a single person: (1) the conquerer who smashes obstacles which would hinder his venture; (2) the organizor who meshes people and materials to accomplish tasks large and small; and (3) the trader who is able to negotiate with and convince others to purchase his products (Sombart 1967 [1915]).

Energetic, creative, and competitive, the capitalist entrepreneur disdains tradition. If he is to realize his goal of making the business venture thrive without limits as to size or duration, he will not tolerate the passive, inhibited, often-inactive exchange process which had once prevailed in the West. Believing in his own power, uncowed by the magic and superstition which held sway in most of the rest of the world and which reinforced conservative behavior (Weber 1927), the capitalist will carefully plan his activity to ensure success in the market. He will be impatient of older, cumbersome methods of distribution. He will be unwilling to tolerate low levels of demand, no matter how strongly sanctioned by religious, social, or political custom those levels were. He will try to push over, under, around, or through restraints established by public policy, e.g., sumptuary legislation. He will seek to discover and meet existing demand, to stimulate latent demand, and even to encourage new demand—because not to do so would be to risk the life of his business enterprise.

Thus the logical outcome of capitalism as defined by Sombart and Weber is an aggressive, rational, and creative variant of marketing—Modern Western Marketing. Capitalism cannot be seen merely as the progenitor of awesome productive forces, as has hitherto been common, but also of awesome distributive forces, forces which have had enormous impact upon nearly every facet of life. Ironically, Weber completely misses this logical implication of his work. Sombart does too, despite writing about marketing activities at some length.

Capitalism and Modern Western Marketing as Historical Phenomena

Both Sombart and Weber depict capitalism as a historical phenomenon, that is, a phenomenon which did not always exist, will not always exist, and undergoes change over the course of its existence. Sombart in particular believes that the full flourishing of capitalist practice took several centuries to evolve. Both emphasize that capitalism, like most historical phenomena, has only existed in a fraction of the world, in their time little beyond Western Europe and part of North America; some of Weber's greatest work endeavors to explain why capitalism did not take root elsewhere.

Since capitalism is a historical phenomenon of less than universal reach, it follows that Modern Western Marketing is, too. The following section illustrates this with historical examples showing that Modern Western Marketing has evolved in tandem with capitalism.

Capitalism and Modern Western Marketing: The Historical Relationship Illustrated

Periodization

Most investigators agree that capitalism has evolved through several historical periods (Berger 1986; Puhle 1984; Sombart 1919–1928): (1) Pre-capitalism—the late Middle Ages (1300–1500 A.D.); conventionally cited to show the contrast with conditions under capitalism. (2) Early capitalism— 1500–1800 A.D.; restrained but growing. (3) High capitalism—1800–1929; unrestrained. (4) Recent capitalism—1930–present; a new synthesis.

Pre-Capitalism: Barriers to Change, ca. 1300–1500 A.D.

Examination of the economic, social, and cultural conditions that prevailed in Western Europe during the 1300s and 1400s strongly confirms that both capitalism and Modern Western Marketing are historical phenomena, for neither was in much evidence then (Heilbroner 1962). The rationality of conduct so central to capitalism had not yet developed (Huizinga 1924), nor had the emphasis on building an ongoing business. Behavior which we would describe today (Etgar 1983) as "bounded rationality" and "opportunism"— and expect to find only in the least developed areas of the third world—was the norm for what minimal economic life there was in Western Europe.

Under the values then prevalent, the energies and ambitions of Europeans had to be channeled into war, romantic love, and Christian devotions. Few would have even wanted to invest their energies in business, since economic life was low in prestige and promise; it was left for the most part to the outcast Jews. Levels of demand were fixed according to social station, which was almost immutable. For the great bulk of Europe's population, low-level self-sufficiency was the normal manner of life, so aggregate demand was low; among the tiny upper order it was erratic as bouts of indulgence alternated erratcially with spells of extreme asceticism (Huizinga 1924, 18).

What little market-oriented production and commerce that did exist was inhibited by powerful traditions. Guilds restricted output, but not to enlarge their profits, the very notion of which was considered suspect in the eyes of God. The widely accepted Christian notion of the "just price" was a strong inhibitor. Efforts to stimulate demand, like efforts to compete with others for business, were simply unthinkable. While trade within local areas was repressed with moral constraints, long-distance trade ran to the other extreme, being conducted according to the ancient principle of *caveat emptor;* no one expected repeat business, the idea was to cheat and escape (Nussbaum 1933, 152; Weber 1976 [1904–1905], 57–58).

Given such beliefs and conditions, the role of marketing activities in, and their impact upon, society were slight. Exchange relationships were infrequent, repressed, and largely confined to a tiny minority of society.

Early Capitalism and Early Modern Western Marketing, 1500–1800

Capitalism began to emerge about 1500, though there had been isolated earlier manifestations. The question of why and how it came into existence, why in Western Europe, and why at this time, is beyond the scope of this chapter.

Western Europe in 1500 showed signs of enormous energy and daring. The long voyages of maritime discovery then under way represented a courageous willingness to burst the bounds of tradition, custom, and superstition that had constrained medieval Europeans and that continued for centuries to constrain the advanced civilizations of the Orient (Weber 1927; Braudel 1973, 300–309). Capitalism partook of the same spirit of daring. With its onset came "the emergence of money-making as an honored occupation," to cite a well-known historical economist (Hirschmann 1977, 129). Energies and ambition could now flow into founding and operating business ventures—which would perforce involve making conscious and purposeful marketing efforts.

The process was slow, however. The old ways were tenacious, the new frequently hesitant. The conservative business practices of the pre-capitalist period still prevailed in much of Western Europe: "In countless cities commerce and industry were mired in lethargy, protected from every innovation by urban trade privileges and guild regulations," writes the historian DeVries (1976, 233) of Western Europe even after a century of capitalism. Instead of working to make his business venture thrive without limits through ceaseless infusions of capital, the early modern entrepreneur frequently misinvested or dissipated his capital, or cashed it in so that he could ape the living style of rentier noblemen. Projects designed to produce quick riches were more numerous and popular than those which would require ongoing effort. There was no overwhelming commitment to the exchange process: Investors were happy to invest openly in voyages of piracy. Price competition was still disapproved of, as were advertising and competitiveness in general (DeVries 1976; Nussbaum 1933; Sombart 1919–1929).

For the entrepreneur who was ambitious and innovative, the environment in much of Europe was indifferent at best, hostile at worst. Publishers trying to develop efficient commercial networks through which to sell books, for example, faced such obstacles as a primitive banking and a wretched transportation system (Febvre and Martin 1976).

Above all, large-scale demand for almost any conceivable product was still minimal, the great peasant bulk of Europeans still living in traditionalistic torpor as thick as that in China or India. Several historians (Nussbaum 1933, 222; DeVries 1976, 179) report as widespread a custom familiar to those who study today's less-developed countries: People would work for wages only until they had earned that bare minimum needed to support their existing, low, living standards, then stop working until penniless. The near-universal desire for material betterment which is so fundamental a part of the twentieth century Western marketing environment simply did not exist then. It would have to be created if capitalism were to flower fully. That, however, would be a major undertaking, difficult and revolutionary. "In the early modern [European] society," according to DeVries (1976, 189), "strongly held beliefs about the permanence and sanctity of the social hierarchy tended to limit the ability of merchants to foster new consumption patterns."

On the other hand, there existed small, usually urban, pockets of society where change could flourish. The then-emerging national governments were strongly interested in promoting prosperity, which would strengthen their states (Dixon 1981). Some merchants and even nobles were willing to establish and operate capitalist enterprises. Slowly, gradually, capitalism began to develop: "A new state of mind was established, broadly that of an early, still-faltering, Western Capitalism—a collection of rules, possibilities, calculations, the art both of getting rich and of living" (Braudel 1973, 400).

Early capitalism was restrained. Its most eloquent advocate to both Sombart and Weber was the American Benjamin Franklin, who counseled that no businessman should spend more than six hours a day on his business. An influential school of thinkers then praised market commerce for its power to polish and civilize man and society (Hirschman 1977, 1982).

The marketing efforts of the time clearly reflect the ethos of early capitalism. Mass marketing and ruthless competition were foreign to entrepreneurs then. But these businesspeople did, often with the encouragement of central governments, work assiduously to develop markets among the nobility, the high clergy, the growing urban bourgeoisie, and the governments themselves. War materials (the biggest market), books, luxury items of all types, town and country mansions, high fashion clothing, sugar, coffee, tea, and cacao—all were products for which lucrative and expanding markets were being consciously fostered and skillfully served (Braudel 1973; DeVries 1976; Nussbaum 1933; Sombart 1913, 1919–1929).

To make these ventures flourish, efforts were made to devise more effective methods of marketing. Sober and honest business practices were found to build and maintain relationships with buyers. Attention was given to demand. Publishers chose texts for which demand was thought to be steady, and strove to fashion more better distribution systems, because they wanted an adequate and ongoing return on their invested capital (Febvre and Martin

1976). Germany's entrepreneurial merchants and peddlers worked to circumvent the cumbersome guild system (Walker 1971, 121–122). Fixed location retail shops were established in cities all over Europe to increase contact with, and consumption by, the growing well-to-do urban public. The influx of exotic goods from Africa, the Americas, and Asia spurred such consumption further; the combined effect seems to have been to create a sustained desire for novelty among the urban public, which in turn opened up ever-new fields for creative marketers to cultivate (McKendrick, Brewer, and Plumb 1982). In France, Louis XIV (1643–1715), the "Sun King," the most grandiloquent of all European monarchs, deliberately used his spectacular court to publicize new French fashions for the export trade (DeVries 1976, 188).

The Transition to High Capitalism: England in the 1700s

The development of the enormous productive powers of the Industrial Revolution is a well-known aspect of eighteenth century England, as is the fact that the pioneers of the Industrial Revolution were such capitalist entrepreneurs as Josiah Wedgewood and Mathew Boulton. The historians McKendrick, Brewer, and Plumb (1982) have now shown that the marketing efforts of some of these same entrepreneurs worked in tandem with their productive breakthroughs. Marketing activities played "a substantial and a positive role" (McKendrick, Brewer, and Plumb 1982, 2) in creating the world's first "consumer society," a society in which for the first time in history large numbers of people could—and would both want to and be permitted to—consume an ever-renewed stream of products on a regular basis, a society in which the process of commercialization extended to leisure and to childhood itself.

The marketing efforts which brought about the commercialization of English life were more vigorous, refined, and efficacious than any seen previously. Advertising exploded all over the urban landscape, fashion cycles were astutely developed and accelerated—demand was purposefully shaped and enlarged. It was in England, during the second half of the eighteenth century, that Modern Western Marketing emerged full force.

High Capitalism, 1800–1929: Modern Western Marketing as a World-Historical Force

During this period of English-style aggressive and creative capitalism, capitalism engendering and allied to aggressive and creative marketing became the exemplar for most of Western Europe, the United States and Canada, and Japan. In bringing about genuine "commercial societies" in these areas,

Modern Western Marketing transformed the material, social, and mental basis of life more thoroughly than any phenomenon since the introduction of agriculture during the Neolithic Revolution thousands of years before.

High capitalism saw the ideals of capitalism carried to their logical conclusion in business behavior. Business ventures were increasingly viewed as ongoing ventures, to be run by aggressive professional managers even if their founding families died out or lost interest (Chandler 1977; Parsons 1929). Weberian "purposefully rational" management became more and more common, aided by improvements in accounting, law, finance and banking, transportation, and communication, and in the education and discipline of the labor pool (Cochran 1974, *passim;* Landes 1969, 3). The legal development of the corporation with limited liability, which is presumed immortal, made it easier to create enduring enterprises. At the same time, technological advances, explosive population growth, and rapid urbanization created new market opportunities. The important point to note here, however, is that these opportunities had to be rationally and energetically acted upon in order to be realized—there was nothing automatic or inevitable about the growth of markets (Cochran 1974). The ancient Greeks had brilliant technological breakthroughs including a steam engine, but these remained curiosities, uncommercialized, with no impact upon the way of life.

The advance of high capitalism meant that opportunities were acted upon consciously, vigorously, and purposefully in order to generate ongoing profits. Early capitalism's restrained goals and demeanor gave way to unrestrained aggression and ambition. Correspondingly, Western marketing underwent a great surge of energy and creativity as the nineteenth century unfolded, according to historical research done so far (Fullerton 1975, 1977, 1979, 1985, 1988; Hollander 1964, 1986; Porter and Livesay 1971; Presbrey 1929; Redlich 1935; Williams 1982). Within many businesses, older, more conservative institutions of production, distribution, pricing, and promotion were openly challenged by aggressive marketers and, after decades of struggle, were usually overmastered by the end of the century. Enraged by the reluctance of many merchant wholesalers and retailers to accept innovative products, especially branded ones, manufacturers broke the near-monopolistic hold of the merchants over intermediate distribution, and circumvented the old-line retailers. They sent forth literal armies of door-to-door salesmen to sell the then-new aluminum cooking utensils in the United States when retailers shunned the product around 1900. When banks refused to grant consumer credit for automobile purchases, Overland and other producers established their own credit arm around 1915. Old ways could not be tolerated, for they threatened the continued growth and prosperity which were central to capitalist businesspeople.

Whole new segments of the population were brought into the market by means of new products, more and better promotion, and more aggressive retail institutions. Amorality was evident in some of the marketing, for example in the rabid practices of James B. Duke's American Tobacco Company.

Yet the overall moral character of business enterprise in its dealing with customers improved markedly during the late nineteenth and early twentieth centuries (Shaw 1916, 109, 201), as businesses saw the marketing value of ethical dealing in sustaining demand. Retailers realized that many people were prone to buy more if not attacked by the sales help.

Modern Western Marketing was intensely proactive during the high capitalist period, with a strong thrust toward discovering and stimulating latent demands as well as towards creating new ones. These marketing efforts at once benefited from and enhanced the pervasive restlessness and discontent with the existing, which was becoming so intrinsic to Western life.

Recent Capitalism, 1930–Present

The Great Depression, which began in 1929, abruptly ended the era of high capitalism. Capitalism's exuberance was rapidly curbed by legislation, by powerful if informal forces of public opinion, and by its own weakened self-confidence. As late as the 1950s capitalism was so restrained-looking that some questioned if there was any vitality left. There was indeed, proclaimed Levitt (1956); the spirit of capitalism, "visionary, innovationary, and developmental" (Levitt 1956), had merely been institutionalized—it was actually the key element in the value system to which the bland-looking businessmen in their gray flannel suits conformed. And there was considerable vitality beneath the overt restraint.

This vitality was seen to be a threat during the 1960s and 1970s, when capitalism came under severe attack in the United States, Canada, Western Europe, and Japan. But during the past decade it has rebounded, particularly in North America and the Far East. The entrepreneur is now lionized in ways reminiscent of the time of high capitalism, and Sombart's great 1915 vision of capitalist entrepreneurship (Sombart 1967 [1915]) seems thoroughly contemporary.

Modern Western Marketing has continued to reflect developments and change in capitalism. During the 1930s and 1940s research and managerial techniques were refined in efforts to enlarge markets which had been severely shrunk by the Great Depression. Formal and ongoing research to understand buyers and their needs became even more widespread than before 1930, and utilized more sophisticated survey and analytical techniques (Hollander 1986). Marketing people led in the effort to justify capitalism—and its distinct variant of marketing. These promotional efforts, aided by advances in public relations, helped business enterprise to regain public confidence. So, too, did the formalizing of the "Marketing Concept" as corporate and academic dogma starting in the decade of the 1950s. Marketing practices have shown considerable vitality and ingenuity; some of them reflect striking advances in marketing research and in the understanding of consumer behavior. There has been an outpouring of new products and new retailing methods. More than they have for decades, Western businesses recognize the importance of marketing to ongoing success ("Fuehrungstauglich" 1986; "Marketing: the New Priority" 1983). But, how long will all this last?

The Future (?) of Capitalism and Modern Western Marketing

Scenarios of Doom

Despite its current strength and proven record of evolving to meet challenges, capitalism is held by many to be inevitably doomed. Even a well-informed recent enthusiast of capitalism such as Berger asserts that it lacks that emotional and mystical capacity to legitimize itself which would guarantee it long life (Berger 1986, 215). Three principle scenarios of the doom of capitalism can be distinguished: (1) the self-destruction thesis, (2) the exhaustion thesis, and (3) the feudal shackles thesis. The self-destruction thesis is by far the best known. It argues that the very energies which capitalism unleashes will eventually, inevitably, corrode and destroy its bases of support just as they destroyed those of the pre-capitalist order. In the classic versions of Karl Marx (Marx and Engels 1978 [1848]) and Joseph Schumpeter (1950), this is an argument of tremendous logical and rhetorical power. The empirical bases of the argument have not been as strong, however; Marx's and Engel's 1848 predictions have yet to be born out by historical realities (Marx and Engels 1978 [1848]).

The exhaustion thesis as advanced by Sombart (1919–1928, 3: 1013–1014) and by Heilbroner (1982), combines logic and historical observation. Capitalism is foreseen to stagnate as its people—its markets—become surfeited with material abundance, for which the physical environment cannot much longer provide resources in any event. Too, capitalism's institutions and value system will burn themselves out with time; there are assumptions of entropy here. Sombart cites the decline of capitalist vigor in Britain as a likely precursor for other countries.

Britain is also the prime example for the feudal shackles thesis described by Albert O. Hirschman (1982, 1474). According to this line of thought, feudal, i.e., pre-capitalist, ideals and mores have not really been extirpated by the advance of capitalist ones. Rather, they, like fire smoldering in the depths of a peat bog, retain latent potency which can erupt with great power to weaken capitalist ideas and behavior. The feudal shackles thesis does fit the British case well (Wiener 1981), but is harder to justify for other countries.

How Valid are the Doom Scenarios?

As against the arguments for capitalism's doom, are the arguments for its indefinite continuation. The German sociologist Simmel (1955, 61–63) reasons that the competitive marketing efforts to woo customers so basic to high and recent capitalism, work to knit societies together and strengthen them rather than tear them apart as Schumpeter and others believed. The descriptions of intense personal commitment to make the business venture succeed which Sombart wrote about over seventy years ago (Sombart 1967 [1915], 176–183) apply as well today; there is no visible exhaustion of spirit and will. Finally, capitalism has demonstrated enormous and consistent resiliency and adaptability (Landes 1969, 3). It has changed over the five centuries of its existence, changed markedly, and the changes have helped it to survive and thrive. Capitalism has again and again shown resurgent vitality even as it seemed to be growing tired or weak; the past decade in the United States is an example.

Yet we cannot be sure that capitalism will always survive. Since it is a historical phenomenon, given a long enough time span, it most likely will not. It will eventually come to an end, replaced by some other compelling structure of attitudes, beliefs, and rules of conduct. Moreover, since historical researchers agree that the pace of fundamental change has been accelerating rapidly during the past century and a half in the West, the end may come sooner than past experience would imply.

The Future of Modern Western Marketing

Marketing in the generic sense may go on forever, but the demise of capitalism will almost surely bring that of Modern Western Marketing. Both are historical rather than eternal phenomena; closely linked since their inception, they have evolved in tandem and should continue to do so until their demise. To be sure, it is conceivable that a belief-attitude-behavior system other than capitalism could provide the impetus for Modern Western Marketing's unique vigor, creativity, and effectiveness. The incentives need not be positive, nor the rewards joyful: one of Weber's (1976 [1904–1905]) most famous images is that of capitalism as an "iron cage" in which people are confined whether they wish it or no. Yet the fact that Modern Western Marketing has never appeared apart from capitalism over a period of five hundred years renders such a scenario highly conjectural. So, too, does the fact that the goals of other systems do not mesh as well with Modern Western Marketing as do those of capitalism. Marketing under Communist, predominantly Socialist, or other statist systems has been quite different in form and results. Aside from statist systems, the only others powerful enough to be considered here are some religious ones, e.g., now-resurgent Islamic fundamentalism. But the goals of such systems are at substantial variance with those realizable under Modern Western Marketing.

Conclusion

Although marketing in the generic sense of voluntary exchange relationships is timeless, specific variants of marketing thought and practice are historical phenomena—they evolve, and change, and can end. The advanced marketing of North America and Western Europe—Modern Western Marketing— is a historical phenomenon. Closely related to the historical development of Western capitalism, it grew up with capitalism, has flourished with it, and will likely end if capitalism does. Using an approach inspired by the classical German social science philosophy of historicism, a theory of the relationship between capitalism and Modern Western Marketing has been proposed and related to long-term historical developments.

Modern Western Marketing has been, and remains, a powerful force which shapes the social, cultural, and economic environment far more than is acknowledged in most of our current U.S. marketing literature (for an exception see Savitt 1986). It has had enormous historical impact, playing a major, perhaps *the* major role in shaping the intensely commercialized and consumption-oriented societies of Western Europe, the United States, Canada, and, recently, parts of Asia. Today many look to it as an agent of economic development for the less-developed parts of the world. Yet since it is so closely allied to capitalism, which does not prevail in most of the world, it may not be transferrable (Dominguez and Fullerton 1986). It is neither universal nor eternal; it is historical, and therefore real.

References

Berger, Peter L. 1986. *The Capitalist Revolution*. New York: Basic Books.

Braudel, Fernand. 1977. *Afterthoughts on Material Civilization and Capitalism*. Translated by P. M. Ranum. Baltimore: Johns Hopkins University Press.

———. 1973. *Capitalism and Material Life 1400–1800*. Translated by M. Kocham. New York: Harper & Row.

Chandler, Alfred D. 1977. *The Visible Hand*. Cambridge: Harvard University Press.

Cochran, Thomas C. 1974. "The Business Revolution." *American Historical Review* 79. 1449–1466.

DeVries, Jan. 1976. *Economy of Europe in an Age of Crisis 1600–1700*. Cambridge: Cambridge University Press.

Dixon, D. F. 1981. "The Role of Marketing in Early Theories of Economic Development." *Journal of Macromarketing* (Fall). 19–27.

Dobb, Maurice. 1962. *Studies in the Development of Capitalism*. Revised ed.. New York: International.

Dominguez, Luis, and Ronald A. Fullerton. 1986. "The Role of Western Practices in the Organizational Structure and Marketing Behavior of Industrial Firms in an Import-Substituting Nation." In E. Kumcu, A. F. Firat, M. Karafakioglu, eds., *The Role of Marketing in Development*. Istanbul: Istanbul University. 39–48.

Etgar, Michael. 1983. "A Failure in Market Technology Transfer." *Journal of Macromarketing* 3 (No. 1). 59–68.

Febvre, Lucien, and H.-J. Martin. 1976 [1958]. *The Coming of the Book*. Translated by D. Gerard. London: NLB.

Fechner, Erich. 1929. "Der Begriff des kapitalistischen Geisten bei Werner Sombart und Max Weber." *Weltwirtschaftliches Archiv* 30. 194–211.

"Fuehrungstauglich? Ueber Marketing an der Unternehmensspitze" (1987), *Absatzwirtschaft* (January), 26–33.

Fullerton, Ronald A. 1977. "Creating a Mass Book Market in Germany 1870–1890." *Journal of Social History* 10. 265–283.

———. 1975. *The Development of the German Book Markets 1815–1888*. Unpublished Ph.D. diss. Department of History, University of Wisconsin—Madison.

———. 1987a. "Historicism: What It Is, And What It Means For Consumer Research." In Wallendorf, M. & P. Anderson, eds., *Advances in Consumer Research* 14. Provo, Utah: Association for Consumer Research. 431–434.

———. 1988. "How Modern is 'Modern' Marketing? Marketing's Evolution and the Myth of the 'Production Era' ". *Journal of Marketing* 52 (February or April).

———. 1987b. "The Poverty of Ahistorical Analysis: Present Weakness and Future Cure in U.S. Marketing Thought" in A. F. Firat, N. Dholakia, and R. Bagozzi, eds., *Philosophical and Radical Thought in Marketing*. Lexington: Lexington Books. 97–116.

———. 1985. "Segmentation Strategies and Practices in the 19th Century German Book Trade: A Case Study in the Development of a Major Marketing Technique." In Chin Tiong Tan and J. N. Sheth, eds., *Historical Perspective in Consumer Research: National and International Perspectives*. Singapore: National University of Singapore. 135–139.

———. 1979. "Towards a Commercial Popular Culture in Germany 1870–1914." *Journal of Social History* 12. 459–511.

Heilbroner, Robert L. 1982. "The Future of Capitalism." *Challenge* 25 (No. 5). 32–39.

———. 1962. *The Making of Economic Society*. Englewood Cliffs: Prentice-Hall.

Hirschman, Albert O. 1977. *The Passions and the Interests*. Princeton: Princeton University Press.

———. 1982. "Rival Interpretations of Market Society." *Journal of Economic Literature* 20 (December). 1463–1484.

Hollander, Stanley C. 1964. "Anti-Salesman Ordinances of the Mid-Nineteenth Century." In Stephen A. Greyser, ed., *Toward Scientific Marketing*. Chicago: American Marketing Association. 344–351.

———. 1986. "The Marketing Concept: A Deja Vu" in G. Fisk, ed., *Marketing: Management Technology as Social Process*. New York: Praeger. 3–28.

Huizinga, Johann. 1924. *The Waning of the Middle Ages*. Translated by F. Hopman. London: Edward Arnold.

Landes, David. S. 1969. *The Unbound Prometheus: Technological Change and Industrial Development in Western Europe from 1750 to the Present*. Cambridge: Cambridge University Press.

Levitt, Theodore. 1956. "The Changing Nature of Capitalism." *Harvard Business Review* 34 (No. 4). 37–47.

Mannheim, Karl. 1924. "Historismus." *Archiv fuer Sozialwissenschaft und Sozialpolitik* 52. 1–60.

"Marketing: The New Priority." 1983. *Business Week* (November 21). 96–106.

Marx, Karl, and F. Engels. 1978 (1848). *Manifesto of the Communist Party*. In R. C. Tucker, ed., *The Marx-Engels Reader*, second ed. New York: Norton. 469–500.

McKendrick, Neil, J. Brewer, and J. H. Plumb. 1982. *The Birth of a Consumer Society*. Bloomington: Indiana University Press.

Meinecke, Friedrich. 1972 (1936). *Historicism*. Translated by J. E. Anderson. London: Routledge & Kegan Paul.

Naor, Jacob. 1986. "Towards a Socialist Marketing Concept—the Case of Romania." *Journal of Marketing* 50 No. 1 (January). 28–39.

Nevett, Terence, and Lisa Nevett. 1987. "The Origins of Marketing: Evidence from Classical and Early Hellenistic Greece (500–300 B.C.)." In Terence Nevett and Stanley C. Hollander, eds., *Marketing in Three Eras: Proceedings of the Third Conference on Marketing History*. East Lansing: Michigan State University. 13–22.

Nussbaum, Frederick L. 1933. *A History of the Economic Institutions of Modern Europe*. New York: F. S. Crofts.

Parsons, Talcott. 1928–1929. "Capitalism in Recent German Literature: Sombart and Weber." *Journal of Political Economy* 36. 641–661; 37, 31–51.

Porter, Glenn, and H. C. Livesay. 1971. *Merchants and Manufacturers: Studies in the Changing Structure of Nineteenth Century Marketing*. Baltimore: Johns Hopkins Press.

Presbrey, Frank. 1929. *The History and Development of Advertising*. Garden City: Doubleday.

Pryor, Frederic L. 1977. *The Origins of the Economy*. New York: Academic Press.

Puhle, Hans-Juergen. 1984. "Historische Konzepte des entwickelten Industriekapitalismus." *Geschichte und Gesellschaft* 10. 165–184.

Redlich, Fritz. 1935. *Reklame. Begriff—Geschichte—Theorie*. Stuttgart: Enke.

Savitt, Ronald. 1986. "Time, Space and Competition: Formulations for the Development of Marketing Strategy." *Managerial and Decision Economics* 7. 11–18.

Schumpeter, Joseph A. 1950. *Capitalism, Socialism, and Democracy*. Third ed., New York: Harper & Row.

Shaw, Arch W. 1916. *An Approach to Business Problems*. Cambridge: Harvard University Press.

Simmel, George. 1955. *Conflict*. Translated by K. Wolff. Glencoe: Free Press.

Sombart, Werner. 1954 (1927). *Die deutsche Volkswirtschaft im 19. Jahrhundert*. Stuttgart: Kohlhammer.

————. 1967 (1913). *Luxury and Capitalism*. Translated by P. Seligman. Ann Arbor: University of Michigan Press.

————. 1919–1928. *Der moderne Kapitalismus*. Three vols. Munich and Leipzig: Duncker & Humblot.

————. 1967 (1915). *The Quintessence of Capitalism*. Translated by M. Epstein. New York: Fertig.

Troeltsch, Ernst. 1923. *Christian Thought*. Translated by F. v. Huegel. London: University of London Press.

————. 1922. *Der Historismus und seine Probleme*. Tuebingen: J. C. B. Mohr.

Walker, Mack. 1971. *German Home Towns*. Ithaca: Cornell University Press.

Walle, Alf. 1987. "Import Wine at a Budget Price: Marketing Strategy and the Punic Wars." In Terence Nevett and Stanley C. Hollander, eds., *Marketing in Three Eras: Proceedings of the Third Conference on Marketing History*. East Lansing: Michigan State University. 13–22.

Wallerstein, Immanuel. 1974, 1980. *The Modern World System*. Two vols. New York: Academic Press.

Weber, Max. 1927. *General Economic History*. Translated by F. H. Knight. Glencoe: Free Press.

————. 1976 (1904–1905). *The Protestant Ethic and the Spirit of Capitalism*. Translated by T. Parsons. New York: Scribners.

Wiener, Martin J. 1981. *English Culture and the Decline of the Industrial Spirit, 1850–1980*. Cambridge: Cambridge University Press.

Williams, Rosalind H. 1982. *Dream Worlds: Mass Consumption in Late Nineteenth Century France*. Berkeley: University of California Press.

6

Evidence of Marketing Strategy in the Early Printed Book Trade: An Application of Hollander's Historical Approach

Kathleen M. Rassuli

Introduction

Many marketing phenomena are not recent cultural artifacts but have existed in one form or another for centuries. This notion is often overlooked by marketers. At an anecdotal level, marketers generally believe that people were probably trading perhaps even in Neanderthal times. But we believe their trade practices were primitive. The techniques used by the ancients, or even those of their more contemporary counterparts, bore little resemblance to current marketing practices.

The repetitive nature of many marketing phenomena is a common theme permeating many of Stanley Hollander's works. Hollander has, on numerous occasions, reminded us that history can be used to gain a better understanding of marketing phenomena. He would reject naive hypotheses about repetition (Hollander 1984, 13). Nevertheless, he believes, by limiting ourselves to the present, many important insights into marketing and its environment are lost. Fundamental micro and macro marketing questions remain unasked.

This chapter highlights Hollander's contribution to marketing thought through his use of history to understand marketing phenomena. An attempt is made to expand on Hollander's work by providing examples of the "actual and potential dimensions" (Hollander 1984) of marketing in the fifteenth century book trade. By showing that the early printers were engaged in practices similar to those of present-day marketers, it is hoped that our marketing time horizon can be expanded.

Themes in Hollander's Work on Marketing History

In his history seminars, Hollander provides his students with the opportunity, for which I am indebted, to explore the existence of marketing in the past. In his teaching and research, Hollander always stresses the necessity and richness of a historical perspective. He recognizes a difference between the history of scholarly work in marketing and the history of marketing itself. However, he always points out that the marketing historian must consider the work of both marketing scholars and marketing practitioners. While the history of marketing scholarship may be a relatively new phenomenon, the practice of marketing is not.

A lack of historical perspective is perhaps understandable in a time and culture where progress is valued as an end in itself. Assuming that progress has been made, the past seems outmoded and gauche. Fortunately, for our profession, a few scholars have taken the time to look back. While Hollander would eschew the honor, his work stands as a monument to historical scholarship in marketing. He has illuminated, in his careful and deliberate manner, the nature of marketing. And in so doing, has pioneered a path and set the standard for future marketing historians. Hollander's work will stand up to the historians' test of validity, the test of time.

Three interrelated themes run through Hollander's work. First, he believes that history provides the discipline with a more balanced look at current phenomena. Secondly, he demonstrates that marketing phenomena existed in the past. Thirdly, by recognizing the history of marketing, Hollander demonstrates that the discipline can gain insights into the relation of marketing to the macroenvironment. Each of these themes will be discussed in turn. Still, the coherent underlying thread which ties each of Hollander's works together is his desire to demonstrate the usefulness of a historic perspective.

The nature of Hollander's historical arguments is complex. His works are richly illustrated; thus, they defy simple classification. Furthermore, the underlying themes in his work are not mutually exclusive. It is beyond the scope of this research to offer more than a tentative summary. A thorough synthesis at this time would be premature. The six articles chosen exemplify the three themes (Hollander 1960; 1963; 1971; 1972–73; 1984; 1987). The articles cover such disparate topics as retailing, consumer behavior, the legal environment, and macromarketing. Moreover, they cover a time span of almost thirty years. Each article has certainly contributed substantively to the body of knowledge of the respective area. But, the focus of this section is not on the topical content. Rather, the focus here is on Hollander's historical approach.

Hollander teaches that history is a guard against the faddish. A historical approach enables us to place current phenomena into their proper perspective. He argues against simplistic theories and hypotheses—that is, a unidimensional approach to marketing questions. As early as 1960, Hollander questioned the existence of a "natural law of retailing" in his classic article "The Wheel of Retailing." Using the history of retail institutions such as supermarkets in underdeveloped countries and vending machines, the author points to examples which do not conform to the wheel hypothesis. He shows that the wheel hypothesis is not inevitable for all retail institutions (1960, 41).

More recently, in an article appropriately titled, "The Marketing Concept—A Déjà Vu," Hollander demonstrates quite conclusively that the typical exposition of the history of the marketing concept is simplistic.[1] He finds most textbook versions of this history to be "oversimplified and platitudinous," and laments that "almost by definition, platitudes are generally accepted beliefs" (1987, 5). Twenty introductory marketing textbooks show similar time frames for the evolution. According to Hollander, practice of the marketing concept is not of recent extraction. Furthermore, the evolution of the marketing concept lacks validity even for twentieth century U.S. marketing history. Numerous examples are given of companies which had a marketing outlook (as opposed to selling or production) early in this century. Hollander points out that the sales of nonsubsistence items and services grew during the early part of this century—which would indicate discretionary spending power well before 1955. He cites the simplification movement of the 1920s as "inverse evidence of the [same] product diversification and segmentation inherent in the conventional marketing concept" (1987, 20). In summary then, in the author's own words, "Caution should temper enthusiasm for any one swift panacea that is supposed to resolve marketing problems" (Ibid., 39).

Once marketing phenomena are placed into historical perspective, it is clear that many current phenomena are not historically unique. If one is able to delineate the underlying dimensions of marketing phenomena, it is a short step to realize the relationship between seemingly unrelated marketing concepts. This is the task which Hollander sets for himself in "She 'Shops for You or With You'" (1971). The author looks at a little-known and largely forgotten marketing functionary—the "professional shopper" or shopping surrogate. Between 1850 and 1940 individuals and independent organizations offered to shop for consumers. Hollander sketches the similarity of these surrogates to more recent specialists, such as travel agents and interior decorators and to such disparate agencies as the United States Department of Agriculture grading service and Consumers' Union. They are similar in that they all "reduce the information gap between producers and purchasers" (1971, 233). The author lists several reasons for the use of various surrogates, for example, improving selection and as an alternative to spending one's own time in the purchase process. Hollander concludes that consumers, in general, are reluctant to give up their role as shoppers to these specialists.

In "Sumptuary Legislation: Demarketing by Edict" (Hollander, 1984), the relatedness of marketing phenomena is dramatically demonstrated by the existence, at various times in the past, of sumptuary laws. These are laws "designed to inhibit specified consumption practices on the part of all or some segments of society" (1984, 4). These regulations, which constitute a form of demarketing, existed with regard to dress, for example, in ancient Greece and Rome and in medieval Europe. For Hollander, prohibitions on the use of alcohol and on gambling are recent manifestations. Hollander concludes that sumptuary laws have failed to stop the intended consumer behavior (ibid., 12). Additionally, the necessity to legislate against consumption implies that a strong consumption urge existed (ibid., 13).

A third theme which unites the various works of Hollander is his emphasis on understanding the relationship between marketing and the macroenvironment. It follows that if marketing existed in the past, then history can be used to gain a richer understanding of the marketing-environment relationship. For Hollander, the question of causality is not a simple one; he deals with this question in two articles. In "Retailing—Cause or Effect?" (1963) the author notes that company histories comprise the typical approach to retailing history. By concentrating on the merchant prince, however, such histories can overlook the contribution of the environment to the merchant's opportunity (1963, 221). In essence, Hollander shows that while merchants may have an effect on the environment (e.g., merchant princes acting as purchasing agents for consumers), the accomplishments of merchants are effectively limited by the environment. Support is found in manufacturers' absorption of influence in old retail strongholds and the limitations in developing countries on the types of acceptable retail institutions.

In a later work, "Consumerism and Retailing: A Historical Perspective," (1972–73), Hollander again focuses on the influence of the environment on marketing. Turning his attention to the history of consumer movements in the United States during this century, he shows that consumer movements are generally middle- and upper-class phenomena, counter to what intuition would dictate (1972–73, 20). In the past, consumeristic movements have not replaced retail institutions (Ibid., 14). Hollander identifies what he calls a "rachet process." That is, "few consumeristic enactments have ever been repealed" (Ibid, 19).

In summary, Stanley Hollander's work demonstrates his unique approach to the study of marketing. Whether it is in the form of a poolside luncheon speech whimsically entitled "Contemplating Our Navels," or in the form of detailed arguments, he asks marketers to step back and look at ourselves and our history. He demonstrates that many of our notions of marketing history are simplistic and that current marketing had its historical equivalents. Further, the relation between marketing and its environment is complex. He boldly asks the discipline to question its assumptions. Moreover, by his example, he provides the guidelines for such research. By not excluding or delimiting the range of "acceptable" marketing concepts, marketers can gain a much richer understanding of the environment and discipline of marketing. At the very least, a historical perspective allows the discipline to pose more interesting questions.

Exploring the Early English Book Trade

If, as Hollander posits, marketing practices pre-date this century, then one would expect to find examples of marketing in earlier centuries. The medieval trade in printed books provides an excellent ground to explore the early application of marketing strategies and techniques. In that market, one can observe conditions prior to the introduction of printed books. The use of a historical example such as this provides an opportunity to witness the choices made by market participants. That is, under a given set of environmental conditions, how did marketers (printers, publishers) approach the market, what kinds of marketing strategies did they use? In discussing priorities in research on strategy, Day and Wensley (1983) note the need for historical industry studies to gain a better understanding of the evolution of a market. According to these authors, industry evolution is probably an adaptive process where consumers respond to marketers' offerings, send feedback, and marketers alter their offering (Ibid., 17). Of course, any observation of the history of a market depends on the availability of data for the period.

Data Sources and Problems

Medieval historians have pondered and investigated in infinite detail the various aspects the early book trade. Innumerable articles and books have been written about the history of printing and printers, bookbinders, booksellers, authorship, and later publishing. Winckler (1972, 4) notes the monumental work of Besterman, who lists 100,000 entries under the heading of "printing" alone. The Newberry Library's six-volume catalog contains 23,000 entries on the history of printing (Ibid., 7). Uncountable biographies have been written on the early printers (e.g. Blake, 1985 lists 301 biographies of William Caxton, England's first printer and hundreds of related works). In fact, historical work on this topic dates back to the mid-sixteenth century.[2] It is difficult to classify these sources on a primary-secondary continuum of historical sources (Savitt 1980). Nevertheless, these histories and "histories of histories" provide much evidence of marketing activity following the introduction of the printing press. This chapter will draw on these sources. From a *historian's* perspective new facts have not been uncovered. But, for the *marketing* discipline, disparate pieces of evidence drawn together illuminate a small portion of marketing history.

Two limitations should be mentioned. First, the period of study has been limited, for the most part, to the years 1470–1535.[3] In some instances details of the book trade prior to, and following, this period are instructive. The chapter touches on both English and Continental printers, with heavier emphasis placed on the former, in particular on William Caxton. The printing press arrived in England relatively late compared to continental countries. (See "Book Market Conditions").

Second, research on this period of history is hampered by problems of language, translation, and interpretation of old documents. Also, cultural values and period biases exist in the varied presentations of bibliographic materials. These problems are compounded by data gaps and disagreements.

General Market Conditions

Notions of early marketing practices are colored by the belief that early marketers followed the selling or production concept. Zikmund and D'Amico (1986) exemplify a somewhat toned-down version of this belief in the evolution: "The marketing concept, common-sensical as it seems, was not practiced extensively by business until the middle of this century" (16). There is no need to reiterate Hollander's (1987) arguments on the validity of this evolution.

Some textbook authors have gone beyond the marketing concept and deal with the history of marketing more generally. Cravens and Woodruff (1987, 14) and McCarthy and Perreault (1987, 26) believe the function of marketing was mainly that of personal selling and distribution until the industrial revolution. In such an atmosphere, one would find little need to use marketing strategy, as the term is used today (Kotler 1980, 80). However, contrary to this hypothesis, McKendrick et al. (1982) provide evidence that Josiah Wedgwood used complex marketing strategies during the eighteenth century.

What of marketing under the guild system? Guilds are generally assumed to have been cartel-like organizations exercising, more or less, strict control over members. Clearly, under such conditions, one would *not* expect the marketing concept to have been practiced; there would have been little room for strategic marketing maneuvering. According to Thorelli (1983) goods were produced locally, there were few middlemen and little need for marketing research. The reputation of sellers was based on user experience and word-of-mouth instead of advertising. Prices were fixed by the guilds and innovation was hampered (Ibid., 8). This may be an accurate portrayal of the guild system in general, but it cannot account for the facts of the market for printed material. Notwithstanding the guilds, the printing press was developed and successfully launched. The section which follows attempts to show that oversimplified hypotheses about marketing and the marketing concept are not sufficient for the early trade in printed books. At least for this case, marketing theory is not justified in characterizing the industry as part of a simple trade era where middlemen sold the surplus output of families (McCarthy and Perreault 1987, 26).

Book Market Conditions

Biographer Lehmann-Haupt (1950, 64) says the temptation is to believe that the early printed book market was a "publisher's paradise." According to that author, an uncritical observer would believe that Peter Schoeffer (successor to Gutenberg 1457–1503) was "equipped to print whatever the public demanded, at incredibly low prices, with practically no competition to fear and the whole of ancient and medieval literature to choose from. Literary property was free, there were no royalty or copyright considerations, no censorhsip regulations, no reviewers to fear or appease" (Ibid., 64). Indeed, Hirsch (1978) says that Fust and Schoeffer were without any competition. Biographers often conclude that in the early years Caxton was virtually without competition in the English market (Blades, 1861).

At first glance, the market might appear to have been favorable for sellers. Momentarily pause to consider some general information about the market for printed books. Up to approximately the 1450s the only books available were in the form of manuscripts which were transcribed by hand. In 1454 the first printing was done; in 1456 Gutenberg's Bible was printed (Lone 1930, 3). Many historians characterize the printing industry of the time as conservative. Both Williamson (1967, 94) and Febvre and Martin (1984, 79) agree that the appearance of the printed book caused very few changes in the market for books. In fact, in Augsburg illiminated manuscripts were being produced as late as 1470–1480 (Lehmann-Haupt 1978, 219). According to Lehmann-Haupt (1950) the market was still heavily influenced by the practices of the manuscript trade. Printed books were designed to be similar to the manuscripts they hoped to replace. Schoeffer was a conservative innovator in relation to the changes he introduced in the format of the book (Lehmann-Haupt 1950). In addition, the content of his productions was conservative; almost 60 percent of his books were of theological content (Ibid., 66). In fact, most books printed in Europe before 1500 (called incunabula) were in Latin, 77 percent according to Febvre and Martin (1984, 249). Of the content matter, 45 percent was religious (Ibid.). According to Boorstin, the Venetian printer Aldus' motto was "make haste slowly" (1983, 525).

Prior to 1471, few cities in Europe had printing presses. Febvre and Martin (1984, 184–5) list presses in Mainz (the birthplace of the press), Nuremburg, Augsburg, Strassbourg, Basel, and Beromunster in Germany, and in Paris, Venice, Rome, Subiaco, Folligno, and Seville. By 1480, Italy had 50 towns with presses, Germany had 30, France had 9, Holland and

Spain had 8 each, Belgium and Switzerland had 5 each, and England had 4 (Ibid., 182). In total there were 110 cities with presses (Ibid.).

Availability of books was important to the major markets for books— clergy, lawyers, professors and students. Febvre and Martin (1984, 20) note that the scarcity of books led to copies being sold and resold. The aristocracy comprised a small luxury market. Lehmann-Haupt (1978) lists environmental changes in the early fifteenth century which led to a need for printed books. These include the rise of universities, the awakening of vernacular literature, the revived interest in classical literature and the "demand of new classes of readers" for "popular, inexpensive books (ibid., 228). Febvre and Martin (1984, 22) list lay advisors of the Court, state officials, rich merchants, and town citizens among the market for books. They note that "no bourgeois household was complete" without copies of devotional works; these were often given as wedding gifts (Ibid., 28).

Literacy, and therefore the number of readers, is difficult to estimate. Plant (1974), Bennett (1969), and Febvre and Martin (1984) all believe that literacy was on the rise. Fifteenth century estimates conflict. By some accounts very few people could read. But a statement by Sir Thomas More tells that approximately 60 percent of people could read (Bennett 1969, 28). Although most historians would seriously doubt this unusually optimistic estimate, Plant notes that enrollment in "grammar schools" was on the rise. "Fees were usually so low as to draw not only the younger sons of the nobility but also the children of tradesmen and small landowners" (1974, 37).

Space limitations do not permit a full discussion European history during the period in question. There is some evidence that, relative to the time after the 1530s, the environment was somewhat more favorable in the late 1400s. Guilds, with all their attendant restrictions, were characteristic of the time. However, the Stationer's Company was not incorporated in England until 1557. The feudal system was in force, but perhaps on the decline (Febvre and Martin 1984, 21 note a gradual decline from the late thirteenth century). There was a small middle class (Wright 1958). Even though government alliances (internally and externally) were being made and broken, 1484 saw legislation to permit the importation of books into England (Plant 1974, 27). It was not until 1534, the book trade in England had successfully petitioned the government to limit the importation of books (Pollard 1978, 21). A law enacted in 1615 limited the number of printers in England to twenty-two (Pollard 1978).

Roberts says the printing press reduced the price of a book by four-fifths (1889, 19). Price may have been important factor, even for the relatively wealthy markets. Bennett quotes Copeland (an assistant and successor to Caxton), who said that customers were unwilling to pay as much as "a fourpence and thought that a penny was enough" (1969, 186). And here is where a number of problems arose in a market otherwise favorable to sellers.

The cost of printing, which entailed acquiring a press and the capital to undertake the printing, was one problem. The press itself was relatively inexpensive (Febvre and Martin 1984, 110). Moreover, the press could be leased, for a small sum, on a yearly basis. The major cost was the paper. In one example from 1771, Febvre and Martin (1984, 114) show that paper made up 65 percent of the total cost of printing an edition 4,250 (they show that this was similar to the fifteenth century). In a Venetian example they show that the paper cost 1½ to 2 times as much as the printing (Ibid., 112).

Moreover, from a marketers perspective the fact that few native printers operated in the English market, does not imply that an English printer would have had no competition. Certainly all printers competed with the manuscript *scriptora* (copiers) and the secondhand market in manuscripts. Lehmann-Haupt notes that manuscript books of hours were "still doing very well" in the early sixteenth century (1978, 220). One could consider this to be "generic competition." Moreover, authors record a flood of books exported from the continent to the English market. Bennett refers to the record of the Port of London which shows 1400 books entering the port in 1479–80 (1969, 185). In the early part of the sixteenth century, as many as 15 percent of the works in vernacular English were printed on the Continent (Bennett 1969, 188). Competitive printing sources were centered in France, the Netherlands and Antwerp (Avis 1973, 234). Since for the most part, notwithstanding their English publications, continental printers printed Latin and liturgical works, these printers could be considered "product form" competitors. Thus, even the first English printer would have had both domestic and foreign competitors. Duff (1948) lists printers. His work shows volatility in the market. Ten printers produced books for the English market, during Caxton's time, three within England and six outside. The three English printers were Rood of Oxford, Lettou and Machlina. Rood printed for the university. Lettou printed five books on his own (Duff, 1948). Machlina, who probably took over Lettou's business, printed twenty-two books, which Duff describes as "of the most careless description" (Ibid.).

Most importantly, however, de Roover (1953) states that princes and nobles first "scorned" what the author refers to as mass produced books (222). One has to wonder to what extent the same was true of other consumers. She notes that two German printers in Rome, Sweynheym, and Pannartz were reduced to begging when after eight years in the trade, they had an inventory of 12,475 unsold books (Ibid.). The point is that the "publisher's paradise" did not exist. A marketer could not simply choose *any* book, print it and then sell it. Boorstin states, "The act of printing itself became an unprecedented unauthorized declaration of a *public* interest . . . A crucial new element in bookmaking was the need and the opportunity for a publisher to estimate the size of the buying public for each book" (1983, 534). In the words of Febvre and Martin, "the crucial problem" was that of finding a market (1984, 172; de Roover 1953, 228).

Caxton's Approach to the Market

Many early printers on the Continent focused their attention on the printing of Latin works, for the most established markets. The printing career of William Caxton of England (printed from 1476 to 1491) is interesting for two reasons. First, he was not an apprentice printer but learned the art of printing in the late years of his life. Second, and more important from a marketing standpoint, Caxton chose *not* to focus on Latin or liturgical books. He printed books in the vernacular English for "popular tastes."

Caxton was a successful merchant for thirty years in Bruges; he was a member of the Mercer's Company (London's leading guild; see Moran 1976, 81) and Governor of the English Merchants abroad. In 1471, he printed his translation of *The Recuyell of the Histoires of Troye,* in Bruges with Colard Mansion. In 1476, Caxton set up a printing press in London (Westminster) and in 1477 he issued his first major book, *The Dictes and Sayinges of the Philosophers.* The previous year he had printed a Papal Bull granting indulgences for those who helped in the battle against the Turks (Lone 1930, 11). Caxton was also a bookseller; Blake (1976) argues that he continued to sell books during his printing career. On at least one occasion, in 1481, Caxton ordered the Sarum *Missal* and the Sarum *Legenda* to be printed for him by Maynyal of Paris. He then stamped the book with his mark (device). Paris printers specialized in beautifully printed works (Bennett 1969, 185). Childs (1976) believes that the importing of books was important to Caxton.

The size of Caxton's funeral expenses is usually cited as evidence of his success as a printer. Historians believe the expenditure was substantial for the time and his position (Roberts 1889, 19; Duff 1948; Blades 1861; Childs 1976). Some have questioned the source of his wealth, suggesting that it possibly could have resulted from his other business activities (Bennett 1969). However, the success of his assistants and successors, as measured by their longevity and output, probably attests to the soundness of his business techniques. Wynkyn de Worde, Caxton's immediate successor, attributed his own business strategy to that of his master (Bennett 1969; Plomer 1925).

Why a successful merchant, in the late years of his life, would turn to printing has drawn attention from historians. His motives have been disputed. The conventional argument relates to the printer's connection with Lady Margaret Beaufort and his translation for her of *The Recuyell of the Histoires of Troye* (he began the translation for himself but finished under her patronage). Having finished the translation, and upon finding it difficult to have the text copied quickly enough to meet demand for additional copies, Caxton set out to learn the new art of printing (Blades 1861; Duff 1948).

Other scholars would emphasize the printer's desire to translate and share the books that he discovered abroad (see Blades 1889, 72 for a list). In the prologue to *Description of Britain* (1480), Caxton writes, since " . . . the nobleness and worthynesse of the same is not knowen, therfor I entende to sette in this booke the discription of this said ile of Britayne . . . " (Blake 1973, 72). This explanation seems plausible since other early printers appear to also have begun publishing books in which they were interested. Schoeffer, at one time a cleric, published mostly liturgical works (Lehmann-Haupt, 1950). Boorstin (1983) points out that the Venetian printer Aldus' interest in Greek classics led him into his early exclusive publishing of Greek works (527–28).

Alternatively, Blake (1969) argues that Caxton was an adept businessman. Caxton's later biographers have tended to focus somewhat more attention on this aspect of his public life (Hellinga 1982; Bennett 1969; Blake 1969; Childs 1976). Blake (1976, 79) argues that perhaps, as a merchant, Caxton could not make sufficient profit on books which were copied by hand. Therefore, while Blake does not go so far, one might speculate that establishing a press constituted backward vertical integration. "In becoming a printer Caxton had not ceased to be a merchant, he had simply adopted another line of merchandise" (Childs 1976, 125; Bennett 1969; and Pollard 1978, 13 would agree). One might further conjecture that Caxton was reacting as an entrepreneur does to a market opportunity.

Certainly, difficulty arises when one attempts to make an accurate posthumous determination of motives. Did Caxton merely stumble onto a new gadget? Was he a patriot? Was he a true entrepreneur in the Misean sense, motivated only by profit; or was he an astute marketer? Caxton was probably a mixture of all of these. But the possibility that he applied marketing strategy to a perceived opportunity is intriguing.

The type of books Caxton published gives some clues to the logic behind his approach to the market. His enterprise was based on books printed in English. On the one hand, as discussed earlier, the trend toward vernacular languages favored such a strategy. On the other hand, since Caxton was first in the English market, it seems the obvious strategy would have been to produce Latin and/or liturgical works for the largest market. Caxton's venture appears risky; historians have not discussed this point. However, Bennett (1969, 14–15) describes Caxton as very conservative, as does Blake (1969, 79). An alternative hypothesis, compatible with the historians' characterization, might be posed. Perhaps Caxton had witnessed the glut of religious books (de Roover, 1953, 223) already on the market in countries on the Continent. Further, he may have recognized the capability of Continental printers in meeting the needs of the liturgical market. By printing English books for popular tastes, he avoided a frontal attack on more entrenched competitors.

To von Mises, an entrepreneur profits from his ability "to anticipate better than other people the future demand of the consumers" (1949, 288). Historians would probably agree that Caxton was well-placed to anticipate demand, particularly among the aristocracy and perhaps secondarily among the "aspiring classes." Caxton's work as a merchant abroad had acquainted him with Lady Margaret Beaufort of Burgundy, who was his patron for a number of his publications. Moreover, he had served on a failed trade mission. So, it is known that he did have some contact with various courts. The most fashionable court at the time was that of Burgundy (Blake 1969). Blake points out that in Bruges, Caxton was most certainly exposed to two great Burgundian secular libraries—those of the Dukes of Burgundy and Louis of Bruges (Ibid., 68).

Hellinga (1982, 101) stresses that as a successful merchant in the Southern Netherlands, he "had come to know the reading public spread among far more layers of society than in England and most other countries at the time." Aside from the typical readers, the author mentions that in Flanders the "secular clergy, the professional classes, merchants and administrators" also read books (Ibid., 101). Lehmann-Haupt points out that even before the advent of the printing press, Augsberg merchants purchased manuscript histories of their town councils (1950, 65). Hellinga (1982, 102) notes that Caxton's choice of English works appealed to aspiring classes.

The importation of books may have been another source of Caxton's knowledge (Blake 1969). That is, Caxton observed sales and then translated and printed those books for which a market existed (ibid, 78). But Caxton's "great advantage" over any potential competitors, according to Blake, was that he "could provide them [the English market] with literature which was in their own language but which was also the courtly reading of the Burgundian court" (Ibid.). Hence, one might conclude that Caxton entered the English market with some knowledge of expected future English tastes. The standardization of tastes is the first reason Gluck (1983, 25) gives for firms entering global competition. With regard to the medieval English book market, one might speculate that Caxton entered because of the anticipated standardization of a taste for reading and collecting.

Caxton used a number of strategic maneuvers to hold competitors at bay, reduce risk and to ensure sales of his product. He appears to have strategically used at least three of the Four Ps. Caxton's "product," the books he chose to print, was tailored to fit his target market (apparently the aristocracy and possibly the aspiring classes). Bennett calls his choices "eminently 'safe' " (1969, 15). He published tales of chivalry, which were popular with readers of the time, histories and translations of the classics among others. Then, as if to insure sale, he carefully referred to the type of reader *suitable for the book*. This is possibly evidence of segmentation. Caxton announces "not for a rude or uplandish man," "for noble, wyse and grete lords," for *"every man,"* for *"alle Englisshmen,"* and for *"yonge children"* (*Eneydos, Of Old Age, Book of Good Manners, Chronicles of England,* and *Caton* respectively. See Blake 1973 for the transcription of Caxton's prologues and epilogues). As to the distribution of Caxton's output among markets, Blake goes so far as to say " . . . that unless you were an author, a nobleman or a mercer you had little chance of appearing there [in Caxton's writings]" (1973, 28).

The support of politically powerful and wealthy backers was sought. Earl Rivers and Lady Margaret Beaufort were long-time patrons. Often these patrons guaranteed the purchase of a sizeable quantity of the books (e.g., the books were given as gifts by nobles to their acquaintances). Caxton announced the sponsorship of each book in its prologue. Blake (1969) uses the dedication of *Caton* (1483) to the merchants of London, to show how Caxton minimized his political risk at a time of the change of British rule. According to that author, this dedication implied that Caxton did not want to mention any royal persons, to avoid associating himself too closely to either side. M.T.C. Lowry (1983) provides fascinating details of how the printing of *St. Winifred* (1485) may have gained Tudor support for Caxton. Lowry argues that Caxton's translation, often labeled sloppy, was a deliberate distortion. The English court was, at that time, attempting to win the support of the Welsh people which was needed in order to conquer France (1983, 111). The translation, biased toward the Schrewsbury (Welsh) version, would have demonstrated the printer's loyalty.

But Caxton appears not to have relied solely on court contacts. Concurrently, he undertook an exercise in simultaneously building and testing the market prior to issuing his major volumes. Childs refers to the Indulgence printed by Caxton as the earliest known, but perhaps not the only, pamphlet issued by Caxton. Bennett describes in detail how, during his first two years, Caxton printed "about twenty smaller volumes in quarto size" (about six by nine inches) ranging in length from 8 to 30 to 78 pages (1969, 13). According to this author, "These we may regard as efforts on his part to establish a market, while he was labouring on his great folio volume" (ibid.). Caxton chose some poems by Chaucer, some translations of the philosophers and "a little *Book of Courtesy*" (ibid.). Moreover, Bennett informs us that these smaller works were printed at Caxton's own risk, that is, without the backing of patrons. Later, he issued major folio volumes of the *Canterbury Tales* and the *Dictes of the Philosophers.* As evidence that this was a premeditated practice, not just fortuitous, Childs cites Copeland (Caxton's assistant and later a printer), who said " 'following the trace of my mayster Caxton, begynnynge with small storyes and pamphletes' " (1976, 149).

Childs also discusses at length Caxton's location in Westminster Abbey as being ideal for his market (1976, 169). He says to reach the Chapter House (meeting place of the House of Commons) "members of the Commons still needed to use the path that went past Caxton's bookshop." Additionally, "the south door into the Abbey was also used by the royal family and courtiers when attending services there" (Ibid., 170). Childs continues that the Sacrist's roll for 1488–89 shows that Caxton also rented a booth for one week while Parliament was in session (Ibid.). Blake would add that the location was also ideal because, aside from noble passersby, "litigants, professional men and merchants," in fact, anyone with dealings at Westminster, would pass by (1969, 80).

The purpose of the dedications to patrons, in Caxton's prologues, has been disputed. Hirsch (1978) discusses the increasing use of the title page as advertisement throughout Europe in the 1400s. Favor among the court certainly helped to engender favor among the reading public (Celebrity endorsement? Perhaps a trickle-down effect). For Blake (1976) the elaborate stories in Caxton's prologues were just one promotional technique. He also used illustrations to promote the purchase of new editions. The second edition of the *Canterbury Tales,* with woodcuts, was meant to promote printings of Chaucer's other texts (Blake 1976). Moreover, a surviving advertisement from 1477 tells the reader to come to the "sign of the Red Pale" where he can acquire materials, printed in the letters similar to those of the ad, and "he shal have them good chepe" (Blake 1973, 55).

Drawing on a variety of sources, then, gives the impression that Caxton did in fact use a number of contemporary market strategies. There is indirect evidence that Caxton had been keeping foreign competition in abeyence. Upon his death, Leeu of Antwerp printed copies of three of Caxton's major works. Bennett says that Wynkyn de Worde, Caxton's immediate successor, was caught by surprise (1969, 185).

Conclusions and Implications

This abbreviated study of the early English market for printed books has shown that market participants could not simply publish indiscriminately. They had to actively seek markets, design their product and tailor their marketing mix to fit the needs of the market. Caxton clearly used marketing techniques to reduce risk and ensure success in his chosen market. Historians tend to support the fact that both marketing and consumer desire existed in the 1400s. Thus this chapter provides further support for the points Hollander makes about the existence of marketing prior to this century.

Caxton's case suggests that strategic marketing variables were the same as they are today. Moreover, the relative emphasis on variables was a function of the type and nature of consumers and competitors. However, consistent with Hollander's findings, use of marketing variables was a function of the environment. The guilds, the government and the relative size of social classes all affected Caxton's strategic use of marketing variables. It is interesting to note that the line between consumer and investor is blurred in the face of Caxton's use of royal patrons. Further, the line between marketing research, market building, and promotion becomes blurred. Caxton used what might be referred to as "proactive" marketing research. Comparisons to present-day marketing techniques would be instructive.

The most important insight, however, comes from witnessing the process of market development under a given set of environmental constraints. Looking backward in time, one can witness marketing dynamics. Caxton took steps to build the market for reading materials, but the actual design of the product (i.e., the selection of texts to translate and print) was dictated by his knowledge of current tastes. Marketers often assume that market building is a prohibitively expensive task. Caxton's strategy shows how one marketer, in a given environment, shifted some of the cost and risk to the market itself. The evolution of the Continental and English markets was only touched on in this study. Future research into that evolution can provide additional insights into the variety of strategic solutions applied by other printers.

Notes

1. The general evolution, briefly stated: prior to 1955, a lack of discretionary spending power led firms to be unconcerned with consumer needs. The post-1955 buyers' market led marketers to follow the marketing concept.

2. See N.F. Blake, *William Caxton: A Bibliographical Guide,* (New York: Garland Publishing, Inc. 1985) p. 63. For example, see John Bale (1557–59) *Scriptorium Illustrium* (Basle: I Oporinum); *Typographical Antiquities* by John Ames and William Herbert (1785); or the *Catalog of Books in the Library of the British Museum,* compiled in 1884.

3. Caxton began printing in 1471; in the 1530s there was legislation to limit importation of books.

References

Avis, Frederick C. 1973. "England's Use of Antwerp Printers 1500–1540." *Gutenberg Jahrbuch* No. 16. 234–240.

Bennett, H.S. 1969. *English Books and Readers 1475–1557*. London: Cambridge University Press.

Blades, William. 1861. *William Caxton*. New York: Burt Franklin.

Blake, N.F. 1985. *William Caxton: A Bibliographical Guide*. New York: Garland Publishing.

———. 1976–77. "William Caxton the Man and His Work." *Journal of the Printing Historical Society* 11. 64–80.

———. 1973. *Caxton's Own Prose*. London: Andre Deutsch.

———. 1965. "William Caxton: His Choice of Texts." *Anglia*. 83; 289–307.

Boorstin, Daniel J. 1983. *The Discoverers*. New York: Random House.

Childs, Edmund. 1976. *William Caxton A Portrait in a Background*. London: Northwood Publications Ltd.

Cravens, David W., and Robert B. Woodruff. 1987. *Marketing*. Reading, Mass.: Addison-Wesley Publishing.

Day, George S., and Robin Wensley. 1983. "Priorities for Research in Strategic Marketing." Report No. 83–103, (April). Marketing Science Institute. Cambridge, Mass.

Duff, E. Gordon. 1948. *A Century of the English Book Trade*. London: The Bibliographical Society.

Febvre, Lucian, and Henri-Jean Martin. 1984. *The Coming of the Book*. Verso Edition. Translated by David Gerard. London: Thetford Press Ltd.

Gluck, Frederick. 1983. "Global Competition in the 1980s." *Journal of Business Strategy* No. 4 (Spring). 3:22–27.

Hellinga, Lotte. 1982. *Caxton in Focus*. London: The British Library.

Hirsch, Rudolf. 1978. *The Printed Word: Its Impact and Diffusion*. London: Variorum Reprints.

Hollander, Stanley C. 1960. "The Wheel of Retailing." *Journal of Marketing* No. 1 (July), 25:37–42.

———. 1963. "Retailing: Cause or Effect?" In S. Decker, ed., *Emerging Concepts in Marketing*. Chicago: American Marketing Association. 220–232.

———. 1971. "She 'Shops for You or With You' Notes on the Theory of the Consumer Purchasing Surrogate." In George Fisk, ed., *New Essays in Marketing Theory*. Boston: Allyn & Bacon. 218–240.

———. 1972–1973. "Consumerism and Retailing: A Historical Perspective." *Journal of Retailing* No. 4 (Winter). 48:6–21.

———. 1984. "Sumptuary Legislation: Demarketing by Edict." *Journal of Macromarketing* Spring. 4–16.

———. 1987. "The Marketing Concept: A Déjà Vu" In George Fisk, ed., *Marketing Management Technology as Social Process*. New York: Praeger.

Kotler, Philip. 1980. *Principles of Marketing*. Englewood Cliffs, N.J.: Prentice-Hall.

Lehmann-Haupt, Helmut. 1950. *Peter Shoeffer of Gernsheim and Mainz*. Rochester, N.Y.: The Printing House of Leo Hart.

———. 1978. "The Heritage of the Manuscript." In Paul A. Winkler, ed., *History of Books Printing*. 179–229.

Lone, E. Miriam. 1930. *Some Noteworthy Firsts in Europe During the Fifteenth Century*. New York; Lathrop C. Harper.

Lowry, M.J.C. 1983. "Caxton, St Winifred and the Lady Margaret Beaufort." *The Library*. Sixth Series. No. 2 (June). 5:101–117.

McCarthy, E. Jerome, and William D. Perreault, Jr. 1987. *Basic Marketing*. Ninth ed. Homewood, Ill.: Richard D. Irwin.

McKendrick, Neil, John Brewer, and J.H. Plumb. 1982. *The Birth of a Consumer Society*. Bloomington: Indiana University Press.

Mises, Ludwig von. 1949. *Human Action*. New Haven: Yale University Press.

Moran, James. 1976–77. "Caxton and the City of London." *Journal of the Printing Historical Society*. 2:81.

Plant, Marjorie. 1974. *The English Book Trade*. Third ed. London: George Allen and Unwin Ltd.

Plomer, Henry R. 1925. *Wyndyn De Worde and His Contemporaries*. London: Grafton & Co.

Pollard, Graham. 1978. "The English Market for Printed Books, The Sandars Lectures, 1959." *Publishing History* No. 4. 7–48.

Roberts, William. 1889;1967. *The Earlier History of English Bookselling*. London: Sampson, Low, Marston, Searle, and Rivington; Detroit: Gale Research Co.

Roover, Florence Edler de. 1953. "New Facets on the Financing and Marketing of Early Printed Books." *Business History Review*. No. 2 (June). 27:222–230.

Savitt, Ronald. 1980. "Historical Research in Marketing." *Journal of Marketing*. (Fall). 44:52–58.

Thorelli, Hans B. 1983. "Concepts of Marketing: A Review, Preview, and Paradigm." In P. Varadarajan, ed., *The Marketing Concept: Perspectives and Viewpoints*. College Station, Tex: Texas A&M University. 2–37.

Williamson, Derek. 1967. *Bibliography*. London: Clive Bingley.

Winckler, Paul A. 1972. "Materials and Sources for Teaching the History of Books and Printing." *Journal of Education for Librarianship*. No. 1 (Summer). Part 1 13:43–71 and No. 2 (Fall). Part 2 13:123–136.

Wright, Louis Booker. 1958. *Middle-Class Culture in Elizabethan England*. Ithaca, N.Y.: Cornell University Press.

Zikmund, William, and Michael D'Amico. 1986. *Marketing*. Second ed. New York: John Wiley and Sons.

Part III
Marketing and Economic Development over Time

Introduction

As with most of this book, this section has a double significance. It represents an area of study to which Hollander himself has made a considerable contribution, and allows the two contributors to demonstrate why adopting a historical perspective is essential if we are to understand evolutionary processes.

Ronald Savitt discusses some of the major issues involved in coming to a historical understanding of marketing's role in economic development. Since development is a historical process, it should be seen from a historical perspective. The current situation leaves something to be desired, however, since those historians working in the area are generally not concerned with marketing as such, and attention tends to be focused on the developing world, ignoring any lessons that the developed nations might provide. The marketing literature, while yielding some valuable studies of individual cases, also shows there to be no clearly defined research tradition, and no conceptual framework within which further work can take place. The work of agricultural economists, while offering some useful insights, tends to focus on questions related to the food supply rather than on industrial development, and on marketing only insofar as it is related to commodities.

Savitt argues that in order to understand marketing's contribution to the development process, we must take marketing functions as the starting point for research, since they may be assumed to be present whenever marketing is present. However, we know little about the way the functions have evolved, either in the developing or the developed world.

The apparent inability of marketing authors to view economic development from a historical perspective is due, Savitt suggests, to the lack of a conceptual model that can describe the effects of marketing change. There is a need for research emphasizing temporal causation, showing what connections—if any—exist between historical events and antecedent phenomena. It should illuminate how and why marketing has affected the course of development, rather then how it *ought* to affect it. It should (as Hollander would certainly agree) make us reconsider those classical questions which are rarely posed, both as regards marketing and the development process itself. And it may use research methods which are not necessarily "historical," so long as the results are of value in a historical context.

Savitt examines the historical research process, identifying the key elements of description, analysis, and synthesis, and suggesting the kinds of issues they might be concerned with in an economic development study. He then turns to the question of causation which, though a contentious issue among historians, represents an essential feature of marketing inquiry. Specifically, as he points out, marketers will need to convince governments to give priority to marketing-related activities when allocating resources. This means they will need to be able to demonstrate a causal connection between marketing and economic development. At present, although marketers generally assume this to be the case, there is little evidence by way of substantiation. Moreover, concentration on causation would allow us to see marketing as part of an ongoing evolutionary process. Too often, Savitt feels, attention tends to focus on the major variables, ignoring the historical context in which they occur, which can lead to a concentration on symptoms rather than underlying causes.

Marketing's contribution to date to the study of economic development has been mainly in the form of limited studies. But if we are to come to an understanding of the role played by marketing, future work must focus on what Savitt calls "the totality of the marketing process" in order to help us formulate theories of change. The ability of marketing scholars to do this, he believes, may well determine the future of marketing itself.

E. Jerome McCarthy also addresses our lack of understanding of the development process, proposing the degree of marketing orientedness as an explanation of economic growth in a particular area, and introducing the concept of a marketing-oriented index (MOI).

He defines the index as the level of marketing orientedness in an area divided by the marketing orientedness of competing areas. The economy of an area will grow when its MOI is greater than one, and contract when the index falls below one. The index will generally tend toward one because a competitive advantage that emerges in a particular area is normally quickly matched by its competitors, so unless improvements in marketing-oriented activities continue, economic growth will cease. Each economy should therefore seek to establish maximum comparative advantage over its competitors, though in practice this may be inhibited by a production orientation on the part of businessmen, or by government protection or the existence of cartels working according to non-market objectives. In order to maximize its advantage, it is also essential that an area's entrepreneurs are able to keep a fair share of the profit they generate.

McCarthy admits that measurement of an area's MOI is no simple task, since so much depends on the attitudes and behavior of the various people involved. He points out, however, that MOI is relevant only insofar as it is greater or smaller than that of a competing area, and in terms of the direction of any movement. Even rough subjective measures may therefore suffice.

Without different marketing institutions and increased marketing orientedness, an economy cannot reach the higher stages of economic development. Growth that depends on a short-run advantage such as limited natural resources can easily change to decline. Even the traditional leaders among industrialized nations have seen competitive advantages eroded as other economies improved their competitiveness. However, the distribution systems of marketing-oriented economies appear to be growing still more marketing-oriented, which will help to reduce costs, improve products, and generally to expand markets. By contrast, the middlemen to be found in most developing economies, which are generally at the surplus-oriented or production-oriented stage, do little to help local firms rise to higher stages of development. They trade surpluses rather than expand markets. They may become rich in the process, but they do little to help national economic growth.

Marketing-oriented producers and middlemen are therefore essential precursors of economic growth. McCarthy stresses, however, that a higher degree of marketing orientation does not of itself offer a guarantee that growth will follow. Continuous innovation and improvement are necessary to ensure that the MOI stays above one by keeping ahead of competitors. Recent history suggests that this competition will become increasingly fierce.

7

A Personal View of Historical Explanation in Marketing and Economic Development

Ronald Savitt

Introduction

This chapter will examine some of the issues in the development of historical understanding of the role of marketing in economic development. The thesis is that economic development is a historical phenomenon and that to understand the role marketing can play we must address the topic with a historical perspective. Such a perspective reflects long sweeps of time and incorporates a wide variety of factors that cause change. These two elements have not been part of marketing thought and must be added if we are to understand what marketing adds to economic development.

This chapter is written in an expressive form that argues for an idea through the openness of expression. I have attempted to put ideas in perspective without looking for attribution from every source. Where necessary and with great parsimony I have used references at the end of the chapter. I hope the reader will allow me to engage him or her in this exercise and accept variations from convention. Further, much of the writing is critical about what has gone before us; it is meant to suggest to those of us working in this important field that we must do better if we are to make the contributions which are so important. Chiding one's colleagues to do better is also part of the spirit of this chapter.

Since this chapter is personal, I have posed each major topic in the form of a question. This is as much a challenge to the reader as to the author, and I am hopeful the questions will engage us in the pursuit of answers, but do not look for explicit and definitive answers; they will come as we complete the work described. My views represent one set of ideas on some important issues.

Before proceeding, I must clearly state my biases. I have a strong belief that in order to understand events as complicated as economic development and institutions as complex as marketing, we must be concerned with evolutionary processes. Such processes provide one, though not the only, means of understanding change. The purpose of an evolutionary approach is to provide explanation. Prediction about what might happen under varying circumstances is a natural outcome, though the creation of deterministic principles is not. Marketing decision-makers—and too often academics—appear to want a high degree of certainty in a world ever in flux. What is known about the past may help us shape the future (Savitt 1987). By suggesting this approach I am asking for new concepts rather than restating old ones. It is my hope that by engaging in this exercise, we will progress faster by becoming more comfortable with our limitations rather than creating more of them.

What do we know?

What do we know about marketing and economic development? In spite of a growing literature, there are few studies which fully explore the relationship. What we have is an isolated set of studies, many of which propose relationships; others provide photographic glimpses of marketing activities, and still others provide discussions of the social consequences of some parts of marketing programs. Recent interest in the area has stimulated some scholars to begin the long, arduous task of understanding marketing and economic development by defining and evaluating the marketing literature (Wood and Vitell 1986). These represent significant efforts in the proper direction.

The comprehensive studies of the relationships of marketing and economic development for the most part have been written by historians whose major interests have not always been with the subtleties of marketing. While they have not examined marketing per se, their work often provides important insights into the process. More importantly, their work can be the basis of more systematic work in marketing. Questions about the evolution of marketing as a social institution generally are ignored within the marketing literature although there are important exceptions, such as Bucklin's study and the classic work of Cox (Bucklin 1965; Cox 1965). Both provide frameworks for conducting further work, though few have responded to the challenges.

Much of the research and writing about marketing and economic development has focused on the developing world; little attention has been paid to that relationship in the developed world. The literature is generally fragmented, ranging in diversity from highly normative discussions to "instant pictures" of events in a variety of economies. Most of the work reflects little theoretical development. While there are important insights, there is no framework bringing ideas and concepts together. Throughout the literature there is a noticeable absence of a clearly developed research tradition with resulting theoretical development and empirical studies. While the study of marketing and economic development in the American setting may not provide specific directives for the developing world, it would have provided an agenda for undertaking such research.

Very little of the work in marketing's sister disciplines has been brought into the discussion of marketing and economic development. While there have been some significant exceptions, this area suffers the general reluctance of marketing to borrow from other disciplines except in the area of psychology (Goldman 1979). In contrast, many of the disciplines from which we might find important concepts to help us in our pursuit of understanding have often borrowed from marketing (Dannhauser 1981; Plattner 1984; Pritz 1983). One of the richest disciplines is history, an area quite foreign to the traditional study in marketing. One of the most important figures in this area is Fernand Braudel, the French historian. His monumental three-volume undertaking examines the six centuries leading up to the industrial revolution. Within these volumes are strong arguments and even stronger evidence about the importance of marketing systems in the development of capitalism (Braudel 1979). Braudel represents only one of many sources which can be important in allowing marketing scholars to make contributions.

Even though Braudel's three-volume work has only recently been available in English, there have been numbers of other important studies which have gone without significant recognition (Shapiro and Doody 1968). Speculation as to the reasons behind this situation is warranted, though there is no clear answer. In great part, it is a function of the parochial view of the contemporary doctoral program in marketing with its concentration on behavioral concepts and methods and its general disregard for economic analysis. What is ironic about the problem is the great number of foreigners (non-North Americans) who have written in the area but who have not brought historical perspectives into their work from their own background and experiences.

As one might expect, there has been substantial work in agricultural economics on the role of marketing in economic development (Abbot 1984). In terms of both quality and quantity, the theoretical developments and empirical work have been insightful. The contributions are substantial, though there are two shortcomings. First, they focus only on part of the development process, namely, that directed at self-sufficiency of food supply; only in a tangential context does it concern itself with later stages of development, those related to industrial development. Secondly, the work focuses only on a limited number of marketing functions and by doing so does not evaluate more substantive marketing issues. Often the scope is limited to "commodities" rather than more marketing-oriented approach of differentiated products, images, and symbols. The importance of advertising, for example, is examined in traditional economic terms. The view that advertising may play an important role in consumer education, the learning of social values, is not generally accepted (Carter and Savitt 1983). To understand this one needs only to compare how economists and marketers evaluate issues such as distribution costs and the workings of the market place.

Agricultural economists have focused their work on basic marketing functions, the universal elements which are a part of every marketing transaction. Marketing functions were most clearly defined in the early works of L. D. H. Weld (1917). His discussion of the marketing functions, buying and selling (the functions of exchange), transportation and storage (the functions of physical supply), and financing, risk-taking, and standardization (the facilitating functions) have in one way or another become the standard format in many marketing textbooks over the past seventy years (Savitt 1984). Although "the marketing functions" take a back seat to more popular issues of consumer behavior in contemporary marketing analysis, they still represent the common denominator of marketing and as such offer an important starting place for understanding marketing in and among environments.

This is an important beginning point for understanding the role of marketing in the economic development process. And it is an important starting point if the role is to be viewed in a historical perspective. My argument is simply that if marketing is the universal institution (in the context of societal institutions which include others such as marriage, families, law, etc.), then we must be concerned with the basic functions. If marketing is universal, then the role of marketing and economic development must use the functions as the critical units of analysis. Using the functions as the basic unit of investigation does not mean that all studies of marketing and economic development must deal with each of the functions, either at a macro or micro stage; all it means is that they represent one starting point for the conceptualization of this historical research. They represent the philosophical primitives which are assumed to be present wherever and whenever marketing occurs. As such they offer a common set of concepts around which historical research can develop. Yet, we know little about the way in which the functions unfold in the developing world, let alone the developed. As we will see later, scholars in other disciplines have used marketing functions to shape their inquiries.

Simplification has its risks but it also has its virtues insofar as it challenges. In the present case I am using it in the form of three hypotheses to summarize what we know about the role of marketing in economic development. These are:

1. Marketing as an institution is part of a larger set of processes that needs to be clearly defined, and the relations between marketing development must be established and clarified (we do not know very much about marketing and economic development).

2. Marketing may be an active force in the process, that is, one that stimulates development; it may be a force which reacts to the development process; or it may be neutral in the process (we do not know how marketing works in the economy).

3. The study of marketing in the development context requires historical evaluation insofar as development is a process that is time-driven: not caused by, but best seen over, time (we know marketing should be viewed historically as other social institutions).

Why are we here?

Within the published scholarship in marketing and economic development, there are vast differences in scope. It is difficult and unfair to assess an entire field; however, something must be said about the merit of the work to date. The field can be characterized as low in volume and low in quality (Dholakia and Dholakia 1984, 57). There are a number of factors that lead to this judgment:

1. A general parochial bias of most marketing scholars toward the topic in contrast to topical areas such as consumer behavior or methodology.

2. The difficulties of undertaking research in the "developing world" and few studies that meet traditional research criteria.

3. The limited horizons of marketing scholars in terms of the use of concepts, data, and research of sister disciplines.

4. The limited theories of marketing development and growth within the marketing discipline and the limited linkages of such theories to the theories of economic development from economics.

5. The general focus on commercial applications of marketing principles rather than those related to the development of the marketing institution.

What we know about marketing and economic development is clouded by failure of the American (educated) observer to fully appreciate the complexities of the development situation. All too often discussions of the role of marketing in economic development refer to the absence of "marketing systems" or to their "primitive nature." Such statements appear to say, first, that the observer does not appreciate the ways in which goods and services are brought into line with consumers' desires. The fact that there is a discrepancy between what buyers and sellers want and what they receive is an evaluation of how well the marketing system operates rather than whether or not it exists (I believe marketing is a universal institution). Second, the observer is making unfair comparisons between what he or she views as a marketing system with sophisticated characteristics, and an "unsophisticated" one. Here the comparative criteria, that is, the factors used in making judgments, often come from the sophisticated perspective from the "primitive system." Bias exists to the extent that perceived newness is somehow better than old and that simpler somehow is less acceptable than more complex. Third, stemming from the second, is the incorrect series of judgments that marketing systems in the developing world or those of the past are less complex than those found in more developed settings or more contemporary periods. An excellent example of the complexity and sophistication of early marketing systems is found in Earle's "Commodity Exchange and Markets in the Inca State; Recent Archaeological Evidence" (Earle 1984).

What we know is probably a lot less than we think we know. The quantity of work does not overshadow the lack of quality. What we have does not point to where we might go, though it can be included as part of further evaluation.

Why historical explanation?

It almost need not be said that economic development is a historical process; yet much theoretical writing and much empirical research in marketing does not treat it in that perspective. While the development of theoretical arguments might generally escape the luxury of attending to measurement issues, they are not luxuries but necessities if we are to understand economic development. Because economic development evolves over time, it is necessary to pay attention to historical explanation.

Much research on the role of marketing in economic development takes the form of the classical experiment. A marketing institution or activity is the intervening or independent variable, and economic development as a whole or some part becomes the dependent variable. The marketing literature abounds with examples of marketing intervention in an ongoing process from which direct results are drawn and cause and effect relationships are made. The experimental design leads the researcher to believe that "cause and effect" have been discovered as the result of marketing intervention. Statistical measurement indicates relationships, although not the relationships of the process. All too often, and unlike the controlled laboratory setting of the biological or physical scientists, the marketing experiment has not been subjected to proper measurement and adequate control.

In order to select appropriate measures, we must consider all environemtnal factors affecting the process. Beyond the issue of what to measure is the more compounding problem of how long to make the measurements. Historical processes take time to evolve, and the fair length of time to reach judgment is not easily specified in advance. It obviously differs among disciplines. Too often, marketing studies are probably too short to fully measure and account for change. What we are concerned with is: Will the change really hold?

What is seen in the literature, with few exceptions, is a collection of studies about what I have come to call "modernization." By modernization I mean superficial, easily arranged, and easily implemented changes. There are examples of new institutional types here and there and new practices scattered about. While the observations may be important, they have not been systematically evaluated—comparative analysis across cases in a meta-analysis approach—nor have there been systematic efforts to go back to the original benchmark and trace the events forward (Arndt 1970). For example, there were a number of studies on marketing and economic development undertaken in South America in the 1970s whose importance is not in question; what is in question, however, is the degree to which the programs really affected economic development. For example, do we know anything about what has taken place in these countries since these studies? I am afraid the answer is no. What we have is random artifacts, but no process to examine them to see what they mean.

Ashton nearly forty years ago argued that there is a strong relationship between economic history and economic theory (Ashton 1946). That relationship comes from the emphasis of economic—in our case marketing—history's focus on events and situations which recur with some degree of regularity (Supple 1963, 8). It is realistic to suggest that the reason marketing has provided so little to the literature of economic development is that there is no theory or model that describes the effects of marketing change. The lack of extensive studies containing a true historical—in this case, time-based perspective—limits the base upon which to develop theory. The descriptive works of what has taken place, even though they provide the data for theory development, are not present in that perspective.

What is the historical perspective?

An important part of the discussion of historical explanation in marketing and economic development is an explanation of the elements that make historical analysis distinctive. This discussion not only helps define what the goals of the research should be but also provides the standards by which each piece of writing can be evaluated (Rabb 1983, 330–332).

There are some elements which represent a historical perspective.

1. *An emphasis on temporal causation.* Causation must be viewed in a wide context that goes beyond events taking place near or at the same time. Context is established by making connections with *antecedent* phenomena (Rabb 1983, 331). Much as the biologist conducting experiments in petri

dishes is obligated to ensure that they are sterile, that they are maintained in a specified environment, and they are maintained over some time period in a constant state, so must the researcher in marketing and economic development provide his research statements about the corollary conditions in the "social experiment." This requirement must be present whether the study is of the introduction of a social change variable, such as the implantation of a new marketing technique, or whether the research is looking at events evolving without direct and purposeful intervention. Only when these conditions are met can the scholar see if what is taking place is truly due to the acting of marketing or as a result of other elements.

An example of this is found in a study of changes in the Egyptian rural marketing system over the past three hundred years. In that study the author acknowledges the persistence of important weekly markets in Egypt over three centuries despite extensive state control (Larson 1985, 495).

Concern for time in marketing analysis has often been disregarded. We are often not given much indication about the conditions affecting events and their movement. Where the process begins, or at least can be first identified, and what factors may be at work moving events must be part of the process of understanding. It is an appreciation of the factors and their movement which give meaning. Paying attention to temporal causation does not mean that time is the motivating or causal force. Rather it suggests that all human activity is linked to time on a moving beltway which must be accounted for.

This does not mean that all events must be described and their effects accounted for, but that some understanding of the circumstances must be offered. Whether it be the introduction of a new retailing institution or new methods of physical distribution, the background of how things moved to where they are when the "innovation" took place is required. All too often, studies in this area do not prepare the groundwork in this fashion and hence the reader is led either to believe the impact of the marketing change or, one hopes, to seriously discount the work. Viewing the development process as a part of an ongoing set of experiments, perhaps, best expresses the point. No researcher in a traditional laboratory setting would fail to discuss conditions surrounding an experiment. The importance of the surroundings and how they change from time to time as the experiment is carried out is part of the responsible adherence to a methodology.

As with all historical research, there is need for the marketing historian to be deeply involved with issues of timing and precedence. In the same way the economic historian must ponder why the Industrial Revolution began in Great Britain in the late eighteenth and early nineteenth century, so must the marketing historian focus on those issues which, for example, have led to the use of market segmentation and its spread. In the case of development, timing and precedence can be seen more clearly in terms of 'why did marketing develop in one environment?' and 'what were the factors that led to its spread from that setting?' Phrased in the more classical development perspective the question might be: What explains, in the case of developing countries, the timing and nature of bursts of development? Supple 25–26).

2. *A focus on the understanding and explanations of situations, processes or events, not on the theoretical means by which that understanding and explanations are reached.* This sharply distinguishes the function of historical work between descriptive (and often thought to be historical research) and analytical historical research. "To pose the difference at its simplest level: a goal for historians might be to explain how and why fertility changed, and what the effects were in various times and places; the demographer's goal would be to know what general mechanisms caused fertility to change. One set of questions may be interesting to historians, another to social scientists" (Rabb, 330).

The corollary for marketing is that historical analysis of marketing and economic development should explain how and why marketing affected the development rather than primarily concentrate on how marketing should affect development. The former is concerned with the larger setting of events and the course of events over time and through space, while the latter would be more interested in *a priori* the modeling of events, causes, and hypothesized effects. (There is room and need for both; however, the point of departure is a critical issue, much like the controversy between inductive and deductive methods.) The difference can be discovered in the description of actions, rather than in the models of action. Here a historical perspective serves as the means by which taxonomy with explanation serves as the means of creating a framework for the derivation of theory. History proves the broad tapestry against which the various events can be woven and from which more general theories can be drawn. The normative theory develops later and from this.

This perspective was once a common approach in marketing, and there are many who would argue that the discipline is worse off as a result of a commitment to a dominantly normative approach. The importance of explanation was perhaps most clearly proclaimed in the preface of *Marketing in the American Economy*:

> . . . in our conviction that students can best be introduced to marketing by a text book whose primary point of view is the transcendent importance of this social institution as a vast and complex function of our free-enterprise economy. We believe that students must be given a clear understanding of why marketing exists as well as how it is carried out in the American economy's dynamic mixture of public and private enterprise, and they must be able to come to some judgment as to how well it discharges both its social and its economic tasks (Vaile, Grether, and Cox 1952).

3. *A determination to enlarge and reinterpret classical questions.* One of the core issues of marketing history is the development of taxonomic and normative models; however, another important one is the reformulation of "existing questions, to cast them in a new light, or to add dimensions not previously seen. A study has to make us reconsider traditional issues, however unlikely its connection to them, if it is to carry worth and purpose. Although the degree of freshness is often the basis for assessing quality, it is the linkage to previous inquiry that establishes a work as history" (Rabb 331).

I will be brash enough to argue in the area of marketing and economic development that only a few of the classical questions have been asked and an even smaller number considered. There are some fundamental decisions, which are part of every marketing system, that represent the source of the classical questions. As suggested, the subtle ones are often ignored and what is also distressing that many of the obvious ones are ignored too. Although the following questions are not comprehensive, they do represent some that need to be asked, reasked, and rephrased: (1) How are goods and services distributed? (2) How are prices set? (3) How is market information dispersed to consumers, distributors, and producers? (4) How are market choices made? Are they free, effective, and efficient? (5) How is the process regulated?

Numerous studies focus on the normative aspects of what the role of marketing should be in the development process, but disregard the underlying process of marketing. While these discussions play important roles in isolating the questions, they do not provide an understanding of what takes place, or more importantly, what must take place. There is lack of understanding about the nature of market development and hence the suggestions that are provided simply do not work. While they may represent theoretical perspectives in the abstract, the test of a theory's goodness is its applicability in more than one case. More importantly, many studies do not show an understanding of the economic development process; it is simply a more complex process than that discussed in much of the marketing literature (Little 1982).

Because we have not taken the time to ask the classical questions, follow them over time, and compare them among a variety of circumstances, we really have little to say about the development process. One classical question that has not been fully explored in marketing is: How do market systems evolve in the development process? While many quote with some frequency Alderson's discussion of the factors governing the development of marketing channels, very few—if any—studies in marketing can be found that either test the propositions in specific development situations or compare such factors and processes among development situations (Alderson 1954). It is interesting to note that others—notably anthropologists, geographers, and some historians—have undertaken such explorations; but, of course, they each bring their own particular discipline and interests into the process (Forman and Riegelhaupt 1970; Hollier 1984; Larson 1985).

In terms of the development process itself there is another set of classical questions to be answered; they are: (1) What is the nature of the development process? (2) What are the elements of change and how do they move through time and space? (3) What are the sources of change, such as natural evolution or informal or formal intervention? Each can be broken down further and further; however, the point remains that there are classical questions.

An important question has to do with how transactions are made more efficient. In a study of medieval fairs, Moore examines how merchants acting as members of an economic, religious, and social community were able to enforce a variety of trading principles. One issue that recurs repeatedly is how and where merchants should be located within the fairgrounds to permit the most efficient operations of large-scale traders and also to assure the health and safety of all fairgoers (Moore 1985, 113). "Another important principle enforced with some rigor by fair owners was the prohibition of forestalling, the practice of buying up goods—usually foodstuffs—just outside the fairgrounds for subsequent resale within the fair" (Moore 1985, 131).

Probably the only area in marketing in which classical questions have been asked is retail change (Savitt 1982). Here there has been a substantial recasting of the classical questions in order to determine the nature of retail change. While there is some controversy as to whether the theories apply to the general or specific case, there has been smoke and fire. While the work has not been fully approached in what might viewed as a historical perspective, it does provide direction as to what might be done in other areas in marketing and economic development. What needs to be accomplished to put these studies in a historical perspective are the following: (1) Testing of the various theories over long time periods. (2) The specific constructs which have been generated in a North American context but which may not be applicable in others. (3) Comparative studies which allow insights into developed areas in developing economies and developing areas in developed economies.

4. *An indifference to method as long as the results are illuminating.* Unlike the previous points, this element is not concerned with determining whether a piece of research is historical. This point is made to prevent the sophistry that often can take place if one subscribes to the view that "if you do not use historical research methodologies a piece of research is not historical."

The choice of methodology does not and should not determine the content of the work. Methodology in the research sense only *determines* the means of collecting and evaluating the data. While there are historical approaches, these are not the same as methodology. It is the temporal perspective and the desire to explain events "over and through time" that makes a work historical or something else. Observations, survey, experimentation, and simulation can all be used in historical research as the driving research design; some of this set will be more appropriate than others, but all of them can be used. Similarly, historical studies should not be defined by the degree to which they use or do not use quantitative analysis.

Issues of scope and assortment of data by historical research vary in the same way they do in other types of research. Some historians, such as Braudel, choose to use a large canvas and fill it in with great detail while others focus on small issues and still others concentrate their efforts on specialized events. The point is that history does not deal solely with the discovery and presentation of facts, "but with the relationships between particular collections of facts. It may, of course, be concerned with a special case, although even here will have to rely upon explanation and hypothesis" (Supple 8).

What does historical research look like?

Historical research incorporates each of three elements, description, analysis, and synthesis, though the amount of emphasis given to each varies in almost every work. There are many pieces of history that are purely descriptive in nature and basically present a chronology of events without any attempt to explain why the events took place or any attempt to place the events in a larger setting in which they can be compared to other events in different settings. Both analytical and synthetic pieces require description of events; however, the emphasis in both is different. In the first case, the primary concern is with explanation, while in the second, the primary concern is the development of generalization as a result of extensive evaluation of many events. Each type of research serves specific purposes and contributes to understanding, though I believe all three must be part of historical research in marketing.

"Descriptive history deals primarily with what happened and to a certain extent with how it happened. It reconstructs the historical situation by narrating the facts as objectively as possible" (Tume 1970, 49). The narrative is a common style of writing history and it is easy to sublimate all descriptive works to simply pieces of narration. The problem of form in historical writing is difficult because the historian not only must represent the complexity of past activities, but also must represent it in movement through time. A strict chronological description of events does not add anything to understanding unless it pauses to sort the important from the unimportant. It must be accompanied by some analysis (Marwick 1970, 144–145).

Analytical history searches for the causes of events and attempts to answer the question "why?" An analytical marketing piece might try to answer why ultimate consumer goods firms moved from a selling to a marketing approach. Such a study would not only want to show what were the precedents to the marketing approach (marketing concept) but also what were the factors that led to its adoption and its effects or lack of effects on other marketing and business activities and the impact on ultimate consumers. In the case of marketing and economic development, we need to be concerned about the changes that have taken place and have either remained permanent fixtures or disappeared as a result of marketing forces on the environment and as a result of environmental forces on marketing. The central search must be for the "causes and meaning of events in order to understand change and discover the truth about behavior" (Tuma 1970, 50). Larson provides a good example of this approach in the introduction to the study of the rural marketing system in Egypt. There she establishes her analytical framework, drawn from regional science models proposed by Carol Smith (1976). Larson organizes her research around a framework that views the evolution of rural marketing systems from solar, administrative in early periods to dendentretic, monopolistic in intermediate periods, and finally to multifaceted systems in latter periods (Larson 1985, 495).

Both descriptive and analytic studies are part of the process of understanding; however, it can only be brought to complete fruition by synthesis. Synthesis in this perspective is primarily the comparison of results rather than the description or narration about events and the explanation of change. The synthesizer must look for the work of others in order to perform this task. And this task is enormous in the case of marketing since there has been little done in the other areas. The quality of synthesis is dependent on the work from which it is drawn and on the ability of the person looking at the problems. Here the ability to cast and recast the classical questions becomes very important.

Although not fully meeting the definition of synthesis presented here, Forman and Riegelhaupt provide significant insights into what the process looks like. They propose a model to describe the stages in the development of marketing systems in developing countries. While much of their evidence and evaluation comes from work in Brazil, there is no reason to believe their generalizations are limited to Brazil. Indeed, an important piece of historical research helping to explain the rule of marketing in economic development could come from extending their work. What the authors do is provide a series of generalizations relating to the formulation of marketing systems (Forman and Riegelhaupt 1970).

Their generalizations describe the actors, stages, processes, marketing inputs, and production outputs related to the movement from local market place domination to prevalence of urban consumer markets. Stage 1, for example, begins with a peasant's retailing his own goods in local market places. By Stage 4, wholesalers begin to bypass the middlemen and go directly to the peasant provider. "This stage is marked by the development of the infrastructure, although a lack of information prevails at the local level. A high degree of capitalization is required in the distributive sector. Prices for the entire system are controlled at this level by wholesalers." (Forman and Riegelhaupt 1970, 209). The generalization found from this type of synthesis is as follows: "We are calling to mind the fact that agricultural development is a two-part process: the marketing system will lead to a restructuring of the production system when the latter is unable to meet consumer demands" (Forman and Riegelhaupt 1970, 211).

Synthetic work is based on comparative methods and strongly implies that generalization is possible. Causal statements and laws can be discerned and discovered; it means that "the uniformity of and similarity between events is frequent enough to permit induction from the unique to the general" (Tuma 1970, 78). Unfortunately, synthetic approach has not been as popular in the marketing discipline as it has been elsewhere in the social sciences; it seemingly is not part of the way marketing scholars look at the world. Whether it will be corrected is difficult to speculate; whether it is or not, its absence will affect both the quantity and the quality of work in marketing history.

Is there historical causation?

There is probably no more controversial area in historical analysis than that of causation. It occupies a significant portion of historical and philosophical writing (Fisher 1970; Popper 1957). The issues range in complexity from the ability to correctly document cause and effect to the relationships between cause and deterministic behavior. Some historians believe their function is in reporting and interpreting events while others believe they must show cause as part of their process. The arguments rage and will continue to do so; a full discussion of them is beyond the purpose of this chapter.

While not all knowledge has to have empirical origins, we do exist with the need to have evidence that some effect can be attributable to some set of circumstances. This is especially so when scholars attempt to convince governments to allocate resources to marketing activities in contrast to others. If a strong case is to be made in a developing country why a sum should be given to the creation of marketing agencies at the same time that infant mortality rates are increasing, then there must be some compelling evidence that the marketing program will enhance development. Some may argue this example is too strong, but it is not if one considers the poorest nations in the world, the low-income economies as defined by The World Bank (The World Bank 1986). Too much of the marketing literature argues that "marketing practices can result in organizing, and accelerating economic development" (Etemad 1984, 51). But where is the evidence that marketing does that?

Whether causation is the proper domain of historical study in the general case does not affect the social sciences and marketing, because the social sciences have as their mission the understanding and determination of events. In order to make beneficial decisions some understanding of cause and effect relationships is mandatory. Even though marketing may be examined in purely historical terms, analysis of marketing's role in economic development must be understood in terms which focus on causal relationships. While the normative concern of marketing may never satisfy Popper, the discipline must pursue explanation through a study of historical methods.

Historical causation in marketing opens up an important avenue which has not been well developed. It provides an important way of looking at marketing as part of an ongoing process rather than as a series of often unconnected points. Too much research in marketing concentrates on a major variable without regard to the grand flow of events. While it is easier to focus on major variables either one at a time or in groups, this approach leaves much to be desired. The major variables are never placed in the context in which they arise nor are they considered as to whether they are part of one or more ongoing processes.

There is no doubt it is much more difficult to look at the total process of something as complicated as marketing; however, unless it is done, the discipline will remain as a string of studies. While marketing has traditionally been defined as a process, this concept has not always been carried into the work in the field of economic development. The latter, of course, is recognized as a process; if we are to understand marketing's role in it, we must approach marketing as a process. In that regard, "cause and effect are not to be confused as distinct events, but are to be regarded as components within some single ongoing process" (Mandlebaum 1977, 63).

The evaluation of an event can be helpful in understanding the complexities of cause and effect. For example, the introduction of supermarkets to a developing economy is regarded by many as an important event. To many it represents a sign of marketing's impact on the development process; namely, out of it come increases in consumption capacity, increases in employment, and development of marketing sophistication. The question is, is the successful implantation of a supermarket or any other marketing innovation a cause or an effect? Namely, do supermarkets work because they are the last element of development in a marketing system? Or are supermarkets the catalyst that produces the conditions by which development takes place? Basically, it should not be viewed as either in the very abstract case which characterizes much of literature; rather it must be viewed as part of a process. But what process?

It is easier to go from that highly complex case to a simpler one, to gain insights into the nature of an ongoing process. Processes are by their very nature composed of a series of events linked in some way with each other. Some are directly linked insofar as doing A causes B, and others appear to be linked. In most cases it is very difficult to find the direct linkage in regard to causality, especially when a number of other events are taking place at the same time or continue to proceed through time. Turning on a light bulb by a wall switch is an interesting case in point. If every time we turn the switch up the light goes on, there appears a direct perception that causality is at work and an effect results. In this case, the perception is of two separate events, but indeed are they? Much the same can said about marketing in the development process. What factors allow for marketing change and are they the same as the change itself? This appears philosophical, but so is the nature of the decisions which are made and especially their consequences.

The perception of separate events stems from three perceptual features which, either working alone or together, give the feeling the events are separate. The first is the lack of spatial continuity between the switch and the light; the event takes place at two different places. The second is the difference in correspondence between the switch and the light; they are two different instruments and hence are viewed in the sense that one affects the other. Finally, there is instantaneous succession, namely, the movement of the switch and the immediacy of the light suggest that the events are separate (Mandelbaum 1977, 63–64). In the supermarket case, can we truly subscribe to the premise that either the supermarket is the cause of further economic development or has been caused by the development process itself?

It seems appropriate to suggest that changes in how goods are marketed at retail are part of the process of overall economic change and that the ability of an entrepreneur or a government to introduce a supermarket is reflective of the state of the process. Is it the supermarket itself which causes or is caused by development? Viewing the appearance of "modern institutions" in a number of contexts needs care so that we do not look for cause and effect, but concentrate on the process. Supermarkets may be the logical end of marketing's role in economic development or they may be isolated events. Whatever they are, they must be examined as part of an ongoing set of activities. What is required is a set of primitive statements or preconditions in the specific sense that will guide the research and provide bases for making judgments. And, if the preconditions can be identified, they must be placed in a historical perspective.

Too often the marketing literature focuses on economic development as a contemporary phenomenon. While this has serious intellectual problems, there are also serious problems in the development of programs. The basis for action must be related to an understanding of the past. In that regard, I urge the reader to consider the excellent study of Barbara K. Larson, "The

Rural Marketing System of Egypt over the Last Three Hundred Years" (Larson 1985). Larson describes and explains the transformations of the rural marketing system in terms of patterns of spatial organization in terms of the various factors that helped to shape it. She concludes: " . . . an understanding of the shape and functions of a rural marketing system does not depend on an appraisal of geographic and narrowly economic factors alone. The institutional framework—political, social, economic—within which such a marketing system, and thus the political economy as a whole, must also be considered" (Larson 1985, 530).

Larson describes how basic marketing functions are performed and what factors affect them over time. The research has a specific set of hypotheses to test; these frame the data, the narration, and the analysis. (Her reliance on the work of C. A. Smith provides a perspective on regional science analysis though Larson's conclusions, as noted above, argue for a wider set of causal factors (Smith 1976).) This study offers the marketing historian an understanding of the elements of historical causation—a concept not well established in the marketing research area. It also provides a fruitful approach to the advancement of public policy in the development area. This is particularly important because much marketing and economic development literature focuses on the role of governments in using marketing to achieve development goals.

Although some might argue it is unfair to compare Larson's piece to the work of Mahmoud and Rice because the objectives of their work is so different, I find the comparison important because it gives credence to the need for greater depth in writings in this area (Mahmoud and Rice 1984). Mahmoud and Rice use Egypt as a case for understanding marketing problems in less-developed countries. Their discussion isolates a number of factors that inhibit the development of marketing activities, then offers a comprehensive set of solutions. They have all but ignored important historical factors that have led to the present marketing environment and whose presence will obviously affect the viability of their proposed solutions. While I do not necessarily disagree with their observations, I do disagree with the way they have defined them. Mahmoud and Rice treat them as symptoms rather than as causes and hence have proposed "symptomatic cures," rather than solutions. While I might be viewed as pedantic, I cannot help but believe that knowing the "whys" of conditions is the proper place to begin. And, obviously, in something as complex as an economy, historical analysis plays an important role in understanding.

Where do we go from here?

Historical analysis can add much to our understanding of the role of marketing in economic development. However, it must be pursued with vigor and enterprise and must go beyond descriptive studies. These are important in providing data for analysis, but they do not always provide the basis for generalization. If we are to know about marketing's role in the development process, historical studies must be used to formulate theories of change. Marketing has gone too far without theoretical development in this area. Some theories of change will be borrowed and at the moment, economic anthropology and regional science appear to offer the strongest concepts.

All of this means a very different perspective for the study of marketing in the development process. We must engage ourselves in the analysis of basic marketing institutions and arrangements, and be constantly aware of the need to have and to test viable hypotheses. Much of this will require an inclusion of concepts from sister disciplines and a clear recognition of the problems of borrowing. We will no longer be able to be content with the "introduction of this or that" into a developing country but focus on the totality of the marketing process. How well we as marketing scholars are able to meet the challenges of this perspective may indicate how well the discipline as a whole will fare.

References

Abbot, J. C. 1984. *Marketing Improvements in the Developed World. What Happens and What Have We Learned.* FAO Agricultural Services Bulletin 58. Rome: Food and Agriculture Administration.

Alderson, W. 1954. "Factors Governing the Development of Marketing Channels." In R. M. Clemett, ed., *Marketing Channels for Manufactured Products.* Homewood, Ill.: Richard D. Irwin. 5–34.

Arndt, J. 1970. "Temporal Lags in Comparative Retailing." *Journal of Marketing* 36 (October). 40–45.

Ashton, T. S. 1946. "The Relation of Economic History to Economic Theory." *Economica.* 12:81–96.

Braudel, F. 1979. *Civilization and Capitalism, 15th – 18th Century,* Vol. 1; *The Structure of Everyday Life,* Vol. 2; *The Wheels of Commerce,* Vol. 3; *The Perspective of the World.* New York: Harper & Row.

Bucklin, L. P. 1972. *Competition and Evolution in the Distributive Trades.* Englewood Cliffs, N.J.: Prentice-Hall

Carter, F. S., and R. Savitt. 1983. "A Resource Allocation Model for Integrating Marketing into Economic Development Plans." In E. Kaynak, ed., *World Marketing Congress: Proceedings.* 79–88.

Cox, R., C. S. Goodman, and T. C. Fichandler. 1965. *Distribution in a High-Level Economy.* Englewood Cliffs, N.J.: Prentice-Hall

Cundiff, E. 1982. "A Macromarketing Approach to Economic Development." *Journal of Macromarketing* 2 (Spring). 14–19.

Dannhauser, N. 1981. "Evolution and Revolution of Downward Channel Integration in the Philippines." *Economic Development and Cultural Change* (April). 584–595.

Dholakia, N. and R.R. Dholakia. 1984. "Missing Links: Marketing and the Newer Theories of Development." In G.S. Kindra, ed., *Marketing in Developing Countries*. London: Croom Helm. 57–75.

Earle, T. 1984. "Commodity Exchange and Markets in the Inca States: Recent Archaeological Evidence." In S. Platner, ed., *Markets and Marketing*. Lanham, Md.: University Press of America. 369–399.

Etemad, H. 1984. "Is Marketing the Catalyst in the Economic Development Process?" In G. S. Kindra, op. cit. 29–56.

Fisher, D. H. 1970. *Historians' Fallacies: Toward a Logic of Historical Thought.* New York: Harper & Row.

Forman, S. and J. F. Riegelhaupt 1970. "Market Place and Marketing System. Toward a Theory of Peasant Economic Integration." *Comparative Studies in Society and History* 12 (2). 188–212.

Goldman, A. 1979. "Publishing Activity in Marketing as an Indicator of Its Structure and Interdisciplinary Boundaries." *Journal of Marketing Research* 16 (Summer). 485–494.

Hollier, G. P. 1984. "The Marketing and Distribution of Palm Oil in North West Province Cameroon." *Scottinsh Geographical Journal* 100 (December). 171–183.

Kindra, G.S., ed 1984. *Marketing in Developing Countries*. London: Croom Helm.

Larson, B. K. 1985. "The Rural Marketing System of Egypt over the Last Three Hundred Years." *Comparative Studies in Society and History* 27 (July). 494–530.

Little, I. M. D. 1982. *Economic Development: Theory, Policy and International Relations*. New York: Basic Books

Mahmoud, E., and G. Rice. 1984. "Marketing Problems in the LDCs: The Case of Egypt." In Kindra, op. cit. 76–94.

Mandelbaum, M. 1977. *The Anatomy of Historical Knowledge*. Johns Hopkins University Press.

Marwick, A. 1970. *The Nature of History*. London: Macmillan.

Moore, E. W. 1985. *The Fairs of Medieval England: An Introductory Study*. Toronto: Pontifical Institute of Medieval Studies.

Plattner, S., ed. 1984 *Markets and Marketing*. Lanham, Md.: University Press of America.

Popper, K. R. 1957. *The Poverty of Historicism*. New York: Harper & Row.

Pritz, S., ed. 1983. *Economic Anthropology: Topics and Theories*. New York: University Press of America.

Rabb, T. K., "Coherence, Synthesis and Quality in History." In T. K. Rabb and R. I. Rothberg, eds., *The New History; the 1980s and Beyond*. Princeton: Princeton University Press.

Savitt, R. 1982. "A Historical Approach to Comparative Retailing." *Management Decision* 20 (4). 16–23.

———. 1984. "Antecedents of Macromarketing: A Brief Review." Ninth Annual

Macromarketing Seminar. Vancouver, British Columbia. University of British Columbia. Unpublished.

———. 1987. "Marketing Competition, Entrepreneurial Behavior and the Development of Strategy." In R. Bagozzi and F. Furat, eds., *Philosophical and Radical Thought in Marketing*. Lexington, Mass.: Lexington Books.

Shapiro, S. J. and A. F. Doody, eds. 1968. *Readings in the History of American Marketing*. Homewood, Ill.: Richard D. Irwin.

Smith, C. A. 1976. "Exchange Systems and the Spatial Distribution of Elites: The Organization of Stratification in Agrarian Societies." In C. A. Smith, ed., *Regional Analysis*. New York: Academic Press. 2:309–374.

Supple, B. E. 1963. "Economic History, Economic Theory, and Economic Growth." In B. E. Supple, ed., *The Experience of Economic Growth: Case Studies in Economic History*. New York: Random House. 1–46.

The World Bank. 1986. *World Development Report 1986*. New York: Oxford University Press.

Tuma, E. H. 1971. *Economic History and the Social Sciences*. Berkeley, Calif.: University of California Press.

Vaile, R. S., E. T. Grether, and R. Cox. 1952. *Marketing in the American Economy*. New York: Ronald Press.

Weld, L. D. H. 1917. "Marketing Functions and Mercantile Organization." *American Economic Review* VII (June). 304–318.

Wood, V. R., and S. J. Vitell. 1986. "Marketing and Economic Development: Review, Synthesis and Evaluation." *Journal of Macromarketing* 6 (Spring). 28–48.

8
Marketing Orientedness and Economic Development

E. Jerome McCarthy

Introduction

Most discussions of the why (or why not) of economic development emphasize production rather than marketing. The implicit assumption is that supply creates its own demand—that somehow, magically, marketing institutions distribute whatever is supplied. In contrast to this conventional wisdom, some economists recognize the intimate relationship between marketing and production. Ragnar Nurkse included demand in his "vicious circle of poverty" concept. He said, "A country is poor because it is poor." This meant to him that not only production efficiency, but also consumer demand must be considered in economic development (Nurske 1952, 4). Simply stated, if a potential producer "for the market" doesn't see an opportunity to sell his specialized production, he will not leave his susistence way of life, and so will not represent potential demand for other possible producers, either. Thus the vicious circle of poverty continues.

Typically, marketing is treated only as a part of the production process. But it may be more correct to think of production as only a part of the marketing process. This may seem only a semantic difference, but it is critical for understanding economic development.

We argue that far too much emphasis is placed on production and far too little on marketing. Even Rostow's "stages of economic growth" are by his own admission based on a "dynamic theory of production" (Rostow 1962, 12–13). Seeing marketing in its proper perspective can help explain past, present, and future levels of economic growth.

Marketing people must offer more than their beliefs and convictions, however. They must show that being marketing oriented plays a major role in economic development. After all, aren't there already plenty of marketing institutions? We have had markets with various kinds of retailers and wholesalers for thousands of years. So why focus on marketing institutions and being marketing oriented? One reason is that emphasis on production has not explained the why of economic development. So a different approach is needed. This chapter presents a new explanation of economic development.

The Marketing-Oriented Index (MOI)

In this chapter we take the position that a geographic area (economy) grows when its marketing-oriented index is greater than one and contracts when its marketing-oriented index is less than one. The MOI is defined as the level of marketing orientedness in an area divided by the marketing orientedness of competing areas. An "area" here can refer to a city, state, region within a country, country, or a world region (e.g., the "Pacific Rim").

Obviously, this index is a relative measure, but it tends toward one. And this means "no-growth" because the competitive advantage of one area (obtained by being or becoming more marketing oriented) is met by competing areas. So continued improvements in marketing-oriented activities are needed for continued growth. And unfortunately, when temporary advantages are neutralized, growth ceases. In other words, continued innovation and market-oriented strategy planning are needed to find new opportunities (needs which can be met by the firms in an area) to keep ahead of competitive firms in other areas.[1]

"Marketing oriented" means trying to carry out the marketing concept—which says that a firm (area) should aim all of its efforts at satisfying its target customers, at a profit (McCarthy and Perrault 1987, 28–31). This is now thought of as a "modern" idea, but many early merchants and traders grasped at least some of the marketing concept and prospered as a result. Early Phoenician and Dutch traders, for example, saw the value of taking goods to foreign markets where they would have greater value. They may not have been as marketing oriented as some of our modern firms. But they didn't have to be, because their competitors were often blindly production oriented—that is, they made whatever products were easy to produce and then tried to sell them in their home areas.

Marketing orientedness is related to how effectively the resources of an area (economy) are organized to satisfy some customers' needs. Ideally, the firms and middlemen in an economy should carefully study the needs of their potential markets and integrate their individual efforts to maximize the output of their production-distribution systems and therefore of the economy. This would mean finding the most strongly felt unsatisfied needs which they can satisfy in exchange for the most output they can earn from anyone. This might mean an economy that is well suited to producing oranges would specialize in oranges and trade with others in the world who want oranges. The desirability and economics of interregional trade is discussed by economists under the title of "comparative advantage." They have shown quite clearly that if economies are interested in maximizing their economic welfare they should seek their maximum comparative advantage. In the absence of a completely planned economy, however, finding this maximum comparative advantage is usually a trial-and-error approach. And production-oriented firms and middlemen do not move a whole economy very quickly to its optimum position. Further, any interference with the search for the optimum position will slow, block, or even reverse the movement toward the optimum position. Government protection of "home industries" or business cartels may lead to short-run advantage for the "protected" but reduce the short-run and long-run MOI and hurt the "unprotected" who suffer from higher prices, less output, and/or unrealized economic growth. This is a common problem in developing and planned economies—where "non-market" objectives lead to resource allocations that block or slow the normal market-directed growth that would occur if individual firms and middlemen were allowed to seek comparative advantage opportunities for their own and the economy's advantage. Note: it is assumed that individuals, firms and middlemen, and areas will work to improve their economic situation if they believe they will receive at least some of the fruits of their efforts. This has been amply demonstrated wherever the returns for work have been related to the amount and value of the work. And here this means the more marketing oriented will receive higher incomes and the very production oriented will not and may even become more impoverished.

An area's MOI is a measure of how effectively the firms and middlemen in an area are moving toward their optimum "comparative advantage" position when compared to competing areas (that often can do approximately the same things). In tradition-bound, typically production-oriented economies, a few political and/or military leaders and their families can live very well.

They have little reason to encourage the economy to move toward a higher level of development. In contrast, in a more marketing-oriented economy, entrepreneurs, traders, and explorers are encouraged to find better strategies (perhaps by public recognition or being allowed to keep some of the fruits of their financial success) and the economy moves more quickly toward its optimum position. Along the way, some efforts are bumbling—and the economy moves ahead in fits and starts. But if some firms combine their resources in a more effective way than competitors in other areas (to provide greater satisfaction to some customers) then they *become* more marketing oriented. This results in a higher MOI for the economy. For example, production-oriented corn farmers are exhibiting more marketing orientedness as they try to use better seed and new fertilizers to grow a more nutritious corn for feeding animals demand. A higher MOI would be deserved because these producers saw the opportunity and were willing to change their production process drastically, including selecting new kinds of seed and hiring human pickers rather than relying on their easy-to-use mechanical pickers.

Note here that we define "production oriented" and "marketing oriented" as opposite ends of a continuum. So if an economy begins to move fron its most extreme production-oriented position toward being marketing oriented, then its measure of marketing orientedness could be greater than that of its production-oriented competitors and therefore its MOI would be greater than one.

Some outstanding examples of greater marketing orientedness leading to greater economic growth are London, (during the 1800s when it was an open city), Taiwan, Japan, the "Pacific Rim" countries (in the last few decades), and China (in the 1980s as government controls have been relaxed or removed).

Measuring the MOI

Measuring an area's MOI is not an easy task because the attitudes and behavior of the people in the area affect how much it will produce and how fast it will grow (assuming governments do not inhibit long-term growth) and it is difficult to measure attitudes. But measurements or judgments are possible—about the vitality of an area's business people and their economic performance. And the rate of growth of an area and the source of the growth can help estimate the area's marketing orientedness, too.

Fortunately, we are mainly concerned with whether an area's MOI is greater than or less than its major competitors and the direction of any changes. So even rough subjective measures will often be adequate for suggesting what is needed to encourage economic growth. That is, if an area's MOI is far below one by whatever measure is used, then it must make some changes or prepare for lower economic growth. Just "hoping" that something "good" will happen will not work in our increasingly competitive, more marketing-oriented world.

Marketing Concept and Marketing Functions are Vital in Economic Development

There are two basic reasons for misunderstanding the role of marketing institutions and marketing orientedness: (1) the marketing concept is poorly understood—even today it commonly means "selling and/or advertising," and (2) marketing institutions are usually all lumped together as "middlemen."

Actually, however, there are many different kinds of middlemen. And each provides a different blend of the necessary basic functions (commonly accepted functions are buying, selling, financing, storing, risk-taking, transporting, grading, and market information) and producer firms need different blends of these functions at different stages of economic development.

Further, in increasingly competitive markets, more effective application of the marketing concept is needed to keep ahead of competition and obtain economic growth. Simply having resources does not mean that these resources will be converted into profitable output. Obvious modern cases are third-world countries with many natural resources but much lower economic growth than might be expected. In contrast, it appears that absence of resources is not a barrier to economic growth. The outstanding example is Japan, which is not blessed with a surplus of land and other resources, and yet has experienced rapid growth.

Stages of Economic Development and the Movement of the MOI

To better understand economic growth and development, we will define four stages of economic development and consider the evolution of producers (firms as defined here) and the marketing institutions they need—and how an area's MOI moves up and down over time.

The four stages of economic development are:

1. Self-sufficient firms and economies (areas)
2. Surplus-oriented economies (areas)
3. Production-oriented economies (areas)
4. Marketing-oriented economies (areas)

These four stages cover the full range of possibilities—from the most non-market-oriented to a completely marketing-oriented economy. Note that different areas within a country could be at different stages, (e.g., "sophisticated" urban areas versus "commodity" producing rural areas).

Stage I: Self-sufficient Firms and Economies

These firms and economies consist basically of "closed" family or extended-family units operating at the subsistence level. They normally do not produce surpluses and have no interest in bartering or trading with others. Marketing is not needed because there is no "exchange"—just "sharing." Examples of such units (and some still exist today) are hunting and gathering tribes. Some feudal manors were self-sufficient. And some simple planned economies (controlled by military or religious leaders) have shared the output of local production in some non-market way.

Stage II: Surplus-oriented Economies

Here, some of the farm family units of Stage I have shifted out of the "closed" stage, but are still primarily self-supporting. The surpluses they offer in the market may be due to especially favorable weather conditions or extra time (above subsistence production needs), which is shifted to producing easy-to-make commodities such as baskets, cloth, or leather work.

Critical Functions: Buying and Selling. At this stage, the producers need at least two marketing functions—buying and selling. There must be a "market" where the producers can trade or sell their surpluses. The producers may provide the selling function (and any other necessary functions) themselves. Farmers' markets and occasional markets meet this need. Or the sellers may find it desirable to sell their surpluses to middlemen who provide this function for them. In this case, the middlemen must assume other functions (including financing, storing, transporting, and risk-taking).

Critical Institutions: Local Markets and Traders. Local markets enable producers to sell their surplus output or find traders who will do it for them. And itinerant peddlers buy some of these surpluses to sell to consumers who do not or cannot come to the markets. If many small producers occasionally develop similar surpluses, then some collecting points—probably run by middlemen—develop.

It is clear that such institutions are helpful, but they are not necessary to the survival of the surplus-oriented "firms." Each firm is still able to provide its own basic needs. These marketing institutions merely enable each producer to sell its surplus and improve its own standard of living.

Marketing-oriented Index Hovers Around One. The marketing-oriented index of each economy hovers near one in Stage II. There are occasional "blips" up and down when some areas are blessed by better weather *and* some middlemen develop to take the surpluses to areas which have not produced such surpluses. Unfortunately, in the absence of such middlemen, bountiful outputs may only result in lower prices, which may lead to lower levels of output as the return from producing for the market declines. On the other hand, the MOI can rise if middlemen are sufficiently marketing oriented to see an opportunity to buy these surpluses and move them elsewhere. Unfortunately many "traditional" production-oriented middlemen do not operate this way. Their philosophy is "buy low and sell high" and they build inventories to sell later. These middlemen "clear the market" (in the classic economic sense) but they do not help producers direct their activities toward more productive activities. A sensible Stage II (self-sufficient) producer will not leave his self-sufficient way of life and try to make a living producing for such a market. And this leads to the tradition-bound economies which we still see in underdeveloped parts of the world.

Stage III: Production-oriented Economies

Here we find farm family units producing specialized crops for the market. We also find cottage and handicraft industries. And in more developed economies, such producers specialize in any of the industrial or consumer products we find in a modern economy.

Producers at this stage are quite production oriented; that is, they produce items which are easy for them to produce. They may not completely ignore market needs, but they tend to produce basic commodities or products for which they feel there is an established and fairly steady demand. Production-oriented firms, both large and small, are found in all developed economies. And if most of an economy's firms and middlemen are production oriented, then it is practical to call it a production-oriented economy.

Functions Needed: All of Them. Production-oriented producers assume there is demand for their product and expect that "someone" will get rid of anything they produce. They may not even have their own sales departments. These producers expect others to provide *all* the marketing functions. And in developing economies, an especially critical function is financing, because money resources are often scarce. In such cases, the typical production-oriented middlemen may provide other functions poorly or grudgingly but still be used if they have sufficient financial resources. Selling, for example, may be treated as "trading" rather than aggressively seeking to expand demand. These middlemen may help "clear the market," but only at lower prices as more production-oriented producers leave their self-sufficient way of life and increase supply as they begin producing "commodities" for the market. This leads to the classic pure competition situation described by economists—and little or no entrepreneurial profit for producers in the long run. Production-oriented middlemen in Stage III may do relatively little promotion. And they seldom provide technical assistance for their customers or allow interested producers to help these customers because they, the middlemen, are reluctant to reveal their customer lists. Some of these middlemen may not even provide the marketing information function—that is, feedback to help producers adjust their efforts to better meet the needs of their end use customers. As a result, the producers may continue making lower quality or inappropriate products—and continue to receive poor returns from a purely competitive market which will clear only at some (low) price. This, of course, discourages producers from trying to increase their output, and, cumulatively, inhibits the growth of the entire economy.

Critical (Adequate) Institutions: Typical Traders and Merchants. The marketing institutions that are "adequate" in Stage III are the typical production-oriented traders and merchants. Traders help markets clear by focusing on buying and selling—as in the typical "farmers' market." Merchants do more storing than traders. But both rely heavily on the critical need for financing—typical of small production-oriented producers. They have never been successful enough to accumulate sufficient capital to finance the production-distribution process, and so must rely on middlemen, perhaps including financial institutions such as banks and moneylenders. Traders and merchants often provide the financing function, as well as other marketing functions.

Unfortunately, the typical middlemen found in production-oriented economies are seeking short-run opportunities. They are more concerned with turnover and a quick profit than in developing effective channels of distribution. In fact they may seek to force prices down (by when and how much they buy) at the producer level so they can "buy low" and (later) take a larger share of the market they are already serving. This, of course, stimulates competition and may contribute to the growth of the economy *in the short run*. But their emphasis is on cutting price to exploit current markets rather than serving present and new markets more effectively. Some of the middlemen's customers might prefer added services or new products rather than just lower and lower prices. Such middlemen are less likely to encourage the development of new or modified products, or to find new markets.

Depending on the product, the marketing institutions needed at this stage include specialists in buying, selling, storing, and transporting output from many producers. Among them are auction companies, commodity exchanges, futures markets, factors, brokers, finance companies, manufacturers' agents, selling agents, merchant wholesalers, and retailers. These middlemen are necessary for the development and operation of production-oriented firms and economies, but they do not stimulate maximum growth.

Marketing-Oriented Index May Hover Near One. Production-oriented producers and middlemen may occasionally "get lucky" and have a competitive advantage due to market changes (such as Brazilian coffee growers' profiting from the growing popularity of coffee. And this may give them (temporarily anyway) an MOI above one. Or some "blips" in growth may occur due to political, technological, or economic factors. For example, some of the early growth in Europe was due to colonial expansion, which provided new resources and markets to develop or "harvest." And wars to win control of other people's territories also gain control of additional resources, perhaps enabling one area to exploit—for its own benefit—the human and other resources of another area. Conversely, natural disasters in one area might make the output of another area more valuable and give it a temporary competitive advantage. But, generally speaking, the MOIs of production-oriented economies hover around one—because all the producers focus on products which can also be produced by firms in competing areas. In other words, no area develops a long-lasting competitive advantage over the others and so we see "no-growth" economies in which output is related to the number of people and how hard they work.

One a more positive note, technological developments which occur as a result of a mostly production-oriented concern with cutting costs may "luckily" match some market needs (for lower cost output if nothing else) and lead to a higher MOI. For example, the Industrial Revolution enabled England and parts of Western Europe to harness power and replace hand labor with machines—thereby lowering costs and greatly expanding output and real incomes. But eventually these developments are copied by competing areas and the initial competitive advantage is lost.

Stage IV: Marketing-oriented Firms and Economies

At this stage, marketing-oriented producers try to develop marketing mixes to satisfy specific target markets rather than just producing whatever it is easy for them to make. While the physical plants of such firms may be similar to Stage III plants, the firms' marketing-orientation is distinguishing.

Critical Functions: All of Them—Well Executed. Here, the producers think of potential customers first and use marketing research to learn more about their markets and how well they and associated middlemen are satisfying their customers. The producers still need marketing institutions which provide all of the functions, but their greatest need is for more marketing-oriented execution of the functions.

Critical Institutions: Marketing-oriented Traders and Merchants. Stage IV middlemen have marketing managers; that is, people who develop whole marketing-oriented strategic plans (including marketing mixes), not just promotion plans to sell what has been produced.

The marketing institutions needed in Stage IV—including their physical and office facilities—may appear similar to those in Stage III. It is the attitudes and methods of operation that are different. These middlemen are more willing to aggressively seek customers and try to understand their needs to help solve their problems. Such middlemen are interested in longer-term relationships, both with their producers and their customers. They are not just interested in "clearing markets."

In recent years, many major producers and middlemen in the United States (and elsewhere) moved into Stage IV. When producers move into Stage IV and find only Stage III marketing institutions, they tend to take over more of the marketing functions—either going "direct" or integrating. This contributed to a temporary decline of wholesaling in the United States, but now wholesalers have made a comeback as they have become more marketing oriented. Food brokers, for example, have grown in importance as they have tailored their efforts to provide not only selling, but also rapid information feedback as well as close cooperation with the manufacturers they serve. And modern supermarkets, mass merchandisers, and discounters have drastically changed production-distribution systems by forming chains and streamlining their operations. Sometimes they have formally integrated—by buying other producers or retailers. In other cases, administered channel systems have developed to help ensure smooth flows all the way from producers to final consumers. More than half of the final consumer products in the United States move through such "integrated" channels.

Marketing-Oriented Index Can Rise Far Above One, For Awhile. Many modern corporations, especially producers of consumer products, are fairly marketing oriented—i.e., they easily earn an MOI above one compared to their many less marketing-oriented (or outright production-oriented) competitors. But few economies have enough marketing-oriented firms to earn an MOI that stays substantially above one for very long.

Marketing Orientedness is Necessary for Economic Growth

As we see, different marketing institutions and greater marketing orientedness are necessary at higher stages of economic development. If these changes do not occur, the economies do not move to higher stages and higher levels of real income. In the extreme this means that some more or less self-sufficient producers stay at the subsistence level indefinitely. We still see such economies in various parts of Latin America, Africa, and Asia.

Some economies grow faster than others for many years because they are able to maintain competitive advantages over other areas based on: (1) the technical skills of their people; (2) the quality of their resources and/or their ability to effectively combine them into marketable output; and/or (3) the military power to dominate trade—requiring other areas to buy the output of their economies in return for "commodities" (as was done during the colonial periods, for example).

Inevitably, however, temporary competitive advantages based on fortuitous things, like good growing seasons, low-cost raw materials, or trading relationships based on military power tend to weaken and firms in other areas match or overcome these earlier competitive advantages. Then the MOIs of the various economies tend toward one. Worse, if the previous growth was based on short-term advantages like a few unusually good growing years, a gold supply that runs out, or military supremacy that shifts to another area, then the MOIs can drop far below one and economic decline can occur. For example, once-wealthy Spain ceased growing and then regressed as England became a world power based first on naval power and then its great success with technical and commercial developments during the Industrial Revolution. That is, Spain's MOI relative to England dropped below one as England's MOI rose above one. England remained a world economic and military power for more than one hundred years. But now England has fallen behind and other economies have grown because they organized themselves to better satisfy the needs of their own people and people in other areas. Similarly, the U.S. economy had a high MOI for several years after World War II because the other major industrial powers had been decimated by war. Also, modern technological developments had not yet spread to all of the other countries. But now "everyone" can make the easy-to-produce "commodities"—and the U.S. MOI has declined closer to one. Similarly, Western Europe and Japan had "economic blips" as their economies recovered from World War II and they made effective use of recent technological developments. But now these nations, too, are moving towards MOIs of one or less as other economies improve *their* competitive advantages based on raw materials, worker effectiveness, managerial sophistication, and (in some cases) greater attention to market-oriented strategy planning than in the economies that got started earlier and faced less competition (leading to higher MOIs than they deserved).

Production-oriented firms and economies may remain at their current levels of economic development. Occasionally there may be spurts of growth when their MOI slips above one due to some fortuitous circumstances. But, basically, they are "stuck" at their present level of economic development because they have no competitive advantage over other areas and no reason for any growth. Or worse, their MOIs may go far below one as competitive economies become more effective.

Stage IV firms and marketing-oriented administered or integrated production-distribution systems seem to be growing. Such systems are able to satisfy customers more effectively than poorly coordinated or uncoordinated systems. This means they can offer lower prices and/or better products, and thereby expand their output by opening new markets or finding entirely new uses for their resources. It is firms and economies like these that help expand markets and find new opportunities and must be contrasted with the production-oriented Stage II and III firms.

In most developing economies, firms and middlemen have been and are at Stage II or just edging into Stage III. Fortunately, more marketing-oriented Stage IV firms and middlemen can help the production-oriented move to Stage II or even be part of a Stage IV production-distribution system. On the other hand, the traders found in most "local" markets do not help production-oriented firms move to higher stages of economic development. They are merely trading surpluses, not expanding markets. They see their job as "clearing markets." More efficient Stage II or III middlemen can increase their own incomes, but their attitudes and methods of operation do not help their production-oriented economies achieve real growth. Instead, more marketing-oriented middlemen are needed. Producers must be encouraged to meet specific needs rather than only producing more of whatever can be produced easily. When such marketing-oriented people are not present in an economy, growth is inhibited. Or it may even lead to a decline in the total economic welfare of an economy.

The point here is that given people and other resources, marketing-oriented institutions help match the use of these resources to market opportunities in the most effective way. Unfortunately, however, many producers and middlemen have been (and still are) production oriented and ineffective resource managers. They lack understanding of the marketing process and market-oriented strategic planning. This results in MOIs of one or less—and "no-growth" or declining economies.

In summary, effective marketing-oriented producers and middlemen are necessary and sufficient conditions for speeding economic growth and development. Marketing-oriented firms and middlemen are necessary because without them, economic growth will be inhibited. They are also sufficient because they stimulate growth *providing it is economically feasible* and is not blocked or inhibited by government.

Being More Marketing Oriented Does Not Completely Solve Economic Growth Problems

Just moving to a marketing orientation does not permanently solve the problem of stimulating growth, however. The MOI model says that an area (economy) will grow when its MOI is greater than one. But competitors' efforts can reduce an area's MOI. This means that continued innovation and market-oriented strategy planning are needed to stay ahead of competition so the MOI stays greater than one. This is a difficult and continuing challenge requiring a dynamic society that rewards entrepreneurs and business-people who encourage long-term growth.

Recent history suggests that competition—to survive and grow—will continue to get tougher. The growth and expansion of multinational corporations, government trading groups, governments interested in encouraging economic development, and better training of business people will cause the competition to escalate—making it more difficult for areas and economies to keep their MOI much above one for very long. People (as consumers) will probably benefit by this continued competitive pressure because they will see better offerings at lower prices, but people (as producers) and firms and economies that try to continue in their production-oriented ways or aren't as aggressive as competitors will find that their "economic miracles" are only "blips" on their economic growth curves—which may only be rising with population growth, or even declining.

Conclusion

Marketing orientedness is necessary and sufficient for survival and growth in increasingly competitive markets. But an economy's marketing-oriented index must stay greater than one for continued growth. This is not easy to accomplish as competitors become more sophisticated and aggressive, and governments try to protect the status quo and/or levy taxes without regard to economic growth. Nevertheless, to keep an economy's MOI from slipping below one, it must continue to find new opportunities which it can satisfy better than competitors (the role of marketing-oriented people!) or its growth will be limited to the growth in its own population, at best. If its MOI slips below one, real income growth may decline, even if its population increases. And unfortunately, this often leads to economic and social misery. This is where many economies have been and are now "stuck". They have: (1) MOIs far below one; (2) production-oriented producers who keep producing commodities the way they always have; and (3) production-oriented middlemen who "buy low and sell high" (relying on their financial resources where money is a scarce resource). These economies are doomed to "no-growth" or even economic decline. And, further, if their government institutions are hopelessly production-oriented, it may be years—if ever—before they can raise their MOIs closer to one. In fact, as more progressive economies become more marketing oriented in order to keep their own MOIs above one, it is likely that really production-oriented economies will see their MOIs continue to slip further below one. In other words, these economies will stay at their current levels, or worse, slip further back to where they were years ago. So it is possible to predict the economic future of many economies by describing their past. And the outlook for some of these economies is not very encouraging, given modern expectations about a reasonable standard of living, and the stubborn refusal of many producers, middlemen, and governments to adopt more marketing-oriented ways of running their economies.

Notes

1. A firm, here, is broadly defined as any production entity which acts as a unit. Thus, farm family units as well as large industrial companies are firms. The weighted average of the marketing orientedness of all the firms and middlemen in an area is the marketing orientedness of that area. And when the marketing orientedness of

one competing area is divided into that of another, the result is the MOI for the area in the numerator.

References

McCarthy, E. Jerome, and William D. Perrault, Jr. 1987. *Basic Marketing: A Managerial Approach*. Ninth ed. Homewood, Ill.: Richard D. Irwin.

Nurkse, Ragnar. 1952. *Problems of Capital Formation in Underdeveloped Countries*. Oxford: Basil Blackwell.

Rostow, W. W. 1962. *The Stages of Economic Growth*. Cambridge: Cambridge University Press.

Part IV
Historical Perspectives on Retailing

Introduction

This section treats the area of marketing with which Stanley Hollander is particularly associated, from his time as a retail manager in the early 1940s, through his famous 1960 "Wheel of Retailing" article on the pattern of retail institutional evolution, and through numerous papers and *Journal of Retailing* articles beginning in 1948. Here, three well-known marketing scholars present complementary analyses of the history of retailing.

Edward W. Cundiff gives us a broad overview of the evolution of retailing across time and cultures, beginning with peddlers and market gatherings in antiquity. This excellent introduction to the subject captures both the inexorable flux of change over time and the sometimes surprising intricacies of that flux. Cundiff shows that some still-vibrant retail institutions like the peddler are millennia old, but most of the institutions familiar to Americans and Europeans today represent adaptive responses to the major economic, demographic, technological, and social changes first unleashed by the Industrial Revolution in the 1800s. These changes led to retail innovations unique to the Western world, particularly the United States, where changes such as mass automobile ownership occurred ahead of Europe and made possible the early success of institutions such as the supermarket and the planned shopping center. Until the Industrial Revolution, argues Cundiff, retail activities had developed along similar lines everywhere in the world.

Philip Kotler echoes the overall picture given by Cundiff, then traces the development of a single retail institution, the U.S. convenience store, from its beginnings in the 1920s to the present. He shows that the convenience store began as a creative amalgam of the old-style "mom and pop" grocery with three concepts that had emerged around the early decades of this century—self-service, cash-and-carry (as opposed to credit) selling, and chain stores. Moreover, its formative decades were influenced by competition from the supermarket, an innovation usually dated to the early 1930s. Kotler makes an important point here: marketing institutions do not emerge out of nothing. Equally important is the next point Kotler makes—that the convenience store has changed, at times significantly, over its history; is undergoing change now; and will change in the future. Sale of gasoline, fast food, and banking services via automatic teller machines are the big changes of the past decade or so, for example.

The continued success of the convenience store, Kotler believes, will depend upon its ability to continue to change astutely. In particular, average sales per customer visit will have to be increased, new demographic groups attracted, and the urge (or even need) to carry new products balanced against the danger that additional products may blur the crucial consumer perception that the stores do offer speed, i.e., convenience.

Our third chapter on retailing history deals with a key activity of any retail institution—pricing. Roger Dickinson has selected six episodes of retail pricing in the United States during the 1950s, describing and evaluating their impact at the time and their implications for today. The episodes cover the then-prevailing thought about pricing, the so-called "fair trade" laws, and such retail practices as "price wars" and Merchandise Management Accounting.

Dickinson reminds us that some of the pricing thought and teaching then was better than today's in its willingness to look beyond the purely quantifiable. He also reminds us that there was considerable price competition among U.S. retailers; their lot was no easier than that of retailers now. Some retailers had a sophisticated awareness of the long-run impacts of pricing decisions, for example upon store image. But others fell victim to simplistic policies, e.g., the inflexible price cutting of Safeway Stores' Lingan Warren, or to in-practice impractical nostrums like Merchandise Management Accounting. Pricing policies that considered only the numbers brought at best modest success, at worst disaster.

Dickinson's overall conclusion is that pricing is far too complex and important to be reduced to an exclusively quantitative science. Yet this is what much marketing thought since the 1950s has attempted to make of it. The fascinating episodes of retail pricing from thirty and more years ago do have a good deal to teach us.

9
The Evolution of Retailing Institutions across Cultures

Edward W. Cundiff

Introduction

From the time mankind learned to live in groups and developed the concept of ownership of personal property, people have felt the need to exchange quantities of one good in excess of their own needs for another good or for money. Archaeologists find evidence of retailing activities long before recorded history. Retailing evolved along similar lines in most human societies. Early in human history, as early as 4000–5000 B.C., mankind developed basic retailing institutions that served consumer needs virtually unchanged for several millennia.

Early Retail Exchanges

One of the earliest retailers was the peddler, who filled in the gaps in what were basically self-sufficient family units. He brought salt to people located away from the ocean or natural salt deposits; he brought flint, amber, and furs from the Baltic Sea region to central Europe and the Mediterranean basin; he brought tropical shells to the temperate regions. Even in prehistoric times the peddler traveled hundreds of miles to bring products to locations where they were in short supply (Hermann 1954; The Influence of Automobiles 1927). This service continued into the twentieth century, e.g., peddlers selling in the towns or cities and bringing goods from the cities to rural and primitive areas. Peddlers were early entrepreneurs who recognized the opportunity for profit in serving the unmet needs of people in other locations (Nystrom 1951, 117–139).

Evolving at the same time as the peddler, but for different reasons, was the community marketplace. When household units experienced imbalances between consumption needs and production, they sought to exchange "excess" quantities of their own production for other households' excess of materials which they lacked. The community marketplace evolved as a place where these exchanges could take place. Both the peddler and the marketplace served as important media of communication with regard to such as exchange of ideas and technology across culture in both Western and Eastern societies. There is evidence of the presence of these retailing institutions in archaeological remains as early as 5000 B.C.

The market was normally located at a convenient place near the center of the community. In the smaller villages the buyers and sellers would gather at the designated spot on a regular basis, seasonally or once a month. As the communities grew larger, more frequent market meetings were needed, and many became weekly events (Mund 1948, 4–5). In the larger communities permanent shelters were often built to protect shoppers and sellers from the elements. For example, in classic Greek times, the major cities each had an agora, or market, that provided covered colonnades for shoppers. Permanent markets flourished even earlier, in 1200 B.C., in China (Wooster 1926).

Specialization—Establishment of Permanent Retail Locations

In the most primitive societies each family unit was basically independent, producing its own food through agriculture, hunting, and fishing, constructing its own shelters, and making its own clothing and weapons. It was only when family production and/or consumption were out of balance that these people turned to the marketplace to dispose of excess or to fill deficiencies. Specialization of effort developed as communities grew larger. As communities grew large enough to support specialization, individuals particularly good at making pottery, shoes, or weaving cloth found that they could spend full time at their specialty, exchanging things they made best for their other needs, and probably ending up with more goods than before.

The development of specialists resulted in the establishment of permanent shops where the proprietor could make and sell his goods, and since they were on the premises making their products every day, they were also available to sell them every day. As a consequence, consumers were able to shop daily at their convenience. For convenience of the customer, these shopkeepers located their establishments near the town center and marketplace. The central city retail location had evolved.

The next logical evolutionary step was to the pure or full-time retailer. As towns continued to grow in size, demand developed for goods not produced in the local community. Entrepreneurs recognized the opportunity to bring products from other areas and sell them at a profit. Like the peddlers, these businessmen did not spend the majority of their time producing goods; they were full-time marketers. Like the producer/retailers they tended to specialize in only one line of goods. These specialty stores sold only shoes, or only bakery products, or only fabrics. Even in ancient societies (2 or 3 millennia B.C.) these shops and retail stores evolved as quickly as the cities grew large enough to support them. As late as the eighteenth century most retailing was dominated by these small shops—England was described as a nation of shopkeepers (Nystrom 1951).

Effects of Population Changes

The specialty store and central market continued to serve human societies in all parts of the world pretty much unchanged until the nineteenth century. Rural areas were served by peddlers and/or village general stores, which sold the essential items the farmers could not produce themselves. These general stores were the next evolutionary step from the peddler in rural areas. They had permanent locations and were available daily, but their merchandise selection was not much better than that of the peddler. Towns and cities continued to be served by public marketplaces and by specialty stores, including food stores.

The retailing developments described thus far were, to a fair degree, caused by demographic changes in the population, the growth in numbers of people and with that growth, the development of town and cities. These changes, in turn, allowed the development of specialization, which shaped the retail structure in the cities (Alexander 1958). This pattern of retail development was essentially the same in all evolving societies. It was not until the eighteenth century that new influences began to shape the structure of retailing. This process of retailing evolution, both in rural and urban locations, is charted in Figure 9–1.

The Industrial Revolution

It was with the advent of the industrial revolution that retailers began to evolve new methods of operation. As industries develop in a society, an increasing number of people move away from the small subsistence farms to jobs in the towns; they no longer produce their own food and retailers fill this need. They also find that other products they used to produce, such as textiles and clothing and home utensils and furnishings, are available through mass production at lower prices, often lower than the costs of materials to make their own. As the proportion of the population living in a money economy and working for wages increases, the importance of retailing increases and the need and opportunity for retailing innovations develop. In Western Europe and North America, the impetus for retailing innovation grew in the latter part of the nineteenth century and the early part of the

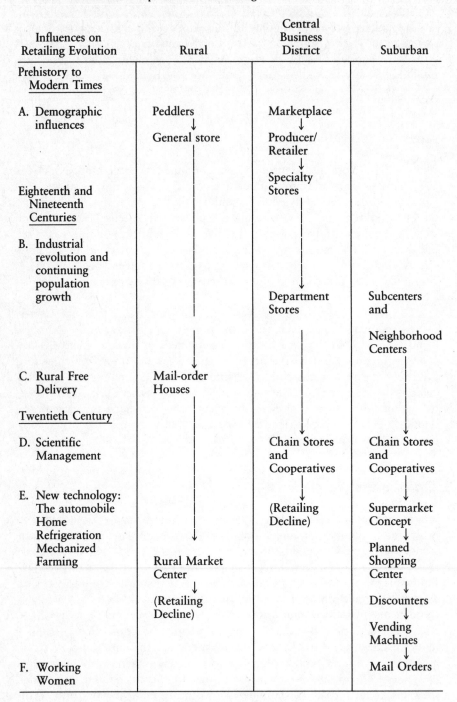

Influences on Retailing Evolution	Rural	Central Business District	Suburban
Prehistory to Modern Times			
A. Demographic influences	Peddlers ↓ General store	Marketplace ↓ Producer/ Retailer ↓ Specialty Stores	
Eighteenth and Nineteenth Centuries			
B. Industrial revolution and continuing population growth		Department Stores	Subcenters and Neighborhood Centers
C. Rural Free Delivery	Mail-order Houses		
Twentieth Century			
D. Scientific Management		Chain Stores and Cooperatives	Chain Stores and Cooperatives
E. New technology: The automobile Home Refrigeration Mechanized Farming	Rural Market Center ↓ (Retailing Decline)	(Retailing Decline)	Supermarket Concept ↓ Planned Shopping Center ↓ Discounters ↓ Vending Machines ↓ Mail Orders
F. Working Women			

Figure 1. Evolution of Retailing Institutions

twentieth century; in less developed countries retailing changes came only as economic development made them possible.

The Emerging Middle Class—The Department Store

The first important new retailing institution in urban areas, one which evolved almost simultaneously in Paris and Philadelphia in the 1860s, was the department store (Bloomfield 1930, 11). These stores were targeted toward the increasing number of middle-class families in the larger cities. They were designed to provide the broad selection of goods found in the public markets but to bring them all under a single roof and a common overall management and one non-bargained price. The exposition-like character and the excitement of the marketplace has always been an important part of the department stores' image. From the first they have operated as a collection of semi-independent shops competing with each other for the attention of the customer (Michel 1963). And they are still organized to give each department executive considerable independence in making merchandising decisions. As cities increased in size, so did the number and size of retailers in the central shopping area. Not only were there increasing numbers of department stores, but many specialty stores broadened their merchandise selection to complete lines of goods, such as women's or men's clothing. This same broadening of merchandise offerings took place in the food stores, as general grocery stores began to replace the specialty green grocers, bakers, and butchers (Phillips 1938a).

Congestion and Development of Suburbs

As cities grew larger and congestion in the central city increased, consumers became reluctant to do all their shopping downtown, and decentralized retailing locations away from the central business district evolved. This was the first step in the movement of retailing out of downtown. Subcenters developed to serve the day-to-day shopping needs of consumers. These subcenters carried a complete range of convenience goods, and the larger centers (which might comprise as many as twenty or thirty stores) also carried a limited selection of shopping goods. Neighborhood centers developed with three to five convenience goods stores, such as groceries, pharmacies, and cleaners. The retailing centers of the central cities were still the major source of shopping goods for all income levels, and public transportation made access available to most shoppers.

Government Services—Mail-Order Houses

The next circumstance that affected the evolution of retailing institutions was an increase and improvement in government mail service—the provision of rural free delivery of parcels. Its influence was mostly on rural retailing. In the United States, the provision by the government of rural free postal delivery spawned a new kind of retail institution, the mail-order house. Farmers, whose only source of merchandise on a regular basis was the general store, found the selection of merchandise much broader and prices much lower in the mail-order catalogues. The growth of the big mail order houses was phenomenal (Clark 1922), and the decline of the general store became inevitable. Figure 9–2, using the first census data available on retail sales shows that by 1939, mail-order house sales had peaked and then very gradually declined until the 1980s.

Scientific Management—The Chain Store

Chains are not new. There were multiple unit retailers in ancient Japan and China (Nystrom 1930, 1:76). But, the twentieth century chain store revolution was the result of applying improved management techniques to the retail store. At the beginning of the twentieth century retailing was inefficient in all parts of the world. Most stores were family-owned "mom and pop" stores characterized by limited merchandise selection, poor physical plants, and high costs of operation. The time was ripe for the application to

	Percent of Total Retail Sales							
	U.S.A.[1]							Europe[2]
	1919	1929	1939	1948	1958	1963	1979	1960
General Stores		6.3%	3.1%	0.9%	—	—	—	
Mail-Order Houses		1.1%	1.3%	1.1%	1%	1%	0.6%	
Department Store		8.0%	9.6%	7.3%	6.7%	8.4%	15.6%	3.6%
Chain Stores (Including food)	5%	29.6%	30.6%	29.6%	33.7%	36.6%	33.7%	8.2%
Supermarkets/ Discount House			3.2%	9.1%	13.5%	17.6%	36.1%	
Consumer Cooperatives			0.4%					6.2%
Vending Machines						0.6%		
All Others		55.0%	51.2%	51.0%	45.1%	35.8%	14%	78%

Sources: [1]United States Department of Commerce, Bureau of the Census.

[2]James B. Jeffrys & Derek Knee, *Retailing in Europe* (London: Macmillan & Co., Ltd., 1962).

Figure 2. Growth Patterns of Types of Retailer

retailing of many of the scientific management techniques developed in mass production. So, mass retailing in the form of chain stores mushroomed. Through the introduction of standardized operating methods, large-scale buying, and reduction of services, chain stores were able to lower their operating costs and, hence, their prices (Bloomfield 1930, 11). In a number of merchandise lines, but particularly in food and drugs, during the 1920s, the small independents were almost totally supplanted by chain outlets. The period of most rapid growth, as shown in figure 2 was the 1920s when sales as a percent of total retail sales increased from 5 percent to 30 percent.

Consumer Cooperatives

Consumers sometimes tried to achieve the cost savings from mass retailing by establishing their own retail stores or cooperatives. By banding together the cooperatives tried to reduce their costs through large-scale buying, while at the same time increasing the efficiency of store operation (Drury 1937; Gide 1922). In the United States co-ops had almost no impact on the market—less than 0.5 percent because they were unable to achieve as great efficiency as the chain stores (Blankertz 1958). However, in Europe and England, where the chain stores were less effective, the co-ops were more successful. In Finland, for example, they accounted for one-third of total retail sales in the 1960s (Hall 1931; Jeffrys & Knee 1962).

Unique American Evolution

It was early in the twentieth century that the evolution of retailing institutions in the United States departed from that in other economically developed nations. Changes affecting retailing in the United States were not taking place in other countries. The population of the European countries was more stable. The technological revolution didn't hit the farms in a major way until after World War II, so rural population was more stable and there was little migration to the cities. Finally, a combination of less middle-class buying power and a superior public transportation system in place in Europe delayed the widespread adoption of the automobile until after World War II.

The Impact of New Technologies

The Automobile and Rural Retailing

A particularly important technological breakthrough for the evolution of retailing was the development of the automobile. In the United States, a combination of factors, such as a very large land area inadequately served by public transportation and a large middle class able to afford the high cost of the automobile, led to widespread adoption of the automobile earlier than in other parts of the world.

This new product transformed rural America in the second quarter of the twentieth century. As rural families acquired automobiles (Hall 1931), the general stores, which had already been hurt by the mail-order houses, were put out of business. Farm families were able to travel by automobile to the nearest county seat or market town as quickly as they could travel to the general store by horse (Converse 1928). The retailing establishments in the towns grew in size and in selection of merchandise. Continued growth of retailing in these market towns, however, was slowed, or sometimes halted, by another technological development—mechanized farming.

Mechanization allowed each farmer to increase his acreage and/or reduce his help. Prior to the introduction of the tractor, one farmer could only plant and manage about one quarter-section of land; with the introduction of more sophisticated farming equipment one farmer could manage a number of sections of land. In successive decades, continuing improvements in automobiles and in the highway system in the United States led the smaller number of remaining rural inhabitants to do more of their shopping in urban areas, causing an even further decline in the retailing institutions in the market towns (Wooster 1926).

Automobiles and Refrigerators—The Supermarket

The first uniquely American retailing institution evolved in the 1930s as the ownership of automobiles became widespread. It was called the supermarket, and it refined the concept successfully introduced by the neighborhood chain store outlets of achieving a high merchandise turnover. But in this case, the higher turnover was achieved through increasing the volume of sales in the outlet instead of through limiting merchandise selection. The high turnover of merchandise allowed the supermarket to earn a large profit even though markup per unit was lower. But, in order to achieve a broad merchandise selection and still keep stockturn low, the supermarket had to be much larger than traditional retail food outlets, and each store had to draw customers from a much larger area than the old neighborhood outlets. It was the automobile that made this possible. Therefore, one necessary requirement of the supermarket was a large parking lot (Nystrom 1951; Phillips 1938b).

Another technological development necessary to ensure the success of the supermarket was home refrigeration. Since the driving time to the supermarket for the average customer was longer, and since the size of the store and congestion increased the time required to shop, use of the supermarket was justified only if the consumer changed his or her shopping habits. Instead of shopping daily for food, a great many supermarket customers gradually extended the time between shopping trips to as much as a week (Nystrom 1951). Supermarkets grew steadily in share of retail sales from 1939 to 1980.

The Planned Shopping Center

The automobile also had a strong impact on the growth patterns and retailing structure in the cities. As automobile ownership increased, many city residents sought to escape the crowding and pollution in the cities by moving to the suburbs. The suburbs were often beyond the services of public transportation, and even when public transportation was available, the typical American's "love affair" with his automobile made him or her choose driving over public transportation to the central city shopping areas.

Traffic congestion and parking problems in the central city became ever worse. The time was ripe for a new retailing innovation, the planned shopping center, which was oriented and designed completely for the convenience of automobile drivers (Rolph 1933). The small neighborhood centers began to mushroom in the rapidly growing perimeters of the cities and neighboring suburbs in the 1930s, but it was not until after World War II that the larger centers became important.

Gradually, during the next forty years, as the cities continued to grow outward from the centers, rings of ever-larger shopping centers developed. Since these centers were large enough to serve the total shopping and convenience goods needs of the consumers, and since they were closer to the concentrations of population, they eventually supplanted the central city shopping areas in most communities for all but the most exotic kinds of merchandise. The central city retailing centers withered to but a small vestige of their former size.

Discounting

During the late 1940s (Korvette was founded in 1948) and the 1950s innovative retailers applied the operating methods of the supermarket to new lines of merchandise, and the discount house was born. During the next two decades, discount houses evolved in several forms, grew larger, and became more numerous, capturing a sizable share of the retail market. The culmination of this supermarket development was the introduction of the discount mall in the early 1980s. These malls offered a broad range of lines of merchandise at lowest possible markups.

Vending Machines

Another technological breakthrough was the development of machines that receive coins, make change, dispense merchandise, and even make change for paper money. These developments made possible the development of the vending machine industry. Vending machines have been around in their simpler forms since early in the twentieth century, but it wasn't until a need for them developed that they really grew as an important type of retailing. They serve consumers' needs by providing convenience goods at places where the consumer doesn't have the time or is unable to travel to a regular retail outlet (Maynard and Beckman 1927). However, their role in the overall retailing structure is small (only 0.6 percent of total retail sales) because they only serve a kind of emergency consumer need.

Working Women—Mail Order

The most recent retailing development in the United States is not an innovation but merely an adaptation of mail order retailing to new types of merchandise and new operating methods. Three new factors encouraged this development: the great increase in the number of working women, the widespread adoption of national credit cards and better delivery systems. Women, who had done most of the family shopping when they were full-time homemakers, when working were much less willing to spend their limited free time shopping. They found the process of selecting fashion merchandise and other shopping goods from catalogues in the home much less time-consuming and more relaxing. The widespread adoption of national credit cards in the 1970s made it easier to handle the process of paying for mail-order merchandise. And third, the development of a better delivery system with a number of private concerns offering competition to parcel post made it possible to increase the speed of delivery of mail-order purchases. During the early 1980s more retailers moved into direct mail selling, and the volume of this type of retail sales increased many times.

Differing Patterns of Development

Prior to the 1930s, retailing evolution throughout the world had followed a fairly standard pattern. The more highly developed nations developed similar innovations more or less at the same time, and the less-developed nations followed along later. However, with the introduction of the supermarket, American retailing developed a unique pattern compared to that in much of the rest of the world.

Canada and Australia

Canada and Australia, both of which adopted the automobile as a major form of transportation early, for much the same reasons as the United States, and both of which have experienced rapid growth in population since 1940, quickly adopted the American retailing innovations. Supermarkets, planned shopping centers, and discount houses quickly became a part of their retail structure.

Europe

Yet, in Western Europe these innovations were not adopted, and retailing remained essentially unchanged until the 1960s. Immediately before and after World War II, scientific management concepts resulted in the development of retail chains and the introduction of more efficient operating methods, but the environment was not right for the introduction of supermarkets or planned shopping centers. Total population was stable, or growing only slowly, and automobile ownership was not widespread. Migration from the farms began in the eighteenth century in England, but only started after World War II in most of Europe, so the population of most European cities was either stable or growing only very slowly (Michel 1963). In addition, cultural conservatism and pressures for protection by existing retailing institutions probably slowed the adoption of new retailing forms.

Also, supermarkets, planned shopping centers, and discount houses all require large tracts of ground to provide space for parking as well as for buildings. It is usually too expensive to obtain such land by razing existing structures in established sections of cities, so they built at the edges of the cities in the direction of population growth. As population continues to grow beyond these locations each becomes the center of its own large market.

But, since growth in most European cities was minimal, new perimeter locations would have remained outside of the consumers' normal travel patterns, even after consumers acquired automobiles. Thus, as recently as 1960, small independent retailers continued to account for 78 percent of total retail sales in Europe. By this time, independent retailers' share had declined to only 36 percent in the United States (See figure 2). Retailing entrepreneurs, reluctant to lose the potential profits offered by the supermarket concept with its strong price appeal, finally devised a new retail institution, the hypermarket. These retail outlets, which combined the merchandise to be found in a supermarket and a discount house, in a floor space two or three times as large as either, were located on inexpensive land beyond the edges of the cities. The appeal of their enormous inventory selection at very low prices was strong enough to draw city dwellers outside the city in their automobiles. Hypermarkets expanded rapidly in a number of European countries in the last half of the 1960s and the 1970s (Langeard & Malsagne 1971).

Other Countries

Basically similar retailing institutions have evolved in other parts of the world. The extent to which these institutions have evolved somewhat differently and the speed of their adoption has been dependent on the variation in the development and impact of the influences described in figure 1. In countries where population growth has been slow, or where the number of people who could afford automobiles and other new technological developments was small, supermarkets and planned shopping centers have not developed. Instead, the discounting concept may have been adapted to the use of existing retailers. The same is true of other retailing innovations.

Summary

Since people first banded together in groups, they have experienced the need to exchange things they own for things possessed by others. This need for exchange has provided the impetus for the development of varied retailing institutions which over the centuries have evolved into ever more complex and sophisticated organizations.

The continuing growth and movement of human population has increased the need for retailers to serve consumption needs. In addition, increasing specialization of human effort, replacing the self-sufficient family unit, created the need for permanent, full-time retailers to fill the growing range of needs not satisfied by personal production.

The Industrial Revolution had a major impact on retailing. The emerging middle class was consumption oriented, and the department store evolved to serve its needs. The migration of population to the cities as a result of the Industrial Revolution created more and more urban congestion, which ultimately helped bring on the movement of retailing toward the suburbs. In the last quarter of the nineteenth century, improvement in governmental postal service in rural areas resulted in the development of mail-order houses.

The continuing development of new technologies has continued to influence the evolution of retailing. The combined effects of mechanized farming and the automobile have gradually reduced the volume and impact of retailing in rural locations. The automobile and the home refrigerator helped make the supermarket viable and successful. The automobile in combination with continuing growth in urban congestion accelerated the movement toward the suburbs, thus making the planned shopping center possible, and ultimately, influenced the decline of urban retailing.

Most recently, in the United States women were drawn into the workplace. These working women were unable to afford the demands placed on their time by existing retailers, so they welcomed the alternative of mail-order shopping in their homes and shopping at other times. Increasing the use of national credit cards made it possible to use mail-order shopping with a minimum of effort and inconvenience and contributed to the development of this form of retailing.

References

Alexander, Ralph S. 1958. "The Changing Structure of Intermediate Markets." In R. V. Mitchell, ed., *Changing Structure and Strategy in Marketing*. Urbana: Bureau of Business and Economic Research, University of Illinois. 66–71.

Blankertz, Donald F. 1958. "Consumer Actions and Consumer Nonprofit Cooperation." In R. V. Mitchell, ed., *Structure and Strategy in Marketing*. Urbana: Bureau of Business and Economic Research, University of Illinois. 66–71.

Bloomfield, Daniel. 1930. *Trends in Retail Distribution.* New York: H. W. Wilson.

Clark, Fred E. 1922. *Principles of Marketing.* New York: Macmillan.

Converse, Paul D. 1928. *The Automobile and the Village Merchant.* Bulletin 19 of the University of Illinois Bureau of Business Research. Urbana: Bureau of Business Research, University of Illinois.

Drury, J. C. 1937. "An Introduction to the History of Consumers' Cooperation." *Annals of the American Academy of Political and Social Science* 191 (May). 4–10.

Gide, Charles. 1922. *Consumers' Cooperative Societies.* New York: Alfred A. Knopf.

Hall, F. 1931. "Consumers' Cooperation in Great Britain and Ireland." *Encyclopedia of the Social Sciences.* Vol. 4. New York: Macmillan.

Hermann, Paul. 1954. *Conquest By Man.* New York: Harper. *The Influence of Automobiles and Good Roads on Retail Trading Centers* (1927). *Nebraska Studies in Business* 18.

Jeffrys, James B., and Derek Knee. 1962. *Retailing in Europe.* London: Macmillan.

Langeard, Eric, and Robert Malsagne. 1971. *Les Magasins de Grande Surface.* Paris: Dunod Economie.

Maynard, H. H., and T. N. Beckman. 1927. *Principles of Marketing.* Part III. New York: Ronald Press.

Michel, Marcel. 1963. *La Distribution des Merchandises en Belgique.* Louvain: Centre de Recherch Economique.

Mund, Vernon. 1948. *Open Markets.* New York: Harper.

Nystrom, P. H. 1930. *Economics of Retailing.* vol. 1. New York: Ronald Press.

———. 1951. "Retailing in Retrospect." In Hugh C. Wales, ed., *Changing Perspectives in Marketing*. Urbana: University of Illinois Press. 117–139.

———. 1931. "Trends in Large Scale Retailing." *Harvard Business Review* 10 (October). 30–37.

Phillips, Charles F. 1938a. "The Supermarkets." *Harvard Business Review* 16 No. 2. 188–200.

———. 1938b. *Marketing,* New York: Houghton Mifflin.

Rolph, I. K. 1933. *The Location and Structure of Retail Trade.* U.S. Department of

Commerce, Bureau of Foreign and Domestic Commerce, Domestic Commerce Series 80.

Wooster, H. A. 1926. "A Forgotten Factor in Industrial History." *American Economic Review* (March).

10
The Convenience Store: Past Developments and Future Prospects

Philip Kotler

Introduction

The convenience store represents a distinct species of food retailing institution whose growth has been phenomenal in the United States and whose potential for worldwide transplantation is enormous. Although it has several earmarks of the old "mom and pop" grocery store—entrepreneurial character, limited assortment, and long working hours—it also combines features not seen before and it represents a unique and viable method of food retailing. The convenience store concept itself has spawned several forms and undergoes continuous evolution.

The purpose of this chapter is to critically review the past, present, and future of this dynamic institution. Specifically, we will examine the following questions:

1. How did the food retailing industry evolve of which convenience stores are a part?
2. What are the major characteristics of the convenience store concept?
3. What consumer segments primarily are served by the convenience store?
4. What are the competitive requirements for the continued success of convenience stores?

Evolution of the Food Retailing Industry

The food retailing industry has exhibited a long and involved history marked by several stages of evolution. In the beginning, primitive man satisfied all his food needs through hunting and fishing. In the next stage, he learned he could grow a variety of fruits, vegetables, and grains to supplement his diet. Over time, food-gathering skills improved, and individual family units found

A special thanks is owed to Kathy Gardner and Larry Wilken, my research assistants, who helped prepare this chapter.

it advantageous to specialize in producing specific food items at a surplus level and trading the surplus level against needed crops. The specialization of labor and resulting surplus gave rise to the exchange of food commodities.

Initially, exchange was most prevalent among dwellings in the immediate vicinity of another. Enterprising individuals would travel to other dwellings to exchange goods. A crucial development in the evolution of the retail food industry occurred when markets or sites of exchange became fixed in one location. A member of the family, usually the wife, would sit in the market to offer her goods in exchange for other goods. Women were the first retailers.

Originally, retailers would spread their goods on a cloth and squat beside them. Later, pushcarts came into existence. Ultimately, permanent stores emerged, when parts of homes in the marketplace became "selling rooms." Each early store specialized in a different type of food item: baked goods, meats, fish, fruits, or vegetables. Shoppers would travel from one store to another to acquire the needed assortment of foods. The advantage of food specialization was fresh merchandise of good quality. The disadvantage was inconvenience in that each shopper had to travel to acquire the desired assortment. The inconvenience factor was not great, however, since shoppers did not have many alternatives competing for their time.

The following stage consisted of a movement toward wider assortment within stores. Individuals specializing in a particular commodity began to add other goods. According to Goldman, a store carrying staple food items— rice, salt, meat—began to carry fruit and vegetables, thus venturing into perishables (Goldman 1974). Bolder store entrepreneurs later added a line of meats, which involved additional skill, cost, and risk in store management. The concept of a grocery store evolved as a means of meeting all of a person's food needs in one location. This greatly reduced the number of stops the shopper had to make when gathering food supplies. At the same time, larger stores required a larger customer volume for success. And the owner/entrepreneur could no longer provide the personalized, expert service which was expected from food specialty stores.

The preceding evolution of the retail food industry has been described from a universal perspective. Many variations appeared in different societies and cultures. The remainder of this chapter will focus on the American food retailing industry to illustrate specific developments.

The early American food retail scene was dominated by general stores and "mom and pop" stores. They were eventually overtaken by the American supermarket, clearly the dominant form today in American food retailing. But the American supermarket did not emerge overnight. It had a background in several key retailing concepts. One of these was cash-and-carry merchandising, which can be traced back to 1912 and John Hartford of the Great Atlantic and Pacific Tea Company, who persuaded his father to let him experiment with the idea of economy stores (Markin 1968). Economy stores offered no delivery service and carried no credit accounts.

Self-service was another innovation necessary for the evolution of the supermarket. In 1912, Clarence Saunders opened the first Piggly Wiggly store in Memphis Tennessee. He influenced the popularization of self-service more than any other individual (Markin 1968).

Supermarkets were first introduced by independent food retailers in the early 1930s. A supermarket was defined, prior to 1962, as a complete departmentalized food store with a minimum sales volume of $375,000 a year and at least the grocery department fully self-service. Before the introduction of supermarkets, independents had had a difficult time competing with the economy stores operated by the chains. As supermarkets grew in consumer popularity, the chains found themselves at a competitive disadvantage and began to adopt supermarket tactics. The late 1930s saw rapid growth and expansion of the supermarket concept. As chains began to again dominate the food retailing industry, independent retailers formed cooperative groups (Certified Grocers) or voluntary merchandising groups (IGA) to improve their competitive viability.

The Concept of a Convenience Store

The convenience store actually had its beginnings in the 1920s with the founding of the Southland Ice Company. The manufacturer opened retail ice stations where "curb service" was provided for its customers. At the request of some customers, the company began stocking a few grocery items such as milk, bread, eggs, cigarettes, and a few canned goods. The need for a store to handle such items was because regular grocery stores were closed on Sundays. The selling of these products greatly increased the profits of the Southland Ice Company and was the start of the convenience-store concept.

Southland called its first retail chain of convenience stores Tote'm. By 1939 the company had sixty retail locations, mostly in the Dallas-Fort Worth area. The profits from these stores surpassed those from the ice operations by a wide margin. In the meantime, Southland had bought out a chain of stores called City Ice Stores. The firm wanted to develop an advertising program for its stores and felt a common identity was needed for the program to succeed.

The Tracy-Locke Company was handling the advertising campaign for Southland and was given the responsibility of creating a new name for all of the stores. The advertising agency created the name "7–11" stores. The idea was that the stores would stay open from 7 A.M. to 11 P.M., seven days a week. Once the store operators agreed to this arrangement in 1946, the name "7-Eleven" became official. This was the start of the modern convenience store era.

Over the next thirty years convenience stores developed a number of characteristics which distinguished them from conventional supermarkets in several ways.

1. Convenience stores were considerably smaller in size. They averaged 1,000–4,500 square feet compared to an average area of 33,000 square feet for new supermarkets being built in 1980.

2. Convenience stores stocked fewer product lines and fewer items within each line. Typically, only the smaller sizes of packaged goods were available in convenience stores.

3. Fresh meat was not found in convenience stores and produce, if offered at all, was carried in very small quantities of a lesser quality.

4. Convenience stores stocked only top-selling brands and often at premium prices. The prices of some items could run 15 percent higher than in supermarkets. For this reason, the average gross margin for convenience stores was typically higher than that of a conventional supermarket. In 1979 convenience stores had an average gross margin of 29.3 percent (*Progressive Grocer* 1980). This margin had risen to 32.2 percent by 1986 (National Association of Convenience Stores 1987).

5. Convenience stores featured a nearby location, longer hours of operations, and quick service. Convenience stores drew most of their customers from within a 1- to 2-mile radius of the store. They began with late evening and early morning business hours beyond those of traditional supermarkets. In 1976, 28 percent of all convenience stores were open around the clock. Quick check-out time was important since customers were only in a convenience store for an average of 3–4 minutes.

Further Evolution—Recent Trends

In the past decade many factors have led to a change from the conventional convenience store described above to what is now a variety/combination convenience store:

1. Increased competition among traditional convenience stores.

2. Increased competition from oil retailers who are opening stores at their service stations.

3. The cost of opening a store, which has increased threefold since the mid 1970s to an average of $370,000 (land, building, and inventory) (Brown 1984).

4. An effort to expand the convenience store customer base beyond the blue-collar male.

5. The trend of many large supermarkets staying open longer hours to gain a competitive edge among themselves. This will make the supermarket more competitive as far as time convenience is concerned, and makes the supermarket an alternative to the convenience store throughout the day.

No longer will milk, bread, and eggs cover the increased overhead. Higher profit margins are needed and more customers must be drawn into the store. Convenience stores can no longer grow by relying on the blue-collar segment. To meet these requirements, the convenience store now offers a variety of products and services in addition to the traditional ones. Efforts have been made to attract a broad customer base, including women and higher-income customers.

The Convenience Store Product Mix

In the early 1970s, with the coming of the oil crises and the high demand for gasoline, convenience stores began installing gasoline pumps. The late 1970s saw an increase in consumer awareness of energy conserving measures and a decline in the consumption of gasoline. Today, gasoline is a big customer draw and is offered by 65 percent of all convenience stores. Gasoline contributes only a 7.3 percent margin while accounting for 33 percent of total convenience store sales (National Association of Convenience Stores 1987).

As the demand for gasoline declined, convenience retailers were forced to look into other revenue producing areas; thus, the emergence of fast food with an average profit margin of 42 percent. This environmental climate also led to the conversion of gas stations into convenience stores/service stations. As of 1985, fast food accounted for 11 percent of convenience store sales (excluding gasoline), representing approximately an 8 percent market share in the fast-food industry (Schoifet 1985). The convenience store is now recognized as a viable competitor in this market. Fast-food offerings range from pastries, donuts, and coffee for the morning crowd to deli sandwiches, pizza, hot dogs, hamburgers, and fountain sodas for generating a brisk lunch and dinner business. These offerings are adjusted based on geographical preferences, e.g., Mexican food is offered in the Southwest, and Polish sausage enjoys a high sale in black and Southern areas. Convenience stores have also been experimenting with a number of service offerings designed to attract new customers. These include dry cleaning, videocassette rentals, flower ordering, mail pick-up, and most recently, automatic teller machines.

Profit margins on gasoline and transaction fees for ATMs are small, but studies show that 25 percent to 40 percent of customers who buy gasoline or use the ATM will buy something else—such as a fast-food product with a high margin (Brown 1984). The convenience store has become a one-stop extravaganza where a person can get cash through an ATM, buy gasoline, eat a meal, and then pick up some convenience items and rent a videocassette before heading home. Where else can a person do all of this in one stop at one location? Almost anything goes under the new convenience store concept and more products/services can and will be added in the future. However, the average customer spent an average of $1.50 per visit in 1977 (*Business Week* 1977) and only spends about $2.00 per visit now—suggesting convenience stores have not been successful in increasing average purchases.

The Role of Franchising

Convenience stores have by and large relied on franchising to create a standardized expectation for the consumer. Southland Corporation, which operates 7-Eleven stores, franchises about 40 percent of its convenience outlets. While providing an opportunity for American entrepreneurial spirit, Southland still manages to exert considerable control by retaining title to the real estate. Franchisee fees vary. For stores that have been in operation for twelve continuous months, the fee is 15 percent of the total gross profit of the store over this period of time. For all other stores, the fee is 15 percent of the annualized average per-store-month gross profit for all stores within the district in which the store is located. Gasoline profits are not included in figuring the franchise fees (The Southland Corporation 1986). In return, the company trains two people and handles all merchandising, advertising, and financial statements. Stores are expected to show a profit after six months in operation. Strict controls are necessary to ensure profitability in a food retailing industry where the average sale is very small.

The Target Markets of a Convenience Store Operation

Since their introduction, convenience stores have been successful at identifying groups and purchase occasions that trigger sales throughout the day. Because the average convenience store carries only 3,000 items, the needs of selected target markets must be carefully considered. In the 1970s, the largest percentage of convenience store sales came from tobacco products. A typical convenience store customer was a man who had just run out of cigarettes. Dairy products were the second largest convenience store category, catering to mothers needing milk for their families. Success of this low-margin category was evidence that more women were frequenting convenience stores to shop for essential household needs. This development was a sign of potential growth for grocery and health and beauty-aid categories. Products such as coffee and 7-Eleven's frozen Slurpee were used to bring customers into the store.

The 1980s have seen a decrease in gasoline prices and a decline in the number of smokers. Yet gasoline now accounts for the largest percentage of convenience store sales while tobacco still holds the second largest category in spite of the adverse publicity given to cigarette smoking.

Grocery, beer, dairy, and soft drink products all have about the same percentage of sales followed by fast-food products (*Nation's Restaurant News* 1983). However, due to the high margins and the power of attracting customers, emphasis is on marketing fast-food products and growth in this category is imminent. Southland Corporation is currently test marketing Hardee's hamburgers as an addition to its fast food line.

Today, the strategies used to attract customers are geared to a broad customer base. Items such as cigarettes, beer, and dairy products are still essential in attracting the traditional blue-collar workers and housewives, along with the new customer mix of working women, white-collar workers, and young men and women. However, the newer and more effective items attracting the needed broad customer base are gasoline, fast food, and ATMs. Convenience stores are also targeting specific segments with fresh and innovative promotions. An example of this is Circle K's introduction of the "Deli Fresh Lite" line of reduced calorie sandwiches aimed at diet-conscious working women and white-collar males (*Nation's Restaurant News* 1985). Store remodeling efforts have been geared toward women since their entry to the work force, especially in the last five years. Efforts are now being directed to young adults (age 20–34) because this age group makes up 63 percent of all convenience store customers and consists of a large number of food service patrons (*Supermarket Business* 1981). The emergence of this segment as the most rapidly growing is a factor favorable to convenience store expansion. Dining areas are now being provided to make the convenience store an even more attractive alternative to other fast-food outlets.

Convenience stores are also turning increasingly to the stimulation of impulse buying. The idea is that once a customer is in the store, he or she will buy more than the item(s) motivating the visit. Thus, a typical convenience store strategy is to use gasoline, fast food, or low prices on staple items to attract more customer volume. When the customer is in the store, the merchandising and store layout help generate impulse purchases. Many high-volume items such as dairy products, beer, and sodas are located in areas where many impulse items must be passed to get to the needed products and also to get to the cashier. Approximately half the products sold in convenience stores are consumed within thirty minutes of the purchase (*Business Week* 1977).

Several studies attempted to profile the convenience store user of the 1970s. In a study by Darden et al., the most common users of convenience stores emerged as families with young children (Darden, Darden, and Lumpkin 1980). These individuals normally had higher incomes, but lower levels of education and lower-status jobs than nonusers. This combination suggested dual breadwinners in the family unit. Heavy users tended to be more family oriented and to put less value on time spent in seeking consumer information and shopping for low prices. To these consumers, gas savings were not as important as time savings, again suggesting that heavy users of convenience stores were less money conscious than time conscious. Others had profiled the typical convenience store user as a man who ran in for a pack of cigarettes or some beer.

With the new product/service mix and strategies of the 1980s attracting a variety of customers, a profile of a typical convenience store user is hard to determine. Besides the users already described, almost anyone is a potential user today. There has been an increase in white-collar workers and working women as users of the convenience store. To be competitive and to increase volume, and to improve their images, convenience stores have increased advertising and promotional expenditures. An example is Southland's backing of the Muscular Dystrophy Association Labor Day Telethon in 1986. The promotion consisted of thirty-second network television spots with the theme, "Making a miracle happen for Jerry's kids," which focused on the convenience of making donations through pledge boxes at 7500 7-Eleven stores (Freeman 1985). As mentioned earlier, store layout is important in creating impulse buying. The convenience industry growth and need for effective store design has led to the emergence and success of companies such as CDI, a New York design company specializing in convenience store creation.

Convenience Stores as Competitors in the Future Retail Food Industry

In their 1980 annual report, *Progressive Grocer* noted that the 34,125 convenience stores in the United States had overtaken supermarkets in terms of number of outlets. This number has grown to more than 60,000 in 1986. Does this mean that supermarkets and convenience stores will be intense competitive rivals during the rest of the 1980s and throughout the 1990s? According to present indications, this seems more likely than in the past. Noteworthy here is the Kroger Company's 1983 acquisition of Dillon Companies, Inc., which ranks among the top ten convenience store operators.

Supermarket owners used to see the main threat as coming from fast food outlets rather than convenience, warehouse, or limited assortment stores. With convenience stores' expansion into the fast-food area, it seems likely that competition with supermarkets will be concentrated on that area, rather than in grocery products where the main competition to supermarkets will come from new superstores. In a survey of supermarket chain executives, prospects for convenience stores were assessed in the fair-to-good category, while prospects for superstores and combinations stores were judged to be in the good-to-excellent category. As convenience stores venture into new areas, their competitors will increase in number. Currently, they face competition from supermarkets offering extended hours on one side and from fast-food outlets on the other, in addition to other convenience stores and service stations with stores. In the future it will be very difficult to distinguish the service station from the pure-bred convenience store.

Each food retailing format appears to have captured a target market segment. Superstores and combination stores provide one-stop shopping for the energy- and time-conscious consumer. However, the recent decline of gasoline prices could lead to more multiple-stop shopping, which would be advantageous for the convenience store. Warehouse and limited-item outlets appeal to the price-conscious, inflation-oriented shopper who wants low prices with only the bare necessities. Again, the present environmental climate of low inflation could help the convenience store become a feasible alternative for these consumers. Convenience stores cater to shoppers of impulse goods and last-minute items at a higher price. Meanwhile, the conventional supermarket struggles to keep its customers from going in all the other directions.

As recently as 1977, convenience store chains did not see themselves in direct competition with the supermarket. Robert E. Hutchinson of Circle K Corporation explained, "We are not in competition for the weekly grocery shopping. We locate close to bedroom communities so that when customers forget something, they can just drop in" (*Business Week* 1977). Because of changes in the marketplace since then, this attitude would be dangerous. As competition intensifies into the 1990s, it appears battles will be most intense not only within each type of food retailing format, but also between the convenience store and other outlets such as service stations, fast food, and supermarkets.

Strategies For Growth

Convenience stores have a number of marketing strategies available to them as we approach the 1990s. At the beginning of the present decade observers believed that the convenience store population in the South was close to the saturation point. Expansion was anticipated in the Middle Atlantic, the Midwest, and the Pacific, where convenience store penetration was low and in central urban areas and smaller towns in the Sunbelt and West. The migration to smaller towns also was expected to provide opportunities for expansion. According to the National Association of Convenience Stores (1987) this picture still generally holds good, though there has been a noticeable movement of younger, higher-income consumers into urban areas which were formerly the home of lower-income families. This has provided the convenience store with a promising new target segment.

Convenience stores are continuing to locate in areas which seem to be saturated, particularly the South. Their philosophy is that people will use convenience stores more in warmer areas, particularly late in the evening. In addition, although 1,000 households is normally accepted as the trade area needed to support a convenience store, areas with fewer than this number of households are attracting convenience stores (National Association of Convenience Stores, 1987).

Attention is also turning to foreign markets, although some express concern over whether the convenience store concept is truly exportable. Nevertheless, Southland Corporation already has franchises in Japan, Canada, and Australia. For example, Ito-Yokado Group in Japan operates more than 500 7-Eleven stores in Japan with great success. Also, Circle K Corporation has signed a licensing agreement with Group Usaha Trisakti calling for the opening of as many as 100 stores throughout Indonesia in the next five years. Circle K also has 260 stores in Japan and Hong Kong, with plans to enter the United Kingdom (*Nation's Restaurant News* 1986).

New products and services also are part of a well-planned strategy for the next decade. Currently, 65 percent of American convenience stores have self-service gasoline pumps. Nearly every future new store is being designed to incorporate the sale of gasoline. It seems likely that major convenience store groups will try to take over some oil companies as indicated by Southland's acquisition of Citgo in 1983. The convenience store industry is particularly interested in the major oil companies because of their prime outlet locations, and vice-versa. In addition, some convenience store chains have credit card arrangements with major oil companies. At the same time, the oil industry has become more involved in the concept of convenience stores. This may eventually include outright ownership of convenience store chains along with the current expansion of existing service stations to carry convenience food items.

A variety of other new product and service categories are also under consideration. Some stores may incorporate photography centers. Greeting cards and magazines have been added to many existing product lines. Some of the larger convenience store chains have added a few private-label products to please the price-conscious consumer. Also under consideration is the use of card-activated gasoline pumps and the use of gasoline pumps that will accept certain denominations of cash. Another innovative idea in connection with electronic funds transfer is the development of an electronic shopping network. National Convenience Stores, in 1984, was negotiating with vendors to develop this system, which could offer sporting event ticketing, airline ticketing, catalogue sales, electronic couponing, and banking services such as bill payment (*Supermarket Business* 1984). Southland is currently experimenting with this idea by offering airline ticketing services at its 7-Eleven stores in Corpus Christi and Houston, Texas (*Convenience Store News* 1987). Current economic trends seem to favor the convenience store. The higher cost of eating out has forced many Americans to use fast-food outlets, where convenience stores are becoming increasingly strong. The reduction in inflation has seen a reduction in the use of list making and food-ad scanning by consumers, together with an increase in impulse purchasing, which convenience stores rely on heavily. But though the current environment is favorable for convenience store operations, more alert management will be needed to effectively deal with the new markets that convenience stores are continuously entering, as this will not only expand the customer base but also the competition base.

In 1979, the convenience store industry reported a sales increase of 14.8 percent over the previous year (*Progressive Grocer* 1980). The industry is still growing but at a slower rate, as evidenced by the 9.7 percent sales increase from 1983 to 1984 (*Supermarket News* 1985) and the 8.5 percent increase from 1984 to 1985 (National Association of Convenience Stores 1987). Some of the factors credited for this continual growth are more professional management, more selective site locations, sharper merchandising strategies, and the introduction of many new products and services including gasoline, fast food, and ATMs. In order for convenience stores to remain a vital segment of both the retail food industry and the fast-food industry, a number of success requirements become apparent. Among these are:

1. Improvement of the selection process for site locations.
2. Careful assessment of potential marketing opportunities and fine tuning of the corresponding marketing strategies.
3. Better selection of franchisees.
4. Better training of franchisees, especially in the area of new products and services.
5. A better knowledge of store design to incorporate all products and services effectively.
6. More sophisticated testing of merchandise and approaches in a sample of existing stores.

7. Continued good research on the evolution of consumer buyers' needs and wants.

8. Awareness of potential for diversification outside the convenience store concept (e.g., warehouse stores, hardware stores, drugstores, etc.).

9. Continued awareness and understanding of competitive forces in the marketplace as the "product" line becomes increasingly diversified.

10. Emphasis on higher store productivity and efficiency.

11. An increase in the convenience store quality image to attract higher income groups.

12. Finding new ways to increase the average customer purchase.

Conclusion

Convenience stores represent a distinct institution in the food retailing industry that caters primarily to the needs of shoppers for quickly acquiring last-minute, unplanned items at a nearby location at almost any hour of the day. Supermarkets and other food retailing forms are not able to economically offer this type of convenience because their costs are higher. As long as consumers are willing and able to afford the higher prices that go along with this convenience, convenience stores will continue to serve distinct needs. The real opportunity for convenience stores is to think carefully through the distinctive convenience needs of various demographic groups—small children, teens, the 20–34-year-old age group, white-collar workers, single men and women, working women, married families, and senior citizens—and to respond to each group with potent and appropriate assortments and services.

Historically, convenience stores have very effectively utilized the present strategy of adding new products and services. However, there may be a point at which this approach will no longer continue to attract "new" customers. There must also be a danger that the proliferation of products and services, together with the use of more sophisticated store layouts, will actually change the consumer's perception of the convenience store by making it less easy to locate specific items, and to get in and out quickly. The key to future success will be to find a way of increasing the consumers' purchases once in the store; in other words, increasing the average purchase of the consumer.

References

Brown, Francis C. III. 1984. "Convenience Stores Moving to Diversify." *Wall Street Journal* (September) 35.

Business Week. 1977. "Convenience Stores: A $7.4 Billion Mushroom." March 21. 61–64.

Convenience Store News. Telephone conversation. 23 March 1987.

Darden, W. R., D. K. Darden, and J. R. Lumpkin. 1980. "Psychographic and Demographic Profile of Convenience Food Store Users: Why People Convenience Shop." Unpublished paper: University of Arkansas, School of Business.

Freeman, Laurie. 1985. "Sponsors Ready for Jerry's Kids." *Advertising Age* (August 26). 4.

Goldman, Arieh. 1974. "Outreach of Consumers and The Modernization of Urban Food Retailing in Developing Countries." *Journal of Marketing* 38 (October). 8–16.

Liles, Allen. 1977. *Oh Thank Heaven! The Story of the Southland Corporation.* Dallas, Tex.: The Southland Corporation.

Markin, R. J. 1968. *The Supermarket: An Analysis of Growth, Development, and Change.* Pullman, Wash: Washington State University Press.

National Association of Convenience Stores. Telephone conversation. 23 March 1987.

National Petroleum News. 1985. "C-Store Sales Up, Gasoline Gains Slow" (September). 60.

Nation's Restaurant News. 1985. "Circle K Adds 'Diet' Items" (March 11). 2.

Nation's Restaurant News. 1986. "Circle K Plans Stores in Indonesia" (February 17). 36.

Nation's Restaurant News. 1983. "Transition to Fast Food Creates New Woes for Many Operators" (January 17). 28.

Progressive Grocer. 1980. "47th Annual Report of the Grocery Industry" (April). 113–14.

Schoifet, Mark. 1985. "C-Stores' Fast-Food Sales Soar" *Nation's Restaurant News* (January 21). 1.

Supermarket Business. 1981. "Study Predicts 188% Convenience Store Growth by 89" (May). 6.

Supermarket Business. 1984. "Video Electronic Shopping Being Planned" (July). 7.

Supermarket News. 1985. "Convenience Store Sales Said to Rise 9.7% in 1984" (August 19). 14.

The Southland Corporation. 1986. *The 7-Eleven Franchise* (brochure). Dallas, Tex.: The Southland Corporation.

11
Lessons from Retailers' Price Experiences of the 1950s

Roger Dickinson

Introduction

There is a rich body of experience in the 1950s with respect to retailer-related pricing that suggests important lessons for today. Indeed, pricing was an important facet of the discipline of marketing in the 1950s. This was only natural. Economics is often perceived as the mother discipline of marketing, and pricing had been and is central to the study of economics. Indeed, much effort in the 1950s was directed to integrate economic pricing theory with marketing and business practice. (Hollander 1957; Adelman 1957; Lanzillotti 1958; Hawkins 1954.)

There were MBA courses on pricing in the 1950s. Indeed, one reviewer of this chapter suggested that more was taught about pricing then and it was probably better taught. Two prominent marketing academics in the 1950s, Alfred R. Oxenfeldt and Ralph Cassady, Jr. (see citations, including F. E. Brown), spent major portions of their research on pricing.

This chapter considers six prominent events, theories, and/or developments related to retail pricing in the 1950s:

1. The policies of Lingan A. Warren of Safeway
2. Price wars
3. Merchandise Management Accounting
4. The Marketing Concept
5. The Wheel of Retailing
6. Fair Trade

Interesting in themselves, they have important ramifications for present day marketing.

The author expresses his appreciation to: Jerome Greenberg, Rutgers; E. T. Grether, the University of California; W. H. Hutt, University of Dallas; and Robert Kahn, *Retailing Today*, for their suggestions and comments. The final product is the sole responsibility of the author.

1950s—Background

Most of what was taught in business schools of the 1950s can be seen as before the Gordon-Howell (1959) and Pierson (1959) reports; i.e., the "quantitative" revolution had not yet occurred. Most of the intellectual efforts in business disciplines emanated from the major colleges of business. Most leading marketing academics were economists. The key analytical tools were traditional statistical analysis, "marginal analysis," and the Keynesean model of macroeconomics. For most research purposes, the basic assumption of academics in the 1950s was that short-term profitability was the most obvious and most important proxy variable to long term profitability, although strategy was generally seen as the dominator of short term activities (Oxenfeldt 1960; Lanzillotti 1958). Clearly, however, if among alternatives being considered, the long-term scenarios are perceived to be uninfluenced by the selection of an alternative, the short-term aspects are correctly seen as all important.

Marginal analysis was the key sophisticated decision tool of management, dominating subjects like managerial economics and capital budgeting (Dean 1951a; 1951b). Marginal analysis was applied economic theory of the nineteenth century. But, interestingly, Hicks (1985) suggests that Alfred Marshall considered three time periods as relevant (see Addendum). Over time, economics and business academics adopted the short- and long-term dichotomies for most analysis.

Much of the world of goods and services was simpler in the 1950s (Kahn 1987). Thus, retailers were more likely then to be pricing products that were directly competitive with products of other suppliers. Further, the consumer was more likely to know the price since there were fewer stockkeeping units to keep in mind while shopping. And the housewife of the period had more time to devote to shopping-related activities. Consequently, retailers often had less discretion in the pricing of individual items.

Department store retailers in the 1950s were often seen as positioned by price from the perspectives of consumers, retail executives, and suppliers. For example, Macy's price policy in 1951 on non-fixed priced goods was as follows (Kahn 1987): undersell by 6 percent stores that offered service and credit (e.g., Gimbel's and A&S); match the price of stores that offered service but no credit (Alexander's, Ohrbach's); oversell by 5 percent stores that offer neither credit nor service (S. Klein). Thus in the 1950s in New York City, these were from low to high (Sears was a minor factor but had a presence in areas such as Brooklyn):

S. Klein

Korvette (a bigger factor in the late 1950s)

Alexanders

Traditional department stores—Macy and Abraham & Straus

Lord & Taylor, Saks

Part of this was conscious "positioning" by retail executives or what Cassady (1961) might call niching. Of course there had always been "automatic" niching in retail in the sense that the purchase votes of the consumer had interacted with the information systems of the store. The more the customer bought in the store, the more that customer counted in the creation of merchandise assortments, price lines, and the like of that store.

Some legal "events" of the 1950s are now described. The Federal Trade Commission's first guidelines against bait advertising were issued effective in 1959 (Howard 1983, 217). The FTC offered "Guides Against Deceptive Pricing" (Monroe 1979, 209). In 1953, the Supreme Court decision in the Automatic Canteen Case outlined some conditions under which the buyer of a firm can be held in violation of section 2F of the Robinson-Patman Act (Howard 1983, 201). Aspects of fair trade decisions are offered later in the paper.

Pricing over the product life cycle had been proposed (Dean 1950).

Particular note should be made of the heterogeneity of retailing (Hollander 1958). Merchants and service enterprises differed in such as size, capitalization, commodities, and services offered, organizational structure, consumer appeals, expense rates, unit of sale, competitive pressures, and motivations (2). Each of these might influence pricing. Extreme care should therefore be exercised in generalizing from a small number of instances or events within retailing.

Episodes of Pricing in the 1950s

Lingan A. Warren and Safeway

Lingan A. Warren of Safeway (about $2 billion in sales in the mid-fifties) was a vigorous price competitor.[1] Warren believed unequivocally in meeting all the prices of competitors at all times. He held that in the grocery business if a firm takes more than a modest profit, it is made vulnerable to competition. He regarded Safeway as a vehicle for the scientific distribution of food. In his Safeway capacity, he fought such potential "deterrents" to competition as coupons, retail milk price laws, trading stamps, supplier allowances, and vendor direct store deliveries.

In the context of today, Warren's fight against supplier couponing is particularly noteworthy. He felt that coupons prevented the consumer from making the most prudent choice and that the amount paid by the manufacturer did not cover the cost to the retailers of handling the coupons. One way he fought coupons was by honoring any coupon for a product that Safeway carried whether the customer actually purchased the product. Other retailers also have done this, provoking numerous legal actions.

Warren, embroiled in numerous legal skirmishes, was displaced in 1955. He might be perceived as the most aggressive price cutter in the food business thus far in this century. Many would suggest Warren acted irrationally on many price matters. But it should be noted that Warren had a compensation arrangement related to profitability, so there presumably were strong profit considerations in his aggressive actions (Kahn 1987). Clearly, over time the idea of meeting all the prices of competitors became out of date (Cassady 1962; Brown and Oxenfeldt 1972) as supermarkets evolved, were introduced to the "science of pricing," and met competitors in most markets mainly on an overall image dimension (Bhasin and Dickinson 1987; Bernhaut 1987).

Discussion. An aggressive price policy communicated "effectively" to relevant competitors and potential competitors can strongly influence industry behavior, including discouraging entry of firms into markets. The adoption of high margins by Safeway (an investment philosophy) after the departure of Warren apparently facilitated the growth of low-price-oriented firms such as Lucky Stores. In the early 1970s, the aggressive pricing of Pathmark and others in the Northeast blunted the expansion of A&P's Warehouse Economy Outlet (WEO) later to become Where Economy Originates (Nagle 1987). A key executive of the Jewel corporation suggested that their Jewel T "experiment" was only successful in those geographic areas where their pricing was not met (American Collegiate Retailing Association 1980). In the Dallas metroplex, Jewel T was met in price item for item by Skaggs, Safeway, and Kroger as Jewel T opened.

Price Wars

Price wars are not easily defined. Cassady (1963, 2) suggests that a price war is an engagement involving two or more vendors seeking to achieve a goal that each is determined to attain and in which rival vendors, using price as a weapon, make successive countermoves in an attempt to gain an advantage or resist any advantage gained by the other. The essence is head-on conflict. Cassady (1964, 11) maintains that a price skirmish is a type of competitive-price encounter that only lasts a short time and that only involves a small segment of a market.

In the 1950s, there were numerous price wars in gasoline (Cassady and Jones 1951; Cassady 1956, 1957a, 1957b, 1963; Howard 1956, 361). Indeed, Cassady devoted a fair portion of his research to the study of price wars among various types of retail and service outlets. Cassady (1963, 49) lists nineteen merchandise categories relevant to price wars. These include gasoline, food, department stores, motels, poker parlor lunches, and taxi service (Cassady 1962, 154 footnote 7; 1957a, 1957b, 1964).

The department store war of 1951 deserves specific mention (Cassady 1957a). Macy had the policy of charging 6 percent less than stores that offered service and credit except on price-fixed items. The Gimbel motto was "Nobody—But Nobody Undersells Gimbel's." The Schwegmann court decision in 1951 (Schwegmann Brothers v. Calvert Distillers Corporation 341 US 384) freed Macy from certain price restrictions. It chose to price 6 percent less. Other stores, e.g., Bloomingdale's, Gimbel's, Abraham and Straus, and Namm's joined in the fray. The war continued for six or so weeks, although the war did not end suddenly. There was no clear-cut explanation of how the war was ended.

An interesting by-product of this war was that department stores learned that suppliers would give substantial price concessions for the potential of volume (Osterweis 1986). Price concessions from suppliers, of course, were commonplace in the early 1930s (Lebhar 1963). But post–World War II price discounts to retailers were not common for department stores (Osterweis 1986).

Discussion. Price wars are likely when: firms or industries have heavy inventories; there is excess capacity; a competitor is trying to expand; there has been a sudden change in market conditions; there has been a decline in demand; a firm is trying to dominate a market; and/or the technological mix has changed substantially (Cassady 1963, 51–52). Thus, price wars can be used by managements to achieve strategic objectives, e.g., gain market share or upset "inevitable" competitive outcomes (Cassady 1963; Cassady 1964, 12; Bhasin and Dickinson 1987). Price wars may hurt, help, or be neutral with respect to society and the competitive environment (Cassady 1963). Price wars can be the inadvertent outcome of a series of actions taken by competitors, e.g., a price skirmish may "degenerate" into a war (Cassady 1964). Wars can result from defensive actions taken by firms with respect to a new competitor (Cassady 1964, 12). Price wars participated in by Safeway during the Warren tenure were apparently defensive in nature (Cassady 1964, 109–11; Kahn 1987).

Everyday low prices that are perceived as low by potential entrants into a market may even help prevent price wars, in that entrance into markets may be forestalled. Clearly aggressive price policies and reputations can have strategic connotations.

In addition to reflecting the strategy of the firm and the personalities of the participants, the literature suggests that price wars will be sporadic in that they come and go frequently (Howard 1956, 361). The wars are more common in certain competitive configurations than in others. An example is that, to the consternation of elected representatives from New York state, gas wars were mainly conducted on the New Jersey side of the New York-New Jersey bridges and tunnels. The New Jersey configuration of gas stations was more conducive to aggressive price competition. Cassady (1957b, 366) suggests that deep price cuts by one competitor might bring a price war to a head promptly. Further, deceit and the dissemination of falsehoods may be useful in attaining tactical superiority (Cassady 1957b, 366). In addition, price actions on weekends (or odd hours) may be less likely to bring competitive responses because firm offices may be closed (Cassady 1964, 13).

A particularly interesting aspect of the interaction among competitors during price wars is the signalling that occurs. For example, in one market a move by a competitor, reacting to a reduction of another, to reduce its price to cost often indicated not only an acceptance of the challenge but also a willingness to fight to the finish (Cassady 1964, 13). Blanking out of signs after heavy price competition may indicate a willingness to increase prices (Cassady 1964, 13).

Insights from the literature may be useful in understanding elements of the food and gas price wars of today. Further, the extra-value couponing activities of supermarkets focus competition on price. And some executives see extra value couponing as an instrument in a price war (Bhasin and Dickinson forthcoming). To the extent that price wars injure all competitors, Cassady's admonition to managers—"Don't let your dollars become angry"—may be useful (Cassady 1963, 54).

Merchandise Management Accounting (Direct Profitability per Unit)

Department store competition in the middle and late 1950s was characterized as intertype competition (a term coined by E. T. Grether). Discount stores like Korvette became threats to the traditional department store (Barmash 1981).

Merchandise Management Accounting (MMA) was the application of the principles of marginal analysis to retail decision making at the level of the item (a refrigerator), specific event (advertising), or activity (increased sales activity). The focus of the effort was to develop contribution to overhead per unit of merchandise sold and relate that contribution to a management decision with respect to such as space, advertising, sales, and price. The initial thrust was in terms of price (McNair and May 1957). The analysis was supposed to reflect whether and/or by how much department stores should lower prices and whether the discount stores were losing money at the prevailing prices of discount stores (May 1986). MMA was developed during the 1950s. Malcolm McNair interacted with executives of the National Retail Merchants Association to propel MMA (with the help of Arthur Andersen and Robert Jones of that firm) to national status (*Journal of Retailing*, 1958).

Despite great efforts by J. L. Hudson in Detroit, Goldblatts in Chicago, and others, MMA failed for many reasons (Dickinson 1966). Korvette opened a large unit across the street from the major unit of Abraham and Straus in Brooklyn in 1956. A&S "met" or "beat" the prices of Korvette for strategic reasons, i.e., to preserve its illustrious base store. This action set the pace for the reaction of other department stores to Korvette's entry in other markets, e.g., G. Fox in Hartford. Thus, survival dominated shorter-term considerations and MMA became irrelevant for its initially conceived purposes.

Discussion. MMA was suspect for various reasons, including that standard costs may be inappropriate in developing marginal costs; the interrelationships of sales (and costs) of items could not be established; the problems attendant to the differential value of "rent" for various departments and parts of departments could not be resolved; and there was no accepted way of developing an imputed interest on inventory (Dickinson 1966).

"Profitability" per item was of limited value for department stores. "Unprofitable items" were often necessary to fill out merchandise selections. While the rule that 20 percent of your items will often account for 80 percent of your sales may be exaggerated and/or distorted, clearly selecting or eliminating items in a merchandise classification in a department store by a rule such as maximizing contribution to overhead of a unit of merchandise was no guarantee of optimality or even reasonableness.

Further, optimizing "profitability" in the short term is just one proxy variable that might be used to develop or foster long-term profitability. Indeed, any one measure of short term profitability is deficient in some respects. Key measures of short-term profitability in retailing would, for most purposes, be with respect to three dimensions: space, inventory, and labor. Measures of these three only have claim to short term "optimality" if the decision maker is willing to make substantial assumptions, e.g., the dollar value of the inventory cannot be increased. For most purposes, a balance is relevant in the same sense that decisions with respect to inventory turn require a balance (Duncan, Hollander, and Savitt 1983, 269).

The value of direct profitability per item to supermarkets today, the new version of MMA, is less obvious (Curhan and Dickinson 1986). Clearly, all the theoretical shortcomings are there. The practical value of item direct profitability for supermarkets is another matter.

The Market Concept

The marketing concept has essentially been an academic phenomenon, at least from the retail perspective. Indeed, the marketing concept generally increased the perceived role of the supplier in the channel. The marketing concept has many antecedents, but GE is often given the credit (Barksdale and Darden 1971). Historically, it has emphasized the importance of the customer or consumer; the integrating facets of the marketing mix; and short-term profitability as a key goal i.e., as a substitute for market share battles (Bell 1966; Oxenfeldt 1966). Lanzillotti (1958) suggested that A&P, Kroger, and Sears used market share as their most important goal in the 1950s.

The marketing concept has been much criticized in recent years for such as: having a short term orientation, impairing innovation, leading to poor social consequences, and having negative organizational implications. In the light of the increasing power of the retailer (Stern 1986) and the multiplicity of goals related to "optimization" (Dickinson, Herbst, and McCormack 1986), it appears that implementation of some interpretations of the marketing concept leads to unfortunate ramifications.

Discussion. The leading impact of the "traditional" interpretation of the marketing concept on price was to suggest to suppliers that they give up their market share wars and pursue short-term profitability as the key proxy variable to long-term profitability. The severe beatings given our corporations in international markets has led to a reassessment of short-term profitability as the key proxy for long-term profitability.

The influence of various interpretations of the marketing concept appears strong even today. On one view, it illustrates the potential for inducing the cooperative solution in the prisoner's dilemma (Axelrod 1984). Today, the same suggested cooperative solutions are seen in the context of the reaction of trade groups to extra-value couponing, i.e., let's get out of these. It may also indicate the ease with which myths can be propagated in an unsuspecting academic community.

The Wheel of Retailing

The wheel of retailing has endured a number of years and has spawned a large number of articles. Hollander's (1960) interpretation of McNair's (1958) wheel emphasized low price and low cost as key ingredients of entrepreneurial formulations in creating new forms of retailing. This theory, despite articulated exceptions, was consistent with the perceived importance of price as a method of niching in retailing in the 1950s and before. Further, the wheel may be useful in describing the development and/or demise of retail forms such as the Levitz innovation, discount catalogue store, the super appliance store, and the various forms of the warehouse concept.

The wheel highlighted the word-of-mouth advantages inherent in developing a dramatic new form of retailing; underlined the inevitability of cost increases and the dangers inherent in the inevitable trade-up policy that historically has been management's reaction to increasing costs and/or lack of sales growth; and emphasized the lack of success of large firms in the important area of creating new forms of retailing. The wheel also communicated the often-reflected inevitability of cycles (Dean 1950; Hirschman 1982; Schlesinger 1986). Thus, the excitement attendant to the new form had to diminish and therefore the word-of-mouth advertising advantage had to be lost—sometime (Dickinson 1983). The entrepreneurial advantages of the creator of the new firm were dissipated as communication within the firm became more difficult, the incentives for the entrepreneur decreased, and executives retired. The low retail price advantage was diminished as intertype competition became secondary to intratype competition. Thus the stage was set for a new twist of the wheel. If an entrepreneur could create a dramatic new retail form, she, too, would have the competitive advantages that accrued to the initial firm. Competition could not only be destructive (Schumpeter 1951), but could offer an inherent set of competitive advantages attendant to particular kinds of entrepreneurship—those that create retail forms that are very different from those existing.

Discussion. Whatever the validity of elements of the wheel,[2] clearly there are valuable lessons that can be learned by students of retailing.

1. High prices offer an umbrella under which competition can prosper, e.g., the Lingan A. Warren position.
2. Watching costs is critical. Increases in costs are normal and in retailing set in process a spiral of increasing prices that can destroy competitive advantage.
3. New forms of competition by retailers are often difficult to classify and react to.
4. In success lie the seeds of failure.

Further, the wheel presents a logic for periods of great growth in a new form of retailing. Changes in various activities may be seen as staccato bursts (Boulding 1981; Anderson 1986; Dean 1950).

Fair Trade

Many retailers in the 1930s and later were not content with the status of the market system. In 1936, the Supreme Court approved the principle of state fair-trade laws, including the nonsigner clause under which all retailers were bound to the established minimum resale price even when just one retailer signed the agreement (Howard 1983, 148).

Federal statutes in 1937 and 1952 exempted fair-trade resale-price maintenance from the Sherman and Federal Trade Commission Acts (Cassady, 1962, 225). Retail trade groups, primarily drug and liquor stores, were quite active in fostering fair trade practices (Howard 1983, 148; Cassady 1962, chapter 8). The effectiveness of fair trade varied with the product line (Hollander 1958, 4).

Going into the 1950s, fair trade was dominant. But during the 1950s, the importance of fair trade diminished (Cassady 1962, 227). The Schwegmann Case invalidated the nonsigner clause and, as suggested previously, set off the department store price war of 1951. In 1952, Congress passed the McGuire act with the intention of legalizing the nonsigner principle in interstate trade (Cassady 1962, 225). But there were many reversals and Cassady (1962, 227) relates that by March 1961, the laws of eighteen states were either struck down completely or had been invalidated in part by a decision that the nonsigner clause was unconstitutional.

Discussion. In many instances there is an inherent conflict between the ramifications of a negatively sloped demand curve to the manufacturer and incentives offered to or demanded by resellers to support a particular line of merchandise or service. The conflict is that, all things being equal, a negatively sloped demand curve implies that a lower price to the consumer will increase the quantity demanded and thus manufacturers generally favor a lower price to the consumer. But often the margin generated by the lower consumer price for the resellers does not offer sufficient economic incentive to satisfy the resellers.

Without legislation or the intercession of groups (e.g., retail trade groups), it would appear natural for many products to fall into two groups from the perspective of the reseller. One group of products has to be handled by the retailer (although it need not always be displayed) because failure to handle a product risks losing customers to other retailers, e.g., Heinz catsup. The assortment of goods at the store is fundamental to the convenience of the customers; and if that mix is not satisfactory to the customer, there is no customer loyalty (Kahn 1987). Thus, the key criterion for the retailer deciding to handle such goods is the relationship of the sales of the item to the sales of other items in the context of what might be termed customer loyalty to the retailer. A second group of items, services, and the like is purchased by the retailer only if the specific goods of a supplier adds directly to the contribution to overhead of the retailer, i.e., selection has to directly increase perceived incremental profits. Some would call these two artificial dichotomies, the push and pull distribution systems.

Fair trade was designed to force a minimum satisfactory (for the resellers) high price for items that were "demanded" by consumers. As such, the manufacturer selected a price that hopefully would permit the product to be handled by "all" relevant retailers at a price that was almost satisfactory to "all." The manufacturer had to "police" the marketplace if fair trade was to be enforced (Cassady 1962, chapter 8).

The death of fair trade was the Consumer Good Pricing Act of 1975, which removed the federal exemptions of fair trade from the antitrust laws (Howard 1983, 149). The channel problems that "caused" fair trade, in general, remain. For goods or services that are not "pulled" through the channel by the consumers, the supplier must find a way to "hold" prices to consumers. The established method is to sell only to resellers who willingly maintain price, e.g., a push distribution system. But there are other ways conducive to price maintenance, e.g., consignment, the various forms of franchising (Hollander 1958, 6–7), and coercion (Kaikati 1987).

Overall Observations

1. Much is to be learned from examining the history of pricing. It would appear (as will be suggested in the next set of observations) that a careful study of pricing would have helped business and academia avoid many pitfalls.

2. The dominance of the long-term aspects in the pricing decision were clearly understood in the 1950s (Lanzillotti 1958), although, as in the eighties, investigators and business individuals usually select either the long-term or the short-term as the basis for analysis. The more pressing problem in the 1980s would appear to be the effective integration of the short and the long term aspects of pricing. (See Addendum.)

3. Many pricing activities of the fifties gave substantial warning to academics about the shortcomings of strictly quantitative measures, which for the most part were and are short-term. Thus, Warren's thrust can be related to the longer term. Price wars had market share and image connotations. Merchandise Management Accounting proved inadequate. The high prices generated in the wheel suggested a protective competitive umbrella under which entrepreneurs could flourish.

The quantitative "stampede" in academia, from a historical perspective, may partially indicate the obvious. In academia, even for Nobel laureates, there apparently is no penalty for being wrong. Walters (1987) suggests that it is doubtful whether any economist has ever been blackballed by the Swedish Academy even for the most egregious errors of simple analysis.

4. Price competition was active in many segments of the marketing and economic systems in the 1950s.

5. Retailers' perceived price competition was intense and difficult to identify in the 1950s. This may lend credence to Oxenfeldt's (1986) suggestion that retailers in all times feel that competition is intense.

6. Niching as a management tool is not new. Niching was clearly a part

of the fifties. And there has always been the automatic positioning as a result of the interaction of the votes of customers and the information systems of the retailers. It is clear, however, that society was not as affluent then as now and that the information systems, while often extensive, could not be "effectively" analyzed because the computer was not yet a tool. Thus, niching in the 1950s was primitive in today's terms.

7. Behavior of firms in an industry appears to depend heavily on the models of competitive behavior held by executives. Therefore, it would appear that substantial knowledge of the behavior of firms in particular markets is important for all executives (Grether 1968; Vaile, Grether, and Cox 1952).

Addendum—Time

The effective integration of time periods into decision making has plagued decision makers over the years, today, and in the fifties. Marshall (1961, vii) suggests that elements of time are at the center of the chief difficulty of every economic problem. Marshall's conception of time is continuous and yet capable of being divided for purposes of economic inquiry into periods of different lengths (Mitchell 1949, 77–8).

For demand, he apparently sees three periods—very quick changes (e.g., inclement weather), moderate-length, and long periods (Marshall 1961, 369-70). For supply, four time periods are considered—in sight; what can be produced with existing facilities; that which can be reproduction with new plants; and secular movements (378–79). Marshall (378–79), however, did emphasize in most of his analyses the short and long term.

Most economists have accepted the long-term–short-term periods or perhaps normal and subnormal periods. And in the context of economic analyses, this seems quite appropriate. During a subnormal period, there is no time for longer-run forces to work themselves out (Grether 1987). In sharp contrast, a normal period allows for such an outcome. However, in a business context, two periods may not be useful. Distinguishing among elements of short term may be important. The discount rates developed by capital budgeting to integrate net-after-tax cash flows of differing periods are not dependable for business purposes (Dickinson and Herbst 1983). Further, in retailing, businesses are just not optimizing for today (e.g., Little and Shapiro 1977). Thus, research that assumes optimization for today may be out of synchronization with goals of the firm related to other time periods.

The increasing sophistication of the tools of analysis available to executives makes the specification of time periods even more important for business entities. The long term has become more accessible to firms. While sophisticated capital budgeting techniques have failed as an overall top-management decision integrating tool, proxy variables for the longer term, formalized into systems, e.g., the Boston Consulting Group model, makes the long term more accessible.

In some sense, there appear to be four different time frames relevant to business decision making, at least retail managements. (1) The immediate term—one day, one week; (2) the reference short-term period for which short-term profitability can be a useful proxy (or constraint) to the longer term, perhaps three months; (3) the longest time period for which modern planning tools are relevant; and (4) the period past that for which planning tools are relevant.

Notes

1. The bases for this section are Sheehan (1958); Robert Kahn, editor of *Retailing Today*; and E. T. Grether, University of California.

2. At least one retailing text does not emphasize the wheel. See Duncan, Hollander, and Savitt (1983).

References

Adelman, M. A. 1957. "The Product and Price in Distribution." *American Economic Review* 47 (May). 266–273.

American Collegiate Retailing Association Meeting. 1980. Chicago (April).

Anderson, Perry. 1986. *Times Literary Supplement* (December 12). 1405.

Arrow, Kenneth J. 1986. "Rationality of Self and Others in an Economic System." *Journal of Business* 59 (October). 5393.

Axelrod, Robert. 1984. *The Evolution of Cooperation.* New York: Basic Books.

Barksdale, Hiram C., and W. Darden. 1971. "Marketers' Attitudes Toward the Marketing Concept." *Journal of Marketing* 35 (October). 29.

Barmash, Isadore. 1981. *More Than They Bargained For.* New York: Lebhar-Friedman.

Bell, Martin L. 1966. *Marketing.* Boston: Houghton Mifflin. 10–25.

Bernhaut, Charles. 1987. Former Director of Research for Supermarkets General and Consultant in the food industry. Conversation with author.

Bhasin, Ajay, and Roger Dickinson 1987. *Agribusiness.* 3(3)(Fall) 293–306.

Boulding, Kenneth E. 1981. *Evolutionary Econnomics.* Beverly Hills: Sage.

Brown, F. E., and Alfred R. Oxenfeldt. 1986. "Should Price Depend on Costs." MSU *Business Topics* 16 (Autumn). 73–77.

Brown, F. E., and Alfred R. Oxenfeldt. 1972. *Misperceptions of Economic Phenomena.* New York: Sperr and Douth.

Cassady, Ralph, R., and William F. Brown. 1961. "Exclusionary Tactics in American Business Competition: An Historical Analysis." *UCLA Law Review.* 8:88–134.

Cassady, Ralph, Jr., and W. L. Jones. 1951. *The Nature of Competition in the Gasoline at the Retail Level.* Berkeley: University of California Press.

Cassady, Ralph, Jr. 1954. *Price Making and Price Behavior in the Petroleum Industry.* New Haven: Yale University Press.

———.1956. "Price Warfare and Armed Conflict: A Comparative Analysis." *Michigan Business Review* (November). 1–5.

———. 1957a. "The New York Department Store Price War of 1951, A Microeconomic Analysis." *Journal of Marketing* 22 (July). 3–11.

———. 1962. "Taxicab Rate War: Counterpart of International Conflict." *The Journal of Conflict Resolution*, 1 (December). 364–368.

———. 1962. *Competition and Price Making in Food Retailing.* New York: Ronald Press.

———. 1963. "Price Warfare in Business Competition." Occasional Paper No. 22, Bureau of Business and Economic Research. Michigan State University, East Lansing, Michigan.

———. 1964. "The Price Skirmish—A Distinctive Pattern of Competitive Behavior." *California Management Review* 6 (Winter). 11–6.

Curhan, Ronald C., and Roger A. Dickinson. 1986. "Optimization: The Supermarket Industry." *Agribusiness* 2 (No. 1). 55–63.

Dean, Joel. 1950. "Pricing Policies for New Products." *Harvard Business Review* 28 (November). 45–53.

———. 1951a. *Capital Budgeting.* New York: Columbia University Press.

———. 1951b. *Managerial Economics.* New York: Prentice-Hall.

Dickinson, Roger A. 1966. "Marginalism in Retailing: the Lessons of a Failure." *Journal of Business* 36 (July). 353–358.

———. 1983. "Innovations in Retailing." *Retail Control* 51 (June-July). 30–54.

Dickinson, Roger A., and Anthony F. Herbst. 1983. "What Retailers Should Know About Discount Rates." *Retail Control* 52 (September). 43–51.

Dickinson, Roger A., Anthony F. Herbst, and Joseph P. McCormack. 1986. "Comments on Value Based Planning." *Journal of Retailing* 62 (Winter). 446–451.

Duncan, Delbert J., Stanley Hollander, and Ronald Savitt. 1983. *Modern Retailing Management.* Homewood, Ill.: Irwin.

Gordon, Robert Aaron, and James Edwin Howell. 1959. *Higher Education for Business.* New York: Columbia University Press.

Grether, E. T. 1968. Conversation with author.

———. 1987. Correspondence with author.

Hawkins, E. R. 1954. "Pricing Policy and Theory." *Journal of Marketing* 18 (January). 233–240.

Hirschman, Albert. 1982. *Shifting Involvements.* Princeton, N.J.: Princeton University Press.

Hicks, John. 1985. *Methods of Dynamic Economics.* Oxford: Clarendon Press.

Hollander, Stanley C. 1957. "Price and Competitive Aspects of the Distributive Trades." *American Economic Review* (May). 252–65.

Hollander, Stanley C. 1958. "Retail Price Policies." Occasional Paper No. 1. Bureau of Business and Economic Research. East Lansing: Michigan State University.

Hollander, Stanley C. 1960. "The Wheel of Retailing." *Journal of Marketing* 25 (July). 37–42.

Howard, Marshall C. 1956. "Interfirm Relations in Oil Products." *Journal of Marketing* 20 (April). 356.

Howard, Marshall C. 1983. *Antitrust and Trade Regulation.* Englewood Cliffs, N.J.: Prentice-Hall.

Journal of Retailing. 1958. 34 (Spring).

Kahn, Robert. 1987. ed., *Retailing Today.* Correspondence with author.

Kaikati, Jack G. 1987. "The Boom in Warehouse Clubs." *Business Horizons* (March-April). 69–70.

Lanzillotti, Robert, F. 1958. "Pricing Objectives of Large Companies." *American Economic Review* (December). 923–40.

Lebhar, Godfrey. 1963. *Chain Stores in America 1859–1962.* New York: Chain Store Age Publishing.

Little, John D. C., and Jeremy F. Shapiro. 1977. "A Theory of Pricing for Non-Featured Products in Supermarkets." Working Paper. 931–77. MIT (May).

McNair, M. P. 1958. "Significant Trends and Developments in the Postwar Period." In A. B. Smith, ed., *Competitive Distribution in a Free, High-Level Economy.* Pittsburgh: University of Pittsburgh Press.

McNair, Malcolm, and Eleanor May. 1957. "Pricing for Profit: A Revolutionary Approach to Retail Accounting." *Harvard Business Review* 35 (May-June). 105–122.

Marshall, Alfred. 1961. *Principles of Economics.* New York: Macmillan.

May, Eleanor. 1986. Professor, University of Virginia. Correspondence with author.

Mitchell, Wesley C. 1949. *Lecture Notes on Types of Economic Theory 1934–5.* Vol. II. New York: Augustus M. Kelley.

Monroe, Kent. 1979. *Pricing.* New York: McGraw-Hill.

Nagle, Thomas T. 1987. *The Strategy and Tactics of Pricing.* Englewood Cliffs, N.J.: Prentice-Hall.

Osterweis, Steve. 1986. Former director, New York University Institute for Retail Research. Correspondence with author.

Oxenfeldt, Alfred R. 1951. *Industrial Pricing and Market Practices.* New York: Prentice-Hall.

———. 1960. "A Multistage Approach to Pricing." *Harvard Business Review* 38 (July-August). 125–133.

———. 1961. *Pricing for Marketing Executives.* Belmont, Calif.: Wadsworth Publishing Co.

———. 1966. "Product Line Pricing." *Harvard Business Review* 44 (July-August). 135–143.

———. 1966. *Executive Action in Marketing.* Belmont, Calif.: Wadsworth.

———. 1986. Correspondence with author.

Pierson, Frank C. 1959. *The Education of American Businessmen: A Study of University-College Programs in Business Administration.* New York: McGraw-Hill.

Schlesenger, Arthur. 1986. *The Cycles of American History.* Boston: Houghton Mifflin.

Schumpeter, J. A. 1951. "The Creative Response in Economic History." In Richard V. Clemence ed., *Essays of J. A. Schumpeter.* Cambridge, Mass.: Addison-Wesley.

Sheehan, Robert. 1958. "Magowan's Way with Safeway." *Fortune*, 58 (October). 115–7.

Stern, Louis. 1986. In Richard P. Bagozzi, *Principles of Marketing Management*. Chicago: Science Research Associates. 613.

Vaile, Roland S., E. T. Grether, and Reavis Cox. 1952. *Marketing in the American Economy*. New York: Ronald Press.

Walters, Alan. 1987. *Times Literary Supplement*. (January 30). 105.

Part V
Advertising: The Archaeology of Marketing

Introduction

For some time now, past **advertisements** have been recognized by social and cultural historians as valuable source materials, and the **business** of advertising recognized as an important topic in the history of the high-level economies that have developed in Western Europe, North America, and parts of Asia in the nineteenth and twentieth centuries. In this section both of these facets are analyzed.

Richard W. Pollay writes from the dual perspective of a consumer researcher of long standing and the working curator of a major archive of advertising history. He characterizes the time from the late nineteenth century onward as the "Pack-Age." It is an age whose way of life is characterized by intentionally enticing packaging and other forms of energetic promotion, including but by no means limited to advertising. If we today, and historians in the future, are to fully understand the ethos of such an age, he argues, there must be adequate source material—there must be extensive and well-run research collections of promotional materials over time. By adequate, Pollay means voluminous; he believes small samples would fail to convey the pervasiveness of modern promotional efforts. Since most promotions are designed to be ephemeral, however, and since most of the advertising industry resolutely (if foolishly) refuses to look back, adequate collections cannot be assumed. A great deal of television and radio advertising, for example, has already been lost.

There are some collections, most begun at the initiative of individuals rather than institutions. The bulk of Pollay's essay is an in-depth look at archival holdings and other collections of promotional materials that have been developed in the United States and Canada. Pollay describes these fully, and critically evaluates the source materials they contain. Advertisements alone are far less valuable than in conjunction with the market research, strategy memoranda, media schedules, and creative notes that lie behind them, in Pollay's judgment. Anyone curious about how historical research is done by experts will learn a great deal from this chapter. It will also be a valuable guide to anyone who undertakes historical research using promotional materials.

Terence Nevett brings the book to a close on an international note with his study of American influences upon British advertising from the early nineteenth century until 1920. He shows these influences to have been significant, especially from about 1900, thereby correcting the myth that the American advertising business only began to have an impact upon Britain in the 1950s.

The strength of the American influence mirrored an influx of American businesses and products during the last decades of the nineteenth century, and the growing social respectability accorded Americans. Earlier, anything American had been equated with boorishness; American promotion had been equated with the excesses of Phineas T. Barnum. Yet Barnum's legacy was ambivalent, for the British recognized that he had shown the value of publicity to business. As Americans became a larger and more respectable presence, the positive side of the Barnum legacy came to the forefront. Americans were seen as the masters of vigorous and effective promotion.

By 1920, U.S. influence had raised creative standards, leading to ads with more appeal to consumers (if less to Oxbridge literati); had eroded newspapers' resistance to display ads and lively copy; had encouraged more use of special events, publicity, and sales promotions such as samples; and had increased the sense of worth and professionalism among British advertising people. American books and periodicals on advertising were avidly read. Numerous British advertising people and ambitious manufacturers went directly to America for ideas and inspiration.

12
Current Events that Are Making Advertising History

Richard W. Pollay

Introduction

This chapter does not discuss those events that future historians will judge important. Rather, it describes those resources that future historians will likely find valuable, and the events in discussion are the several institutional developments of the past decade that may make their job easier: the establishment and growth of several museums, libraries, archives, and collections of advertising. Thus this title, like some advertising, is totally defensible as accurate, yet may have created a false impression that attracted attention.

A decade ago the literature on the history of advertising, and the resources that could be called upon were thin (Pollay 1978). But since then there has been a surge of interest in advertising history from many disciplines and perspectives. As a historian of broadcasting, Barnouw (1978) wrote on the powerful role the sponsor plays in electronic media. Pope (1983) described the institutional developments in the early part of the century as advertising took on its current creative and consulting role. Both Schudson (1984), a sociologist, and Marchand (1985), a historian, discuss the social milieu of agencies, and the social content and impact of ads with focus on the 1920s and 1930s. Fox (1984) describes the various styles of advertising that emerged from various agencies headed by strong personalities in his "group biography" of *The Mirror Makers*. Other historians, most notably Fox and Lears (1983), have worked on the culture of consumption, sparking a growing interest among allied fields such as popular culture, modern anthropology, and archaeology.

The interest from business studies has been modest, but the more general

Generous cooperation and informative correspondence of many individuals aided this review. Especially noteworthy were the efforts of the various staff of the Archives Center of the National Museum of American History (Smithsonian): John A. Fleckner, Stacey Flaherty, Barbara Griffiths, and Carol Dreyfus. Other assistance was received from Anna Marie Sandecki of N. W. Ayer, Sarah Paulson of the American Advertising Museum, Diana Foxhill Carothers of the Communications Library at the University of Illinois, and Eleanor Tanin of the Film and TV Archive at UCLA.

field of marketing history is expanding as this very volume evidences. Some of the work on advertising has been guided by methodological, not substantive, interests as in the many conflicting 'lydiametric' analyses of the data for the female tonic of the Lydia Pinkham Company (Pollay 1984b). Descriptive analyses of systematic samples of advertising since the turn of the century have been produced for their information content (Pollay 1984c), values (Pollay 1984a), strategies, and tactics (Pollay 1985b). To provoke more interest, essays have also examined the cultural consequences of advertising (Pollay 1986a, 1986b) and the partnership of advertising and the editorial function to create a "BUY-ological urge" (Pollay 1985c).

While there has been far more produced than one might have expected a decade ago, we still lack at least two major components to our understanding of advertising's role in modern society. There is still no history of the evolving technologies of advertising research, which range from the casual focus groups and field interviews to the very elaborate and psychologically sophisticated segmentation studies. Methods used in copy testing, media planning models, intrusiveness and recall studies, and "Behaviorscan" computer tracking of purchasing, for examples, all need careful discussion to document the shift from advertising as commercial art to being more of a commercial science. We need far more on advertising since World War II. At the moment the postwar period is still best described by the journalist Mayer (1958) and the insider Seldin's (1963) undervalued *Golden Fleece*.

We also need more agencies to open up their archives or to donate relevant manuscript materials, especially on the planning processes. But future historians will have a somewhat easier time of it thanks to the current efforts of several institutions described here.

The Smithsonian's Collection on Advertising History

The Archives Center of the National Museum of American History, in Washington, D.C., maintains a large and growing holding on advertising. This organizational unit was established in 1983 to both maintain existing holdings and to acquire new materials. The Archives Center holds historical photographs and other manuscript materials, especially on the history of science and technology, but the advertising collection figures prominently in its holdings, functioning, and purpose. This is due in part to their size and scope. These holdings also attract 75 percent of the traffic to the Archives Center and are often highly useful to the larger Smithsonian Institution for both research and display.

The established significant holdings are the Warshaw Collection of Business Americana, a massive collection of nineteenth and early twentieth century print ads and ephemera, and the more than 400,000 proofsheets produced from 1889 to 1970 by the prominent N. W. Ayer advertising agency of Philadelphia. The Archives Center has been supplementing this material through aggressive acquisition efforts to document more modern advertising campaigns. So far the promotional efforts of Pepsi-Cola, Marlboro, and Alka-Seltzer have been documented with oral histories, trade publications, manuscript materials and, of course, ads themselves.

Warshaw Collection of Business Americana

With more than a million pieces, requiring nearly 1,000 linear feet for storage room in approximately 3,000 archival boxes, cabinets, shelves, and drawers, this collection contains vast numbers of trade cards, catalogs, pamphlets, labels, letterheads, lithographs, and other material. It is the largest, most varied, and visually rich collection of advertising materials now publicly available. The bulk of the materials comes from the late nineteenth and early twentieth centuries, but there is a cluster of items from 1930s to 1950s and a few from the late eighteenth century. The materials are cross-sectional in nature, providing glimpses into thousands of concerns in hundreds of product categories, but no complete history for any specific firm.

Assembled by a New York "PAC-rat" (Paper and Advertising Collector) beginning in 1920, the size of the collection prohibited careful organization by its assembler. Reorganization, cataloging and preservation has been an awesome and ongoing effort since its acquisition in 1967 (Bliss 1984). It is now divided into some 500 subject areas, from abrasives to zoology, generally clustered by product. Intriguing exceptions include files on civil defense, phrenology, hypnotism, salesmanship, the devil, the Boy Scouts, the YMCA, and the Ku Klux Klan. The largest categories, with roughly 20 or more boxes of material, include agriculture, automobiles, banks, drugs, dry goods, electricity, foods, hotels, insurance, newspapers, patent medicines (55 boxes!), politics, railroads, schools, seeds, shoes, steamboats, stoves, textiles, theater, tobacco, whiskey, and world expositions. For 116 of these categories, but not necessarily the largest, narrative descriptions are now available discussing the scope and contents. Ultimately, narrative descriptions of the contents of each subject area are planned.

While not a systematic sampling, the mere bulk of the holding makes it arguably characteristic of the genre of printing and commercial communication. Containing almost no companion documentary material, the strength of the Warshaw holding is in its richness of images and associated texts. These illustrate work and leisure, home and the marketplace, providing a visual social history on how Americans perceived themselves. With captions and copy, the ads convey information about the values and social practices often not otherwise documented. Social portrayals of women, children, and ethnic minorities are abundant. Our material culture is very well displayed in the often excellently detailed images of products offered for sale, like clothing, tools, appliances, furniture, or decor. And of course it is rich material for a history of printing and ad production, or of commercial art or typography.

N. W. Ayer Advertising Agency

This holding is most valuable because Ayer is one of the nation's oldest agencies, one with a well-described early history (Hower 1939) and one of only a few with a long-ongoing archival activity. The agency was innovative, especially up through the twenties when agencies were first acquiring their modern role. This record covers the emergence—"Out of the Cracker Barrel" (Cahn 1969)—of the National Biscuit Company and its major success with a packaged and branded Uneeda Biscuit. Since modern marketing emerges from the cracker-barrel era, and this distinction explains much about the role of advertising, this firm's history is symbolically significant. For stable clients, there is a longitudinal view of the evolution of campaigns. The collection also displays the transformation from ads rich in verbal copy to ones rich in visual art, the early use of photography and fine art, many new product introductions, and "initial efforts to identify positive cultural symbols and values with the product" (Crew and Fleckner 1987).

The Ayer holding is primarily the some 400,000 proofsheets of ads for the many hundreds of campaigns done by the prominent Ayer agency from 1889 to 1970. The product/client index has more than 2500 entries. Prominent clients include Acme Paint, whose "Acme Quality" slogan's success led to many smaller Acme firms. The boxes of ads on behalf of the agency itself also show the use of "Acme Quality" as the agency's own promotional promise. Other clients were American Telephone and Telegraph, Atlantic Refining, Canada Dry Ginger Ale, Cannon Towels, Columbia Records, Container Corporation of America, Dole (Hawaiian Pineapple Co.), Eveready Batteries (22 boxes), Ford, Heinz Foods, Hires Root Beer, International Silver(ware), Kellogg's (eight boxes), Nabisco (28 boxes), Pittsburgh Plate Glass, Reynold's Tobacco, Sani-Flush, Steinway Pianos, United Airlines, U.S. Rubber, Victrola, Welch's Grape Juice, and ZuZu Gingersnaps. Unfortunately, this massive holding is not well supplemented here with planning documents, correspondence, or other manuscript materials.

The agency is ongoing and until the summer of 1987 maintained a library and archives in New York. The archive is being closed for reasons of economy and the disposition of the holdings are uncertain. They have another 50,000 non-duplicating proofsheets from 1890 to the present, plus the ongoing files of tearsheets for print ads. This includes a series of *Printer's Ink* covers outlining agency success stories from 1922 to 1926. The holdings of company newsletters, agency publicity, corporate records and biographical information, and more is both old and recent, and currently strongest for 1930 to the 1960s.

The Modern Advertising History Program

As substantial as those holdings are, they have the shortcoming of including little documentation on the processes by which advertising strategies are decided and ads are produced. Nor, because of their print focus, do they illuminate the transformation of advertising as it entered the electronic media. The Archives Center, therefore, has initiated acquisition efforts and documentation projects, particularly where oral histories can be obtained from living participants. To date, three corporate projects are underway, each with corporate cooperation and financial support: Pepsi-Cola, Marlboro (Phillip Morris), and Alka-Seltzer (Miles Laboratories). Planned are projects centered on topical themes such as early television advertising, or the 'creative revolution' of the 1960s.

The Pepsi Generation. Pepsi-Cola USA donated a collection of posters, displays, signs, photos, videotapes, ad catalogs, and promotional items to the Smithsonian, as part of its seventy-fifth anniversary activity in 1983. While some materials date from 1902, most of the 300 objects and tapes came from the period since 1960. This period is of interest for the emergence of television advertising in color, the so-called "creative revolution" and related changes in ad style and production technologies, and the common and corporate focusing on the youth market. But the ideal documentation for this period and these issues apparently no longer exists (Dreyfus and Connors 1985). The corporate records and memos outlining market research, rationalizing copy premise choices, specifying media plans, and the like were either nonexistent or unavailable.

But because it was recent history, people were still alive and active who could be interviewed, so with corporate cooperation Pepsi became the first oral history project for the Archives Center. Dr. Scott Ellsworth, the staff oral historian, interviewed 26 people during 1984–85 for durations from half an hour to 4 hours, producing a total of more than 38 hours of tape. A broad range of personnel were interviewed: bottlers, songwriters, producers, directors, performers, publishers, and, of course, many senior executives from Pepsi and its agencies, most notably BBD&O and McCann-Erickson. Notables include John Bergin, president of McCann-Erikson, Tom Dillon, Phil Dusenberry and Allen Rosenshine of BBD&O, and the creative director of Pepsi, Allan Pottasch. These interviews are abstracted and indexed with the timed access to pertinent excerpts (TAPE) system. Thus files on paper permit scanning of the tape contents and a timing track greatly simplifies access to passages of interest on the actual tapes for verbatims, or auditing for color and emphasis. There are a few restrictions on the quotability of some tapes, but these will diminish in time. The finding aids also include some brief biographical and scope notes.

Holdings of some 100 television ads from 1946 to 1984 illustrate the ads discussed in the interviews. (The strength of this run of television spots is reportedly due to the good fortune of an employee in a production house having more historical foresight than either the client or its agencies. He saved masters of ads, while they did not.) Between the spots and the interviews, there are insights and illustrations of the shifts in campaign thrusts from the economy of "Twice as Much for a Nickel" to a reduced-in-calories promise of "Light Refreshment," to the status appeal of "Be Sociable," to the "Taste That Beats the Others Cold." Most notable, perhaps, is the successful and innovative evolution of the exuberant, youthful "Pepsi Generation" with its precursor themes "Now it's Pepsi . . . For Those Who Think Young," "Come Alive . . ." and "You've got a Lot to Live, and Pepsi's Got a Lot to Give." These spots display early use of action scenes, acting spontaneity, and editing techniques that are still imitated two decades later.

The interviews also illuminate issues of corporate politics, the role of advertising in competition and marketing strategy, the role of periodic new themes in revitalizing bottler enthusiasm, the failure of the status appeal of "Be Sociable," and the importance of the imagery of California to the "Pepsi Generation" message. One also encounters incidentals on advertising theory, aesthetics, and production, like learning about the role that serendipity sometimes plays in acting and filming to create 'discoveries' rather than planned executions according to prior strategies.

The challenge of transporting the Pepsi Generation campaign into international markets is evident as interviewees suggest that it wouldn't work except where market share was already substantial. Those with international interests and language skills will appreciate a reel of television spots from Japan and various common-market countries. These are surprisingly diverse, like an Italian spot selling Pepsi as a means of encouraging picky children to eat well. The creative executions also vary in style, but include high-quality items, like a simple charmer from Japan featuring a baby struggling to open a bottle, and a humorous, fast-paced Danish spot for "lipsmakin', thirst-quenchin', acetastin', motivatin', goodbuzzin', cooltalkin', high-walkin', fastlivin', evergivin', coolfizzin' Pepsi." Only some show the influence of the U.S. theme lines, although several seem youth-focused and some even use English embedded in the native language spots.

The limits of memory and selective sharing always makes oral histories a somewhat thin source needing supplementation with paper records for their greater detail and fidelity. While the research files supporting the Pepsi ads and interviews are not deep, they do include advertising catalogs for

1969 to 1983, annual reports, and a nearly complete run of the company publication, *Pepsi-Cola World*.

Because the soft drink business has quite independent local bottlers who needed to be sold ad campaign ideas and objects, brand management creates a full catalog of advertising, a historically interesting compilation that doesn't exist in many other industries. The roughly 200 pages of the average ad catalog shows how varied are the materials produced in a full-blown campaign. The pages offer local dealers examples and purchase opportunities of not only storyboards and rich storyline descriptions of the prominent television spots, but also newspaper, radio, theater, outdoor ads, signage, point-of-purchase displays, and specialty items.

The most interesting research file is the run of the employee magazine, *Pepsi-Cola World*, from 1941 to 1984. While it becomes a little less informative in its later years as it becomes more of a bottler's network magazine, its pages are rich with stories and illustrations of sales promotional activities, trade advertising, export market activities, miscellaneous promotions like skywriting, backstage activity in ad production, public relations activities especially in Hollywood and among high society, and the regular feature, "Ad of the Month," which endured despite changes in the editorial thrust. This is a good source of illustrations as well as research information, as good quality photography and printing were common, including color originals on fine paper in the later years.

These pages deserve browsing for serendipitous discoveries on both advertising and other aspects of marketing history. One can see the job and tools of the district sales manager of the 1940s, with photos showing him loading his car with a dozen pieces of luggage of the "vital tools of his job:" forms and memos, a "bible" of sales data, correspondence files, census and competitive data on territories, product-testing equipment, samples of current promotions, a bottler's catalog, specification and service manuals for dispensing equipment, cameras, dictating equipment, activity and expense log books, and so forth.

Although unsupported by documents, the audiovisual files also include a presentation tape from a jingle supplier, with unused 1976 jingle examples in diverse styles.

The Marlboro Man. The jut-jawed, oft-tattooed independent cowboy horseman created by the Leo Burnett agency for the Philip Morris brand of Marlboro cigarettes has been called the greatest ad campaign of the last fifty years. It started with a luxury woman's brand of filter cigarettes with "ivory tipped" and red "beauty tipped" filters to mask lipstick stains, and enjoyed a mere quarter of a percent market share in 1954. After some intermediary stages of changing color package designs, jingles sung seductively by Julie London sighing "Filter, Flavor, Flip-Top Box," and using male models with tattooed wrists and backs of hands, it finally and indelibly became associated with the rugged individualism of frontier masculinity, the mythic Marlboro Man. With this imagery, it held a domestic market share of more than 20 percent in the 1970s in a market crowded with many brands.

Using this image and the fact of its popularity, the firm penetrated markets in the rest of the world. It is offering this brand in more than 170 countries now. There it symbolizes America and Western affluence, in addition to any inkling of our cultural understanding of "cowboys." It is the largest exporter of cigarettes in the world, with Marlboro the largest-selling brand in the world. Thus, Marlboro is significant, both as a success story and also as the implanting of rich imagery into popular cultures at home and overseas.

The creative work that is the operational campaign is sampled by 13 hours of domestic and two hours of international television ads, 1500 slides of print ads, some reaching back to the 1920s, proofsheets of 1980s ads, some posters, a *Merchandising Materials Catalog* for the sales force and retailers of the 1980s, and miscellany like the *Country Store Catalog* of promotional items with Marlboro branding retailed to consumers.

The second oral history project interviews respondents about this campaign's origins, development, creative executions, and internationalization from the 1950s to the 1970s. The core of the Marlboro holding is the many interviews, with people performing many roles and operating in many countries. The original 30 interviews done domestically are being matched with 30 more done internationally. Most respondents are agency or client account executives, but the domestic sample is quite broad and includes creative personnel, actors, and production people like cameramen, directors, gaffers, and grips. Notables whose personal success followed that of the brand were Norman Muse, the agency creative director with the brand for 24 years who became chairman and creative head, worldwide, and Jack Landry, the original account man who became senior vice-president of Philip Morris. All oral history interviews are cataloged and coded using the TAPE system, and a small audit sample suggests care, consistency, and intelligence in the coding and extracting.

These interviews provide anecdotal insights into topics such as the nature of agency-client relations and how decisions were made and conflicts resolved; the role of research in indicating the superior recall for the cowboy among all previously used tattooed images; the resistance of creative staff and the delay of nine months from screening of first spot to its public use on-air; the consistency of creative over time and across media, and forms of display and merchandising materials; how not all creative personnel were conscious of the shifts from pastoral to hostile environments and back; how, as the campaign matured, ads became able to be assumptive and subtle, evoking the established image with a glimpse of the famous tattooed hand

and needing no verbal claims nor even explicit brand mention; how faith, not science, was required as early sales and forecasts in the first year of the campaign were disappointing: how modest and informal was the creative strategy, with no articulated copy platform statement until after several years of execution, with only crude layouts guiding the still photography, and only very rough storyboards guiding filming; how policies constrained creative work, like the forbidding of exhaling of smoke, the rare and restricted use of cows as opposed to horses; how cameramen shot multiple takes with various packages, shown in various ways to conform to regulations in the various jurisdictions where film might be used; how understanding survives of the reasons for the failure of the menthol product line extension while a "light" version succeeded; how the veterans distrust the modern brand manager system and how young brand managers are perceived as misunderstanding the stoic and heroic "soul" of the Marlboro Man because of suggestions to make him more joyous with lighthearted laughter; and how varied are the conceptions of this "soul" of the brand image held by various people, and how varied their attributions for its commercial success; and lastly, how the image has greater success among the young, naïve residents of urban centers than among the towns of the true West.

It is the international dimension that gives the Marlboro material its greatest value, for this is not easily duplicated in other campaigns. This illuminates the globalization of advertising strategy and creative that is so hotly debated now (Levitt 1983). It would seem that Marlboro represents an ideal example of the feasibility and desirability of an invariant image used successfully on a global basis. But the interviews suggest the still-substantial amount of tailoring of this campaign to suit the needs of other national and cultural markets.

The international perspective is being developed through 29 interviews (oral histories) done overseas. Six countries were chosen to provide a cross-section of cultures, regulatory environments, market development, competitive intensity, and market success. These, and their dominant attributes, are: Argentina, with substantial regulation, a conversion of the campaign focus from cowboys to sports like motorcar racing realizing only modest success; Brazil, with lighter regulation, a similar shift from a cowboy to a sports focus but with greater success; the Dominican Republic, an example of undeveloped countries with absolutely no regulations, political families in the midst of the tobacco industry and a whopping 36 percent market share for Marlboro; Germany, a large market in both volume and per capita consumption, where Marlboro has been sold since the 1960s and now enjoys the largest market share; Hong Kong, representative of Asian markets, with almost duty-free entry but difficult distribution systems to penetrate and cultural contrasts with the West; and lastly Switzerland, the first overseas market for Marlboro.

Because of the legal conservatism of tobacco companies and their attorneys, there is no documentary record to validate or enrich the interviews. This is unfortunate, for the interviews are often mythic in their anecdotes, but too often lacking in specifics. Thus there are mentions, but minimal evidence, of the kinds of market research studies done by the firm, the agency, or contract researchers, like Elmo Roper's original study on consumer perceptions of filters and package designs. Nor is there any formal statement of the competitive situation, target market(s), copy strategy or its rationale, media strategies, ad testing procedures, effectiveness measures, and operational tactics.

A few associated documents are informative. *Smoking Issues* is a 1986 descriptive analysis of 138 different countries around the world for their legal requirements regarding warning labels, public smoking, constituent listing, use of visual and verbal depictions in ads, product sampling, sponsorship, protection of vulnerable audiences (youth), use of brand name on nontobacco products, and media restraints. *Call News* (1960–1977) and *The Force* (1978ff) are the sales force magazines for Philip Morris. In these pages are lots of brief stories about merchandising, promotions and consumer contact by salesforce members, and the retailers or distributors to whom they sell. Sometimes this is very informative, as in a 1983 enumeration of the successful placing of 360,000 units of a dozen types of point of sale items, such as standing ashtrays, coffee servers, perpetual calendars, message boards, personalized signs, metal signs and logos, pencil caddies, clocks, and "sold here" signs.

Alka-Seltzer. Given the snake-oil pitchman history and popular reputation of marketing, no collection of advertising documents would seem complete without something on patent medicines in the modern era. Fortunately, Miles Laboratories has long had a serious view of itself and its history as a leading supplier of proprietary medicines, and lets its record stand in evidence.

Begun in 1882 with a sedative product, Dr. Miles' Nervine, the Miles firm soon had a full line of "restorative remedies" such as pills, tonics, blood purifiers, and even a Cure for the Heart. From its early days, the firm was committed to aggressive marketing and much promotional literature. In 1884 they launched *Medical News,* a publication for the layman of blended science and advertising. At this time they also began massive direct mail campaigns and use of newspapers. They bought a printing press and in 1889 published 100,000 copies of sixteen-page pamphlets offering "Hints for Households" and almanac information, as well as advertising in some 800 newspapers. By the turn of the century the almanac was an annual production of an estimated 18 to 24 million (!) copies distributed to some 90 percent of RFD homes and through all dealer druggists. Miles was buying printing presses in bulk and offering them to publishers of small town newspapers in exchange for future advertising space.

Newspaper ads offering free in-store samples launched the brand in 1931. Tasters who answered questions were given further take-home product samples. Very shortly after the launching, the brand was one of the pioneer radio advertisers, sponsoring "Songs of Home Sweet Home." The first broadcast in January 1932 offered more free samples and received 33,000 mail-in requests from every state in the union. Sponsoring the "National Barn Dance" a year later was also effective on sales, as the firm could see the growth of the radio network paralleled in their regional sales expansion. Also during the 1930s, the firm developed merchandising displays and short promotional films for theaters. It also pioneered in television in 1949 and by 1954, television was getting 60 percent of the ad budget. This would grow to 80 percent by 1959 with much spot buying and sponsorship of twelve shows, including the popular "Wednesday Night Fights," "Leave it to Beaver," and "The Rifleman," which obtained an impressive 49.9 share of viewers.

It was not until 1946 that Miles started a market research department, although they had run tests in 1934 of the theatre films. Neither Miles nor its traditional ad agency, Wade, used very disciplined approaches to early marketing and advertising decisions, content probably in their success with casual research and sales assessments. But by 1959 they were apparently quite sold on the value of external market research services, buying analyses from Ernest Dichter, Social Research, Schwerin, and Elrick and Lavidge.

The advertising history of their Alka-Seltzer brand is potentially the most informative of the brand histories in the archives at this date, for the reels of 31 television spots for 1950 to 1983 are being supplemented with written documentary records. Already complete are an Alka-Seltzer chronology, a full collection of storyboards for 1950 to 1983; directories to these ads via titles, dates, slogans, or characters employed.

Accession of supporting documentation from Miles headquarters is ongoing, but in hand are valuable holdings like a set of 1930s scripts for radio ads; all television scripts for 1955; in-house histories of the market research efforts; sundry sales and advertising data; and market research reports over the years and from various contract suppliers; a 1963 "fact book" which includes information on competitive ads; retailers and salesmen surveys; and the text of a medical briefing of the ad agency personnel. Some of this material is fascinating and relatively rare, like the 1959 research proposal and promises of Dichter's Institute for Motivation Research. Other smaller documents yield insight, like a 1959 executive request to initiate an annual marketing planning process which acknowledges possession of a competitive marketing plan.

These files are backed up with corporate archives of considerable depth, a veritable treasure trove for a corporate historian with marketing interests.

These archives are currently managed by a scholar, who is also responsible for corporate communications. The Smithsonian retrieval of copies of some key documents for the files in Washington will no doubt have to leave many interesting materials remaining in Elkhart. Among the Miles files they will scan and extract, but which might still deserve additional scrutiny, are: seven volumes of data including ad and sales records; three volumes of promotional artifacts; Wade advertising agency scrapbooks, 1928–1966; fifty-seven boxes of market research to 1972; seventy-five boxes of advertising from 1952 on; five boxes of public relations files, 1954–1979; and one box of President's Office correspondence on advertising, and perhaps agency searches and shifts. This is but a sampling of the large corporate archives that Miles Laboratories has had the foresight to retain.

The Alkalizer, a quarterly house organ, is held for 1960 to 1986, and scattered holdings exist of *Miles Ahead,* a salesforce magazine. The first now serves the personnel department announcing arrivals, departures, and activities of Elkhart staff. In the earlier days it featured a regular column, "Sales Promotions at Work from Coast to Coast," and these still occur occasionally. There one can learn of a 1960s merchandising mass display made up of battery-operated spinning tablets mounted on jumbo-sized cartons, a large talking Speedy doll, giant paper glasses filled with merchandise, and the more common end-of-aisle supermarket display bins in custom wrapping. In 1986 you can learn about an "Alka-Seltzer to the Rescue" fire truck that visits state fairs and festivals like chili cook-offs distributing 11 million (!) product samples. There are also occasional columns on "Alka-Seltzer Around the World," of note because the brand contributed 80 percent of all foreign revenues. Occasional articles also look backward with nostalgia at early advertising in print, on radio, in films, or via promotional events such as parade participation or contests. The issues of the early sixties also contain information on the media buys of television shows, or the signing of a star like singer Jaye P. Morgan to appear in ads or to give testimonials.

The product's history is interesting for several reasons beyond its representation of the product class of patent medicines. The product has always been offered at a broad audience offering relief from various defined symptoms like "acidosis," sleeplessness, hangovers, "that dragged-out feeling," stuffiness, or "the blahs," all without being too specific about the medical ingredients or specific reasons for product superiority. Sometimes references were simply to "magic spirals," or Speedy's magic wand. This varied "positioning" history runs aside a history of changing media strategies and changing creative. They pioneered in both radio and television, being astute in seeing electronic media as reaching the large audience desired. The creative includes the use of the animated Speedy mnemonic character and many, many famous and funny television ads that display the "creative revolution" of the late 1960s and 1970s.

The creative history is also a veritable archetype for the infidelities of agency-client relations. The relatively small Wade agency of Chicago was the agency of record for Alka-Seltzer from 1931. Its founder was for ten years the first foreman of Miles' printing operation, leaving Miles in 1909 to start his own agency working on other brands for Miles. It handled the original launch of the product, and its pioneering onto television in 1949 with still-recognizable slogans like "Relief is just a swallow away" and the famous stop-motion animated puppet character, Speedy, first seen in 1952. Despite prizes won and increased sales, Miles reassigned the account to one of the era's best known creative boutiques, Jack Tinker and Associates, in 1963, perhaps seeking the glamor of big-league New York "hot" agencies. Here Mary Wells worked on the account and retired Speedy, but only for a while. This agency's creative is best remembered for the humorous, highly recalled spot featuring many tummies, "No matter what shape your stomach's in." The account moved again in 1968 to Doyle, Dane Bernbach, Inc., who sold Alka-Seltzer as relief for "the blahs" and made the famous and funny "Mamma Mia, that's a spicy meatball" spot of a poor actor doing multiple takes of a scene eating meatballs and evidencing greater and greater need for relief. The account moved yet again in 1971 to Wells, Rich, and Greene (back to Mary Wells) where still-famous lines were entered into the popular culture such as: "I can't believe I ate the whole thing," "Try it, you'll like it," "You're making a big mistake," and "plop, plop, fizz, fizz. Oh what a relief it is!" The account was shifted once more in 1983 to McCann Erickson where it now resides, probably insecurely and temporarily.

The recent history may also vivify more than the problems and processes of agency turnover. Many of the television spots were notoriously funny, earning many creative awards and much public comment and appreciation. But the value and limitations of the use of humor in advertising seems questioned by the very fickleness of agency relations despite this success. Also of interest is the apparent avoidance of direct references to hangovers and alcohol drinking. Even in the permissive 1970s, the copy is coy and refers only to overindulgence in general. Interviews with participants may also have disclosures on the problems of product-line extensions and how much promotional support they receive, the changing competitive climate as new headache preparations enter the market, or the balancing and coordinating of advertising with sales promotion activities.

Future Plans

Future plans for the Smithsonian's Archives Center's advertising activity revolve around several goals. They would like to supplement the current documentation of modern campaigns with a research agenda for topics not well documented when focused on single firms. Possible topics might include the emergence of television advertising and its impact on clients, agencies, media structure; the so-called "creative revolution" of the 1960s; the role of women in ads and the advertising industry; the prevalence and impact of market segmentation as a strategic practice; the interplay between advertising and music, film, or other aspects of popular culture.

They appreciate the need to know their customers, academic but with varied interests, and seek closer connections with the advertising industry so that their efforts are "guided by the best available professional advice and contribute to the educational goals of the industry" (Fleckner 1986). They welcome learning about the needs and interests of the research scholars from business, communications, or journalism schools who teach advertising and might therefore have highly specific research interests or want educational aids, and those for whom advertising is a document that informs an allied subject of interest in economics, history, modern anthropology, popular culture, American studies, sociology, and the like.

They would also like to create a greater number of interpretive products to reach a broader public. Now primarily a resource for display materials for the Smithsonian and a supplier of research information and illustration for scholars and their publications, they hope to produce their own books, films, videotapes, and sundry classroom materials. Ideally, more people will come to better appreciate both advertising and, through advertising, American social and economic history. The first of these products will probably be a book drawn from the Modern Advertising History Program, telling some of the story of the Marlboro Man, Speedy Alka-Seltzer, and the Pepsi Generation.

The American Advertising Museum. America's first museum dedicated entirely to advertising is not in New York, or Chicago, or for that matter, Los Angeles. It is in Portland, Oregon, the home of one of America's oldest and largest professional associations, the Portland Advertising Federation, the group of 900 members who sponsor the museum. The members have donated $115,000, many artifacts and many hours of professional time for activities such as design and production of displays, researching of artifacts, and soliciting of cash and in-kind contributions from other businesses and foundations. More than three years of effort preceded the museum's opening in June 1986.

The American Advertising Museum occupies a 6,000-square-foot space in a renovated historical building in the city's "Old Town" district, a space whose renovation expenses and first year's rent have also been donated. It was conceived of as an educational center to collect, maintain, and display advertising with "high educational, curatorial, and interpretive standards" to serve professionals, students, educators, and the general public.

To this end, it maintains a now-small reference library, and has a meeting room and auditorium in addition to its exhibit space. The library holds 1500 texts, directories, reference books, periodicals, indexes, and career guides, all donated, but this has the potential to grow substantially from continuing donations from members. The museum's collections consist of more than 5,000 print ads dating from 1683, including a large collection donated by Walter Weir, and more than 1000 radio commercials and 1000 television spots. Donations to the collections and the current displays have come from major agencies, clients, national industry associations and other curatorial institutions like the Warshaw Business Americana Collection of the Smithsonian and the History of Advertising Archives in Vancouver.

The exhibits, the sum and substance of the museum experience for most of the public, include both permanent and temporary or traveling elements. Currently they are: (1) Advertising Timeline, a chronological journey through the industry's significant developments since the 1600s through the advent of outdoor, newspapers, magazines, direct mail, radio, and television; (2) The Advertising Process, a look at the evolution of an award-winning campaign from concept through creative execution to implementation; (3) The Evolution of a Logo, a similar presentation of logo development; (4) Advertising Specialties, a borrowed display of 200 items from the Smithsonian; (5) The Advertising Council, examples of public service campaigns, the most famous of which is the enduring Smokey the Bear forest-fire prevention effort; (6) Vintage Radio and Television Ads, a continuous playback of early and famous ones; and last, but not least; (7) a Presentation Room, which celebrates "advertising excellence on the local, national, and international level."

This year, as one example, they will display the traveling exhibit of early twentieth century commercial art, accidentally rediscovered by Nabisco. More than one hundred original paintings were found wrapped, stashed, and then forgotten in an office of one of the original Minneapolis mills. There the stable environmental conditions preserved the work of the many famous artists and illustrators who did commissioned work for the firm, primarily for their famous Cream of Wheat magazine campaigns.

The sponsoring federation also plans to develop outreach programs to include traveling exhibits, seminars, a national lending library, special publications, and production of audio-video cassettes.

The Museum of Modern Mythology

Although smaller in size, purpose, and scope, this new San Francisco museum preserves the corporate and advertising use of various symbols and trade marks. It includes the anthropomorphic humanoids like the Jolly Green Giant, Mr. Peanut, Chiquita Banana, Charlie the Tuna, Elsie the Cow, Smokey the Bear, or the Poppin' Fresh Dough Boy. Fictional human characters are also represented here, such as the Marlboro Man, Betty Crocker, the Man from Glad, Aunt Jemima, or Mr. Whipple, the fastidious storekeeper who for years has been harassing shoppers for squeezing toilet paper to check for softness.

Upon reflection, there is an enormous menagerie of such beasts and spokespeople for myths. Just in the cat family there are Morris the Cat plugging cat food, Tony the Tiger selling sweetened cereal, the Pink Panther now selling pink insulation, a cougar pitching cars of the same name, and a tiger in your (gas) tank as symbolically a brand of gasoline. Thus this small museum, founded in 1982, has a surprisingly rich bestiary and pantheon to draw upon.

The facility was founded by a trio of graphic designers—one of whom was a collector of advertising dolls—who disclaim any intent to be solely a museum of advertising. But while they would like to expand to areas such as comic books, television shows, or record-album cover art, they are primarily concerned with a museum of commercial creations. Currently their exhibits are only three: "Tell Me a Story," composed of advertising symbols that come out of folklore; "Meet Mr. Product," with anthropomorphic products; and "Television Made Me What I Am Today." They do not maintain research files in support of the displays, but the principals would be worth interviewing for the lore of anecdotes they've no doubt collected about the use of the characters. The museum board includes some academics, which may in time encourage the creation of more formal research resources.

The D'Arcy Collection

This is an enormous holding of about 2 million print ads clipped by the D'Arcy, McManus, and Masius agency of St. Louis. It was donated in 1983 to the Communications Library of the University of Illinois. It includes ads from the turn of the century, but is strongest for the 1930s through the 1950s. The firm has committed itself to adding the files for 1960 to 1983 at a later date. The virtue of this holding, in contrast to the Ayer or J. Walter Thompson sets of proofsheets, is that it also contains competitive ads, thereby profiling advertising activity for many product categories.

The sheer size of the collection, some thirty-seven file cabinets full, has made the processing task substantial. Originally grouped by product categories, they were in some disarray. They are now alphabetized by product, and then by brand name. A grant has been received for microfilming preservation, needed especially for the deteriorating newsprint. Indexes are being prepared for both on-line and printed formats permitting ready retrieval by brand, year, or product. Most of the clippings were both dated and gave the name of the source magazine or newspaper.

For more information see Carothers (1987).

The History of Advertising Archives

The History of Advertising Archives at the University of British Columbia are devoted to the study, preservation, and occasional exhibition of advertising documents and artifacts. They hold a historical library of printed and audiovisual materials, research and reference collections of advertisements in various media, display items, slides for presentations, manuscripts materials, and artifacts and advertiques. All of the holdings outlined next are being cataloged, indexed, and assembled onto a master file disk readable on a personal computer.

Users. The archives are a unique resource for a number of different users, such as: (1) media, who are provided reels, ideas, comments, interviews, and reference to others; (2) researchers, who access the data bases, library, or the reference and research collections. These include professionals, university scholars, and those with operations like the new Ogilvy Foundation in San Francisco; (3) art directors or set designers who want to recreate a historical ambience with advertiques. Similar help has also gone to retail display designers and museums; (4) educators, who are supplied reels and films about advertising, or guest speakers; (5) entertainers, for script consulting and technical assistance on pitches, announcers styles, or sales techniques; (6) lawyers, most recently for analysis of old cigarette ads relevant to product liability prosecutions.

Access. The History of Advertising Archives are open to all researchers, although circulation is controlled. Office space is available for extended visits, as is assistance. Facilities include all necessary video and audio tape equipment. Mail inquiries as to holdings are answered promptly.

Holdings

Books and Journals. Most titles listed within the bibliographic sections of *Information Sources in Advertising History* (Pollay 1978) and most academic advertising journals are held, as are sundry working papers, dissertations, and publications by national advertising associations. Included are many rare and obscure titles, especially items not often found in academic libraries such as: table books of reproductions of ads, collectors' illustrated price guides, items like J. Walter Thompson's "Blue Book" on advertising media from 1904, *Sears' Advertising Policies* for 1955; the *Madison Avenue Handbook,* a New York professional directory, for 1980; and the *Media Guide* for the 1976 Virginia Slims Pro Tennis circuit. Among the convenient secondary sources are the dissertations studying advertising's history, or using advertising as data.

Manuscripts. The volume of manuscript material held is small, making the archives designation more reflective of aspirations than current reality. In hand are: (1) Western Washington Power Company, primarily ephemera for the 1920s to 1940s promoting appliances and electric use; (2) The Green and Huckvale Papers consists of eight boxes of papers and four boxes of audiovisuals for a medium-sized Vancouver agency with various accounts, for 1977 to 1981. Well represented are hotels, government agencies, especially those concerned with real estate and development, and retail accounts, including files for litigations over fee collection; (3) Several files of procedures and policies in operation at the Benton & Bowles offices in Manhattan, 1984; (4) A Beef Information Centre "Jack Spratt" campaign promoting beef as a lean meat, 1985, includes various creative but no planning documents; and (5) The Expo '86 file, a collection of publicity, advertising, souvenirs, and oddments collected by local citizens, plus samples of the advertising to the trade (travel agents). Included is a media plan for the trade advertising, and examples of some cooperative programs with sponsors.

Artifacts. The archival and manuscript collection includes a large collection of advertising artifacts, particularly curious specialty items, and advertiques illustrative of junctures in advertising history. The most extensive holding is a collection of nineteenth century patent medicine artifacts, including much printed ephemera. Substantial numbers of specialty advertising items are also held, like buttons, lapel pins, or embroidered badges. Many items and promotional materials are kept for any and all firms named Acme, as these are deemed to symbolize the grassroots of the economy (Pollay 1987). Other artifacts collected are those showing the diversity of forms of advertising, clones to existing products like candy copies of cigarette brands, and oddities like "widgets and gizmos."

As specific illustrations, recently purchased for both personal use and ultimately the archives' collection are: a nineteenth century letter opener advertising itself as an advertising specialty item; a fruit crate label for "Visitor" brand lemons placed in the guest room for visiting scholars; a Davey Crockett Bread pin; a shaped cutting board featuring a brand name of mushrooms; a set of soup tureens whose design is based on old versions of the Tabasco and oyster-can labels; a Campbell Soup instant lunch appliance that heats coffee; a coffee cup shaped like a battery labelled "Energizer;" a "Ritz-watch" whose baby-talk pun appeals; a "Takoma (Take-home-a) Biscuit" pin for an early twentieth century competitor to Uneeda Biscuits, the cornerstone to Nabisco's transformation of cracker distribution from barrels to packages; and a World War II playing card featuring a Coke ad and silhouettes of airplanes to train air-raid wardens.

Audio-Visual Library. The collection includes 3,000 35mm slides on advertising and business history, and six feet of videotapes of television ads. The videotapes include samples of two hundred or more ads for most years since 1973, and irregular holdings that predate that. Irregular holdings of audiotapes of radio ads are also held. Most of them are either award-winning reels, samplers from production houses, writers of agencies, or collectors' oddities, such as "bloopers." Promotional phonograph albums or sales training materials exist as well. Shows, speeches, and interviews related to advertising and related arts (market research, package design, etc) are on both video and audiotapes. These include both primary and secondary sources, such as interviews with advertising copy testers or with historians.

Research Collections. Carefully drawn samples of advertisements in print, television, and direct mail have been drawn for data-base development and use by others. The most thoroughly explored to date is the collection of print advertising from 1900 to 1980. It has been studied for its information content (Pollay 1984c), images of the "good life," (Belk and Pollay 1985), values (Pollay 1984a), and changing strategies (Pollay 1985b). Largely unanalyzed is the set of television ads taped annually since the early 1970s. Every year 200 or more ads are taped and filed, yielding a very large sample for historical purposes. Few alternative sources exist for systematic sampling of the ephemeral advertising on electronic media. A collection of direct mail assembled by a U.S. resident and purchaser by mail covers all items received during one calendar year, 1981–82, with duplicates purged.

Data-Base Availability. The data bases developed under the auspices of the archives are generally readily available at cost for scholarly research. They are typically stored on SPSS data files on disk and tape, and access can usually be arranged for on-line direct linkage or tape duplication. Use is subject to some limitations. The data bases are for bona fide scholarly research, and neither the raw data nor analytic results based upon the data may be sold, leased, or given to commercial users. Access to the data base typically involves efforts by staff members or research associates of the History of Advertising Archives. In addition, most of the data exists because of grants from supporting agencies. Acknowledgements and offers of co-authorship are expected. Application for access should involve at least a letter outlining the research planned, the data needed, and the contemplated research product(s). Supportive materials ought to include a résumé, bibliography, and relevant reprints.

Acquisitions. Acquisition efforts include purchase of advertiques and book titles and receipt of donations from benefactors, including students and colleagues who find Acme artifacts and other ephemera. Potential contributions of libraries and archival material are evaluated without obligation. The History of Advertising Archives respond promptly to donors regarding all plans and proposals for special events, posters, new releases, audiovisual materials, or other publicity concerning any donation. The archives cooperate in all promotional activities deemed appropriate and consistent with the maintenance of the archives' reputation.

Other Archives

There are few major collections of documents to become part of public archives since Pollay (1978). No doubt there may be many valuable corporate records of advertising activity, now minimally processed, which may be entering corporate archives and which might someday be publicly accessible. Existing major holdings, like that on communications in Madison, Wis. may be expanding and accumulating their advertising papers. Fairleigh Dickinson University is the official repository for the outdoor advertising industry. Duke University is reported to be building a collection, in part by extracting from existing holdings.

Darrell B. Lucas Papers. The Archives of the History of American Psychology at the University of Akron hold fourteen boxes for Dr. Lucas, consisting of drafts and correspondence related to his important books, *Advertising Psychology and Research* (1950) and *Measuring Advertising Effectiveness* (1963). While the correspondence includes the trivial, related to quotation permissions and the like, it also includes unpublished detail on techniques in use by advertisers at that time. Lucas is also cross-referenced with seven other holdings in this archive, one of which is no doubt the unspecified volume of papers for Harry Hollingworth.

J. Walter Thompson Proofsheets. The corporate Information Center of the Chicago office has a collection of over 100,000 print ads, according to Williamson (1980). If available to scholars, this is potentially as valuable as the D'Arcy files at Illinois and rivals the Ayer proofsheets at the Smithsonian. Either might serve as good data for a study of the evolution of ad style and sophistication from a single agency over a long span of time. The New York office also maintains an archives with some files open to the public.

Other Collections

Smaller collections are scattered here and there. Fine graphics, especially as seen in trade cards and other nineteenth century ephemera can be found at the New York Historical Society, the Chicago Historical Society, the Cincinnati Art Museum Library, the American Antiquarian Society, Harvard Business School's Baker Library, and at Yale. The University of Michigan Library has a holding of political ads and posters. For any particular product, one can look for corporate and special library holdings in Young (1977).

Who knows how many private collections there may be of advertising materials? Many collectors seem to exist with various interests in advertising items. Some collect around themes, like everything with a cat, or railroad, or ethnic image. Some collect for brands and companies, like Coca-Cola or General Electric, or for product classes, like beer memorabilia. Some collect advertising in specific object forms, like business cards, serving trays, paperweights, dolls, or thimbles. I am an eclectic collector (Pollay 1987a) by comparison to these, and despite appearances because of the public nature of my holdings, my collection is modest compared to many.

Happily, some are even collecting the most ephemeral but the most important of mass advertising forms, television spots. We have learned from the paucity of radio ad collections that survive just how little trace electronic advertising leaves. The Museum of Broadcasting (N.Y.) and the NBC Archives at the Library of Congress have preserved little if any advertising.

Diamant Memorial Library of Classic Television Commercials. This was a pioneering assembly, but is of modest size. It consists of sixty-nine classic spots aired before 1948–1958, available for purchase on a two-hour reel. At Brooklyn College, it is sold by the Department of Television and Radio. Hopefully this small collection will act as a seed crystal for a larger collection in the New York region.

CLIO Collection. All CLIO award winners since 1960 to present are available for rental from the American TV and Radio Commercial Festivals Group in New York. The group also has a number of short films presenting "witty studies" of trends in various years of the 1960s. More substantial are the more than forty undated reels for specific product categories, and those demonstrating techniques of editing, optical effects, graphics, animation, cinematography, direction, musical scoring, and use of humor. They also have reels of radio ads since 1967 for both award winners and eleven product categories, and slides of award-winning print advertising and package design. Presumably any of these can be played at the New York office. This office also has records for the "Effies," awards given by the New York chapter of the American Marketing Association for marketing effectiveness, and with whom they merged in 1971. The choice of the Greek goddess of history, Clio, as their symbol, suggests that these will be preserved for posterity.

These publishers of CLIO magazine coordinate the judging for "advertising excellence worldwide" by some 500 judges. In actuality it is dominated by U.S. creative, so for worldwide scope one should see the Cannes Festival reels of spots where creative from Europe, Asia, or Australia often dominate the American entries. Both award reels have the problem of considering only those who enter the competition by application, so they draw from an incomplete and repetitive list of agencies and clients interested in these sorts of distinctions.

Harry Wayne McMahan Collection. The largest inventory of television ads is apparently the claimed 23,000 commercials of this former *Advertising Age* columnist. This private library in Escondido, Calif. is updated constantly as the author continues his personal selecting of the 200 best from each year. Because privately and jealously held, these are very difficult to access and to assess. Some have been rented by groups such as NBC for "New and Improved—Television's Greatest Commercials," and these are available at UCLA.

UCLA Television Archives. The best current accessible source for television spots is the Film and TV Archive of the Department of Theater Arts, UCLA. They hold more than 500 reels of film and tape that consist entirely of ads. While there is no separate listing of individual ads yet, the whole archive has a purchasable catalog. Among their holdings are the CLIO reels since 1960, and many other tapes of programs with the ads still embedded. Also notable is the collection of old ads made by James Hall for Carson Productions television specials on classic commercials. Assembled in 1982 from agencies, sponsors, production companies, the CLIO organization, and individuals, much was transferred to tape given to UCLA before the originals were returned.

Coda: The Pack-Age Revisited

Archaeology looks backward even further than historians, and often describes people or ages by the tools and technologies that most characterize them, as in the Bronze Age or the Beaker People. Whether future historians or archaeologists consider the consumer culture of developed nations as the "Pack-Age" remains to be seen. There is much to suggest that the term is a strong candidate for typifying modern society and the core position of its marketplace to its culture.

The throw-away can, carton, bottle, foil, or plastic package is disposable but indispensible to our modern life. It carries the brand name, which is simultaneously the reservoir for all of the firm's good will created by advertising and product reputation, and the embodiment of what the consumer buys. Especially for undifferentiated products, the brand and its image are the determining factors for both the anticipated or perceived satisfactions for the consumer and also the market share enjoyed by the manufacturers.

The shift from the unpackaged goods sold to middlemen resellers and retailers to packaged goods presold to consumers by advertising has been virtually revolutionary. Previously, the local merchant controlled the trade, staking his reputation by giving personal endorsement to the products he sold, there being no other identification. This was a labor-intensive task, part of the extended personal service offered from shopkeeper to store patron. Today's market, with advertised goods dispensed through self service, could have been seen as an inevitability once the process of packaging and branding had begun. With standardized quality and quantity, the packaged, branded good both permitted and required the manufacturer to have direct contact, through advertising, with his consumers taking over the bulk of the promotional function. This has meant a major shift in balance of power in the market from the middlemen's control of the nineteenth century to manufacturer control in the twentieth century.

As recently as the 1930s, the affluent in traditional centers like London continued to look down upon those plebeians who used "shop" jam or tinned salmon, for these elites were still paying dearly for the luxury and class distinction of having customized service and selection. But they were the dying breed, as prepackaged and branded goods have become the standard of the economy. There is no longer any social stigma to their use. Poor and rich alike are able to buy the "best-selling," "prize-winning," or "gold-medal" products, and buy them at the same prices from the same stores. Future historians might suggest that the package, in the Pack-Age, did more to level society and produce an equality of at least some consumption experiences, than did the arguments of Karl Marx and various political implementations based upon ideals of equality.

But because the packages of today are for the most part designed to be ephemeral, and because most advertising, especially electronic, is also ephemeral in nature, we risk having a very thin record for future historians or archaeologists to consider. Few cartons are intended to be kept once they are opened by the consumer. The future archaeologist unearthing garbage dumps and finding those items made of non-biodegradable materials, such as plastic yogurt cups, may fail to appreciate the extent to which such packaging predominates in our market. Such a discovery, even in multiples, seems unlikely to suggest, for example, the amount, scope, and purpose of the various activities involved as millions of yogurt cartons are manufactured, filled, shipped, sold, emptied, and discarded every year. Nor will the few television ads preserved accidentally on videotapes of other programming indicate the extent to which advertising is omnipresent in modern life.

But thanks to the efforts of the various museum, archives, special libraries, and private collectors, some decent record should survive. Several of these have been outlined, and this listing is by no means exhaustive. Archival records related to advertising exist elsewhere, such as the communications holdings of the University of Wisconsin, or the biographical and correspondence files of David Ogilvy at the Library of Congress (Pollay 1978). The individual collecor, the unheralded "PAC-rat," is also owed a debt of gratitude. Individual initiative is what created most of those holdings, not the actions of large organizations. Even the activities of the bigger institutions, like the Smithsonian, have their impetus in seed collections gathered and contributed by private collectors. Optimally, more and more private collections will be donated to public institutions as estates are transferred between generations.

Classic Americana and notable marketing stories could be preserved through collections for products such as Tide laundry detergent, Hershey's chocolate, Swanson's TV Dinners, McDonald's fast foods, Campbell's soups, Maytag washing machines, Sony electronics, Volkswagen automobiles, Levi's (or Pierre Cardin) jeans, or any feminine sanitary products.

The institutions of advertising are still notoriously indifferent to their own histories (Pollay 1977). While a few firms, like N. W. Ayer, or a few individuals like David Ogilvy, have a greater perspective and sense of themselves in a historical context, the typical agency cares not at all about yesterday. The short-term focus, shared with clients, is on what's happening right now and what should happen next. The planning and strategy process makes them look ahead somewhat, but this is rarely guided by looks in their rear-view mirrors. Pressed for time, few practitioners even take the time to understand the history of their own client or brands. Even relatively recent advertising or market research reports are hardly looked at, precipitating much re-invention and rediscovery of lessons lost for the lack of historical perspective.

The larger organizations, like the American Association of Advertising Agencies or the American Advertising Federation, exist primarily as legislative lobbies, being both advocates and watchdogs, advancing or retarding governmental actions they desire or detest. Because of the politically sensitive and possibly scandalous nature of this work, even their own written records are probably minimal and unlikely to ever become intentionally public. These organizations are hardly likely to facilitate a preservation of advertising history. Just recently they balked at cooperating with the Smithsonian's efforts, despite the prestige involved, when it appeared that doing so might put on the payroll a distinguished academic they considered "unfriendly."

This timid display of defensiveness suggests that at least the current industry leadership has neither the foresight nor the self-confidence to support historical scholarship. They presumably fear that any truths exposed through an accurate history will be even more damaging than the popular myths about Madison Avenue hucksters carrying on the traditions and morality of snake-oil salesmen.

Fortunately, there are those with more faith in the advances and accomplishments of advertising, and the role it plays in furthering the advances and accomplishments of the rest of society.

References

Alka-Seltzer Oral History and Documentation Project: Project Handbook. 1986. Washington, D.C.: National Museum of American History, Smithsonian Institution, Archives Center.

Barnouw, Erik. 1978. *The Sponsor: Notes on a Modern Potentate.* N.Y.: Oxford University Press.

Bliss, Susan D. 1984. "Conserving and Cataloging 150 Years of U.S. Business Ephemera." *Research Reports* (Winter). 1–3.

Cahn, William. 1969. *Out of the Cracker Barrel.* N.Y.: Simon and Schuster.

Carothers, Diane Foxhill. 1987. "Eighty-Plus Years of Advertising History Through the D'Arcy Collection." *Proceedings.* American Academy of Advertising. In press.

Crew, Spencer R., and John A. Fleckner. 1987. "Archival Sources for Business History at the National Museum of American History." *Business History Review.* Vol. 61. In press.

Dreyfus, Carol, and Thomas Connors. 1985. "Oral History and American Advertising: How the 'Pepsi Generation' Came Alive." *International Journal of Oral History.* No. 3 (November). 6:191–197.

Ellsworth, Scott. 1986. "Inventing Marlboro: A Historical Context." *Marlboro Oral History and Documentation Project: Project Handbook.* Washington, D.C.: National Museum of American History, Archives Center.

Fleckner, John A. 1986. Interview with author. Washington, D.C.. October.

Fox, Richard W., and T. J. Jackson Lears, eds. 1983. *The Culture of Consumption: Critical Essays in American History, 1880–1980.* N.Y.: Pantheon.

Fox, Stephen. 1984. *The Mirror Makers: A History of Twentieth Century American Advertising.* N.Y.: William Morrow.

Hower, Ralph M. 1939. *"The History of an Advertising Agency: N. W. Ayer & Son at Work, 1869–1939.* Cambridge: Harvard University Press.

Levitt, Theodore. 1983. "Globalization of Markets." *The Marketing Imagination.* N.Y.: Free Press.

Lucas, Darrell B., and Stuart Henderson Britt. 1950. *Advertising Psychology and Research.* N.Y.: McGraw-Hill.

Lucas, Darrell B., and Stuart Henderson Britt. 1963. *Measuring Advertising Effectiveness.* N.Y.: McGraw-Hill.

Marchand, Roland. 1985. *Advertising The American Dream: Making Way for Modernity, 1920–1940*. Berkeley: University of California Press.

Mayer, Martin. 1958. *Madison Avenue, U.S.A.* N.Y.: Harper & Row.

Pollay, Richard W. 1987a. "The History of Advertising Archives: Confessions of a PAC-Rat." *Advances in Consumer Research*. Vol. XIV. Paul F. Anderson and Melanie Wallendorf, eds. In press.

———. 1987b. "Insights into Consumer Behavior from Historical Studies of Advertising." *Advances in Consumer Research*, Vol. XIV. Paul F. Anderson and Melanie Wallendorf, eds. In press.

———. 1987c. "On the Value of Reflections on the Values in "The Distorted Mirror." *Journal of Marketing*. Vol. 51. In press.

———. 1987d. "Tracking the Marlboro Man, Speedy Alka-Seltzer and the Pepsi Generation Through the Smithsonian Archives." *Proceedings*. American Academy of Advertising. In press.

———. 1986a. "The Distorted Mirror: Reflections on the Unintended Consequences of Advertising." *Journal of Marketing*, (Spring). 50:18–36.

———. 1986b. "The Quality of Life in 'The Padded Sell': Common Criticisms of Advertising's Cultural Character and International Public Policies." *Current Issues and Research in Advertising*. No. 2 (Reviews). 9:173–250.

———. 1985a. "History of Advertising." In Charles F. Fraser, ed., *Defining the Core of the Discipline*. Urbana, Ill.: University of Illinois.

———. 1985b. "The Subsiding Sizzle: Shifting Strategies in Print Advertising, 1900–1980." *Journal of Marketing*. No. 3 (Summer). 49:24–37.

———. 1985c. "Thank the Editors for the BUY-ological Urge! American Magazines, Advertising and the Promotion of the Consumer Culture, 1920–1980." In Stanley C. Hollander and Terence Nevett, eds., *Marketing in the Long Run*. Michigan State University Press. 54–68.

———. (1984a). "The Identification and Distribution of Values Manifest in Print Advertising, 1900–1980." In Robert E. Pitts and Arch G. Woodside, eds., *Personal Values and Consumer Behavior*. Lexington, Mass.: Lexington Books. 60–71.

———. 1984b. "The Languishing of Lydiametrics: The Ineffectiveness of Econometric Research on Advertising Effects." *Journal of Communication*. No. 2 (Spring). 34:8–23.

———. 1984c. "Twentieth Century Magazine Advertising: Determinants of Informativeness." *Written Communication*. No. 1. 1:56–77.

———. 1978. *Information Sources in Advertising History*. Riverside, Conn.: Greenwood Press. 328.

———. 1977. "The Importance, and the Problems, of Writing the History of Advertising." *Journal of Advertising History*. No. 1. 1:3–5.

Pope, Daniel. 1983. *The Making of Modern Advertising*. N.Y.: Basic Books.

Schudson, Michael. 1984. *Advertising, The Uneasy Persuasion: Its Dubious Impact on American Society*. N.Y.: Basic Books.

Seldin, Joseph. 1963. *The Golden Fleece: Selling the Good Life to Americans*. N.Y.: Macmillan.

Williamson, Elizabeth. 1980. "Advertising." In M. Thomas Inge, ed., *American Popular Culture*. Vol. 2. Wesport, Conn.: Greenwood Press.

Young, Margaret Labash, et al. 1977. *Subject Directory of Special Libraries and Information Centers*. Detroit: Gale Research.

Appendix: Addresses of Advertising Archives and Collections

American Advertising Museum
9 N.W. Second Avenue
Portland, Oregon 97209

D'Arcy Collection
Communications Library
University of Illinois 61801

CLIO Awards
American TV and Radio Commercial Festivals Group
New York, NY 10022

Darrell B. Lucas Papers
The Archives of the History of American Psychology
University of Akron, Ohio 44325

Diamant Memorial Library of Classic Television Commercials
Department of Television and Radio
Brooklyn College, CUNY, 11210

The History of Advertising Archives
Faculty of Commerce, UBC
Vancouver, BC, Canada V6T 1Y8

Miles Laboratories Archives
Elkhart, Indiana 46515

Smithsonian Institution, Archives Center
National Museum of American History (NMAH)
Washington, DC 20560

Film & TV Archive
Department of Theater Arts, UCLA
1015 N. Cahuenga Blvd.
Hollywood, CA 90038

13
American Influences on British Advertising before 1920

Terence Nevett

Introduction: Britain and the Americans

In the 1950s the marketing opportunities offered by resurgent European economies proved a powerful attraction for American manufacturers and service organizations. With them went their advertising agents, who found London a convenient center for a European agency operation. The period witnessed considerable activity as American agencies opened London offices, bought partial or complete control of existing agencies, or set up joint ventures with local partners. Yet although this "invasion" is normally regarded as marking the beginning of American interest and influence, it was in fact the culmination of a movement of ideas and practices across the Atlantic that had begun at least a hundred years earlier. This chapter examines the origins of that movement and assesses its effects on British advertising of the time.

The full extent of American influence in the nineteenth century can only be appreciated in the context of contemporary British views about America and the Americans generally. In the early decades of the century, "the British attitude toward America was one of condescension. They saw the Americans as boorish citizens of a fourthrate country . . . Above all, they detested the boastfulness, the passion for making money and the love of smart dealing that were the special characteristics of the Yankees" (Fitzsimons 1969). The same writer notes that between 1820 and 1844 at least one hundred books on America were written by British travelers, their consensus being overwhelmingly unfavorable.

To be American was therefore a considerable handicap in business, as well as socially. Americans made much of "smartness," which in British eyes was simply a euphemism for fraud. It appeared to be extolled as a virtue greater than honesty, which was a reversal of values the British could neither

The research presented here was completed with the assistance of a Central Michigan University Summer Research Fellowship. The author wishes to acknowledge his indebtedness to the university for that award.

understand nor accept. It is not surprising, in the light of such perceptions, that the American business presence in Britain was extremely limited. When John Morgan Richards arrived in London in 1867 there were still "not exceeding a dozen firms of American origin, including the American banking houses" (Richards 1905, 177).

The situation changed gradually toward the end of the century. By 1883 the American, Colonial, and British Exchange Club had been founded with premises in Old Bond Street, "with the object of providing a central rendez-vous, at the West End of London, for mutual intercourse between the Old and New Worlds. An institution of this description has long been wanted in London, for whilst Indian, Clerical, Naval, Military, University, and other classes have their Clubs, where men of similar social position and tastes assemble, American and Colonial gentlemen, many thousands of whom visit London annually, have hitherto been confined to small and inconvenient newsrooms" (ABC Exchange Club 1883).

It must be assumed that the "many thousands" came mainly from the colonies, rather than the United States. The information contained in the Exchange's *Handy Book* relates especially to Australia, and there are still relatively few American banks listed. Only eight American newspapers were represented in London.

Twenty years later there had been a dramatic change. "Today there are many hundreds of firms engaged exclusively in American manufactures and productions" (Richards 1905, 177). This came about partly through the innovative nature of American industry, which was able to generate a variety of products for which there was an immediate demand in Britain. These included agricultural implements, printing presses, typesetting machines, tramways, air brakes, typewriters, sewing machines, keyless watches, Yale locks, Kodak cameras, cash registers, canned goods, telephones, and gram-ophones (Richards 1905, 217–218). It had become easier to sell these prod-ucts because of improvements in transportation and communications. The Atlantic cable had been completed in 1866, and regular steamship sailings made it possible for businessmen to make regular trips between the conti-nents. John Morgan Richards crossed the Atlantic forty times between 1867 and 1905, while Brent Good, a principal of a firm he represented in Britain, had made the crossing at least sixty times. Equally important, however, was the fact that Americans had become accepted socially. Lord Randolph Churchill took an American wife in 1874. William Waldorf, with an inher-itance valued at $200 million, settled in London, bought the *Pall Mall Ga-zette,* founded the *Pall Mall Magazine,* took British citizenship, was made a peer, and subsequently became Viscount Astor. His son John Jacob was given a classic English upper-class background—Eton, the Life Guards, ADC to the Viceroy of India—and later entered Parliament. When he succeeded to his father's title, his wife, Nancy, became the first woman member of

Parliament. John Morgan Richards, although engaged in business that was still not accepted at the highest levels of society and involved with patent medicines, which certainly carried a stigma, was nevertheless able to gain a foothold in English society. It may be that he bought his way in, since he rented a castle from Lord Ampthill, near to Queen Victoria's estate in the Isle of Wight, and later bought another castle on the Isle. Nevertheless, his daughter married the son of General Sir Harry Prendergast VC, GCB. His son Nelson, after an education that included Trinity Hall Cambridge, married the daughter of their neighbor, Captain Edgar Bishop. Little wonder that, looking back to the time when he first arrived in England, Richards was able to detect a marked improvement in the standing of Americans generally. "I do certainly consider that Americans have won their way to exceeding popularity amongst the English people, and there is no social function of distinction or privilege at which they would not be welcome guests" (Richards 1905, 220).

The Barnum Legacy

One of the main factors in coloring British perceptions of the Americans was the impact of Phineas T. Barnum during his visits to London, and particularly his first in 1844. Barnum has been described as "the embodiment of all the Yankee characteristics most detested by the British" (Fitzsimons 1969, 36). But if his name became synonymous with sharp practice, he was indisputably a master publicist. As he himself wrote, "I thoroughly understood the art of advertising, not merely by printer's ink, which I have always used freely, and to which I confess myself so much indebted for my success, but by turning every possible circumstance to my account" (Fitzsimons 1969, 57).

Barnum arrived in England in 1844 with the midget he styled General Tom Thumb. His first tactic was to try to negotiate with the editors of the Liverpool newspapers on the basis of placing advertising in return for editorial "puffs." Though he had done this with considerable success in the United States, the Liverpool press was not interested.

When he reached London, he tried taking the midget on a series of visits to meet newspaper editors. Only the *Illustrated London News* found the "General" worth a mention. Barnum therefore had to resort to less orthodox means of obtaining publicity. Before leaving New York he had obtained a letter of introduction from Horace Greeley of the *New York Tribune* to Edward Everett, U.S. ambassador in London. Everett arranged a meeting with Charles Augustus Murray, Master of the Queen's Household, who had spent two years in the United States living with the Pawnees. Murray in turn arranged for the "General" to be presented at Court, where he played with the royal children and was given presents by Queen Victoria. Barnum announced this in the Court Circular, a calendar of events carried by the leading newspapers, breaking with accepted practice in that he wrote the announcements himself. He also launched Tom Thumb in London society by means of a series of receptions attended exclusively by members of the aristocracy.

The public flocked to see the midget on display at London's Egyptian Hall, where the takings averaged five hundred pounds a day. In due course, however, a reaction set in against Barnum and all that he stood for, which seems to have been caused by two particular events. The first was the suicide of the English painter Benjamin Haydon. Deeply in debt and with failing eyesight, Haydon had mounted an exhibition of his works at the Egyptian Hall at the same time Tom Thumb was on display there. While the public flocked to see the midget, they ignored poor Haydon, who subsequently committed suicide under especially horrible circumstances. A national outcry followed, in which Haydon's widow was voted a pension by Parliament, and much of the blame for Haydon's misfortunes was attributed to Barnum.

The second event contributing to Barnum's unpopularity was the appearance of his autobiography, in which he revealed details of the various shady dealings with which he had been associated, including exploiting the English affection for their queen in order to promote Tom Thumb. The reaction was predictable. An anonymous reviewer in *Fraser's Magazine* was typical in his views of Barnum and his tactics: "It must be a strange taste, indeed, which leads a man to gibbet himself for contempt, and to court the rotten eggs and dead cats of a moral pillory. Strange, however, as it is, the phenomenon is presented in perfection in the person of Mr. Phineas T. Barnum, who having made an immense fortune by what he terms 'management', has, in the volume before us, made the public the confidant of the discreditable 'dodges' by which he made it. Not only does he tell his story without a blush, but he is even proud of his rascalities, and winds up a sickening tale of falsehood and duplicity by claiming credit to himself as a public benefactor . . . In this country we believe no man would have had the effrontery to put his name to a work containing disclosures so disgraceful . . . The book is an offence and a nuisance" (*Fraser's Magazine* 1855).

Barnum's legacy was twofold. First, everything he did seemed to confirm the worst British suspicions about the American character, thus making it even harder for American companies to trade successfully in Britain. As the reviewer in *Fraser's Magazine* commented, "Nowhere does the universal adoration of the 'almighty dollar' appear more conspicuous as the prevailing taint of the national character of the United States than in the pages of the book before us."

Second, "Barnum was the first man to appreciate the supreme, the ultimate value of publicity: that any kind of publicity was better than none, and that it did not matter what the newspapers said about you so long as they mentioned your name" (Fitzsimons 1969, 16). In particular his name became linked with promotional stunts of a kind rarely found in Britain before his visit. Later writers were to describe them as "Barnum-like" or "Barnumesque," which could be either attributive or pejorative, depending on the writer's viewpoint.

The Dissemination of Ideas

There are several channels by which American influences were disseminated during the later decades of the century, helping to overcome the general mistrust of Americans and to affect the way British advertisers and their agencies promoted goods and services to the public.

Americans in Britain

One of the most important means by which ideas were spread was through the activities of American businessmen operating in London. It is only possible to comment about such activities in fairly broad terms, since the records of several American societies active in London at this period, deposited with the British Library, are missing, believed destroyed by German bombing during World War II. As mentioned earlier, however, we know that the American, Colonial, and British Exchange Club existed in 1883. John Morgan Richards also mentions his connection with the American Round Table, which in 1905 had been meeting for twenty years, and the American Society Benevolent Fund, set up in London by Americans to help their fellow countrymen who crossed the Atlantic on cattleboats expecting easy pickings on their arrival.

The chairman of the American Society in 1896 was Henry Solomon Wellcome, partner in the pharmaceutical firm of Burroughs Wellcome. Originally the firm represented American pharmaceutical manufacturers such as Wyeth and McKesson and Robins, but gradually moved into manufacturing on its own account. Wellcome was an active publicist; one of his favorite methods was to supply medical chests to famous people. This proved particularly effective in the case of H. M. Stanley, the reporter who tracked down African explorer Dr. Livingstone. Wellcome took British citizenship in 1906 and was later knighted (DBB 1984).

By 1903 Funk and Wagnalls had set up an office in London. In an interview that year with the trade journal *Advertising World,* their advertising manager made a comment which may well have reawakened some British fears about dealing with Americans: "I regret to say that the standards of commercial integrity appear to be generally higher in this country than in my own." He noted however, that the British were lowering their standards to meet the increasing foreign competition. The firm's American origin was clearly not a major handicap since he mentioned that they had sold copies of their dictionary to members of the royal family, including a deal with Queen Victoria which gave her a 5 percent discount for cash (March 1903, 242–243). It is difficult to imagine a British firm of this period attempting to do business with the monarch on such presumptuous terms.

The advent of the twentieth century marked a dramatic increase in the volume of publicity generated by American firms selling in the British market. In 1902 *Advertising World* noted that "during the last twelve months the volume of American business has leapt suddenly into enormous figures, and assumed such proportions as to make American advertisers amongst the chief users of advertising space in this country" (August 1902, 133). The British were being offered Quaker Oats, Grape Nuts, Instant Postum, Force Food, Shredded Wheat, and Heinz Baked Beans, in addition to a range of household products such as Fairbank's Gold Dust Soap Powder and Glycerine-Tar Soap, and a variety of patent medicines of questionable efficacy. Some of these were marketed by the proprietors directly, and some through agents. In either case, it seems to have become increasingly common for the proprietors to visit London to check on progress. In February 1903, for example, Mr. C. W. Post, president of the Postum Cereal Company was interviewed by *Advertising World,* and took advantage of the opportunity to give his views on the uncooperative attitude of many British publishers (February 1903, 179–180).

An indication of the confidence felt by Americans resident in Britain in the prospects for business generally is the mounting of the American Exhibition at the Crystal Palace in 1903. By that time, clearly, the old antagonisms had been forgotten, and the legacy of Phineas T. Barnum successfully overcome. One of the promoters of the exhibition was John Morgan Richards, who had done so much to foster trading links between the two countries for almost forty years. Barely a decade later they were to become even more firmly joined as British and American troops fought side by side in the trenches during World War I.

American Advertising Agents

Since we are concerned with advertising, the role of advertising agents will be considered separately from that of businessmen in general. Several agencies were active in London in the 1890s, having moved there to service the demands of their clients who were expanding their selling operations into the British market. This motivation is clear from an interview given by agency head Charles H. Fuller to *Advertising World* in August 1902. Fuller stated categorically that he was only interested in handling American business in

London, and that he did not want British clients. He also made it clear that he would not take "any account previously handled by another agency," adding that if his policy on British business ever changed, the same rule would apply (214). In an article the previous month the journal had noted that Fuller's agency "has introduced a large number of clients to the English public," including the Postum Cereal Company and the F. A. Stuart Remedies Company (136).

Paul E. Derrick opened a London branch of his agency in 1896 to meet the needs of such clients as Quaker Oats, the Regal Boot Company, and Fairbank's Gold Dust Soap Powder and Glycerine Tar-Soap. From the outset the agency seems to have handled advertising in the United States for British clients as well as in Britain and other European countries for American clients (*Advertising World* July 1902, 88–89, 113). Initially the London branch was under the management of H. Powell Rees, a Briton who had learned the business in the United States, having spent fifteen years handling advertising for such celebrated British products as Van Houtens cocoa, Pears soap, and Beechams pills. Rees, however, decided he could do better on his own, and set up another agency in opposition to Derricks. This prompted Paul Derrick himself to sail from New York to see what remedial action was needed. He was to remain in London until his retirement in the early 1930s, becoming a widely respected and influential figure on the advertising scene. As well as producing a book and a number of articles in the trade press on the role of advertising and the status of the advertising agent, he was to play an important role as a government adviser on publicity during World War I. He was also greatly loved by this staff, introducing to London such revolutionary concepts as the five-day week.

Derrick and Fuller operated as normal advertising agents, though they differed as to the markets they served and the clients they would accept. Albert L. Teele, who arrived in London in 1891, was careful to point out that his services were rather more specialized. He was neither an agent nor a contractor, and did not accept commission from publishers as was the case with both types of business. His concern was with "the writing of advertisements, and with it everything which pertains to the preparation of advertising matter." Teele had worked in the business for twelve years before setting up in London, and considered himself unique in the way he operated: "I believe that I am the only advertising expert in England with an office distinct and separate from an advertising agency" (Teele 1892, 11–15).

American and British advertising agents had evolved in different ways. The American agents date from the 1840s and had developed as sellers of advertising space, owing allegiance to the media rather than to advertisers. Their British counterpart first appeared at the end of the eighteenth century, and from the outset acted for the advertiser, booking space in any publication (not just in those he was trying to sell) and writing copy if required.

This distinction is important with regard to two other businesses which were set up at the turn of the century. The first was opened by Louis B. Porter, who acted as London representative for a group of American magazine publishers. He was, in fact, operating as a space broker on the American pattern, even though he took great pains to present himself to the British as something quite different. In an interview with *Advertising World* he declared that his purpose was not just to sell advertising space but to help British exporters, "to work with them over the many problems that had to be solved, to familiarize them with local trade conditions, the character and extent of the competition they would have to meet, and to ascertain whether it was possible or not to build up an American trade on a profitable basis" (June 1902, 22–23).

Porter opened his office in 1900. The previous year saw the arrival of what was to become one of the most famous names in advertising when the J. Walter Thompson Company set up its London operation. Thompson had made his mark selling space in magazines, originally religious journals and later the growing field of women's publications. His London office functioned solely as a sales office for his American space broking business, and was intended to induce English firms to advertise in the United States. It did not handle advertising or placement in Europe for Americans. The office was to close in 1916 because of World War I, reopening on the same basis in 1919. It did not become a full service advertising agency until 1927 (*Advertising Age* 1964).

British Initiatives

American influence was by no means confined to Americans taking promotional concepts and practices to Britain. It is clear that the traffic was two-way, with British advertisers and agents actively seeking out ideas from the United States for use in their home market, and gaining experience in American methods that would put them in a stronger competitive position. As noted earlier, H. Powell Rees, manager of Paul Derrick's London office, made much of the fact that he had worked in the United States for fifteen years. In April 1902 *Advertising World* reported the launching of another agency headed by H. J. King-Potter, a Briton with twelve years of American experience. The most famous figure to return to Britain, however, was Charles Higham, the first advertising agent to receive a knighthood. After emigrating with his mother at the age of thirteen, he worked unsuccessfully at some sixty jobs. Returning to London, he was able to put his experience to good use selling advertising space on theater curtains and then in the agency business.

American experience was not the only means by which American influence was transferred. English advertising agents around the turn of the century were reported to be making expeditions across the Atlantic in search of clients wishing to advertise in Britain, as well as in other overseas markets their American counterparts were unwilling to tackle. In February 1902 *Advertising World* carried an interview from the American trade journal *Printer's Ink* with Mr. Wann, head of the T. B. Browne agency of London. Wann pointed out that Brownes were handling American advertising not only for the British market, but also for Continental Europe, South Africa, and Australia (46–48).

Leading advertisers were also being exposed to American ideas, particularly if they had export interests there. Thomas Barratt of Pears Soap made a number of trips to promote the product in the American market, enjoying the distinction of persuading the celebrated preacher Henry Beecher Stowe to write a testimonial for use in advertising. Barratt was subsequently elected to membership of the Sphinx Club of New York, an exclusive association of advertising professionals, other British members of which included soap manufacturer William Lever and medical products manufacturer Thomas Beecham. There was clearly a very direct American influence on the campaigns mounted by some of these firms in the British market, since in 1902 both Pears and Van Houten Cocoa were using advertisements prepared in New York for American use by H. Powell Rees (*Advertising World* June 1902, 88–89).

It seems, too, that merely associating with American organizations could bring about a noticeable change in attitude. In September 1902 *Advertising World* carried a portrait of Harold S. Durrant, advertising manager for Force Food. Though British, Durrant had worked as special correspondent in Europe for the *New York Herald,* with the result that "Mr. Durrant has all the energy and smartness of a Yankee, and is usually taken as such" (215). Far from being a pejorative association with the excesses of Barnum, this appears to have been intended as a compliment.

Knowledge For Sale

So far this chapter has been concerned with the way people connected with advertising were exposed to methods and attitudes characteristic of the United States. Another important factor to consider, however, is that the American advertising business clearly felt itself to be in advance of that in Britain, and therefore to have knowledge and skills which the British would be prepared to buy. The earliest effort along these lines seems to have been the Page-Davis Correspondence School of Advertising, which was set up in Chicago in 1895 and opened a London branch in 1900. Interestingly, the impetus here came not from the proprietors of the school but from the Thomas Dixon advertising agency of London. Dixon's brother was traveling in the United States in search of business for the agency, saw advertisements for the school, and after corresponding with Thomas, signed a deal to offer courses in Britain. In reporting the opening, *Advertising World* commented unfavorably on one aspect of the school's activities which it did not care to see introduced across the Atlantic: namely, the pushing of employment opportunities for women, whom the journal declared to be unsuited by nature to a business life. It did concede, however, that they might conceivably have a role to fill in copywriting, where there was a distinct shortage of talent.

The British advertising business constituted a ready market for relevant books and periodicals. *Advertising World* carried advertisements for the trade journal *Profitable Advertising,* publication of which was later undertaken by the Charles Vernon agency in London. There also seems to have been a considerable demand for *Printers Ink,* that most famous of advertising journals, since an English edition was launched under the editorship of S. H. Benson, probably the best known and certainly the most widely respected advertising agent of the day. Publication ceased with the outbreak of World War I and was not to resume. Among the influential books offered for sale in the early years of the century were the works of Professor Walter Dill Scott, at that time director of the Psychological Laboratory at Northwestern University, and *Good Advertising* and *Short Talks on Advertising* by Charles Austin Bates.

Contemporary advertising agents sometimes use regular newsletters as a means of keeping in touch with present and prospective clients. These publications may include updates on the agency and its activities, and often contain items related to research undertaken by agency personnel or expressions of opinion on matters of current interest. American agents around the turn of the century were using the same tactic, exploiting the British eagerness to learn about American methods by catering to that desire in newsletters. The well-known New York agency of Calkins and Holden, for example, offered to put any British manufacturer on its mailing list, presumably in the hope that the firm in question might some day wish to advertise in the United States. The same agency also wrote a monthly American Newsletter for *Advertising World,* which doubtless was responding to a detected need on the part of the publication's readers.

The Effects of American Influence

Easing of Creative Restrictions by Media

When John Morgan Richards arrived in Britain, he was dismayed to find that newspapers would not accept display advertisements, which meant that no advertisement could be wider than a single column, no illustrations were permitted, and the choice of type faces was severely restricted. "The old-fashioned system was regulated by the conservative taste of the editor, and not with a view to fall in with the wishes of the advertiser" (Richards 1905, 47). He accordingly set out to try and change such conventions, and to induce papers to accept display advertisements. "This was a difficult task, and a sad disappointment, so strongly were the newspaper proprietors esconced behind the barriers of what they considered to be the proper and seemly method of English advertising" (Richards 1905, 47). To make matters worse, the daily newspapers insisted on editing advertisers' copy. Richards was eventually successful to the extent that he became the first advertiser to take a full column advertisement in a daily paper, and the first to take the whole back page of a London weekly. It must be said, however, that he was by no means alone in fighting this particular battle, since British advertisers were becoming equally incensed at what they felt to be the publishers' obscurantist attitude, and were themselves bringing considerable pressure to bear. When the breakthrough came in the last few years of the nineteenth century, the results were inevitably compared with the kind of advertising which appeared in American publications. "It is true that of late years American methods of advertising in newspapers have been introduced into this country, and the eye is often forced to read a particular advertisement by the boldness of the type or the extent of the space occupied" (Moran 1905, 5).

If American influence helped loosen the shackles that constrained press advertising, it had the opposite effect with regard to billboards. In 1901 a public outcry greeted the erection on Dover Cliffs of a huge sign for Quaker Oats. The position was symbolic, the white cliffs of Dover being the first sight of England to greet travelers arriving from Continental Channel ports. In spite of widespread protests, "the men of Chicago," as Moran referred to them, refused to take it down. Dover Corporation accordingly promoted its own Act of Parliament to enable it to tackle this and any future abuses. In 1907 Parliament passed more general legislation in the form of the Advertisements Regulation Act, which enabled local authorities to make bylaws for the regulation of hoardings and the protection of certain amenities.

The opposition would seem to have been motivated not only by the placing of the sign, and the strange insensitivity of the advertiser to British feelings, but also by the fact that the advertiser was American. Moran's reference to "the men of Chicago" was noted before. Rather than name the product, he described it as "a certain Chicago commodity" (171). Yet reference to a photograph of the site, included in Moran's book, shows quite clearly there were actually two signs on the cliffs. The second, though much smaller than the Quaker Oats sign, can be read quite easily, and is for Pextons, a local department store. Throughout the debates and correspondence which surrounded the Dover affair, no mention of Pextons' billboard has been found.

Higher Creative Standards

There is little doubt that the creative standard of American advertising was higher than that in Britain. J. E. Garratt, an agent in Britain for American companies, wrote to *Advertising World* in November 1902: "Of course, anybody who knows anything about it has got to admit that in many respects American advertising is ahead of English" (333). This seems to have been true particularly in the industrial sector, according to a writer in the *Magazine of Commerce* in 1907: "It is a melancholy fact that the best advertisements in the foremost British technical periodicals come from America. It is still more melancholy to note that the announcements of American firms are, in the case of some British journals, actually greater in number than those of their British counterparts."

To some extent, the appeal of American advertising to the British advertiser was probably linked to the greater freedom offered by American publishers, and which John Morgan Richards and others were fighting to secure in Britain. As a contributor to *Advertising World* commented, "Looking through the pages of a couple of American magazines the other day, I was struck by the great advantage the writer has over his English confrere in the superiority of the type used. The faces are far more interesting and attractive in appearance, and make the general effect more pleasing and effective than is the case with the type used in this country" (December 1901, 5).

But this was by no means the whole story. Even allowing for the advantages they enjoyed in terms of mechanical production, American advertisements seem to have been more creative; that is to say, they were written and designed in such a way as to be more likely to appeal to the consumer. Alexander McNab, advertising manager for the Liptous grocery chain and therefore an important figure on the British scene, was interviewed by *Advertising World*. "Asked what he thought about the style of American Advertising, Mr. McNab said: Some American advertisers have a system of talking through their advertisements to the public in a simple but forcible manner which I like very much" (December 1901, 13).

English advertisers acknowledged American superiority by copying American designs. In 1902 the anonymous writer of "Our American Letter" in *Advertising World* looked through a collection of English magazines and found eleven examples of designs used for some time in the United States but that he had never seen before in Britain. Four of these he claimed to know for a fact had been created in the United States. Some of the advertisements he had seen used in London had been condemned on the other side of the Atlantic. He observed: "I should imagine that our advertising paper must have quite a large circulation in London, created just by the desire to get hold of smart designs without having to do a lot of brain-racking, or paying someone to do it for you" (February 1902, 44).

American expertise was particularly apparent in the area of mail order advertising. Freer (1921) told advertising students that "the American catalogue is a thing of wonder. To glance through it is to covet, and to covet is usually to acquire, for the American sales merchant takes good care to remove all obstacles from your path and to make you feel that you can afford to buy" (117). He believed American advertisements set a standard to aim for, declaring, "I believe students of advertising will be well repaid for studying the advertisements of American mail order houses" (241).

As well as looking at American advertisements, some advertisers went to the United States making no secret of the fact that they were looking for ideas. One such was Mr. Wack, managing director of A. J. White Ltd., who, ironically, was American. "Every year Mr. Wack visits the large cities in the United States to observe what the largest or the smallest successful American advertiser is doing . . . Then he quietly returns to undertake those fresh, original conceptions which are sending up the prosperity of A. J. White Ltd. in leaps and bounds" (*Advertising World* May 1902, 169). We can only speculate at the curious logic whereby pirated ideas could be described as fresh and original.

Although the view of American superiority in advertising was widely held, there were some dissenting voices. In June 1902, for example, *Advertising World* commented on the standard of advertising for American firms which was appearing in the British press. "It is true that the number of American advertisers over here is rapidly increasing, and from what we hear, it is likely to be very largely increased indeed before the end of 1902. But to ascribe the improvement which has taken place in British advertising to the example set by the American firms is not correct. As a matter of fact, up to the present, there has been nothing done by these firms that home firms could advantageously imitate, or learn from." (12).

British advertising agent F. E. Coe, though scarcely an objective witness, took advertisements for his agency in *Advertising World,* claiming that American agents did not understand the English scene well enough. There may well be some truth in this, since differences in taste and culture between the two countries could well have meant that while ideas and general creative approaches could cross the Atlantic successfully, actual advertisements could not. Another British agent, Mr. Wann, head of the T. B. Browne agency, was interviewed by *Printers Ink* while on a visit to the United States. Asked about the suitability of American advertisements for the British market, he replied, "Naturally American advertisements have to be toned down some-what to suit the English market, in the same way that English advertisements have to be considerably smartened up to suit America" (*Advertising World* February 1902, 46).

American creative influence did not extend to the poster, even though it became regarded as an art form with an estimated 6000 poster collections in the United States by 1896 (Hillier 1974, 135). Edward McKnight Kauffer, who settled in London in 1914, was to be an important figure in London in the inter-war period, but he was not a typical product of the American school, having studied in Munich and Paris. America's first woman poster artist, Ethel Read, also moved to London, but worked there as an illustrator of children's books. Moran appears to have been correct when he wrote in 1905 that although American poster artists had produced "much interesting work . . . they can scarcely be said as yet to have produced any new influence of their own" (105).

Lower Standards of Taste

British advertising people sometimes objected to the way American advertisements were written. This is hardly surprising, perhaps, when one remembers that British copywriters of the time were being urged to model themselves on Shakespeare, Milton, and Macaulay. *Advertising News* took the Grape Nuts Company to task for using the abbreviation "don't." Apart from being bad grammar, the publication observed acidly, it would put the product at a disadvantage by identifying it as American (15 April 1904, 1).

Howard Bridgewater, editor of the *Magazine of Commerce,* in a speech to the System Club of London, launched a vigorous attack on "Americanisms": "Another point to which I would like to draw attention is the use—or perhaps, I should say abuse—of Americanisms in British advertising. We have learned a great deal from the Americans, but their method of addressing themselves to the public is not always suitable for adoption on this side. For example, I noticed recently an announcement which asked whether the reader was in a rut so deep that he couldn't see over the top, suggesting that if so the advertiser was the man to help him out. Now the ordinary man of business greatly—and, I think, very properly—resents this sort of talk, and I am confident that it will never result in good business in this country" (*Magazine of Commerce* May 1907, 323).

Bridgewater's audience included Mr. R. M. Fairbanks of the Fairbanks Company, a leading American advertiser in the British market, who was not prepared to concede the point: "While I object as strongly as anyone to what I term "would-be Americanisms," I also object to their being confounded with the real article, and I must strongly contend that forcible effects do not necessarily imply bad taste. Some of the most striking advertising anywhere originated by the English soap manufacturers" (*Magazine of Commerce* May 1907, 323).

It would seem Bridgewater and Fairbanks were talking about British advertisers' attempting to imitate the American style of copywriting, which is certainly evidence of American influence, and scarcely supports *Advertising News'* contention that to be regarded as American was a disadvantage.

Complaints about lack of taste were directed not only at the way advertisements were written, but also at the products themselves. In July 1902 *Advertising World* published a letter from a correspondent calling himself "Advt. Manager" and entitled "Noxious Advertisements": "It is a matter of common knowledge that within the last few months there has been an extraordinary rush of American advertising in this country. Much of it is good, clean business, but there is also a lot of the other sort." He complained in particular about "an American 'doctor'" whose advertisements had been rejected by many British journals (85). Three years later, Moran was drawing attention to "advertisements of an improper and objectionable kind well known in the American Press which have recently shown a marked tendency to increase in this country" (Moran 1905, 91).

While there certainly were American patent medicines appearing on the British market, it would be hypocritical to suggest that this was a new phenomenon. Quack doctors and their advertisements had been a source of complaints for some two centuries, and had even provoked Parliament to pass legislation aimed at curbing their activities (Nevett 1982). American remedies had been available in Britain at least since the middle of the nineteenth century, when Franklin's Pill of Health was being advertised as "Infallible Life Preserver. A safe and certain cure for every disease . . . prepared by an eminent American chemist from the original recipe of Dr. Benjamin Franklin." Furthermore, it was claimed that the medicine trade had originally spread from Britain to the United States with the export of such products as Dr. Morison's Hygiene Pills and Old Parr's Life Pills (claimed to have enabled their inventor to live to 150) (Freedley 1853), so that the Americans might be said to be replying in kind.

Increased Use of Promotions

The main influence here was undoubtedly Barnum, and although he may have done some harm to the image of Americans generally, his approach to promotion was being followed by many advertisers later in the century. His methods were controversial, but this seems to have been the result of a belief that the customer would be cheated, rather than any disagreement with the method per se. "An Adept" sounded this note of caution: "We are free to admit that a Barnum-like course of publicity may occasionally be attended with success, and chiefly by the amusing absurdity by which such a system is generally accompanied; but we maintain that unless the object or matter advertised before the public has a substratum of truth, honesty and propriety, then loss and not gain will ensue. Moreover, the superstructure and promise held forth to the world must be capable of bearing reasonable and even rigid inquiry" ("An Adept" 1875, 26).

British retailers in particular seem to have owed a debt to Barnum. Jesse Boot was said to have been copying the American's methods when he opened new shops to the accompaniment of a brass band, a Salvation Army man with a bell, a bevy of sandwich-board men, and a coach and four festooned with placards. Thomas Lipton, whose advertising manager has already been noted as admiring American methods, had pigs driven through the streets under a banner saying "Lipton's orphans"; had thin men carrying signs saying "Going to Lipton's" and fat men carrying signs reading "Coming from Lipton's"; had monster cheeses towed through the streets to his shops by steam engines; and tried to give Queen Victoria a five-ton cheese for her Golden Jubilee in 1885 (Nevett 1982).

The introduction of new food products to the British market provided American firms with further opportunities for promotional ingenuity. H. J. Heinz seem to have pioneered the distribution of free samples in Britain, distributing them from stalls in retail outlets as early as 1904, and sent women representatives to call on newspaper editors to induce them to write about the company's products. The Grape Nuts Company, meanwhile, sent out recipes to women's magazines, in which its product was the main ingredient.

Increased Professionalism

Among the most notable results of American influence was a growing sense of professionalism among advertising people in Britain. Advertising traditionally had been regarded by the upper classes as unnecessary and unsuitable for a respectable business. In contrast to the British view, as expressed by such writers as Carlyle and Macaulay, Americans seem to have accepted advertising as an essential part of commercial activity: "Mercantile men have certainly never entertained the idea that all that is necessary, in order to do business, is to open a shop or store and stock it with merchandise. To take some means to inform the public of the nature of their business, and solicit their patronage, has ever been a matter of primary importance" (Freedley 1853, 96). John Morgan Richards, too, commented that when he started in his first job, "any novelty in the way of presenting one's business was then, as now, regarded as desirable." Accordingly, "My chief training in the United States was the preparation of advertisements" (Richards 1905, 41, 46). Richards himself was no doubt ample testimony to the value of such a training.

The difference was nowhere more apparent than in what British and American advertisers were prepared to pay to secure good advertising. *Advertising World* admonished its readers: "Don't pay a big price for space in a medium, and then be afraid to spend a couple of guineas for the matter you fill it with" (December 1905, 7). W. Teignmouth Shore, writing in the *Fortnightly Review,* made a pointed comparison between the practices in the two countries: "The Englishman believes he can obtain the service of a first-class advertising man for the salary of a chief cook. The American will pay a salary which would be startling if offered to the manager of a business in this country" (Shore 1907).

Considerable credit for bringing about a change in British attitudes must go to Paul Derrick, the American advertising agent who worked in London for many years. He attacked what he called the "paralyzing prejudice" against advertising which he detected in British business, manifested in the way British companies treated their advertising agent like a valet or errand boy. Derrick was extremely successful and highly respected, as might be expected of the creator of the Johnny Walker whisky symbol and the benign-looking quaker of Quaker Oats. His views therefore carried considerable weight—even more so when the government made him comptroller of publicity for the National Service Department during World War I. The very fact that advertising agents and consultants such as Derrick, Thomas Russell, and Charles Higham were called in to help with advertising campaigns in the national interest is testimony to the acceptance of advertising as a profession. The fact that Derrick was American is evidence that the longstanding British distrust and the legacy of Phineas T. Barnum had finally been overcome.

Summary and Conclusion

There is considerable evidence of American influence on British advertising during the second half of the nineteenth century. The first major impact was undoubtedly made by Barnum, but although his methods may have been effective for him in the short term, they appeared to the British to be part of the perceived desire on the part of Americans generally to cheat the public. If Barnum had imitators in terms of his approach to promotion, he also left an unfortunate legacy of resentment which took several decades to overcome.

British knowledge of American advertising methods was linked to the increase in trade between the two countries, which followed upon improvements in communications and transportation. American businessmen crossed the Atlantic, sometimes to stay. As American products were introduced to the British market, American advertising agents began to follow to serve the needs of their clients. They expected British publishers to offer the same facilities in terms of space sizes and type faces as those in the United States, and to be treated as skilled professionals. When the conditions they found did not accord with such expectations, they exerted considerable pressure to change them.

British advertisers and agents, meanwhile, were being exposed to American methods through reading American books and journals, or crossing the Atlantic themselves. Generally they seem to have liked what they found, in press advertising if not on poster hoardings, and used American ideas and styles of writing—with varying degrees of adaptation—in their British campaigns.

On a more general level, it should be remembered that by personal example, and by winning social and political acceptance, American businessmen in London helped to overcome British suspicions about the American people, and made acceptance of American methods that much easier.

References

ABC Exchange Club. 1883. *Handy Book*. London: ABC Exchange Club.

"An Adept." 1878. *Publicity. An Essay with Ancient and Modern Instances*. London: G. S. Brown.

Advertising Age. 1964. Supplement: "The Centennial of the J. Walter Thompson Co." Vol. 35 (49) 7 December.

Advertising News. Various issues.

Advertising World. Various issues.

Dictionary of American Biography. 1928. Vol. 1. Entry on Phineas T. Barnum. New York: Scribner.

Dictionary of Business Biography. 1986. Vol. 5. Entry on Sir Henry Solomon Wellcome. London: Butterworth.

Fitzsimons, Raymund. 1969. *Barnum in London*. London: Geoffrey Bles.

Fraser's Magazine. 1855. "Barnum," cccxii (February). 213–223.

Freedley, Edwin T. 1853. *How to Make Money*. London: George Routledge.

Freer, Cyril. 1921. *The Inner Side of Advertising*. London: The Library Press.

Hillier, Bevis. 1974. *Posters*. London: Spring Books.

Magazine of Commerce. Various issues.

Moran, Clarence. 1905. *The Business of Advertising*. London: Methuen.

Nevett, T. R. 1982. *Advertising in Britain. A History*. London: Heinemann.

Peppin, Brigid, and Lucy Micklethwait. 1983. *Dictionary of British Book Illustrators of the Twentieth Century*. Entry on Edward McKnight Kauffer, London: John Murray.

Richards, John Morgan. 1905. *With John Bull and Jonathan*. London: T. Werner Laurie.

Shore, W. Teignmouth. 1907. "The Craft of the Advertiser." *Fortnightly Review* (February).

Teele, Albert L. 1892. *Ideal Advertising*. London: Albert L. Teele.

Turner, E. S. 1965. *The Shocking History of Advertising*. Harmondsworth: Penguin Books.

About the Contributors

Edward W. Cundiff is chairman and John A. Beck Centennial Professor in Communication in the Advertising Department of the University of Texas at Austin. A former editor of the *Journal of Marketing*, he has written extensively on international retailing and marketing. His five books include well-known texts on sales management, international marketing, and basic marketing.

Isabella C. M. Cunningham is the Ernest A. Sharpe Centennial Professor in Communication at the University of Texas at Austin, where she has taught since 1974. Dr. Cunningham has authored and co-authored six books and numerous articles. She received J.D. and M.B.A. degrees from universities in Brazil, and her Ph.D. from Michigan State University.

William H. Cunningham is president of the University of Texas at Austin. He also holds the Regents Chair in Higher Education Leadership and is professor of marketing. Dr. Cunningham is a nationally known marketing scholar, a former editor of the *Journal of Marketing*, and author of seven books. His research interests include marketing management, marketing research, and strategic market planning. He came to the University of Texas in 1971 from Michigan State University, where he earned his B.A., M.B.A., and Ph.D.

Roger Dickinson has a Ph.D. from the Columbia Graduate School of Business. He is a professor of marketing at the University of Texas at Arlington and a member of the board of Tandycrafts, Inc. He is the author of about fifty refereed publications. He was a research assistant to both Professors Oxenfeldt and Cassady.

George Fisk serves as Georgia Power Professor of Marketing in the School of Business Administration at Emory University, Atlanta, Ga. Among his books are *Marketing Systems* and *Marketing and the Ecological Crisis*. He has also edited a number of books including *New Essays in Marketing Theory* and *Marketing Management Technology as a Social Process*. His interest in marketing history stems from a concern with the need to develop long-time runs for the testing of behavioral and structural hypotheses explaining the emergence of marketing as a form of economic specialization.

Jerry Goolsby is an assistant professor of marketing at Oklahoma State University. His current research interests lie in the areas of marketing ethics and cognitive moral development.

Barbara L. Gross is a doctoral candidate in marketing at the University of Southern California, Graduate School of Business Administration. She previously taught at California State University, Los Angeles.

Shelby D. Hunt is the Paul Whitefield Horn Professor of Marketing at Texas Tech University and a past editor of the *Journal of Marketing*. He is a recipient of the 1987 Academy of Marketing Science Distinguished Educators Award. His articles have appeared in the *Journal of Marketing, Journal of Marketing Research, Journal of Consumer Research, Journal of Business Research, Journal of Macromarketing, Journal of Retailing,* and the *Journal of Marketing Education*. His articles on marketing theory have twice received the *Journal of Marketing* Harold H. Maynard Award for the best theory article. He is also the author of *Marketing Theory: The Philosophy of Marketing Science*.

Philip Kotler is one of the world's leading authorities and consultants on marketing. He is the Harold T. Martin Professor of Marketing at the J. L. Kellogg Graduate School of Management, Northwestern University. A graduate of the University of Chicago and the Massachusetts Institute of Technology, Dr. Kotler is the author of the world's most widely used graduate textbook in marketing, *Marketing Management,* now in its fifth edition. He has also published *Marketing Professional Services* and *Marketing For Health Care Organizations*. Dr. Kotler has won several prizes for his original contributions to marketing, including the *Leader in Marketing Thought Award* (1975), the *Distinguished Marketing Educator Award* (1985), and the *Award for Excellence in Health Care Marketing* (1985).

Dr. E. Jerome McCarthy, Michigan State University, pioneered the Four Ps of Managerial marketing in his *Basic Marketing: A Managerial Approach*. He also wrote texts on data processing and social issues in marketing, as well as various articles and monographs. As a Ford Foundation Fellow he did research on the role of marketing in economic development. In 1987 he received the American Marketing Association's Trailblazer Award.

Richard W. Pollay is curator of the History of Advertising Archives at the University of British Columbia. In addition to his many historical studies, like "The Subsiding Sizzle," he also has raised many concerns about the social and cultural impacts of advertising in "The Distorted Mirror," and "The Quality of Life in 'The Padded Sell'." These are generating much debate and discussion within the fields of marketing and advertising.

Kathleen M. Rassuli is Professor Hollander's student and a doctoral candidate at Michigan State University. She holds a B.A. in Business Administration from the University of Nebraska-Lincoln. Mrs. Rassuli represented Michigan State at the 1985 AMA Doctoral Consortium. She is currently assistant professor of marketing at Indiana-Purdue University at Fort Wayne and wrote an article entitled "Desire—Induced, Innate, Insatiable?" with Professor Hollander, for the Fall 1986 *Journal of Macromarketing*.

Ronald Savitt is the John L. Beckley Professor of American Business at the University of Vermont. He holds an A.B. and M.B.A. from the University of California-Berkeley and a Ph.D. from the University of Pennsylvania. Professor Savitt has taught at Boston University, the University of Alberta, and Michigan State University; he was a Fulbright Scholar at Bogazici University in Turkey and the International Scholar in Retailing at Stirling University in Scotland. He has been author and/or editor in ten books; his research has been published in the *European Journal of Marketing, Journal of Marketing, Managerial and Decision Economics, California Management Review*, and several books. His most recent publication is "Entrepreneurial Behavior and Marketing Strategy" in *Philosophical and Radical Thought in Marketing*, published by Lexington Books in 1987.

Jagdish N. Sheth is the Robert E. Brooker Distinguished Professor of Marketing and Research at the University of Southern California, Graduate School of Business Administration. He previously was the Walter H. Stellnar Distinguished Professor of Marketing at the University of Illinois from 1975 to 1984, and has also taught at Columbia University and the Massachusetts Institute of Technology. He received his doctorate from the University of Pittsburg under Professor John A. Howard.

About the Editors

Terence Nevett, who holds a Ph.D. from the University of London, is professor of marketing at Central Michigan University. His publications in the area of marketing history include *Advertising in Britain. A History* (Heinemann 1982); four entries on famous admen for Britain's *Dictionary of Business Biography* (Butterworth 1984); a chapter on "Advertising and Editorial Integrity in the Nineteenth Century" in *The Press in English Society,* edited by M. Harris and A. Lee (Fairleigh Dickinson University Press 1986); and a number of articles and papers. His *Voluntary Regulation of Advertising,* coauthored with Gordon E. Miracle, was published by Lexington Books in 1987.

Dr. Nevett is coeditor with Stanley C. Hollander of two volumes of conference proceedings (*Marketing in the Long Run* 1985, and *Marketing in Three Eras* 1987), and of *Retrospectives in Marketing,* a marketing history newsletter. He is also a governor of the History of Advertising Trust, London. In 1983 he was named Procter and Gamble Distinguished Professor by Michigan State University.

Ronald A. Fullerton began studying marketing history during a Harvard seminar in 1965; it has been a major focus of all his subsequent work. His articles on marketing history have appeared in the *International Journal of Advertising, International Journal of Research in Marketing, Journal of Marketing, Journal of Social History,* and several conference proceedings. He is currently assistant professor of marketing at Southeastern Massachusetts University. He received his B.A. from Rutgers, M.A. (history) from Harvard, M.B.A. from Cornell, and Ph.D. from the University of Wisconsin-Madison. He was a member of the Seminar on the History of the Book Trade at Johannes Gutenberg University in Mainz, Germany. His "The Poverty of Ahistorical Analysis: Present Weakness and Future Cure in U.S. Marketing Thought" was published in Lexington Books' *Philosophical and Radical Thought in Marketing* in 1987.